Magill's Bibliography of Literary Criticism

Magill's
Bibliography
of
Literary Criticism

SELECTED SOURCES FOR THE STUDY OF MORE THAN
2,500 OUTSTANDING WORKS OF WESTERN LITERATURE

Edited by
FRANK N. MAGILL

Associate Editors

STEPHEN L. HANSON
PATRICIA KING HANSON

Volume One
Abe - Eliot
1 - 608

SALEM PRESS

Englewood Cliffs

173337

R
016.809
M145
v. 1

LIBRARY OF CONGRESS CATALOG CARD NUMBER: 79-63017

Complete Set: ISBN 0-89356-188-6
Volume 1:   ISBN 0-89356-189-4

PRINTED IN THE UNITED STATES OF AMERICA

PREFACE

INFORMATION that lies fallow serves no purpose; it is only when information is put to use that it earns its right to be collected and saved. A prime example of this concept is the bibliography, the latchkey to the knowledge bank in a given field—the combination to the safe, so to speak. Without a listing of sources for specialized areas of knowledge, such as literature or science, for example, it would be almost impossible for scholars or researchers to examine in depth the contributions of other specialists in their field. MAGILL'S BIBLIOGRAPHY OF LITERARY CRITICISM is the result of a team effort by a score of researchers who have made an exhaustive study of the literature of scholarly criticism in the fields of fiction, drama, and poetry and structured the findings in a format we hope will be convenient and easy to use. The expertise of the staff is beyond question—all have graduate degrees in librarianship or literature, or both, and are experienced librarians in their own right.

In the beginning certain guidelines were provided for the staff members, and these were augmented by staff suggestions as the work progressed. Our plan was to develop a work useful to librarians who serve undergraduates and generalists rather than highly specialized scholars—experts who often have limited, even exotic, requirements. Thus we have been broad in our coverage of titles and generous in our selection of sources for individual titles. There are 613 authors represented, 2,546 literary works covered, and 36,137 individual citations listed. Major novels and plays usually have about twenty-five sources listed, while minor works average about a dozen.

The time span of this work runs from the Gilgamesh Epic to the the present, some material published as late as September, 1978, being included. Literally thousands of volumes have been scanned to find the sources included here. All types of citations are used: articles in periodicals, articles or chapters from books, and entire books. Emphasis has been on citations published in the 1960's and 1970's so that this work will augment if not supersede older bibliographies that every library already has. Thus librarians who gain access to MAGILL'S BIBLIOGRAPHY OF LITERARY CRITICISM may soon find that this is the *first* place they will look and often the *only* place because of the set's comprehensive and current nature.

The page format of this work has been designed with the librarian's time and convenience of utmost concern. Authors appear alphabetically with their dates. Each of their titles to be dealt with then appears alphabetically. Under the individual works the authors of the citations are listed alphabetically with no divisions that separate works in periodicals from works in various other forms. Upon examination of the citation as listed it is usually clear enough as to which medium has been used. There are no abbreviations of journals or publishers to confuse the unwary and require reference to a "legend" or, even worse, another visit to the librarian's desk for assistance. All the works of "multiple" authors (poets who also write drama, dramatists who also write novels) appear together. The work is not divided into sections covering (1) novels, (2) short stories, (3) plays, (4) poetry, and the like.

Two complete indexes provide quick and easy access to the thirty-six thousand entries herein: a title index at the end of Volume Four and an author and title index at the beginning of each volume, covering the citations in that volume. If the author is known, the user merely selects the proper alphabetical volume and all that author's citations will be found following his name—though assembled separately by book title. If the researcher does not know the author of a work, he may refer to the alphabetical title index in Volume Four which will reveal the volume and page number of the title desired.

MAGILL'S BIBLIOGRAPHY OF LITERARY CRITICISM has been prepared *by* librarians *for* librarians. It is comprehensive and up-to-date. It will provide the undergraduate with adequate sources for his term paper; it will provide the graduate student or professor with a sound basis for further research; it will provide the busy librarian with a single resource that will save hours of daily digging for years to come. Nobody deserves such a boon more.

FRANK N. MAGILL

RESEARCH ASSOCIATES

Glenna Dunning
Linda Edgington
Patricia King Hanson
Stephen L. Hanson
Julia Johnson
Timothy Johnson
Robert Mitchell

RESEARCH ASSISTANTS

Paul Christopher
Janet Curry
Ray Ford
Christine Gladish
Carolyn McIntosh
Susan Mackall
Frank Mason
Steven Robertson
Don Thompson
Dunning Wilson
Patricia Yan

Magill's
Bibliography
of
Literary Criticism

LIST OF AUTHORS AND TITLES—VOLUME ONE

List of Authors and Titles—Volume One

List of Authors and Titles—Volume One

List of Authors and Titles—Volume One

KOBO ABE
(1924–   )

The Woman in the Dunes

Currie, William. "Abe Kobo's Nightmare World of Sand," in his *Approaches to the Modern Japanese Novel*. Tokyo, Japan: Sophia University, 1976, pp. 1–18.

Hardin, Nancy S. "An Interview with Abe Kobo," in *Contemporary Literature*. XV (1974), pp. 439–456.

Kauffmann, Stanley. "Novels from Abroad," in *New York Review of Books*. III (January 14, 1965), p. 21.

Marks, Alfred H. and Barry D. Bort. *Guide to Japanese Prose*. Boston: G.K. Hall, 1975, pp. 117–120.

Miner, Earl. "Life Is a Sandpit," in *Saturday Review*. XLVII (September 5, 1964), p. 32.

Richey, Clarence W. "Abe's *The Woman in the Dunes*," in *Explicator*. XXXI (1973), item 77.

Ross, N.W. "Captives in the Sands of Fate," in *New York Times Book Review*. (August 30, 1964), pp. 4–5.

Williams, Philip. "Abe Kobo and Symbols of Absurdity," in *Studies on Japanese Culture*, Volume I. Edited by Saburo Ota and Rikutaro Fukuda. Tokyo, Japan: P.E.N. Club, 1973, pp. 477–482.

Yamanouchi, H. "Abe Kobo and Oe Kenzaburo: The Search for Identity in Contemporary Japanese Literature," in *Modern Japan: Aspects of History, Literature and Society*. Edited by William G. Beasley. Berkeley: University of California Press, 1975, pp. 166–186.

HENRY ADAMS
(1838–1918)

The Education of Henry Adams

Bell, Daniel. *The Coming of the Post-Industrial Society: A Venture in Social Forecasting.* New York: Basic Books, 1973, pp. 168–170.

Bercovitch, Sacvan. "Horologicals to Chronometricals: The Rhetoric of the Jeremiad," in *Literary Monographs.* III (1970), pp. 1–124.

Blasing, Mutlu Konuk. "Henry Adams, Connoisseur of Chaos," in *The Art of Life: Studies in American Autobiographical Literature.* Edited by Mutlu Konuk Blasing. Austin: University of Texas Press, 1977, pp. 77–111.

Cooley, Thomas. *Educated Lives: The Rise of Modern Autobiography in America.* Columbus: Ohio State University Press, 1976, pp. 27–49.

Cox, James M. "Autobiography and America," in *Virginia Quarterly Review.* XLVII (Spring, 1971), pp. 252–277.

Downs, Robert Bingham. *Famous American Books.* New York: McGraw-Hill, 1972, pp. 234–239.

Gidley, M. "One Continuous Farce: Notes on Faulkner's Extra-Literary Reading," in *Mississippi Quarterly.* XXIII (Summer, 1970), pp. 299–314.

Guttmann, Allen. "*The Education of Henry Adams,*" in *Landmarks in American Writing.* Edited by Hennig Cohen. New York: Basic Books, 1969, p. 252–260.

Harbert, Earl N. "The Education of Henry Adams: The Confessional Mode as Heuristic Experiment," in *Journal of Narrative Technique.* IV (January, 1974), pp. 3–18.

Levenson, J.C. "Henry Adams and the Art of Politics," in *Southern Review.* IV (Winter, 1968), pp. 50–58.

Loewenberg, Bert James. *American History in American Thought.* New York: Simon and Schuster, 1972, pp. 520–545.

Miller, Ross Lincoln. "Henry Adams: Making It Over Again," in *Centennial Review.* XVIII (Summer, 1974), pp. 288–305.

Minter, David L. *The Interpreted Design as a Structural Principle in American Prose.* New Haven, Conn.: Yale University Press, 1969, pp. 103–133.

Muller, H.J. *In Pursuit of Relevance.* Bloomington: Indiana University Press, 1971, pp. 197–207.

Roelofs, Gerrit H. "Henry Adams: Pessimism and the Intelligent Use of Doom," in *Journal of English Literary History.* XVII (September, 1950), pp. 214–239.

Rule, Henry B. "Henry Adams' Satire on Human Intelligence: Its Method and Purpose," in *Centennial Review.* XV (Fall, 1971), pp. 430–444.

Scheick, William J. "Symbolism in *The Education of Henry Adams,*" in *Arizona Quarterly.* XXIV (Winter, 1968), pp. 350–360.

Shaw, Peter. "The Success of Henry Adams," in *Yale Review.* L (Autumn, 1969), pp. 71–78.

Sklar, Judith N. "*The Education of Henry Adams* by Henry Adams," in *Daedalus.* CIII (Winter, 1974), pp. 59–66.

Vandersee, C.A. "The Hamlet in Henry Adams," in *Shakespeare Survey.* XXIV (1971), pp. 87–104.

————. "Henry Adams and 1905: Prolegomena to the *Education,*" in *Journal of American Studies.* II (October, 1968), pp. 199–224.

————. "Henry Adams and the Invisible Negro," in *South Atlantic Quarterly.* LXVI (Winter, 1967), pp. 13–30.

Waterston, Elizabeth. "The Gap in Henry Adams' Education," in *Canadian Review of American Studies.* VII (1976), pp. 132–138.

JOSEPH ADDISON
(1672–1719)

Cato

Boas, Frederick. *An Introduction to Eighteenth-Century Drama, 1700–1780.* Oxford: Clarendon Press, 1953, pp. 117–123.

Courthope, W.J. *Addison.* London: Macmillan, 1919, pp. 115–130.

Dobrée, Bonamy. "The First Victorian," in *Essays in Biography, 1680–1726.* Freeport, N.Y.: Books for Libraries Press, 1925, pp. 287–299.

Donaldson, Ian. "Cato in Tears: Stoical Guises of the Man of Feeling," in *Studies in the Eighteenth Century*, Volume II. Edited by R.F. Brissenden. Toronto: University of Toronto Press, 1973, pp. 377–395.

Johnson, Samuel. "Joseph Addison," in *Lives of the English Poets*, Volume I. New York: Dutton, 1925, pp. 337–339.

Kelsall, M.M. "The Meaning of Addison's *Cato*," in *Review of English Studies.* XVII (1966), pp. 149–162.

Krutch, Joseph Wood. *Comedy and Conscience After the Restoration.* New York: Russell and Russell, 1967, pp. 230–231.

Loftis, John. "The Reform Movement and the Theory of Dramatic Genres," in *The Revels: History of Drama in English*, Volume V: 1660–1750. Edited by John Loftis, Richard Southern, Marion Jones and A.H. Scouten. London: Methuen, 1976, pp. 60–62.

Nettleton, George H. *English Drama of the Restoration and Eighteenth Century (1642–1780).* New York: Macmillan, 1914, pp. 179–182.

Nicoll, Allardyce. *A History of Early Eighteenth Century Drama, 1700–1750.* Cambridge: Cambridge University Press, 1929, pp. 87–89.

Noyes, Robert Gale. "Augustan Tragedy," in *The Neglected Muse: Restoration and Eighteenth-Century Tragedy in the Novel (1740–1780).* Providence, R.I.: Brown University Press, 1958, pp. 122–135.

Rogers, Donald O. "Addison's *Cato*: Teaching Through Imagery," in *CEA Critic.* XXXVI (March, 1974), pp. 17–18.

Smithers, Peter. *The Life of Joseph Addison.* Oxford: Clarendon Press, 1954, pp. 250–269.

Ward, Adolphus William. *A History of English Dramatic Literature to the Death of Queen Anne*, Volume III. London: Macmillan, 1899, pp. 439–442.

The Sir Roger de Coverley Papers

Abbott, Herbert Vaughan. "Introduction," in The Sir Roger de Coverley Papers *from* The Spectator. New York: Scott, Foresman, 1919, pp. 13–48.

Bolton, J.H. *A Commentary and Questionnaire on the* Coverley Papers *(Addison and Steele)*. London: Pitman, 1927.

Duke, R.E.H. *Reflections on the Character and Doings of Sir Roger de Coverley of Addison*. London: Elliott Stock, 1900.

Evans, James E. and John N. Wall, Jr. "Introduction," in *A Guide to Prose Fiction in* The Tatler *and* The Spectator. New York: Garland, 1977, pp. 34–39.

Frazer, Sir James George. "Sir Roger de Coverley," in Sir Roger de Coverley, *and Other Literary Pieces*. New York: Macmillan, 1920, pp. 3–61. Reprinted in *The Gorgon's Head, and Other Literary Pieces*. New York: Macmillan, 1927, pp. 35–96.

Freeman, Phyllis. "Who Was Sir Roger de Coverley?," in *Quarterly Review*. CCLXXXV (1947), pp. 592–604.

Furtwangler, Albert. "Mr. Spectator, Sir Roger, and Good Humour," in *University of Toronto Quarterly*. XLVI (Fall, 1976), pp. 31–50.

Kay, Donald. *Short Fiction in* The Spectator. University: University of Alabama Press, 1975, pp. 91–96.

Pocock, Guy Noel. "Sir Roger de Coverley," in *Little Room*. New York: Dutton, 1926, pp. 21–31.

Winchester, C.T. "Introduction," in *The Sir Roger de Coverley Papers*. New York: American Book Company, 1904, pp. 29–32.

The Spectator

Beljame, Alexandre. *Men of Letters and the English Public in the Eighteenth Century, 1660–1744: Dryden, Addison, Pope*. London: Routledge and Kegan Paul, 1948, pp. 263–316.

Bond, Donald F. "Introduction," in *The Spectator*, Volume I. Oxford: Clarendon Press, 1965, pp. xiii–cix.

Boyce, Benjamin. "English Short Fiction in the Eighteenth Century," in *Studies in Short Fiction*. V (1968), pp. 95–112.

Butt, John. "Addison," in *The Augustan Age*. London: Hutchinson's, 1950, pp. 36–45.

Chambers, Robert D. "Addison at Work on *The Spectator*," in *Modern Philology*. LVI (1959), pp. 145–153.

Connely, Willard. *Sir Richard Steele*. New York: Scribner's, 1934, pp. 182–216.

Courthope, W.J. *Addison*. London: Macmillan, 1919, pp. 81–114.

Dobrée, Bonamy. "The First Victorian," in *Essays in Biography, 1680–1726*. Freeport, N.Y.: Books for Libraries Press, 1925, pp. 273–286. Reprinted as "Joseph Addison: *The Spectator*," in *Milton to Ouida: A Collection of Essays*. New York: Barnes & Noble, 1970, pp. 64–76.

Dobson, Austin. "The Story of *The Spectator*," in *Side-Walk Studies.* London: Chatto and Windus, 1902, pp. 208–229.

Evans, James, E. and John N. Wall, Jr. "Introduction," in *A Guide to Prose Fiction in* The Tatler *and* The Spectator. New York: Garland, 1974, pp. 9–70.

Furtwangler, Albert, "The Making of Mr. Spectator," in *Modern Language Quarterly.* XXXVIII (March, 1977), pp. 21–39.

Gay, Peter. "The Spectator as Actor: Addison in Perspective," in *Encounter.* XXIX (1967), pp. 27–32.

Humphreys, H.R. *Steele, Addison and Their Periodical Essays.* London: Longmans, Green, 1959.

Irving, William Henry. "Augustan Attitudes—Steele and Addison," in *The Providence of Wit in the English Letter Writers.* Durham, N.C.: Duke University Press, 1955, pp. 164–177.

Johnson, Samuel. "Joseph Addison," in *Lives of the English Poets*, Volume I. New York: Dutton, 1925, pp. 333–337.

Lewis, C.S. "Addison," in *Essays on the Eighteenth Century Presented to David Nichol Smith in Honour of His Seventieth Birthday.* Oxford: Clarendon Press, 1945, pp. 1–14. Reprinted in *Eighteenth-Century English Literature: Modern Essays in Criticism.* Edited by James L. Clifford. New York: Oxford University Press, 1959, pp. 144–157.

Macaulay, Thomas Babington. *Essay on Addison.* Edited by Charles Flint McClumpha. New York: American Book Company, 1904, pp. 114–128.

Marr, George S. "The *Tatler* and *Spectator*, and Other Periodical Essay Work of Addison and Steele," in *The Periodical Essayists of the Eighteenth Century.* New York: Appleton, 1924, pp. 21–63.

Routh, Harold. "Steele and Addison," in *Cambridge History of English Literature*, Volume IX. Edited by A.W. Ward and A.R. Waller. New York: Putnam's, 1913, pp. 29–72.

Smithers, Peter. *The Life of Joseph Addison.* Oxford: Clarendon Press, 1954, pp. 202–245.

Thorpe, Clarence D. "Addison's Contribution to Criticism," in *The Seventeenth Century: Studies in the History of English Thought and Literature from Bacon to Pope.* Edited by Richard F. Jones. Stanford, Calif.: Stanford University Press, 1951, pp. 318–329.

Walker, Hugh. "The Queen Anne Essayists," in *The English Essay and Essayists.* New York: Dutton, 1923, pp. 99–128.

Watson, Melvin. "*The Spectator* Tradition and the Development of the Familiar Essay," in *Journal of English Literary History.* XIII (1946), pp. 189–215.

Winton, Calhoun. "The Years of *The Spectator*," in *Captain Steele: The Early Years of Richard Steele*. Baltimore: Johns Hopkins University Press, 1964, pp. 131–153.

Woolf, Virginia. "Addison," in *The Common Reader. First Series*. New York: Harcourt, Brace and World, 1953, pp. 98–108.

The Tatler

Aitken, George A. *The Life of Richard Steele*, Volume I. London: William Isbister, 1889, pp. 239–258.

Beljame, Alexandre. *Men of Letters and the English Public in the Eighteenth Century, 1660–1744: Dryden, Addison, Pope*. London: Routledge and Kegan Paul, 1948, pp. 260–263.

Bond, Richmond P. "Isaac Bickerstaff, Esq.," in *Restoration and Eighteenth-Century Literature: Essays in Honor of Alan Dugald McKillop*. Edited by Carroll Camden. Chicago: University of Chicago Press, 1963, pp. 103–124.

————. The Tatler: *The Making of a Literary Journal*. Cambridge, Mass.: Harvard University Press, 1971.

Boyce, Benjamin. "English Short Fiction in the Eighteenth Century," in *Studies in Short Fiction*. V (1968), pp. 95–112.

Connely, Willard. *Sir Richard Steele*. New York: Scribner's, 1934, pp. 143–181.

Courthope, W.J. *Addison*. London: Macmillan, 1919, pp. 81–114.

Dobrée, Bonamy. *English Literature in the Early Eighteenth Century, 1700–1740*. Oxford: Clarendon Press, 1959, pp. 74–84.

Dobson, Austin. *Richard Steele*. London: Longmans, 1886, pp. 89–126.

Evans, James E. and John N. Wall, Jr. "Introduction," in *A Guide to Prose Fiction in* The Tatler *and* The Spectator. New York: Garland, 1977, pp. 9–70.

Furtwangler, Albert. "The Making of Mr. Spectator," in *Modern Language Quarterly*. XXXVIII (March, 1977), pp. 21–39.

Graham, Walter. "The *Tatler, Spectator*, and *Guardian*," in *English Literary Periodicals*. New York: Thomas Nelson, 1930, pp. 65–84.

Greenough, C.N. "The Development of *The Tatler*, Particularly in Regard to News," in *PMLA*. XXXI (1916), pp. 633–663.

Humphreys, A.R. *Steele, Addison and Their Periodical Essays*. London: Longmans, Green, 1959.

Irving, William Henry. "Augustan Attitudes—Steele and Addison," in *The Providence of Wit in the English Letter Writers*. Durham, N.C.: Duke University Press, 1955, pp. 164–177.

Johnson, Samuel. "Joseph Addison," in *Lives of the English Poets*, Volume I. New York: Dutton, 1925, pp. 333–337.

Macaulay, Thomas Babington. *Essay on Addison.* Edited by Charles Flint McClumpha. New York: American Book Company, 1904, pp. 101–114.

Marr, George S. "The *Tatler* and *Spectator*, and Other Periodical Essay Work of Addison and Steele," in *The Periodical Essayists of the Eighteenth Century.* New York: Appleton, 1924, pp. 21–63.

Mayo, Robert D. *The English Novel in the Magazines, 1740–1815.* Evanston, Ill.: Northwestern University Press, 1962, pp. 33–39, 41–43.

Routh, Harold. "Steele and Addison," in *Cambridge History of English Literature*, Volume IX. Edited by A.W. Ward and A.R. Waller. New York: Putnam's, 1913, pp. 29–72.

Sherburn, George and Donald F. Bond. "Addison, Steele, and the Periodical Essay," in *A Literary History of England.* Edited by Albert C. Baugh. New York: Appleton-Century-Crofts, 1967, pp. 870–882.

Smithers, Peter. *The Life of Joseph Addison.* Oxford: Clarendon Press, 1954, pp. 192–200.

Walker, Hugh. "The Queen Anne Essayists," in *The English Essay and Essayists.* New York: Dutton, 1923, pp. 99–128.

Waller, A.R. "Richard Steele, Gazeteer and Bickerstaff," in *Studies in the Early English Periodical.* Edited by Richmond P. Bond. Chapel Hill: University of North Carolina Press, 1957, pp. 49–72.

Winton, Calhoun. "Isaac Bickerstaff's *Tatler*," in *Captain Steele: The Early Career of Richard Steele.* Baltimore: Johns Hopkins University Press, 1964, pp. 101–130.

AESCHYLUS
(c.525 B.C.–c.456 B.C.)

Agamemnon

Anderson, F.M. "Character of Clytemnestra," in *Transactions of the American Philological Association.* LX (1929), pp. 136–154.

Baldry, H.C. "House of Atriade (in the *Agamemnon*)," in *Classical Review.* V (March, 1955), pp. 16–17.

Denniston, J.D. and D. Page. *Aeschylus:* Agamemnon. Oxford: Clarendon Press, 1957.

Diggle, J. "Notes on the *Agamemnon* and *Persae* of Aeschylus," in *Classical Review.* XVIII (March, 1968), pp. 1–4.

Earp, F.R. "Studies in Character: Agamemnon," in *Greece and Rome.* XIX (June, 1950), pp. 49–61.

Fitton-Brown, A.D. "Some Notes on *Agamemnon*," in *Classical Philology.* XLVII (July, 1952), pp. 150–156.

Fletcher, F. *Notes on the* Agamemnon *of Aeschylus.* Oxford: Blackwell, 1949.

Fraenkel, Eduard. *Agamemnon.* Oxford: Clarendon Press, 1950.

Golden, Leon. *In Praise of Prometheus.* Chapel Hill: University of North Carolina Press, 1966, pp. 113–126.

Hooker, J.T. "The Sacrifice of Iphigeneia in the *Agamemnon*," in *Agon.* II (1968), pp. 59–65.

Kitto, H.D.F. "Damn the Tragic Hero," in *Studies in Theatre and Drama.* The Hague: Mouton, 1972, pp. 21–47.

Lawrence, S.E. "Artemis in the *Agamemnon*," in *American Journal of Philology.* XCVII (Summer, 1976), pp. 97–110.

Lawson, J.C. "The *Agamemnon* of Aeschylus," in *Journal of Hellenic Studies.* LIII (1933), p. 112.

Leahy, D.M. "Representation of the Trojan War in Aeschylus' *Agamemnon*," in *American Journal of Philology.* XCV (Spring, 1974), pp. 1–23.

Lebeck, A. *Image and Idea of the* Agamemnon *of Aeschylus.* New York: Columbia University Press, 1964.

Lloyd-Jones, H. "The Guilt of Agamemnon," in *Classical Quarterly.* XII (1962), pp. 187–199.

Olson, E. "The *Agamemnon*," in *Tragedy and the Theory of Drama.* Detroit: Wayne State University Press, 1966, pp. 171–194.

Pope, M. "Merciful Heavens? A Question in Aeschylus' *Agamemnon*," in *Journal of Hellenic Studies.* XCIV (1974), pp. 100–113.

Quincey, J.H. "The Beacon-sites in the *Agamemnon*," in *Journal of Hellenic Studies*. LXXXIII (1963), pp. 118–132.

Sidgwick, Arthur. *Aeschylus:* Agamemnon. Oxford: Clarendon Press, 1898.

Smethurst, M.J. "Authority of the Elders (the *Agamemnon* of Aeschylus)," in *Classical Philology*. LXVII (July, 1972), pp. 89–93.

Tracy, H.L. "Dramatic Art in Aeschylus' *Agamemnon*," in *Classical Journal*. XLVII (December, 1951), pp. 151, 215–218.

Whallon, W. "Why Is Artemis Angry?" in *American Journal of Philology*. LXXXII (January, 1961), pp. 78–88.

Young, D.C.C. "Gentler Medicines in the *Agamemnon*," in *Classical Quarterly*. XIV (1964), pp. 1–14.

Libation Bearers

Diggle, J. "Transposition in the *Choephori*," in *Classical Review*. XX (December, 1970), pp. 267–269.

Golden, Leon. *In Praise of Prometheus*. Chapel Hill: University of North Carolina Press, 1966, pp. 79–87.

Hamburger, K. "Electra," in *From Sophocles to Sartre*. New York: Frederick Ungar, 1969, pp. 45–68.

————. "Orestes," in *From Sophocles to Sartre*. New York: Frederick Ungar, 1969, pp. 22–44.

Kenna, J.E.G. "The Return of Orestes," in *Journal of Hellenic Studies*. LXXXI (1961), pp. 99–104.

Lebeck, A. "First Stasimon of Aeschylus' *Choephori*: Myth and Mirror Image," in *Classical Philology*. LXII (July, 1967), pp. 182–185.

Lloyd-Jones, H. *The Libation Bearers*. Englewood Cliffs, N.J.: Prentice-Hall, 1970.

Sidgwick, Arthur. *Choephori*. Oxford: Clarendon Press, 1892.

Oresteia

Barthes, Roland. "Putting on the Greeks," in *Critical Essays*. Evanston, Ill.: Northwestern University Press, 1972, pp. 60–66.

Burke, Kenneth. "Form and Persecution in the *Oresteia*," in *Language as Symbolic Action*. Berkeley: University of California Press, 1966, pp. 125–138.

Cole, J.R. "The *Oresteia* and Cimon," in *Harvard Studies in Classical Philology*. LXXXI (1977), pp. 99–111.

Conacher, D.J. "Interaction Between Chorus and Characters in the *Oresteia*," in *American Journal of Philology*. XCV (Winter, 1974), pp. 323–343.

Dodds, E.R. "Morals and Politics in the *Oresteia*," in *Proceedings of the Cambridge Philological Society*. VI (1960), pp. 19–31.

Downs, R.B.   "Father of Tragedy: Aeschylus," in *Famous Books, Ancient and Medieval.* New York: Barnes & Noble, 1964, pp. 43–48.

Gassner, John.   *"Oresteia*: Dramatic Form and Vision," in *Dramatic Soundings.* Edited by Glenn Loney. New York: Crown, 1968, pp. 3–20.

Golden, Leon.   *In Praise of Prometheus.* Chapel Hill: University of North Carolina Press, 1966, pp. 79–97.

Hamburger, K.   *"Orestes,"* in *From Sophocles to Sartre.* New York: Frederick Ungar, 1969, pp. 22–44.

Harris, G.   "Furies, Witches, and Mothers," in *The Character of Kinship.* Edited by Jack Goody. New York: Cambridge University Press, 1974, pp. 145–159.

Kott, J.   *"Orestes, Electra, Hamlet,"* in *The Eating of the Gods.* New York: Random House, 1973, pp. 240–267.

Lattimore, R.   *Oresteia: Agamemnon, The Libation Bearers, The Eumenides.* Chicago: University of Chicago Press, 1958.

Miller, D.L.   "Orestes: Myth and Dream as Catharsis," in *Myths, Dreams, and Religion.* Edited by Joseph Campbell. New York: Dutton, 1970, pp. 26–47.

Peradotto, J.J.   "Cledonomancy in the *Oresteia,*" in *American Journal of Philology.* XC (January, 1969), pp. 1–21.

Reiter, Seymour.   "The Trilogy as a Dramatic Form," in *World Theater; The Structure and Meaning of Drama.* New York: Horizon Press, 1973, pp. 138–145.

Rexroth, Kenneth.   "Aeschylus: The *Oresteia,*" in *Classics Revisited.* Chicago: Quadrangle Books, 1968, pp. 46–50.

Vellacott, P.   "Has Good Prevailed? A Further Study of the *Oresteia,*" in *Harvard Studies in Classical Philology.* LXXXI (1977), pp. 113–122.

Versenyi, L.   "The *Oresteia,"* in *Man's Message.* Albany: State University of New York Press, 1974, pp. 162–207.

Warner, Rex.   *The Oresteia.* New York: A. Colish, 1961.

The Persians

Avery, Harry C.   "Dramatic Devices in Aeschylus' *Persians,*" in *American Journal of Philology.* LXXXV (1964), pp. 173–184.

Bernhardt, W.W.   "Note on the Structure and Rhetoric in Aeschylus' *Persae,*" in *Essays in Criticism.* XVI (April, 1966), pp. 207–211.

Broadhead, Henry Dan.   Persae *of Aeschylus.* London: Cambridge University Press, 1960.

Clifton, G.   "The mood of the *Persai* of Aeschylus," in *Greece and Rome.* X (October, 1963), pp. 111–116.

Diggle, J. "Notes on the *Agamemnon* and *Persae* of Aeschylus," in *Classical Review.* XVIII (March, 1968), pp. 1–4.

Gagarin, Michael. *Aeschylean Drama.* Berkeley: University of California Press, 1976, pp. 31–56.

Golden, Leon. *In Praise of Prometheus.* Chapel Hill: University of North Carolina Press, 1966, pp. 31–41.

Harmon, A.M. "The Scene of the *Persians* of Aeschylus," in *Transactions of the American Philological Association.* LXIII (1932), pp. 7–19.

Ireland, S. "Dramatic Structure in the *Persae* and *Prometheus* of Aeschylus," in *Greece and Rome.* XX (1973), pp. 162–168.

Murray, Gilbert. "The *Persea*," in *Aeschylus: A Collection of Critical Essays.* Englewood Cliffs, N.J.: Prentice-Hall, 1972, pp. 29–39.

————. *The Persians.* New York: Oxford University Press, 1939.

Sidgwick, Arthur. *Aeschylus' Persae.* Oxford: Clarendon Press, 1903.

Winnington-Ingram, R.P. "Zeus in the *Persae*," in *Journal of Hellenic Studies.* XCIII (1973), pp. 210–229.

Prometheus Bound

Ballard, E.G. "The Unbinding of Prometheus," in *Classical Journal.* L (1955), pp. 217–220.

Downs, R.B. "Father of Tragedy: Aeschylus" in *Famous Books, Ancient and Medieval.* New York: Barnes & Noble, 1964.

Farnell, L.R. "The Paradox of the *Prometheus Vinctus*," in *Journal of Hellenic Studies.* LIII (1933), pp. 40–50.

Fitton-Brown, A.D. "*Prometheia*," in *Journal of Hellenic Studies.* LXXIX (1959), pp. 52–61.

Fowler, Barbara H. "The Imagery of the *Prometheus Bound*," in *American Journal of Philology.* LXXVIII (1957), pp. 173–184.

Gagarin, Michael. *Aeschylean Drama.* Berkeley: University of California Press, 1976, pp. 132–136.

Golden, Leon. *In Praise of Prometheus.* Chapel Hill: University of North Carolina Press, 1966, pp. 100–113.

Herington, C.J. *The Author of the* Prometheus Bound. Austin: University of Texas Press, 1970.

————. "A Study in the *Prometheia*: Part I: The Elements in the Trilogy," in *Phoenix.* XVII (1963), pp. 180–199.

————. "A Study in the *Prometheia*: Part II: Birds and the *Prometheia*, in *Phoenix.* XVII (1963), pp. 236–243.

Ireland, S. "Dramatic Structure in the *Persae* and *Prometheus* of Aeschylus," in *Greece and Rome.* XX (1973), pp. 162–168.

Konstan, D. "The Ocean Episode in the *Prometheus Bound*," in *History of Religions*. XVII (August, 1977), pp. 61–72.

Kott, J. "The Vertical Axis, or, The Ambiguities of *Prometheus*," in *The Eating of the Gods*. New York: Random House, 1973, pp. 3–42.

Musurillo, H. "Particles in the *Prometheus Bound*," in *Classical Philology*. LXV (July, 1970), pp. 175–177.

Thompson, George. "*Prometheia*," in *Aeschylus: A Collection of Critical Essays*. Edited by Marsh H. McCall. Englewood Cliffs, N.J.: Prentice-Hall, 1972, pp. 124–147.

Tracy, S.V. "*Prometheus Bound*," in *Harvard Studies in Classical Philology*. LXXV, (1971), pp. 59–62.

Robertson, D.S. "Prometheus and Chiron," in *Journal of Hellenic Studies*. LXXI (1951), pp. 150–155.

Yu, A.C. "New Gods and Old. Tragic Theology in the *Prometheus Bound*," in *Journal of the American Academy of Religion*. XXXIX (1971), pp. 19–42.

Seven Against Thebes

Brown, A.L. "The End of *Seven Against Thebes*," in *Classical Quarterly*. XXVI (1976), pp. 206–219.

Burnett, A.P. "Curse and Dream in Aeschylus' *Septem*," in *Greek, Roman, and Byzantine Studies*. XIV (1973), pp. 343–368.

Cameron, H.D. "The Debt to Earth in the *Seven Against Thebes*," in *Transactions of the American Philological Association*. XCV (1964), pp. 1–8.

————. "The Power of Words in the *Seven Against Thebes*," in *Transactions of the American Philological Association*. CI (1970), pp. 95–118.

————. *Studies of the* Seven Against Thebes *of Aeschylus*. New York: Humanities Press, 1968.

Dawe, R.D. "The End of *Seven Against Thebes*," in *Classical Quarterly*. XVII (1967), pp. 16–28.

Gagarin, Michael. *Aeschylean Drama*. Berkeley: University of California Press, 1976, pp. 120–127, 151–162.

Golden, Leon. *In Praise of Prometheus*. Chapel Hill: University of North Carolina Press, 1966, pp. 42–61.

Lloyd-Jones, H. "The End of the *Seven Against Thebes*," in *Classical Quarterly*. IX (1959), pp. 80–115.

Otis, Brooks. "The Unity of *Seven Against Thebes*," in *Greek, Roman, and Byzantine Studies*. III (1960), pp. 145–174.

Podlecki, A.J. "The Character of Eteocles in Aeschylus' *Septem*," in *Transactions of the American Philological Association*. XCV (1964), pp. 283–299.

Rosenmeyer, T. "*Seven Against Thebes*: The Tragedy of War," in *Arion.* I (Spring, 1962), pp. 48–78.

Sidgwick, Arthur. *Aeschylus:* Septem Contra Thebas. Oxford: Clarendon Press, 1903.

Solmsen, F. "The Erinys in Aeschylus' *Septem*," in *Transactions of the American Philological Association.* LXVIII (1937), pp. 197–220.

Stothard, P. "*Seven Against Thebes*: Criticism," in *Plays and Players.* XXIV (July, 1977), pp. 24–25.

Tucker, T.G. *The* Seven Against Thebes *of Aeschylus.* Cambridge, Mass.: Harvard University Press, 1908.

The Suppliants

Caldwell, R.S. "The Psychology of Aeschylus' *Supplices*," in *Arethusa.* VII (1974), pp. 45–70.

Finley, John Huston. "The *Suppliants*," in *Aeschylus: A Collection of Critical Essays.* Edited by Marsh H. McCall. Englewood Cliffs, N.J.: Prentice-Hall, 1972, pp. 63–72.

Gagarin, Michael. *Aeschylean Drama.* Berkeley: University of California Press, 1976, pp. 127–132.

Garvie, A.F. *Aeschylus'* Supplices*: Play and Trilogy.* London: Cambridge University Press, 1969.

Golden, Leon. *In Praise of Prometheus.* Chapel Hill: University of North Carolina Press, 1966, pp. 100–113.

Lembke, J. "Aeschylus' *Suppliants*: Design in a Beholder's Eye," in *Arion.* I (1973–74), pp. 627–639.

Murray, Gilbert. *The Suppliant Women (Supplices).* London: Allen and Unwin, 1959.

Murray, R.D. *Motif of Io in Aeschylus'* Suppliants. Princeton, N.J.: Princeton University Press, 1958.

Podlecki, A.J. "Politics in Aeschylus' *Supplices*," in *Classical Folia.* XXVI (1972), pp. 64–71.

Spier, H. "The Motive for the Suppliants' Flight," in *Classical Journal.* LVII (April, 1962), pp. 315–317.

AESOP
(fl. Sixth century B.C.)

Aesop's Fables

Chesterton, G.K. "Aesop's *Fables*," in *The Spice of Life and Other Essays.* Chester Springs, Penn.: Dufour, 1966, pp. 61–65.

Clark, G. "Henryson and Aesop: The Fable Transformed," in *ELH.* XLIII (Spring, 1976), pp. 1–18.

Downs, Robert Bingham. "Famed Fabulist; Aesop," in *Famous Books, Ancient and Medieval.* New York: Barnes & Noble, 1964, pp. 31–35.

Jacobs, Joseph, Editor. *The Fables of Aesop.* New York: Burt Franklin, 1889.

Kovacs, R.C.D. *The Aesopic Fable in Ancient Rhetorical Theory and Practice.* Urbana: University of Illinois Press, 1950.

Kubler, G. *The Shape of Time.* New Haven, Conn.: Yale University Press, 1962.

Noel, Thomas. "Aesop As a Popular Figure and the Fable in England," in *Theories of the Fable in the Eighteenth Century.* New York: Columbia University Press, 1975, pp. 25–37.

Perry, Ben Edwin. *Studies in the Text History of the Life and* Fables *of Aesop.* Haverford, Pa.: American Philological Association, 1936.

JAMES AGEE
(1909–1955)

A Death in the Family

Dupee, F.W. "The Prodigious James Agee," in *New Leader*. XL (December 9, 1957), pp. 20–21.

Frohock, W.M. *The Novel of Violence in America*. Dallas: Southern Methodist University Press, 1957, pp. 225–229.

Hoffman, F.J. *The Art of Southern Fiction*. Carbondale: Southern Illinois University Press, 1967, pp. 75–77.

Kazin, Alfred. *Contemporaries*. Boston: Little, Brown, 1962, pp. 185–187.

MacDonald, Dwight. "Death of a Poet," in *New Yorker*. XXXIII (November 16, 1957), pp. 224–241.

Milner, J.O. "Autonomy and Communion in *A Death in the Family*," in *Tennessee Studies in Literature*. XXI (1977), pp. 105–113.

Ohlin, Peter H. *Agee*. New York: McDowell, McDowell, Oblensky, 1966, pp. 194–214.

Perry, J. Douglas, Jr. "Thematic Counterpoint in *A Death in the Family*: The Function of the Six Extra Scenes," in *Novel*. V (1972), pp. 234–241.

Roe, Michael Morris. "A Point of Focus in James Agee's *A Death in the Family*," in *Twentieth Century Literature*. XII (October, 1966), pp. 149–153.

Rorse, J. "James Agee, Southern Literature and the Domain of Literature," in *South Atlantic Quarterly*. LXXVI (Summer, 1977), pp. 309–317.

Ruhe, Edward. "*A Death in the Family*," in *Epoch*. VIII (Winter, 1958), pp. 247–251.

Ruoff, Gene W. "*A Death in the Family*: Agee's 'Unfinished Novel,' " in *The Fifties: Fiction, Poetry, Drama*. Edited by Warren French. Deland, Fla.: Everett/Edwards, 1973, pp. 121–132.

Seib, Kenneth. *James Agee: Promise and Fulfillment*. Pittsburgh: University of Pittsburgh Press, 1968, pp. 73–96.

Shepherd, Allen. "A Sort of Monstrous Grinding Beauty: Reflections on Character and Theme in James Agee's *A Death in the Family*," in *Iowa English Yearbook*. XIV (1969), pp. 17–24.

Sosnoski, James J. "Craft and Intention in James Agee's *A Death in the Family*," in *Journal of General Education*. XX (October, 1968), pp. 170–183.

Stuckey, W.J. *The Pulitzer Prize Novels: A Critical Backward Look*. Norman: University of Oklahoma Press, 1966, pp. 181–184.

Trilling, Lionel. "The Story and the Novel," in *The Griffin*. VII (January, 1958), pp. 4–12.

Let Us Now Praise Famous Men

Chesnick, Eugene. "The Plot Against Fiction: *Let Us Now Praise Famous Men*," in *Southern Literary Journal*. IV (1971), pp. 48–67.

Holder, Alan. "Encounter in Alabama: Agee and the Tenant Farmer," in *Virginia Quarterly Review*. XLII (1966), pp. 189–206.

Hynes, Samuel. "James Agee: *Let Us Now Praise Famous Men*," in *Landmarks of American Writing*. Edited by Henig Cohen. New York: Basic Books, 1969, pp. 328–340.

Kramer, Victor A. "Agee's *Let Us Now Praise Famous Men*: Image of Tenant Life," in *Mississippi Quarterly*. XXV (1972), pp. 405–417.

Rewak, W.J. "James Agee's *Let Us Now Praise Famous Men*: The Shadow over America," in *Tennessee Studies in Literature*. XXI (1977), pp. 91–104.

CONRAD AIKEN
(1899–1973)

The Poetry of Aiken

Aldrich, Jennifer. "The Deciphered Heart: Conrad Aiken's Poetry and Prose Fiction," in *Sewanee Review*. LXXV (Summer, 1967), pp. 485–520.

Beach, Joseph Warren. "Conrad Aiken and T.S. Eliot: Echoes and Overtones," in *PMLA*. LXIX (1954), pp. 753–762.

Blackmur, Richard P. *The Expense of Greatness*. New York: Arrow Editions, 1940, pp. 199–223.

Blanshard, Rufus A. "Pilgrim's Progress: Conrad Aiken's Poetry," in *Texas Quarterly*. I (Winter, 1958), pp. 135–148.

Brown, Calum S. "The Achievement of Conrad Aiken," in *Georgia Review*. XXVII (1973), pp. 477–488.

Denney, Reuel. *Conrad Aiken*. Minneapolis: University of Minnesota Press, 1964.

Gregory, Horace and Marya Zaturenska. *A History of American Poetry: 1900–1940*. New York: Harcourt Brace, 1946, pp. 217–225.

Hoffman, Frederick J. *Conrad Aiken*. New York: Twayne, 1962, pp. 69–139.

Kunitz, Stanley. "The Poetry of Conrad Aiken," in *Nation*. CXXXIII (October 14, 1931), pp. 393–394.

Lerner, Arthur. *Psychoanalytically Oriented Criticism of Three American Poets: Poe, Whitman, and Aiken*. Cranbury, N.J.: Fairleigh Dickinson University Press, 1970, pp. 84–107.

Martin, Jay. *Conrad Aiken: A Life of His Art*. Princeton, N.J.: Princeton University Press, 1962, pp. 3–66, 102–187.

Peterson, Houston. *The Melody of Chaos*. New York: Longmans, Green, 1931.

Tate, Allen. "Conrad Aiken's Poetry," in *Nation*. CXXII (January 13, 1926), pp. 38–39.

PEDRO ANTONIO DE ALARCÓN
(1833–1891)

The Three-Cornered Hat

Colford, William E. "Introduction," in *The Three-Cornered Hat*. By Pedro de Alarcón. Woodbury, New York: Barron's Educational Series, 1958, pp. i–xiii.

Hodge, H.S. Vere. "*The Three-Cornered Hat*," in *Saturday Review*. CLVI (July 22, 1933), p. 104.

Medina, Jeremy T. "Structural Techniques of Alarcon's *El sombrero de tres picos*," in *Romance Notes*. XIV (1972), pp. 83–85.

Place, Edwin B. "The Antecedents of *El sombrero de tres picos*," in *Philological Quarterly*. VIII (January, 1929), pp. 39–42.

Turner, H.F. "Introduction," in *The Three-Cornered Hat*. By Pedro Antonio de Alarcón. London: John Calder, 1959, pp. 1–5.

Warren, L.A. *Modern Spanish Literature*, Volume I. London: Brentano's, 1929, pp. 113–114.

Winslow, Richard W. "The Distinction of Structure in Alarcón's *El sombrero de tres picos* and *El capitan veneno*," in *Hispania*. XLVI (December, 1963), pp. 715–720.

EDWARD ALBEE
(1928–   )

The American Dream

Balliett, Whitney.   "Three Cheers for Albee," in *New Yorker*. XXXVI (February 4, 1961), pp. 62, 64–66.

Bigsby, C.W.E.   *Confrontation and Commitment, A Study of Contemporary American Dreams, 1959–1966*. Columbia: University of Missouri Press, 1968, pp. 71, 75–79.

Brustein, Robert.   "Fragments from a Cultural Explosion," in *New Republic*. CXLIV (March 27, 1961), p. 30.

Canaday, Nicholas.   "Albee's *The American Dream* and the Existential Vacuum," in *South Central Bulletin*. XXVI (1966), pp. 28–34.

Clurman, Harold.   "Theatre," in *Nation*. CXCII (February 11, 1961), pp. 125–126.

Debusscher, Gilbert.   *Edward Albee, Tradition and Renewal*. Brussels: American Studies Center, 1967, pp. 35–46.

Driver, Tom.   "A Milestone and a Fumble," in *Christian Century*. LXXVIII (March 1, 1961), p. 275.

Gassner, John.   "Broadway in Review," in *Educational Theatre Journal*. XIII (May, 1961), pp. 109–110.

Gelbert, Roger.   "Albee et al," in *New Statesman*. LXII (November 3, 1961), pp. 667–668.

Hamilton, Kenneth.   "Mr. Albee's Dream," in *Queen's Quarterly*. LXX (August, 1963), pp. 393–399.

Hatch, Robert.   "Arise Ye Playgoers of the World," in *Horizon*. III (July, 1961), pp. 116–117.

Hewes, Henry.   "On Our Bad Behaviour," in *Saturday Review*. XLIV (February 11, 1961), p. 54.

Popkin, Henry.   "Theatre Chronicle," in *Sewanee Review*. LXIX (1961), pp. 342–343.

Pryce-Jones, Alan.   "Alan Pryce-Jones at the Theatre," in *Theatre Arts*. XLV (March, 1961), p. 68.

Rutenberg, Michael.   *Edward Albee: Playwright in Protest*. New York: D.B.S. Publications, 1969, pp. 61–76.

Samuels, Charles T.   "The Theatre of Edward Albee," in *Massachusetts Review*. VI (1964–1965), pp. 191–193.

Trotta, G.   "On Stage: Edward Albee," in *Horizon*. IV (September, 1961), p. 79.

Wellworth, George.   *The Theatre of Protest and Paradox: Development in the Avant-Garde Drama.* New York: New York University Press, 1964, pp. 278–282.

The Ballad of the Sad Café

Bigsby, C.W.E.   "Edward Albee's Georgia Ballad," in *Twentieth Century Literature.* XIII (January, 1968), pp. 229–236.

Brustein, Robert.   "The Playwright as Impersonator," in *New Republic.* CXLIX (November 16, 1963), pp. 28–29.

Clurman, Harold.   "Theatre," in *Nation.* CXCVII (November 23, 1963), pp. 353–354.

Gilman, Richard.   "Albee's Sad Ballad," in *Commonweal.* LXXIX (November 22, 1963), pp. 256–257.

Hewes, Henry.   "Dismemberment of the Wedding," in *Saturday Review.* XLVI (November 16, 1963), p. 54.

Kostelanetz, Richard.   "Albee's Sad Cafe," in *Sewanee Review.* LXXII (1964), pp. 724–726.

Lewis, Theophilus.   "Theatre," in *America.* CX (January 4, 1964), p. 26.

McCarten, John.   "Tormented Trio," in *New Yorker.* XXXIX (November 9, 1963), p. 95.

Morse, Ben.   "Three Ballads," in *Players Magazine.* XL (1964), p. 138.

Simon, John.   "Theatre Chronicle," in *Hudson Review.* XVII (Spring, 1964), pp. 81–83.

Sontag, Susan.   "Going to the Theatre," in *Partisan Review.* XXXI (Winter, 1964), pp. 97–98.

Von Dreele, W.H.   "A Master Carpenter," in *National Review.* XVI (January 14, 1964), pp. 34–35.

The Death of Bessie Smith

Balliett, Whitney.   "Empress of the Blues," in *New Yorker.* XXXVII (March 11, 1961), p. 114.

Brustein, Robert.   "Fragments from a Cultural Explosion," in *New Republic.* CXLIV (March 27, 1961), pp. 29–30.

————.   *Seasons of Discontent.* New York: Simon and Schuster, 1965, pp. 46–48.

Clurman, Harold.   "Theatre," in *Nation.* CXCII (March 18, 1961), p. 242.

————.   *The Naked Image; Observations on the Modern Theatre.* New York: Macmillan, 1966, pp. 17–18.

Daniel, W.C.   "Absurdity in *The Death of Bessie Smith*," in *College Language Association Journal.* VIII (September, 1964), pp. 78–80.

Debusscher, Gilbert. *Edward Albee, Tradition and Renewal.* Brussels: American Studies Center, 1967, pp. 21–30.

Gelbert, Roger. "Albee et al," in *New Statesman.* LXII (November 3, 1961), pp. 667–668.

Grande, Luke M. "Edward Albee's *Bessie Smith*: Alienation, The Color Problem," in *Drama Critique.* V (1962), pp. 66–69.

Hatch, Robert. "Arise Ye Playgoers of the World," in *Horizon.* III (July, 1961), pp. 116–117.

Hayes, Richard. "At the Albee,' in *Commonweal.* LIV (August 25, 1961), pp. 471–472.

Lukas, Mary. "*The Death of Bessie Smith* and *The American Dream,*" in *Catholic World.* CXCIII (August, 1961), pp. 335–336.

Rutenberg, Michael. *Edward Albee: Playwright in Protest.* New York: D.B.S. Publications, 1969, pp. 79–92.

Samuels, Charles T. "The Theatre of Edward Albee," in *Massachusetts Review.* VI (1964–1965), pp. 189–190.

Wellworth, George. *The Theatre of Protest and Paradox.* New York: New York University Press, 1964.

Witherington, Paul. "Language of Movement in Albee's *The Death of Bessie Smith,*" in *Twentieth Century Literature.* XIII (July, 1967), pp. 84–88.

A Delicate Balance

Bierhaus, E.G., Jr. "Strangers in a Room: *A Delicate Balance* Revisited," in *Modern Drama.* XVII (1974), pp. 199–206.

Bigsby, C.W. "The Strategy of Madness: An Analysis of Edward Albee's *A Delicate Balance,*" in *Wisconsin Studies in Contemporary Literature.* IX (Spring, 1968), pp. 223–235.

Brown, Terence. "Harmonic Discord and Stochastic Process: Edward Albee's *A Delicate Balance,*" in *Re: Arts and Letters.* III (1970), pp. 54–60.

Brustein, Robert. "Albee Decorates an Old House," in *New Republic.* CLV (October 8, 1966), pp. 35–36.

Clurman, Harold. "Theatre," in *Nation.* CCIII (October 10, 1966), pp. 361–363.

Croce, Arlene. "New-Old, Old-New, and New," in *National Review.* XIX (January 24, 1967), pp. 99–100.

Hardwick, Elizabeth. "Straight Play: *A Delicate Balance,*" in *New York Review of Books.* VII (October 20, 1966), pp. 4–5.

Nelson, Gerald. "Edward Albee and His Well-Made Plays," in *Tri-Quarterly.* V (1966), pp. 182–188.

Post, Robert M. "Fear Itself: Edward Albee's *A Delicate Balance*," in *College Language Association Journal*. XIII (1969), pp. 163–171.

Pryce-Jones, Alan. "The Theatre of Edward Albee," in *Listener*. LXXVI (November 24, 1966), pp. 763–764.

Sheed, Wilfred. "*A Delicate Balance*," in *The Morning After: Selected Essays and Reviews*. New York: Farrar, Straus, 1971, pp. 165–167.

————. "Liquor Is Thicker," in *Commonweal*. LXXXV (October 14, 1966), pp. 55–56.

Simon, John. "Should Albee Have Said 'No Thanks?,' " in *Singularities: Essays on the Theatre/1964–1973*. New York: Random House, 1975, pp. 58–64.

————. "Theatre Chronicle," in *Hudson Review*. XIX (Winter, 1966–1967), pp. 627–629.

Szeliski, John J. Von. "Albee: A Rare Balance," in *Twentieth Century Literature*. XVI (1970), pp. 123–130.

Tiny Alice

Ballew, L.M. "Who's Afraid of Tiny Alice?" in *Georgia Review*. XX (1966), pp. 292–299.

Bigsby, C.W. "Curiouser and Curiouser: A Study of Edward Albee's *Tiny Alice*," in *Modern Drama*. X (1967), pp. 258–266.

Brustein, Robert. *Seasons of Discontent*. New York: Simon and Schuster, 1965, pp. 307–311.

————. "Three Plays and a Protest," in *New Republic*. CLII (January 23, 1965), pp. 33–34.

Davison, Richard Alan. "Edward Albee's *Tiny Alice*: A Note of Re-examination," in *Modern Drama*. XI (May, 1968), pp. 54–60.

Dukore, B.F. "*Tiny Albee*," in *Drama Survey*. V (1966), pp. 60–66.

Hewes, Henry. "The *Tiny Alice* Caper," in *Saturday Review*. XLVII (January 30, 1964), pp. 38–39, 65.

————. "Through the Looking Glass, Darkly," in *Saturday Review*. XLVIII (January 16, 1965), p. 40.

Lipton, Edward. "The *Tiny Alice* Enigma," in *Saturday Review*. XLVIII (February 20, 1965), p. 21.

Lucey, William F. "Albee's Tiny Alice: Truth and Appearance," in *Renascence*. XXI (1969), pp. 76–80, 110.

McCarten, John. "Mystical Manipulations," in *New Yorker*. XL (January 9, 1965), p. 84.

Markson, J.W. "Tiny Alice: Edward Albee's Negative Oedipal Enigma," in *American Imago*. XXIII (1966), pp. 3–21.

Markus, T.B.   "Tiny Alice and Tragic Catharsis," in *Educational Theatre Journal.* XVII (October, 1965), pp. 225–233.

Martin, Paulette.   "A Theatre of Mystery," in *Commonweal.* LXXXIV (September 16, 1966), pp. 582–585.

Rogoff, Gordon.   "The Trouble with Alice," in *Reporter.* XXXII (January 28, 1965), pp. 53–54.

Roth, Phillip.   "The Play That Dare Not Speak Its Name," in *New York Review of Books.* IV (February 25, 1965), p. 4.

Rutenberg, Michael.   *Edward Albee: Playwright in Protest.* New York: D.B.S. Publications, 1969, pp. 119–134.

Sheed, Wilfred.   "The Stage," in *Commonweal.* LXXXI (January 22, 1965), p. 543.

Simon, John.   "Theatre Chronicle," in *Hudson Review.* XVIII (Spring, 1965), pp. 81–84.

Valgemae, Mardi.   "Albee's Great God Alice," in *Modern Drama.* X (December, 1967), pp. 267–273.

Who's Afraid of Virginia Woolf?

Adler, Thomas P.   "Albee's *Who's Afraid of Virginia Woolf?*: A Long Day's Journey into Night," in *Educational Theatre Journal.* XXV (1973), pp. 66–70.

Bigsby, C.W.   "*Who's Afraid of Virginia Woolf?*: Edward Albee's Morality Play," in *Journal of American Studies.* I (October, 1967), pp. 257–268.

Dollard, John.   "The Hidden Meaning of *Who's Afraid. . .?*," in *Connecticut Review.* VII, (1973), pp. 24–48.

Dozier, Richard J.   "Adultery and Disappointment in *Who's Afraid of Virginia Woolf?*," in *Modern Drama.* XI (1969), pp. 432–436.

Fischer, Gretl K.   "Edward Albee and Virginia Woolf," in *Dalhousie Review.* XLIX (1969), pp. 196–207.

Gilman, Richard.   Here We Go Round the Albee Bush," in *Common and Uncommon Masks: Writings on the Theatre, 1961–1970.* New York: Random House, 1971, pp. 133–136.

Halperen, Max.   "What Happens in *Who's Afraid. . .?*," in *Modern American Drama: Essays in Criticism.* Edited by William E. Taylor. DeLand, Fla.: Everett/Edwards, 1968, pp. 129–143.

Hazard, Forrest E.   "The Major Theme in *Who's Afraid of Virginia Woolf?*," in *CEA Critic.* XXXI, (December, 1968), pp. 10–11.

Hilfer, Anthony C.   "George and Martha: Sad, Sad, Sad," in *Seven Contemporary Authors: Essays on Cozzens, Miller, West, Golding, Heller, Albee, and Powers.* Austin: University of Texas Press, 1966, pp. 119–139.

Holtan, Orly. *"Who's Afraid of Virginia Woolf?* and the Patterns of History," in *Educational Theatre Journal.* XXV, 1973, pp. 46–52.

McDonald, Daniel. "Truth and Illusion in *Who's Afraid of Virginia Woolf?,"* in *Renascence.* XVII (Winter, 1964), pp. 63–69.

Meyer, Ruth. "Language: Truth and Illusion in *Who's Afraid of Virginia Woolf?,"* in *Educational Theatre Journal.* XX (1968), pp. 60–69.

Norton, Rictor. "Folklore and Myth in *Who's Afraid of Virginia Woolf?,"* in *Renascence.* XXIII (1971), pp. 159–167.

Paul, Louis. "A Game Analysis of Albee's *Who's Afraid of Virginia Woolf?:* The Core of Grief," in *Literature and Psychology.* XVII (November, 1967), pp. 47–51.

Porter, Thomas E. "Fun and Games in Surburbia: *Who's Afraid of Virginia Woolf?,"* in *Myth and Modern American Drama.* Detroit: Wayne State University Press, 1969, pp. 225–247.

Quinn, James P. "Myths and Romance in Albee's *Who's Afraid of Virginia Woolf?,"* in *Arizona Quarterly.* XXX (1974), pp. 197–204.

Roy, Emil. *"Who's Afraid of Virginia Woolf?* and the Tradition," in *Bucknell Review.* XIII (March, 1965), pp. 27–36.

Samuels, C.T. "The Theatre of Edward Albee," in *Massachusetts Review.* VI (1964–1965), pp. 187–201.

Schechner, Richard. "Who's Afraid of Edward Albee?," in *Tulane Drama Review.* VII (1963), pp. 7–10.

Schneider, Alan. "Why So Afraid?," in *Tulane Drama Review.* VII (1963), pp. 10–13.

Simon, John. "Theatre Chronicle," in *Hudson Review.* XV (Winter, 1962–1963), pp. 571–573.

Von Dreele, W.H. "The Twentieth Century and All That," in *National Review.* XIV (January 15, 1963), pp. 35–36.

Weatherby, W.J. "Albee on Broadway," in *Manchester Guardian* (October 15, 1962), p. 7.

The Zoo Story

Bigsby, C.W.E. *Confrontation and Commitment: A Study of Contemporary American Drama.* Columbia: University of Missouri Press, 1968, pp. 71–75, 84–85.

Brustein, Robert. *Seasons of Discontent.* New York: Simon and Schuster, 1965, pp. 28–29.

Clurman, Harold. "Theatre," in *Nation.* CXC (February 13, 1966), pp. 153–154.

————. *The Naked Image; Observations on the Modern Theatre.* New York: Macmillan, 1966, pp. 14–15.

Debusscher, Gilbert. *Edward Albee: Tradition and Renewal.* Brussels: American Studies Center, 1967, pp. 9–20.

Kostelanetz, Richard. *The New American Arts.* New York: Horizon Press, 1965, pp. 50–55.

Lester, Bill. "*This Property Is Condemned* and *The Zoo Story*," in *Plays and Players.* VIII (October, 1960), p. 13.

Levine, Mordecai H. "Albee's Liebestod," in *College Language Association Journal.* X (1967), pp. 252–255.

Lewis, Theophilus. "Theatre," in *America.* CVIII (June 22, 1963), pp. 891–892.

Macklin, Anthony. "The Flagrant Albatross," in *College English.* XXVIII (1966), pp. 58–59.

Malcolm, Donald. "Off-Broadway," in *New Yorker.* XXXV (January 23, 1960), pp. 75–76.

Newman, David. "Four Make a Wave," in *Esquire.* LV (April, 1961), pp. 48–58.

Platinsky, M.L. "The Transformations of Understanding: Edward Albee in the Theatre of the Irresolute," in *Drama Survey.* IV (1965), pp. 220–232.

Richards, Stanley. "On and Off Broadway," in *Players Magazine.* XXXVII (October, 1960), p. 10.

Rutenberg, Michael. *Edward Albee: Playwright in Protest.* New York: D.B.S. Publications, 1969, pp. 15–37.

Sheed, Wilfred. "Back to the Zoo," in *Commonweal.* LXXXII (July 9, 1965), pp. 501–502.

Spielberg, Peter. "The Albatross in Albee's Zoo," in *College English.* XXVII (1966), pp. 562–565.

Wellworth, George. *The Theatre of Protest and Paradox: Developments in the Avant-Garde Drama.* New York: New York University Press, 1964, pp. 275–279.

Zimbardo, R.A. "Symbolism and Naturalism in Edward Albee's *The Zoo Story*," in *Twentieth Century Literature.* VIII (April, 1962), pp. 10–17.

LOUISA MAY ALCOTT
(1832–1888)

Little Women

Auerbach, Nina. "Austen and Alcott on Matriarchy: New Women or New Wives?," in *Novel, a Forum on Fiction.* X (Fall, 1976), pp. 6–26.

Brophy, Brigid. *Don't Never Forget: Collected Views and Reviews.* New York: Holt, Rinehart, 1966, pp. 113–120.

Crompton, Margaret. "*Little Women*: The Making of a Classic," in *Contemporary Review.* CCXVIII (February, 1971), pp. 99–104.

Janeway, Elizabeth. "Meg, Jo, Beth, Amy and Louisa," in *New York Times Book Review.* LXXIII (September 29, 1968), p. 42.

CIRO ALEGRIA
(1909–1967)

Broad and Alien Is the World

Endres, Valeria. "The Role of Animals in *El Mundo es Ancho y Ajeno*," in *Hispania*. XLVIII (1965), pp. 67–69.

Escabar, Alberto. "Ciro Alegria's Worlds," in *Americas*. XV (1963), pp. 7–10.

McGourn, Francis T. "The Priest in *El Mundo es Ancho y Ajeno*," in *Romance Notes*. IX (1968), pp. 224–233.

Mate, Hubert E. "Some Aspects of Novels of Lopez y Fuentes and Ciro Alegria," in *Hispania*. XXXIX (1956), pp. 287–292.

Schwartz, Kessel. *A New History of Spanish American Fiction*, Volume II. Coral Gables, Fla.: University of Miami Press, 1971, pp. 60–61.

Spell, Jefferson Rea. "Ciro Alegria, Criollista of Peru," in *Contemporary Spanish-American Fiction*. Chapel Hill: University of North Carolina Press, 1944, pp. 253–268.

Wolfe, Bertram D. "The Novel in Latin America," in *Antioch Review*. III (1943), pp. 191–208.

MATEO ALEMÁN
(1547–1615)

Guzmán de Alfarache

Berberfall, Lester. "The Picaro, in Context," in *Hispania*. XXXVII (September, 1954), pp. 289–292.

Chandler, Richard E. and Kessel Schwartz. *A New History of Spanish Literature*. Baton Rouge: Louisiana State University Press, 1961, pp. 183–184.

Davis, Barbara. "The Style of Mateo Alemán's *Guzmán de Alfarache*," in *Romanic Review*. LXVI (1975), pp. 199–213.

Del Piero, R.A. "The Picaresque Philosophy in *Guzmán de Alfarache*," in *Modern Language Forum*. XLII (December, 1957), pp. 152–156.

Eoff, Sherman. "A Galdosian Version of Picaresque Psychology," in *Modern Language Forum*. XXXVIII (March–June, 1953), pp. 5–9.

————. "The Picaresque Psychology of *Guzmán de Alfarache*," in *Hispanic Review*. XXI (April, 1953), pp. 107–119.

Grass, Roland. "Morality in the Picaresque Novel," in *Hispania*. XLII (May, 1959), pp. 194–196.

Jones, J.A. "The Duality and Complexity of *Guzmán de Alfarache*: Some Thoughts on the Structure and Interpretation of Alemán's Novel," in *Knaves and Swindlers: Essays on the Picaresque Novel in Europe*. Edited by Christine B. Whitborn. London: Oxford University Press, 1974, pp. 24–47.

Merimee, Ernest. *A History of Spanish Literature*. New York: Holt, 1930, pp. 314–316.

Norval, M.N. "Original Sin and the 'Conversion' in the *Guzmán de Alfarache*," in *Bulletin of Hispanic Studies*. LI (1974), pp. 346–364.

Perez, Rosa Perelmuter. "The Rogue as Trickster in *Guzmán de Alfarache*," in *Hispania*. LIX (1976), pp. 820–826.

Randall, Dale. *The Golden Tapestry*. Durham, N.C.: Duke University Press, 1963, pp. 132–134, 174–184.

Stamm, James R. "The Uses and Types of Humor in the Picaresque Novel," in *Hispania*. XLII (December, 1959), pp. 482–485.

Williams, Robert H. "Satirical Rules of Etiquette in the 'Siglo de Oro,' " in *Hispania*. XIII (October, 1930), pp. 293–300.

NELSON ALGREN
(1909–   )

The Man with the Golden Arm

Bluestone, George. "Nelson Algren," in *Western Review*. XXII (1957), pp. 35–39.

Cox, Martha Heasley and Wayne Chatterton. *Nelson Algren*. Boston: Twayne, 1975, pp. 111–133.

Eisinger, Chester E. *Fiction of the Forties*. Chicago: University of Chicago Press, 1963, pp. 81–85.

Geismar, Maxwell. "Nelson Algren: The Iron Sanctuary," in *College English*. XIV (1953), pp. 311–315. Reprinted in *American Moderns: From Rebellion to Conformity*. By Maxwell Geismar. New York: Hill and Wang, 1958, pp. 191–192.

Gelfant, Blanche Housman. *The American City Novel*. Norman: University of Oklahoma Press, 1954, pp. 252–257.

Never Come Morning

Appel, Benjamin. "Labels," in *Tough Guy Writers of the Thirties*. Edited by David Madden. Carbondale: Southern Illinois University Press, 1968, pp. 16–17.

Bluestone, George. "Nelson Algren," in *Western Review*. XXII (1957), pp. 30–33.

Cox, Martha Heasley and Wayne Chatterton. *Nelson Algren*. Boston: Twayne, 1975, pp. 94–110.

Eisinger, Chester E. "Character and Self in the Fiction of the Left," in *Proletarian Writers of the Thirties*. Edited by David Madden. Carbondale: Southern Illinois University Press, 1968, pp. 174–175.

————. *Fiction of the Forties*. Chicago: University of Chicago Press, 1963, pp. 77–80.

Geismar, Maxwell. "Nelson Algren: The Iron Sanctuary," in *College English*. XIV (1953), pp. 312–313. Reprinted in *American Moderns: From Rebellion to Conformity*. By Maxwell Geismar. New York: Hill and Wang, 1958, pp. 189–190.

Umphlett, Wiley Lee. *The Sporting Myth and the American Experience: Studies in Contemporary Fiction*. Lewisburg, Pa.: Bucknell University Press, 1975, pp. 102–109.

Somebody in Boots

Bluestone, George. "Nelson Algren," in *Western Review.* XXII (1957), pp. 27–30.

Cox, Martha Heasley and Wayne Chatterton. *Nelson Algren.* Boston: Twayne, 1975, pp. 59–73.

Eisinger, Chester E. "Character and Self in the Fiction of the Left," in *Proletarian Writers of the Thirties.* Edited by David Madden. Carbondale: Southern Illinois University Press, 1968, pp. 174–175.

————. *Fiction of the Forties.* Chicago: University of Chicago Press, 1963, pp. 76–77.

Ferguson, Otis. "On the Bum," in *New Republic.* LXXXIII (July 17, 1935), p. 286.

A Walk on the Wild Side

Bluestone, George. "Nelson Algren," in *Western Review.* XXII (1957), pp. 40–42.

Cox, Martha Heasley and Wayne Chatterton. *Nelson Algren.* Boston: Twayne, 1975, pp. 73–92.

Farrell, James T. "On the Wrong Side of Town," in *New Republic.* CXXXIV (May 21, 1956), pp. 18–19.

Geismar, Maxwell. "Against the Tide of Euphoria," in *Nation.* CLXXXII (June 2, 1956), p. 473.

Howe, Irving. "Mass Society and Post Modern Fiction," in *The American Novel Since World War II.* Edited by Marcus Klein. Greenwich, Conn.: Fawcett, 1969, pp. 136–137.

Kelly, James. "Sin-Soaked in Storyville," in *Saturday Review.* XXXIX (May 26, 1956), p. 16.

Podhoretz, Norman. "The Man with the Golden Beef," in *New Yorker.* XXXII (June 2, 1956), pp. 120–127.

Rolo, Charles J. "Fiction Chronicle," in *Atlantic.* CXCVII (June, 1956), p. 79.

Widmer, Kingsley. *The Literary Rebel.* Carbondale: Southern Illinois University Press, 1965, pp. 130–131.

JORGE AMADO
(1912–   )

Dona Flor and Her Two Husbands

Clements, R.J. "*Dona Flor and Her Two Husbands*," in *Saturday Review*. LII (August 16, 1969), pp. 22–23.

Fernandez, Oscar. "*Dona Flor and Her Two Husbands*," in *Modern Language Journal*. LIV (May, 1970), pp. 386–387.

Gallagher, David. "*Dona Flor and Her Two Husbands*," in *New York Times Book Review*. (August 17, 1969), p. 33.

Hill, William B. "*Dona Flor and Her Two Husbands*," in *America*. CXXI (November 29, 1969), p. 531.

Wain, John. "The Very Thing," in *New York Review of Books*. XIV (February 26, 1970), pp. 37–38.

Home Is the Sailor

Adams, Phoebe. "Jorge Amado's *Home Is the Sailor*," in *Atlantic*. CCXIII (April, 1964), p. 149.

Grossman, W.L. "The Captain Was All at Sea," in *Saturday Review*. XLVII (March 28, 1964), p. 43.

Peterson, Virgilia. "The Captain and the Sea," in *New York Times Book Review*. (March 22, 1964), p. 4.

West, Anthony. "*Home Is the Sailor*," in *New Yorker*. XL (August 8, 1964), pp. 89–90.

Shepherds of the Night

Duncan, John. "The World of the People," in *New York Times Book Review*. (January 22, 1967), p. 4, 38.

Gerassi, M.N. "The Glory of Poor Living," in *Nation*. CCIV (June 5, 1967), pp. 733–734.

Hales, David. "The Peaceable Kingdom of Bahia," in *Saturday Review*. L (February 4, 1967), p. 45.

Parker, Robert Anthony. "*Shepherds of the Night*," in *America*. CXVI (March 25, 1967), p. 470.

Wain, John. "Versions of Pastoral," in *New York Review of Books*. VIII (May 4, 1967), p. 35–36.

KINGSLEY AMIS
(1922–   )

The Green Man

Bell, Pearl K. "A Tough Act to Follow," in *New Statesman.* LIII (September 21, 1970), pp. 17–18.

Coleman, John. "Mixed Spirits," in *Observer.* (October 12, 1969), p. 33.

Cooper, William. "Away from This Body," in *Listener.* LXXXII (October 9, 1969), pp. 489–490.

Davenport, Guy. "On the Edge of Being," in *National Review.* XXII (August 25, 1970), pp. 903–904.

"Drunk and the Dead," in *Times Literary Supplement.* (London) (October 9, 1969), p. 1145.

Freud, Clement. "Mine Ghost," in *Spectator.* CCXXIII (October 11, 1969), pp. 480–481.

Hope, Francis. "Sobering," in *New Statesman.* LXXVIII (October 10, 1969), pp. 503–504.

McDowell, Frederick P.W. "Time of Plenty: Recent British Novels," in *Contemporary Literature.* XIII (Summer, 1972), pp. 366–368.

Sissman, L.E. "The Aftermath of Anger," in *New Yorker.* XLVI (November 14, 1970), p. 206.

Weeks, Edward. "The Peripatetic Reviewer," in *Atlantic.* CCXXVI (September, 1970), p. 127.

Yardley, Jonathan. "After the One Book," in *New Republic.* CLXIII (September 19, 1970), pp. 27–28.

Lucky Jim

Allen, Walter. *Beat Generation and the Angry Young Men.* London: Souvenir Press, 1959, pp. 339–341.

Alsop, Kenneth. *Angry Decade: A Survey of the Cultural Revolt of the Nineteen-fifties.* London: Peter Owen, 1964, pp. 51–66.

Boyle, Ted and Terence Brown. "The Serious Side of Kingsley Amis's *Lucky Jim,*" in *Critique: Studies in Modern Fiction.* IX (1966), pp. 100–107.

Brophy, Brigid. *Don't Never Forget; Collected Views and Reviews.* New York: Holt, Rinehart & Winston, 1967, pp. 217–222.

———. "Just Jim," in *London Sunday Times Magazine.* (January 26, 1964), pp. 11–13.

Conquest, Robert. "Christian Symbolism in *Lucky Jim,*" in *Critical Quarterly.* VII (Spring, 1965), pp. 87–92.

Dixon, Terrell F. "Chance and Choice in *Lucky Jim*," in *Ball State University Forum.* XVII (1976), pp. 75–80.

Dobrée, Bonamy. "English Poetry Today: The Younger Generation," in *Sewanee Review.* LXII (Autumn, 1954), pp. 598–620.

Fallis, Richard. "*Lucky Jim* and Academic Wishful Thinking," in *Studies in the Novel.* IX (Spring, 1977), pp. 65–72.

Feldman, Gene and Max Gartenberg. *Beat Generation and the Angry Young Men.* New York: Citadel Press, 1958, pp. 339–341.

Gibson, Walker. "You Mustn't Say Things Like That," in *Nation.* CLXXXVII (November 20, 1958), pp. 410–412.

Harkness, Bruce. "The Lucky Crown—Contemporary British Fiction," in *English Journal.* XLVII (October, 1958), pp. 387–397.

Hurrell, John D. "Class and Conscience in John Braine and Kingsley Amis," in *Critique: Studies in Modern Fiction.* II (Spring-Summer, 1958), pp. 39–53.

Lebowitz, Naomi. "Kingsley Amis: The Penitent Hero," in *Perspective.* X (Summer-Autumn, 1957/1959), pp. 129–136.

Lodge, David. "The Modern, the Contemporary and the Importance of Being Kingsley Amis," in *Critical Quarterly.* V (1963), pp. 335–354.

Meckier, Jerome. "Looking Back in Anger: The Success of a Collapsing Stance," in *Dalhousie Review.* LII (1972), pp. 47–58.

Montgomery, John. "Young? Angry? Typical?" in *Books & Bookmen.* XI (December, 1965), pp. 86–89.

Morgan, W. John. "Authentic Voices," in *Twentieth Century.* CLXI (February, 1957), pp. 138–144.

Noon, William T. "Satire: Poison and the Professor," in *English Record.* XI (Fall, 1960), pp. 53–56.

O'Connor, William Van. "Two Types of 'Heroes' in Post-War British Fiction," in *PMLA.* LXXVII (March, 1962), pp. 168–174.

Voorhees, Richard J. "Kingsley Amis: Three Hurrahs and a Reservation," in *Queen's Quarterly.* LXXIX (1972), pp. 40–46.

Wain, John. "A Young Man Who Is Not Angry: How It Strikes a Contemporary," in *Twentieth Century.* CLXI (March, 1957), pp. 227–236.

Webster, Harvey Curtis. "A Scholar's Quest," in *Saturday Review.* XXXVII (February 20, 1954), p. 20.

One Fat Englishman

Barrett, William. "Angry Englishman," in *Atlantic.* CCXIII (April, 1964), pp. 144–145.

Degnan, J.P. "Scourge of the Establishment," in *Commonweal.* LXXX (June 19, 1964), pp. 402–403.

DeMott, Benjamin. "Of Snobs and Taxes and Unimpressed Men," in *Harper's.* CCXXVIII (April, 1964), pp. 106–107.

Furbank, P.N. "Western Approaches," in *Encounter.* XXII (January, 1964), pp. 74–77.

Gardiner, H.C. *"One Fat Englishman,"* in *America.* CX (April 11, 1964), p. 515.

Hamilton, Kenneth. "Kingsley Amis, Moralist," in *Dalhousie Review.* XLIV (Autumn, 1964), pp. 339–347.

Hartley, Anthony. "Everyman in America," in *New Leader.* XLVII (April 27, 1964), pp. 26–27.

Hoyt, Charles Alva. "Pans Across the Sea," in *Saturday Review.* XLVII (March 7, 1964), pp. 38–39.

Jones, D.A.N. "Amis's English Usage," in *New York Review of Books.* II (April 16, 1964), pp. 13–14.

Kelly, Edward. "Satire and Word Games in Amis's *Englishman,*" in *Satire Newsletter.* IX (1972), pp. 132–138.

Kreutz, Irving. "Mrs. Trollope, Move Over," in *Arts in Society.* III (Summer, 1966), pp. 604–608.

Levine, Paul. "Individualism and the Traditional Talent," in *Hudson Review.* XVII (Autumn, 1964), pp. 470–471.

Panter-Downes, Mollie. "That Certain Missing Feeling," in *New Yorker.* XL (June 20, 1964), pp. 134–136.

Powell, Anthony. "Kingsley's Heroes," in *Spectator.* CCXI (November 29, 1963), pp. 709–710.

Ricks, Christopher. "Cant Trap," in *New Statesman.* LXVI (November 19, 1963), pp. 790–792.

Soule, George. "The High Cost of Plunging," in *Carleton Miscellany.* V (Fall, 1964), pp. 106–111.

Weightman, John. "Mr. Amis Goes Metaphysical," in *Observer.* (November 17, 1963), p. 24.

Wood, F.T. "Current Literature 1963," in *English Studies.* XLV (June, 1964), pp. 260–261.

Take a Girl Like You

Bergonzi, Bernard. *The Situation of the Novel.* London: Macmillan 1970, pp. 165–168.

Birstein, Ann. "Round Peg, Square World," in *Reporter.* XXIV (April 13, 1961), pp. 55–56.

Chinneswararao, G.J. "Amis's *Take a Girl Like You,*" in *Indian Journal of English Studies.* XII (December, 1971), pp. 110–114.

Coleman, John. "King of Shaft," in *Spectator*. CCV (September 23, 1960), pp. 445–446.

Cosman, Max. "Take a Novelist Like Amis," in *Commonweal*. LXXIII (March 10, 1961), pp. 615–616.

Enright, D.J. "The New Pastoral-Comical," in *Spectator*. CCVI (February 3, 1961), pp. 154–155.

Fraser, George Sutherland. *The Modern Writer and His World*. London: Deutsch, 1964, pp. 175–179.

Lodge, David. "The Modern, the Contemporary, and the Importance of Being Amis," in *Critical Quarterly*. V (1963), pp. 335–354.

Moers, Ellen. "Still Angry," in *Commentary*. XXXI (June, 1961), pp. 542–544.

Parker, R.B. "Farce and Society: The Range of Kingsley Amis," in *Wisconsin Studies in Contemporary Literature*. II (Fall, 1961), pp. 27–38.

Ross, T.J. "Lucky Jenny, or Affluent Times," in *New Republic*. CXLIV (March 27, 1961), pp. 21–23.

Sissman, L.E. "Kingsley Amis at Halfway House," in *New Yorker*. XLV (April 26, 1969), pp. 163–170.

Weightman, J.G. *"Take a Girl Like You,"* in *Twentieth Century*. CLXVIII (December, 1960), pp. 581–584.

That Uncertain Feeling

Corke, Hilary. "Bad Conscience," in *Encounter*. V (October, 1955), pp. 85–88.

Hurrell, John D. "Class and Conscience in John Braine and Kingsley Amis," in *Critique*. II (Spring-Summer, 1958), pp. 39–53.

Lebowitz, Naomi. "Kingsley Amis; the Penitent Hero," in *Perspective*. X (Summer, 1957–Autumn, 1959), pp. 129–136.

O'Connor, William Van. "Parody as Criticism," in *College English*. XXV (1964) pp. 241–248.

Quigly, Isabel. "New Novels: *That Uncertain Feeling*," in *Spectator*. CVC (September 2, 1955), pp. 316–317.

Rees, David. "That Petrine Cock," in *Spectator*. CCXV (August 27, 1965), pp. 268–269.

Simpson, Louis. "Fiction Chronicle," in *Hudson Review*. IX (Summer, 1956), pp. 302–309.

Stern, James. "Some Unpleasant People," in *New York Times Book Review*. (February 26, 1956), p. 4.

Toynbee, Philip. "Class Comedy," in *Observer*. (August 21, 1955), p. 9.

Voorhees, Richard J. "Kingsley Amis: Three Hurrahs and a Reservation," in *Queen's Quarterly.* LXXIX (1972), pp. 40–46.

Webster, Harvey Curtis. "The Gay, Good-Bad People," in *Saturday Review.* XXXIX (February 25, 1956), p. 17.

Wilson, Edmund. "Is It Possible to Pat Kingsley Amis?" in *New Yorker.* XXXII (March 24, 1956), pp. 140–142. Reprinted in *The Bit Between My Teeth: A Literary Chronicle of 1950–1965.* New York: Farrar, Strauss, 1965, pp. 274–281.

Wright, David. "Beginning with Amis," in *Time & Tide.* XXXVI (August 27, 1955), pp. 1114–1115.

MAXWELL ANDERSON
(1888–1959)

Barefoot in Athens

Brown, John M. *As They Appear.* New York: McGraw, 1952, pp. 199–206.

Herschbell, Jackson K. "The Socrates and Plato of Maxwell Anderson," in *North Dakota Quarterly.* XXXVIII (Winter, 1970), pp. 45–59.

Nathan, George Jean. *Theatre in the Fifties.* New York: Knopf, 1953, pp. 40–42.

Shivers, Alfred S. *Maxwell Anderson.* Boston: Twayne, 1976, pp. 66–71.

Both Your Houses

Avery, Laurence G. "Maxwell Anderson and *Both Your Houses,*" in *North Dakota Quarterly.* XXXVIII (Winter, 1970), pp. 5–24.

Bailey, Mabel D. *Maxwell Anderson: The Playwright as Prophet.* New York: Abelard-Schuman, 1957.

Brown, John M. *Two on the Aisle: Ten Years of the American Theatre in Performance.* New York: Norton, 1938, pp. 208–211.

Himelstein, Morgan Y. *Drama Was a Weapon, the Left-Wing Theatre in New York, 1929–1941.* New Brunswick, N.J.: Rutgers University Press, 1963, pp. 129–130.

Rabkin, Gerald. *Dogma and Commitment; Politics in the American Theatre of the Thirties.* Bloomington: Indiana University Press, 1964, pp. 263–288.

Shivers, Alfred S. *Maxwell Anderson.* Boston: Twayne, 1976, pp. 96–100.

Elizabeth the Queen

Bailey, Mabel D. *Maxwell Anderson: The Playwright as Prophet.* New York: Abelard-Schuman, 1957, pp. 45–54.

Carmer, Carl. "Maxwell Anderson, Poet and Champion," in *Theatre Arts.* XVII (June, 1933), pp. 437–446.

Downer, Alan S. *American Drama and Its Critics.* Chicago: University of Chicago Press, 1965, pp. 151–154.

Flexner, Eleanor. *American Playwrights: 1918–1938.* New York: Simon and Schuster, 1938, pp. 88–93.

Knepler, Henry W. "Maxwell Anderson: A Historical Parallel," in *Queen's Quarterly.* LXIV (1957), pp. 250–263.

Miller, Jordan Y. "Maxwell Anderson: Gifted Technician," in *The Thirties: Fiction, Poetry, Drama.* Edited by Warren French. Deland, Fla.: Everett/Edwards, 1967, pp. 186–187.

Rabkin, Gerald. *Dogma and Commitment; Politics in the American Theatre of the Thirties.* Bloomington: Indiana University Press, 1964, pp. 274–276.

Shivers, Alfred S. *Maxwell Anderson.* Boston: Twayne, 1976, pp. 85–89.

Watts, Harold H. "Maxwell Anderson: The Tragedy of Attrition," in *College English.* IV (January, 1943), pp. 220–230.

Gods of the Lightning

Avery, Laurence G. "Maxwell Anderson: A Changing Attitude Toward Love," in *Modern Drama.* X (December, 1967), pp. 241–248.

Block, Anita. *The Changing World in Plays and Theatre.* Boston: Little, Brown, 1939, pp. 230–239.

Flexner, Eleanor. *American Playwrights: 1918–1938.* New York: Simon and Schuster, 1938, pp. 85–88.

Rabkin, Gerald. *Dogma and Commitment; Politics in the American Theatre of the Thirties.* Bloomington: Indiana University Press, 1964, pp. 266–268.

Shivers, Alfred S. *Maxwell Anderson.* Boston: Twayne, 1976, pp. 105–107.

High Tor

Bailey, Mabel D. *Maxwell Anderson: The Playwright as Prophet.* New York: Abelard-Schuman, 1957, pp. 146–149.

Brown, John M. *Two on the Aisle: Ten Years of the American Theatre in Performance.* New York: Norton, 1938, pp. 152–155.

Krutch, Joseph Wood. *The American Drama Since 1918.* New York: Braziller, 1957, pp. 301–305.

Miller, Jordan Y. "Maxwell Anderson: Gifted Technician," in *The Thirties: Fiction, Poetry, Drama.* Edited by Warren French. Deland, Fla.: Everett/ Edwards, 1967, p. 190.

Rabkin, Gerald. *Dogma and Commitment; Politics in The American Theatre of the Thirties.* Bloomington: Indiana University Press, 1964, pp. 284–286.

Shivers, Alfred S. *Maxwell Anderson.* Boston: Twayne, 1976, pp. 114–122.

Young, Stark. *Immortal Shadows.* New York: Scribner's, 1948, pp. 185–188.

Key Largo

Bailey, Mabel D. *Maxwell Anderson: The Playwright as Prophet.* New York: Abelard-Schuman, 1957, pp. 106–114.

Brown, John. *Broadway in Review.* New York: Norton, 1940, pp. 67–71.

Downer, Alan S. *American Drama and Its Critics.* Chicago: University of Chicago Press, 1965, pp. 162–164.

Miller, Jordan Y. "Maxwell Anderson: Gifted Technician," in *The Thirties: Fiction, Poetry, Drama*. Edited by Warren French. Deland, Fla.: Everett/ Edwards, 1967, p. 191.

Rabkin, Gerald. *Dogma and Commitment; Politics in the American Theatre of the Thirties*. Bloomington: Indiana University Press, 1964, pp. 286–288.

Rodell, John S. "Maxwell Anderson: A Criticism," in *Kenyon Review*. V (Spring, 1943), pp. 272–277.

Shivers, Alfred S. *Maxwell Anderson*. Boston: Twayne, 1976, pp. 52–56.

Sievers, W. David. *Freud on Broadway*. New York: Hermitage House, 1955, pp. 177–178.

Watts, Harold H. "Maxwell Anderson: The Tragedy of Attrition," in *College English*. IV (January, 1943), pp. 220–230.

Mary of Scotland

Bailey, Mabel D. *Maxwell Anderson: The Playwright as Prophet*. New York: Abelard-Schuman, 1957, pp. 36–45.

Flexner, Eleanor. *American Playwrights: 1918–1938*. New York: Simon and Schuster, 1938, pp. 93–97.

Gabriel, Gilbert W. "Maxwell Anderson's *Mary of Scotland*," in *The American Theatre as Seen by Its Critics, 1752–1934*. Edited by Montrose J. Moses and John M. Brown. New York: Cooper Square, 1934.

Halline, Allan G. "Maxwell Anderson's Dramatic Theory," in *American Literature*. XVI (May, 1944), pp. 68–81.

Knepler, Henry W. "Maxwell Anderson: A Historical Parallel," in *Queen's Quarterly*. LXIV (1957), pp. 250–263.

Maguire, C.E. "The Divine Background," in *Drama Critique*. II (February, 1959), pp. 18–33.

Miller, Jordan Y. "Maxwell Anderson: Gifted Technician," in *The Thirties: Fiction, Poetry, Drama*. Edited by Warren French. Deland, Fla.: Everett/ Edwards, 1967, pp. 186–187.

Quinn, Arthur H. *A History of the American Drama from the Civil War to the Present Day*. New York: Appleton-Century-Crofts, 1936.

Rabkin, Gerald. *Dogma and Commitment; Politics in the American Theatre of the Thirties*. Bloomington: Indiana University Press, 1964, pp. 274–276.

Shivers, Alfred S. *Maxwell Anderson*. Boston: Twayne, 1976, pp. 80–85.

Watts, Harold H. "Maxwell Anderson: The Tragedy of Attrition," in *College English*. IV (January, 1943), pp. 220–230.

The Masque of Kings

Bailey, Mabel D. *Maxwell Anderson: The Playwright as Prophet*. New York: Abelard-Schuman, 1957, pp. 67–76.

Downer, Alan S. *American Drama and Its Critics*. Chicago: University of Chicago Press, 1965, pp. 169–170.

Flexner, Eleanor. *American Playwrights: 1918–1938*. New York: Simon and Schuster, 1938, pp. 120–125.

Himelstein, Morgan Y. *Drama Was a Weapon, the Left-Wing Theatre in New York, 1929–1941*. New Brunswick, N.J.: Rutgers University Press, 1963, p. 140.

Rabkin, Gerald. *Dogma and Commitment; Politics in the American Theatre of the Thirties*. Bloomington: Indiana University Press, 1964, pp. 279–281.

Shivers, Alfred S. *Maxwell Anderson*. Boston: Twayne, 1976, pp. 93–96.

Night Over Taos

Avery, Laurence G. "The Conclusion of *Night Over Taos*," in *American Literature*. XXXVII (November, 1965), pp. 318–321.

Bailey, Mabel D. *Maxwell Anderson: The Playwright as Prophet*. New York: Abelard-Schuman, 1957, pp. 128–131.

Miller, Jordan Y. "Maxwell Anderson: Gifted Technician," in *The Thirties: Fiction, Poetry, Drama*. Edited by Warren French. Deland, Fla.: Everett/Edwards, 1967, pp. 186–187.

Shivers, Alfred S. *Maxwell Anderson*. Boston: Twayne, 1976.

Sievers, W. David. *Freud on Broadway*. New York: Hermitage House, 1955, pp. 174–175.

Star-Wagon

Bailey, Mabel D. *Maxwell Anderson: The Playwright as Prophet*. New York: Abelard-Schuman, 1957, pp. 149–151.

Brown, John M. *Two on the Aisle: Ten Years of the American Theatre in Performance*. New York: Norton, 1938, pp. 155–159.

McCarthy, Mary. *Sights and Spectacles, 1937–1956*. New York: Farrar, Straus and Cudahy, 1956, pp. 3–8.

Shivers, Alfred S. *Maxwell Anderson*. Boston: Twayne, 1976, pp. 122–125.

Valley Forge

Bailey, Mabel D. *Maxwell Anderson: The Playwright as Prophet*. New York: Abelard-Schuman, 1957, pp. 61–67.

Flexner, Eleanor. *American Playwrights: 1918–1938*. New York: Simon and Schuster, 1938, pp. 98–102.

Himelstein, Morgan Y. *Drama Was a Weapon, the Left-Wing Theatre in New York, 1929–1941*. New Brunswick, N.J.: Rutgers University Press, 1963, p. 130.

Rabkin, Gerald. *Dogma and Commitment; Politics in the American Theatre of the Thirties.* Bloomington: Indiana University Press, 1964, pp. 282–284.

Shivers, Alfred S. *Maxwell Anderson.* Boston: Twayne, 1976, pp. 44–49.

Young, Stark. *Immortal Shadows.* New York: Scribner's, 1948, pp. 165–168.

What Price Glory?

Bailey, Mabel D. *Maxwell Anderson: The Playwright as Prophet.* New York: Abelard-Schuman, 1957, pp. 98–102.

Block, Anita. *The Changing World in Plays and Theatre.* Boston: Little, Brown, 1939, pp. 306–310.

Brown, John M. *Still Seeing Things.* New York: McGraw, 1950, pp. 227–232.

Downer, Alan S. *American Drama and Its Critics.* Chicago: University of Chicago Press, 1965, pp. 149–150.

Krutch, Joseph Wood. *The American Drama Since 1918.* New York: Braziller, 1957, pp. 29–44.

Miller, Jordan Y. "Maxwell Anderson: Gifted Technician," in *The Thirties: Fiction, Poetry, Drama.* Edited by Warren French. Deland, Fla.: Everett/Edwards, 1967, pp. 186–195.

Shivers, Alfred S. *Maxwell Anderson.* Boston: Twayne, 1976, pp. 49–52.

Woollcott, Alexander. *Portable Woollcott.* New York: Viking, 1946, pp. 441–443.

The Wingless Victory

Bailey, Mabel D. *Maxwell Anderson: The Playwright as Prophet.* New York: Abelard-Schuman, 1957, pp. 142–145.

Belli, Angela. "Leormand's *Asie* and Anderson's *The Wingless Victory*," in *Comparative Literature.* XIX (1967), pp. 226–239.

Flexner, Eleanor. *American Playwrights: 1918–1938.* New York: Simon and Schuster, 1938, pp. 116–120.

MacCarthy, Desmond. "A Tragedy of Race," in *New Statesman.* XXVI (September 18, 1943), p. 184.

Shivers, Alfred S. *Maxwell Anderson.* Boston: Twayne, 1976, pp. 103–105.

Young, Stark. *Immortal Shadows.* New York: Scribner's, 1948, pp. 185–187.

Winterset

Abernethy, Francis E. "*Winterset*: A Modern Revenge Tragedy," in *Modern Drama.* VII (September, 1964), pp. 185–189.

Adler, Jacob H. "Shakespeare in *Winterset*," in *Educational Theatre Journal.* VI (October, 1954), pp. 241–248.

Bailey, Mabel D. *Maxwell Anderson: The Playwright as Prophet.* New York: Abelard-Schuman, 1957, pp. 132–142.

Block, Anita. *The Changing World in Plays and Theatre.* Boston: Little, Brown, 1939, pp. 239–245.

Brown, John M. *Dramatis Personae; a Retrospective Show.* New York: Viking, 1963, pp. 73–76.

————. *Two on the Aisle: Ten Years of the American Theatre in Performance.* New York: Norton, 1938, pp. 148–152.

Dusenbury, Winifred L. *The Theme of Loneliness in Modern American Drama.* Gainesville: University of Florida Press, 1960, pp. 113–134.

Flexner, Eleanor. *American Playwrights: 1918–1938.* New York: Simon and Schuster, 1938, pp. 102–116.

Gilbert, Robert L. "Mio Romagna: A New View of Maxwell Anderson's *Winterset*," in *North Dakota Quarterly.* XXXVIII (Winter, 1970), pp. 33–43.

Harris, Ainslie. "Maxwell Anderson," in *Madison Quarterly.* IV (January, 1944), pp. 30–44.

Heilman, Robert B. *Tragedy and Melodrama.* Seattle: University of Washington Press, 1968, pp. 276–278.

Jones, John B. "Shakespeare as Myth and the Structure of *Winterset*," in *Educational Theatre Journal.* XXV (1973), pp. 34–45.

Kliger, Samuel. "Hebraic Lore in Maxwell Anderson's *Winterset*," in *American Literature.* XVIII (November, 1946), pp. 219–232.

Krutch, Joseph Wood. *The American Drama Since 1918.* New York: Braziller, 1957, pp. 295–301.

O'Hara, Frank H. *Today in American Drama.* Chicago: University of Chicago Press, 1939, pp. 1–52.

Pearce, Howard D. "Job in Anderson's *Winterset*," in *Modern Drama.* VI (May, 1963), pp. 32–41.

Rabkin, Gerald. *Drama and Commitment: Politics in the American Theatre of the Thirties.* Bloomington: Indiana University Press, 1964, pp. 263–288.

Roby, Robert C. "Two Worlds: Maxwell Anderson's *Winterset*," in *College English.* XVIII (January, 1957), pp. 195–202.

Shivers, Alfred S. *Maxwell Anderson.* Boston: Twayne, 1976, pp. 107–114.

Tees, Arthur T. "*Winterset*: Four Influences on Mio," in *Modern Drama.* XIV (1971), pp. 408–412.

Wilson, Edmund. *The Shores of Light.* New York: Farrar, Straus and Giroux, 1952, pp. 670–674.

ROBERT ANDERSON
(1917–   )

Tea and Sympathy

Adler, Thomas P.   *Robert Anderson.* Boston: Twayne, 1978, pp. 69–81.

Bentley, Eric Russell.   *The Dramatic Event: An American Chronicle.* New York: Horizon Press, 1954, pp. 150–153.

Gassner, John.   *Theatre at the Crossroads; Plays and Playwrights of the Mid-Century American Stage.* New York: Holt, Rinehart and Winston, 1960, pp. 288–293.

Hewes, Henry.   "Broadway Postscript: Orange Pekoe," in *Saturday Review.* XXXVI (October 17, 1953), p. 35.

Kerr, Walter.   *How Not to Write a Play.* New York: Simon and Schuster, 1955, pp. 108–111.

Sievers, W. David.   *Freud on Broadway: A History of Psychoanalysis and the American Drama.* New York: Hermitage House, 1955, pp. 410–411.

"Some Notes on *Tea and Sympathy*," in *The Exonian.* CCXXIV (March 3, 1954), pp. 14–16.

Tynan, Kenneth.   *Curtains; Selections from the Drama Criticism and Related Writings.* New York: Atheneum, 1961, p. 172.

Weales, Gerald.   *American Drama Since World War II.* New York: Harcourt, Brace and World, 1962, pp. 49–56.

SHERWOOD ANDERSON
(1876–1941)

Dark Laughter

Anderson, David D. *Sherwood Anderson: An Introduction and Interpretation.* New York: Barnes & Noble, 1967, pp. 122–129.

Cargill, Oscar. *Intellectual America: Ideas on the March.* New York: Macmillan, 1941, pp. 322–331, 676–685.

Chase, Cleveland B. *Sherwood Anderson.* New York: Robert M. McBride, 1927, pp. 16–27.

Howe, Irving. "Sherwood Anderson and D.H. Lawrence," in *Furioso.* V (Fall, 1950), pp. 21–33.

Krutch, Joseph Wood. *American Criticism.* New York: Harcourt, 1926, pp. 108–111.

Lovett, Robert Morss. "Sherwood Anderson, American," in *Virginia Quarterly Review.* XVII (Summer, 1941), pp. 379–388.

McHaney, Thomas L. "Anderson, Hemingway, and Faulkner's *The Wild Palms,*" in *PMLA.* LXXXVII (May, 1972), pp. 465–474.

Rahv, Philip. *Image and Idea: Fourteen Essays on Literary Themes.* Norfolk, Conn.: New Directions, 1949, pp. 3–5.

Sherman, Stuart P. *Critical Woodcuts.* New York: Scribner's, 1926, pp. 3–17.

Tugwell, Rexford Guy. "An Economist Reads *Dark Laughter,*" in *New Republic.* XLV (December 9, 1925), pp. 87–88.

White, Ray Lewis. "Hemingway's Private Explanation of *The Torrents of Spring,*" in *Modern Fiction Studies.* XIII (Summer, 1967), pp. 261–263.

Wickham, Harvey. *The Impuritans.* New York: L. MacVeagh, 1929, pp. 268–282.

Poor White

Anderson, David D. "The Uncritical Critics: American Realists and the Lincoln Myth," in *Midamerica II.* Edited by David D. Anderson. East Lansing, Mich.: Midwestern Press, 1975, pp. 17–23.

Burbank, Rex. *Sherwood Anderson.* New York: Twayne, 1964, pp. 48–60.

Gelfant, Blanche Housman. *The American City Novel.* Norman: University of Oklahoma Press, 1954, pp. 95–132.

Hoffman, Frederick John. *The Twenties.* New York: Viking, 1955, pp. 302–306.

Howe, Irving. "Sherwood Anderson and the American Myth of Power," in *Tomorrow.* VII (August, 1949), pp. 52–54.

Rideout, Walter B. "Introduction," in *Poor White*. By Sherwood Anderson. New York: Viking, 1966, pp. ix–xx.

Ward, A.C. *American Literature, 1880–1930.* New York: Dial Press, 1932, pp. 111–113, 120–133.

Winesburg, Ohio

Abcarian, Richard. "Innocence and Experience in *Winesburg, Ohio,*" in *University Review.* XXXV (December, 1968), pp. 95–105.

Anderson, David D. *Barron's Simplified Approach to* Winesburg, Ohio. Woodbury, N.Y.: Barron's Educational Series, 1967.

Baker, Carlos. "Sherwood Anderson's Winesburg: A Reprise," in *Virginia Quarterly Review.* XLVIII (Autumn, 1972), pp. 568–579.

Bluefarb, Sam. *The Escape Motif in the American Novel: Mark Twain to Richard Wright.* Columbus: Ohio State University Press, 1972, pp. 42–58.

Bort, Barry D. "*Winesburg, Ohio*: The Escape from Isolation," in *Midwest Quarterly.* XII (Summer, 1970), pp. 443–456.

Ciancio, Ralph. " 'The Sweetness of the Twisted Apples': Unity of Vision in *Winesburg, Ohio,*" in *PMLA.* LXXXVII (October, 1972), pp. 994–1006.

Ferres, John H. "*Winesburg, Ohio* at Fifty," in *Hofstra Review.* IV (Autumn, 1969), pp. 5–10. Reprinted as "The Nostalgia of *Winesburg, Ohio,*" in *Newberry Library Bulletin.* VI (July, 1971), pp. 235–242.

Frank, Waldo. "*Winesburg, Ohio* after Twenty Years," in *Story.* XIX (September–October, 1941), pp. 29–33.

Fussell, Edwin. " 'Winesburg, Ohio': Art and Isolation," in *Modern Fiction Studies.* VI (Summer, 1960), pp. 106–114.

Gochberg, Donald. "Stagnation and Growth: The Emergence of George Willard," in *Expression.* IV (Winter, 1960), pp. 29–35.

Howe, Irving. "Sherwood Anderson: *Winesburg, Ohio,*" in *The American Novel from James Fenimore Cooper to William Faulkner.* Edited by Wallace Stegner. New York: Basic Books, 1965, pp. 154–165.

Ingram, Forrest L. "American Short Story Cycles: Foreign Influences and Parallels," in *Proceedings of the Comparative Literature Symposium, V: Modern American Fiction. Insights and Foreign Lights.* Edited by Wolodymyn T. Zyla and Wendell M. Aycock. Lubbock: Texas Tech University, 1972, pp. 19–37.

Laughlin, Rosemary M. "Godliness in the American Dream in *Winesburg, Ohio,*" in *Twentieth Century Literature.* XIII (July, 1967), pp. 97–103.

Lawry, Jon S. "The Artist in America: The Case of Sherwood Anderson," in *Ball State University Forum.* VII (Spring, 1966), pp. 15–26.

Lorch, Thomas M. "The Choreographic Structure of *Winesburg, Ohio,*" in *College Language Association Journal.* XII (September, 1968), pp. 56–65.

Love, Glen A. "*Winesburg, Ohio* and the Rhetoric of Silence," in *American Literature.* XL (March, 1968), pp. 38–57.

Maresca, Carol J. "Gestures as Meaning in Sherwood Anderson's *Winesburg, Ohio,*" in *College Language Association Journal.* IX (March, 1966), pp. 279–283.

Mellard, James M. "Narrative Forms in *Winesburg, Ohio,*" in *PMLA.* LXXXIII (October, 1968), pp. 1304–1312.

Murphy, George D. "The Theme of Sublimation in Anderson's *Winesburg, Ohio,*" *Modern Fiction Studies.* XIII (Summer, 1967), pp. 237–246.

Pawlowski, Robert S. "The Process of Observation: *Winesburg, Ohio* and *The Golden Apples,*" in *University Review.* XXXVII (June, 1971), pp. 292–298.

Rogers, Douglas R. "Development of the Artist in *Winesburg, Ohio,*" in *Studies in the Twentieth Century.* X (Fall, 1972), pp. 91–99.

San Juan, Epifanio, Jr. "Vision and Reality: A Reconsideration of Sherwood Anderson's *Winesburg, Ohio,*" in *American Literature.* XXXV (May, 1963), pp. 137–155.

Somers, Paul P., Jr. "Anderson's Twisted Apples and Hemingway's Crips," in *Midamerica I.* Edited by David P. Anderson. East Lansing, Mich.: Midwestern Press, 1974, pp. 82–97.

Stouck, David. "*Winesburg, Ohio* and the Failure of Art," in *Twentieth Century Literature.* XV (October, 1969), pp. 145–151.

Tanner, Tony. *The Reign of Wonder: Naïvety and Reality in American Literature.* Cambridge: Cambridge University Press, 1965, pp. 205 –227.

IVO ANDRIĆ
(1892–1975)

Bosnian Chronicle

Barac, Antun. *A History of Yugoslav Literature.* Ann Arbor: Michigan Slavic Publications, 1973, pp. 245–248.

Ferguson, Alan. "Public and Private Worlds in *Travnik Chronicle,*" in *Modern Language Review.* LXX (1975), pp. 830–838.

Hitrec, Joseph. "Translator's Note," in *Bosnian Chronicle.* By Ivo Andrić. New York: Knopf, 1964, pp. v–viii.

Johnstone, Kenneth. "Translator's Note," in *Bosnian Chronicle.* By Ivo Andrić. New York: London House & Maxwell, 1959, pp. 9–12.

Kadic, Ante. *Contemporary Serbian Literature.* London: Mouton, 1964, pp. 61–64.

Loud, John. "Between Two Worlds: Andrić the Storyteller," in *Review of National Literatures.* V (1974), pp. 112–126.

The Bridge on the Drina

Barac, Antun. *A History of Yugoslav Literature.* Ann Arbor: Michigan Slavic Publications, 1973, pp. 245–248.

Curcin, Ivo. "Andrić's *Bridge on the Drina* and the Problem of Genre," in *Proceedings: Pacific Northwest Conference on Foreign Languages.* Edited by Walter E. Kraft. Corvallis: Oregon State University, XXIII (1972), pp. 307–324.

della Fazia, Alba. "Nobel Prize, 1962, and *The Bridge on the Drina* Revisited," in *Books Abroad.* XXXVII (Winter, 1963), pp. 24–26.

Edwards, Lovett F. "Translator's Foreword," in *The Bridge on the Drina.* By Ivo Andrić. New York: Macmillan, 1959, pp. 7–9.

Kadic, Ante. *Contemporary Serbian Literature.* London: Mouton, 1964, pp. 60–63.

McNeill, William H. "Introduction," in *The Bridge on the Drina.* By Ivo Andrić. Chicago: University of Chicago Press, 1977, pp. 1–5.

Moravcevich, Nicholas. "Ivo Andrić and the Quintessence of Time," in *Slavic and East European Journal.* XVI (1972), pp. 313–318.

Pribic, Nikola R. "Ivo Andrić and His Historical Novel *The Bridge on the Drina,*" in *Florida State University Slavic Papers.* III (1969), pp. 77–80.

MAYA ANGELOU
(1928–   )

I Know Why the Caged Bird Sings

Arensburg, Liliane K.   "Death as Metaphor of Self in *I Know Why the Caged Bird Sings*," in *College Language Association Journal*. XX (1976), pp. 273–291.

Hiers, John T.   "Fatalism in Maya Angelou's *I Know Why the Caged Bird Sings*," in *Notes on Contemporary Literature*. VI (1976), pp. 5–7.

Kent, George E.   "Maya Angelou's *I Know Why the Caged Bird Sings* and Black Autobiographical Tradition," in *Kansas Quarterly*. VII (1975), pp. 72–78.

McMurray, Myra K.   "Role Playing as Art in Maya Angelou's Caged Bird," in *South Atlantic Bulletin*. XLI (1976), pp. 106–111.

Smith, Sidonie A.   "The Song of a Caged Bird: Maya Angelou's Quest After Self Acceptance," in *Southern Humanities Review*. VII (1973), pp. 365–375.

JEAN ANOUILH
(1910–   )

Antigone

Archer, Marguerite. *Jean Anouilh.* New York: Columbia University Press, 1971, pp. 18–24.

Belli, Angela. *Ancient Greek Myths and Modern Drama: A Study in Continuity.* New York: New York University Press, 1971, pp. 97–111.

Burdick, Dolores M. "Antigone Grown Middle-Aged: Evolution of Anouilh's Hero," in *Michigan Academician.* VII (1974), pp. 137–147.

Calin, William. "Patterns of Imagery in Anouilh's *Antigone*," in *French Review.* XLI (1967), pp. 76–83.

DeLaura, David J. "Anouilh's Other Antigone," in *French Review.* XXXV (1961), pp. 36–41.

Deutsch, R. "Anouilh's *Antigone*," in *Classical Journal.* XLII (October, 1946), pp. 14–16.

Dickinson, Hugh. *Myth on the Modern Stage.* Urbana: University of Illinois Press, 1969, pp. 260–266.

Falb, Lewis W. *Jean Anouilh.* New York: Frederick Ungar, 1977, pp. 50–69.

Grossvogel, David I. *Twentieth Century French Drama.* Ithaca, N.Y.: Cornell University Press, 1961, pp. 162–164, 174–187.

Hamburger, Kate. *From Sophocles to Sartre: Figures from Greek Tragedy, Classical and Modern.* New York: Frederick Ungar, 1969, pp. 147–166.

Heiney, Donald. "Jean Anouilh: The Revival of Tragedy," in *College English.* XVI (1955), pp. 331–335.

Hudson, Lynton. *Life and the Theatre.* London: George G. Harrap, 1949, pp. 137–139.

Ince, W. "Prologue and Chorus in Anouilh's *Antigone*," in *Forum for Modern Language Studies.* IV (1968), pp. 277–285.

Joseph, Sister E. "The Two *Antigones*: Sophocles and Anouilh," in *Thought.* XXXVIII (1963), pp. 586–593, 601–606.

Lenski, B.A. *Jean Anouilh: Stages in Rebellion.* Atlantic Highlands, N.J.: Humanities Press, 1975, pp. 35–46.

Lumley, Frederick. *New Trends in Twentieth Century Drama: A Survey Since Ibsen and Shaw.* London: Oxford University Press, 1967, pp. 170–181.

Marsh, E.O. *Jean Anouilh, Poet of Pierrot and Pantaloon.* London: Allen, 1953, pp. 107–120.

Pronko, Leonard Cabell. *The World of Jean Anouilh.* Berkeley: University of California Press, 1961, pp. 24–28, 200–207.

Saisselin, Remy G. "Is Tragic Drama Possible in the Twentieth Century?," in *Theatre Annual.* (1960), pp. 12–21.

Schlesinger, A. "Anouilh's *Antigone* Again," in *Classical Journal.* XLII (January, 1947), pp. 207–209.

Sherrell, R. "The Case Against God in Modern French Drama," in *Religion in Life.* XXXI (Autumn, 1962), pp. 616–618.

Siepmann, E.O. "The New Pessimism in France," in *Nineteenth Century.* CXLIII (1948), pp. 275–278.

Spingler, Michael. "Anouilh's Little Antigone: Tragedy, Theatricalism, and the Romantic Self," in *Comparative Drama.* VIII (1974), pp. 228–238.

Thody, Philip. *Anouilh.* Edinburgh: Oliver and Boyd, 1968, pp. 31–34.

Varty, K. "The Future Tense in Anouilh's *Antigone*," in *Modern Languages.* XXXIII (1957), pp. 99–101.

Ardèle

Archer, Marguerite. *Jean Anouilh.* New York: Columbia University Press, 1971, pp. 32–33.

Benedict, S. "Anouilh in America," in *Modern Language Journal.* XLV (December, 1961), pp. 341–342.

Bishop, Thomas. *Pirandello and the French Theatre.* New York: New York University Press, 1960, pp. 113–114.

Chiari, Joseph. *The Contemporary French Theatre: The Flight from Naturalism.* New York: Macmillan, 1959, pp. 199–202.

Clurman, Harold. *Lies Like Truth: Theatre Reviews and Essays.* New York: Macmillan, 1958, pp. 202–203.

della Fazia, Alba. *Jean Anouilh.* New York: Twayne, 1969, pp. 86–90.

Falb, Lewis W. *Jean Anouilh.* New York: Frederick Ungar, 1977, pp. 85–88.

Harvey, John. *Anouilh: A Study in Theatrics.* New Haven, Conn.: Yale University Press, 1964, pp. 105–106.

Hewes, Henry. "The Tried and the Untried," in *Saturday Review.* LII (May 10, 1969), p. 40.

Hobson, Harold. *The Theatre Now.* London: Longmans, Green, 1953, pp. 34–36.

Howarth, W.D. "Anouilh," in *Forces in Modern French Drama: Studies in Variations on the Permitted Lie.* Edited by John Fletcher. New York: Frederick Ungar, 1972, pp. 97–98.

John, S. "Obsession and Technique in the Plays of Jean Anouilh," in *French Studies.* XI (1957), pp. 108–109.

Lenski, B.A. *Jean Anouilh: Stages in Rebellion.* Atlantic Highlands, N.J.: Humanities Press, 1975, pp. 17–24.

Luce, S.   "The Whimsical and the Sordid in Jean Anouilh," in *Kentucky Foreign Language Quarterly*. XII (1965), p. 90.

Lumley, Frederick.   *New Trends in Twentieth Century Drama: A Survey Since Ibsen and Shaw*. London: Oxford University Press, 1967, pp. 170–181.

Marsh, E.O.   *Jean Anouilh, Poet of Pierrot and Pantaloon*. London: Allen, 1953, pp. 139–149.

Pronko, Leonard Cabell.   *The World of Jean Anouilh*. Berkeley: University of California Press, 1961, pp. 44–45.

Styan, J.L.   *The Dark Comedy*. London: Cambridge University Press, 1962, pp. 199–206.

————.   *The Elements of Drama*. London: Cambridge University Press, 1960, pp. 198–204.

Worsley, T.C.   *The Fugitive Art*. London: John Lehmann, 1952, pp. 234–236.

Becket

Archer, Marguerite.   *Jean Anouilh*. New York: Columbia University Press, 1971, pp. 39–41.

Aylen, Leo.   *Greek Tragedy and the Modern World*. London: Methuen, 1964, pp. 290–292.

Browne, E. Martin.   "The Two Beckets," in *Drama*. LX (Spring, 1961), pp. 27–30.

Cismaru, Alfred.   "*Becket*: Anouilh as Devil's Advocate," in *Renascence*. XVIII (Winter, 1966), pp. 81–88.

Clurman, Harold.   *The Naked Image: Observations on the Modern Theatre*. New York: Macmillan, 1966, pp. 27–30.

Cohn, Ruby.   *Currents in Contemporary Drama*. Bloomington: Indiana University Press, 1969, pp. 104–106.

Cubeta, Paul M.   *Modern Drama for Analysis*. Chicago: University of Chicago Press, 1964, pp. 513–522.

Gassner, John.   *Dramatic Soundings: Evaluations and Retractions Culled from Thirty Years of Dramatic Criticism*. New York: Crown, 1968, pp. 497–499.

Gatlin, J.C.   "Becket and Honor: A Trim Reckoning," in *Modern Drama*. VIII (December, 1965), pp. 277–283.

Guicharnaud, Jacques.   *Modern French Theatre from Giraudoux to Genet*. New Haven, Conn.: Yale University Press, 1961, pp. 117–134.

Harvey, John.   *Anouilh: A Study in Theatrics*. New Haven, Conn.: Yale University Press, 1964, pp. 97–98.

Harvitt, Helene.   "The Translation of Anouilh's *Becket*," in *French Review*. XXXIV (May, 1961), pp. 569–571.

Kerr, Walter. *The Theater in Spite of Itself.* New York: Simon and Schuster, 1963, pp. 154–157.

Lenski, B.A. *Jean Anouilh: Stages in Rebellion.* Atlantic Highlands, N.J.: Humanities Press, 1975, pp. 35–46.

Milne, Tom. "*Becket,*" in *Encore.* VIII (September–October, 1961), pp. 37–40.

Pronko, Leonard Cabell. "The Prelate and the Pachyderm: Rear Guard and Vanguard Drama in the French Theatre," in *Modern Drama.* IV (May, 1961), pp. 63–71.

————. *The World of Jean Anouilh.* Berkeley: University of California Press, 1961, pp. 56–61.

Reiter, Seymour. *World Theater: The Structure and Meaning of Drama.* New York: Horizon Press, 1973, pp. 13–35.

Roy, Emil. "The Becket Plays: Eliot, Fry, and Anouilh," in *Modern Drama.* VIII (December, 1965), pp. 268–276.

Sochatoff, A. "Four Variations on the Becket Theme," in *Modern Drama.* XII (May, 1969), pp. 84–85.

Thody, Philip. *Anouilh.* Edinburgh: Oliver and Boyd, 1968, pp. 52–56.

Tynan, Kenneth. *Tynan Right and Left: Plays, Films, People, Places and Events.* New York: Atheneum, 1967, pp. 99–100.

Colombe

Bentley, Eric. *The Dramatic Event: An American Chronicle.* New York: Horizon Press, 1954, pp. 182–185.

Bishop, Thomas. *Pirandello and the French Theatre.* New York: New York University Press, 1960, pp. 110–111.

Clurman, Harold. "Theatre," in *Nation.* CLXXVIII (January, 30, 1954), pp. 98–99.

della Fazia, Alba. *Jean Anouilh.* New York: Twayne, 1969, pp. 83–85.

Falb, Lewis W. *Jean Anouilh.* New York: Frederick Ungar, 1977, pp. 73–84.

Gassner, John. *Theatre at the Crossroads: Plays and Playwrights of the Mid-Century American Stage.* New York: Holt, Rinehart and Winston, 1960, pp. 245–247.

Harvey, John. *Anouilh: A Study in Theatrics.* New Haven, Conn.: Yale University Press, 1964, pp. 73–75, 86–88.

Hatch, Robert. "Theatre," in *Nation.* CLXXVIII (January 23, 1954), pp. 77–78.

Howarth, W.D. "Anouilh," in *Forces in Modern French Drama: Studies in Variations on the Permitted Lie.* Edited by John Fletcher. New York: Frederick Ungar, 1972, pp. 96–97.

Lumley, Frederick. *New Trends in Twentieth Century Drama: A Survey Since-Ibsen and Shaw.* London: Oxford University Press, 1967, pp. 170–181.

Marsh, E.O. *Jean Anouilh, Poet of Pierrot and Pantaloon.* London: Allen, 1953, pp. 157–164.

Nelson, Robert James. *Play Within a Play: The Dramatist's Conception of His Art, Shakespeare to Anouilh.* New Haven, Conn.: Yale University Press, 1958, pp. 145–154.

Pickering, Jerry V. "The Several Worlds of Anouilh's *Colombe,*" in *Drama Survey.* V (Winter, 1966–1967), pp. 267–275.

Pronko, Leonard Cabell. *The World of Jean Anouilh.* Berkeley: University of California Press, 1961, pp. 47–49.

Scott-James, Paule. "The Theatre of Jean Anouilh," in *Contemporary Review.* CLXXIX (1951), pp. 302–308.

Styan, J.L. *The Dark Comedy.* London: Cambridge University Press, 1960, pp. 206–217.

Thody, Philip. *Anouilh.* Edinburgh: Oliver and Boyd, 1968, pp. 25–28.

Dinner with the Family

Bishop, Thomas. *Pirandello and the French Theatre.* New York: New York University Press, 1960, p. 117.

della Fazia, Alba. *Jean Anouilh.* New York: Twayne, 1969, pp. 71–74.

Falb, Lewis W. *Jean Anouilh.* New York: Frederick Ungar, 1977, pp. 35–47.

Harvey, John. *Anouilh: A Study in Theatrics.* New Haven, Conn.: Yale University Press, 1964, pp.129–130.

Howarth, W.D. "Anouilh," in *Forces in Modern French Drama: Studies in Variations on the Permitted Lie.* Edited by John Fletcher. New York: Frederick Ungar, 1972, pp. 92–93.

Lawrence, Ralph. "Theatre Notes," in *English.* XII (Summer, 1958), pp. 59–60.

Lenski, B.A. *Jean Anouilh: Stages in Rebellion.* Atlantic Highlands, N.J.: Humanities Press, 1975, pp. 17–24.

Marsh, E.O. *Jean Anouilh, Poet of Pierrot and Pantaloon.* London: Allen, 1953, pp. 77–78.

Nelson, Robert James. *Play Within a Play: The Dramatist's Conception of His Art, Shakespeare to Anouilh.* New Haven, Conn.: Yale University Press, 1958, pp. 136–137.

Pronko, Leonard Cabell. *The World of Jean Anouilh.* Berkeley: University of California Press, 1961, pp. 15–16, 185–188.

The Ermine

Archer, Marguerite. *Jean Anouilh.* New York: Columbia University Press, 1971, pp. 9–10.

Chiari, Joseph. *The Contemporary French Theatre: The Flight from Naturalism.* New York: Macmillan, 1959, pp. 176–178.

Falb, Lewis W. *Jean Anouilh.* New York: Frederick Ungar, 1977, pp. 21–23.

Harvey, John. *Anouilh: A Study in Theatrics.* New Haven, Conn.: Yale University Press, 1964, pp. 103–104.

John, S. "Obsession and Technique in the Plays of Jean Anouilh," in *French Studies.* XI (1957), pp. 99–100.

Knowles, Dorothy. *French Drama of the Inter-War Years, 1918–1939.* London: George G. Harrap, 1967, pp. 167–168.

Lumley, Frederick. *New Trends in Twentieth Century Drama: A Survey Since Ibsen and Shaw.* London: Oxford University Press, 1967, p. 171.

Marsh, E.O. *Jean Anouilh, Poet of Pierrot and Pantaloon.* London: Allen, 1953, pp. 103–104.

Pronko, Leonard Cabell. *The World of Jean Anouilh.* Berkeley: University of California Press, 1961, pp. 4–6.

Stevens, Linton C. "Hybris in Anouilh's *L'Hermine* and *La Sauvage*," in *French Review.* XXXVII (1964), pp. 658–663.

Thody, Philip. *Anouilh.* Edinburgh: Oliver and Boyd, 1968, pp. 15–16.

Eurydice

Archer, Marguerite. *Jean Anouilh.* New York: Columbia University Press, 1971, pp. 11–12.

Aylen, Leo. *Greek Tragedy and the Modern World.* London: Methuen, 1964, pp. 286–288, 291.

Chiari, Joseph. *The Contemporary French Theatre: The Flight from Naturalism.* New York: Macmillan, 1959, pp. 185–187.

della Fazia, Alba. *Jean Anouilh.* New York: Twayne, 1969, pp. 110–112.

Dickinson, Hugh. *Myth on the Modern Stage.* Urbana: University of Illinois Press, 1969, pp. 250–260.

Free, Mary G. "On the Function of the Two Waiters in Anouilh's *Eurydice*," in *Notes on Contemporary Literature.* II (1972), pp. 13–15.

Harvey, John. *Anouilh: A Study in Theatrics.* New Haven, Conn.: Yale University Press, 1964, pp. 119–120.

Heiney, Donald. "Jean Anouilh: The Revival of Tragedy," in *College English.* XVI (1955), pp. 331–335.

Henn, Thomas R. *The Harvest of Tragedy.* London: Methuen, 1956, pp. 240–242.

Hobson, Harold. *The Theatre Now.* New York: Longmans, Green, 1953, pp. 36–39.

Ingham, Patricia. "The Renaissance of Hell," in *Listener.* LXII (September 3, 1959), pp. 349–351.

Lenski, B.A. *Jean Anouilh: Stages in Rebellion.* Atlantic Highlands, N.J.: Humanities Press, 1975, pp. 25–34.

Lumley, Frederick. *New Trends in Twentieth Century Drama: A Survey Since Ibsen and Shaw.* London: Oxford University Press, 1967, pp. 170–181.

Marsh, E.O. *Jean Anouilh: Poet of Pierrot and Pantaloon.* London: Allen, 1953, pp. 91–106.

Nathan, George Jean. *Theatre in the Fifties.* New York: Knopf, 1953, pp. 161–164.

Porter, David H. "Ancient Myth and Modern Play: A Significant Counterpoint," in *Classical Bulletin.* XLVIII (November, 1971), pp. 1–9.

Pronko, Leonard Cabell. *The World of Jean Anouilh.* Berkeley: University of California Press, 1961.

Scott-James, Paule. "The Theatre of Jean Anouilh," in *Contemporary Review.* CLXXIX (1951), pp. 302–308.

Styan, J.L. *The Dark Comedy.* London: Cambridge University Press, 1962, pp. 130–131, 193–199.

_____. *The Elements of Drama.* London: Cambridge University Press, 1960, pp. 217–227.

Thody, Philip. *Anouilh.* Edinburgh: Oliver and Boyd, 1968, pp. 29–30.

Worsley, T.C. *The Fugitive Art.* London: John Lehmann, 1952, pp. 172–174.

The Fighting Cock

Brustein, Robert. *Seasons of Discontent.* New York: Simon and Schuster, 1965, pp. 101–104.

Clurman, Harold. *The Naked Image: Observations on the Modern Theatre.* New York: Macmillan, 1966, pp. 25–27.

della Fazia, Alba. *Jean Anouilh.* New York: Twayne, 1969, pp. 95–99.

Falb, Lewis W. *Jean Anouilh.* New York: Frederick Ungar, 1977, pp. 114–115.

Harvey, John. *Anouilh: A Study in Theatrics.* New Haven, Conn.: Yale University Press, 1964, pp. 44–49, 149–150, 162–163.

Hooker, Ward. "Irony and Absurdity in the Avant-Garde Theatre," in *Kenyon Review.* XXII (1960), pp. 436–454.

Howarth, W.D. "Anouilh," in *Forces in Modern French Drama: Studies in Variations on the Permitted Lie.* Edited by John Fletcher. New York: Frederick Ungar, 1972, pp. 106–107.

Knowles, Dorothy. *French Drama of the Inter-War Years, 1918–1939.* London: George G. Harrap, 1967, p. 178.

Lenski, B.A. *Jean Anouilh: Stages in Rebellion.* Atlantic Highlands, N.J.: Humanities Press, 1975, pp. 58–66.

Lumley, Frederick. *New Trends in Twentieth Century Drama: A Survey Since Ibsen and Shaw.* London: Oxford University Press, 1967, pp. 170–181.

Pronko, Leonard Cabell. *The World of Jean Anouilh.* Berkeley: University of California Press, 1961, pp. 53–56.

Thody, Philip. *Anouilh.* Edinburgh: Oliver and Boyd, 1968, pp. 76–81.

The Lark

Archer, Marguerite. *Jean Anouilh.* New York: Columbia University Press, 1971, pp. 39–41.

Aylen, Leo. *Greek Tragedy and the Modern World.* London: Methuen, 1964, pp. 287–290.

Bermel, Albert. *The Genius of the French Theatre.* New York: Mentor, 1961, pp. 21–22, 443–444.

Champigney, R. "Theatre in a Mirror: Anouilh," in *Yale French Studies.* XIV (Winter, 1954–1955), pp. 61–63.

Chiari, Joseph. *The Contemporary French Theatre: The Flight from Naturalism.* New York: Macmillan, 1959, pp. 187–195.

Cohn, Ruby. *Currents in Contemporary Drama.* Bloomington: Indiana University Press, 1969, pp. 110–122.

Falb, Lewis W. *Jean Anouilh.* New York: Frederick Ungar, 1977, pp. 102–113.

Fowlie, Wallace. *Dionysus in Paris: A Guide to Contemporary French Theater.* New York: Meridian Books, 1960, pp. 119–122.

Gassner, John. *Theatre at the Crossroads: Plays and Playwrights of the Midcentury American Stage.* New York: Holt, 1960, pp. 247–249.

Harvey, John. *Anouilh: A Study in Theatrics.* New Haven, Conn.: Yale University Press, 1964, pp. 94–96.

Howarth, W.D. "Anouilh," in *Forces in Modern French Drama: Studies in Variations on the Permitted Lie.* Edited by John Fletcher. New York: Frederick Ungar, 1972, pp. 101–102.

Hunter, F.J. "The Value of Time in Modern Drama," in *Journal of Aesthetics and Art Criticism.* XVI (1957), pp. 194–201.

Jamieson, D.M. "Anouilh's *Lark*: Aptness and Functionality," in *Modern Languages.* LVII (1976), pp. 105–116.

Knepler, Henry. "*The Lark.* Translation vs. Adaptation: A Case History," in *Modern Drama.* I (1958), pp. 15–28.

Lenski, B.A. *Jean Anouilh: Stages in Rebellion.* Atlantic Highlands, N.J.: Humanities Press, 1975, pp. 35–46.

Lumley, Frederick. *New Trends in Twentieth Century Drama: A Survey Since Ibsen and Shaw.* London: Oxford University Press, 1967, pp. 170–181.

Moore, Harry T. *Twentieth Century French Literature to World War II,* Volume II. Carbondale: Southern Illinois University Press, 1966, pp. 17–22.

Pronko, Leonard Cabell. *The World of Jean Anouilh.* Berkeley: University of California Press, 1961, pp. 37–40.

Styan, J.L. *The Dark Comedy.* London: Cambridge University Press, 1962, pp. 5–7.

Thody, Philip. *Anouilh.* Edinburgh: Oliver and Boyd, 1968, pp. 48–52.

Williamson, Audrey. *Contemporary Theatre, 1953–1956.* London: Rockliff, 1956, pp. 51–53.

Medea

Archer, Marguerite. *Jean Anouilh.* New York: Columbia University Press, 1971, pp. 25–26.

Aylen, Leo. *Greek Tragedy and the Modern World.* London: Methuen, 1964, pp. 284–286.

della Fazia, Alba. *Jean Anouilh.* New York: Twayne, 1969, pp. 110–112.

Hamburger, Kate. *From Sophocles to Sartre: Figures from Greek Tragedy, Classical and Modern.* New York: Frederick Ungar, 1969, pp. 123–134.

Harvey, John. *Anouilh: A Study in Theatrics.* New Haven, Conn.: Yale University Press, 1964, pp. 96–97.

Heiney, Donald. "Jean Anouilh: The Revival of Tragedy," in *College English.* XVI (1955), pp. 331–335.

Lapp, John C. "Anouilh's *Medea*: A Debt to Seneca," in *Modern Language Notes.* LXIX (1954), pp. 183–187. Reprinted in Medea: *Myth and Dramatic Form.* Edited by James L. Sanderson. Boston: Houghton Mifflin, 1967, pp. 309–313.

Lyons, Charles R. "The Ambiguity of the Anouilh *Medea*," in *French Review.* XXXVII (1964), pp. 312–319.

Marsh, E.O. *Jean Anouilh, Poet of Pierrot and Pantaloon.* London: Allen, 1953, pp. 131–134.

Naughton, H. "The Heroines of Giraudoux and Anouilh," in *Renascence.* XIX (1966), pp. 17–20.

Pronko, Leonard Cabell. *The World of Jean Anouilh.* Berkeley: University of California Press, 1961, pp. 30–33, 207–210. Reprinted in Medea: *Myth and Dramatic Form.* Edited by James L. Sanderson. Boston: Houghton Mifflin, 1967, pp. 314–320.

Scott-James, Paule. "The Theatre of Jean Anouilh," in *Contemporary Review.* CLXXIX (1951), pp. 302–308.

Thody, Philip. *Anouilh.* Edinburgh: Oliver and Boyd, 1968, p. 35.

Poor Bitos

Archer, Marguerite. *Jean Anouilh.* New York: Columbia University Press, 1971, pp. 36–38.

Bishop, Thomas. *Pirandello and the French Theatre.* New York: New York University Press, 1960, pp. 111–113.

Brustein, Robert. *The Third Theatre.* New York: Knopf, 1969, pp. 91–95.

Clurman, Harold. *The Naked Image: Observations on the Modern Theatre.* New York: Macmillan, 1966, pp. 33–36.

della Fazia, Alba. *Jean Anouilh.* New York: Twayne, 1969, pp. 118–120.

Falb, Lewis W. *Jean Anouilh.* New York: Frederick Ungar, 1977, pp. 85–87.

Fowlie, Wallace. *Dionysus in Paris: A Guide to Contemporary French Theater.* New York: Meridian Books, 1960, pp. 110–112.

Harvey, John. *Anouilh: A Study in Theatrics.* New Haven, Conn.: Yale University Press, 1964, pp. 106–110, 163–164.

Howarth, W.D. "Anouilh," in *Forces in Modern French Drama: Studies in Variations on the Permitted Lie.* Edited by John Fletcher. New York: Frederick Ungar, 1972, pp. 103–104.

Knowles, Dorothy. *French Drama of the Inter-War Years, 1918–1939.* London: George G. Harrap, 1967, pp. 177–178.

Lenski, B.A. *Jean Anouilh: Stages in Rebellion.* Atlantic Highlands, N.J.: Humanities Press, 1975, pp. 47–57.

Lumley, Frederick. *New Trends in Twentieth Century Drama: A Survey Since Ibsen and Shaw.* London: Oxford University Press, 1967, pp. 170–181.

Novick, Julius. *Beyond Broadway: The Quest for Permanent Theatres.* New York: Hill and Wang, 1968, pp. 59–61.

Pronko, Leonard Cabell. *The World of Jean Anouilh.* Berkeley: University of California Press, 1961, pp. 52–53.

Thody, Philip. *Anouilh.* Edinburgh: Oliver and Boyd, 1968, pp. 56–63.

The Rehearsal

Bentley, Eric. *The Dramatic Event: An American Chronicle.* New York: Horizon Press, 1954, pp. 66–69.

Bishop, Thomas. *Pirandello and the French Theatre.* New York: New York University Press, 1960, pp. 114–115.

della Fazia, Alba. *Jean Anouilh.* New York: Twayne, 1969, pp. 80–83.

Falb, Lewis W.   *Jean Anouilh.* New York: Frederick Ungar, 1977, pp. 71–72.

Harvey, John.   *Anouilh: A Study in Theatrics.* New Haven, Conn.: Yale University Press, 1964, pp. 111–112, 130–131, 148–149.

Hobson, Harold.   *The Theater Now.* London: Longmans, Green, 1953, pp. 24–26.

Howarth, W.D.   "Anouilh," in *Forces in Modern French Drama: Studies in Variations on the Permitted Lie.* Edited by John Fletcher. New York: Frederick Ungar, 1972, pp. 95–107.

Lenski, B.A.   *Jean Anouilh: Stages in Rebellion.* Atlantic Highlands, N.J.: Humanities Press, 1975, pp. 17–24.

Marsh, E.O.   *Jean Anouilh, Poet of Pierrot and Pantaloon.* London: Allen, 1953, pp. 152–156.

Pronko, Leonard Cabell.   *The World of Jean Anouilh.* Berkeley: University of California Press, 1961, pp. 45–47.

Thody, Philip.   *Anouilh.* Edinburgh: Oliver and Boyd, 1968, pp. 66–70.

The Restless Heart

Archer, Marguerite.   *Jean Anouilh.* New York: Columbia University Press, 1971, p. 10.

Chiari, Joseph.   *The Contemporary French Theatre: The Flight from Naturalism.* New York: Macmillan, 1959, pp. 179–183.

della Fazia, Alba.   *Jean Anouilh.* New York: Twayne, 1969, pp. 49–52.

Falb, Lewis W.   *Jean Anouilh.* New York: Frederick Ungar, 1977, pp. 21–23.

Gascoigne, Bamber.   *Twentieth Century Drama.* London: Hutchinson's, 1962, pp. 144–146.

Jones, Robert Emmet.   *The Alienated Hero in Modern French Drama.* Athens: University of Georgia Press, 1962, pp. 65–67.

Knowles, Dorothy.   *French Drama of the Inter-War Years, 1918–1939.* London: George G. Harrap, 1967, pp. 170–172.

Lenski, B.A.   *Jean Anouilh: Stages in Rebellion.* Atlantic Highlands, N.J.: Humanities Press, 1975, pp. 25–34.

Lumley, Frederick.   *New Trends in Twentieth Century Drama: A Survey Since Ibsen and Shaw.* London: Oxford University Press, 1967, pp. 176–177.

Marsh, E.O.   *Jean Anouilh, Poet of Pierrot and Pantaloon.* London: Allen, 1953, pp. 48–60.

Pronko, Leonard Cabell.   *The World of Jean Anouilh.* Berkeley: University of California Press, 1961, pp. 9–11.

Scott-James, Paule.   "The Theatre of Jean Anouilh," in *Contemporary Review.* CLXXIX (1951), pp. 302–308.

Stevens, Linton C. "Hybris in Anouilh's *L'Hermine* and *La Sauvage*," in *French Review.* XXXVII (1964), pp. 658–663.

Thody, Philip. *Anouilh.* Edinburgh: Oliver and Boyd, 1968, pp. 16–19.

Ring Round the Moon

Archer, Marguerite. *Jean Anouilh.* New York: Columbia University Press, 1971, pp. 29–30.

Howarth, W.D. "Anouilh," in *Forces in Modern French Drama: Studies in Variations on the Permitted Lie.* Edited by John Fletcher. New York: Frederick Ungar, 1972, pp. 94–95.

Marsh, E.O. *Jean Anouilh, Poet of Pierrot and Pantaloon.* London: Allen, 1953, pp. 135–139.

Moore, Harry T. *Twentieth Century French Literature to World War II,* Volume II. Carbondale: Southern Illinois University, 1966, pp. 17–22.

Nathan, George Jean. *Theatre Book of the Year, 1950–51.* New York: Knopf, 1951, pp. 126–129.

Nelson, Robert James. *Play Within a Play: The Dramatist's Conception of His Art, Shakespeare to Anouilh.* New Haven, Conn.: Yale University Press, 1958, pp. 140–141.

Pronko, Leonard Cabell. *The World of Jean Anouilh.* Berkeley: University of California Press, 1961, pp. 41–44.

Styan, J.L. *The Elements of Drama.* London: Cambridge University Press, 1960, pp. 256–257.

Thody, Philip. *Anouilh.* Edinburgh: Oliver and Boyd, 1968, pp. 42–45.

Valency, Maurice. "The World of Jean Anouilh," in *Theatre Arts.* XLI (1957), pp. 31–32, 92–93.

Worsley, T.C. *The Fugitive Art.* London: John Lehmann, 1952, pp. 119–121.

Thieves' Carnival

Archer, Marguerite. *Jean Anouilh.* New York: Columbia University Press, 1971, pp. 27–28.

della Fazia, Alba. *Jean Anouilh.* New York: Twayne, 1969, pp. 68–71.

Falb, Lewis W. *Jean Anouilh.* New York: Frederick Ungar, 1977, pp. 34–35.

Knowles, Dorothy. *French Drama of the Inter-War Years, 1918–1939.* London: George G. Harrap, 1967, pp. 172–173.

Lenski, B.A. *Jean Anouilh: Stages in Rebellion.* Atlantic Highlands, N.J.: Humanities Press, 1975, pp. 17–24.

Luce, S. "The Whimsical and the Sordid in Jean Anouilh," in *Kentucky Foreign Language Quarterly.* XII (1965), pp. 93–95.

Lumley, Frederick. *New Trends in Twentieth Century Drama: A Survey Since Ibsen and Shaw.* London: Oxford University Press, 1967, p. 171.

Marsh, E.O. *Jean Anouilh, Poet of Pierrot and Pantaloon.* London: Allen, 1953, pp. 43–48.

Nelson, Robert James. *Play Within a Play: The Dramatist's Conception of His Art, Shakespeare to Anouilh.* New Haven, Conn.: Yale University Press, 1958, pp.134–136.

Pronko, Leonard Cabell. *The World of Jean Anouilh.* Berkeley: University of California Press, 1961, pp. 14–15.

Thody, Philip. *Anouilh.* Edinburgh: Oliver and Boyd, 1968, pp. 38–39.

Valency, Maurice. "The World of Jean Anouilh," in *Theatre Arts.* XLI (1957), pp. 31–32, 92–93.

Time Remembered

Archer, Marguerite. *Jean Anouilh.* New York: Columbia University Press, 1971, pp. 28–29.

Bishop, Thomas. *Pirandello and the French Theatre.* New York: New York University Press, 1960, pp. 118–119.

della Fazia, Alba. *Jean Anouilh.* New York: Twayne, 1969, pp. 74–77.

Falb, Lewis W. *Jean Anouilh.* New York: Frederick Ungar, 1977, pp. 34–35.

Howarth, W.D. "Anouilh," in *Forces in Modern French Drama: Studies in Variations on the Permitted Lie.* Edited by John Fletcher. New York: Frederick Ungar, 1972, pp. 93–94.

Kerr, Walter. *The Theater in Spite of Itself.* New York: Simon and Schuster, 1963, pp. 151–154.

Luce, S. "The Whimsical and the Sordid in Jean Anouilh," in *Kentucky Foreign Language Quarterly.* XII (1965), p. 95.

Marsh, E.O. *Jean Anouilh, Poet of Pierrot and Pantaloon.* London: Allen, 1953, pp. 88–91.

Nelson, Robert James. *Play Within a Play: The Dramatist's Conception of His Art, Shakespeare to Anouilh.* New Haven, Conn.: Yale University Press, 1958, pp. 137–140.

Pronko, Leonard Cabell. *The World of Jean Anouilh.* Berkeley: University of California Press, 1961, p. 16.

Thody, Philip. *Anouilh.* Edinburgh: Oliver and Boyd, 1968, pp. 39–41.

Traveller Without Luggage

Bishop, Thomas. *Pirandello and the French Theatre.* New York: New York University Press, 1960, pp. 109–110.

Champigney, R. "Theater in a Mirror," in *Yale French Studies.* XIV (Winter, 1954/1955), pp. 59–60.

Chiari, Joseph. *The Contemporary French Theatre: The Flight from Naturalism.* New York: Macmillan, 1959, pp. 195–196.

Clurman, Harold. *The Naked Image: Observations on the Modern Theatre.* New York: Macmillan, 1966, pp. 31–33.

della Fazia, Alba. *Jean Anouilh.* New York: Twayne, 1969, pp. 53–56.

Falb, Lewis W. *Jean Anouilh.* New York: Frederick Ungar, 1977, pp. 23–32.

Grossvogel, David I. *The Blasphemers.* Ithaca, N.Y.: Cornell University Press, 1962, pp. 76–77.

Harvey, John. *Anouilh: A Study in Theatrics.* New Haven, Conn.: Yale University Press, 1964, pp. 17–18.

Hobson, Harold. *The Theater Now.* London: Longmans, Green, 1953, pp. 39–43.

Howarth, W.D. "Anouilh," in *Forces in Modern French Drama: Studies in Variations on the Permitted Lie.* Edited by John Fletcher. New York: Frederick Ungar, 1972, pp. 91–92.

Knowles, Dorothy. *French Drama of the Inter-War Years, 1918–1939.* London: George G. Harrap, 1967, pp. 169–170.

Marsh, E.O. *Jean Anouilh, Poet of Pierrot and Pantaloon.* London: Allen, 1953, pp. 65–76.

Milne, Tom. "Traveller Without Commitment," in *Encore.* VI (March–April, 1959), pp. 37–39.

Pronko, Leonard Cabell. *The World of Jean Anouilh.* Berkeley: University of California Press, 1961, pp. 12–14.

Thody, Philip. *Anouilh.* Edinburgh: Oliver and Boyd, 1968, pp. 19–22.

The Waltz of the Toreadors

Archer, Marguerite. *Jean Anouilh.* New York: Columbia University Press, 1971, pp. 33–35.

Benedict, S. "Anouilh in America," in *Modern Language Journal.* XLV (December, 1961), pp. 342–343.

della Fazia, Alba. *Jean Anouilh.* New York: Twayne, 1969, pp. 90–95.

Falb, Lewis W. *Jean Anouilh.* New York: Frederick Ungar, 1977, pp. 88–99.

Fowlie, Wallace. *Dionysus in Paris: A Guide to Contemporary French Theater.* New York: Meridian Books, 1960, pp. 116–119.

Gassner, John. *Dramatic Soundings: Evaluations and Retractions Culled from Thirty Years of Dramatic Criticism.* New York: Crown, 1968, pp. 294–296.

Grossvogel, David I. *Twentieth Century French Drama.* Ithaca, N.Y.: Cornell University Press, 1961, pp. 202–204.

Harvey, John. *Anouilh: A Study in Theatrics.* New Haven, Conn.: Yale University Press, 1964, pp. 18–19, 25–26, 31–32, 110–111.

Howarth, W.D. "Anouilh," in *Forces in Modern French Drama: Studies in Variations on the Permitted Lie.* New York: Frederick Ungar, 1972, pp. 98–99.

Kauffmann, Stanley. "Family Life Here and There," in *New Republic.* CXLVII (July 30, 1962), pp. 29–30.

Kerr, Walter. *The Theater in Spite of Itself.* New York: Simon and Schuster, 1963, pp. 144–145.

Lambert, J.W. *"Waltz of the Toreadors,"* in *Plays and Players.* XXI (1974), pp. 43–44.

Lenski, B.A. *Jean Anouilh: Stages in Rebellion.* Atlantic Highlands, N.J.: Humanities Press, 1975, pp. 17–24.

Lumley, Frederick. *New Trends in Twentieth Century Drama: A Survey Since Ibsen and Shaw.* London: Oxford University Press, 1967, pp. 170–181.

Marsh, E.O. *Jean Anouilh, Poet of Pierrot and Pantaloon.* London: Allen, 1953, pp. 164–175.

Nelson, Robert James. *Play Within a Play: The Dramatist's Conception of His Art, Shakespeare to Anouilh.* New Haven, Conn.: Yale University Press, 1958, pp. 134–135.

Pronko, Leonard Cabell. *The World of Jean Anouilh.* Berkeley: University of California Press, 1961, pp. 59–62.

Thody, Philip. *Anouilh.* Edinburgh: Oliver and Boyd, 1968, pp. 23–25.

Valency, Maurice. "The World of Jean Anouilh," in *Theatre Arts.* XLI (1957), pp. 31–32, 92–93.

Walker, Roy. "Another Anouilh," in *Theatre.* VII (January 17, 1953), pp. 8–10.

Williamson, Audrey. *Contemporary Theatre, 1953–1956.* London: Rockliff, 1956, pp. 73–75.

LUCIUS APULEIUS
(c.125–c.175)

Metamorphoses, or The Golden Ass

Birley, A. "Apuleius: Roman Provincial Life," in *History Today*. XVIII (September, 1968), pp. 629–636.

Cherpack, C. "Ideas and Prose Fiction in Antiquity," in *Comparative Literature Studies*. XI (Spring, 1974), pp. 185–203.

Dietrich, B.C. "The Golden Art of Apuleius," in *Greece and Rome*. XIII (October, 1966), pp. 189–206.

Drake, G.C. "Candidus. A Unifying Theme in Apuleius' *Metamorphoses*," in *Classical Journal*. LXIII (1968), pp. 266–267.

————. "Ghost Story in *The Golden Ass* by Apuleius," in *Papers in Language and Literature*. XIII (Winter, 1977), pp. 3–15.

Ebel, H. "Apuleius and the Present Time," in *Arethusa*. III (1970), pp. 155–176.

Haight, E.H. "Comparison of the Greek Romance and Apuleius' *Metamorphoses*," in *Essays on The Greek Romances*. New York: Longmans, Green, 1936, pp. 86–120.

————. *Apuleius and His Influence*. New York: Cooper Square Press, 1963.

Mackay, L.A. "The Sin of The Golden Ass," in *Arion*. IV (Autumn, 1965), pp. 474–480.

Massey, Irving. "*The Golden Ass*: Character Versus Structure," in *The Gaping Pig*. Berkeley: University of California Press, 1976, pp. 34–75.

Nethercut, W.A. "Apuleius' Literary Art: Resonance and Depth in the *Metamorphoses*," in *Classical Journal*. LXIV (December, 1968), pp. 110–119.

————. "Apuleius' *Metamorphoses*: The Journey," in *Agon*. III (1968), pp. 97–134.

Rexroth, Kenneth. "Apuleius: *The Golden Ass*," in *Classics Revisited*. Chicago: Quadrangle Books, 1968, pp. 116–120.

Rubino, C.A. "Literary Intelligibility in Apuleius' *Metamorphoses*," in *Classical Bulletin*. XLII (1966), pp. 65–69.

Sandy, G.N. "Knowledge and Curiosity in Apuleius' *Metamorphoses*," in *Latomus*. XXXI (1972), pp. 179–183.

Schlam, C.C. "The Curiosity of *The Golden Ass*," in *Classical Journal*. LXIV (December, 1968), pp. 120–125.

Smith, W.S. "The Narrative Voice in Apuleius' *Metamorphoses*," in *Transactions of The American Philological Association*. CIII (1972), pp. 513–534.

Summers, R.J.   "Roman Justice and Apuleius' *Metamorphoses*," in *Transactions of The American Philological Association*. CI (1970), pp. 511–531.

Todd, F.A.   "*Golden Ass*," in *Some Ancient Novels*. New York: Oxford University Press, 1940, pp. 102–140.

Walsh, P.G.   *The Roman Novel*: The Satyricon *of Petronius and* The Metamorphoses *of Apuleius*. London: Cambridge University Press, 1970.

THOMAS AQUINAS
(c.1225–1274)

Summa Theologica

Armstrong, Arthur Hilary. *The Greek Philosophical Background of the Psychology of St. Thomas.* London: Blackfriars, 1952.

Chenu, Marie Dominique. *Toward Understanding St. Thomas.* Translated by A.M. Landry and D. Hughes. Chicago: H. Regnery, 1964.

Colish, M.L. "Saint Thomas in Historical Perspective: The Modern Period," in *Church History.* XLIV (December, 1975), pp. 433–449.

Copleston, Frederick. *A History of Philosophy.* London: Search Press, 1976, Volume II, pp. 302–434.

————. *Thomas Aquinas.* New York: Barnes & Noble, 1977.

Ferrell, Walter. *A Companion to the* Summa. New York: Sheed and Ward, 1938–1942.

Gilson, Etienne Henry. *The Christian Philosophy of St. Thomas Aquinas.* Translated by L.K. Shook. New York: Random House, 1956.

————. "Thomas Aquinas," in *A History of Christian Philosophy in the Middle Ages.* New York: Random House, 1955, pp. 361–383.

————. *The Philosophy of Saint Thomas Aquinas.* Folcroft, Pa.: Folcroft Library Editions, 1924.

Kenny, Anthony, Compiler. *Aquinas: A Collection of Critical Essays.* Garden City, N.Y.: Anchor Books, 1969.

Klocker, Harry R., Editor. *Thomism and Modern Thought.* New York: Irvington Publications, 1962.

Kristeller, Paul O. "Thomism and the Italian Thought of the Renaissance," in *Medieval Aspects of Renaissance Learning.* Edited by Edward P. Mahoney. Durham: North Carolina Press, 1974, pp. 29–91.

Levi, Albert William. "Medieval Philosophy: The Age of the Saints," in *Philosophy as Social Expression.* Chicago: University of Chicago Press, 1974, pp. 101–162.

Maritain, Jacques. *The Angelic Doctor.* Translated by J.F. Scanlan. New York: Dial, 1931.

Pegis, Anton. *Saint Thomas and Philosophy.* Milwaukee: Marquette University Press, 1964.

————. *Saint Thomas and the Greeks.* Milwaukee: Marquette University Press, 1939.

Pieper, Josef. *Guide to Thomas Aquinas.* Translated by Richard Winston and Clara Winston. New York: Pantheon, 1962.

Riley, Isaac W. "Ecclesiastical Morals: St. Thomas Aquinas," in *Men and Morals*. New York: Frederick Ungar, 1960, pp. 179–192.

Robb, James Harry. *Man as Infinite Spirit*. Milwaukee: Marquette University Press, 1974.

Vann, G. *Saint Thomas Aquinas*. New York: Benzinger Brothers, 1947.

Weisheipl, James A. *Friar Thomas D'Aquino: His Life, Thought, and Work*. Garden City, N.Y.: Doubleday, 1974.

Wheeler, Mary Cecelia. *Philosophy and the* Summa Theologica *of Saint Thomas Aquinas*. Washington, D.C.: Catholic University of America Press, 1956.

PIETRO ARETINO
(1492–1556)

The Courtesan

Damiani, Bruno M. "Delicado and Aretino: Aspects of a Literary Profile," in *Kentucky Romance Quarterly*. XVII (1970), pp. 309–324.

El-Gabalawy, Saad. "Aretino's Pornography and Renaissance Satire," in *Rocky Mountain Review of Language and Literature*. XXX (1976), pp. 87–99.

Herrick, Marvin T. *Italian Comedy in the Renaissance*. Urbana: University of Illinois Press, 1960, pp. 85–95.

Wright, Jules N., "The Hypocrite in Aretino and in Molière," in *Forum Italicum*. VI (1972), pp. 393–397.

LUDOVICO ARIOSTO
(1474–1533)

Orlando Furioso

Brand, C.P. *Ludovico Ariosto: A Preface to the* Orlando Furioso. Edinburgh: Edinburgh University Press, 1974.

Carne-Ross, D.S. "The One and the Many: A Reading of the *Orlando Furioso*," in *Arion*. III (1976), pp. 146–219.

Durling, R.M. *The Figure of the Poet in Renaissance Epic*. Cambridge, Mass.: Harvard University Press, 1965, pp. 112–181.

Edwards, Ernest W. *The* Orlando Furioso *and Its Predecessor*. Folcroft, Pa.: Folcroft Library Editions, 1976.

Gibaldi, Joseph. "Will Ariosto Be the Next Tolkien?," in *College Literature*. II (1975), pp. 138–142.

Griffin, Robert. *Ludovico Ariosto*. New York: Twayne, 1974.

Hanning, Robert W. "Sources of Illusion: Plot Elements and Their Thematic Uses in Ariosto's Ginevra Episode," in *Forum Italicum*. V (1971), pp. 514–535.

Hough, Graham G. *A Preface to the* Faerie Queene. London: Duckworth, 1962, pp. 25–47.

Kennedy, W.J. "Ariosto's Ironic Allegory," in *Modern Language Notes*. LXXXVIII (January, 1973), pp. 44–67.

Marinelli, P.V. "Redemptive Laughter: Comedy in the Italian Romances," in *Versions of Medieval Comedy*. Edited by P.G. Ruggiers. Norman: University of Oklahoma Press, 1977, pp. 227–248.

Molinaro, Julius A. "Ariosto and the Seven Deadly Sins," in *Forum Italicum*. III (June, 1969), pp. 252–269.

———. "Sin and Punishment in the *Orlando Furioso*," in *MLN*. LXXXIX (January, 1974), pp. 35–46.

———. "Avarice and Sloth in the *Orlando Furioso*," in *Renaissance and Reformation*. X (1974), pp. 103–115.

Quadri, Franco. "*Orlando Furioso*," in *Tulane Drama Review*. XIV (1969/70), pp. 116–124.

Tommaso, Andrea di. "*Insania* and *Furor*: A Diagnostic Note on Orlando's Malady," in *Romance Notes*. XIV (1972/73), pp. 583–588.

Wilkins, Ernest H. *A History of Italian Literature*. Revised by Thomas G. Bergin. Cambridge, Mass.: Harvard University Press, 1974, pp. 185–195.

ARISTOPHANES
(c. 448 B.C.—c. 385 B.C.)

The Acharnians

Henderson, J. "Note on Aristophanes' *Acharnians*," in *Classical Philology*. LXVIII (October, 1968), pp. 289–290.

Melchinger, S. *Euripides*. New York: Frederick Ungar, 1973, pp. 17–19.

Merry, W.W. Acharnians; *with Introduction, Notes, and Dialectical Glossary*. Oxford: Clarendon Press, 1925.

Mitchell, T. Acharnians, *with Notes, Critical and Explanatory*. London: John Murray, 1835.

Rogers, B. *Acharnians*. London: G. Bell, 1930.

Ruck, C. "Euripides' Mother: Vegetables and the Phallus in Aristophanes," in *Arion*. II (1975), pp. 13–57.

Sandbach, F.H. "An Athenian Comedy," in *The Comic Theatre of Greece and Rome*. New York: Norton, 1977, pp. 15–25.

Solomos, Alexis. *The Living Aristophanes*. Ann Arbor: University of Michigan Press, 1974, pp. 67–85.

Sommerstein, A.H. *Acharnians, The Clouds, Lysistrata*. Baltimore: Penguin, 1974.

Starkie, W.J.M. The Acharnians, *with Introduction, English Prose Translation, Critical Notes, and Commentary*. London: Macmillan, 1909.

Stothard, P. "*Acharnians*," in *Plays and Players*. XXIV (July, 1977), pp. 24–25.

Walcot, P. "Aristophanes and Other Audiences," in *Greece and Rome*. XVIII (1971), pp. 35–50.

West, M.L. "Aristophanes' *Acharnians* 1178–86," in *Classical Review*. XXI (June, 1971), pp. 157–158.

The Birds

Arrowsmith, W. "Aristophanes' *Birds*: The Fantasy Politics of Eros," in *Arion*. I (Spring, 1973), pp. 119–167.

Blake, W.E. "The Aristophanic Bird Chorus—a Riddle," in *American Journal of Philology*. LXIV (January, 1943), pp. 87–91.

Borthwick, E.K. "Two Notes on the *Birds* of Aristophanes," in *Classical Review*. XVII (December, 1967), pp. 248–250.

Dale, A.M. "Hoopoe's Song (Aristophanes, *Birds* 227 ff)," in *Classical Review*. XIX (December, 1969), pp. 199–200.

Downs, R.B. "Greek Comic Genius: Aristophanes," in *Famous Books, Ancient and Medieval*. New York: Barnes & Noble, 1974, pp. 76–81.

Henry, A.S. "Aristophanes, *Birds* 268–93," in *Classical Philology*. LXXII (January, 1977), pp. 52–53.

Hines, P. "Translation of Aristophanes' *Birds*," in *Notes and Queries*. XVIII (October, 1971), pp. 378–379.

Lawler, L.B. "Four Dances in *The Birds* of Aristophanes," in *Transactions of the American Philological Association*. LXXIII (1942), pp. 58–63.

McCollum, W.G. "The Ambiguities of *The Birds*," in *The Divine Average; a View of Comedy*. Cleveland: The Press of Case Western Reserve University, 1971, pp. 125–138.

Maxmim, J. "*Meniskoi* and the *Birds*," in *Journal of Hellenic Studies*. XCV (1975), pp. 175–180.

Murray, Gilbert. *The Birds*. New York: Oxford University Press, 1950.

Pollard, J.R.T. "*The Birds* of Aristophanes—a Source Book for Old Beliefs," in *American Journal of Philology*. LXIX (October, 1948), pp. 353–376.

Quain, E.A. "Aristophanes: *Lysistrata, Birds, Clouds*," in *Great Books: A Christian Appraisal; a Symposium on the First Year's Program of the Great Books Foundation*. Old Greenwich, Conn.: Devin-Adair, 1949, pp. 19–24.

Rosenmeyer, T.G. "Notes on Aristophanes' *Birds*," in *American Journal of Philology*. XCIII (January, 1972), pp. 223–238.

Schreiber, F. "Double-barreled Joke: Aristophanes, *Birds*, 38," in *American Journal of Philology*. XCV (Summer, 1974), pp. 95–99.

Solomos, Alexis. *The Living Aristophanes*. Ann Arbor: University of Michigan Press, 1974, pp. 165–180.

Wycherly, R.E. "*Birds*," in *Classical Quarterly*. XXXI (January, 1937), pp. 22–31.

The Clouds

Adkins, A.W.H. "*Clouds*, Mysteries, Socrates and Plato," in *Antichthon*. IV (1970), pp. 13–24.

Brumbaugh, Robert S. "Scientific Apparatus on Stage in 423 B.C.," in *Yale Classical Studies*. XXII (1972), pp. 215–221.

Downs, R.B. "Greek Comic Genius: Aristophanes," in *Famous Books, Ancient and Medieval*. New York: Barnes & Noble, 1974, pp. 76–81.

Haslan, M.W. "Attribution and Action in Aristophanes, *Clouds* 723–796," in *Harvard Studies in Classical Philology*. LXXX (1976), pp. 45–47.

Havelock. E.A. "The Socratic Self as It Is Parodied in Aristophanes' *Clouds*," in *Yale Classical Studies*. XXII (1972), pp. 1–18.

Karavites, P. "Socrates in the *Clouds*," in *Classical Bulletin*. L (1973–1974), pp. 65–69.

Quain, E.A. "Aristophanes: *Lysistrata, Birds, Clouds*," in *Great Books: A Christian Appraisal; a Symposium on the First Year's Program of the Great Books Foundation.* Old Greenwich, Conn.: Devin-Adair, 1949, pp. 19–24.

Segal, C. "Aristophanes' Cloud Chorus," in *Areth.* II (Fall, 1969), pp. 143–161.

Solomos, Alexis. *The Living Aristophanes.* Ann Arbor: University of Michigan Press, 1974, pp. 105–125.

Sommerstein, A.H. *Acharnians, The Clouds, Lysistrata.* Baltimore: Penguin, 1974.

The Frogs

Borthwick, E.K. "Seeing Weasels: The Superstitious Background of the Empusa Scene in the *Frogs*," in *Classical Quarterly*. XVIII (1968), pp. 200–206.

Campbell, A.Y. "Aristophanes' *Frogs*," in *Classical Review*. III (December, 1953), pp. 137–138.

Cary, A.L.M. "The Appearance of Charon in the *Frogs*," in *Classical Review*. LI (May, 1937), pp. 52–53.

Demand, N. "Identity of the *Frogs*," in *Classical Philology*. LXV (April, 1970), pp. 83–87.

Denniston, J.D. "Technical Terms in the *Frogs* of Aristophanes," in *Classical Quarterly*. (July, 1927), pp. 113–121.

Dickerson, G.W. "Aristophanes' *Renae* 862. A Note on the Anatomy of Euripidean Tragedy," in *Harvard Studies in Classical Philology*. LXXVIII (1974), pp. 177–188.

Downs, R.B. "Greek Comic Genius: Aristophanes," in *Famous Books, Ancient and Medieval*. New York: Barnes & Noble, 1974, pp. 76–81.

Hooker, G.T.W. "The Topography of the *Frogs*," in *Journal of Hellenic Studies*. LXXX (1960), pp. 112–117.

Littlefield, D.J., Editor. *Twentieth Century Interpretations of* The Frogs; *a Collection of Critical Essays.* Englewood Cliffs, N.J.: Prentice-Hall, 1961.

MacDowell, D.M. "*Frogs* Chorus," in *Classical Review*. XXII (March, 1972), pp. 3–5.

Russo, C.F. "The Revision of Aristophanes' *Frogs*," in *Greece and Rome*. XIII (April, 1966), pp. 1–13.

Solomos, Alexis. *The Living Aristophanes.* Ann Arbor: University of Michigan Press, 1974, pp. 208–227.

Taplin, O.   "Aeschylean Silences and Silences in Aeschylus," in *Harvard Studies in Classical Philology*. LXXVI (1972), pp. 57–97.

Walcot, P.   "Aristophanes and Other Audiences," in *Greece and Rome*. XVIII (1971), pp. 35–50.

Wills, G.   "Aeschylus' Victory in the *Frogs*," in *American Journal of Philology*. XC (January, 1969), pp. 48–51.

Wilson, A.M.   "Euripolidean Precedent for the Rowing Scene in Aristophanes' *Frogs*?," in *Classical Quarterly*. XXIV (December, 1974), pp. 250–252.

Young, A.M.   "*The Frogs* of Aristophanes as a Type of Play," in *Classical Journal*. XX (October, 1933), pp. 23–32.

Lysistrata

Downs, R.B.   "Greek Comic Genius: Aristophanes," in *Famous Books, Ancient and Medieval*. New York: Barnes & Noble, 1974, pp. 76–81.

Elderkin, G.W.   "Aphrodite and Athena in the *Lysistrata* of Aristophanes," in *Classical Philology*. XXXV (October, 1935), pp. 387–396.

Hulton, A.O.   "The Woman on the Acropolis. A Note on the Structure of the *Lysistrata*," in *Greece and Rome*. XIX (1972), pp. 32–36.

Quain, E.A.   "Aristophanes: *Lysistrata, Birds, Clouds*," in *Great Books: A Christian Appraisal; a Symposium on the First Year's Program of the Great Books Foundation*. Old Greenwich, Conn.: Devin-Adair, 1949, pp. 19–24.

Solomos, Alexis.   *The Living Aristophanes*. Ann Arbor: University of Michigan Press, 1974, pp. 181–190.

Sommerstein, A.H.   *Acharnians, The Clouds, Lysistrata*. Baltimore: Penguin, 1974.

Vaio, J.   "The Manipulation of Theme and Action in Aristophanes' *Lysistrata*," in *Greek, Roman, and Byzantine Studies*. XIV (1973), pp. 369–380.

Thesmophoriazusae

Miller, H.W.   "Euripides' *Telephus* and the *Thesmophoriazusae* of Aristophanes," in *Classical Philology*. XLIII (July, 1948), pp. 174–183.

————.   "On the Parabasis of the *Thesmophoriazusae*," in *Classical Philology*. XLII (July, 1947), pp. 180–181.

————.   "Some Tragic Influences in the *Thesmophoriazusae* of Aristophanes," in *Transactions of the American Philological Association*. LXXVII (1946), pp. 171–182.

Ruck, C.   "Euripides' Mother: Vegetables and the Phallus in Aristophanes," in *Arion*. II (1975), pp. 13–57.

Solomos, Alexis.   *The Living Aristophanes*. Ann Arbor: University of Michigan Press, 1974, pp. 191–207.

The Wasps

Borthwick, E.K. "The Dances of Philocleon and the Sons of Carninus in Aristophanes' *Wasps*," in *Classical Quarterly*. XVIII (1968), pp. 44–51.

Dale, A.M. "An Interpretation of Aristophanes' *Vespae* 130–210 and Its Consequences for the Stage of Aristophanes," in *Journal of Hellenic Studies*. LXXVII (1957), pp. 205–211.

Killeen, J.F. "The Comic Costume Controversy," in *Classical Quarterly*. XXI (1971), pp. 51–54.

Long, T. "Two Generations of Attribution in Aristophanes' *Vespae*," in *American Journal of Philology*. XCIII (July, 1972), pp. 462–467.

————. "The Parados of Aristophanes' *Wasps*," in *Illinois Classical Studies*. I (1976), pp. 15–21.

Platnauer, M. "Three Notes on Aristophanes' *Wasps*," in *Classical Review*. LXIII (May, 1949), pp. 6–7.

Post, L.A. "Catana the Cheese-Grater in Aristophanes' *Wasps*," in *American Journal of Philology*. LIII (July, 1932), p. 265.

Ruck, C. "Euripides' Mother: Vegetables and the Phallus in Aristophanes," in *Arion*. II (1975), pp. 13–57.

Solomos, Alexis. *The Living Aristophanes*. Ann Arbor: University of Michigan Press, 1974, pp. 126–136.

Vaio, J. "Aristophanes' *Wasps*. The Relevance of the Final Scenes," in *Greek, Roman, and Byzantine Studies*. XII (1971), pp. 335–351.

ARISTOTLE
(384 B.C.–322 B.C.)

The Poetics

Abercrombie, L. "Aristotle's *Poetics*," in *Principles of Literary Criticism*. New York: Barnes & Noble, 1960, pp. 63–117.

Brereton, G. "The Legacy of Aristotle," in *Principles of Tragedy*. Coral Gables, Fla.: University of Miami Press, 1968, pp. 21–47.

Butcher, S.H. *Aristotle's Theory of Poetry and Fine Art*. New York: Dover, 1951.

Cooper, L. Poetics *of Aristotle, Its Meaning and Influence*. Ithaca, N.Y.: Cornell University Press, 1956.

Devereux, G. "The Structure of Tragedy and the Structure of the Psyche in Aristotle's *Poetics*," in *Psychoanalysis and Philosophy*. Edited by Charles Hanly and Morris Lazerowitz. New York: International Universities Press, 1971, pp. 46–75.

Else, G.F. *Aristotle's* Poetics: *The Argument*. Cambridge, Mass.: Harvard University Press, 1958.

Fergusson, Francis. "*The Poetics* of Aristotle," in *Literary Landmarks*. Rutgers: Rutgers University Press, 1975, pp. 3–36.

Gassner, J. "Aristotelian Literary Criticism," in *Dramatic Soundings*. New York: Crown, 1968, pp. 133–152.

Gilbert, A.H. "Aristotle's Four Species of Tragedy (*Poetics* 18) and Their Importance for Dramatic Criticism," in *American Journal of Philology*. LXVIII (October, 1947), pp. 363–381.

Golden, L. "Aristotle and the Audience for Tragedy," in *Mnemosyne*. XXIX, Part IV (1976), pp. 351–359.

————. "Epic, Tragedy and Catharsis," in *Classical Philology*. LXXI (January, 1976), pp. 77–85.

Golden, L. and O. Hardison. *Aristotle's* Poetics. Englewood Cliffs, N.J.: Prentice-Hall, 1967.

Gomme, A.W. "Some Problems in Aristotle's *Poetics*," in *Greek Attitudes to Poetry and History*. Berkeley: University of California Press, 1954, pp. 49–72.

Howell, Wilbur Samuel. "Aristotle and Horace on Rhetoric and Poetics," in *Poetics, Rhetoric and Logic; Studies in the Basic Disciplines of Criticism*. Ithaca, N.Y.: Cornell University Press, 1975, pp. 45–72.

Jones, H.J.F. "Aristotle's *Poetics*," in *On Aristotle and Greek Tragedy*. Oxford: Clarendon Press, 1962, pp. 11–62.

Kitto, H.D.F. "Criticism and Chaos," in *Poiesis; Structure and Plot.* Berkeley: University of California Press, 1966, pp. 1–32.

Lucas, F.L. *Tragedy: Serious Drama in Relation to Aristotle's* Poetics. New York: Macmillan, 1958.

Myers, H.A. "Aristotle's Study of Tragedy," in *Tragedy: A View of Life.* Ithaca, N.Y.: Cornell University Press, 1956, pp. 28–53.

Olson, Elder, Editor. *Aristotle's* Poetics *and English Literature.* Chicago: University of Chicago Press, 1965.

Wheelwright, P.E. "Mimesis and Katharsis: An Archetypal Consideration," in *English Institute Essays, 1946–1952.* New York: Columbia University Press, 1951, pp. 3–30.

Wimsatt, W.K. and C. Brooks. "Aristotle: Tragedy and Comedy," in their *Literary Criticism.* New York: Knopf, 1957, pp. 21–34.

MATTHEW ARNOLD
(1822–1888)

Culture and Anarchy

Alexander, Edward. *Matthew Arnold, John Ruskin and the Modern Temper.* Columbus: Ohio State University Press, 1973.

Anderson, Warren D. *Matthew Arnold and the Classical Tradition.* Ann Arbor: University of Michigan Press, 1965.

Arnold Newsletter. Volume 1– Spring 1973– Ypsilanti: Eastern Michigan University Press.

Bush, Douglas. *Matthew Arnold: A Survey of His Poetry and Prose.* New York: Macmillan, 1971.

Connell, William F. *The Educational Thought and Influence of Matthew Arnold.* London: Routledge and Kegan Paul, 1950.

Coulling, Sidney M. "The Evolution of *Culture and Anarchy*, in *Studies in Philology.* LX (October, 1963), pp. 637–688.

_____. *Matthew Arnold and His Critics: A Study of Arnold's Controversies.* Athens: Ohio University Press, 1974.

DeLaura, David J., Editor. *Matthew Arnold: A Collection of Critical Essays.* Englewood Cliffs, N.J.: Prentice-Hall, 1973.

Goldberg, J.F. "*Culture and Anarchy* and the Present Tense," in *Kenyon Review.* XXXI (1969), pp. 583–611.

Johnson, Wendell S. *The Voices of Matthew Arnold: An Essay in Criticism.* Westport, Conn.: Greenwood Press, 1973. Reprint of 1961 Edition.

Madden, William A. *Matthew Arnold: A Study of the Aesthetic Temperament in Victorian England.* Bloomington: Indiana University Press, 1967.

Neiman, Fraser. *Matthew Arnold.* New York: Twayne, 1968.

Raleigh, John H. *Matthew Arnold and American Culture.* Berkeley: University of California Press, 1957.

Rowse, Alfred L. *Matthew Arnold: Poet and Prophet.* London: Thames and Hudson, 1976.

Super, Robert H. *The Time-Spirit of Matthew Arnold.* Ann Arbor: University of Michigan Press, 1970.

Thorpe, Michael. *Matthew Arnold.* London: Evans, 1969.

Trilling, Lionel. *Matthew Arnold.* New York: Columbia University Press, 1949.

Walcott, Fred G. *The Origins of* Culture and Anarchy*: Matthew Arnold and Popular Education in England.* Toronto: University of Toronto Press, 1970.

The Poetry of Arnold

Allott, Kenneth, Editor. *Matthew Arnold.* Athens: Ohio State University Press, 1976.

Anderson, Warren D. *Matthew Arnold and the Classical Tradition.* Ann Arbor: University of Michigan Press, 1965.

Arnold Newsletter. Volume 1– Spring 1973– Ypsilanti: Eastern Michigan University Press.

Buckler, William E. *The Major Victorian Poets: Tennyson, Browning, Arnold.* Boston: Houghton Mifflin, 1973.

Bush, Douglas. *Matthew Arnold: A Survey of His Poetry and Prose.* New York: Macmillan, 1971.

Connell, William F. *The Educational Thought and Influence of Matthew Arnold.* London: Routledge and Kegan Paul, 1950.

Coulling, Sidney M. *Matthew Arnold and His Critics: A Study of Arnold's Controversies.* Athens: Ohio University Press, 1974.

Culler, Arthur D. *Imaginative Reason: The Poetry of Matthew Arnold.* Westport, Conn.: Greenwood Press, 1976. Reprint of 1966 Edition.

Dawson, Carl, Editor. *Matthew Arnold, the Poetry.* London: Routledge and Kegan Paul, 1973.

DeLaura, David J., Editor. *Matthew Arnold: A Collection of Critical Essays.* Englewood Cliffs, N.J.: Prentice-Hall, 1973.

Johnson, Wendell S. *The Voices of Matthew Arnold: An Essay in Criticism.* Westport, Conn.: Greenwood Press, 1973. Reprint of 1961 Edition.

Latham, Jacqueline, Editor. *Critics of Matthew Arnold.* London: Allen and Unwin, 1973.

Madden, William A. *Matthew Arnold: a Study of the Aesthetic Temperament in Victorian England.* Bloomington: Indiana University Press, 1967.

Malder, F.B. "Matthew Arnold and the Circle of Recurrence," in *Victorian Poetry.* XIV (Winter, 1976), pp. 293–309.

Neiman, Fraser. *Matthew Arnold.* New York: Twayne, 1968.

Rowse, Alfred L. *Matthew Arnold: Poet and Prophet.* London: Thames and Hudson, 1976.

Super, Robert H. *The Time-Spirit of Matthew Arnold.* Ann Arbor: University of Michigan Press, 1970.

Thorpe, Michael. *Matthew Arnold.* London: Evans, 1969.

Tinker, Chauncey R. *The Poetry of Matthew Arnold: A Commentary.* New York: Russell and Russell, 1970. Reprint of 1940 Edition.

Trilling, Lionel. *Matthew Arnold.* New York: Columbia University Press, 1949.

Trotter, D. "Hidden Ground Within: Matthew Arnold's Lyric and Elegaic Poetry," in *ELH*. XLIV (January, 1977), pp. 526–553.

LOUIS AUCHINCLOSS
(1917–   )

The Embezzler

Hicks, Granville. "A Bad Legend in His Lifetime," in *Saturday Review.* XLIX (February 5, 1966), pp. 35–36. Reprinted in *Literary Horizons: A Quarter Century of American Fiction.* New York: New York University Press, 1970, pp. 201–204.

Knickerbocker, Conrad. "The Crooked and the Straight," in *New York Times Book Review.* (February 6, 1966), pp. 1, 38.

Lehan, Richard. "The American Novel—A Survey of 1966," in *Wisconsin Studies in Contemporary Literature.* VIII (Summer, 1967), pp. 442–444.

Milne, W. Gordon. "Auchincloss and the Novel of Manners," in *University of Kansas City Review.* XXIX (March, 1963), pp. 177–185. Reprinted in *The Sense of Society: A History of the American Novel of Manners.* Cranbury, N.J.: Fairleigh Dickinson University Press, 1977, pp. 236–253.

Pickrel, Paul. "The Double Vision of Society," in *Harper's.* CCXXXII (March, 1966), pp. 148–149.

Sullivan, Richard. "Primer's Past," in *Critic.* XXIV (April–May, 1966), pp. 61–62.

Weeks, Edward. "After the Market Broke," in *Atlantic.* CCXVII (February, 1966), p. 129.

Westbrook, Wayne W. "Louis Auchincloss' Vision of Wall Street," in *Critique.* XV (1973), pp. 57–66.

The Great World and Timothy Colt

Bliven, Bruce, Jr. "*The Great World and Timothy Colt,*" in *Saturday Review.* XXXIX (October 20, 1956), p. 17.

Brooks, John. "Ideals on Trial," in *New York Times Book Review.* (October 21, 1956), pp. 4, 50.

Brudney, Victor. "*The Great World and Timothy Colt,*" in *Yale Law Journal.* LXVII (November, 1957), pp. 176–178.

Gutwillig, Robert. "Honorable Failure," in *Commonweal.* LXIX (December 12, 1958), pp. 296–297.

Kane, Patricia. "Lawyers at the Top: The Fiction of Louis Auchincloss," in *Critique.* VII (Winter, 1964–1965), pp. 36–46.

Kaplan, Benjamin. "*The Great World and Timothy Colt,*" in *Harvard Law Review.* LXX (April, 1957), pp. 1132–1135.

Milne, W. Gordon. "Auchincloss and the Novel of Manners," in *University of Kansas City Review*. XXIX (March, 1963), pp. 177–185. Reprinted in *The Sense of Society: A History of the American Novel of Manners*. Cranbury, N.J.: Fairleigh Dickinson University Press, 1977, pp. 236–253.

West, Anthony. "At Home and Abroad," in *New Yorker*. XXXII (November 10, 1956), pp. 219–220.

White, G. Edward. "Human Dimensions of Wall Street Fiction," in *American Bar Association Journal*. LVIII (February, 1972), pp. 175–180.

The House of Five Talents

Boroff, David. "Saga of the Silver Spoon Set," in *Saturday Review*. XLIII (September 10, 1960), p. 25.

Chandler, David. "*The House of Five Talents*," in *America*. CIV (October 1, 1960), pp. 22–23.

Chapin, Victor. "What the Rich Can't Buy," in *New Leader*. XLIII (October 31, 1960), pp. 24–25.

DeMott, Benjamin. "Fiction Chronicle," in *Partisan Review*. XXVII (Fall, 1960), pp. 751–753.

Janeway, Elizabeth. "Augusta Millinder Looks Backward," in *New York Times Book Review*. (September 11, 1960), p. 5.

Macauley, Robie. "Let Me Tell You About the Rich," in *Kenyon Review*. XXVII (Autumn, 1965), pp. 653–655.

Mizener, Arthur. "Some Kinds of Modern Novel," in *Sewanee Review*. LXIX (Winter, 1961), pp. 158–159.

Paulding, Gouverneur. "The Four Hundred," in *Reporter*. XXIII (September 15, 1960), p. 55.

Pickrel, Paul. "Old Lady's Home," in *Harper's Magazine*. CCXXI (October, 1960), pp. 102, 104.

Tuttleton, James W. "Cozzens and Auchincloss—The Legacy of Form," in his *The Novel of Manners in America*. Chapel Hill: University of North Carolina Press, 1972, pp. 245–261.

Weeks, Edward. "A Story of a Fortune," in *Atlantic*. CCVI (December, 1960), pp. 114, 116.

Portrait in Brownstone

Barrett, William. "Once Affluent Society," in *Atlantic*. CCX (August, 1962), pp. 142–143.

Hicks, Granville. "The Good Society of Stocks and Bonds," in *Saturday Review*. XLV (July 14, 1962), pp. 21, 33. Reprinted in *Literary Horizons: A Quarter Century of American Fiction*. New York: New York University Press, 1970, pp. 188–191.

Janeway, Elizabeth. "Ugly Duckling in a Gilded World," in *New York Times Book Review.* (July 15, 1962), pp. 1, 29.

Paulding, Gouverneur. "A Constant Woman," in *Reporter.* XXVII (September 13, 1962), pp. 44, 46.

Pickrel, Paul. "The Changes That Time Brings," in *Harper's Magazine.* CCXXV (August, 1962), p. 91.

Tuttleton, James W. "Cozzens and Auchincloss—The Legacy of Form," in *The Novel of Manners in America.* Chapel Hill: University of North Carolina Press, 1972, pp. 245–261.

The Rector of Justin

Adams, J. Donald. "Louis Auchincloss and the Novel of Manners," in *New York Times Book Review.* (September 29, 1963), p. 2. Reprinted in *Speaking of Books—And Life.* New York: Holt, Rinehart and Winston, 1965, pp. 11–14.

Adams, Robert M. "Saturday Night and Sunday Morning," in *New York Review of Books.* II (July 9, 1964), pp. 14–15.

Auchincloss, Louis. "Writing *The Rector of Justin,*" in *Afterwords: Novelists on Their Novels.* Edited by Thomas McCormack. New York: Harper, 1968, pp. 3–9.

Balliett, Whitney. "A Model Novel," in *New Yorker.* XL (August 1, 1964), pp. 76–77.

Hicks, Granville. "Headmaster for Hero," in *Saturday Review.* XLVII (July 11, 1964), pp. 27–28. Reprinted in *Literary Horizons: A Quarter Century of American Fiction.* New York: New York University Press, 1970, pp. 195–198.

Levine, Paul. "Individualism and the Traditional Talent," in *Hudson Review.* XVII (Autumn, 1964), pp. 476–477.

Peterson, Virgilia. "A Crucible Covered with Ivy," in *New York Times Book Review.* (July 12, 1964), pp. 1, 20.

Pickrel, Paul. "Manners of Mammon," in *Harper's Magazine.* CCXXIX (July, 1964), pp. 97–98.

Spender, Stephen. "Traditional vs. Underground Novels," in *Great Ideas Today.* New York: Atheneum, 1965, pp. 186–187.

Sullivan, Richard. "Auchincloss in Academe," in *Critic.* XXIII (August–September, 1964), pp. 75–76.

Weeks, Edward. "The Making of a Headmaster," in *Atlantic.* CCXIV (July, 1964), pp. 132–133.

Romantic Egoists

Hay, Sara Henderson. "Instinctive Non-Conformist," in *Saturday Review.* XXXVII (July 10, 1954), p. 35.

Kane, Patricia. "Lawyers at the Top: The Fiction of Louis Auchincloss," in *Critique.* VII (Winter, 1964–1965), pp. 36–46.

Quinton, Anthony. "The Errors of Formalism," in *Encounter.* IV (February, 1955), pp. 85–86.

Rolo, Charles J. "Reflections in Mirrors," in *Atlantic.* CXCIV (July, 1954), pp. 83–84.

Stern, James. "Reflections in a Mirror," in *New York Times Book Review.* (May 16, 1954), p. 4.

Wilson, Angus. "The Short Story Changes," in *Spectator.* CXCIII (October 1, 1954), pp. 401–402.

Tales of Manhattan

Geisler, Thomas. "A Novel View of the Law and Lawyers," in *Harvard Law Record.* XLVI (April 25, 1968), pp. 15, 19.

Hatch, Robert. "A Cruel Note," in *Harper's Magazine.* CCXXXIV (April, 1967), p. 110.

Hicks, Granville. "Perspectives on Prosperity," in *Saturday Review.* L (April 8, 1967), p. 39. Reprinted in *Literary Horizons: A Quarter Century of American Fiction.* New York: New York University Press, 1970, pp. 205–208.

Sayre, Nora. "Lampshades," in *Reporter.* XXXVII (July 13, 1967), pp. 60–61.

Schott, Webster. "Beneath the Smooth Surface," in *New York Times Book Review.* (March 19, 1967), p. 5.

Tucker, Martin. "*Tales of Manhattan,*" in *Commonweal.* LXXXVI (June 16, 1967), pp. 372–373.

Weeks, Edward, "The Sheen of Society," in *Atlantic.* CCXIX (May, 1967), pp. 126–127.

White, G. Edward. "Human Dimensions of Wall Street Fiction," in *American Bar Association Journal.* LVIII (February, 1972), pp. 175–180.

W.H. AUDEN
(1907–1973)

The Poetry of Auden

Bahlke, George W. *The Later Auden: From* "New Year Letter" *to* About the House. New Brunswick, N.J.: Rutgers University Press, 1970.

Beach, Joseph Warren. *The Making of the Auden Canon.* Minneapolis: University of Minnesota Press, 1957.

————. "The Poems of Auden and the Prose Diathesis," in *Virginia Quarterly Review.* XXV (Summer, 1949), pp. 369–383.

Blair, John G. *The Poetic Art of W.H. Auden.* Princeton, N.J.: Princeton University Press, 1965.

Cox, R.G. "The Poetry of W.H. Auden," in *The Modern Age: The Pelican Guide to English Literature*, Volume VII. Edited by Boris Ford. Harmondsworth, England: Penguin, 1961, pp. 373–393.

Davison, Dennis. *W.H. Auden.* London: Evans, 1970.

Day Lewis, Cecil. *A Hope for Poetry.* Oxford: Blackwell, 1934.

Dewsmap, Terence. *The Poetry of W.H. Auden.* New York: Monarch Press, 1965.

Everett, Barbara. *Auden.* Edinburgh: Olmer and Boyd, 1966.

Fuller, John. *A Reader's Guide to W.H. Auden.* London: Thames and Hudson, 1970.

Greenberg, Herbert. *Quest for the Necessary: W.H. Auden and the Dilemma of Divided Consciousness.* Cambridge, Mass.: Harvard University Press, 1968.

Hoggart, Richard. *Auden: An Introductory Essay.* London: Chatto and Windus, 1951.

————. *W.H. Auden.* London: Longmans, 1957.

Nelson, Gerald. *Changes of Heart: A Study of the Poetry of W.H. Auden.* Berkeley: University of California Press, 1969.

Replogle, Justin. *Auden's Poetry.* Seattle: University of Washington Press, 1969.

Scarfe, Francis. *W.H. Auden.* Monaco: Lyrebird Press, 1949.

Sitwell, Edith. *Aspects of Modern Poetry.* London: Duckworth, 1934, pp. 238–245.

Spears, Monroe K., Editor. *Auden: A Collection of Critical Essays.* Englewood Cliffs, N.J.: Prentice-Hall, 1964.

————. *The Poetry of W.H. Auden: The Disenchanted Island.* New York: Oxford University Press, 1963.

Spender, Stephen. "Five Notes on W.H. Auden's Writing," in *Twentieth Century*. III (July, 1932), pp. 13–15.

_____. "The Importance of W.H. Auden," in *London Mercury*. XXXIX (April, 1939), pp. 613–618.

Stall, John E. *W.H. Auden; A Reading*. Muncie, Ind.: Ball State University, 1970.

Wright, George T. *W.H. Auden*. New York: Twayne, 1969.

SAINT AUGUSTINE
(354–430)

The City of God

Barker, E. *Essays on Government.* New York: Oxford University Press, 1951, pp. 234–269.

Baynes, N.H. *Byzantine Studies and Other Essays.* London: Athlone Press, 1955, pp. 288–306.

Brookes, E.H. The City of God *and the Politics of Crisis.* London: Oxford University Press, 1960.

Burleigh, J.H. The City of God; *A Study of St. Augustine's Philosophy.* London: Nisbet, 1949.

Figgis, J.N. *The Political Aspects of St. Augustine's* City of God. London: Peter Smith, 1963.

Hearnshaw, F.J.C. *Some Great Political Idealists of the Christian Era.* London: Harrap, 1937, pp. 9–21.

Horton, J.T. "The *De Civitate Dei* as Religious Satire," in *Classical Journal.* LX (February, 1965), pp. 193–203.

Lowith, Karl. *Meaning in History; The Theological Implications of the Philosophy of History.* Chicago: University of Chicago Press, 1949, pp. 160–173.

Marshall, R.T. *Studies in the Political and Socio-Religious Terminology of the* De Civitate. Washington, D.C.: Catholic University of America Press, 1952.

Mommsen, T.E. *Medieval and Renaissance Studies.* Ithaca, N.Y.: Cornell University Press, 1959, pp. 265–298, 325–348.

Niebuhr, R. *Christian Realism and Political Problems.* New York: Scribner's, 1953, pp. 119–146.

O'Grady, J.F. "Priesthood and Sacrifice in *City of God,*" in *Augustiniana.* XXI (1971), pp. 27–44.

O'Meara, J.J. *Charter of Christendom.* New York: Macmillan, 1961.

Russell, B.R. *History of Western Philosophy.* New York: Simon and Schuster, 1945, pp. 352–366.

Versfeld, M. *Guide to* The City of God. New York: Sheed and Ward, 1958.

Confessions

Bainton, R.H. *Early and Medieval Christianity.* Boston, Mass.: Beacon Press, 1962, pp. 39–44.

Burke, K.   *The Rhetoric of Religion; Studies in Logology*. Berkeley: University of California Press, 1970.

Burrell, D.   "Reading the *Confessions* of Augustine: An Exercise in Theological Understanding," in *Journal of Religion*. L (October, 1970), pp. 327–351.

Downs, R.B.   *Famous Books, Ancient and Medieval*. New York: Barnes & Noble, 1964, pp. 253–259.

Findlay, J.N.   "Time: A Treatment of Some Puzzles," in *Essays on Logic*. Edited by A.G.N. Fleu. Oxford, England: Blackwell, 1960, pp. 37–54.

Harvey, J.F.   *Moral Theology of the* Confessions *of Saint Augustine*. Washington, D.C.: Catholic University of America Press, 1951.

O'Brien, W.J.   "Toward Understanding Original Sin in Augustine's *Confessions*," in *Thought*. XLIX (December, 1974), pp. 436–446.

O'Connell, R.J.   *St. Augustine's* Confessions; *The Odyssey of Soul*. Cambridge, Mass.: Belknap Press, 1969.

Ramage, Carol I.   "The *Confessions* of St. Augustine: The Aenid Revisited," in *Pacific Coast Philology*. V (1970), pp. 54–60.

Taylor, J.H.   "St. Augustine, and the Hortensius of Cicero," in *Studies in Philology*. LX (July, 1963), pp. 487–498.

Vance, Eugene.   "Augustine's *Confessions* and the Grammar of Selfhood," in *Genre*. VI (1973), pp. 1–28.

Wagner, M.M.   "Plan in the *Confessions* of St. Augustine," in *Philological Quarterly*. XXIII (January, 1944), pp. 1–23.

Zacher, C.K.   *Curiosity and Pilgrimage; The Literature of Discovery in Fourteenth-Century England*. Baltimore: Johns Hopkins University Press, 1976, pp. 18–41.

JANE AUSTEN
(1775–1817)

Emma

Beer, Patricia. *Reader, I Married Him: A Study of the Women Characters of Jane Austen, Charlotte Brontë, Elizabeth Gaskell and George Eliot.* London: Macmillan, 1974, pp. 49–82.

Bramer, George R. "The Setting in *Emma*," in *College English.* XXII (December, 1960), pp. 335–346.

Drew, Elizabeth A. *The Novel; A Modern Guide to Fifteen English Masterpieces.* New York: Norton, 1963, pp. 792–821.

Duckworth, Alistair M. *The Improvement of the Estate; A Study of Jane Austen's Novels.* Baltimore: Johns Hopkins University Press, 1971, pp. 145–178.

Duffy, Joseph M. "*Emma*: The Awakening from Innocence," in *Journal of English Literary History.* XXI (1954), pp. 39–53.

Edge, Charles. "*Emma*: A Technique of Characterization," in *The Classic British Novel.* Edited by Howard Harper and Charles Edge. Athens: University of Georgia Press, 1972, pp. 51–64.

Hagen, John. "The Closure of *Emma*," in *Studies in English Literature, 1500–1900.* XV (1975), pp. 546–561.

Halperin, John and Janet Kunert. *Plots and Characters in the Fiction of Jane Austen, the Brontës, and George Eliot.* Hamden, Conn.: Shoe String Press, 1976.

Hamouchene, Ulla, Gerd Lemvig and Else Thomsen. "Aspects of Three Novels by Jane Austen, Part Two: *Emma.* Love and Marriage, or How the Rigid Class Division Should Be Mollified a Little," in *Language and Literature.* II, (1973), pp. 56–71.

Harvey, W.J. "The Plot of *Emma*," in *Essays in Criticism.* XVII (January, 1967), pp. 48–63.

Jones, Evan. "Characters and Values: *Emma* and *Mansfield Park*," in *Quadrant.* XII (1968), pp. 35–45.

Karl, Frederick R. *An Age of Fiction; The Nineteenth Century British Novel.* New York: Farrar, Straus and Giroux, 1964, pp. 27–62.

Kissane, James D. "Comparison's Blessed Felicity: Character Arrangement in *Emma*," in *Studies in the Novel.* II (1969), pp. 173–184.

Kooiman-Van Middendorp, Gerarda M. *The Hero in the Feminine Novel.* New York: Haskell House, 1966, pp. 49–59.

Kroeber, Karl. *Styles in Fictional Structure: The Art of Jane Austen, Charlotte Brontë, George Eliot.* Princeton, N.J.: Princeton University Press, 1971, pp. 15–26, 75–79, 151–180.

Lawry, J.S. " 'Decided and Open': Structure in *Emma*," in *Nineteenth-Century Fiction.* XXIV (June, 1969), pp. 1–15.

Leeming, Glenda. *Who's Who in Jane Austen and the Brontës.* London: Elm Tree Books, 1974.

Lodge, David. *Emma: A Casebook.* Nashville, Tenn.: Aurora, 1970.

Mansell, Darrel. *The Novels of Jane Austen: An Interpretation.* London: Macmillan, 1973, pp. 146–184.

Moore, E. Margaret. "*Emma* and Miss Bates: Early Experience of Separation and the Theme of Dependency in Jane Austen's Novels," in *Studies in English Literature.* IX (Autumn, 1969), pp. 573–585.

Pinion, F.B. *A Jane Austen Companion: A Critical Survey and Reference Book.* London: Macmillan, 1973, pp. 114–122.

Swingle, L.J. "The Perfect Happiness of the Union: Jane Austen's *Emma* and English Romanticism," in *Wordsworth Circle.* VII (1976), pp. 312–319.

Tomlinson, T.B. "Jane Austen's Originality: *Emma*," in *Critical Review.* IX (1966), pp. 22–37.

Weissman, Judith. "Evil and Blunders: Human Nature in *Mansfield Park* and *Emma*," in *Women and Literature.* IV (1976), pp. 5–17.

White, Edward M. "*Emma* and the Parodic Point of View," in *Nineteenth-Century Fiction.* XVIII (June, 1963), pp. 55–63.

Mansfield Park

Anderson, Walter E. "The Plot of *Mansfield Park*," in *Modern Philology.* LXXI (1973), pp. 13–17.

Beer, Patricia. *Reader, I Married Him: A Study of the Women Characters of Jane Austen, Charlotte Brontë, Elizabeth Gaskell and George Eliot.* London: Macmillan, 1974, pp. 63–82.

Bush, Douglas. *Jane Austen.* New York: Collier, 1975, pp. 108–135.

Colby, Robert A. *Fiction with a Purpose; Major and Minor Nineteenth-Century Novels.* Bloomington: Indiana University Press, 1967, pp. 66–104.

Draffan, Robert A. "*Mansfield Park*: Jane Austen's Bleak House," in *Essays in Criticism.* XIX (October, 1969), pp. 371–384.

Duckworth, Alistair M. *The Improvement of the Estate; A Study of Jane Austen's Novels.* Baltimore: Johns Hopkins University Press, 1971, pp. 35–80.

Edge, Charles E. "*Mansfield Park* and Ordination," in *Nineteenth-Century Fiction.* XVI (1961), pp. 269–274.

Edwards, Thomas R., Jr. "The Difficult Beauty of *Mansfield Park*," in *Nineteenth-Century Fiction*. XX (June, 1965), pp. 51–67.

Fleishman, Avrom. "*Mansfield Park* in Its Time," in *Nineteenth-Century Fiction*. XXII (June, 1967), pp. 1–18.

————. *A Reading of Mansfield Park: An Essay in Critical Synthesis*. Baltimore: Johns Hopkins University Press, 1970.

Fowler, Marian E. "The Courtesy-Book Heroine of *Mansfield Park*," in *University of Toronto Quarterly*. XLIV (1974), pp. 31–46.

Goldberg, Annemette, Margit Mortensen and Marianne Sorensen. "Aspects of Three Novels by Jane Austen, Part One: *Mansfield Park*. Love and Marriage, or How to Catch a Husband Without Really Trying," in *Language and Literature*. II (1973), pp. 39–56.

Halperin, John and Janet Kunert. *Plots and Characters in the Fiction of Jane Austen, the Brontës, and George Eliot*. Hamden, Conn.: Shoe String Press, 1976.

Jones, Evan. "Characters and Values; *Emma* and *Mansfield Park*," in *Quadrant*. XII (1968), pp. 35–45.

Lauber, John. "Heroes and Anti-Heroes in Jane Austen's Novels," in *Dalhousie Review*. LI (1971–72), pp. 489–503.

Lodge, David. *Language of Fiction; Essays in Criticism and Verbal Analysis of the English Novel*. New York: Columbia University Press, 1966, pp. 94–113.

Mansell, Darrel. *The Novels of Jane Austen: An Interpretation*. London: Macmillan, 1973, pp. 108–145.

Nardin, Jane. *Those Elegant Decorums: The Concept of Propriety in Jane Austen's Novels*. Albany: State University of New York Press, 1973, pp. 82–108.

Pinion, F.B. *A Jane Austen Companion: A Critical Survey and Reference Book*. London: Macmillan, 1973, pp. 101–113.

Sherry, Norman. *Jane Austen*. New York: Arco, 1969, pp. 70–76.

Simon, Irene. "Jane Austen and the Art of the Novel," in *English Studies*. XLIII (1962), pp. 225–239.

Tave, Stuart M. *Some Words of Jane Austen*. Chicago: University of Chicago Press, 1973, pp. 158–204.

Weissman, Judith. "Evil and Blunders: Human Nature in *Mansfield Park* and *Emma*," in *Women and Literature*. IV (1976), pp. 5–17.

White, Edward M. "A Critical Theory of *Mansfield Park*," in *Studies in English Literature, 1500–1900*. VII (Autumn, 1967), pp. 659–677.

Zimmerman, Everett. "Jane Austen and *Mansfield Park*: A Discrimination of Ironies," in *Studies in the Novel*. I (Fall, 1969), pp. 347–356.

Northanger Abbey

Beer, Patricia. *Reader, I Married Him: A Study of the Women Characters of Jane Austen, Charlotte Brontë, Elizabeth Gaskell and George Eliot.* London: Macmillan, 1974, pp. 66–77.

Burlin, Katrin R. " 'The Pen of the Contriver': The Four Fictions of *Northanger Abbey*," in *Jane Austen: Bicentenary Essays.* Edited by John Halperin. New York: Columbia University Press, 1975, pp. 89–111.

Bush, Douglas. *Jane Austen.* New York: Collier, 1975, pp. 57–70.

Chard, Leslie F., II. "Jane Austen and the Obituaries: The Names of *Northanger Abbey*," in *Studies in the Novel.* VII (1975), pp. 133–136.

Duckworth, Alistair M. *The Improvement of the Estate; A Study of Jane Austen's Novels.* Baltimore: Johns Hopkins University Press, 1971, pp. 81–85, 91–102.

Emden, Cecil S. "The Composition of *Northanger Abbey*," in *Review of English Studies.* XIX (August, 1968), pp. 279–287.

Fleishman, Avrom. "The Socialization of Catherine Morland," in *Journal of English Literary History.* XLI (1974), pp. 649–667.

Gallon, D.N. "Comedy in *Northanger Abbey*," in *Modern Language Review.* LXIII (October, 1968), pp. 802–809.

Gooneratne, Yasmine. *Jane Austen.* New York: Cambridge University Press, 1970, pp. 49–62.

Griffin, Cynthia. "The Development of Realism in Jane Austen's Early Novels," in *Journal of English Literary History.* XXX (1963), pp. 36–52.

Halperin, John and Janet Kunert. *Plots and Characters in the Fiction of Jane Austen, the Brontës, and George Eliot.* Hamden, Conn.: Shoe String Press, 1976.

Hennedy, Hugh L. "Acts of Perception in Jane Austen's Novels," in *Studies in the Novel.* V (1973), pp. 25–30.

Kearful, Frank J. "Satire and the Form of the Novel: The Problem of Aesthetic Unity in *Northanger Abbey*," in *Journal of English Literary History.* XXXII (1965), pp. 511–527.

Kiely, Robert. *The Romantic Novel in England.* Cambridge, Mass.: Harvard University Press, 1972, pp. 118–135.

McKillop, Alan D. "Critical Realism in *Northanger Abbey*," in *Jane Austen: A Collection of Critical Essays.* Edited by Ian Watt. Englewood Cliffs, N.J.: Prentice-Hall, 1963.

Mansell, Darrel. *The Novels of Jane Austen: An Interpretation.* London: Macmillan, 1973, pp. 1–45.

Mathison, John K. "*Northanger Abbey* and Jane Austen's Conception of the Value of Fiction," in *Journal of English Literary History.* XXIV (1957), pp. 138–152.

Nardin, Jane. *Those Elegant Decorums: The Concept of Propriety in Jane Austen's Novels.* Albany: State University of New York Press, 1973, pp. 62–81.

Page, Norman. *The Language of Jane Austen.* Oxford: Blackwell, 1972, pp. 15–20.

Pinion, F.B. *A Jane Austen Companion: A Critical Survey and Reference Book.* London: Macmillan, 1973, pp. 76–83.

Rothstein, Eric. "The Lessons of *Northanger Abbey*," in *University of Toronto Quarterly.* XLIV (1974), pp. 14–30.

Rubinstein, E. "*Northanger Abbey*: The Elder Morlands and 'John Home-spun,' " in *Papers in Language and Literature.* V (1969), 434–440.

Shenfield, Margaret. "Jane Austen's Point of View," in *Quarterly Review.* CCXCVIII (July, 1958), pp. 296, 298–306.

Sherry, Norman. *Jane Austen.* New York: Arco, 1969, pp. 46–56.

Tave, Stuart. *Some Words of Jane Austen.* Chicago: University of Chicago Press, 1973, pp. 36–73.

Persuasion

Auerbach, Nina. "O Brave New World: Evaluation and Revolution in *Persuasion*," in *Journal of English Literary History.* XXXIX (1972), pp. 112–128.

Beer, Patricia. *Reader, I Married Him: A Study of the Women Characters of Jane Austen, Charlotte Brontë, Elizabeth Gaskell and George Eliot.* London: Macmillan, 1974, pp. 45–82.

Bogh, Kirsten. "Aspects of Three Novels by Jane Austen, Part Three: *Persuasion.* Love and Marriage, or 'Bad Morality to Conclude With?,'" in *Language and Literature.* II (1973), pp. 72–94.

Bush, Douglas. *Jane Austen.* New York: Collier, 1975, pp. 169–186.

Collins, K.K. "Mrs. Smith and the Morality of *Persuasion*," in *Nineteenth-Century Fiction.* XXX (1975), pp. 383–397.

Duckworth, Alistair M. *The Improvement of the Estate; A Study of Jane Austen's Novels.* Baltimore: Johns Hopkins University Press, 1971, pp. 179–208.

Duffy, Joseph M. "Structure and Idea in *Persuasion*," in *Nineteenth-Century Fiction.* VIII (1954), pp. 272–289.

Gomme, Andor. "On Not Being Persuaded," in *Essays in Criticism.* XVI (April, 1966), pp. 170–184.

Halperin, John and Janet Kunert. *Plots and Characters in the Fiction of Jane Austen, the Brontës, and George Eliot.* Hamden, Conn.: Shoe String Press, 1976.

Kaul, A.N.   *The Action of English Comedy; Studies in the Encounter of Abstraction and Experience from Shakespeare to Shaw.* New Haven, Conn.: Yale University Press, 1970, pp. 237–249.

McMaster, Juliet.   "Surface and Subsurface in Jane Austen's Novels," in *Aerial.* V (1974), pp. 15–20.

Mansell, Darrel.   *The Novels of Jane Austen: An Interpretation.* London: Macmillan, 1973, pp. 185–221.

Monaghan, David M.   "The Decline of the Gentry: A Study of Jane Austen's Attitude to Formality in *Persuasion,*" in *Studies in the Novel.* VII (1975), pp. 73–87.

Nardin, Jane.   *Those Elegant Decorums: The Concept of Propriety in Jane Austen's Novels.* Albany: State University of New York Press, 1973, pp. 129–154.

Pinion, F.B.   *A Jane Austen Companion: A Critical Survey and Reference Book.* London: Macmillan, 1973, pp. 123–129.

Rackin, Donald.   "Jane Austen's Anatomy of *Persuasion,*" in *The English Novel in the Nineteenth-Century: Essays on the Literary Mediation of Human Values.* Edited by George Goodin. Urbana: University of Illinois Press, 1972, pp. 52–80.

Ruoff, Gene W.   "Anne Elliot's Dowry: Reflections on the Ending of *Persuasion,*" in *Wordsworth Circle.* VII (1976), pp. 342–351.

Sherry, Norman.   *Jane Austen.* New York: Arco, 1969, pp. 83–88.

Simon, Irene.   "Jane Austen and the Art of the Novel," in *English Studies.* XLIII (1962), pp. 225–239.

Tave, Stuart.   *Some Words of Jane Austen.* Chicago: University of Chicago Press, 1973, pp. 256–287.

Walling, William A.   "The Glorious Anxiety of Motion: Jane Austen's *Persuasion,*" in *Wordsworth Circle.* VII (1976), pp. 333–341.

Wiesenfarth, Joseph.   "*Persuasion*: History and Myth," in *Wordsworth Circle.* II (1971), pp. 160–168.

Wolfe, Thomas P.   "The Achievement of *Persuasion,*" in *Studies in English Literature, 1500–1900.* XI (1971), pp. 687–700.

Zeitlow, Paul N.   "Luck and Fortuitous Circumstance in *Persuasion*: Two Interpretations," in *Journal of English Literary History.* XXXII (1965), pp. 179–195.

Pride and Prejudice

Anderson, Walter E.   "Plot, Character, Speech, and Place in *Pride and Prejudice,*" in *Nineteenth-Century Fiction.* XXX (1975), pp. 367–382.

Beer, Patricia. *Reader, I Married Him: A Study of the Women Characters of Jane Austen, Charlotte Brontë, Elizabeth Gaskell and George Eliot.* London: Macmillan, 1974, pp. 47–75.

Booth, Bradford. Pride and Prejudice*: Text, Backgrounds, Criticism.* New York: Houghton, Mifflin, 1963.

Bush, Douglas. *Jane Austen.* New York: Collier, 1975, pp. 91–107.

Dooley, D.J. "Pride, Prejudice and Vanity in Elizabeth Bennet," in *Nineteenth-Century Fiction.* XX (September, 1965), pp. 185–188.

Duckworth, Alistair M. *The Improvement of the Estate: A Study of Jane Austen's Novels.* Baltimore: Johns Hopkins University Press, 1971, pp. 115–143.

Duffy, Joseph M. "The Politics of Love: Marriage and the Good Society in *Pride and Prejudice*," in *University of Windsor Review.* XI (1976), pp. 5–26.

Fox, Robert C. "Elizabeth Bennet: Prejudice or Vanity?," in *Nineteenth-Century Fiction.* XVII (September, 1962), pp. 185–187.

Gooneratne, Yasmin. *Jane Austen.* New York: Cambridge University Press, 1970, pp. 81–103.

Gray, Donald J. Pride and Prejudice*: An Authoritative Text, Backgrounds, Reviews, and Essays in Criticism.* New York: Norton, 1966.

Griffin, Cynthia. "The Development of Realism in Jane Austen's Early Novels," in *Journal of English Literary History.* XXX (1963), pp. 36–52.

Halperin, John and Janet Kunert. *Plots and Characters in the Fiction of Jane Austen, the Brontës, and George Eliot.* Hamden, Conn.: Shoe String Press, 1976.

Karl, Frederick R. *An Age of Fiction; The Nineteenth-Century British Novel.* New York: Farrar, Straus and Giroux, 1964, pp. 27–62.

Kooiman-Van Middendorp, Gerarda M. *The Hero in the Feminine Novel.* New York: Haskell House, 1966, pp. 49–59.

Lauber, John. "Heroes and Anti-Heroes in Jane Austen's Novels," in *Dalhousie Review.* LI (1971–72), pp. 489–503.

McCann, Charles J. "Setting and Character in *Pride and Prejudice*," in *Nineteenth-Century Fiction.* XIX (June, 1964), pp. 65–75.

Marcus, Mordecai. "A Major Thematic Pattern in *Pride and Prejudice*," in *Nineteenth-Century Fiction.* XVI (December, 1961), pp. 274–279.

Maugham, William Somerset. *Art of Fiction; An Introduction to Ten Novels and Their Authors.* Garden City, N.Y.: Doubleday, 1955, pp. 55–78.

Moler, Kenneth L. "*Pride and Prejudice*: Jane Austen's 'Patrician Hero,' " in *Studies in English Literature, 1500–1900.* VII (Summer, 1967), pp. 491–508.

Nash, Ralph. "The Time Scheme for *Pride and Prejudice*," in *English Language Notes*. IV (1967), pp. 194–198.

Orum, Tania. "Love and Marriage, or How Economy Becomes Internalized: A Study of Jane Austen's *Pride and Prejudice*," in *Language and Literature*. II (1973), pp. 3–37.

Pinion, F.B. *A Jane Austen Companion: A Critical Survey and Reference Book*. London: Macmillan, 1973, pp. 92–100.

Rubinstein, E. *Twentieth Century Interpretations of* Pride and Prejudice; *A Collection of Critical Essays*. Englewood Cliffs, N.J.: Prentice-Hall, 1969.

Shapiro, Charles. *Twelve Original Essays on Great English Novels*. Detroit: Wayne State University Press, 1960, pp. 69–85.

Weinsheimer, Joel. "Chance and the Hierarchy of Marriages in *Pride and Prejudice*," in *Journal of English Literary History*. XXXIX (1972), pp. 404–419.

Zimmerman, Everett. "Pride and Prejudice in *Pride and Prejudice*," in *Nineteenth-Century Fiction*. XXIII (June, 1968), pp. 64–73.

Sandition

Bush, Douglas. *Jane Austen*. New York: Collier, 1975, pp. 187–193.

Butler, Marilyn. "*Persuasion* and *Sandition*," in *Jane Austen and the War of Ideas*. Edited by Marilyn Butler. Oxford: Clarendon Press, 1975, pp. 275–291.

Kestner, Joseph. "*Sandition* or *The Brothers*: Nature into Art," in *Papers on Language and Literature*. XII (1976), pp. 161–166.

Lauber, John. "*Sandition*: The Kingdom of Folly," in *Studies in the Novel*. IV (Fall, 1972), pp. 353–363.

Lock, F.P. "'The Neighborhood of Tombuctoo': A Note on *Sandition*," in *Notes and Queries*. XIX (1972), pp. 97–99.

Mudrick, Marvin. *Jane Austen*. Princeton, N.J.: Princeton University Press, 1952, pp. 241–258.

Pinion, F.B. *A Jane Austen Companion: A Critical Survey and Reference Book*. London: Macmillan, 1973, pp. 130–134.

Rubinstein, E. "Jane Austen's Novels: The Metaphor of Rank," in *Literary Monographs*. II (1969), pp. 187–190.

Southam, B.C. "*Sandition*: The Seventh Novel," in *Jane Austen's Achievement, Papers Delivered at the Jane Austen Bicentennial Conference at the University of Alberta*. Edited by Juliet McMaster. New York: Barnes & Noble, 1976, pp. 1–26.

Sense and Sensibility

Brown, Lloyd W. "The Comic Conclusion in Jane Austen's Novels," in *PMLA*. LXXXIV (1969), pp. 1582–1587.

Bush, Douglas. *Jane Austen.* New York: Collier, 1975, pp. 78–88.

Cecil, Lord David. *Fine Art of Reading; And Other Literary Studies.* Indianapolis: Bobbs-Merrill, 1957, pp, 149–160.

Duckworth, Alistair M. *The Improvement of the Estate; A Study of Jane Austen's Novels.* Baltimore: Johns Hopkins University Press, 1971, pp. 81–91, 102–114.

Gillie, Christopher. "*Sense and Sensibility*: An Assessment," in *Essays in Criticism.* IX (January, 1959), pp. 1–9.

Gooneratne, Yasmin. *Jane Austen.* New York: Cambridge University Press, 1970, pp. 63–80.

Gornall, F.G. "Marriage, Property, and Romance in Jane Austen's Novels," in *Hibbert Journal.* LXV (1967), pp. 151–156.

Griffin, Cynthia. "The Development of Realism in Jane Austen's Early Novels," in *Journal of English Literary History.* XXX (1963), pp. 36–52.

Halperin, John and Janet Kunert. *Plots and Characters in the Fiction of Jane Austen, the Brontës, and George Eliot.* Hamden, Conn.: Shoe String Press, 1976.

Kooiman-Van Middendorp, Gerarda M. *The Hero in the Feminine Novel.* New York: Haskell House, 1966, pp. 49–59.

Kroeber, Karl. *Styles in Fictional Structure: The Art of Jane Austen, Charlotte Brontë, George Eliot.* Princeton, N.J.: Princeton University Press, 1971, pp. 65–68.

Lauber, John. "Heroes and Anti-Heroes in Jane Austen's Novels," in *Dalhousie Review.* LI (1971–72), pp. 489–503.

————. "Jane Austen's Fools," in *Studies in English Literature, 1500–1900.* XIV (1974), pp. 513–515.

Leeming, Glenda. *Who's Who in Jane Austen and the Brontës.* London: Elm Tree Books, 1974.

Lerner, Laurence. "*Sense and Sensibility*: A Mixed-Up Book," in *Critics on Jane Austen.* Edited by Judith O'Neill. Coral Gables, Fla.: University of Miami Press, 1970, pp. 97–101.

————. *The Truthtellers: Jane Austen, George Eliot, D.H. Lawrence.* New York: Schocken, 1967, pp. 137–139, 160–166.

McKillop, Alan D. "The Context of *Sense and Sensibility*," in *Rice Institute Pamphlets.* XLIV (1957), pp. 65–78.

Mansell, Darrel. *The Novels of Jane Austen: An Interpretation.* London: Macmillan, 1973, pp. 46–77.

Morgan, Susan. "Polite Lies: The Veiled Heroine of *Sense and Sensibility*," in *Nineteenth-Century Fiction.* XXXI (1976), pp. 188–205.

Nardin, Jane. *Those Elegant Decorums: The Concept of Propriety in Jane Austen's Novels.* Albany: State University of New York Press, 1973, pp. 24–46.

Page, Norman. *The Language of Jane Austen.* Oxford: Blackwell, 1972, pp. 20–24.

Pinion, F.B. *A Jane Austen Companion: A Critical Survey and Reference Book.* London: Macmillan, 1973, pp. 84–91.

Rubinstein, E. "Jane Austen's Novels: The Metaphor of Rank," in *Literary Mongraphs.* II (1969), pp. 107–117.

Sherry, Norman. *Jane Austen.* New York: Arco, 1969, pp. 56–63.

Zimmerman, Everett. "Admiring Pope No More Than Is Proper: *Sense and Sensibility*," in *Jane Austen, Bicentenary Essays.* Edited by John Halperin. New York: Cambridge University Press, 1975, pp. 112–122.

MARIANO AZUELA
(1873–1952)

The Fireflies

Langford, Walter M. "Mariano Azuela: A Break with the Past," in *The Mexican Novel Comes of Age*. Notre Dame, Ind.: University of Notre Dame Press, 1971, pp. 14–33.

Leal, Luis. *Mariano Azuela.* New York: Twayne, 1971, pp. 70–74, 113–119.

Levy, K.L. "*La luciérnaga*: Title; Leitmotif and Structural Unity," in *Philological Quarterly*. LI (January, 1972), pp. 321–328.

Mullen, E.J. "Towards a Prototype of Mariano Azuela's *La luciérnaga*," in *Romance Notes*. II (1970), pp. 518–521.

Spell, Jefferson Rea. "*Contemporary Spanish-American Fiction.* Chapel Hill: University of North Carolina Press, 1944, pp. 88–92.

The Underdogs

Berler, Beatrice. "The Mexican Revolution as Reflected in the Novel," in *Hispania*. XLVII (1964), pp. 41–46.

Blom, Frans. "*The Underdogs*," in *Saturday Review*. VI (1929), p. 179.

Carter, Boyd G. "The Mexican Novel at Mid-Century," in *Prairie Schooner*. XXVIII (1954), pp. 143–156.

Dulsey, Bernard M. "The Mexican Revolution as Mirrored in the Novels of Mariano Azuela," in *Modern Language Journal*. XXXV (1951), pp. 382–386.

Englekirk, John E. "The Discovery of *Los de Abajo*," in *Hispania*. XVIII (1935), pp. 53–62.

————. "Fortunes of *Los de Abajo*," in *Books Abroad*. XXI (1947), pp. 399–400.

Gruening, Ernest. "*The Underdogs*," in *The New World Monthly*. I (January, 1930), pp. 66–68.

Jerome, Judson. "Judson Jerome on Mariano Azuela's *Los de Abajo (The Underdogs)*," in *Rediscoveries*. Edited by David Madden. New York: Crown, 1971, pp. 179–189.

Langford, Walter M. "Mariano Azuela: A Break with the Past," in *The Mexican Novel Comes of Age*. Notre Dame, Ind.: University of Notre Dame Press, 1971, pp. 14–33.

Leal, Luis. *Mariano Azuela.* New York: Twayne, 1971, pp. 101–103, 110–113.

Spell, Jefferson Rea. "Mariano Azuela, Portrayer of the Mexican Revolution," in *Contemporary Spanish-American Fiction*. Chapel Hill: University of North Carolina, 1944, pp. 82–89.

Torres-Rioseco, A. "Spanish American Novel," in *Epic of Latin American Literature*. New York: Oxford University Press, 1944, pp. 168–208.

ISAAC BABEL
(1894–1941)

Red Cavalry

Apple, M. "History and Case History in *Red Cavalry* and *The Day of the Locust*," in *Nathanael West: The Cheaters and the Cheated*. Edited by David Madden. Deland, Fla.: Everett/Edwards, 1973, pp. 235–247.

Carden, Patricia. *The Art of Isaac Babel*. Ithaca, N.Y.: Cornell University Press, 1972, pp. 86–151.

Falchikov, M. "Conflict and Contrast in Isaak Babel's *Konarmiya*," in *Modern Language Review*. LXXII (January, 1977), pp. 125–133.

Falen, James E. *Isaac Babel: Russian Master of the Short Story*. Knoxville: University of Tennessee Press, 1974, pp. 115–199.

Hallett, Richard. *Isaac Babel*. New York: Frederick Ungar, 1972, pp. 32–43.

Klotz, Martin B. "Poetry of the Present: Isaak Babel's *Red Cavalry*," in *Slavic and East European Journal*. XVIII (1974), pp. 160–169.

Lee, Alice. "Epiphany in Babel's *Red Cavalry*," in *Russian Literature Triquarterly*. III (1972), pp. 249–260.

Marcus, Steven. "The Stories of Isaac Babel," in *Partisan Review*. XXII (Summer, 1955), pp. 400–411.

Mathewson, Rufus W., Jr. *The Positive Hero in Russian Literature*. Stanford, Calif.: Stanford University Press, 1975, pp. 201–214.

Poggioli, Renato. *The Phoenix and the Spider*. Cambridge, Mass.: Harvard University Press, 1957, pp. 229–238.

Terros, Victor. "Line and Color: The Structure of Isaac Babel's Short Stories in *Red Cavalry*," in *Studies in Short Fiction*. II (1966), pp. 141–156.

Thomson, Boris. *Lot's Wife and the Venus de Milo; Conflicting Attitudes to the Cultural Heritage in Modern Russia*. Cambridge: Cambridge University Press, 1978, pp. 98–122.

Trilling, Lionel. *Beyond Culture; Essays on Literature and Learning*. New York: Viking, 1965, pp. 119–144.

SIR FRANCIS BACON
(1561-1626)

Essays

Bowen, Catherine Drinker. *Francis Bacon; The Temper of a Man.* Boston: Little, Brown, 1963.

Crowther, James Gerold. *Francis Bacon, the First Statesman of Science.* London: Cresset, 1960.

Eisley, Loren C. *Francis Bacon and the Modern Dilemma.* New York: Scribner's, 1973.

Farrington, Benjamin. *Francis Bacon, Philosopher of Industrial Science.* New York: Collier, 1961.

Fish, Stanley E. "Georgics of the Mind: The Experience of Bacon's *Essays*," in *Self Consuming Artifacts: The Experience of the Seventeenth Century.* Berkeley: University of California Press, 1972, pp. 78–155.

Green, Adwin Wigfall. *Sir Francis Bacon.* New York: Twayne, 1966.

Hopkins, Vivian C. "Emerson and Bacon," in *American Literature.* XXIX (1958), pp. 408–430.

Jardine, Lisa. *Francis Bacon: Discovery and the Art of Discourse.* New York: Cambridge University Press, 1974.

Patrick, J. Max. *Francis Bacon.* London: Longmans, Green, 1961.

Tittotson, Geoffrey. "Words for Princes: Bacon's *Essays*," in *Essays in Criticism and Research.* Cambridge: Cambridge University Press, 1942, pp. 31–40.

Vickers, Brian. *Francis Bacon and Renaissance Prose.* Cambridge: Cambridge University Press, 1968.

Wallace, Karl R. *Francis Bacon on the Nature of Man.* Urbana: University of Illinois Press, 1967.

Zeitlin, Jacob. "The Development of Bacon's *Essays*—with Special Reference to the Questions of Montaigne's Influence upon Them," in *Journal of English and Germanic Philology.* XXVII (1928), pp. 496–519.

History of the Reign of King Henry VII

"Bacon as an Historian," in *Times Literary Supplement.* (April 8, 1926), pp. 253–254.

Benjamin, Edwin B. "Bacon and Tacitus," in *Classical Philology.* LX (1965), pp. 102–110.

Bowen, Catherine Drinker. *Francis Bacon; The Temper of a Man.* Boston: Little, Brown, 1963.

Clark, S. "Bacon's Henry VII: A Case Study in the Science of Man," in *History and Theory*. XIII (1974), pp. 97–118.

Crowther, James Gerold. *Francis Bacon, the First Statesman of Science*. London: Cresset, 1960.

Dean, Leonard F. "Sir Francis Bacon's Theory of Civil History Writing," in *Journal of English Literary History*. VIII (1941), pp. 161–183.

Eisley, Loren C. *Francis Bacon and the Modern Dilemma*. New York: Scribner's, 1973.

Ferguson, A.B. "Non-Political Past in Bacon's Theory of History," in *Journal of British Studies*. XIV (November, 1974), pp. 4–20.

Green, Adwin Wigfall. *Sir Francis Bacon*. New York: Twayne, 1966.

Kirkwood, James J. "Bacon's *Henry VII*: A Model of a Theory of Historiography," in *Renaissance Papers*. (1966), pp. 51–55.

Patrick, J. Max. *Francis Bacon*. London: Longmans, Green, 1961.

Wheeler, Thomas. "Bacon's Henry VII as a Machiavellian Prince," in *Renaissance Papers*. (1958), pp. 111–117.

————. "The Purpose of Bacon's *History of Henry the Seventh*," in *Studies in Philology*. LIV (1957), pp. 1–13.

————. "Sir Francis Bacon's Concept of the Historian's Task," in *Renaissance Papers*. (1955), pp. 40–46.

White, Howard B. "The English Solomon: Francis Bacon on Henry VII," in *Social Research*. XXIV (1957), pp. 457–481.

The New Atlantis

Bierman, Judah. "*The New Atlantis*, Bacon's Utopia of Science," in *Papers on Language and Literature*. CI (1967), pp. 99–110.

————. "*The New Atlantis* Revisited," in *Studies in the Literary Imagination*. IV (1971), pp. 121–141.

————. "Science and Society in *The New Atlantis* and Other Essays," in *PMLA*. LXXVIII (1963), pp. 492–500.

Bowen, Catherine Drinker. *Francis Bacon; The Temper of a Man*. Boston: Little, Brown, 1963.

Crowther, James Gerold. *Francis Bacon, the First Statesman of Science*. London: Cresset, 1960.

Eisley, Loren C. *Francis Bacon and the Modern Dilemma*. New York: Scribner's, 1973.

Green, Adwin Wigfall. *Sir Francis Bacon*. New York: Twayne, 1967.

Jardine, Lisa. *Francis Bacon: Discovery and the Art of Discourse*. New York: Cambridge University Press, 1974.

McCutcheon, Elizabeth. "Bacon and the Cherubim: An Iconographical Reading of *The New Atlantis*," in *Journal of English Literary History*. II (1972), pp. 334–355.

Reiss, T.J. "Structure and Mind in Two Seventeenth Century Utopias: Campanella and Bacon," in *Yale French Studies*. XLIX (1973), pp. 82–95.

Vickers, Brian. *Francis Bacon and Renaissance Prose*. Cambridge: Cambridge University Press, 1968.

Weinberger, J. "Science and Rule in Bacon's Utopia: An Introduction to the Reading of *The New Atlantis*," in *American Political Science Review*. LXX (1976), pp. 865–885.

Weiner, Harvey S. " 'Science or Providence': Theory and Practice in Bacon's *New Atlantis*," in *Enlightenment Essays*. III (1972), pp. 85–92.

JAMES BALDWIN
(1924–   )

Another Country

Alexander, Charlotte. "The Stink of Reality: Mothers and Whores in James Baldwin's Fiction," in *Literature and Psychology*. XVIII (1968), pp. 15–21.

Berry, Boyd. "Another Man Done Gone: Self Pity in Baldwin's *Another Country*," in *Michigan Quarterly Review*. V (Fall, 1966), pp. 285–290.

Bone, Robert A. *The Negro Novel in America*. New Haven, Conn.: Yale University Press, 1965, pp. 228–239.

————. "The Novels of James Baldwin," in *Tri-Quarterly*. II (Winter, 1965), pp. 12–20.

Collier, Eugenia. "The Phrase Unbearably Repeated," in *Phylon*. XXV (Fall, 1964), pp. 288–296.

Dane, Peter. "Baldwin's Other Country," in *Transition*. V (1966), pp. 38–40.

Gross, Theodore. "The World of James Baldwin," in *Critique*. VII (1965), pp. 142–146.

Harper, Howard M. *Desperate Faith*. Chapel Hill: University of North Carolina Press, 1967, pp. 151–159.

Hyman, S.E. "No Country of Young Men," in *Standards: A Chronicle of Books for Our Times*. New York: Horizon Press, 1966, pp. 78–82.

Klein, Marcus. *After Alienation: American Novels in Mid-Century*. Cleveland: World, pp. 184–188.

Littlejohn, David. *Black on White; A Critical Survey of Writing by American Negroes*. New York: Grossman, 1966, pp. 125–133.

MacInnes, Colin. "Dark Angel: The Writings of James Baldwin," in *Encounter*. XXI (August, 1963), pp. 28–31.

Margolies, Edward. *Native Sons: A Critical Study of Twentieth Century Negro-American Authors*. New York: Lippincott, 1968, pp. 118–120.

Thelwell, M. "*Another Country*: Baldwin's New York Novel," in *The Black American Writer*, Volume I. Deland, Fla: Everett/Edwards, 1969, pp. 181–198.

Watson, Edward. "The Novels and Essays of James Baldwin," in *Queen's Quarterly*. LXXII (Summer, 1965), pp. 305–307.

Giovanni's Room

Alexander, Charlotte. "The Stink of Reality: Mothers and Whores in James Baldwin's Fiction," in *Literature and Psychology*. XVIII (1968), pp. 9–15.

Bone, Robert A.   *The Negro Novel in America*. New Haven, Conn.: Yale University Press, 1965, pp. 226–228.

————. "The Novels of James Baldwin," in *Tri-Quarterly*. II (Winter, 1965), pp. 10–12.

Klein, Marcus.   *After Alienation: American Novels in Mid-Century*. Cleveland: World, 1962, pp. 184–188.

MacInnes, Colin.   "Dark Angel: The Writings of James Baldwin," in *Encounter*. XXI (August, 1963), pp. 25–28.

Margolies, Edward.   *Native Sons: A Critical Study of Twentieth-Century Negro-American Authors*. New York: Lippincott, 1968, pp. 114–118.

Noble, David W.   *The Eternal Adam and the New World Garden*. New York: Braziller, 1968, pp. 212–215.

Sayre, Robert F.   "James Baldwin's Other Country," in *Contemporary American Novelists*. Edited by H.T. Moore. Carbondale: Southern Illinois University Press, 1964, pp. 163–165.

Watson, Edward.   "The Novels and Essays of James Baldwin," in *Queen's Quarterly*. LXXII (Summer, 1965), pp. 391–392.

Go Tell It on the Mountain

Alexander, Charlotte.   *Baldwin's* Go Tell It on the Mountain, Another Country, *and Other Works: A Critical Commentary*. New York: Monarch, 1968.

————. "The 'Stink' of Reality: Mothers and Whores in James Baldwin's Fiction," in *Literature and Psychology*. XVIII (1968), pp. 21–23.

Allen, Shirley S.   "The Ironic Voice in Baldwin's *Go Tell It on the Mountain*," in *James Baldwin: A Critical Evaluation*. Edited by Therman B. O'Daniel. Washington, D.C.: Howard University Press, 1977, pp. 30–37.

————. "Religious Symbolism and Psychic Reality in Baldwin's *Go Tell It on the Mountain*," in *College Language Association Journal*. XIX (December, 1975), pp. 173–199.

Bell, G.E.   "Dilemma of Love in *Go Tell It on the Mountain*," in *College Language Association Journal*. XVII (March, 1974), pp. 397–406.

Bone, Robert.   *The Negro Novel in America*. New Haven, Conn.: Yale University Press, 1965, pp. 216–225.

————. "The Novels of James Baldwin," in *Tri-Quarterly*. II (Winter, 1965), pp. 3–20.

Cartey, Wilfred.   "The Realities of Four Negro Writers," in *Columbia University Forum*. IX (Summer, 1966), pp. 34–42.

Fabre, Michel.   "Fathers and Sons in James Baldwin's *Go Tell It on the Mountain*," in *Modern Black Novelists*. Edited by M.G. Cooke. Englewood Cliffs, N.J.: Prentice-Hall, 1971, pp. 88–104.

Gerard, Albert.   "Humanism and Negritude: Notes on the Contemporary Afro-American Novel," in *Diogenes*. XXXVII (Spring, 1962), pp. 127–132.

Graves, Wallace. "The Question of Moral Energy in James Baldwin's *Go Tell It on the Mountain*," in *College Language Association Journal*. VII (March, 1964), pp. 215–223.

Harper, Howard M., Jr. *Desperate Faith*. Chapel Hill: University of North Carolina Press, 1967, pp. 142–147.

Kent, George E. "Baldwin and the Problem of Being," in *College Language Association Journal*. VII (March, 1964), pp. 215–223.

Klein, Marcus. *After Alienation: American Novels in Mid-Century*. Cleveland: World, 1962, pp. 178–184.

Littlejohn, David. *Black on White: A Critical Survey of Writings by American Negroes*. New York: Grossman, 1966, pp. 121–124.

MacInnes, Colin. "Dark Angel: The Writings of James Baldwin," in *Encounter*. XXI (August, 1963), pp. 23–25.

Margolies, Edward. "The Negro Church: James Baldwin and the Christian Vision," in *Native Sons: A Critical Study of Twentieth Century Negro-American Authors*. Philadelphia: Lippincott, 1968, pp. 109–114.

JOHN BALE
(1495–1563)

King John

Adams, Barry B. "Doubling in Bale's *King Johan*," in *Studies in Philology*. LXII (1965), pp. 111–120.

————. "Introduction," in *John Bale's* King Johan. San Marino, Calif.: Huntington Library, 1969, pp. 1–69.

Elson, John. "Studies in the King John Plays," in *Joseph Quincey Adams Memorial Studies*. Edited by James G. McManaway. Washington, D.C.: Folger Shakespeare Library, 1948, pp. 191–197.

Farnham, Willard. *The Medieval Heritage of Elizabethan Tragedy*. Berkeley: University of California Press, 1936, pp. 225–226, 248–249.

Johnson, S.F. "The Tragic Hero in Early Elizabethan Drama," in *Studies in the English Renaissance Drama in Memory of Karl Julius Holzknecht*. Edited by Josephine W. Bennett, Oscar Cargill and Vernon Hall, Jr. New York: New York University Press, 1959, pp. 157–163.

McCusker, Honor C. *John Bale: Dramatist and Antiquary*. Freeport, N.Y.: Books for Libraries Press, 1971, pp. 86–95.

Miller, Edwin S. "The Roman Rite in Bale's *King John*," in *PMLA*. LXIV (1949), pp. 802–822.

Pafford, John Henry Pyle "Introduction," in *King Johan*. By John Bale. London: Oxford University Press, 1931, pp. v–xxxiv.

————. "Two Notes on Bale's *King John*," in *Modern Language Review*. LVI (1961), pp. 553–555.

Ribner, Irving. *The English History Play in the Age of Shakespeare*. Princeton, N.J.: Princeton University Press, 1957, pp. 37–41, 49–54.

HONORÉ DE BALZAC
(1799–1850)

César Birotteau

Bertault, Philippe. *Balzac and* The Human Comedy. New York: New York University Press, 1963, pp. 24–25, 138–141.

Bowen, Ray P. *The Dramatic Construction of Balzac's Novels.* Eugene: University of Oregon Press, 1946, pp. 45–48, 88–90, 115–116.

Dedinsky, Brucia L. "Development of the Scheme of the *Comedie humaine*: Distribution of the Stories," in *The Evolution of Balzac's* Comedie humaine. Edited by E. Preston Dargan and Bernard Weinberg. Chicago: University of Chicago Press, 1942, pp. 148–150.

Fess, G.M. "Balzac's First Thought of *César Birotteau*," in *Modern Language Notes.* XLIX (December, 1934), pp. 516–519.

Giraud, R. *Unheroic Heroes.* New Brunswick, N.J.: Rutgers University Press, 1957, pp. 101–114, 119–123.

Maurois, Andre. *Prometheus: The Life of Balzac.* London: Bodley Head, 1965, pp. 345–348.

The Chouans

Barnes, Helen E. *A Study of the Variations Between the Original and the Standard Edition of Balzac's* Les Chouans. Chicago: University of Chicago Press, 1923.

Bertault, Philippe. *Balzac and* The Human Comedy. New York: New York University Press, 1963, pp. 25–29.

Bowen, Ray P. *The Dramatic Construction of Balzac's Novels.* Eugene: University of Oregon Press, 1946, pp. 17–20, 77–79, 104–105.

Dargan, E. Preston. "Balzac and Cooper: *Les Chouans*," in *Modern Philology.* XIII (August, 1915), pp. 1–21.

Dargan, E. Preston and W.L. Crain. "The First Monument: *Les Chouans*," in *Studies in Balzac's Realism.* By E. Preston Dargan, W.L. Crain and others. Chicago: University of Chicago Press, 1932, pp. 33–67.

Fess, Gilbert M. "The Documentary Background of Balzac's *Les Chouans*," in *Modern Language Notes.* LXIX (December, 1954), pp. 601–605.

Haggis, D.R. "Scott, Balzac, and the Historical Novel as Social and Political Analysis: *Waverley* and *Les Chouans*," in *Modern Language Review.* LXVIII (1973), pp. 51–68.

Ham, Edward B. "The Vimont *Chouans*," in *Romance Notes.* I (November, 1959), pp. 2–6.

Hamilton, James F. "The Novelist as Historian: A Contrast Between Balzac's *Les Chouans* and Hugo's *Quatrevingt-treize*," in *French Review*. XLIX (1976), pp. 661–668.

Hemmings, F.W.J. "Balzac's *Les Chouans* and Stendhal's *De l'amour*," in *Balzac and the Nineteenth Century: Studies in French Literature Presented to Herbert J. Hunt by Pupils, Colleagues and Friends*. Leicester, England: Leicester University Press, 1972, pp. 99–110.

Hunt, Herbert J. *Honoré de Balzac: A Biography*. London: Athlone Press, 1957, pp. 24–26.

Oliver, E.J. *Honoré de Balzac*. New York: Macmillan, 1964, pp. 47–48.

Rogers, Samuel. *Balzac & the Novel*. Madison: University of Wisconsin Press, 1953, pp. 173–174.

Shepherd, James L., III. "Balzac's Debt to Cooper's *Spy* in *Les Chouans*," in *French Review*. XXVIII (December, 1954), pp. 145–152.

The Country Doctor

Bertault, Philippe. *Balzac and* The Human Comedy. New York: New York University Press, 1963.

Bowen, Ray P. *The Dramatic Construction of Balzac's Novels*. Eugene: University of Oregon Press, 1946.

Hunt, Herbert J. *Honoré de Balzac: A Biography*. London: Athlone Press, 1957, pp. 51–56.

Maurois, Andre. *Prometheus: The Life of Balzac*. London: Bodley Head, 1965, pp. 226–228.

Oliver, E.J. *Honoré de Balzac*. New York: Macmillan, 1964, pp. 123–131.

Plomer, William. "Lenin's Favorite Novel," in *Spectator*. CLIX (August 6, 1937), pp. 248–249.

Cousin Bette

Bertault, Philippe. *Balzac and* The Human Comedy. New York: New York University Press, 1963, pp. 63–64, 175–176.

Bowen, Ray P. *The Dramatic Construction of Balzac's Novels*. Eugene: University of Oregon Press, 1946, pp. 60–65, 96–98.

Dedinsky, Brucia L. "Development of the Scheme of the *Comedie humaine*: Distribution of the Stories," in *The Evolution of Balzac's* Comedie humaine. Edited by E. Preston Dargan and Bernard Weinberg. Chicago: University of Chicago Press, 1942, pp. 155–156.

Jameson, Frederic. "*La cousine Bette* and Allegorical Realism," in *PMLA*. LXXXVI (1971), pp. 241–254.

Maurois, Andre. *Prometheus: The Life of Balzac*. London: Bodley Head, 1965, pp. 486–487, 498–499.

Oliver, E.J. *Honoré de Balzac*. New York: Macmillan, 1964, pp. 132–146.

Ortali, Helene. "Images of Women in Balzac's *La cousine Bette*," in *Nineteenth-Century French Studies*. IV (1976), pp. 194–205.

Prendergast, C.A. "Antithesis and Moral Ambiguity in *La cousine Bette*," in *Modern Language Review*. LXVIII (1973), pp. 315–332.

Pritchett, V.S. "Books in General," in *New Statesman and Nation*. XXVI (December 11, 1943), p. 387.

Turnell, Martin. *The Novel in France*. New York: New Directions, 1951, pp. 241–245.

Cousin Pons

Adamson, Donald. "*Le cousin Pons*: The 'Paragraphic Compose,' " in *Modern Language Review*. LIX (April, 1964), pp. 209–213.

Bertault, Philippe. *Balzac and* The Human Comedy. New York: New York University Press, 1963, pp. 171–172, 187–188.

Bowen, Ray P. *The Dramatic Construction of Balzac's Novels*. Eugene: University of Oregon Press, 1946, pp. 65–68, 98–99.

Dedinsky, Brucia L. "Development of the Scheme of the *Comedie humaine*: Distribution of the Stories," in *The Evolution of Balzac's* Comedie humaine. Edited by E. Preston Dargan and Bernard Weinberg. Chicago: University of Chicago Press, 1942, pp. 155–156.

Maurois, Andre. *Prometheus: The Life of Balzac*. London: Bodley Head, 1965, pp. 496–498.

Pritchett, V.S. "Books in General," in *New Statesman and Nation*. XXVI (December 11, 1943), p. 387.

————. *The Living Novel and Later Appreciations*. New York: Random House, 1964, pp. 332–339.

Rosaire, Forrest. "Slice of Somber Life: *Le cousin Pons*," in *Studies in Balzac's Realism*. By Edwin Preston Dargan, W.L. Crain and others. Chicago: University of Chicago Press, 1932, pp. 191–213.

Eugénie Grandet

Bowen, Ray P. *The Dramatic Construction of Balzac's Novels*. Eugene: University of Oregon Press, 1946, pp. 26–31, 81–82, 106.

Lush, Adaline Lincoln. "The House of the Miser: *Eugénie Grandet*," in *Studies in Balzac's Realism*. By E. Preston Dargan, W.L. Crain and others. Chicago: University of Chicago Press, 1932, pp. 121–135.

Rogers, Samuel. *Balzac & the Novel*. Madison: University of Wisconsin Press, 1953, pp. 168–169.

Saintsbury, George. *A History of the French Novel to the Close of the 19th Century*. London: Macmillan, 1919, pp. 163–164.

Sandwith, M.T.E. *"Jane Eyre* and *Eugénie Grandet,"* in *Nineteenth Century.* XCII (August, 1922), pp. 235–240.

Turnell, Martin. *The Novel in France.* New York: New Directions, 1951, pp. 235–238.

Wetherill, P.M. "A Reading of *Eugénie Grandet,"* in *Modern Languages.* LII (1971), pp. 166–176.

Father Goriot

Auerbach, Erich. "In the Hotel de la Mole," in *Partisan Review.* XVIII (May–June, 1951), pp. 280–284. Reprinted in *Mimesis.* By Erich Auerbach. New York: Doubleday, 1957, pp. 413–417.

Berman, Ronald. "Analogies and Realities in *Père Goriot,"* in *Novel.* III (1969), pp. 7–16.

Besser, Gretchen R. "Lear and Goriot: A Re-evaluation," in *Orbis Litterarum.* XXVII (1972), pp. 28–36.

Bowen, Ray P. *The Dramatic Construction of Balzac's Novels.* Eugene: University of Oregon, 1946, pp. 36–42, 85–86, 107–115.

Conner, J. Wayne. "On Balzac's *Goriot,"* in *Symposium.* VIII (Summer, 1954), pp. 68–73.

Downing, George E. "A Famous Boarding-House: *Le père Goriot,"* in *Studies in Balzac's Realism.* By E. Preston Dargan, W.L. Crain and others. Chicago: University of Chicago Press, 1932, pp. 136–150.

Fanger, Donald. *Dostoevsky and Romantic Realism.* Cambridge, Mass.: Harvard University Press, 1965, pp. 38–56.

Hunt, Joel. "Balzac and Dostoevskij: Ethics and Eschatology," in *Slavic and East European Journal.* XVI (Winter, 1958), pp. 307–323.

Maugham, W. Somerset. *Great Novelists and Their Novels.* Philadelphia: Winston, 1948, pp. 41–58.

Oliver, E.J. *Honoré de Balzac.* New York: Macmillan, 1964, pp. 53–68.

Pugh, A.R. "Recurring Characters in *Le père Goriot,"* in *Modern Language Review.* LVII (October, 1962), pp. 518–522.

Savage, Catharine H. "The Romantic *père Goriot,"* in *Studies in Romanticism.* V (Winter, 1966), pp. 104–112.

Sobel, Margaret. "Balzac's *Le père Goriot* and Dickens' *Dombey and Son*: A Comparison," in *Rice University Studies.* LIX (1973), pp. 71–81.

Turnell, Martin. *The Novel in France.* New York: New Directions, 1951, pp. 228–235.

Yarrow, P.J. *"Le père Goriot* Re-considered," in *Essays in Criticism.* VII (October, 1957), pp. 363–373.

The Human Comedy

Antoniadis, Roxandria V. "Faulkner and Balzac: The Poetic Web," in *Comparative Literature Studies*. IX (1972), pp. 303–325.

Auerbach, Erich. "In the Hotel de la Mole," in *Partisan Review*. XVIII (May–June, 1951), pp. 285–293.

Bays, Gwendolyn. "Balzac as Seer," in *Yale French Studies*. XIII (Spring–Summer, 1954), pp. 83–92.

Bertault, Philippe. *Balzac and* The Human Comedy. New York: New York University Press, 1963.

Blackburn, Bonnie. "Master and Apprentice: A Realistic Relationship," in *Studies in Balzac's Realism*. By E. Preston Dargan, W.L. Crain and others. Chicago: University of Chicago Press, 1932, pp. 151–189.

Bowen, Ray P. "Balzac's Interior Descriptions as an Element in Characterization," in *PMLA*. XL (June, 1925), pp. 289–301.

Brombert, Victor. "Balzac and the Caricature of the Intellect," in *French Review*. XXXIV (October, 1960), pp. 3–12.

Canfield, Arthur Graves. *The Reappearing Characters in Balzac's* Comedie humaine. Chapel Hill: University of North Carolina Press, 1961.

Clark, Priscilla P. "Balzac and the Bourgeoise," in *Tennessee Studies in Literature*. XIV (1969), pp. 51–60.

Cook, Albert. *The Meaning of Fiction*. Detroit: Wayne State University Press, 1960, pp. 64–82.

Crampton, Hope. "Melmoth in *La Comedie humaine*," in *Modern Language Review*. LXI (January, 1966), pp. 42–50.

Dargan, E. Preston. "Balzac's General Method: An Analysis of His Realism," in *Studies in Balzac's Realism*. Edited by E. Preston Dargan, W.L. Crain and others. Chicago: University of Chicago Press, 1932, pp. 1–31.

————. *Honoré de Balzac: A Force of Nature*. Chicago: University of Chicago Press, 1932, pp. 42–75.

Dedinsky, Brucia L. "Development of the Scheme of the *Comedie humaine*," in *The Evolution of Balzac's* Comedie humaine. Edited by E. Preston Dargan and Bernard Weinberg. Chicago: University of Chicago Press, 1942, pp. 22–181.

Galpin, Alfred. "A Balzac Centenary: The Avant-Propos of the *Comedie humaine*," in *French Review*. XXXIX (January, 1943), pp. 213–222.

Garnand, H.J. *The Influence of Walter Scott on the Works of Balzac*. New York: Carranza, 1926, pp. 90–134.

Hunt, Hubert J. *Balzac's* Comedie humaine. London: Athlone Press, 1959.

Levin, Harry. *The Gates of Horn: A Study of Five French Realists*. New York: Oxford University Press, 1963, pp. 156–213.

Lock, Peter W. "Hoarders and Spendthrifts in *La Comedie humaine*," in *Modern Language Review*. LXI (January, 1966), pp. 29–41.

————. "Point of View in Balzac's Short Stories," in *Balzac and the Nineteenth Century*. Edited by D.G. Charlton, J. Gaudon and Anthony R. Pugh. Leicester, England: Leicester University Press, 1972, pp. 57–69.

Moss, Martha Neiss. "Balzac's Villains: The Origins of Destructiveness in *La Comedie humaine*," in *Nineteenth-Century French Studies*. VI (Fall–Winter, 1977–1978), pp. 36–51.

Oliver, E.J. *Balzac the European*. London: Sheed and Ward, 1959, pp. 47–204.

Rogers, Samuel. *Balzac & the Novel*. Madison: University of Wisconsin Press, 1953, pp. 43–187.

Turnell, Martin. *The Novel in France*. New York: New Directions, 1951, pp. 216–227.

Weinberg, Bernard. "Summaries of Variants in Twenty-Six Stories," in *The Evolution of Balzac's* Comedie humaine. Edited by E. Preston Dargan and Bernard Weinberg. Chicago: University of Chicago Press, 1942, pp. 368–421.

Lost Illusions

Bart, B.F. "Balzac and Flaubert: Energy Versus Art," in *Romanic Review*. XLII (October, 1951), pp. 198–204.

Beebe, Maurice. "The Lesson on Balzac's Artists," in *Criticism*. II (Summer, 1960), pp. 231–232.

Bertault, Philippe. *Balzac and* The Human Comedy. New York: New York University Press, 1963, pp. 42–44.

Bowen, Ray P. *The Dramatic Construction of Balzac's Novels*. Eugene: University of Oregon Press, 1946, pp. 48–51, 90–91.

Chaikin, Milton. "Maupassant's *Bel-Ami* and Balzac," in *Romance Notes*. II (Spring, 1960), pp. 109–112.

Dedinsky, Brucia L. "Development of the Scheme of the *Comedie humaine*: Distribution of the Stories," in *The Evolution of Balzac's* Comedie humaine. Edited by E. Preston Dargan and Bernard Weinberg. Chicago: University of Chicago Press, 1942, pp. 89–90, 102–105.

Maurois, Andre. *Prometheus: The Life of Balzac*. London: Bodley Head, 1965, pp. 298–300, 362–363.

Pritchett, V.S. "Books in General," in *New Statesman and Nation*. XLII (October 6, 1951), pp. 383–384.

Rogers, Samuel. *Balzac & the Novel*. Madison: University of Wisconsin Press, 1953, pp. 166–168.

Spitzer, Leo. "Balzac and Flaubert Again," in *Modern Language Notes*. LXVIII (December, 1953), pp. 583–590.

Tolley, Bruce. "The 'Cenacle' of Balzac's *Illusions Perdues*," in *French Studies*. XV (October, 1961), pp. 324–334.

Warren, F.M. "Was Balzac's *Illusions Perdues* Influenced by Stendhal?," in *Modern Language Notes*. XLIII (March, 1928), pp. 179–180.

The Wild Ass's Skin

Beebe, Maurice. "The Lesson of Balzac's Artists," in *Criticism*. II (Summer, 1960), pp. 228–231.

Bertault, Philippe. *Balzac and* The Human Comedy. New York: New York University Press, 1963, pp. 59–63.

Bowen, Ray P. *The Dramatic Construction of Balzac's Novels*. Eugene: University of Oregon Press, 1946, pp. 20–23, 79–80.

Dedinsky, Brucia L. "Development of the Scheme of the *Comedie humaine*: Distribution of the Stories," in *The Evolution of Balzac's* Comedie humaine. Edited by E. Preston Dargan and Bernard Weinberg. Chicago: University of Chicago Press, 1942, pp. 36–50, 69–72.

Gregg, Richard A. "Balzac and Women in *The Queen of Spades*," in *Slavic and East European Journal*. X (Fall, 1966), pp. 279–281.

Hunt, H.J. "Balzac's Pressmen," in *French Studies*. XI (July, 1957), pp. 230–244.

Maurois, Andre. *Prometheus: The Life of Balzac*. London: Bodley Head, 1965, pp. 173–180.

Millott, H.H. "*La Peau de Chagrin*: Method in Madness," in *Studies in Balzac's Realism*. By E. Preston Dargan, W.L. Crain and others. Chicago: University of Chicago Press, 1932, pp. 68–89.

Nozick, Martin. "Unamuno and *La Peau de Chagrin*," in *Modern Language Notes*. LXV (April, 1950), pp. 255–256.

Nykl, Alois Richard. "The Talisman in Balzac's *La Peau de Chagrin*," in *Modern Language Notes*. XXXIV (December, 1919), pp. 479–481.

Rudwin, Maximilian. "Balzac and the Fantastic," in *Sewanee Review*. XXXIII (January, 1925), pp. 14–17.

PÍO BAROJA
(1872–1956)

Caesar or Nothing

Barrow, Leo. *Negation in Baroja: A Key to His Novelistic Creativity.* Tucson: University of Arizona Press, 1971.

Bell, Aubrey F. *Contemporary Spanish Literature.* New York: Knopf, 1925, pp. 107–120.

Boyd, E.A. "Pío Baroja," in *Studies from Ten Literatures.* New York: Scribner's, 1925, pp. 72–86.

Madariaga, Salvador de. "Pío Baroja," in *Genius of Spain.* New York: Oxford University Press, 1923, pp. 111–127.

Patt, Beatrice. *Pío Baroja.* New York: Twayne, 1971, pp. 73–75, 106–110.

Shaw, D.L. "Two Novels of Baroja: An Illustration of His Technique," in *Bulletin of Hispanic Studies.* XL (July, 1963), pp. 156–158.

The Restlessness of Shanti Andia

Barrow, Leo. *Negation in Baroja: A Key to His Novelistic Creativity.* Tucson: University of Arizona Press, 1971.

Bell, Aubrey. *Contemporary Spanish Literature.* New York: Knopf, 1925, pp. 107–120.

Drake, W.A. "Pío Baroja," in *Contemporary European Writers.* New York: Day, 1928, pp. 114–123.

Madariaga, Salvador de. "Pío Baroja," in *Genius of Spain.* New York: Oxford University Press, 1923, pp. 111–127.

Patt, Beatrice. *Pío Baroja.* New York: Twayne, 1971, pp. 46–47, 110–112.

Pritchett, V.S. "Pío Baroja: An Independent Temper," in *New Statesman.* LVIII (September 26, 1959), pp. 396–397.

The Tree of Knowledge

Barrow, Leo. *Negation in Baroja: A Key to His Novelistic Creativity.* Tucson: University of Arizona Press, 1971.

Eoff, S.H. "The Persuasion to Passivity," in *The Modern Spanish Novel.* New York: New York University Press, 1961, pp. 148–185.

Fox, E. Inman. "Baroja and Schopenhauer," in *Revue de Litterature Comparee.* XXXVII (1963), pp. 350–359.

Patt, Beatrice. *Pío Baroja.* New York: Twayne, 1971, pp. 112–121.

Reid, John T. *Modern Spain and Liberalism: A Study in Literary Contrasts.* Stanford, Calif.: Stanford University Press, 1937, pp. 102–104.

Zalacaín the Adventurer

Barrow, Leo. *Negation in Baroja: A Key to His Novelistic Creativity.* Tucson: University of Arizona Press, 1971.

Eoff, Sherman. "The Persuasion to Passivity," in *The Modern Spanish Novel.* New York: New York University Press, 1961, pp. 148–185.

Jones, R.L. "Laguardia," in *Canadian Modern Language Review.* XXII (March, 1966), pp. 25–26.

————. "Urbia and Zaro: Birth and Burial of Zalacain," in *Canadian Modern Language Review.* XXII (March, 1966), pp. 29–35.

Patt, Beatrice. *Pío Baroja.* New York: Twayne, 1971, pp. 105–106.

JAMES M. BARRIE
(1860–1937)

The Admirable Crichton

Beerbohm, Max. *Around Theatres.* Elmsford, N.Y.: British Book Centre, 1953, pp. 231–234.

Clark, Barrett H. *A Study of the Modern Drama.* New York: Appleton, 1928, pp. 316–320.

Darlington, William A. *J.M. Barrie.* London: Blackie, 1938, pp. 90–92.

Dorton, F.J. Harvey. *J.M. Barrie.* New York: Holt, 1929, pp. 62–69.

Geduld, Harry M. *Sir James Barrie.* New York: Twayne, 1971, pp. 113–120.

McGraw, William R. "Barrie and the Critics," in *Studies in Scottish Literature.* I (October, 1963), pp. 129–130.

———. "James M. Barrie's Concept of Dramatic Action," in *Modern Drama.* V (September, 1962), pp. 133–141.

Phelps, William L. *Essays on Modern Dramatists.* New York: Macmillan, 1921, pp. 19–27.

———. "Plays of J.M. Barrie," in *North American Review.* CCXII (December, 1920), pp. 829–843.

Walkley, Arthur B. *Drama and Life.* New York: Brentano Book Store, 1908, pp. 198–208.

Alice Sit-by-the-Fire

Dorton, F.J. Harvey. *J.M. Barrie.* New York: Holt, 1929, pp. 56–57.

Geduld, Harry M. *Sir James Barrie.* New York: Twayne, 1971, pp. 124–130.

Green, Roger L. *J.M. Barrie.* New York: Walck, 1960.

McGraw, William R. "James M. Barrie's Concept of Dramatic Action," in *Modern Drama.* V (September, 1962), pp. 133–141.

Wright, Allen. *J.M. Barrie, Glamour of Twilight.* Edinburgh: Ramsey, Head, 1976.

Auld Licht Idylls

Chapple, J.A.V. *Documentary and Imaginative Literature, 1880–1920.* New York: Barnes & Noble, 1970, pp. 55–58.

Dorton, F.J. Harvey. *J.M. Barrie.* New York: Holt, 1929, pp. 24–25.

Geduld, Harry M. *Sir James Barrie.* New York: Twayne, 1971, pp. 16–19.

Green, Roger L. *J.M. Barrie.* New York: Walck, 1960.

Wright, Allen. *J.M. Barrie, Glamour of Twilight.* Edinburgh: Ramsey, Head, 1976.

The Boy David

Darlington, William A. *J.M. Barrie.* London: Blackie, 1938, pp. 143–147.

Geduld, Harry M. *Sir James Barrie.* New York: Twayne, 1971, pp. 164–168.

McGraw, William. "Barrie and the Critics," in *Studies in Scottish Literature.* I (October, 1963), pp. 129–130.

Roston, Murray. *Biblical Drama in England from the Middle Ages to the Present Day.* Evanston, Ill.: Northwestern University Press, 1968, pp. 285–286.

Weales, Gerald. *Religion in Modern English Drama.* Philadelphia: University of Pennsylvania Press, 1961, pp. 35–36.

Wright, Allen. *J.M. Barrie, Glamour of Twilight.* Edinburgh: Ramsey, Head, 1976.

Dear Brutus

Darlington, William A. *J.M. Barrie.* London: Blackie, 1938, pp. 123–128.

Dorton, F.J. Harvey. *J.M. Barrie.* New York: Holt, 1929, pp. 96–103.

Geduld, Harry M. *Sir James Barrie.* New York: Twayne, 1971, pp. 144–157.

Green, Roger L. *J.M. Barrie.* New York: Walck, 1960.

Jelliffe, Smith E. "*Dear Brutus*: The Dramatist's Use of the Dream," in *New York Medical Journal.* CIX (1919), pp. 577–583.

MacCarthy, Desmond. *Drama* . . . London: Putnam's, 1940, pp. 315–321.

————. *Theatre* . . . New York: Oxford University Press, 1955, pp. 144–149.

McGraw, William R. "Barrie and the Critics," in *Studies in Scottish Literature.* I (October, 1963), pp. 124–127.

Mais, Stuart P.B. *Some Modern Authors.* New York: Richards, 1923, pp. 252–263.

Miller, Nellie B. *The Living Drama.* New York: Century, 1924, pp. 313–316.

A Kiss for Cinderella

Dorton, F.J. Harvey. *J.M. Barrie.* New York: Holt, 1929, pp. 85–88.

Geduld, Harry M. *Sir James Barrie.* New York: Twayne, 1971, pp. 137–143.

Hackett, Frances. *Horizons: A Book of Criticism.* Munich: Heubsch, 1918, pp. 208–212.

Wright, Allen. *J.M. Barrie, Glamour of Twilight.* Edinburgh: Ramsey, Head, 1976.

Young, Stark. *Immortal Shadows; A Book of Criticism.* New York: Scribner's, 1948, pp. 227–229.

The Little Minister

Darlington, William A. *J.M. Barrie*. London: Blackie, 1938, pp. 77–79.

Dorton, F.J. Harvey. *J.M. Barrie*. New York: Holt, 1929, pp. 39–49.

Geduld, Harry M. *Sir James Barrie*. New York: Twayne, 1971, pp. 39–45.

Phelps, William L. *Essays on Modern Dramatists*. New York: Macmillan, 1921, pp. 15–18.

Wright, Allen. *J.M. Barrie, Glamour of Twilight*. Edinburgh: Ramsey, Head, 1976.

Little White Bird

Dorton, F.J. Harvey. *J.M. Barrie*. New York: Holt, 1929, pp. 70–75.

Geduld, Harry M. *Sir James Barrie*. New York: Twayne, 1971, pp. 53–70.

Green, Roger L. *Fifty Years of Peter Pan*. London: Davies, 1954, pp. 16–19.

————. *J.M. Barrie*. New York: Walck, 1960.

Wright, Allen. *J.M. Barrie, Glamour of Twilight*. Edinburgh: Ramsey, Head, 1976.

Mary Rose

Baring, M. *Punch and Judy and Other Essays*. London: Heineman, 1924, pp. 349–354.

Darlington, William A. *J.M. Barrie*. London: Blackie, 1938, pp. 130–134.

Dorton, F.J. Harvey. *J.M. Barrie*. New York: Holt, 1929, pp. 103–111.

Geduld, Harry M. *Sir James Barrie*. New York: Twayne, 1971, pp. 157–164.

Goitein, P.L. "A New Approach to an Analysis of *Mary Rose*," in *British Journal of Medical Psychology*. VI (1926), pp. 178–208.

Karpe, Marietta and Richard Karpe. "The Meaning of Barrie's *Mary Rose*," in *International Journal of Psycho-Analysis*. XXXVIII (1957), pp. 408–411.

Langdon-Brown, Sir Walter. *Thus We Are Men*. London: Kegan Paul, 1938, pp. 123–151.

Lewisohn, L. *Drama and the Stage*. New York: Harcourt, 1922, pp. 174–178.

McGraw, William R. "Barrie and the Critics," in *Studies in Scottish Literature*. I (October, 1963), pp. 127–128.

Peter and Wendy

Geduld, Harry M. *Sir James Barrie*. New York: Twayne, 1971, pp. 65–69.

Green, Roger L. *J.M. Barrie*. New York: Walck, 1960.

Wright, Allen. *J.M. Barrie, Glamour of Twilight*. Edinburgh: Ramsey, Head, 1976.

Peter Pan

Beerbohm, Max. *Around Theatres.* Elmsford, N.Y.: British Book Centre, 1953, pp. 357–361.

Darlington, William A. *J.M. Barrie.* London: Blackie, 1938, pp. 97–103, 148–150.

Dorton, F.J. Harvey. *J.M. Barrie.* New York: Holt, 1929, pp. 70–82.

Geduld, Harry M. *Sir James Barrie.* New York: Twayne, 1971, pp. 53–70.

Green, Roger L. *Fifty Years of Peter Pan.* London: Davies, 1954.

Karpe, Marietta. "The Origins of *Peter Pan*," in *Psychoanalytic Review.* XLIII (1956), pp. 104–110.

McGraw, William R. "Barrie and the Critics," in *Studies in Scottish Literature.* I (October, 1963), pp. 109–120.

————. "James M. Barrie's Concept of Dramatic Action," in *Modern Drama.* V (September, 1962), pp. 133–141.

Orcutt, W.D. "Barrie and the Birth of *Peter Pan*," in *From My Library Walls.* New York: Longmans, Green, 1945, pp. 8–12.

Phelps, William L. *Essays on Modern Dramatists.* New York: Macmillan, 1921, pp. 31–34.

Skinner, John. "James M. Barrie or the Boy Who Wouldn't Grow Up," in *American Imago.* XIV (1957), pp. 111–141.

Williams, David P. "Hook and Ahab: Barrie's Strange Satire on Melville," in *PMLA.* LXXX (December, 1965), pp. 483–488.

Quality Street

Beerbohm, Max. *Around Theatres.* Elmsford, N.Y.: British Book Centre, 1953, pp. 220–223.

Darlington, William A. *J.M. Barrie.* London: Blackie, 1938, pp. 87–90.

Dorton, F.J. Harvey. *J.M. Barrie.* New York: Holt, 1929, pp. 60–61.

Geduld, Harry M. *Sir James Barrie.* New York: Twayne, 1971, pp. 107–113.

Walkley, Arthur B. *Drama and Life.* New York: Brentano Book Store, 1908, pp. 194–197.

Wright, Allen. *J.M. Barrie, Glamour of Twilight.* Edinburgh: Ramsey, Head, 1976.

Sentimental Tommy

Dorton, F.J. Harvey. *J.M. Barrie.* New York: Holt, 1929, pp. 50–55.

Geduld, Harry M. *Sir James Barrie.* New York: Twayne, 1971, pp. 45–49.

Green, Roger L. *J.M. Barrie.* New York: Walck, 1960.

Wright, Allen. *J.M. Barrie, Glamour of Twilight.* Edinburgh: Ramsey, Head, 1976.

Tommy and Grizel

Dorton, F.J. Harvey. *J.M. Barrie*. New York: Holt, 1929, pp. 50–55.

Geduld, Harry M. *Sir James Barrie*. New York: Twayne, 1971, pp. 49–51.

Green, Roger L. *J.M. Barrie*. New York: Walck, 1960.

Wright, Allen. *J.M. Barrie, Glamour of Twilight*. Edinburgh: Ramsey, Head, 1976.

The Twelve Pound Look

Clark, Barrett H. *A Study of the Modern Drama*. New York: Appleton, 1928, pp. 312–316.

Darlington, William A. *J.M. Barrie*. London: Blackie, 1938, pp. 109–111.

Dorton, F.J. Harvey. *J.M. Barrie*. New York: Holt, 1929, pp. 90–91.

Geduld, Harry M. *Sir James Barrie*. New York: Twayne, 1971, pp. 77–79.

MacGowan, Kenneth. *Primer on Playwriting*. New York: Random House, 1951, pp. 172–173.

Wright, Allen. *J.M. Barrie, Glamour of Twilight*. Edinburgh: Ramsey, Head, 1976.

What Every Woman Knows

Darlington, William A. *J.M. Barrie*. London: Blackie, 1938, pp. 104–105.

Dorton, F.J. Harvey. *J.M. Barrie*. New York: Holt, 1929, pp. 57–58.

Geduld, Harry M. *Sir James Barrie*. New York: Twayne, 1971, pp. 130–137.

McGraw, William R. "Barrie and the Critics," in *Studies in Scottish Literature*. I (October, 1963), pp. 122–123.

————. "James M. Barrie's Concept of Dramatic Action," in *Modern Drama*. V (September, 1962), pp. 133–141.

Phelps, William L. *Essays on Modern Dramatists*. New York: Macmillan, 1921, pp. 41–47.

JOHN BARTH
(1930–   )

The End of the Road

Barnes, Hazel E.   *The Literature of Possibility: A Study in Humanistic Existentialism.* Lincoln: University of Nebraska Press, 1959, p. 380.

Bluestone, George.   "John Wain and John Barth: The Angry and the Accurate," in *Massachusetts Review.* I (1960), pp. 582–589.

Boyers, Robert.   "Attitudes Toward Sex in American 'High Culture,' " in *The Annals of the American Academy of Political and Social Science.* CCCLXXVI (1968), pp. 47–49.

Brooks, Peter.   "John Barth," in *Encounter.* XXVIII (1967), pp. 71–75.

Bryant, Jerry H.   *The Open Decision: The Contemporary American Novel and Its Intellectual Background.* New York: Free Press, 1970, pp. 283–303.

Davis, Robert Murray.   "The Shrinking Garden and New Exits: The Comic-Satire Novel in the Twentieth Century," in *Kansas Quarterly.* I (1969), pp. 13–15.

Graff, Gerald E.   "Mythotherapy and Modern Poetics," in *Tri-Quarterly.* XI (Winter, 1968), pp. 76–90.

Gross, Beverly.   "The Anti-Novels of John Barth," in *Chicago Review.* XX (1968), pp. 95–109.

Hassan, Ihab.   "The Existential Novel," in *Massachusetts Review.* III (1962), p. 796.

Hirsch, David.   "John Barth's Freedom Road," in *Mediterranean Review.* II (1972), pp. 38–47.

Kennard, Jean E.   *Number and Nightmare: Forms of Fantasy in Contemporary Fiction.* Hamden, Conn.: Archon Books, 1975, pp. 65–67.

Kerner, David.   "Psychodrama in Eden," in *Chicago Review.* XIII (Spring, 1959), pp. 59–67.

Kostelanetz, Richard.   *The New American Arts.* New York: Horizon Press, 1965, pp. 203–212.

Majdiak, Daniel.   "Barth and the Representation of Life," in *Criticism.* XII (1970), pp. 51–67.

Noland, Richard W.   "John Barth and the Novel of Comic Realism," in *Wisconsin Studies in Contemporary Literature.* VII (1966), pp. 239–257.

Raban, Jonathan.   *The Technique of Modern Fiction: Essays in Practical Criticism.* Notre Dame, Ind.: University of Notre Dame Press, 1968, pp. 76–78.

Smith, Herbert F. "Barth's Endless Road," in *Critique: Studies in Modern Fiction.* VI (1963), pp. 68–76.

Stubbs, John C. "John Barth as a Novelist of Ideas: The Themes of Value and Identity," in *Critique: Studies in Modern Fiction.* VIII (Winter, 1965–1966), pp. 105–108.

Tanner, Tony. "The Hoax That Joke Bilked," in *Partisan Review.* XXXIV (1967), pp. 102–109.

Trachtenberg, Alan. "Barth and Hawkes: Two Fabulists," in *Critique: Studies in Modern Fiction.* VI (Fall, 1963), pp. 11–15.

Verzosa, Guillermina L. "The Unsayable and Its Expression in John Barth's *The End of the Road*," in *St. Louis University Research Journal of the Arts and Sciences.* V (1974), pp. 131–187.

The Floating Opera

Aarseth, Inger. "Absence of Absolutes: The Reconciled Artist in John Barth's *The Floating Opera*," in *Studia Neophilologica.* XLVII (1975), pp. 53–68.

Bluestone, George. "John Wain and John Barth: The Angry and the Accurate," in *Massachusetts Review.* I (1960), pp. 582–589.

Gross, Beverly. "The Anti-Novels of John Barth," in *Chicago Review.* XX (1968), pp. 95–109.

Harris, Charles B. "Todd Andrews: Ontological Insecurity and *The Floating Opera*," in *Critique: Studies in Modern Fiction.* XVIII (1976), pp. 34–50.

Hawkes, John. "*The Floating Opera* and *Second Skin*," in *Mosaic.* VIII (1974), pp. 17–28.

Jordan, Enoch P. "*The Floating Opera* Restored," in *Critique: Studies in Modern Fiction.* XVIII (1976), pp. 5–16.

Kennard, Jean E. *Number and Nightmare: Forms of Fantasy in Contemporary Fiction.* Hamden, Conn.: Archon Books, 1975, pp. 60–65.

Kostelanetz, Richard. *The New American Arts.* New York: Horizon Press, 1965, pp. 209–210.

Le Clair, Thomas. "Death and Black Humor," in *Critique: Studies in Modern Fiction.* XVII (1975), pp. 17–19.

———. "John Barth's *The Floating Opera*: Death and the Craft of Fiction," in *Texas Studies in Literature and Language.* XIV (1973), pp. 711–730.

Martin, Dennis M. "Desire and Disease: The Psychological Pattern of *The Floating Opera*," in *Critique: Studies in Modern Fiction.* XVIII (1976), pp. 17–33.

Noland, Richard. "John Barth and the Novel of Comic Realism," in *Wisconsin Studies in Contemporary Literature.* VII (Autumn, 1966), pp. 239–244.

Ryan, Marjorie. "Four Contemporary Satires and the Problem of Norms," in *Satire Newsletter.* VI (1969), pp. 40–46.

Schickel, Richard. *"The Floating Opera,"* in *Critique: Studies in Modern Fiction.* VI (1963), pp. 53–67.

Stubbs, John C. "John Barth as Novelist of Ideas: The Themes of Value and Identity," in *Critique: Studies in Modern Fiction.* VIII (Winter, 1965–1966), pp. 102–105.

Tatham, Campbell. "John Barth and the Aesthetics of Artifice," in *Contemporary Literature.* XII (1971), pp. 60–73.

Voelker, Joseph C. "The Drama of Digression: Narrative Technique in John Barth's *The Floating Opera,"* in *Cimarron Review.* XXIX (1974), pp. 34–44.

Giles Goat-Boy

Byrd, Scott. *"Giles Goat-Boy* Visited," in *Critique: Studies in Modern Fiction.* IX (1967), pp. 108–112.

Garis, Robert. "What Happened to John Barth?," in *Commentary.* XLII (1966), pp. 189–195.

Gresham, James T. *"Giles Goat-Boy*: Satyr, Satire, and Tragedy Twined," in *Genre.* VII (1974), pp. 148–163.

Gross, Beverly. "The Anti-Novels of John Barth," in *Chicago Review.* XX (1968), pp. 95–109.

Kennard, Jean E. "John Barth: Imitations of Imitations," in *Mosaic.* III (1970), pp. 116–131.

————. *Number and Nightmare: Forms of Fantasy in Contemporary Fiction.* Hamden, Conn.: Archon Books, 1975, pp. 73–78.

Kiely, Benedict. "Ripeness Was Not All: John Barth's *Giles Goat-Boy,"* in *Hollins Critic.* III (December, 1966), pp. 1–12. Reprinted in *The Sounder Few.* Edited by R.H.W. Dillard, George Garrett and John Rees Moore. Athens: University of Georgia Press, 1971, pp. 195–210.

McColm, Pearlmarie. "The Revised New Syllabus and the Unrevised Old," in *Denver Quarterly.* I (Autumn, 1966), pp. 136–138.

McDonald, James L. "Barth's Syllabus: The Frame of *Giles Goat-Boy,"* in *Critique: Studies in Modern Fiction.* XIII (1972), pp. 5–10.

Mercer, Peter. "The Rhetoric of *Giles Goat-Boy,"* in *Novel: A Forum on Fiction.* IV (1971), pp. 147–158.

Olderman, Raymond M. *Beyond the Waste Land: A Study of the American Novel in the Nineteen-Sixties.* New Haven, Conn.: Yale University Press, 1972, pp. 72–93.

Rodrigues, Eusebio L. "The Living Sakhyan in Barth's *Giles Goat-Boy,"* in *Notes on Contemporary Literature.* II (1972), pp. 7–8.

Samuels, Charles T. "John Barth: A Buoyant Denial of Relevance," in *Commonweal.* LXXXV (October 21, 1966), pp. 80–82.

Scholes, Robert. *The Fabulators.* New York: Oxford University Press, 1967, pp. 135–173.

Slethaug, Gordon E. "Barth's Refutation of the Idea of Progress," in *Critique: Studies in Modern Fiction.* XIII (1972), pp. 11–29.

Stark, John O. *The Literature of Exhaustion: Borges, Nabokov, and Barth.* Durham, N.C.: Duke University Press, 1974, pp. 118–175.

Tanner, Tony. "The Hoax That Joke Bilked," in *Partisan Review.* XXXIV (Winter, 1967), pp. 102–109.

Tatham, Campbell. "The Gilesian Monomyth: Some Remarks on the Structure of *Giles Goat-Boy*," in *Genre.* III (1970), pp. 364–375.

Tilton, John W. "*Giles Goat-Boy*: An Interpretation," in *Bucknell Review.* XVIII (1970), pp. 92–119.

Ziolkowski, Theodore. *Fictional Transfigurations of Jesus.* Princeton, N.J.: Princeton University Press, 1972, pp. 256–298.

The Sot-Weed Factor

Bean, John C. "John Barth and Festive Comedy: The Failure of Imagination in *The Sot-Weed Factor*," in *Xavier University Studies.* X (1971), pp. 3–15.

Brooks, Peter. "John Barth," in *Encounter.* XXVIII (1967), pp. 71–75.

Bryant, Jerry H. *The Open Decision: The Contemporary American Novel and Its Intellectual Background.* New York: Free Press, 1970, pp. 283–303.

Dippie, Brian W. " 'His Visage Wild; His Form Exotick': Indian Themes and Cultural Guilt in John Barth's *The Sot-Weed Factor*," in *American Quarterly.* XXI (1969), pp. 113–121.

Diser, Philip E. "The Historical Ebenezer Cooke," in *Critique: Studies in Modern Fiction.* X (1968), pp. 48–59.

Fiedler, Leslie. "John Barth: An Eccentric Genius," in *On Contemporary Literature.* Edited by Richard Kostelanetz. New York: Avon Books, 1964, pp. 238–243.

————. *The Return of the Vanishing American.* New York: Stein and Day, 1968, pp. 150–153.

Holder, Alan. " 'What Marvelous Plot . . . Was Afoot?': History in Barth's *The Sot-Weed Factor*," in *American Quarterly.* XX (1968), pp. 596–604.

Hyman, Stanley Edgar. *Standards: A Chronicle of Books for Our Time.* New York: Horizon Press, 1966, pp. 204–208.

Jones, D. Allan. "The Game of the Name in Barth's *The Sot-Weed Factor*," in *Research Studies.* XL (1972), pp. 219–221.

Kennard, Jean E. "John Barth: Imitations of Imitations," in *Mosaic.* III (1970), pp. 116–131.

Kostelanetz, Richard. *The New American Arts.* New York: Horizon Press, 1965, pp. 203–212.

Lee, L.L. "Some Uses of *Finnegans Wake* in John Barth's *The Sot-Weed Factor*," in *James Joyce Quarterly.* V (Winter, 1968), pp. 177–178.

Lewis, R.W.B. *Trials of the Word: Essays in American Literature and the Humanistic Tradition.* New Haven, Conn.: Yale University Press, 1965, pp. 220–226.

Miller, Russell H. "*The Sot-Weed Factor*: A Contemporary Mock-Epic," in *Critique: Studies in Modern Fiction.* VIII (1965–1966), pp. 88–100.

Morrell, David. "Ebenezer Cooke, Sot-Weed Factor Redivivus: The Genesis of John Barth's *The Sot-Weed Factor*," in *Bulletin of the Midwest Modern Language Association.* VIII (1975), pp. 32–47.

Noland, Richard W. "John Barth and the Novel of Comic Realism," in *Wisconsin Studies in Contemporary Literature.* VII (1966), pp. 247–256.

Rovit, Earl. "The Novel as Parody: John Barth," in *Critique: Studies in Modern Fiction.* VI (1963), pp. 77–85.

Rubin, Louis D., Jr. "Notes on the Literary Scene: Their Own Language," in *Harper's Magazine.* CCXXX (April, 1965), pp. 173–175.

Slethaug, Gordon E. "Barth's Refutation of the Idea of Progress," in *Critique: Studies in Modern Fiction.* XIII (1972), pp. 11–29.

Stubbs, John C. "John Barth as a Novelist of Ideas: The Themes of Value and Identity," in *Critique: Studies in Modern Fiction.* VIII (Winter, 1965–1966), pp. 108–113.

Sutcliffe, Denham. "Worth a Guilty Conscience," in *Kenyon Review.* XXIII (Winter, 1961), pp. 181–186.

Tanner, Tony. "The Hoax That Joke Bilked," in *Partisan Review.* XXXIV (1967), pp. 102–109.

Trachtenburg, Alan. "Barth and Hawkes: Two Fabulists," in *Critique: Studies in Modern Fiction.* VI (Fall, 1963), pp. 15–18.

DONALD BARTHELME
(1931–   )

City Life

Algren, Nelson. *"City Life,"* in *Critic*. XXIX (September, 1970), p. 86.

Berek, Peter. "Disenchanted Symbols," in *Nation*. CCX (May 25, 1970), p. 630.

Dickstein, Morris. *"City Life,"* in *New York Times Book Review*. (April 26, 1970), p. 1.

Hendin, Josephine. *"City Life,"* in *Saturday Review*. LIII (May 9, 1970), p. 34.

The Short Stories of Barthelme

Aldridge, John W. *The Devil in the Fire: Retrospective Essays on American Literature and Culture, 1951–1971*. New York: Harper & Row, 1972, pp. 261–266.

Ditsky, John M. " 'With Ingenuity and Hard Work, Distracted': The Narrative Style of Donald Barthelme," in *Style*. IX (1975), pp. 388–400.

Gillen, Francis. "Donald Barthelme's City: A Guide," in *Twentieth Century Literature*. XVIII (January, 1972), pp. 37–44.

Johnson, R.E. " 'Bees Barking in the Night': The End and Beginning of Donald Barthelme's Narrative," in *Boundary*. V (1976), pp. 71–92.

_____. "Structuralism and the Reading of Contemporary Fiction," in *Soundings*. LVIII (1975), pp. 281–306.

Kazin, Alfred. *Bright Book of Life: American Novelists and Storytellers from Hemingway to Mailer*. Boston: Little, Brown, 1973, pp. 271–274.

Klinkowitz, Jerome. *Literary Disruptions: The Making of a Post-Contemporary American Fiction*. Urbana: University of Illinois Press, 1975, pp. 70–87.

Peden, William. *The American Short Story*. Boston: Houghton Mifflin, 1975, pp. 177–179.

Samuels, Charles Thomas. "Moving Through 'The Indian Uprising,' " in *The Process of Fiction*. Edited by Barbara McKenzie. New York: Harcourt, 1974, pp. 529–537.

Schmitz, Neil. "What Irony Unravels," in *Partisan Review*. XL (1973), pp. 482–490.

Shorris, Earl. "Donald Barthelme's Illustrated Wordy-Gurdy," in *Harper's*. CCXLVI (January, 1973), pp. 92–94, 96.

Stevick, Phillip. "Lies, Fictions, and Mock Facts," in *Western Humanities Review.* XXX (Winter, 1976), pp. 1–12.

Tanner, Tony. *City of Words.* New York: Harper & Row, 1971, pp. 400–406.

Vidal, Gore. *Matters of Fact and of Fiction: Essays, 1973–1976.* New York: Random House, 1977, pp. 102–107.

Whalen, Thomas D. "Wonderful Elegance: Barthelme's 'The Party,' " in *Critique.* XVI (1975), pp. 44–48.

Wilde, Alan. "Barthelme Unfair to Kirkegaard: Some Thoughts on Modern and Post Modern Irony," in *Boundary.* V (1976), pp. 45–70.

Snow White

Adams, R.R.M. "With English on the English," in *New York Times Book Review.* (May 21, 1967), p. 4.

Crinklaw, Don. *"Snow White,"* in *Commonweal.* LXXXVII (December 29, 1967), p. 416.

Donoghue, D. "What's Your Inner Reality?," in *New York Review of Books.* (August 24, 1967), pp. 12–13.

Epstein, Seymour. "Beauty and the Building Washers," in *Saturday Review.* L (July 1, 1967), p. 24.

Flowers, Betty. "Barthelme's *Snow White*: The Reader-Patient Relationship," in *Critique.* XVI (1975), pp. 33–43.

Gilman, Richard. "Barthelme's Fairy Tale," in *New Republic.* CLVI (June 3, 1967), pp. 27–30. Reprinted in *Confusion of Realms.* New York: Random House, 1969, pp. 42–52.

Harris, Charles B. *Contemporary American Novelists of the Absurd.* New Haven, Conn.: Yale University Press, 1971, pp. 124–127.

Klinkowitz, Jerome. *Literary Disruptions: The Making of a Post-Contemporary American Fiction.* Urbana: University of Illinois Press, 1975, pp. 66–69.

Longleigh, Peter L., Jr. "Donald Barthelme's *Snow White,*" in *Critique.* XI (1969), pp. 30–34.

McCaffery, Larry. "Barthelme's *Snow White*: The Aesthetics of Trash," in *Critique.* XVI (1975), pp. 19–32.

McNall, Sally Allen. " 'But Why am I Troubling Myself About Cans?': Style, Reaction, and Lack of Reaction in Barthelme's *Snow White,*" in *Language and Style.* VIII (1975), pp. 81–94.

O'Connel, Shaun. "Good Dirty Fun and Games," in *Nation.* CCIV (June, 1967), pp. 794–795.

Shadoian, Jack. "Notes on Donald Barthelme's *Snow White,*" in *Western Humanities Review.* XXIV (Winter, 1970), pp. 73–75.

Unspeakable Practices, Unnatural Acts

Aldridge, J.W. "Dance of Death," in *Atlantic.* CCXXII (July, 1968), pp. 89–91.

Benient, Calvin. "No Pretense to Coherency," in *Nation.* CCVI (May 27, 1968), pp. 703–704.

Broyard, Anatole. "Metaphors for Madness," in *New York Times Book Review.* (May 12, 1968), p. 7.

Corke, Hilary. "Whistling in a Gale," in *New Republic.* CLVIII (June 1, 1968), p. 34.

Gass, William H. "The Leading Edge of the Trash Phenomenon," in *New York Review of Books.* (April 25, 1968), pp. 5–6.

Murray, J.G. *"Unspeakable Practices, Unnatural Acts,"* in *Critic.* XXVI (June, 1968), p. 74.

Silver, A.Z. "The Many Uses of Faces," in *Saturday Review.* LI (May 11, 1968), p. 81.

Tucker, Martin. *"Unspeakable Practices, Unnatural Acts,"* in *Commonweal.* LXXXVIII (June 21, 1968), p. 414.

CHARLES BAUDELAIRE
(1821–1867)

Flowers of Evil

Avri, Abraham. "A Revaluation of Baudelaire's '*Le Vin*'; Its Originality and Significance for *Les Fleurs du Mal*," in *French Review*. XLIV (December, 1970), pp. 310–321.

Barlow, Norman H. *Sainte-Beuve to Baudelaire; A Poetic Legacy*. Durham, N.C.: Duke University Press, 1964, pp. 84–138.

Bennett, Joseph D. *Baudelaire: A Criticism*. Princeton, N.J.: Princeton University Press, 1944.

Benson, Eugene. "Charles Baudelaire, Poet of the Malign," in *Atlantic Monthly*. XXIII (February, 1869), pp. 171–177.

Bertocci, Angelo Philip. *From Symbolism to Baudelaire*. Carbondale: Southern Illinois University Press, 1964, pp. 75–168.

Bogan, Louise. *Selected Criticism: Prose, Poetry*. New York: Noonday, 1955, pp. 332–334.

Cowley, Malcolm. *Think Back on Us . . . A Contemporary Chronicle of the 1930's*. Carbondale: Southern Illinois University Press, 1967, pp. 283–287.

Fowlie, Wallace. "Baudelaire and Eliot: Interpreters of Their Age," in *Sewanee Review*. LXXIV (Winter, 1966), pp. 293–309.

————. *Climate of Violence; The French Literary Tradition from Baudelaire to the Present*. New York: Macmillan, 1967, pp. 3–19.

Friedrich, Hugh. *The Structure of Modern Poetry; From the Mid-Nineteenth to the Mid-Twentieth Century*. Evanston, Ill.: Northwestern University Press, 1974, pp. 19–38.

Hambly, Peter. "The Structure of *Les Fleurs du Mal*: Another Suggestion," in *Australian Journal of French Studies*. VIII (September–December, 1971), pp. 269–296.

James, Henry. "Charles Baudelaire," in *Nation*. XXII (April 27, 1876), pp. 279–281.

Peyre, Henri. "Baudelaire as a Love Poet," in *Baudelaire as a Love Poet and Other Essays*. Edited by Lois Hyslop. University Park: Pennsylvania State University Press, 1969, pp. 3–39.

————, **Editor.** *Baudelaire; a Collection of Critical Essays*. Englewood Cliffs, N.J.: Prentice-Hall, 1962.

Saintsbury, George. "Charles Baudelaire," in *Fortnightly Review*. XXIV (1875), pp. 500–518.

FRANCIS BEAUMONT
(1584–1616)

The Knight of the Burning Pestle

Appleton, William W. *Beaumont and Fletcher: A Critical Study.* London: Allen and Unwin, 1956, pp. 13–16.

Boas, Frederick S. *An Introduction to Stuart Drama.* London: Oxford University Press, 1946, pp. 252–254.

Cunningham, John E. *Elizabethan and Early Stuart Drama.* London: Evans, 1965, pp. 86–88.

Doebler, John. "Beaumont's *The Knight of the Burning Pestle* and *The Prodigal Son*," in *Studies in English Literature, 1500–1900.* I (1965), pp. 333–344.

———. "Introduction," in *The Knight of the Burning Pestle.* By Francis Beaumont. Lincoln: University of Nebraska Press, 1967, pp. xi–xxiv.

———. "The Tone of the Jasper and Luce Scenes in Beaumont's *The Knight of the Burning Pestle*," in *English Studies.* LVI (1975), pp. 108–113.

Doran, Madeleine. *Endeavors of Art: A Study of Form in Elizabethan Drama.* Madison: University of Wisconsin Press, 1954, pp. 344-345.

Fletcher, Ian. *Beaumont and Fletcher.* London: Longmans, Green, 1967, pp. 17–19.

Gayley, Charles Mills. *Beaumont, the Dramatist: A Portrait.* New York: Century, 1914, pp. 310–332.

Greenfield, Thelma N. *The Induction of Elizabethan Drama.* Eugene: University of Oregon Books, 1969, pp. 4–6, 113–116.

Gurr, Andrew. "Critical Introduction," in *The Knight of the Burning Pestle.* By Francis Beaumont. Berkeley: University of California Press, 1968, pp. 1–9.

Hattaway, Michael. "Introduction," in *The Knight of the Burning Pestle.* By Francis Beaumont. London: Ernest Benn, 1969, pp. ix–xix.

Maxwell, Baldwin. *Studies in Beaumont, Fletcher, and Massinger.* Chapel Hill: University of North Carolina Press, 1939, pp. 14–16.

———. " 'Twenty Good-Nights'—*The Knight of the Burning Pestle*," in *Modern Language Notes.* LXIII (1948), pp. 233–237.

Moorman, F.W. "Introduction," in *The Knight of the Burning Pestle.* By Francis Beaumont and John Fletcher. London: Aldine House, 1909, pp. v–xii.

Oliphant, E.C.H. *The Plays of Beaumont and Fletcher.* New Haven, Conn.: Yale University Press, 1927, pp. 169–179.

Olive, W.J. "Twenty Good Nights," in *Studies in Philology.* XLVII (April, 1950), pp. 182–189.

Silvette, Herbert.   *The Doctor on the Stage: Medicine and Medical Men in Seventeenth-Century England.* Knoxville: University of Tennessee Press, 1967, pp. 228–229.

Taylor, Marion A.   "Lady Arabella Stuart and Beaumont and Fletcher," in *Papers on Language and Literature.* VIII (1972), pp. 252–260.

Wallis, Lawrence B.   *Fletcher, Beaumont and Company: Entertainers to the Jacobean Gentry.* Morningside Heights, N.Y.: King's Crown Press, 1947, pp. 177–199.

Wells, Henry W.   *Elizabethan and Jacobean Playwrights.* New York: Columbia University Press, 1964, pp. 233–235.

Withington, R.   " 'F.S., Which Is to Say . . . ' The First Act of *The Knight of the Burning Pestle*," in *Studies in Philology.* XXII (1925), pp. 226–233.

The Woman Hater

Appleton, William W.   *Beaumont and Fletcher: A Critical Study.* London: Allen and Unwin, 1956, pp. 11–13.

Gayley, Charles Mills.   *Beaumont, the Dramatist: A Portrait.* New York: Century, 1914, pp. 72–79, 307–311.

Levin, Richard.   *The Multiple Plot in English Renaissance Drama.* Chicago: University of Chicago Press, 1971, pp. 151–154.

Maxwell, Baldwin.   "The Hungry Knave in the Beaumont and Fletcher Plays," in *Philological Quarterly.* V (1926), pp. 299–305.

Oliphant, E.C.H.   *The Plays of Beaumont and Fletcher.* New Haven, Conn.: Yale University Press, 1927, pp. 214–219.

Upton, A.W.   "Allusions to James I and His Court in Marston's *Fawn* and Beaumont's *Woman Hater*," in *PMLA.* XLIV (1929), pp. 1048–1065.

FRANCIS BEAUMONT
(1584–1616)
AND
JOHN FLETCHER
(1579–1625)

The Coxcomb

Appleton, William W. *Beaumont and Fletcher: A Critical Study.* London: Allen and Unwin, 1956, pp. 44–47.

Gayley, Charles Mills. *Beaumont, the Dramatist: A Portrait.* New York: Century, 1914, pp. 96–101, 332–341.

Gossett, Suzanne. "The Term 'Masque' in Shakespeare and Fletcher, and *The Coxcomb*," in *Studies in English Literature, 1500–1900.* XIV (1974), pp. 285–295.

Harbage, Alfred. *Shakespeare and the Rival Traditions.* New York: Barnes & Noble, 1952, pp. 242–243, 247–248.

Oliphant, E.C.H. *The Plays of Beaumont and Fletcher.* New Haven, Conn.: Yale University Press, 1927, pp. 265–274.

Shaw, George Bernard. *Plays and Players: Essays on the Theatre.* New York: Oxford University Press, 1952, pp. 307–312.

Ward, C.E. "Note on Beaumont and Fletcher's *Coxcomb*," in *Philological Quarterly.* IX (1930), pp. 73–76.

Cupid's Revenge

Appleton, William W. *Beaumont and Fletcher: A Critical Study.* London: Allen and Unwin, 1956, pp. 19–22.

Boas, Frederick S. *An Introduction to Stuart Drama.* London: Oxford University Press, 1946, pp. 267–269.

Bowers, Fredson. "Textual Introduction," in *The Dramatic Works in the Beaumont and Fletcher Canon,* Volume II. Cambridge: Cambridge University Press, 1970, pp. 317–332.

Brodwin, Leonora Leet. *Elizabethan Love Tragedy, 1587–1625.* New York: New York University Press, 1971, pp. 125–129.

Dyce, Alexander. "Some Account of the Lives and Writings of Beaumont and Fletcher," in *The Works of Beaumont and Fletcher,* Volume I. London: Edward Moxon, 1843, pp. xxxvi–xxxvii.

Gabler, Hans W. "*Cupid's Revenge* (Q1) and Its Compositors Part I: Composition and Painting," in *Studies in Bibliography.* XXIV (1971), pp. 69–90.

Gayley, Charles Mills. *Beaumont, the Dramatist: A Portrait.* New York: Century, 1914, pp. 111–112.

Oliphant, E.C.H. *The Plays of Beaumont and Fletcher.* New Haven, Conn.: Yale University Press, 1927, pp. 348–353.

Savage, J.E. "Beaumont and Fletcher's *Philaster* and Sidney's *Arcadia*; Also the Use They Made of the Material in *Cupid's Revenge*," in *Journal of English Literary History.* XIV (1947), pp. 194–206.

Thorndike, Ashley H. *The Influence of Beaumont and Fletcher on Shakespeare.* New York: Russell and Russell, 1965, pp. 109–132.

Wells, W. "Birth of Merlin," in *Modern Language Review.* XVI (1921), pp. 129–137.

A King and No King

Appleton, William W. *Beaumont and Fletcher: A Critical Study.* London: Allen and Unwin, 1956, pp. 41–44.

Bluestone, Max and Norman Rabkin. *Shakespeare's Contemporaries: Modern Studies in English Renaissance Drama.* Englewood Cliffs, N.J.: Prentice-Hall, 1970, pp. 342–362.

Boas, Frederick S. *An Introduction to Stuart Drama.* London: Oxford University Press, 1946, pp. 263–266.

Doran, Madeleine. *Endeavors of Art: A Study of Form in Elizabethan Drama.* Madison: University of Wisconsin Press, 1954, pp. 186–187.

Fletcher, Ian. *Beaumont and Fletcher.* London: Longmans, Green, 1967, pp. 35–38.

Gabler, Hans W. "John Beale's Compositors in *A King and No King*," in *Studies in Bibliography.* XXIV (1971), pp. 138–143.

Gayley, Charles Mills. *Beaumont, the Dramatist: A Portrait.* New York: Century, 1914, pp. 109–110, 361–367, 386–396.

Griffiths, L.M. "Shakespearian Qualities of *A King and No King*," in *Poet-Lore.* III (1891), pp. 169–177.

Knights, L.C. *Drama and Society in the Age of Jonson.* London: Chatto and Windus, 1947, pp. 292–295.

Leech, Clifford. *The John Fletcher Plays.* London: Chatto and Windus, 1962, pp. 16–21, 78–83.

Mizener, A. "High Design for *A King and No King*," in *Modern Philology.* XXXVIII (1940), pp. 133–154.

Ornstein, Robert. *The Moral Vision of Jacobean Tragedy.* Madison: University of Wisconsin Press, 1960, pp. 168–169.

Tomlinson, T.B. *A Study of Elizabethan and Jacobean Tragedy.* Cambridge: Cambridge University Press, 1964, pp. 251–252.

Turner, Robert K., Jr. "Introduction," in *A King and No King*. By Francis Beaumont and John Fletcher. Lincoln: University of Nebraska Press, 1963, pp. xi–xxx.

————. "The Morality of *A King and No King*," in *Renaissance Papers*. (1958–60), pp. 93–103.

Waith, Eugene M. *Ideas of Greatness: Heroic Drama in England*. London: Routledge and Kegan Paul, 1971, pp. 151–153.

Wells, Henry W. *Elizabethan and Jacobean Playwrights*. New York: Columbia University Press, 1964, pp. 120–122.

The Maid's Tragedy

Appleton, William W. *Beaumont and Fletcher: A Critical Study*. London: Allen and Unwin, 1956, pp. 34–41, 68–69.

Berry, Francis. *Poet's Grammar*. London: Routledge, 1958, pp. 93–96.

Boas, Frederick S. *An Introduction to Stuart Drama*. London: Oxford University Press, 1946, pp. 260–263.

Bowers, Fredson T. *Elizabethan Revenge Tragedy*. Princeton, N.J.: Princeton University Press, 1940, pp. 169–176.

Brodwin, Leonora Leet. *Elizabethan Love Tragedy, 1587–1625*. New York: New York University Press, 1971, pp. 129–147.

Cunningham, John E. *Elizabethan and Early Stuart Drama*. London: Evans, 1965, pp. 77–82.

Danby, J.F. *Poets on Fortune's Hill*. London: Faber and Faber, 1952, pp. 184–210.

Feldman, A.B. "The Yellow Malady: Short Studies of Five Tragedies of Jealousy," in *Literature and Psychology*. V (May, 1956), pp. 46–49, 51–52.

Fletcher, Ian. *Beaumont and Fletcher*. London: Longmans, Green, 1967, pp. 31–35.

Gayley, Charles Mills. *Beaumont, the Dramatist: A Portrait*. New York: Century, 1914, pp. 107–109, 349–359, 386–395.

Gossett, Suzanne. "Masque Influence on the Dramaturgy of Beaumont and Fletcher," in *Modern Philology*. LXIX (1971–1972), pp. 199–208.

Gurr, Andrew. "Critical Introduction," in *The Maid's Tragedy*. By Francis Beaumont and John Fletcher. Berkeley: University of California Press, 1969, pp. 1–7.

Herndl, George C. *The High Design: English Renaissance Tragedy and the Natural Law*. Lexington: University of Kentucky Press, 1970, pp. 244–247.

Leech, Clifford. *The John Fletcher Plays*. London: Chatto and Windus, 1962, pp. 120–127.

_____. *Shakespeare's Tragedies and Other Studies in Seventeenth Century Drama*. London: Chatto and Windus, 1961, pp. 87–89, 94–95, 107–108.

Neill, Michael. " 'The Simetry, Which Gives a Poem Grace': Masque, Imagery, and the Fancy of *The Maid's Tragedy*," in *Renaissance Drama*. III (1970), pp. 111–135.

Norland, Howard B. "Introduction," in *The Maid's Tragedy*. By Francis Beaumont and John Fletcher. Lincoln: University of Nebraska Press, 1968, pp. xi–xxviii.

Ornstein, Robert. *The Moral Vision of Jacobean Tragedy*. Madison: University of Wisconsin Press, 1960, pp. 173–184.

Prior, Moody E. *The Language of Tragedy*. New York: Columbia University Press, 1947, pp. 101–104.

Reed, Robert Rentoul, Jr. *Bedlam on the Jacobean Stage*. Cambridge, Mass.: Harvard University Press, 1952, pp. 93–96.

Ribner, Irving. *Jacobean Tragedy: The Quest for Moral Order*. New York: Barnes & Noble, 1962, pp. 15–17.

Tomlinson, Thomas Brian. *A Study of Elizabethan and Jacobean Tragedy*. Cambridge: Cambridge University Press, 1964, pp. 243–250.

Wallis, Lawrence B. *Fletcher, Beaumont and Company: Entertainers to the Jacobean Gentry*. Morningside Heights, N.Y.: King's Crown Press, 1947, pp. 200–240.

Wells, Henry W. *Elizabethan and Jacobean Playwrights*. New York: Columbia University Press, 1964, pp. 124–127.

Philaster

Adkins, Mary G. "The Citizens of *Philaster*: Their Function and Significance," in *Studies in Philology*. XLIII (April, 1946), pp. 203–212.

Appleton, William W. *Beaumont and Fletcher: A Critical Study*. London: Allen and Unwin, 1956, pp. 29–34.

Ashe, Dora Jean. "Introduction," in *Philaster*. By Francis Beaumont and John Fletcher. Lincoln: University of Nebraska Press, 1974, pp. xi–xxxii.

Bluestone, Max and Norman Rabkin. *Shakespeare's Contemporaries: Modern Studies in English Renaissance Drama*. Englewood Cliffs, N.J.: Prentice-Hall, 1970, pp. 330–342.

Boas, Frederick S. *An Introduction to Stuart Drama*. London: Oxford University Press, 1946, pp. 257–260.

Bradbrook, M.C. *The Growth and Structure of Elizabethan Comedy*. Berkeley: University of California Press, 1956, pp. 177–186.

Cunningham, John E. *Elizabethan and Early Stuart Drama*. London: Evans, 1965, pp. 82–86.

Danby, John. "Beaumont and Fletcher: Jacobean Absolutists," in *Elizabethan Drama: Modern Essays in Criticism*. Edited by R.J. Kaufmann. New York: Oxford University Press, 1961, pp. 277–296.

————. *Poets on Fortune's Hill*. London: Faber and Faber, 1952, pp. 162–183.

Davison, P. "Serious Concerns of *Philaster*," in *Journal of English Literary History*. XXX (1963), pp. 1–15.

Fletcher, Ian. *Beaumont and Fletcher*. London: Longmans, Green, 1967, pp. 26–31.

Gayley, Charles Mills. *Beaumont, the Dramatist: A Portrait*. New York: Century, 1914, pp. 101–107, 341–349, 386–396.

Gossett, Suzanne. "Masque Influence on the Dramaturgy of Beaumont and Fletcher," in *Modern Philology*. LXIX (1971–1972), pp. 199–208.

Gurr, Andrew. "Introduction," in *Philaster*. By Francis Beaumont and John Fletcher. London: Methuen, 1969, pp. xix–lxxxiv.

Leech, Clifford. *The John Fletcher Plays*. London: Chatto and Windus, 1962, pp. 78–94.

Oliphant, E.C.H. *The Plays of Beaumont and Fletcher*. New Haven, Conn.: Yale University Press, 1927, pp. 201–206.

Ornstein, Robert. *The Moral Vision of Jacobean Tragedy*. Madison: University of Wisconsin Press, 1960, pp. 178–179.

Savage, James E. "Beaumont and Fletcher's *Philaster* and Sidney's *Arcadia*; Also the Use They Made of the Material in *Cupid's Revenge*," in *Journal of English Literary History*. XIV (1947), pp. 194–206.

————. "The 'Gaping Wounds' in the Text of *Philaster*," in *Philological Quarterly*. XXVIII (1949), pp. 443–457.

Schutt, J.H. "*Philaster* Considered as a Work of Literary Art," in *English Studies*. VI (1924), pp. 81–87.

Tomlinson, Thomas Brian. *A Study of Elizabethan and Jacobean Tragedy*. Cambridge: Cambridge University Press, 1964, pp. 253–255.

Wells, Henry W. *Elizabethan and Jacobean Playwrights*. New York: Columbia University Press, 1964, pp. 122–124.

White, D. Jerry. "Irony and the Three Temptations in *Philaster*," in *Toth*. XV (1975), pp. 3–8.

Wilson, Harold S. "*Philaster* and *Cymbeline*," in *English Institute Essays*. (1951), pp. 146–167.

The Scornful Lady

Appleton, William W. *Beaumont and Fletcher: A Critical Study*. London: Allen and Unwin, 1956, pp. 48–49.

Boas, Frederick S.   *An Introduction to Stuart Drama.* London: Oxford University Press, 1946, pp. 266–267.

Bradbrook, M.C.   *The Growth and Structure of Elizabethan Comedy.* Berkeley: University of California Press, 1956, pp. 177–186.

Gayley, Charles Mills.   *Beaumont, the Dramatist: A Portrait.* New York: Century, 1914, pp. 111–113, 368–378.

Masefield, John.   "Beaumont and Fletcher," in *Atlantic Monthly.* CXCIX (June, 1957), pp. 173–174.

Maxwell, Baldwin.   *Studies in Beaumont, Fletcher, and Massinger.* Chapel Hill: University of North Carolina Press, 1939, pp. 17–28.

Oliphant, E.C.H.   *The Plays of Beaumont and Fletcher.* New Haven, Conn.: Yale University Press, 1927, pp. 207–213.

SIMONE DE BEAUVOIR
(1908–   )

All Said and Done

Annan, Gabrielle. "Serious Lady," in *Listener*. XCI (June 6, 1974), pp. 740–741.

Cottrell, Robert D. *Simone de Beauvoir*. New York: Frederick Ungar, 1975, pp. 146–149.

Davidon, Ann Morrissett. "A Life Well Lived for All That," in *Nation*. CCXX (June 14, 1975), pp. 732–734.

Dick, Kay. "La Bonne Bouche," in *Spectator*. CCXXXII (June 8, 1974), p. 708.

Gallant, Mavis. "*All Said and Done*," in *New York Times Book Review*. (July 21, 1974), p. 4.

Pritchett, V.S. "Simone Says," in *New York Review of Books*. (August 8, 1974), p. 24.

Strickland, G.R.S. "Beauvoir's Autobiography," in *Cambridge Quarterly*. I (1965/1966), pp. 43–60.

Warnock, Mary. "The Paths of Freedom," in *New Statesman*. LXXXVII (May 24, 1974), pp. 731–732.

The Coming of Age

Cismaru, Alfred. "Enduring Existentialists: Sartre and de Beauvoir in Their Golden Age," in *Antioch Review*. XXXI (1971/1972), pp. 557–564.

Coles, Robert. "Old Age," in *New Yorker*. XLVIII (August 19, 1972), pp. 68–80.

Cottrell, Robert D. *Simone de Beauvoir*. New York: Frederick Ungar, 1975, pp. 143–146.

Grossman, Edward. "Beauvoir's Last Revolt," in *Commentary*. LIV (August, 1972), pp. 56–59.

Grumback, Doris. "Disposing of 'Mystical Twaddle,' " in *New Republic*. CLXVI (May 20, 1972), pp. 31–33.

Hardwick, Elizabeth. "A Limited Future and a Frozen Past—Such Is the Situation," in *New York Times Book Review*. (May 14, 1972), pp. 1, 40–42.

Huelsbeck, Charles J. "*Coming of Age*," in *America*. CXXVII (July 22, 1972), pp. 47–48.

Meades, Jonathan. "The Ghostly Intruder," in *Books and Bookmen*. XVIII (May, 1972), pp. 50–51.

The Mandarins

Alpert, Hollis. "The World of Ideas and Love," in *Saturday Review*. XXXIX (May 26, 1956), pp. 17, 27.

Brophy, Brigid. *Don't Never Forget: Collected Views and Reviews*. New York: Holt, Rinehart and Winston, 1966, pp. 285–289.

Cottrell, Robert D. *Simone de Beauvoir*. New York: Frederick Ungar, 1975, pp. 107–121.

Ehrmann, Jacques. "Simone de Beauvoir and the Related Destinies of Woman and the Intellectual," in *Yale French Studies*. XXVII (Spring-Summer, 1961), pp. 29–32.

Getlein, Frank. "Extended Comment on French Intellectuals," in *Commonweal*. LXIV (June 15, 1956), pp. 279–280.

Hatzfield, Helmut. *Trends and Styles in Twentieth Century French Literature*. Washington, D.C.: Catholic University of America Press, 1957, pp. 155–156.

Malcolm, Donald. "Simone Go Home," in *New Republic*. CXXXIV (June 18, 1956), pp. 18–19.

Podhoretz, Norman. "Experience of Our Time," in *New Yorker*. XXXII (September 15, 1956), pp. 145–150.

Reck, Rima Drell. "*Les Mandarins*: Sensibility, Responsibility," in *Yale French Studies*. XXVII (1961), pp. 33–40.

Rolo, C.J. "Fiction Chronicle," in *Atlantic*. CXCVII (June, 1956), pp. 77–79.

Timon. "The Troubled Mandarins," in *Masses and Mainstream*. IX (August, 1956), pp. 35–47.

Memoirs of a Dutiful Daughter

Adams, Phoebe. "Reader's Choice," in *Atlantic*. CCIV (July, 1959), p. 80.

Bree, Germaine. "Being of 'The Beaver,' " in *Saturday Review*. XLII (June 6, 1959), p. 19.

Cottrell, Robert D. *Simone de Beauvoir*. New York: Frederick Ungar, 1975, pp. 5–18, 24–25.

Laing, Dilys. "From God to Sartre," in *Nation*. CLXXXVIII (June 27, 1959), pp. 579–580.

Pritchett, V.S. "Catholic or Intellectual?," in *New Statesman*. LVII (June 6, 1959), p. 805.

Sargeant, Winthrop. "Growing Pains," in *New Yorker*. XXXV (September 26, 1959), pp. 178–182.

The Second Sex

Cottrell, Robert D. *Simone de Beauvoir.* New York: Frederick Ungar, 1975, pp. 93–107.

Gill, Brendan. "No More Eve," in *New Yorker.* XXIX (February 28, 1953), pp. 97–99.

Madsen, Axel. *Hearts and Minds: The Common Journey of Simone de Beauvoir and Jean-Paul Sartre.* New York: William Morrow, 1977, pp. 131–133.

Mullahy, Patrick. "Woman's Place," in *Nation.* CLXXVI (February 21, 1953), pp. 171–172.

Radford, C.B. "Simone de Beauvoir: Feminism's Friend or Foe?," in *Nottingham French Studies.* VI (October, 1967), pp. 87–102.

Rolo, C.J. "Cherchez la Femme," in *Atlantic.* CXCI (April, 1953), p. 86.

Rossi, Alice S. *The Feminist Papers: From Adams to de Beauvoir.* New York: Columbia University Press, 1973, pp. 672–674.

Shuster, George N. "Woman," in *Commonweal.* LVII (January 23, 1953), pp. 409–410.

SAMUEL BECKETT
(1906–   )

Endgame

Alvarez, Alfred. *Samuel Beckett*. New York: Viking, 1973, pp. 87–94.

Barnard, G.C. *Samuel Beckett: A New Approach*. London: J.M. Dent, 1970, pp. 101–109.

Cohn, Ruby. *Samuel Beckett: The Comic Gamut*. New Brunswick, N.J.: Rutgers University Press, 1962, pp. 226–242.

Diamond, Elin. "What? . . . Who? . . . No! . . . She!: The Fictionalizers in Beckett's Plays," in *Samuel Beckett: A Collection of Criticism*. Edited by Ruby Cohn. New York: McGraw-Hill, 1975, pp. 111–113.

Glicksberg, Charles I. *The Self in Modern Literature*. University Park: Pennsylvania State University Press, 1963, pp. 117–121.

Hayman, Ronald. *Samuel Beckett*. New York: Frederick Ungar, 1973, pp. 38–62.

Karl, Frederick R. "Waiting for Beckett: Quest and Request," in *A Reader's Guide to the Contemporary English Novel*. New York: Farrar, Straus, 1962, pp. 19–39.

Mayoux, Jean-Jacques. *Samuel Beckett*. London: Longmans, 1974, pp. 31–33.

Mercier, Vivian. *Beckett/Beckett*. New York: Oxford University Press, 1977.

Robinson, Michael. *The Long Sonata of the Dead*. London: Rupert Hart-Davis, 1969, pp. 261–276.

Spurling, John. "Son of Oedipus: *Endgame*," in *Beckett: A Study of His Plays*. Edited by John Fletcher and John Spurling. New York: Hill and Wang, 1972, pp. 69–81.

Webb, Eugene. *The Plays of Samuel Beckett*. Seattle: University of Washington Press, 1972, pp. 54–65.

Wellworth, George. "Samuel Beckett: Life in the Void," in *The Theatre of Protest and Paradox*. New York: New York University Press, 1964, pp. 37–51.

Krapp's Last Tape

Alvarez, Alfred. *Samuel Beckett*. New York: Viking, 1973, pp. 95–98.

Barnard, G.C. *Samuel Beckett: A New Approach*. London: J.M. Dent, 1970, pp. 113–116.

Hayman, Ronald. *Samuel Beckett*. New York: Frederick Ungar, 1973, pp. 72–80.

Karl, Frederick R.   "Waiting for Beckett: Quest and Request," in *A Reader's Guide to the Contemporary English Novel*. New York: Farrar, Straus, 1962, pp. 19–39.

Mercier, Vivian.   *Beckett/Beckett*. New York: Oxford University Press, 1977, pp. 196–236.

Pilling, John.   *Samuel Beckett*. London: Routledge and Kegan Paul, 1976, pp. 83–88.

Robinson, Michael.   *The Long Sonata of the Dead*. London: Rupert Hart-Davis, 1969, pp. 283–285.

Rosen, Steven J.   *Samuel Beckett and the Pessimistic Tradition*. New Brunswick, N.J.: Rutgers University Press, 1976, pp. 114–118.

Spurling, John.   "Death and the Maiden: *Krapp's Last Tape*," in *Beckett: A Study of His Plays*. Edited by John Fletcher and John Spurling. New York: Hill and Wang, 1972, pp. 88–94.

Webb, Eugene.   *The Plays of Samuel Beckett*. Seattle: University of Washington Press, 1972, pp. 66–76.

The Lost Ones

Alvarez, Alfred.   *Samuel Beckett*. New York: Viking, 1973, pp. 127–129.

Brienza, Susan D.   "*The Lost Ones*: The Reader as Searcher," in *Journal of Modern Literature*. VI (February, 1977), pp. 148–168.

Finney, Brian.   "*Assumption to Lessness*: Beckett's Shorter Fiction," in *Beckett the Shape Changer*. Edited by Katherine Worth. London: Routledge and Kegan Paul, 1975, pp. 63–64, 74–78.

McElroy, Joseph.   "*The Lost Ones*," in *New York Time Book Review*. (October 29, 1972), pp. 4, 20.

Mercier, Vivian.   *Beckett/Beckett*. New York: Oxford University Press, 1977, pp. 179–180, 226–229.

Pilling, John.   *Samuel Beckett*. London: Routledge and Kegan Paul, 1976, pp. 29–39.

Ricks, Christopher.   "Beckett First and Last," in *New York Review of Books*. XIX (December 12, 1972), pp. 42–44.

Malone Dies

Abbott, H. Porter.   *The Fiction of Samuel Beckett*. Berkeley: University of California, 1973, pp. 110–123.

Alvarez, Alfred.   *Samuel Beckett*. New York: Viking, 1973, pp. 52–57.

Barnard, G.C.   *Samuel Beckett: A New Approach*. London: J.M. Dent, 1970, pp. 45–56.

Cmarada, Geraldine.   "*Malone Dies*: A Round of Consciousness," in *Symposium*. XIV (Fall, 1960), pp. 199–212.

Coe, Richard N. "God and Samuel Beckett," in *Twentieth Century Interpretations of* Molloy, Malone Dies, The Unnamable. Edited by James D. O'Hara. Englewood Cliffs, N.J.: Prentice-Hall, 1970, pp. 91–111. Also in *Meanjin Quarterly.* XXIV (March, 1965), pp. 66–85.

Cohn, Ruby. *Samuel Beckett: The Comic Gamut.* New Brunswick, N.J.: Rutgers University Press, 1962, pp. 114–168.

Fletcher, John. "Malone 'Given Birth to into Death,' " in *Twentieth Century Interpretations of* Molloy, Malone Dies, The Unnamable. Edited by James D. O'Hara. Englewood Cliffs, N.J.: Prentice-Hall, 1970, pp. 58–61.

————. *The Novels of Samuel Beckett.* New York: Barnes & Noble, 1970, pp. 151–176.

Glicksberg, Charles I. *The Self in Modern Literature.* University Park: Pennsylvania State University Press, 1963, pp. 127–129.

Hoffman, Frederick J. *Samuel Beckett: The Language of Self.* Carbondale: Southern Illinois University Press, 1962, pp. 127–132.

Mayoux, Jean-Jacques. *Samuel Beckett.* London: Longmans, 1974, pp. 22–23.

Oates, Joyce Carol. "The Trilogy of Samuel Beckett," in *Renascence.* XIV (Spring, 1962), pp. 160–165.

O'Hara, J.D. "About Structure in *Malone Dies,*" in *Twentieth Century Interpretations of* Malloy, Malone Dies, The Unnamable. Edited by James D. O'Hara. Englewood Cliffs, N.J.: Prentice-Hall, 1970, pp. 62–70.

Peake, Charles. "The Labours of Poetical Excavation," in *Beckett: The Shape Changer.* Edited by Katherine Worth. London: Routledge and Kegan Paul, 1975, pp. 50–58.

Pilling, John. *Samuel Beckett.* London: Routledge and Kegan Paul, 1976, pp. 30–66.

Robinson, Michael. *The Long Sonata of the Dead.* London: Rupert Hart-Davis, 1969, pp. 170–190.

Webb, Eugene. *Samuel Beckett: A Study of His Novels.* Seattle: University of Washington Press, 1973, pp. 72–150.

Mercier and Camier

Abbott, H. Porter. *The Fiction of Samuel Beckett.* Berkeley: University of California, 1973, pp. 75–91.

Auster, Paul. "*Mercier and Camier,*" in *Commentary.* LX (July, 1975), p. 39.

Blair, Deirde. "*Mercier and Camier,*" in *New York Times Book Review.* (March 9, 1975), p. 19.

Brater, Enoch. "*Mercier and Camier,*" in *New Republic.* CLXXII (March 8, 1975), p. 25.

Cohn, Ruby. "Inexhaustible Beckett: An Introduction," in *Samuel Beckett: A Collection of Criticism.* Edited by Ruby Cohn. New York: McGraw-Hill, 1975, pp. 5–6.

Fletcher, John. *The Novels of Samuel Beckett.* New York: Barnes & Noble, 1970, pp. 110–118.

Kilroy, Thomas. "*Mercier and Camier,*" in *Times Literary Supplement.* (December 13, 1974), p. 1405.

Mayoux, Jean-Jacques. *Samuel Beckett.* London: Longmans, 1974, p. 19.

Updike, John. "*Mercier and Camier,*" in *New Yorker.* LI (September 1, 1975), p. 62.

Molloy

Abbott, H. Porter. *The Fiction of Samuel Beckett.* Berkeley: University of California, 1973, pp. 92–115.

Alvarez, Alfred. *Samuel Beckett.* New York: Viking, 1973, pp. 46–52.

Barnard, J.C. *Samuel Beckett: A New Approach.* London: J.M. Dent, 1970, pp. 31–44.

Cohn, Ruby. *Samuel Beckett: The Comic Gamut.* New Brunswick, N.J.: Rutgers University Press, 1962, pp. 114–168.

Fletcher, John. *The Novels of Samuel Beckett.* New York: Barnes & Noble, 1970, pp. 119–150.

Frye, Northrop. "The Nightmare Life in Death," in *Twentieth Century Interpretations of* Molloy, Malone Dies, The Unnamable. Edited by James D. O'Hara. Englewood Cliffs, N.J.: Prentice-Hall, 1970, pp. 26–34.

Glicksberg, Charles I. *The Self in Modern Literature.* University Park: Pennsylvania State University Press, 1963, pp. 124–127.

Hamilton, Carol. "Portrait in Old Age: The Image of Man in Beckett's Trilogy," in *Western Humanities Review.* XVI (Spring, 1962), pp. 157–165.

Hamilton, Kenneth. "Boon or Thorn? Joyce Cary and Samuel Beckett on Human Life," in *Dalhousie Review.* XXXVIII (Winter, 1959), pp. 433–442.

Hayman, David. "*Molloy* or the Quest for Meaninglessness: A Global Interpretation," in *Samuel Beckett Now.* Edited by Melvin J. Friedman. Chicago: University of Chicago Press, 1970, pp. 129–156.

Hoffman, Frederick J. *Samuel Beckett: The Language of Self.* Carbondale: Southern Illinois University Press, 1962, pp. 119–127.

Hokenson, Jan. "Three Novels in Large Black Pauses," in *Samuel Beckett: A Collection of Criticism.* Edited by Ruby Cohn. New York: McGraw-Hill, 1975, pp. 74–84.

Janvier, Ludovic. "*Molloy,*" in *Twentieth Century Interpretations of* Molloy, Malone Dies, The Unnamable. Edited by James D. O'Hara. Englewood Cliffs, N.J.: Prentice-Hall, 1970, pp. 46–57.

Kern, Edith. "Moran-Molloy: The Hero as Author," in *Twentieth Century Interpretations of* Molloy , Malone Dies, The Unnamable. Edited by James D. O'Hara. Englewood Cliffs, N.J.: Prentice-Hall, 1970, pp. 35–45. Also in *Perspective*. II (Autumn, 1959), pp. 183–193.

Oates, Joyce Carol. "The Trilogy of Samuel Beckett," in *Renascence*. XIV (Spring, 1962), pp. 160–165.

Peake, Charles. "The Labours of Poetical Excavation," in *Beckett: The Shape Changer*. Edited by Katharine Worth. London: Routledge and Kegan Paul, 1975, pp. 50–58.

Pilling, John. *Samuel Beckett*. London: Routledge and Kegan Paul, 1976, pp. 42–65.

Robinson, Michael. *The Long Sonata of the Dead*. London: Rupert Hart-Davis, 1969, pp. 132–169.

Rosen, Steven J. *Samuel Beckett and the Pessimistic Tradition*. New Brunswick, N.J.: Rutgers University Press, 1976, pp. 10–12, 110–113.

Webb, Eugene. *Samuel Beckett: A Study of His Novels*. Seattle: University of Washington Press, 1973, pp. 72–150.

Stories and Texts for Nothing

Abbott, H. Porter. *The Fiction of Samuel Beckett*. Berkeley: University of California, 1973, pp. 124–126, 131–134.

Ackroyd, Peter. "Baubles, Bangles, Pearl Beads," in *The Spectator*. CCXXXIII (March 30, 1974), pp. 393–394.

Coe, Richard N. "God and Samuel Beckett," in *Twentieth Century Interpretations of* Molloy, Malone Dies, The Unnamable. Edited by James D. O'Hara. Englewood Cliffs, N.J.: Prentice-Hall, 1970, pp. 91–111.

Cohn, Ruby. *Samuel Beckett: The Comic Gamut*. New Brunswick, N.J.: Rutgers University Press, 1962, pp. 169–179.

Esslin, Martin. "Samuel Beckett," in *The Novelist as Philosopher*. Edited by John Cruickshank. New York: Oxford University Press, 1962, pp. 143–144.

————. "Worth the 'Wait,' " in *Books and Bookmen*. XIX (June, 1974), pp. 91–92.

Federman, Raymond. "Beckettian Paradox," in *Samuel Beckett Now*. Edited by Melvin J. Friedman. Chicago: University of Chicago Press, 1970, pp. 112–114.

Finney, Brian. "*Assumption to Lessness*: Beckett's Shorter Fiction," in *Beckett: The Shape Changer*. Edited by Katherine Worth. London: Routledge and Kegan Paul, 1975, pp. 63–81.

Fletcher, John. *The Novels of Samuel Beckett*. New York: Barnes & Noble, 1970, pp. 196–205.

Mayoux, Jean-Jacques. *Samuel Beckett*. London: Longmans, 1974, pp. 24–25.

Robinson, Michael. *The Long Sonata of the Dead*. London: Rupert Hart-Davis, 1969, pp. 208–212.

Unnamable

Abbott, H. Porter. *The Fiction of Samuel Beckett*. Berkeley: University of California Press, 1973, pp. 110–112, 124–137.

Alvarez, Alfred. *Samuel Beckett*. New York: Viking, 1973, pp. 57–65.

Barnard, G.C. *Samuel Beckett: A New Approach*. London: J.M. Dent, 1970, pp. 57–66.

Blanchot, Maurice. "Where Now? Who Now?," in *On Contemporary Literature*. Edited by Richard Kostelanetz. New York: Avon Books, 1969, pp. 249–254. Also in *Evergreen Review*. II (Winter, 1959), pp. 224–229.

Chambers, Ross. "Samuel Beckett and the Padded Cell," in *Meanjin Quarterly*. XXI (April, 1962), pp. 451–462.

Cohn, Ruby. *Samuel Beckett: The Comic Gamut*. New Brunswick, N.J.: Rutgers University Press, 1962, pp. 114–168.

Cornwell, Ethel J. "Samuel Beckett: The Flight from Self," in *PMLA*. LXXXVIII (January, 1973), pp. 41–51.

Fletcher, John. *The Novels of Samuel Beckett*. New York: Barnes & Noble, 1970, pp. 179–194.

Glicksberg, Charles I. *The Self in Modern Literature*. University Park: Pennsylvania State University Press, 1963, pp. 129–133.

Hassan, Ihab. *The Literature of Silence*. New York: Knopf, 1968, pp. 162–168.

Hoffman, Frederick J. *Samuel Beckett: The Language of Self*. Carbondale: Southern Illinois University Press, 1962, pp. 132–137.

Karl, Frederick. "Waiting for Beckett: Quest and Request," in *The Contemporary English Novel*. New York: Farrar, Straus, 1962, pp. 19–39.

Oates, Joyce Carol. "The Trilogy of Samuel Beckett," in *Renascence*. XIV (Spring, 1962), pp. 160–165.

Peake, Charles. "The Labours of Poetical Excavation," in *Beckett: The Shape Changer*. Edited by Katherine Worth. London: Routledge and Kegan Paul, 1975, pp. 50–58.

Pilling, John. *Samuel Beckett*. London: Routledge and Kegan Paul, 1976, pp. 26–68.

Rickels, Milton. "Existential Themes in Beckett's *Unnamable*," in *Criticism*. IV (Spring, 1962), pp. 134–147.

Robinson, Michael. *The Long Sonata of the Dead.* London: Rupert Hart-Davis, 1969, pp. 191–207.

Tindall, William Y. *Samuel Beckett.* New York: Columbia University Press, 1964, pp. 29–32.

Webb, Eugene. *Samuel Beckett: A Study of His Novels.* Seattle: University of Washington Press, 1973, pp. 72–150.

Waiting for Godot

Alvarez, Alfred. *Samuel Beckett.* New York: Viking, 1973, pp. 76–86.

Ashomore, Jerome. "Philosophical Aspects of *Godot*," in *Symposium.* XVI (Winter, 1962), pp. 296–306.

Barnard, G.C. *Samuel Beckett: A New Approach.* London: J.M. Dent, 1970, pp. 89–100.

Brereton, Geoffrey. *Principles of Tragedy.* Miami: University of Miami Press, 1968, pp. 244–265.

Chadwick, C. "*Waiting for Godot*: A Logical Approach," in *Symposium.* XIV (Winter, 1960), pp. 252–257.

Cohn, Ruby. *Samuel Beckett: The Comic Gamut.* New Brunswick, N.J.: Rutgers University Press, 1962, pp. 208–225.

Dukore, Bernard F. "The Other Pair in *Waiting for Godot*," in *Drama Survey.* VII (Winter, 1968–1969), pp. 133–137.

Esslin, Martin. *The Theatre of the Absurd.* Garden City, N.Y.: Doubleday, 1961, pp. 13–27.

Fletcher, John. "Bailing Out the Silence," in *Beckett: A Study of His Plays.* Edited by John Fletcher and John Spurling. New York: Hill and Wang, 1972, pp. 55–68.

Flood, Ethelbert. "A Reading of Beckett's *Godot*," in *Culture.* XXII (September, 1961), pp. 257–262.

Gilliat, Penelope. "Beckett," in *Unholy Fools.* New York: Viking, 1973, pp. 20–23.

Glicksberg, Charles I. *The Self in Modern Literature.* University Park: Pennsylvania State University Press, 1963, pp. 117–121.

Guicharnaud, Jacques. "Existence on Stage," in *On Contemporary Literature.* Edited by Richard Kostelanetz. New York: Avon Books, 1969, pp. 262–285.

Harvey, Lawrence E. "Art and the Existential in *En Attendant Godot*," in *PMLA.* LXXV (March, 1960), pp. 137–145.

Hayman, Ronald. *Samuel Beckett.* New York: Frederick Ungar, 1973, pp. 7–37.

Hoffman, Frederick J.   *Samuel Beckett: The Language of Self.* Carbondale: Southern Illinois University Press, 1962, pp. 138–161.

Hooker, Ward.   "Irony and Absurdity in the Avant-Garde Theatre," in *Kenyon Review.* XXII (Summer, 1960), pp. 436–454.

Karl, Frederick R.   "Waiting for Becket: Quest and Request," in *A Reader's Guide to the Contemporary English Novel.* New York: Farrar, Straus, 1962, pp. 19–39.

Kenner, Hugh.   *Samuel Beckett: A Critical Study.* Berkeley: University of California, 1968, pp. 133–139, 146–155, 185–186.

Mathews, Honor.   *The Primal Curse.* New York: Schocken, 1967, pp. 154–168.

Michalyi, Gabor.   "Beckett's *Godot* and the Myth of Alienation," in *Modern Drama.* IX (December, 1966), pp. 277–282.

O'Casey, Sean.   "Not Waiting for Godot," in *Blasts and Benedictions.* New York: St. Martin's Press, 1967, pp. 51–52.

Rechtien, Brother John, S.M.   "Time and Eternity Meet in the Present," in *Texas Studies in Literature and Language.* VI (Spring, 1964), pp. 5–21.

Robinson, Michael.   *The Long Sonata of the Dead.* London: Rupert Hart-Davis, 1969, pp. 245–260.

Scott, Nathan A.   *Samuel Beckett.* New York: Hillary House, 1965, pp. 83–94, 100–101, 105–111.

Styan, J.L.   *The Dark Comedy.* Cambridge: Cambridge University Press, 1962, pp. 218–234.

Webb, Eugene.   *The Plays of Samuel Beckett.* Seattle: University of Washington Press, 1972, pp. 26–41.

Wellworth, George.   "Samuel Beckett: Life in the Void," in *The Theatre of Protest and Paradox.* New York: New York University Press, 1964, pp. 37–51.

MAX BEERBOHM
(1872–1956)

The Essays of Max Beerbohm

Braybrooke, Patrick. *Peeps at the Mighty.* London: Henry J. Drane, 1927, pp. 43–58.

McElderry, Bruce R., Jr. "Max Beerbohm: Essayist, Caricaturist, Novelist," in *On Stage and Off: Eight Essays in English Literature.* Edited by John W. Ehrstine, John R. Elwood and Robert C. McLean. Pullman: Washington State University Press, 1968, pp. 76–86.

Scott-James, Rolfe Arnold. *Fifty Years of English Literature, 1900–1950, with a Postscript, 1951 to 1955.* London: Longmans, Green, 1956, pp. 47–53.

Swinnerton, Frank. "The Special Genius of Sir Max," in *Saturday Review of Literature.* XLI (August 2, 1958), pp. 13–14.

Tuell, Anne Kimball. *Victorian at Bay.* Freeport, N.Y.: Books for Libraries Press, 1966, pp. 81–94.

Wilson, Edmund. *The Bit Between My Teeth; A Literary Chronicle of 1950–1965.* New York: Farrar, Straus, 1965, pp. 41–62.

Woolf, Virginia. *The Common Reader. First Series.* London: Hogarth Press, 1948, pp. 274–276.

Seven Men

L., P. "Books and Things," in *New Republic.* XXI (February 25, 1920), p. 386.

Lago, Mary M. and Karl Beckson. *Max and Will.* Cambridge, Mass.: Harvard University Press, 1975, pp. 108–109.

McElderry, Bruce R., Jr. *Max Beerbohm.* New York: Twayne, 1972, pp. 112–115.

McFee, William. *Swallowing the Anchor.* New York: Doubleday, Doran, 1925, pp. 56–69.

Riewald, J.G. *Sir Max Beerbohm; Man and Writer.* The Hague: Martinus Nijhoff, 1953, pp. 109–114, 224–225, 243–245.

Zuleika Dobson

Empson, William. *Seven Types of Ambiguity.* London: Chatto and Windus, 1949, pp. 176–177.

Forster, E.M. *Aspects of the Novel.* London: Edward Arnold, 1927, pp. 152–156.

Lago, Mary M. and Karl Beckson. *Max and Will.* Cambridge, Mass.: Harvard University Press, 1975, pp. 86–91.

McElderry, Bruce R., Jr. *Max Beerbohm.* New York: Twayne, 1972, pp. 100–108.

Nicolson, Harold. "*Zuleika Dobson*—A Revaluation," in *The Surprise of Excellence: Modern Essays on Max Beerbohm.* Edited by J.G. Riewald. Hamden, Conn.: Archon, 1974, pp. 30–37.

Riewald, J.G. *Sir Max Beerbohm; Man and Writer.* The Hague: Martinus Nijhoff, 1953, pp. 116–126, 137–139.

"*Zuleika Dobson*," in *Spectator.* CVII (November 11, 1911), p. 801.

BRENDAN BEHAN
(1923–1964)

Borstal Boy

Hatch, Robert. "The Critic's View: The Roaring Presence of Brendan Behan," in *Horizon*. III (January, 1961), pp. 113–114.

Jeffs, Rae. *Brendan Behan: Man and Showman*. New York: World, 1968, pp. 25–51.

Kazin, Alfred. "Brendan Behan: The Causes Go, the Rebels Remain," in *Contemporaries*. New York: Harcourt, 1961, pp. 240–246.

Kearney, C. "*Borstal Boy*: A Portrait of the Artist as a Young Prisoner," in *Ariel*. VII (April, 1976), pp. 47–62.

MacIntyre, Thomas. "This Dying Lark," in *Kenyon Review*. XXVII (Winter, 1965), pp. 152–155.

O'Conner, Ulick. *Brendan*. Englewood Cliffs, N.J.: Prentice-Hall, 1970, pp. 208–213.

The Hostage

Brustein, R.S. "Libido at Large," in *Seasons of Discontent*. New York: Simon and Schuster, 1965, pp. 177–180.

Clurman, Harold. "*The Hostage*," in *The Naked Image*. New York: Macmillan, 1958, pp. 43–44.

Flanner, Janet. *Paris Journal, 1944–1965*. New York: Atheneum, 1965, p. 417.

Gilliatt, Penelope. "Brendan Beano," in *Encore*. V (November–December, 1958), pp. 35–36.

Hatch, Robert. "The Critic's View: The Roaring Presence of Brendan Behan," in *Horizon*. III (January, 1961), pp. 113–114.

Hogan, Robert. *After the Irish Renaissance*. Minneapolis: University of Minnesota Press, 1967, pp. 203–205.

Jeffs, Rae. *Brendan Behan: Man and Showman*. New York: World, 1968, pp. 55–59, 91–94.

Kerr, Walter. "*The Hostage*," in *The Theatre in Spite of Itself*. New York: Simon and Schuster, 1963, pp. 108–112.

Kitchin, Laurence. *Mid-Century Drama*. London: Faber and Faber, 1960, p. 111.

Kleinstuck, J. "Brendan Behan's '*The Hostage*,'" in *Essays and Studies*. Edited by English Association. Atlantic Highlands, N.J.: Humanities Press, 1971, pp. 69–82.

MacIntyre, Thomas. "This Dying Lark," in *Kenyon Review*. XXVI (Winter, 1965), pp. 154–155.

O'Connor, Ulick. *Brendan.* Englewood Cliffs, N.J.: Prentice-Hall, 1970, pp. 192–208.

Ryan, Stephen P. "*The Hostage*," in *Catholic World*. CXCII (November, 1960), pp. 126–127.

Simon, John. "*The Hostage*," in *Hudson Review*. XIII (Winter, 1960–1961), pp. 587–588.

Taylor, John Russell. *Anger and After.* London: Methuen, 1963, pp. 104–107.

———. "Brendan Behan," in *The Angry Theatre*. New York: Hill and Wang, 1969, pp. 123–130.

Tynan, Kenneth. "*The Hostage*," in *Curtains*. New York: Atheneum, 1961, pp. 218–220.

Wall, R. "*An Giall* and the *Hostage*," in *Modern Drama*. XVIII (June, 1975), pp. 165–172.

Wellwarth, George. *The Theatre of Protest and Paradox.* New York: New York University Press, 1964, pp. 258–261.

The Quare Fellow

Hogan, Robert. *After the Irish Renaissance.* Minneapolis: University of Minnesota Press, 1967, pp. 199–203.

Hynes, Sam. "An Irish Success," in *Commonweal*. LXXI (March 4, 1960), pp. 627–629.

Jeffs, Rae. *Brendan Behan: Man and Showman.* New York: World, 1968, pp. 61–63, 74–76.

MacInnes, Colin. "The Writings of Brendan Behan," in *The London Magazine*. II (August, 1962), pp. 58–61.

MacIntyre, Thomas. "This Dying Lark," in *Kenyon Review*. XXVI (Winter, 1965), p. 155.

O'Conner, Ulick. *Brendan.* Englewood Cliffs, N.J.: Prentice-Hall, 1970, pp. 166–169.

Taylor, John Russell. "Brendan Behan," in *The Angry Theatre*. New York: Hill and Wang, 1969, pp. 123–130.

———. *Anger and After.* London: Methuen, 1963, pp. 102–104.

Tynan, Kenneth. "*The Quare Fellow*," in *Curtains*. New York: Atheneum, 1961, pp. 136–138.

Wellwarth, George. *The Theatre of Protest and Paradox.* New York: New York University Press, 1964, pp. 258–261.

MRS. APHRA BEHN
(1640–1689)

Oroonoko

Allen, Walter. *The English Novel: A Short Critical History*. New York: Dutton, 1954, pp. 20–22.

Duffy, Maureen. *The Passionate Shepherdess: Aphra Behn, 1640–1689*. London: Jonathan Cape, 1977, pp. 265–270.

Guffey, George. "Aphra Behn's *Oroonoko*: Occasion and Accomplishment," in *Two English Novelists: Aphra Behn and Anthony Trollope*. By George Guffey and Andrew Wright. Los Angeles: William Andrews Clark Memorial Library, University of California at Los Angeles, 1974, pp. 3–41.

Hargreaves, Henry A. "New Evidence on the Realism of Mrs. Behn's *Oroonoko*," in *Bulletin of the New York Public Library*. LXXIV (1970), pp. 437–444.

Johnson, R. Brimley. *The Woman Novelist*. London: W. Collins, 1918, pp. 3–5.

Jusserand, J.J. *The English Novel in the Time of Shakespeare*. London: Unwin, 1890, pp. 414–417.

Link, Frederick M. *Aphra Behn*. New York: Twayne, 1968, pp. 139–142.

Neill, S. Diana. *A Short History of the English Novel*. New York: Macmillan, 1952, pp. 39–41.

Ramsaran, J.A. "*Oroonoko*: A Study of Factual Elements," in *Notes and Queries*. VII (1960), pp. 142–145.

Sackville-West, V. *Aphra Behn: The Incomparable Astrea*. New York: Viking, 1928, pp. 29–49, 141–147.

Sypher, Wylie. "A Note on the Realism of Mrs. Behn's *Oroonoko*," in *Modern Language Quarterly*. III (1942), pp. 401–405.

Woodcock, George. *The Incomparable Aphra*. London: T.V. Boardman, 1948, pp. 16–26, 202–206, 223–238.

Sir Patient Fancy

Duffy, Maureen. *The Passionate Shepherdess: Aphra Behn, 1640–1689*. London: Jonathan Cape, 1977, pp. 156–165.

Gagen, Jean Elisabeth. *The New Woman: Her Emergence in English Drama, 1600–1730*. New York: Twayne, 1954, pp. 44–46.

Link, Frederick M. *Aphra Behn*. New York: Twayne, 1968, pp. 52–56.

Mignon, Elisabeth. *Crabbed Age and Youth: The Old Men and Women in the Restoration Comedy of Manners*. Durham, N.C.: Duke University Press, 1947, pp. 24–25, 87–89.

Wilcox, John. *The Relation of Moliere to Restoration Comedy.* New York: Benjamin Blom, 1964, pp. 146–149.

Woodcock, George. *The Incomparable Aphra.* London: T.V. Boardman, 1948, pp. 131–136.

EDWARD BELLAMY
(1850–1898)

Looking Backward: 2000–1887

Aaron, Daniel. "Edward Bellamy: Village Utopian," in *Men of Good Hope: A Story of American Progressives.* New York: Oxford University Press, 1951, pp. 92–132.

Becker, George J. "Edward Bellamy: Utopia, American Plan," in *Antioch Review.* XIV (June, 1954), pp. 181–194.

Berneri, Marie L. "Utopias of the Nineteenth Century," in her *Journey Through Utopia.* Boston: Beacon, 1951, pp. 207–292.

Bleich, David. "Eros and Bellamy," in *American Quarterly.* XVI (Fall, 1964), pp. 445–459.

Boggs, W. Arthur. "*Looking Backward* at the Utopian Novel, 1888–1900," in *Bulletin of the New York Public Library.* LXIV (June, 1960), pp. 329–336.

Bowman, Sylvia E. *The Year 2000: A Critical Biography of Edward Bellamy.* New York: Bookman, 1958, pp. 112–122.

Downs, Robert B. "American Utopia," in *Books That Changed America.* New York: Macmillan, 1970, pp. 100–109.

Eastman, Max F., Jacques Barzun and Mark Van Doren. "Bellamy: *Looking Backward,*" in *New Invitation to Learning.* Edited by Mark Van Doren. New York: Random House, 1942, pp. 414–427.

Harris, W.T. "Edward Bellamy's Vision," in *The American Hegelians: An Intellectual Episode in the History of Western America.* Edited by William H. Goetzmann. New York: Knopf, 1973, pp. 193–201.

Hicks, Granville. "Struggle and Flight," in *The Great Tradition: An Interpretation of American Literature Since the Civil War.* New York: Macmillan, 1935, pp. 131–163.

Howells, William Dean. "Edward Bellamy," in *Criticism and Fiction and Other Essays.* Edited by Clara Marburg Kirk and Rudolph Kirk. New York: New York University Press, 1959, pp. 246–255.

Ketterer, David. "Utopian Fantasy as Millennial Motive and Science-Fictional Motif," in *New Worlds for Old: The Apocalyptic Imagination, Science Fiction, and American Literature.* Bloomington: Indiana University Press, 1974, pp. 96–122.

Martin, Jay. *Harvests of Change: American Literature, 1865–1914.* Englewood Cliffs, N.J.: Prentice-Hall, 1967, pp. 220–223.

Morgan, Arthur E. *Edward Bellamy.* New York: Columbia University Press, 1944, pp. 204–244.

Mott, Frank. L.   "Crusaders Four," in *Golden Multitudes: The Story of Best Sellers in the United States.* New York: Macmillan, 1947, pp. 165–171.

Parrington, Vernon L.   "Bellamy and His Critics," in *American Dreams: A Study of American Utopias.* Providence, R.I.: Brown University Press, 1947, pp. 69–97.

Sadler, Elizabeth.   "One Book's Influence: Edward Bellamy's *Looking Backward,*" in *New England Quarterly.* XVII (December, 1944), pp. 530–555.

Schiffman, J.H.   "Edward Bellamy and the Social Gospel," in *Intellectual History in America*, Volume II. Edited by Cushing Strout. New York: Harper, 1968, pp. 10–27.

Seager, Allan.   "Edward Bellamy," in *They Worked for a Better World.* New York: Macmillan, 1929, pp. 97–116.

Shurter, Robert L.   "The Literary Work of Edward Bellamy," in *American Literature.* V (November, 1933), pp. 229–234.

————.   "The Writing of *Looking Backward,*" in *South Atlantic Quarterly.* XXXVIII (1939), pp. 255–261.

Taylor, Walter F.   "Edward Bellamy," in *The Economic Novel in America.* Chapel Hill: University of North Carolina Press, 1942, pp. 184–213.

Thomas, John L.   "Introduction," in *Looking Backward: 2000–1887.* By Edward Bellamy. Edited by John L. Thomas. Cambridge, Mass.: Harvard University Press, 1967, pp. 1–88.

Ticknor, Caroline.   "Bellamy and *Looking Backward,*" in *Glimpses of Authors.* New York: Houghton Mifflin, 1922, pp. 112–121.

Westmeyer, Russell E.   "Modern Literary Utopias," in *Modern Economic and Social Systems.* New York: Farrar, 1940, pp. 78–93.

HILAIRE BELLOC
(1870–1953)

The Path to Rome

Belloc, Hilaire. "To Maurice Baring," in *Letters from Hilaire Belloc*. Edited by Robert Speaight. London: Hollis & Carter, 1958, pp. 30–32.

Haynes, Renee. *Hilaire Belloc*. London: Longmans, Green, 1953, pp. 16–19.

Lowndes, Marie Belloc. *The Young Hilaire Belloc*. New York: P.J. Kenedy, 1956, pp. 156–159.

Mandell, C. Creighton and Edward Shanks. *Hilaire Belloc*. London: Methuen, 1916, pp. 71–88, 126–138.

Poynter, J.W. *Hilaire Belloc Keeps the Bridge*. London: Watts, 1929.

Speaight, Robert. *The Life of Hilaire Belloc*. New York: Farrar, Straus & Cudahy, 1957, pp. 116–164.

Wilhelmsen, Frederick. *Hilaire Belloc: No Alienated Man*. New York: Sheed and Ward, 1953, pp. 27–48.

SAUL BELLOW
(1915–   )

The Adventures of Augie March

Aldridge, John W. "The Society of Three Novels," in his *In Search of Heresy*. New York: Greenwood, 1956, pp. 126–148.

Alter, Robert. "Heirs of the Tradition," in *Rogue's Progress: Studies in the Picaresque Novel*. Cambridge, Mass.: Harvard University Press, 1964, pp. 106–132.

Amis, Kingsley. "*The Adventures of Augie March*," in *Spectator*. CXCII (May 21, 1954), p. 626.

Breit, Harvey. "Saul Bellow," in his *The Writer Observed*. New York: World, 1956, pp. 271–274.

Cohen, Sarah Blacher. "Sex: Saul Bellow's Hedonistic Joke," in *Studies in American Fiction*. II (1974), pp. 223–229.

Crozier, Robert D. "Themes in *Augie March*," in *Critique*. VII (Spring–Summer, 1965), pp. 18–32.

Fiedler, Leslie A. "Saul Bellow," in *Saul Bellow and the Critics*. Edited by Irving Malin. New York: New York University Press, 1967, pp. 1–9.

Frank, Reuben. "Saul Bellow: The Evolution of a Contemporary Novelist," in *Western Review*. XVIII (Winter, 1954), pp. 101–112.

Frohock, W.M. "Saul Bellow and His Penitent Picaro," in *Southwest Review*. LII (Winter, 1968), pp. 36–44.

Galloway, David P. "The Absurd Man as Picaro: The Novels of Saul Bellow," in his *The Absurd Hero in American Fiction: Updike, Styron, Bellow, Salinger*. Austin: University of Texas Press, 1966, pp. 82–139.

Goldberg, Gerald J. "Life's Customer: Augie March," in *Critique*. III (Summer, 1960), pp. 15–27.

Guerard, Albert J. "Saul Bellow and the Activists: On *The Adventures of Augie March*," in *Southern Review*. III (July, 1967), pp. 582–596.

Harwell, Meade. "Picaro from Chicago," in *Southwest Review*. XXXIX (Summer, 1954), pp. 273–276.

Hoffman, Frederick J. "The Fool of Experience: Saul Bellow's Fiction," in *Contemporary American Novelists*. Edited by Harry T. Moore. Carbondale: Southern Illinois University Press, 1964, pp. 80–94.

Jones, David R. "The Disappointment of Maturity: Bellow's *The Adventures of Augie March*," in *The Fifties: Fiction, Poetry, Drama*. Edited by Warren French. Deland, Fla.: Everett/Edwards, 1970, pp. 83–92.

Lewis, R.W.B. "Recent Fiction: Picaro and Pilgrim," in *A Time of Harvest: American Literature, 1910–1960*. Edited by Robert E. Spiller. New York: Hill and Wang, 1962, pp. 144–153.

Meyers, J. "Brueghel and Augie March," in *American Literature*. XLIX (March, 1977), pp. 113–119.

Podhoretz, Norman. *Making It*. New York: Random House, 1967.

————. "The Adventures of Saul Bellow," in his *Doings and Undoings*. New York: Farrar, Straus and Giroux, 1964, pp. 205–227.

Priestley, J.B. "*The Adventures of Augie March*," in *Sunday Times* (London). (May 9, 1954), p. 5.

Rupp, Richard H. "Saul Bellow: Belonging to the World in General," in *Celebration in Post-War American Fiction*. Coral Gables, Fla.: University of Miami Press, 1970, pp. 189–208.

Schorer, Mark. "A Book of Yes and No," in *Hudson Review*. VII (Spring, 1954), pp. 136–141.

Tanner, Tony. "A Mode of Motion," in *City of Words: American Fiction, 1950–1970*. New York: Harper, 1971, pp. 64–84.

Way, Brian. "Character and Society in *The Adventures of Augie March*," in *British Association for American Studies Bulletin*. VIII (1964), pp. 36–44.

Weinberg, Helen. *The New Novel in America: The Kafkan Mode in Contemporary Fiction*. Ithaca, N.Y.: Cornell University Press, 1970, pp. 29–107.

Dangling Man

Axthelm, Peter M. "The Full Perception: Saul Bellow," in *The Modern Confessional Novel*. New Haven, Conn.: Yale University Press, 1967, pp. 128–177.

Bain, Joseph. "Escape from Intellection: Saul Bellow's *Dangling Man*," in *University Review*. XXXVII (1970), pp. 28–34.

Clayton, John J. *Saul Bellow: In Defense of Man*. Bloomington: Indiana University Press, 1968.

Donoghue, Denis. "Commitment and the Dangling Man," in *Studies: An Irish Quarterly*. LIII (Summer, 1964), pp. 174–187.

Eisinger, Chester E. "Saul Bellow: Love and Identity," in *Accent*. XVIII (Summer, 1968), pp. 183–188.

Galloway, David D. *The Absurd Hero in American Fiction: Updike, Styron, Bellow, Salinger*. Austin: University of Texas Press, 1966, pp. 82–89.

Geismar, Maxwell. "Saul Bellow: Novelist of the Intellectuals," in *American Moderns: From Rebellion to Conformity*. New York: Hill and Wang, 1958, pp. 210–224.

Glicksberg, Charles I. "The Theme of Alienation in the American Jewish Novel," in *Reconstructionist*. XXIII (November, 1957), pp. 8–13.

Guttmann, Allen. "Mr. Bellow's America," in *The Jewish Writer in America.* New York: Oxford University Press, 1971, pp. 178–221.

Harper, Howard M., Jr. *Desperate Faith: A Study of Bellow, Salinger, Mailer, Baldwin and Updike.* Chapel Hill: University of North Carolina Press, 1967, pp. 8–16.

Kulshrestha, Chirantan. "Affirmation in Saul Bellow's *Dangling Man*," in *Indian Journal of American Studies.* V (1976), pp. i–ii, 21–36.

Malin, Irving. "Saul Bellow: Reputations XIV," in *London Magazine.* X (January, 1965), pp. 43–54.

_____, **Editor.** *Saul Bellow's Fiction.* New York: New York University Press, 1967, pp. 71–76, 139–140.

Mellard, James. "*Dangling Man:* Saul Bellow's Lyrical Experiment," in *Ball State University Forum.* XV (1974), pp. 67–74.

Opdahl, Keith M. *The Novels of Saul Bellow: An Introduction.* University Park: Pennsylvania State University Press, 1967, pp. 28–50.

Podhoretz, Norman. "The Adventures of Saul Bellow," in *Doings and Undoings: The Fifties and After in American Writing.* New York: Farrar, Straus and Giroux, 1964, pp. 206–211.

Trachtenberg, Stanley. "Saul Bellow's Luftmenschen: The Compromise with Reality," in *Critique.* IX (Summer, 1967), pp. 62–73.

Henderson the Rain King

Allen, Michael. "Idiomatic Language in Two Novels by Saul Bellow," in *Journal of American Studies.* I (October, 1967), pp. 275–280.

Bradbury, Malcolm. "Saul Bellow's *Henderson the Rain King*," in *Listener.* LXXI (January 30, 1964), pp. 187–188.

Campbell, Jeff H. "Bellow's Intimation of Immortality: *Henderson the Rain King*," in *Studies in the Novel.* I (1969), pp. 323–333.

Cecil, L. Moffitt. "Bellow's Henderson as American Imago of the 1950's," in *Research Studies.* XL (1972), pp. 296–300.

Chase, Richard. "The Adventures of Saul Bellow: Progress of a Novelist," in *Commentary.* XXVII (April, 1959), pp. 326–330.

Clayton, J.J. *Saul Bellow: In Defense of Man.* Bloomington: Indiana University Press, 1968, pp. 166–185, 251–252.

Detweiler, Robert. "Patterns of Rebirth in *Henderson the Rain King*," in *Modern Fiction Studies.* XII (Winter, 1966–1967), pp. 405–414.

Edwards, Duane. "The Quest for Reality in *Henderson the Rain King*," in *Dalhousie Review.* LIII (1973), pp. 246–255.

Galloway, David O. *The Absurd Hero in American Fiction: Updike, Styron, Bellow, Salinger.* Austin: University of Texas Press, 1966, pp. 110–123.

————. "The Absurd Man as Picaro: The Novels of Saul Bellow," in *Texas Studies in Literature and Language.* VI (Summer, 1964), pp. 244–253.

Guttmann, Allen. "Bellow's Henderson," in *Critique.* VII (Spring-Summer, 1965), pp. 33–42.

Hughes, Daniel J. "Reality and the Hero: *Lolita* and *Henderson the Rain King,*" in *Modern Fiction Studies.* VI (Winter, 1960–1961), pp. 345–364.

Leach, Elsie. "From Ritual to Romance Again: *Henderson the Rain King,*" in *Western Humanities Review.* XIV (Spring, 1961), pp. 223–224.

Majdiak, Daniel. "The Romantic Self and *Henderson the Rain King,*" in *Bucknell Review.* XIX (Fall, 1971), pp. 125–146.

Markos, Donald W. "Life Against Death in *Henderson the Rain King,*" in *Modern Fiction Studies.* XVII (1971), pp. 193–205.

Morrow, Patrick. "Threat and Accommodation: The Novels of Saul Bellow," in *Midwest Quarterly.* VIII (Summer, 1967), pp. 403–406.

Opdahl, Keith M. *The Novels of Saul Bellow: An Introduction.* University Park: Pennsylvania State University Press, 1967, pp. 118–139.

Podhoretz, Norman. "The Adventures of Saul Bellow," in *Doings and Undoings: The Fifties and After in American Writing.* New York: Farrar, Straus and Giroux, 1964, pp. 224–227.

Quinton, Anthony. "The Adventures of Saul Bellow," in *London Magazine.* VI (December, 1959), pp. 55–59.

Rodrigues, Eusebio L. "Saul Bellow's Henderson as America," in *Centennial Review.* XX (1976), pp. 189–195.

Stock, Irvin. "The Novels of Saul Bellow," in *Southern Review.* III (Winter, 1967), pp. 31–36.

Symons, J. "Bellow Before *Herzog,*" in *Critical Occasions.* London: Hamish Hamilton, 1966, pp. 112–118.

Tanner, Tony. *Saul Bellow.* Edinburgh: Oliver and Boyd, 1965, pp. 71–86.

Toliver, Harold E. "Bellow's Idyll of the Tribe," in *Pastoral Forms and Attitudes.* Berkeley: University of California Press, 1971, pp. 323–333.

Whittemore, R. "*Henderson the Rain King,*" in *The Critic as Artist: Essays on Books, 1920–1970.* Edited by Gilbert A. Harrison. New York: Liveright, 1972, pp. 382–387.

Herzog

Aldridge, John. "The Complacency of Herzog," in *Time to Murder and Create.* New York: David McKay, 1966, pp. 133–138.

Atkins, Anselm. "The Moderate Optimism of Saul Bellow's *Herzog,*" in *Person.* L (1969), pp. 117–129.

Axthelm, Peter M. "The Full Perception: Saul Bellow," in *The Modern Confessional Novel.* New Haven, Conn.: Yale University Press, 1967, pp. 128–177.

Bailey, Jennifer. "A Qualified Affirmation of Saul Bellow's Recent Work," in *Journal of American Studies.* VII (April, 1973), pp. 67–76.

Bezanker, Abraham. "The Odyssey of Saul Bellow," in *Yale Review.* LVIII (Spring, 1969), pp. 359–371.

Bradbury, Malcolm. "Saul Bellow's *Herzog*," in *Critical Quarterly.* VII (Autumn, 1965), pp. 269–278.

Clayton, John J. *Saul Bellow: In Defense of Man.* Bloomington: Indiana University Press, 1968.

Cohen, Sarah Blacher. "Sex: Saul Bellow's Hedonistic Joke," in *Studies in American Fiction.* II (1974), pp. 223–229.

Fisch, Harold. "The Hero as Jew: Reflections on *Herzog*," in *Judaism.* XVII (1968), pp. 42–54.

Howe, Irving. "*Herzog*," in *The Critic as Artist: Essays on Books, 1920–1970.* Edited by Gilbert A. Harrison. New York: Liveright, 1972, pp. 181–191.

Josipovici, Gabriel. "Bellow's *Herzog*," in *Encounter.* XXXVII (November, 1971), pp. 49–55.

Kaplan, Harold. "The Second Fall of Man," in *Salmagundi.* XXX (1975), pp. 66–89.

Malin, Irving. *Saul Bellow's Fiction.* Carbondale: Southern Illinois University Press, 1969.

Moser, Harold F., Jr. "The Synthesis of Past and Present in Saul Bellow's *Herzog*," in *Wascana Review.* VI (1971), pp. 28–38.

Rahv, Philip. "Saul Bellow's Progress," in *Literature and the Sixth Sense.* Boston: Houghton Mifflin, 1969, pp. 392–397.

Read, Forrest. "*Herzog*," in *Saul Bellow and the Critics.* New York: New York University Press, 1967, pp. 184–206.

Richter, David H. "Bellow's *Herzog*," in *Fable's End: Completeness and Closure in Rhetorical Fiction.* Chicago: University of Chicago Press, 1974, pp. 185–192.

Rovit, Earl. "Bellow in Occupancy," in *American Scholar.* XXXIV (Spring, 1965), pp. 292–298.

Solotaroff, Theodore. "Napoleon Street," in *The Red Hot Vacuum and Other Pieces on the Writing of the Sixties.* New York: Atheneum, 1970, pp. 94–102.

Uphaus, Suzanne Henning. "From Innocence to Experience: A Study of *Herzog*," in *Dalhousie Review.* XLVI (1966), pp. 67–78.

Vogel, Dan. "Saul Bellow's Vision Beyond Absurdity: Jewishness in *Herzog*," in *Tradition.* IX (Spring, 1968), pp. 65–79.

Weinstein, Norman. "*Herzog*, Order and Entropy," in *English Studies.* LIV (1973), pp. 336–346.

Wise, Ruth R. "The Schlemiel as Liberal Humanist," in *The Schlemiel as Modern Hero.* Chicago: University of Chicago Press, 1971, pp. 92–107.

Young, James Dean. "Bellow's View of the Heart," in *Critique.* VII (Spring–Summer, 1965), pp. 5–17.

Humboldt's Gift

Baker, C. "Bellow's Gift," in *Theology Today.* XXXII (January, 1976), pp. 411–413.

Bradbury, Malcolm. "The It and the We," in *Encounter.* XLV (November, 1975), pp. 61–67.

Casey, J.B. "Bellow's Gift," in *Virginia Quarterly Review.* V (Winter, 1976), pp. 150–154.

McSweeny, Kerry. "Saul Bellow and the Life to Come," in *Critical Quarterly.* XVIII (Spring, 1976), pp. 67–72.

Shattuck, Roger. "A Higher Selfishness?," in *New York Review of Books.* XVIII (September 18, 1975), pp. 21–25.

Stern, Daniel. "The Bellow-ing of the Culture," in *Commonweal.* CII (October 24, 1975), pp. 502–504.

Updike, John. "Draping Radiance with a Worn Veil," in *New Yorker.* LI (September 15, 1975), pp. 122–130.

Mr. Sammler's Planet

Alter, Robert. "Jewish Humor and the Domestication of Myth," in his *Defenses of the Imagination; Jewish Writers and Modern Historical Crisis.* Philadelphia: Jewish Publication Society of America, 1978, pp. 155–167.

Atchity, John Kenneth. "Bellow's Mr. Sammler: The Last Man Given for Epitome," in *Research Studies.* XXXVIII (March, 1970), pp. 46–54.

Berryman, John. "A Note on Augie," in his *The Freedom of the Poet.* New York: Farrar, Straus, 1976, pp. 22–24.

Bolling, Douglass. "Intellectual and Aesthetic Dimensions of *Mr. Sammler's Planet*," in *Journal of Narrative Technique.* IV (1974), pp. 188–203.

Boyers, Robert. "Nature and Social Reality in Bellow's *Sammler*," in *Salmagundi.* XXX (1975), pp. 34–56. Reprinted in *Excursions; Selected Literary Essays.* Port Washington, N.Y.: Kennikat, 1977, pp. 25–46.

Cushman, K. "Mr. Bellow's *Sammler*: The Evolution of a Contemporary Text," in *Studies in the Novel.* VII (Fall, 1975), pp. 425–444.

Grossman, Edward. "The Bitterness of Saul Bellow," in *Midstream*. XVI (August–September, 1970), pp. 3–15.

Guttmann, Allen. "Saul Bellow's Mr. Sammler," in *Contemporary Literature*. XIV (1973), pp. 157–168.

————. "Mr. Bellow's America," in his *The Jewish Writer in America: Assimilation and the Crisis of Identity*. New York: Oxford University Press, 1971, pp. 178–221.

Harris, James N. "One Critical Approach to *Mr. Sammler's Planet*," in *Twentieth Century Literature*. XVIII (1972), pp. 235–250.

Jones, Roger. "Artistry and the Depth of Life: Aspects of Attitude and Technique in *Mr. Sammler's Planet*," in *Anglo-Welsh Review*. XXV (1976), pp. 138–153.

Kar, Prafulla C. "What It Means to Be Exactly Human: A Study of Bellow's *Mr. Sammler's Planet*," in *Studies in American Literature: Essays in Honor of William Mulder*. Edited by Jagdish Chander and Narinder S. Pradhan. Delhi, India: Oxford University Press, 1976, pp. 97–109.

Richter, David H. "Bellow's Herzog," in his *Fable's End; Completeness and Closure in Rhetorical Fiction*. Chicago: University of Chicago Press, 1974, pp. 185–192.

Schulz, Max F. "Mr. Bellow's Perigee, or the Lowered Horizon of *Mr. Sammler's Planet*," in *Contemporary American-Jewish Literature*. Edited by Irving Malin. Bloomington: Indiana University Press, 1973, pp. 117–133.

Siegel, Ben. "Saul Bellow and Mr. Sammler: Absurd Seekers of High Qualities," in *Saul Bellow: A Collection of Critical Essays*. Edited by Earl Rovit. Englewood Cliffs, N.J.: Prentice-Hall, 1975, pp. 122–134.

Stock, Irwin. "Man in Culture," in *Commentary*. XLIX (May, 1970), pp. 89–94.

Towner, D. "Brill's Ruins and Henderson's Rain," in *Critique*. XVII (1976), pp. 96–104.

Vernier, J. "Mr. Sammler's Lesson," in *Les Américanistes; New French Criticism on Modern American Fiction*. Edited by Ira D. Johnson and Christiane Johnson. Port Washington, N.Y.: Kennikat, 1978, pp. 16–36.

Seize the Day

Ciancio, Ralph. "The Achievement of Saul Bellow's *Seize the Day*," in *Literature and Theology*. Edited by Thomas F. Staley and Lester F. Zimmerman. Tulsa: University of Oklahoma Press, 1969, pp. 49–80.

Clayton, J.J. *Saul Bellow: In Defense of Man*. Bloomington: Indiana University Press, 1968.

Davis, Robert G. *The Creative Present: Notes on Contemporary American Fiction*. Edited by Nona Balakian and Charles Simmons. New York: Doubleday, 1963, pp. 124–127.

Eisinger, Chester E. "Saul Bellow: Love and Identity," in *Accent*. XVIII (Summer, 1958), pp. 199–203.

Fossum, Robert R. "The Devil and Saul Bellow," in *Comparative Literature Studies*. III (1966), pp. 200–204.

Galloway, David D. *The Absurd Hero in American Fiction: Updike, Styron, Bellow, Salinger*. Austin: University of Texas Press, 1966, pp. 104–110.

Giannone, Richard. "Saul Bellow's Idea of Self: A Reading of *Seize the Day*," in *Renascence*. XXVII (1975), pp. 193–205.

Hassan, Ihab. *Radical Innocence: Studies in the Contemporary American Novel*. Princeton, N.J.: Princeton University Press, 1961, pp. 311–316.

Jefchak, Andrew. "Family Struggles in *Seize the Day*," in *Studies in Short Fiction*. XI (Summer, 1974), pp. 297–302.

Levine, Paul. "Saul Bellow: The Affirmation of the Philosophical Fool," in *Perspective*. X (Winter, 1959), pp. 172–176.

Mathis, James C. "The Theme of *Seize the Day*," in *Critique*. VII (Spring/ Summer, 1965), pp. 43–45.

Morrow, Patrick. "Threat and Accommodation: The Novels of Saul Bellow," in *Midwest Quarterly*. VIII (Summer, 1967), pp. 391–394.

Nelson, Gerald B. "Tommy Wilhelm," in *Ten Versions of America*. New York: Knopf, 1972, pp. 129–145.

Opdahl, Keith M. *The Novels of Saul Bellow: An Introduction*. University Park: Pennsylvania State University Press, 1967, pp. 96–117.

Podhoretz, Norman. *Doings and Undoings: The Fifties and After in American Writing*. New York: Farrar, Straus and Giroux, 1964, pp. 219–224.

Porter, M. Gilbert. "The Scene as Image: A Reading of *Seize the Day*," in *Saul Bellow: A Collection of Critical Essays*. Edited By Earl Rovit. Englewood Cliffs, N.J.: Prentice-Hall, 1975, pp. 52–71.

Raper, J.R. "Running Contrary Ways: Saul Bellow's *Seize the Day*," in *Southern Humanities Review*. X (1976), pp. 157–168.

Richmond, Lee J. "The Maladroit, the Medico and the Magician: Saul Bellow's *Seize the Day*," in *Twentieth Century Literature*. XIX (1973), pp. 15–26.

Stern, Richard G. "*Seize the Day*," in *Kenyon Review*. XXI (Autumn, 1959), pp. 655–661.

Stock, Irvin. "The Novels of Saul Bellow," in *Southern Review*. III (Winter, 1967), pp. 27–31.

Tanner, Tony. *Saul Bellow*. Edinburgh: Oliver and Boyd, 1965, pp. 58–70.

Trachtenberg, Stanley. "Saul Bellow's Luftmenschen: The Compromise with Reality," in *Critique*. IX (1967), pp. 49–52.

Trowbridge, Clinton W. "Water Imagery in *Seize the Day*," in *Critique*. IX (1967), pp. 62–73.

Weiss, Daniel. "Caliban on Prospero: A Psychoanalytical Study on the Novel *Seize the Day*," in *Saul Bellow and the Critics*. Edited by Irving Malin. New York: New York University Press, 1967, pp. 114–141.

West, Ray B., Jr. *"Seize the Day,"* in *Sewanee Review*. LXIV (Summer, 1957), pp. 498–508.

The Victim

Allen, Walter. *The Modern Novel in Britain and the United States*. New York: Dutton, 1964, pp. 324–325.

Baumbach, Jonathan. "The Double Vision: *The Victim* by Saul Bellow," in *The Landscape of Nightmare*. New York: New York University Press, 1965, 1965, pp. 35–54.

Bradbury, Malcolm. "Saul Bellow's *The Victim*," in *Critical Quarterly*. V (Summer, 1963), pp. 119–128.

Burns, Robert. "The Urban Experience: The Novels of Saul Bellow," in *Dissent*. XXIV (Winter, 1969), pp. 18–24.

Clayton, John J. *Saul Bellow: In Defense of Man*. Bloomington: Indiana University Press, 1968, pp. 139–165, 240–241.

Fiedler, Leslie A. *Love and Death in the American Novel*. New York: Criterion, 1960, pp. 360–361.

Frank, Reuben. "Saul Bellow: The Evolution of a Contemporary Novelist," in *Western Review*. XVIII (Winter, 1954), pp. 105–108.

Galloway, David D. *The Absurd Hero in American Fiction: Updike, Styron, Bellow, Salinger*. Austin: University of Texas Press, 1966, pp. 89–94.

Geismar, Maxwell. "Saul Bellow: Novelist of the Intellectuals," in *American Moderns: From Rebellion to Conformity*. New York: Hill and Wang, 1958, pp. 213–216.

Glicksberg, Charles I. "The Theme of Alienation in the American Jewish Novel," in *Reconstructionist*. XXIII (November, 1957), pp. 8–13.

Hall, James. *The Lunatic Giant in the Drawing Room: The British and American Novel Since 1930*. Bloomington: Indiana University Press, 1968, pp. 138–149.

Harper, Howard M., Jr. *Desperate Faith: A Study of Bellow, Salinger, Mailer, Baldwin and Updike*. Chapel Hill: University of North Carolina Press, 1967, pp. 16–23.

Hassan, Ihab. *Radical Innocence: Studies in the Contemporary American Novel*. Princeton, N.J.: Princeton University Press, 1961, pp. 299–303.

Jensen, Emily. "Saul Bellow's *The Victim*: A View of Modern Man," in *Literature*. IV (1963), pp. 38–44.

Malin, Irving. *Saul Bellow's Fiction*. Carbondale: University of Southern Illinois Press, 1969, pp. 59–63.

Morrow, Patrick. "Threat and Accommodation: The Novels of Saul Bellow," in *Midwest Quarterly*. VIII (Summer, 1967), pp. 395–397.

Opdahl, Keith M. *The Novels of Saul Bellow: An Introduction*. University Park: Pennsylvania State University Press, 1967, pp. 51–69.

Podhoretz, Norman. "The Adventures of Saul Bellow," in *Doings and Undoings: The Fifties and After in American Writing*. New York: Farrar, Straus and Giroux, 1964, pp. 211–215.

Rans, Geoffrey. "The Novels of Saul Bellow," in *Review of English Literature*. IV (October, 1963), pp. 20–22.

Ross, Theodore J. "Notes on Saul Bellow," in *Chicago Jewish Forum*. XVIII (1959), pp. 21–27.

Stock, Irvin. "The Novels of Saul Bellow," in *Southern Review*. III (Winter, 1967), pp. 19–23.

Tanner, Tony. *Saul Bellow*. Edinburgh: Oliver and Boyd, 1965, pp. 26–37.

JACINTO BENAVENTE Y MARTÍNEZ
(1866–1954)

The Bonds of Interest

Boyd, Ernest. *Studies from Ten Literatures.* New York: Scribner's, 1925, pp. 96–105.

Chandler, Frank W. *Modern Continental Playwrights.* New York: Harper & Row, 1931, pp. 503–528.

Clark, Barrett H. *A Study of the Modern Drama.* New York: Appleton, 1925, pp. 215–218.

Gassner, John W. *Masters of the Drama.* New York: Random House, 1940, pp. 428–430.

Glass, E. "*Bonds of Interest,*" in *Poet Lore.* XXXII (June, 1921), pp. 244–250.

Goldberg, Isaac. *The Drama of Transition, Native and Exotic Playcraft.* Cincinnati, Oh.: Stewart Kidd, 1922, pp. 115–120.

Hamilton, Clayton. *Seen on the Stage.* New York: Henry Holt, 1920, pp. 132–137.

Jameson, Storm. *Modern Drama in Europe.* New York: Harcourt, Brace and Howe, 1920, pp. 239–245.

Lumley, Frederick. *New Trends in Twentieth Century Drama: A Survey Since Ibsen and Shaw.* New York: Oxford University Press, 1967, pp. 366–367.

Miller, Nellie Burget. *The Living Drama, Historical Development and Modern Movement Visualized: A Drama of the Drama.* New York: Century, 1924, pp. 362–364.

Nicoll, Allardyce. *World Drama, from Aeschelus to Anouilh.* London: Harrap, 1976, pp. 573–574.

Peñuelas, Marcelino C. *Jacinto Benavente.* New York: Twayne, 1968, pp. 103–111.

Stamm, James R. *A Short History of Spanish Literature.* Garden City, N.Y.: Doubleday, 1967, pp. 180–185.

Starkie, Walter. *Jacinto Benavente.* New York: Oxford University Press, 1924, pp. 151–167.

Underhill, John Garrett. "Introduction," in *Plays by Jacinto Benavente.* New York: Scribner's, 1917, pp. vii–xxv.

Young, Raymond A. "Benavente and the Emancipation of Spanish Women," in *Modern Languages.* XLIX (December, 1968), pp. 157–160.

Young, Robert J., Jr. "Unpredictable Features in the Style of Benavente's *Los Intereses Creados*," in *Language and Style*. IX (1976), pp. 108–117.

The Passion Flower

Gassner, John W. *Masters of the Drama*. New York: Random House, 1940, pp. 430–431.

Hamilton, Clayton. *Seen on the Stage*. New York: Henry Holt, 1920, pp. 132–137.

Marquerie, Alfredo. "A Centenary of Spanish Theatre," in *Topic*. XV (Spring, 1968), p. 34.

Peñuelas, Marcelino C. *Jacinto Benavente*. New York: Twayne, 1968, pp. 120–124.

Rehder, Ernest C. "The Obscure Motives of Rubio in Benavente's *La Malquerida*," in *South Atlantic Bulletin*. XLI (1976), pp. 16–21.

Stamm, James R. *A Short History of Spanish Literature*. Garden City, N.Y.: Doubleday, 1967, pp. 180–185.

Starkie, Walter. "Benavente, the Winner of the Nobel Prize," in *Contemporary Review*. CXXIII (1923), pp. 93–100.

————. *Jacinto Benavente*. New York: Oxford University Press, 1924, pp. 91–103.

Underhill, John Garrett. "Introduction," in *Plays by Jacinto Benavente*. New York: Scribner's, 1917, pp. vii–xxv.

Young, Raymond A. "Benavente and the Emancipation of Spanish Women," in *Modern Language*. XLIX (December, 1968), pp. 157–160.

STEPHEN VINCENT BENÉT
(1898–1943)

John Brown's Body

Catton, Bruce. *Prefaces to History.* New York: Doubleday, 1970, pp. 7–12.

Daniels, S. "Saga of the American Civil War," in *Contemporary Review.* (October, 1934), pp. 466–467.

Fitts, Dudley. "*John Brown's Body,*" in *Hound and Horn.* II (September, 1928), pp. 85–86.

Flanagan, J. "Folk Elements in *John Brown's Body,*" in *New York Folklore Quarterly.* (1964), pp. 243–256.

Jackson, Frederick H. "Stephen Vincent Benet and American History," in *Historian.* XVII (Autumn, 1954), pp. 67–75.

Kreymborg, Alfred. *Our Singing Strength: A History of American Poetry.* New York: Tudor, 1929, pp. 607–611.

Moffett, J. "Some Corrections of Stephen Vincent Benet," in *Notes & Queries.* XIII (1966), pp. 420–421.

Monroe, Harriet. "A Cinema Epic," in *Poetry.* XXXIII (1928), pp. 91–96.

Montgomery, N. "The Homeric Epithet in Contemporary Literature," in *Classical Journal.* XXXIX (1943–1944), pp. 229–230.

Morese, R. "*John Brown's Body,*" in *Invitation to Learning.* II (1952), pp. 359–365.

Nathan, R. "Stephen Vincent Benet and His America," in *Mark Twain Quarterly.* (Winter, 1943–Spring, 1944), pp. 4–5.

O'Neill, Eugene, Jr. "Stephen Vincent Benet's *John Brown's Body,*" in *Saturday Review of Literature.* XXXII (August 6, 1949), pp. 34–35.

Richardson, M. "The Historical Authenticity of John Brown's Raid in Stephen Vincent Benet's *John Brown's Body,*" in *West Virginia History.* XXIV (1963), pp. 168–175.

Stroud, Parry. *Stephen Vincent Benet.* New York: Twayne, 1962, pp. 46–80.

Tate, Allen. "The Irrepressible Conflict," in *Nation.* CXXVII (September 19, 1928), p. 274.

Wiley, Paul L. "The Phaeton Symbol in *John Brown's Body,*" in *American Literature.* XVII (November, 1945), pp. 231–242.

ARNOLD BENNETT
(1867–1931)

Anna of the Five Towns

Drabble, Margaret. *Arnold Bennett.* New York: Knopf, 1974, pp. 91–92, 94–96, 111–112.

Hall, James. *Arnold Bennett: Primitivism and Taste.* Seattle: University of Washington Press, 1959, pp. 32–39.

Lucas, John. *Arnold Bennett, A Study of His Fiction.* London: Methuen, 1974, pp. 40–52.

Simons, J.B. *Arnold Bennett and His Novels: A Critical Study.* Oxford: Blackwell, 1936.

Wright, Walter F. *Arnold Bennett: Romantic Realist.* Lincoln: University of Nebraska Press, 1971.

Young, Kenneth. *Arnold Bennett.* New York: British Book Centre, 1976, pp. 18–19.

The Clayhanger Trilogy

Allen, Walter E. *Arnold Bennett.* Denver: A. Swallow, 1949, pp. 76–82.

Ball, David. "Some Sources for Bennett's *Clayhanger Trilogy,*" in *English.* XXI (Spring, 1972), pp. 13–17.

Barker, Dudley. *Writer by Trade: A Portrait of Arnold Bennett.* New York: Atheneum, 1966, pp. 163–170, 186–189.

Bellamy, William. *The Novels of Wells, Bennett, and Galsworthy: 1890–1910.* New York: Barnes & Noble, 1971, pp. 150–161.

Bequette, M.K. "The Structure of Bennett's *Trilogy,*" in *Arnold Bennett Newsletter.* II (1976), pp. 9–18.

Hackett, Francis. *Horizons; A Book of Criticism.* New York: Huebsch, 1919, pp. 147–162.

Hall, James. *Arnold Bennett: Primitivism and Taste.* Seattle: University of Washington Press, 1959, pp. 84–129.

Hepburn, James G. *The Art of Arnold Bennett.* Bloomington: Indiana University Press, 1963, pp. 81–94.

————. "The Two Worlds of Edwin Clayhanger," in *Boston University Studies in English.* V (1961), pp. 246–255.

Lafourcade, Georges. *Arnold Bennett.* London: Muller, 1939, pp. 121–147.

Lucas, John. *Arnold Bennett, A Study of His Fiction.* London: Methuen, 1974, pp. 132–165.

Scott-James, Rolfe A. *Personality in Literature, 1913–1931.* New York: Holt, 1932, pp. 87–95.

Wright, Walter F. *Arnold Bennett: Romantic Realist.* Lincoln: University of Nebraska Press, 1971.

Young, Kenneth. *Arnold Bennett.* New York: British Book Centre, 1976, pp. 29–31.

The Old Wives' Tale

Allen, Walter E. *Arnold Bennett.* Denver: A. Swallow, 1949, pp. 61–74.

Brewster, Dorothy. *Modern Fiction.* New York: Columbia University Press, 1934, pp. 94–101.

Hackett, Francis. *Horizons; A Book of Criticism.* New York: Huebsch, 1919, pp. 139–146.

Hall, James. *Arnold Bennett: Primitivism and Taste.* Seattle: University of Washington Press, 1959, pp. 47–83.

Hepburn, James G. *The Art of Arnold Bennett.* Bloomington: Indiana University Press, 1963, pp. 17–32, 55–65, 143–149.

Kettle, Arnold. *An Introduction to the English Novel,* Volume II. London: Hutchinson's, 1951–1953, pp. 85–89.

Lafourcade, Georges. *Arnold Bennett.* London: Muller, 1939, pp. 96–120.

Lodge, David. *The Modes of Modern Writing; Metaphor, Metonymy, and the Typology of Modern Literature.* Ithaca, N.Y.: Cornell University Press, 1977, pp. 27–35.

Lucas, John. *Arnold Bennett, A Study of His Fiction.* London: Methuen, 1974, pp. 97–116.

McCullough, Bruce W. *Representative English Novelists: Defoe to Conrad.* New York: Harper, 1946, pp. 310–319.

Scott-James, Rolfe A. *Personality in Literature, 1913–1931.* New York: Holt, 1932, pp. 81–86.

Siegal, Paul N. "Revolution and Evolution in Bennett's *The Old Wives' Tale*," in *Clio.* IV (1975), pp. 159–172.

Simons, J.B. *Arnold Bennett and His Novels.* Oxford: Blackwell, 1936, pp. 99–151.

Swinden, Patrick. *Unofficial Selves: Character in the Novel from Dickens to the Present Day.* New York: Barnes & Noble, 1973, pp. 120–157.

Wright, Walter F. *Arnold Bennett: Romantic Realist.* Lincoln: University of Nebraska Press, 1971, pp. 178–182, 185–186.

Young, Kenneth. *Arnold Bennett.* New York: British Book Centre, 1976, pp. 21–28.

Riceyman Steps

Allen, Walter E.   *Arnold Bennett*. Denver: A. Swallow, 1949, pp. 90–98.

Barker, Dudley.   *Writer by Trade: A Portrait of Arnold Bennett*. New York: Atheneum, 1966, pp. 215–218.

Durkin, Brian.   "Some New Lights on *Riceyman Steps*," in *English Literature in Transition, 1880–1920*. X (1967), pp. 66–80.

Hall, James.   *Arnold Bennett: Primitivism and Taste*. Seattle: University of Washington Press, 1959, pp. 130–138.

Hepburn, James G.   *The Art of Arnold Bennett*. Bloomington: Indiana University Press, 1963, pp. 34–44.

———.   "Some Curious Realism in *Riceyman Steps*," in *Modern Fiction Studies*. VIII (Summer, 1962), pp. 116–126.

Lafourcade, Georges.   *Arnold Bennett*. London: Muller, 1939, pp. 184–195.

Lucas, John.   *Arnold Bennett, A Study of His Fiction*. London: Methuen, 1974, pp. 194–204.

Wright, Walter F.   *Arnold Bennett: Romantic Realist*. Lincoln: University of Nebraska Press, 1971, pp. 152–153, 169–170.

Young, Kenneth.   *Arnold Bennett*. New York: British Book Centre, 1976, pp. 34–36.

THOMAS BERGER
(1924–   )

Little Big Man

Dippie, Brian W.   "Jack Crabb and the Sole Survivors of Custer's Last Stand," in *Western American Literature.* IV (Fall, 1969), pp. 189–202.

Fetrow, Fred M.   "The Function of the External Narrator in Thomas Berger's *Little Big Man,*" in *Journal of Narrative Technique.* V (1975), pp. 57–65.

Gurian, Jay.   "Style in the Literary Desert: *Little Big Man,*" in *Western American Literature.* III (Winter, 1969), pp. 285–296.

Lee, L.L.   "American, Western, Picaresque: Thomas Berger's *Little Big Man,*" in *South Dakota Review.* IV (Summer, 1966), pp. 285–296.

Wylder, Delbert E.   "Thomas Berger's *Little Big Man* as Literature," in *Western American Literature.* III (Winter, 1969), pp. 273–284.

WENDELL BERRY
(1934–   )

The Poetry of Berry

Carruth, Hayden. "Three Poets," in *Poetry*. CVI (July, 1965), pp. 310–311.

Cooper, Jane. "*Openings*," in *New York Times Book Review*. (December 22, 1968), pp. 10–11.

Ditsky, John M. "Wendell Berry: Homage to the Apple Tree," in *Modern Poetry Studies*. II (1971), pp. 7–15.

Fields, Kenneth. "The Hunter's Trail: Poems by Wendell Berry," in *Iowa Review*. I (1970), pp. 90–99.

Martz, L.L. "Recent Poetry: The Substance of Change," in *Yale Review*. LIV (June, 1965), pp. 615–617.

Morgan, Speer. "Wendell Berry: A Fatal Singing," in *Southern Review*. X (1974), pp. 865–877.

Pack, Robert. "Each in His Own Voice," in *New York Times Book Review*. (January 17, 1965), p. 32.

Shaw, Robert B. "Both Sides of the Water," in *Poetry*. CXVII (November, 1970), pp. 112–113.

JOHN BERRYMAN
(1914–1972)

Berryman's Sonnets

Bewley, Marius. "Poetry Chronicle," in *Hudson Review*. XX (August, 1967), pp. 500–504.

Gilman, Milton. "Berryman and the Sonnets," in *Chelsea*. XXII/XXIII (June, 1968), pp. 158–167.

Howell, Anthony. "A Question of Form," in *Poetry Review*. LX (Spring, 1969), pp. 41–49.

Lieberman, Laurence. "The Expansional Poet: A Return to Personality," in *Yale Review*. LVII (Winter,1968), pp. 258–271.

Linebarger, J.M. "*Berryman's Sonnets*: Tradition and the Individual Talent," in *Concerning Poetry*. VI (Spring, 1973), pp. 19–29.

_____. "A Commentary on *Berryman's Sonnets*," in *John Berryman Studies: A Scholarly and Critical Journal*. I (January, 1975), pp. 13–24.

Mazzocco, Robert. "Harlequin in Hell," in *New York Review of Books*. VIII (June 29, 1967), pp. 12–16.

Meredith, William. "A Bright Surviving Actual Scene: *Berryman's Sonnets*," in *Harvard Advocate*. CIII (Spring, 1969), pp. 19–22.

Delusions, Etc., of John Berryman

Baumgaertner, Jill. "Four Poets: Blood Type New," *Cresset*. XXXVI (April, 1973), pp. 16–19.

Brown, John Alan. "Berryman Agonistes," in *New Statesman*. LXXXV (February 16, 1973), pp. 238–239.

Engles, John. "Berryman's Last Poems," in *Country Measures*. II (1973), pp. 177–179.

Harrison, Keith. "Out There and in Here: Berryman, Ponge and Transtromer," in *Carleton Miscellany*. XIII (Spring-Summer, 1973), pp. 111–121.

Harsent, David. "Intimations of Mortality," in *Spectator*. CCXXX (March 24, 1973), p. 368.

Hayes, Ann. "*Delusions, Etc.* and the Art of Distance," in *John Berryman Studies: A Scholarly and Critical Journal*. I (January, 1975), pp. 6–10.

Linebarger, J.M. *John Berryman*. New York: Twayne, 1974.

Meredith, William. "Swan Songs," in *Poetry*. CXXII (May, 1973), pp. 98–103.

Stitt, Peter. "Berryman's Last Poems," in *Concerning Poetry*. VI (Spring, 1973), pp. 5–12.

"His Toy, His Dream, His Rest"

Atlas, James. *"The Dream Songs*: To Terrify and Comfort," in *Poetry.* CXV (October, 1969), pp. 43–46.

Connelly, Kenneth. "Henry Pussycat, He Come Home Good," in *Yale Review.* LVIII (Spring, 1969), pp. 419–427.

Dickey, William. "A Place in the Country," in *Hudson Review.* XXII (Summer, 1969), pp. 347–364.

Eshelman, Clayton. " 'His Toy, His Dream, His Rest,' " in *Minnesota Review.* X (January-April, 1970), pp. 79–80.

Ewart, Gavin. "Making a Language," in *Ambit.* XL (1969), pp. 44–46.

Goldman, Michael. "Berryman: Without Impudence and Vanity," in *Nation.* CCVIII (February 24, 1969), pp. 245–246.

Hazman, Ronald. "The City and the House," in *Encounter.* XXIV (February 1, 1970), pp. 84–91.

Johnson, Carol. "John Berryman: *The Dream Songs*," in *Harvard Advocate.* CIII (Spring, 1969), pp. 23–25.

McMichael, James. "Barges and Strand, Weak Henry, Philip Levine," in *Southern Review.* VIII (Winter, 1972), pp. 213–224.

Mazzaro, Jerome. "Berryman's Dream World," in *Kenyon Review.* XXXI (Spring, 1969), pp. 259–263.

Ricks, Christopher. "Recent American Poetry," in *Massachusetts Review.* XI (Spring, 1970), pp. 313–338.

Sheehan, Donald. "The Silver Sensibility: Five Recent Books of American Poetry," in *Contemporary Literature.* XII (Winter, 1971), pp. 98–121.

Homage to Mistress Bradstreet

Armstrong, Robert. "Uncharted Territories," in *Poetry Review.* I (July–September, 1959), pp. 175–176.

Arpin, Gary Q. "Mistress Bradstreet's Discontent," in *John Berryman Studies: A Scholarly and Critical Journal.* I (1975), pp. 2–7.

Gelpi, Albert. *"Homage to Mistress Bradstreet,"* in *Harvard Advocate.* CIII (Spring, 1969), pp. 14–17.

Gordon, Ambrose, Jr. *"Homage to Mistress Bradstreet,"* in *Yale Review.* XLVI (Winter, 1957), pp. 298–300.

Holder, Alan. "Anne Bradstreet Resurrected," in *Concerning Poetry.* II (Spring, 1969), pp. 11–18.

Johnson, Carol. "John Berryman and Mistress Bradstreet: A Relation of Reason," in *Essays in Criticism.* XIV (October, 1964), pp. 388–396.

Kunitz, Stanley. "No Middle Flight," in *Poetry.* XC (July, 1957), pp. 244–249.

Langland, Joseph. *"Homage to Mistress Bradstreet,"* in *Northwest Review.* I (Spring, 1967), pp. 56–60.

Nims, John Frederick. "Homage in Measure to Mr. Berryman," in *Prairie Schooner.* XXXII (Spring, 1958), pp. 1–7.

Perosa, Sergio. "A Commentary on *Homage to Mistress Bradstreet,"* in *John Berryman Studies: A Scholarly and Critical Journal.* II (1976), pp. 4–25.

Rosenthal, M. L. "Other Confessional Poets," in *The New Poets: American and British Poetry Since World War II.* New York: Oxford University Press, 1967, pp. 118–130.

Stitt, Peter. " 'Bitter Sister, Victim! I Miss You': John Berryman's *Homage to Mistress Bradstreet,"* in *John Berryman Studies: A Scholarly and Critical Journal.* I (April, 1975), pp. 2–11.

White, Elizabeth Wade. *"Homage to Mistress Bradstreet,"* in *New England Quarterly.* XXIX (December, 1956), pp. 545–548.

Love & Fame

Dunn, Douglas. "A Bridge in Minneapolis," in *Encounter.* XXXVIII (May, 1972), pp. 73–78.

Fraser, G.S. "The Magicians," in *Partisan Review.* XXXVIII (Winter, 1971–1972), pp. 469–478.

Lindop, Grevel. *"Love & Fame,"* in *Critical Quarterly.* XIV (Winter, 1972), pp. 379–381.

Linebarger, J.M. *John Berryman.* New York: Twayne, 1974.

Meredith, William. "Swan Songs," in *Poetry.* CXXII (May, 1973), pp. 98–103.

Neill, Edward. "Ambivalence of Berryman: An Interim Report," in *Critical Quarterly.* XVI (Autumn, 1974), pp. 267–276.

Oberg, Arthur. "Deer, Doors, Dark," in *Southern Review.* IX (Winter, 1973), pp. 243–256.

Perloff, Marjorie G. "Poetry Chronicle 1970–71," in *Contemporary Literature.* XIV (Winter, 1973), pp. 97–131.

Phillips, Robert. *The Confessional Poets.* Carbondale: Southern Illinois University Press, pp. 92–106.

Stefanik, Ernest C. "A Cursing Glory: John Berryman's *Love & Fame,"* in *Renascence.* XXV (Summer, 1973), pp. 115–127.

Wilson, R. Patrick. "The Ironic Title of Berryman's *Love & Fame,"* in *Notes on Contemporary Literature.* V (1975), pp. 10–12.

The Poetry of Berryman

Arpin, Gary Q.   *John Berryman: A Reference Guide.* Boston: Hall, 1975.

Beach, Joseph Warren.   *Obsessive Images.* Minneapolis: University of Minnesota Press, 1960.

Berryman, John.   "Changes," in *Poets on Poetry.* Edited by Howard Nemerov. New York: Basic Books, 1966, pp. 94–103.

Carley, Dorothy Myren.   *Modern American Literature.* New York: Frederick Ungar, 1969, pp. 101–104.

Catt, Jonathan.   "The New Poetry," in *The New American Arts.* Edited by Richard Kostelanetz. New York: Horizon Press, 1965, pp. 119–128.

Dodsworth, Martin.   *The Survival of Poetry.* London: Faber and Faber, 1970, pp. 100–132.

Fitzgerald, Robert.   "Poetry and Perfection," in *Saturday Review.* LVI (August, 1948), pp. 685–697.

Hamilton, Jan.   *A Poetry Chronicle.* New York: Harper & Row, 1973, pp. 111–121.

Hassan, Ihab.   *Contemporary American Literature 1945–1972: An Introduction.* New York: Frederick Ungar, 1973, pp. 99–101.

Hayes, Ann.   "The Voice of John Berryman," in *John Berryman Studies: A Scholarly and Critical Journal.* I (July, 1975), pp. 17–20.

Jackson, Bruce.   "Berryman's Chaplinesque," in *Minnesota Review.* V (1965), pp. 90–94.

Lieberman, Laurence.   "The Expansional Poet; A Return to Personality," in *Yale Review.* LVII (1968), pp. 258–271.

Linebarger, J. M.   *John Berryman.* New York: Twayne, 1973.

Lowell, Robert.   "The Poetry of John Berryman," in *New York Review of Books.* II (May 28, 1964), pp. 2–3.

Martz, William J.   *John Berryman.* Minneapolis: University of Minnesota Press, 1969.

Mazzocco, Robert.   "Harlequin in Hell," in *New York Review of Books.* VIII (June 29, 1967), pp. 12–16.

Pearson, Gabriel.   "John Berryman," in *The Modern Poet.* Edited by Jan Hamilton. New York: Horizon Press, 1969, pp. 111–124.

Phillips, Robert.   *The Confessional Poets.* Carbondale: Southern Illinois University Press, 1973, pp. 92–106.

Rosenthal, M. L.   *The New Poets: American and British Poetry Since World War II.* New York: Oxford University Press, 1967, pp. 118–130.

Sergeant, Howard.   "Poetry Review," in *English.* XV (1965), pp. 154–157.

77 Dream Songs

Arpin, Gary Q. "Forward to the End: Berryman's First Dream Song," in *John Berryman Studies: A Scholarly and Critical Journal.* I (1975), pp. 7–11.

_____. " 'I am Their Musick': Lamentations and *The Dream Songs*," in *John Berryman Studies: A Scholarly and Critical Journal.* I (January, 1975), pp. 2–6.

Barbera, Jack Vincent. "Shape and Flow in *The Dream Songs*," in *Twentieth Century Literature.* XXII (1976), pp. 146–162.

Bayley, John. "John Berryman: *A Question of Imperial Sway,"* in *Salmagundi.* XXII–XXIII (Spring–Summer, 1973), pp. 84–102.

Cott, Jonathan. "Theodore Roethke and John Berryman: Two Dream Poets," in *On Contemporary Literature.* Edited by Richard Kostelanetz. New York: Avon Books, 1964, pp. 520–531.

Elliott, George P. "Poetry Chronicle," in *Hudson Review.* XVIII (Autumn, 1964), pp. 451–464.

Glauber, Robert H. "The Poet's Intention," in *Prairie Schooner.* XXXIX (Fall, 1965), pp. 276–280.

Lowell, Robert. "The Poetry of John Berryman," in *New York Review of Books.* V (May 28, 1964), pp. 2–3.

Mendelson, E. "How to Read Berryman's *Dream Songs*," in *American Poetry Since 1960—Some Critical Perspectives.* Edited by Robert B. Shaw. Chester Springs, Pa.: Dufour Editions, 1973, pp. 29–43.

Meredith, William. "Henry Tasting all the Secret Bits of Life: Berryman's *Dream Songs*," in *Wisconsin Studies in Contemporary Literature.* VI (Winter–Spring, 1965), pp. 27–33.

Molesworth, Charles. "Shining the Start: Some Gloss on Berryman's First Dream Song," in *John Berryman Studies: A Scholarly and Critical Journal.* I (1975), pp. 17–22.

Oberg, Arthur. "John Berryman: *The Dream Songs* and the Horror of Unlove," in *University of Windsor Review.* VI (Fall, 1970), pp. 1–11.

Patrick, W.B. "Berryman's *77 Dream Songs*: 'Spare Now a Cagey John/A Whilom,' " in *Southern Humanities Review.* V (Spring, 1971), pp. 113–119.

Pavlovcak, Michael. "The Method of *The Dream Songs*," in *John Berryman Studies: A Scholarly and Critical Journal.* I (January, 1975), pp. 27–29.

Pearson, Gabriel. "John Berryman—Poet as Medium," in *The Review* (Oxford). No. 15 (April, 1965), pp. 3–17.

Porterfield, Jo. "The Melding of a Man: Berryman, Henry, and the Ornery Mr. Bones," in *Southwest Review.* LVIII (Winter, 1973), pp. 30–46.

Ramsey, Paul. "In Exasperation and Gratitude," in *Sewanee Review.* LXXIV (Autumn, 1966), pp. 936–938.

Seidel, Frederick. "Berryman's *Dream Songs*," in *Poetry*. CV (January, 1965), pp. 257–259.

Smith, William Jay. "Pockets of Thought," in *Harper's*. CCXXIX (August, 1964), pp. 100–102.

Stefanik, Ernest C., Jr. "Knowing Henry: A Reading of Dream Song One," in *John Berryman Studies: A Scholarly and Critical Journal*. I (1975), pp. 23–29.

Thornburg, Charles W. "The Significance of Dreams in *The Dream Songs*," in *Literature and Psychology*. XXV (1975), pp. 93–107.

Vonalt, Larry P. "Berryman's *The Dream Songs*," in *Sewanee Review*. LXXIX (1971), pp. 464–469.

————. "Dream Songs First and Last," in *John Berryman Studies: A Scholarly and Critical Journal*. I (1975), pp. 30–35.

Walsh, Malachy. "John Berryman: A Novel Interpretation," in *Viewpoint*. X (Spring, 1969), pp. 5–12.

Warner, Anne B. "Berryman's Elegies: One Approach to *The Dream Songs*," in *John Berryman Studies: A Scholarly and Critical Journal*. II (1976), pp. 5–22.

Wasserstrom, William. "Cagey John: Berryman as Medicine Man," in *Centennial Review*. XII (Summer, 1968), pp. 334–354.

JOHN BETJEMAN
(1906–   )

The Poetry of Betjeman

Brooke, Jocelyn. *Ronald Firbank and John Betjeman.* London: Longmans, 1962.

Larkin, Philip. "Introduction," in John Betjeman's *Collected Poems.* Boston: Houghton Mifflin, 1971, pp. xvii–xli.

Press, John. *John Betjeman.* London: Longmans, 1974.

Sparrow, John. "The Poetry of John Betjeman," in his *Independent Essays.* London: Faber and Faber, pp. 166–179.

Spender, Stephen. "Poetry for Poetry's Sake and Poetry Beyond Poetry," in *Horizon (London).* XIII (April, 1946), pp. 221–238.

Stanford, Derek. *John Betjeman: A Study.* London: Neville Spearman, 1961.

Wain, John. "Four Observer Pieces: John Betjeman," in his *Essays on Literature and Ideas.* New York: St. Martin's, 1971, pp. 168–171.

Waugh, Auberon. "Royal Rhymster," in *The New York Times Magazine.* January 6, 1974, pp. 18–26.

Wiehe, R.E. "Summoned by Nostalgia: John Betjeman's Poetry," in *Arizona Quarterly.* XIX (Spring, 1963), pp. 37–49.

AMBROSE BIERCE
(1842–1914?)

In the Midst of Life

Beer, Thomas. *The Mauve Decade.* New York: Knopf, 1926, pp. 95–96.

Brooks, Van Wyck. "San Francisco: Ambrose Bierce," in *Confident Years: 1885–1915.* New York: Dutton, 1952, pp. 201–215.

Crane, John Kenny. "Crossing the Bar Twice: Post-Mortem Consciousness in Bierce, Hemingway, and Golding," in *Studies in Short Fiction.* VI (Summer, 1969), pp. 361–376.

Fatout, Paul. *Ambrose Bierce: The Devil's Lexicographer.* Norman: University of Oklahoma Press, 1951, pp. 185–186.

Grattan, C. Hartley. *Bitter Bierce.* Garden City, N.Y.: Doubleday, Doran, 1929, pp. 138–151.

Grenander, Mary E. *Ambrose Bierce.* New York: Twayne, 1971, pp. 84–99, 115–130, 138–147.

Jordan, David Starr. *The Days of a Man,* Volume I. New York: World, 1922, p. 461.

Nations, Leroy J. "Ambrose Bierce: The Gray Wolf of American Letters," in *South Atlantic Quarterly.* XXV (1926), pp. 264–268.

O'Brien, Mathew C. "Ambrose Bierce and the Civil War," in *American Literature.* XLVIII (1976), pp. 377–381.

Pollard, Percival. *Their Day in Court.* New York: Neale, 1909, pp. 259–269.

Starrett, Vincent. *Ambrose Bierce.* Chicago: Walter M. Hill, 1920, pp. 26–32. Reprinted in *Buried Ceasars.* Chicago: Covici-McGee, 1923.

Sterling, George. "Introduction," in *In the Midst of Life.* By Ambrose Bierce. New York: Modern Library, 1927, pp. xii–xvi.

Weimer, David R. "Ambrose Bierce and the Art of War," in *Essays in Literary History.* Edited by Rudolph Kirk and C.F. Main. New Brunswick, N.J.: Rutgers University Press, 1960, pp. 229–238.

Wiggins, Robert A. *Ambrose Bierce.* New York: McGraw-Hill, 1964, pp. 23–31.

ROBERT MONTGOMERY BIRD
(1806–1854)

Nick of the Woods

Bryant, James C. "The Fallen World in *Nick of the Woods*," in *American Literature*. XXXVIII (November, 1966), pp. 352–364.

Dahl, Curtis. *Robert Montgomery Bird*. New York: Twayne, 1963, pp. 91–102.

Dibble, R.F. "Reborn Youth; Criticism of *Nick of the Woods*," in *Sewanee Review*. XXVII (October, 1919), pp. 496–499.

Gilman, William H. "Hero and the Heroic in American Literature," in *Patterns of Commitment in American Literature*. Edited by Marston La France. Toronto: University of Toronto Press, 1967, p. 5.

Hall, Joan Joffe. "*Nick of the Woods*: An Interpretation of the American Wilderness," in *American Literature*. XXXV (May, 1963), pp. 173–182.

Richardson, Charles F. *American Literature, 1607–1885,* Volume II. New York: G.P. Putnam, 1889, pp. 394–396.

Van Doren, Carl. *The American Novel*. New York: Macmillan, 1922, p. 66.

Williams, Cecil B. "R.M. Bird's Plans for Novels of the Frontier," in *American Literature*. XXI (November, 1949), pp. 321–324.

BJÖRNSTJERNE BJÖRNSON
(1832–1910)

Beyond Human Power

Beerbohm, Max. *Around Theatres.* Elmsford, N.Y.: British Book Centre, 1953, pp. 175–179.

Björkman, Edwin. "Introduction," in *Plays by Björnstjerne Björnson.* Second Series. New York: Scribner's, 1914, pp. 7–9.

Boyesen, Hjalmar Hjorth. *Essays on Scandinavian Literature.* New York: Scribner's, 1895, pp. 81–84.

Downs, Brian W. *Modern Norwegian Literature, 1860–1918.* Cambridge: Cambridge University Press, 1966, pp. 35–37.

Lamm, Martin. *Modern Drama.* Oxford: Basil Blackwell, 1952, pp. 87–93.

Larson, Harold. *Björnstjerne Björnson: A Study in Norwegian Nationalism.* Morningside Heights, N.Y.: King's Crown, 1944, pp. 141–143.

McFarlane, James Walter. *Ibsen and the Temper of Norwegian Literature.* London: Oxford University Press, 1960, pp. 86–87.

Madsen, Borge Gedso. "Björnstjerne Björnson's *Beyond Human Power* and Kaj Munk's *The Word*," in *Modern Drama.* III (May, 1960), pp. 30–36.

WILLIAM BLAKE
(1757–1827)

The Poetry of Blake

Aers, D. "William Blake and the Dialectics of Sex," in *ELH*. XLIV (Fall, 1977), pp. 500–514.

Bentley, Gerald E., Editor. *William Blake: The Critical Heritage.* Boston: Routledge and Kegan Paul, 1975.

_____. *Blake Records.* Oxford: Clarendon Press, 1969.

Bronowski, Jacob. *William Blake and the Age of Revolution.* London: Routledge and Kegan Paul, 1972.

Chayes, I.H. "Blake and the Seasons of the Poet," in *Studies in Romanticism.* XI (Summer, 1972), pp. 225–240.

Damon, Samuel F. *William Blake: His Philosophy and Symbols.* London: Dawsons, 1969.

Erdman, David V. *Blake, Prophet Against Empire: A Poet's Interpretation of the History of His Own Times.* Princeton, N.J.: Princeton University Press, 1969.

Fisher, Peter F. "Blake's Attacks on the Classical Tradition," in *Philological Quarterly.* XL (1961), pp. 1–18.

Frye, Northrop. *Fearful Symmetry: A Study of William Blake.* Princeton, N.J.: Princeton University Press, 1969.

Gilchrist, Alexander. *The Life of William Blake.* New York: Phaeton Press, 1969.

Gleckner, R.F. "Most Holy Forms of Thought: Some Observations on Blake's Language," in *ELH*. XLI (Winter, 1974), pp. 555–577.

Heinzelmann, K. "Blake's Golden Word," in *English Language Notes.* XV (1977), pp. 33–38.

Hirst, Désirée. *Hidden Riches: Traditional Symbolism from the Renaissance to Blake.* New York: Barnes & Noble, 1964.

Lefcowitz, B.F. "Blake and the Natural World," in *PMLA*. LXXXIX (January, 1974), pp. 121–131.

Murray, R. "Blake and the Ideal of Simplicity," in *Studies in Romanticism.* XIII (Spring, 1974), pp. 89–104.

Paley, Morton D., Editor. *William Blake: Essays in Honor of Sir Geoffrey Keynes.* Oxford: Clarendon Press, 1973.

Raine, Kathleen. *Blake and Tradition.* London: Routledge and Kegan Paul, 1969.

————. "Blake's Christ-consciousness," in *Studies in Comparative Religion.* X (Autumn, 1976), pp. 213–218.

Rosenfeld, Alvin H., Editor. *William Blake: Essays for Samuel Foster Damon.* Providence, R.I.: Brown University Press, 1969.

Sutherland, J. "Blake: A Crisis of Love and Jealousy," in *PMLA.* LXXXVII (May, 1972), pp. 424–431.

Wilson, Mona. *The Life of William Blake.* New York: Oxford University Press, 1971.

Witcutt, William D. *Blake: A Psychological Study.* Folcroft, Pa.: Folcroft Library Editions, 1974.

Witke, J. " 'Jerusalem': A Synoptic Poem," in *Comparative Literature.* XXII (Summer, 1970), pp. 265–278.

Wright, Thomas. *The Life of William Blake.* New York: A. Schram, 1972.

ROBERT BLY
(1926–   )

The Light Around the Body

Brownjohn, Alan. "Pre-Beat," in *New Statesman*. LXXVI (August 2, 1968), p. 146.

Carruth, Hayden. "Comment," in *Poetry*. CXII (September, 1968), p. 423.

Davidson, Peter. "New Poetry: The Generation of the Twenties," in *Atlantic*. CCXXI (February, 1968), p. 141.

Goldman, Michael. "Joyful in the Dark," in *New York Times Book Review*. (February 18, 1968), pp. 10, 12.

Heyden, William. "Inward to the World: The Poetry of Robert Bly," in *Far Point*. III (Fall/Winter, 1969), pp. 42–47.

Howard, Richard. *Alone with America: Essays on the Art of Poetry in the United States Since 1950*. New York: Atheneum, 1969, pp. 42–43.

Leibowitz, Herbert. "Questions of Reality," in *Hudson Review*. XXI (Autumn, 1968), pp. 554–557.

Lensing, George S. and Ronald Moran. *Four Poets and the Emotive Imagination: Robert Bly, James Wright, Louis Simpson, and William Stafford*. Baton Rouge: Louisiana State University Press, 1976, pp. 77–80.

Libby, Anthony. "Robert Bly Alive in Darkness," in *Iowa Review*. III (Summer, 1972), pp. 81–89.

Mazzocco, Robert. "Jeremiads at Half-Mast," in *New York Review of Books*. X (June 20, 1968), pp. 22–24.

Mersman, James F. *Out of the Vietnam Vortex: A Study of Poets and Poetry Against the War*. Lawrence: University of Kansas Press, 1974, pp. 121–157.

Simpson, Louis. "New Books of Poems," in *Harper's*. CCXXXVII (August, 1968), p. 74.

Zinnes, Harriet. "Two Languages," in *Prairie Schooner*. XLII (Summer, 1968), pp. 176–178.

Zweig, Paul. "A Sadness for America," in *Nation*. CCVI (March 25, 1968), pp. 418–420.

The Poetry of Bly

Cavich, David. "Poet as Victim and Victimizer," in *New York Times Book Review*. (February 18, 1973), pp. 2–3.

Faas, Ekbert. "Robert Bly," in *Boundary*. IV (1976), pp. 707–726.

Gitzen, Julian. "Floating on Solitude: The Poetry of Robert Bly," in *Modern Poetry Studies.* VII (1976), pp. 231–241.

Heyden, William. "Inward to the World: The Poetry of Robert Bly," in *Far Point.* III (Fall/Winter, 1969), pp. 42–47.

Howard, Richard. *Alone with America: Essays on the Art of Poetry in the United States Since 1950.* New York: Atheneum, 1969, pp. 38–48.

Leibowitz, Herbert. "Questions of Reality," in *Hudson Review.* XXI (Autumn, 1968), pp. 554–557.

Lensing, George S. and Ronald Moran. *Four Poets and the Emotive Imagination: Robert Bly, James Wright, Louis Simpson, and William Stafford.* Baton Rouge: Louisiana State University Press, 1976, pp. 71–85.

Libby, Anthony. "Robert Bly Alive in Darkness," in *Iowa Review.* III (Summer, 1972), pp. 78–89.

Mersman, James F. *Out of the Vietnam Vortex: A Study of Poets and Poetry Against the War.* Lawrence: University of Kansas Press, 1974, pp. 113–157.

Molesworth, Charles. "Thrashing in the Depths: The Poetry of Robert Bly," in *Rocky Mountain Review of Language and Literature.* XXIX (1975), pp. 95–117.

Stepanchev, Stephen. *American Poetry Since 1945.* New York: Harper & Row, 1965, pp. 185–187.

Silence in the Snowy Fields

Gunn, Thom. "Poems and Books of Poems," in *Yale Review.* LIII (October, 1963), pp. 142–144.

Heyden, William. "Inward to the World: The Poetry of Robert Bly," in *Far Point.* III (Fall/Winter, 1969), pp. 42–47.

Howard, Richard. "Poetry Chronicle," in *Poetry.* CII (June, 1963), pp. 184–186.

Hughes, D.J. "The Demands of Poetry," in *Nation.* CXCVI (January 5, 1963), p. 17.

Lensing, George S. and Ronald Moran. *Four Poets and the Emotive Imagination: Robert Bly, James Wright, Louis Simpson, and William Stafford.* Baton Rouge: Louisiana State University Press, 1976, pp. 72–77.

Libby, Anthony. "Robert Bly Alive in Darkness," in *Iowa Review.* III (Summer, 1972), pp. 79–81.

Logan, John. "Poetry Shelf," in *Critic.* XXI (December, 1962–January, 1963), pp. 84–85.

Mersman, James F. *Out of the Vietnam Vortex: A Study of Poets and Poetry Against the War.* Lawrence: University of Kansas Press, 1974, pp. 118–120.

Simmons, Charles.   "Poets in Search of a Public," in *Saturday Review*. XLVI (March 30, 1963), p. 48.

Stepanchev, Stephen.   *"Silence in the Snowy Fields,"* in *New York Herald Tribune Books*. (August 11, 1963), p. 7.

GIOVANNI BOCCACCIO
(1313–1375)

The Decameron

Almansi, Guido. *The Writer as Liar: Narrative Technique in the* Decameron. London: Routledge, 1975.

Brown, Marshall. "In the Valley of the Ladies," in *Italian Quarterly*. XVIII (1975), pp. 33–52.

Chandler, S. Bernard. "Man, Emotion and Intellect in the *Decameron*," in *Philological Quarterly*. XXXIX (October, 1960), pp. 400–412.

Cole, Howard. C. "Dramatic Interplay in the *Decameron*: Boccaccio, Neifile and Giletta di Nerbona," in *Modern Language Notes*. XC (1975), pp. 38–57.

Cottino-Jones, Marga. "Magic and Superstition in Boccaccio's *Decameron*," in *Italian Quarterly*. LXXII (1975), pp. 5–32.

————. "Observations on the Structure of the *Decameron* Novella," in *Romance Notes* (University of North Carolina). XV (1973), pp. 378–387.

Deligiorgis, Stavros. *Narrative Intellection in the* Decameron. Iowa City: University of Iowa Press, 1975.

De Negri, Enrico. "The Legendary Style of the *Decameron*," in *Romanic Review*. XLIII (1952), pp. 166–189.

Downs, Robert Bingham. "Storyteller Supreme: *The Decameron*," in *Famous Books, Ancient and Medieval*. New York: Barnes & Noble, 1964, pp. 303–306.

Ferrante, Joan. "The Frame Characters of the *Decameron*: A Progression of Virtues," in *Romance Philology*. XIX (1965), pp. 212–226.

Hastings, Robert. *Nature and Reason in the* Decameron. (Publications of the Faculty of Arts, University of Manchester, XXI). Manchester, England: Manchester University Press, 1975.

Kern, Edith G. "The Gardens in the *Decameron* Cornice," in *PMLA*. LXVI (June, 1951), pp. 505–523.

Krutch, Joseph Wood. "Boccaccio and His *Decameron*," in *Atlantic*. CXLV (May, 1930), pp. 656–660.

Lipari, Angelo. "The Structure and Real Significance of the *Decameron*," in *Essays in Honor of Albert Feuillerat* (Yale Romanic Studies XXII, 1943), pp. 43–83.

Mazzotta, Giuseppe. "*The Decameron*: The Literal and the Allegorical," in *Italian Quarterly*. LXXII (1975), pp. 53–73.

————. "*The Decameron*: The Marginality of Literature," in *University of Toronto Quarterly*. XLII (1972), pp. 64–81.

Nelson, John Charles. "Love and Sex in the *Decameron*," in *Philosophy and Humanism: Renaissance Essays in Honor of Paul Oskar Kristeller*. New York: Columbia University Press, 1976, pp. 339–351.

Potter, Joy Hambuechen. "Boccaccio as Illusionist: The Plays of Frames in the *Decameron*," in *Humanities Association Review*. XXVI (1975), pp. 327–345.

Schofield, William Henry. "The Source and History of the Seventh Novel of the Seventh Day in the *Decameron*," in *Harvard Studies and Notes in Philology and Literature*. II (1893), pp. 185–212.

Singleton, Charles S. "On 'Meaning' in the *Decameron*," in *Italica*. XXI (September, 1944), pp. 117–124.

Il Filostrato

apRoberts, R. "Notes on *Troilus and Criseyde*, IV, 1397–1414," in *Modern Language Notes*. LVII (1942), pp. 92–97.

Baum, P. "Chaucer's Nautical Metaphors," in *South Atlantic Quarterly*. XLIX (1950), pp. 67–73.

Bloomfield, Morton Wilfred. "The Source of Boccaccio's *Filostrato* III, 74–79 and Its Bearing on the MS Tradition of Lucretius, *De rerum natura*," in *Classical Philology*. XLVII (1952), pp. 162–165.

Clogan, Paul M. "Two Verse Commentaries on the Ending of Boccaccio's *Filostrato*," in *Medievalia et Humanistica* (North Texas State University). VII (1976), pp. 147–152.

Davis, N. "The *Litera Troili* and English Letters," in *Review of English Studies*. XVI (1965), pp. 233–244.

Frank. R.W. "*Troilus and Criseyde*: The Art of Amplification," in *Medieval Literature and Folklore Studies*. Edited by Jerome Mandel and Bruce A. Rosenberg. New Brunswick, N.J.: Rutgers University Press, 1971, pp. 155–171.

Lewis, Clive Staples. "What Chaucer Really Did to *Il Filostrato*," in *Selected Literary Essays*. Edited by Walter Hooper. New York: Cambridge University Press, 1969, pp. 27–44.

Lumiansky, Robert Mayer. "Aspects of the Relationship of Boccaccio's *Il Filostrato* with Benoit's *Roman de Troie* and Chaucer's *Wife of Bath's Tale*," in *Italica*. XXXI (1954), pp. 1–7.

Mizener, Arthur. "Character and Action in the Case of Criseyde," in *PMLA*. LIV (1939), pp. 65–81.

Owen, C. "Significance of a Day in *Troilus and Criseyde*," in *Medieval Studies*. (1960), pp. 366–370.

Roberts, Robert Pigott. "The Boethian God and the Audience of the *Troilus*," in *Journal of English and Germanic Philology*. LXIX (1970), pp. 425–436.

————. "Love in the *Filostrato*," in *Chaucer Review*. VII (1972), pp. 1–26.

Silber, Gordon Rutledge. "Alleged Imitations of Petrarch in the *Filostrato*," in *Modern Philology*. XXXVII (1939/1940), pp. 113–124.

Steadman, John M. "The Age of Troilus," in *Modern Language Notes*. LXXII (1957), pp. 89–90.

Stroud, T. "Boethius' Influence on Chaucer's *Troilus*," in *Modern Philology*. XLIX (1951/1952), pp. 1–9.

Walker, Ian C. "Chaucer and *Il Filostrato*," in *English Studies*. XLIX (1968), pp. 318–326.

Williams, G. "Who Were Troilus, Criseyde, and Pandarus?," in *Rice Institute Pamphlets*. XLIV (1957), pp. 126–129.

L' Amorosa Fiammetta

Coulter, Cornelia C. "Statius, *Silvae*, V, 4 and Fiammetta's Prayer to Sleep," in *American Journal of Philology*. LXXX (1959), pp. 390–395.

Griffin, Robert. "Boccaccio's *Fiammetta*: Pictures at an Exhibition," in *Italian Quarterly*. XVIII (1975), pp. 75–94.

Waley, Pamela. "Fiammetta and Panfilo Continued," in *Italian Studies*. XXIV (1969), pp. 15–31.

————. "The Nurse in Boccaccio's *Fiammetta*: Source and Invention," in *Neophilologus*. LVI (1972), pp. 164–174.

Whitfield, J.H. "Boccaccio and Fiammetta in the *Teseide*," in *Modern Language Review*. XXXIII (1938), pp. 29–30.

La Teseide

Brewer, D. "The Ideal of Feminine Beauty in Medieval Literature, Especially 'Harley Lyrics,' Chaucer, and Some Elizabethans," in *Modern Language Review*. L (1955), pp. 264–266.

Clark, J. "Dante and the Epilogue of *Troilus*," in *Journal of English and Germanic Philology*. L (1951), pp. 1–10.

Haller, R. "*The Knight's Tale* and the Epic Tradition," in *Chaucer Review*. I (1966), pp. 67–84.

Hollander, Robert. "The Validity of Boccaccio's Self-Exegesis in His *Teseida*," in *Medievalia et Humanistica* (North Texas State University). VIII (1977), pp. 147–152.

Kahane, Henry and Renee Kahane. "Akritas and Arcita: A Byzantine Source of Boccaccio's *Teseida*," in *Speculum*. XX (1945), pp. 415–425.

Pratt, Robert Armstrong. "Chaucer's Use of the *Teseida*," in *PMLA*. LXII (1947), pp. 598–621.

————. "Conjectures Regarding Chaucer's Manuscript of the *Teseida*," in *Studies in Philology*. XLII (1945), pp. 745–763.

Samuel, Irene. "Semiramis in the Middle Ages: The History of a Legend," in *Medievalia et Humanistica* (North Texas State University). II (1944), pp. 32–44.

ANICIUS MANLIUS SEVERINUS BOETHIUS
(c.480–524)

The Consolation of Philosophy

Anderson, William. "Boethius: His Influence and Some of His Translators," in *The Consolation of Philosophy*. By Boethius. Carbondale: Southern Illinois University Press, 1963, pp. 7–16.

Barrett, Helen M. *Boethius: Some Aspects of His Times and Work.* Cambridge: Cambridge University Press, 1940.

Burch, George Bosworth. *Early Medieval Philosophy.* New York: King's Crown Press, 1951, pp. 48–49.

Coolidge, J.S. "Boethius and 'That Last Infirmity of Noble Mind,' " in *Philological Quarterly*. XLII (1962), pp. 176–182.

Ebin, L.A. "Boethius, Chaucer, and *The King Is Quair*," in *Philological Quarterly*. LII (1974), pp. 321–341.

Edman, Irwin. "Introduction," in *The Consolation of Philosophy*. By Boethius. New York: Random House, 1943, pp. x–xvi.

Green, Richard. "Translator's Introduction," in *The Consolation of Philosophy*. Indianapolis: Bobbs-Merrill, 1962, pp. ix–xxiii.

Hawkins, D.J.B. *A Sketch of Mediaeval Philosophy.* London: Sheed & Ward, 1946, pp. 17–21.

Hyman, Arthur and James J. Walsh. *Philosophy in the Middle Ages: The Christian, Islamic, and Jewish Traditions.* New York: Harper & Row, 1967, pp. 114–117.

Patch, Howard Rollin. *The Tradition of Boethius.* New York: Oxford University Press, 1935.

Payne, F. Anne. *King Alfred & Boethius: An Analysis of the Old English Version of* The Consolation of Philosophy. Madison: University of Wisconsin Press, 1968.

Roper, A.H. "Boethius and the Three Fates of Beowulf," in *Philological Quarterly*. XLI (1962), pp. 386–400.

Watts, V.E. "Introduction," in *The Consolation of Philosophy*. By Boethius. Baltimore: Penguin, 1969, pp. 7–32.

Wiltshire, S.F. "Boethius and the summum bonum," in *Classical Journal*. LXVII (1972), pp. 216–220.

Wippel, John F. and Allan B. Wolter. *Medieval Philosophy: From St. Augustine to Nicholas of Cusa.* New York: Free Press, 1969, pp. 4–5.

Wulf, Maurice de. *History of Mediaeval Philosophy.* New York: Dover, 1952, pp. 106–114.

MATTEO MARIA BOIARDO
(1440–1494)

Orlando Innamorato

De Sanctis, Francesco. *History of Italian Literature*, Volume I. New York: Harcourt, Brace, 1931, pp. 403–406.

Di Tommaso, Andrea. *Structure and Ideology of Boiardo's* Orlando Innamorato. Chapel Hill: University of North Carolina Press, 1972.

Donadoni, Eugenio. *A History of Italian Literature*, Volume I. New York: New York University Press, 1969, pp. 161–164.

Fletcher, Jefferson Butler. *Literature of the Italian Renaissance*. Port Washington, N.Y.: Kennikat, 1964, pp. 150–164.

Gardner, Edmund G. *The Arthurian Legend in Italian Literature*. London: Dent, 1930, pp. 274–282.

Griffin, Robert. *Ludvico Ariosto*. New York: Twayne, 1974, pp. 53–54, 143–144.

Hall, Robert A., Jr. *A Short History of Italian Literature*. Ithaca, N.Y.: Linguistica, 1951, pp. 170–175.

Luciani, Vincent. *A Brief History of Italian Literature*. New York: S.F. Vanni, 1967, pp. 75–77.

Trail, Florence. *A History of Italian Literature*. Boston: Badger, 1914, pp. 73–75.

Weaver, Elissa Barbara. "Francesco Berni's *Refacimento* of the *Orlando Innamorato*: Why and How," in *Pacific Coast Philology*. X (1975), pp. 53–58.

Whitfield, J.H. *A Short History of Italian Literature*. Westport, Conn.: Greenwood Press, 1976, pp. 129–142.

Wilkins, Ernest Hatch. *A History of Italian Literature*. Cambridge, Mass.: Harvard University Press, 1954, pp. 172–174.

HEINRICH BÖLL
(1917–   )

Acquainted with the Night

Coupe, W.A. "Heinrich Böll's *Acquainted with the Night*—an Analysis," in *German Life and Letters*. XVII (April, 1964), pp. 238–249.

Demetz, Peter. *Postwar German Literature*. New York: Pegasus, 1970, pp. 191–192.

Kurz, Paul Konrad. "Heinrich Böll: Not Reconciled," in *On Modern German Literature, Vol 4*. University: University of Alabama Press, 1977, pp. 3–36.

Moore, Harry T. *Twentieth Century German Literature*. New York: Basic Books, 1967, p. 194.

Waidson, H.M. *Modern German Novel, 1945–1965*. London: Oxford University Press, 1971, p. 111.

————. "The Novels and Stories of Heinrich Böll," in *German Life and Letters*. XII (July, 1959), pp. 267–270.

Ziolkowski, Theodore. "Heinrich Böll: Conscience and Craft," in *Books Abroad*. XXXIV (Summer, 1960), pp. 218–219.

Billiards at Half Past Nine

Bauke, Joseph P. "*Billiards at Half Past Nine*," in *Saturday Review*. XLV (July 28, 1962), p. 39.

Demetz, Peter. *Postwar German Literature*. New York: Pegasus, 1970, pp. 190–191.

Horst, Karl August. *The Quest of Twentieth Century German Literature*. New York: Frederick Ungar, 1971, p. 150.

Kurz, Paul Konrad. "Heinrich Böll: Not Reconciled," in *On Modern German Literature, Vol 4*. University: University of Alabama Press, 1977, pp. 3–36.

Mandel, Siegfried. *Group 47: The Reflected Intellect*. Carbondale: Southern Illinois University Press, 1973, p. 42.

Moore, Harry T. *Twentieth Century German Literature*. New York: Basic Books, 1967, pp. 194–196.

Reid, James R. "*Billiards at Half Past Nine*," in *Modern Language Review*. XLIX (1967), pp. 477–478.

Sokel, Walter. "Perspective and Dualism in the Works of Heinrich Böll," in *The Contemporary Novel in Germany*. Edited by Robert R. Heitner. Austin: University of Texas, 1967, pp. 111–138.

Waidson, H.M. "Billiards at Nine O'Clock," in *German Life and Letters*. London: Oxford University Press, 1960, p. 311.

———. *Modern German Novel, 1945–1965*. London: Oxford University Press, 1971, pp. 112–113.

Yuill, W.E. "Heinrich Böll," in *Essays on Contemporary German Literature, Vol 4.* Edited by Brian Keith-Smith. London: Oswald Wolff, 1966, pp. 145–153.

Ziolkowski, Theodore. *Dimensions of the Modern Novel.* Princeton, N.J.: Princeton University Press, 1969, pp. 337–342.

The Clown

Cook, Bruce. *"The Clown,"* in *Commonweal.* LXXXI (February 12, 1965), pp. 645–646.

Demetz, Peter. *Postwar German Literature.* New York: Pegasus, 1970, pp. 193–194.

Duroche, L.L. "Böll's Clowns in Existentialist Perspective," in *Symposium.* XXV (Winter, 1971), pp. 347–358.

Enright, Dennis J. "Three New Germans," in *Conspirators and Poets.* Chester Springs, Pa.: Dufour, 1966, pp. 190–200.

Kurz, Paul Konrad. "Heinrich Böll: Not Reconciled," in *On Modern German Literature, Vol 4.* University: University of Alabama Press, 1977, pp. 3–36.

Mandel, Siegfried. *Group 47: The Reflected Intellect.* Carbondale: Southern Illinois University Press, 1973, p. 43.

Moore, Harry T. *Twentieth Century German Literature.* New York: Basic Books, 1967, pp. 196–198.

Waidson, H.M. *Modern German Novel, 1945–1965.* London: Oxford University Press, 1971, pp. 113–114.

Yuill, W.E. "Heinrich Böll," in *Essays on Contemporary German Literature, Vol 4.* Edited by Brian Keith-Smith. London: Oswald Wolff, 1966, pp. 146–153.

PHILIP BOOTH
(1925–   )

The Poetry of Booth

Bennett, Joseph. "Voices Three," in *New York Times Book Review*. (April 30, 1967), p. 24.

Carruth, Hayden. "Opposite Methods," in *Poetry*. CIX (March, 1967), pp. 400–401.

Dickey, James. "Neither Maddeningly Genteel Nor Bawling," in *New York Times Book Review*. (December 24, 1961), pp. 4–5.

Donnelly, Dorothy. "Five Poets," in *Poetry*. C (September, 1962), pp. 399–400.

Hazo, Samuel. "*The Islanders*," in *Commonweal*. LXXV (December 22, 1961), pp. 346–347.

O'Connor, William Van. "Recent Contours of the Muse," in *Saturday Review*. XLV (January 6, 1962), p. 70.

Stern, Milton R. "Halfway House: The Poems of Philip Booth," in *Twentieth Century Literature*. IV (January, 1959), pp. 148–153.

JORGE LUIS BORGES
(1899–   )

The Aleph

Alazraki, James. "Kabbalistic Traits in Borges' Narration," in *Studies in Short Fiction*. VIII (1971), pp. 90–92.

Barrenechea, Ana Maria. *Borges, the Labyrinth Maker*. New York: New York University Press, 1965, pp. 19–35.

Christ, Ronald. "Borges Translated," in *Nation*. CCXII (March 1, 1971), pp. 282–284.

Dauster, Frank. "Notes on Borges' Labyrinths," in *Hispanic Review*. XXX (1962), pp. 142–148.

Finn, James. "Fantasist of the Intellect," in *New Republic*. CLXVIII (December 5, 1970), pp. 28–32.

Murillo, L.A. "The Labyrinths of J.L. Borges: An Introduction to the Stories of *El Aleph*," in *Modern Language Quarterly*. XX (1959), pp. 259–266.

Scholes, Robert. "*The Aleph*," in *Saturday Review*. LIV (January 23, 1971), pp. 72–73.

Stabb, Martin S. *Jorge Luis Borges*. New York: Twayne, 1970, pp. 108–111.

Stark, John O. *The Literature of Exhaustion: Borges, Nabokov, and Barth*. Durham, N.C.: Duke University Press, 1974, pp. 34–35.

Wheelock, Carter. *The Mythmaker: A Study of Motif and Symbol in the Short Stories of Jorge Luis Borges*. Austin: University of Texas Press, 1969, pp. 32–39.

"The Approach to Almostasim"

Alazraki, Jaime. "Borges and the Kabbalah," in *Prose for Borges*. Edited by Charles Newman and Mary Kinzie. Evanston, Ill.: Northwestern University Press, 1974, pp. 199–201.

————. "Kabbalistic Traits in Borges' Narration," in *Studies in Short Fiction*. VIII (1971), pp. 83–84.

Christ, Ronald. *The Narrow Act: Borges' Art of Allusion*. New York: New York University Press, 1969, pp. 94–130.

Enguidanos, Miguel. "Imagination and Escape in the Short Stories of Jorge Luis Borges," in *Texas Quarterly*. IV (Winter, 1961), p. 123.

Stabb, Martin S. *Jorge Luis Borges*. New York: Twayne, 1970, pp. 106–208.

Stark, John O. *The Literature of Exhaustion: Borges, Nabokov, and Barth*. Durham, N.C.: Duke University Press, 1974, pp. 23–25.

Wheelock, Carter. *The Mythmaker: A Study of Motif and Symbol in the Short Stories of Jorge Luis Borges.* Austin: University of Texas Press, 1969, pp. 149–153.

"The Babylonian Lottery"

Barrenechea, Ana Maria. *Borges, the Labyrinth Maker.* New York: New York University Press, 1965, pp. 51–53.

Isaacs, Neil D. "The Labyrinth of Art in Four 'Ficciones' of Jorge Luis Borges," in *Studies in Short Fiction.* VI (1969), pp. 383–386.

Lang, Berel. "On Borges: The Compleat Solipsist," in *Columbia Forum.* I (Summer, 1972), pp. 7–9.

Stabb, Martin S. *Jorge Luis Borges.* New York: Twayne, 1970, pp. 115–117.

Stark, John O. *The Literature of Exhaustion: Borges, Nabokov, and Barth.* Durham, N.C.: Duke University Press, 1974, pp. 38–39.

Weber, Frances W. "Borges's Stories: Fiction and Philosophy," in *Hispanic Review.* XXXVI (1968), pp. 130–132.

Wheelock, Carter. *The Mythmaker: A Study of Motif and Symbol in the Short Stories of Jorge Luis Borges.* Austin: University of Texas Press, 1969, pp. 108–119.

Zaniello, Thomas. "Outopia in Jorge Luis Borges' Fiction," in *Extrapolation.* IX (1967), pp. 9–11.

"Death and the Compass"

Alazraki, Jaime. "Borges and the Kabbalah," in *Prose for Borges.* Edited by Charles Newman and Mary Kinzie. Evanston, Ill.: Northwestern University Press, 1974, pp. 185–188.

Murillo, L.A. *The Cyclical Night: Irony in James Joyce and Jorge Luis Borges.* Cambridge, Mass.: Harvard University Press, 1968, pp. 135–184.

Stabb, Martin S. *Jorge Luis Borges.* New York: Twayne, 1970, pp. 125–127.

Stark, John O. *The Literature of Exhaustion: Borges, Nabokov, and Barth.* Durham, N.C.: Duke University Press, 1974, pp. 36–37.

Weber, Frances W. "Borges's Stories: Fiction and Philosophy," in *Hispanic Review.* XXXVI (1968), pp. 135–138.

Wheelock, Carter. *The Mythmaker: A Study of Motif and Symbol in the Short Stories of Jorge Luis Borges.* Austin: University of Texas Press, 1969, pp. 119–121.

Doctor Brodie's Report

Alegria, Fernando. "Blind Master of the Guided Dream," in *Saturday Review.* LV (February 26, 1972), pp. 59–61.

Christ, Ronald. "All Fiction Is Feigning," in *Nation.* CCIV (February 21, 1972), pp. 251–253.

Kretz, Thomas. "*Doctor Brodie's Report,*" in *America.* CXXVI (February 12, 1972), p. 159.

Magliola, Robert. "Jorge Luis Borges and the Loss of Being: Structuralist Themes in *Doctor Brodie's Report,*" in *Studies in Short Fiction.* XV (Winter, 1968), pp. 25–31.

Weeks, Edward. "*Doctor Brodie's Report,*" in *Atlantic.* CCXXIX (February, 1972), p. 107.

Wheelock, Carter. "Borges' New Prose," in *Prose for Borges.* Edited by Charles Newman and Mary Kinzie. Evanston, Ill.: Northwestern University Press, 1974, pp. 361–370.

"Emma Zunz"

Barrenechea, Ana Maria. *Borges, the Labyrinth Maker.* New York: New York University Press, 1965, pp. 141–142.

Lewald, H.E. "The Labyrinth of Time and Place in Two Stories by Borges," in *Hispania.* XLV (1962), pp. 634–635.

Murillo, L.A. *The Cyclical Night: Irony in James Joyce and Jorge Luis Borges.* Cambridge, Mass.: Harvard University Press, 1968, pp. 195–203.

Stabb, Martin S. *Jorge Luis Borges.* New York: Twayne, 1970, pp. 133–134.

Wheelock, Carter. *The Mythmaker: A Study of Motif and Symbol in the Short Stories of Jorge Luis Borges.* Austin: University of Texas Press, 1969, pp. 139–143.

"Funes the Memorious"

Barrenechea, Ana Maria. *Borges, the Labyrinth Maker.* New York: New York University Press, 1965, pp. 42–43.

Hollander, Robert and Sidney E. Lind. *The Art of the Story: An Introduction.* New York: American Book, 1968, pp. 385–387.

Howard, Daniel F. *Manual to Accompany the Modern Tradition: An Anthology of Short Stories.* Boston: Little, Brown, 1972, pp. 28–29.

Kinzie, Mary. "Recursive Prose," in *Prose for Borges.* Edited by Charles Newman and Mary Kinzie. Evanston, Ill.: Northwestern University Press, 1974, pp. 22–32.

Stabb, Martin S. *Jorge Luis Borges.* New York: Twayne, 1970, pp. 94–95.

Wheelock, Carter. *The Mythmaker: A Study of Motif and Symbol in the Short Stories of Jorge Luis Borges.* Austin: University of Texas Press, 1969, pp. 121–122.

The Garden of Forking Paths

Barrenechea, Ana Maria. *Borges, the Labyrinth Maker.* New York: New York University Press, 1965, pp. 14–15.

Isaacs, Neil D. "The Labyrinth of Art in Four 'Ficciones' of Jorge Luis Borges," in *Studies in Short Fiction.* VI (1969), pp. 392–394.

Murillo, L.A. *The Cyclical Night: Irony in James Joyce and Jorge Luis Borges.* Cambridge, Mass.: Harvard University Press, 1968, pp. 135–184.

Weber, Frances W. "Borges's Stories: Fiction and Philosophy," in *Hispanic Review.* XXXVI (1968), pp. 135–138.

Wheelock, Carter. *The Mythmaker: A Study of Motif and Symbol in the Short Stories of Jorge Luis Borges.* Austin: University of Texas Press, 1969, pp. 119–121.

"The Immortal"

Ayora, Jorge. "Gnosticism and Time in *El Immortal,*" in *Hispania.* LVI (1973), pp. 593–596.

Barrenechea, Ana Maria. *Borges, the Labyrinth Maker.* New York: New York University Press, 1965, pp. 58–61.

Christ, Ronald. *The Narrow Act: Borges' Art of Allusion.* New York: New York University Press, 1969, pp. 192–228.

Murillo, L.A. *The Cyclical Night: Irony in James Joyce and Jorge Luis Borges.* Cambridge, Mass.: Harvard University Press, 1968, pp. 215–242.

Stabb, Martin S. *Jorge Luis Borges.* New York: Twayne, 1970, pp. 129–132.

Stark, John O. *The Literature of Exhaustion: Borges, Nabokov, and Barth.* Durham, N.C.: Duke University Press, 1974, pp. 40–41, 44–46.

Weber, Frances W. "Borges's Stories: Fiction and Philosophy," in *Hispanic Review.* XXXVI (1968), pp. 132–135.

Wheelock, Carter. *The Mythmaker: A Study of Motif and Symbol in the Short Stories of Jorge Luis Borges.* Austin: University of Texas Press, 1969, pp. 129–134.

"The Library of Babel"

Barrenechea, Ana Maria. *Borges, the Labyrinth Maker.* New York: New York University Press, 1965, pp. 44–48.

Garzilli, Enrico. *Circle Without a Center.* Cambridge, Mass.: Harvard University Press, 1972, pp. 101–102.

Huck, Wilbur and William Shanahan. *The Modern Short Story.* New York: American Book, 1968, pp. 115–116.

Isaacs, Neil D. "The Labyrinth of Art in Four 'Ficciones' of Jorge Luis Borges," in *Studies in Short Fiction.* VI (1969), pp. 386–387.

Stabb, Martin S. *Jorge Luis Borges.* New York: Twayne, 1970, pp. 112–115.

Stark, John O. *The Literature of Exhaustion: Borges, Nabokov, and Barth.* Durham, N.C.: Duke University Press, 1974, pp. 38–40, 45–46.

Wheelock, Carter. *The Mythmaker: A Study of Motif and Symbol in the Short Stories of Jorge Luis Borges.* Austin: University of Texas Press, 1969, pp. 158–160.

Zaniello, Thomas. "Outopia in Jorge Luis Borges' Fiction," in *Extrapolation.* IX (1967), pp. 11–13.

"Theme of the Traitor and the Hero"

Barrenechea, Ana Maria. *Borges, the Labyrinth Maker.* New York: New York University Press, 1965, pp. 33–34.

Scholes, Robert. *Elements of Fiction.* New York: Oxford University Press, 1968, pp. 83–88.

Stabb, Martin S. *Jorge Luis Borges.* New York: Twayne, 1970, pp. 118–119.

Wheelock, Carter. *The Mythmaker: A Study of Motif and Symbol in the Short Stories of Jorge Luis Borges.* Austin: University of Texas Press, 1969, pp. 173–174.

Whiston, J. "An 'Irish' Story of Jorge Luis Borges: 'Tema del traidor y del heroe,' " in *Hermathena.* CXIV (1972), pp. 23–28.

"Tlon, Uqbar, Orbis Tertius"

Barrenechea, Ana Maria. *Borges, the Labyrinth Maker.* New York: New York University Press, 1965, pp. 123–124.

Brivic, Sheldon. "Borges' *Orbis Tertius,*" in *Massachusetts Review.* XVI (1975), pp. 387–399.

Caviglia, John. "The Tales of Borges: Language and the Private Eye," in *Modern Language Notes.* LXXXIX (March, 1974), pp. 219–231.

Enguidanos, Miguel. "Imagination and Escape in the Short Stories of Jorge Luis Borges," in *Texas Quarterly.* IV (Winter, 1961), pp 121–123.

Harss, Luis and Barbara Dohmann. *Into the Mainstream.* New York: Harper & Row, 1967, pp. 125–126.

Irby, James E. "Borges and the Idea of Utopia," in *The Cardinal Points of Borges.* Edited by Lowell Dunham and Ivar Ivask. Norman: University of Oklahoma Press, 1971, pp. 35–45.

Isaacs, Neil D. "The Labyrinth of Art in Four 'Ficciones' of Borges," in *Studies in Short Fiction.* VI (1969), pp. 387–392.

Lewald, H.E. "The Labyrinth of Time and Place in Two Stories of Borges," in *Hispania.* XLV (1962), p. 631.

Littlejohn, David. "The Anti-Realists," in *Daedalus.* XCII (1963), p. 255.

Mills, R.S. "The Theme of Scepticism in Borges' 'Tlon, Uqbar, Orbis Tertius,' " in *Studies in Modern Spanish Literature and Art, Presented to Helen F. Grant.* Edited by Nigel Glendinning. London: Tamesis, 1972, pp. 127–138.

Stabb, Martin S. *Jorge Luis Borges.* New York: Twayne, 1970, pp. 100–106.

Stark, John O. *The Literature of Exhaustion: Borges, Nabokov, and Barth.* Durham, N.C.: Duke University Press, 1974, pp. 12–15, 26–29, 43–44.

Weber, Frances W. "Borges's Stories: Fiction and Philosophy," in *Hispanic Review.* XXXVII (1968), pp. 127–130.

Wheelock, Carter. *The Mythmaker: A Study of Motif and Symbol in the Short Stories of Jorge Luis Borges.* Austin: University of Texas Press, 1969, pp. 93–98.

Wright, John. "Borges and Hawthorne," in *Prose for Borges.* Edited by Charles Newman and Mary Kinzie. Evanston, Ill.: Northwestern University Press, 1974, pp. 296–299.

Zaniello, Thomas. "Outopia in Jorge Luis Borges' Fiction," in *Extrapolation.* IX (1967), pp. 13–15.

Zlotchew, Clark M. *"Tlon,* Llhuros, N. Daly and J.L. Borges," in *Modern Fiction Studies.* XIX (1973), pp. 453–460.

"The Writing of the Lord" ("The God's Script")

Alazraki, James. "Kabbalistic Traits in Borges' Narration," in *Studies in Short Fiction.* VIII (1971), pp. 86–87.

Belitt, Ben. "The Enigmatic Predicament: Some Parables of Kafka and Borges," in *Prose for Borges.* Edited by Charles Newman and Mary Kinzie. Evanston, Ill.: Northwestern University Press, 1974, pp. 231–237.

Enguidanos, Miguel. "Imagination and Escape in the Short Stories of Jorge Luis Borges," in *Texas Quarterly.* IV (Winter, 1961), p. 124.

Monegal, Emir Rodriguez. "Borges: The Reader as Writer," in *Prose for Borges.* Edited by Charles Newman and Mary Kinzie. Evanston, Ill.: Northwestern University Press, 1974, pp. 116–119.

Murillo, L.A. "The Labyrinths of Jorge Luis Borges: An Introduction to the Stories of *El Aleph,*" in *Modern Language Quarterly.* XX (1959), pp. 264–266. Reprinted in *The Cyclical Night: Irony in James Joyce and Jorge Luis Borges.* Edited by L.A. Murillo. Cambridge, Mass.: Harvard University Press, 1968, pp. 203–213.

Sosnowski, Saul. " 'The God's Script' — A Kabbalistic Quest," in *Modern Fiction Studies.* XIX (1973), pp. 381–394.

Wheelock, Carter. *The Mythmaker: A Study of Motif and Symbol in the Short Stories of Jorge Luis Borges.* Austin: University of Texas Press, 1969, pp. 32–39.

JAMES BOSWELL
(1740–1795)

The Life of Samuel Johnson, LL.D.

Alkon, Paul K. "Boswell's Control of Aesthetic Distance," in *University of Toronto Quarterly*. XXXVIII (January, 1969), pp. 174–191. Reprinted in *Twentieth Century Interpretations of Boswell's* Life of Johnson: *A Collection of Critical Essays*. Edited by James L. Clifford. Englewood Cliffs, N.J.: Prentice-Hall, 1970, pp. 51–65.

Altick, Richard D. "Johnson and Boswell," in *Lives and Letters*. New York: Knopf, 1965, pp. 60–70. Reprinted in *Twentieth Century Interpretations of Boswell's* Life of Johnson: *A Collection of Critical Essays*. Edited by James L. Clifford. Englewood Cliffs, N.J.: Prentice-Hall, 1970, pp. 104–111.

Bronson, Bertrand H. "Boswell's Boswell," in *Johnson Agonistes and Other Essays*. Cambridge: Cambridge University Press, 1946, pp. 53–99.

Brooks, A. Russell. *James Boswell*. New York: Twayne, 1971, pp. 83–125.

Carlyle, Thomas. "Boswell's *Life of Johnson*," in *Critical and Miscellaneous Essays, Volume II*. London: Chapman and Hall, 1888, pp. 49–104. Reprinted in *Macaulay's and Carlyle's Essays on Samuel Johnson*. Edited by William Strunk, Jr. New York: Henry Holt, 1895, pp. 65–158.

Chapman, R.W. "The Making of the *Life of Johnson*," in *Johnsonian and Other Essays and Reviews*. Oxford: Clarendon Press, 1953, pp. 20–36.

Clifford, James L. "Introduction," in *Twentieth Century Interpretations of Boswell's* Life of Johnson: *A Collection of Critical Essays*. Edited by James L. Clifford. Englewood Cliffs, N.J.: Prentice-Hall, 1970, pp. 1–26.

Collins, P.A.W. *James Boswell: Writers and Their Works*. London: Longmans, Green, 1956, pp. 28–37.

Edel, Leon. *Literary Biography*. Toronto: University of Toronto Press, 1957, pp. 13–20.

Fussell, Paul, Jr. "The Memorable Scenes of Mr. Boswell," in *Encounter*. XXVIII (May, 1967), pp. 70–77.

Gow, A.S.F. "The Unknown Johnson," in *Twentieth Century Interpretations of Boswell's* Life of Johnson: *A Collection of Critical Essays*. Edited by James L. Clifford. Englewood Cliffs, N.J.: Prentice-Hall, 1970, pp. 79–89.

Greene, Donald J. "Reflections on a Literary Anniversary," in *Queen's Quarterly*. LXX (Summer, 1963), pp. 198–208. Partly reprinted in *Twentieth Century Interpretations of Boswell's* Life of Johnson: *A Collection of Critical Essays*. Edited by James L. Clifford. Englewood Cliffs, N.J.: Prentice-Hall, 1970, pp. 97–103.

Hart, Francis R. "Boswell and the Romantics, A Chapter in the History of Biographical Theory," in *Journal of English Literary History.* XXVII (March, 1960), pp. 44–65.

Lewis, L.B. Wyndham. *The Hooded Hawk or the Case of Mr. Boswell.* New York: Longmans, Green, 1947, pp. 189–251.

Longaker, John Mark. "Boswell's *Life of Johnson,*" in *English Biography in the Eighteenth Century.* Philadelphia: University of Pennsylvania Press, 1931, pp. 407–476.

Mallory, George. *Boswell the Biographer.* London: Smith, Elder, 1912, pp. 227–326.

Nicolson, Harold. "The Boswell Formula, 1791," in *The Development of English Biography.* London: Hogarth Press, 1927, pp. 87–108. Reprinted in *Twentieth Century Interpretations of Boswell's* Life of Johnson: *A Collection of Critical Essays.* Edited by James L. Clifford. Englewood Cliffs, N.J.: Prentice-Hall, 1970, pp. 74–78.

Pottle, Frederick A. "The *Life of Johnson:* Art and Authenticity," in *Twentieth Century Interpretations of Boswell's* Life of Johnson: *A Collection of Critical Essays.* Edited by James L. Clifford. Englewood Cliffs, N.J.: Prentice-Hall, 1970, pp. 66–73.

Rader, Ralph W. "Literary Form in Factual Narrative: The Example of Boswell's *Johnson,*" in *Essays in Eighteenth Century Biography.* Edited by Philip B. Daghlian. Bloomington: Indiana University Press, 1968, pp. 3–42.

Reid, B.L. "Johnson's Life of Boswell," in *Kenyon Review.* XVIII (Autumn, 1956), pp. 546–575. Reprinted in *The Long Boy.* Athens: University of Georgia Press, 1969, pp. 1–30.

Siebenschuh, William R. *Form and Purpose in Boswell's Biographical Works.* Berkeley: University of California Press, 1972, pp. 51–77.

Stauffer, Donald R. "The Great Names," in *The Art of Biography in Eighteenth Century England.* Princeton, N.J.: Princeton University Press, 1941, pp. 411–455.

Tinker, Chauncey Brewster. *Young Boswell: Chapters on James Boswell the Biographer.* Boston: Atlantic Monthly Press, 1922, pp. 220–238.

Waingrow, Marshall. "Boswell's Johnson," in *The Correspondence and Other Papers of James Boswell Relating to the Making of the Life of Johnson.* Edited by Marshall Waingrow. New York: McGraw-Hill, 1969, pp. xliv–1. Reprinted in *Twentieth Century Interpretations of James Boswell's* Life of Johnson: *A Collection of Critical Essays.* Edited by James L. Clifford. Englewood Cliffs, N.J.: Prentice-Hall, 1970, pp. 45–50.

Wimsatt, William K., Jr. "James Boswell: The Man and the Journal," in *Yale Review.* XLIX (Autumn, 1959), pp. 80–92. Reprinted (revised) as "The Fact Imagined: James Boswell," in *Hateful Contraries.* Lexington: University of Kentucky Press, 1965, pp. 165–183.

VANCE BOURJAILY
(1922–   )

Brill Among the Ruins

Kelly, James. "*Brill Among the Ruins*," in *Saturday Review.* LIII (December 5, 1970), p. 40.

Towner, Daniel. "Brill's Ruins and Henderson's Rain," in *Critique: Studies in Modern Fiction.* XVII (1976), pp. 96–104.

Weeks, Edward. "*Brill Among the Ruins*," in *Atlantic.* CCXXVII (January, 1971), pp. 103–104.

Confessions of a Spent Youth

Adams, Phoebe. "No Heights, No Depths," in *Atlantic.* CCVII (January, 1961), pp. 156–157.

Bourjaily, Vance. "A Certain Kind of Work," in *Afterwords: Novelists on Their Novels.* Edited by Thomas McCormack. New York: Harper & Row, 1969, pp. 177–191.

Curley, Thomas. "One Man's Story," in *Commonweal.* LXXIII (March 17, 1961), pp. 641–643.

Davis, Janice. "The Materialism of Vance Bourjaily," in *New Republic.* CXLIII (December 19, 1960), pp. 17–18.

Dienstfrey, Harris. "The Novels of Vance Bourjaily," in *Commentary.* XXXI (April, 1961), pp. 360–363.

Hicks, Granville. "The Average Sinner," in *Saturday Review.* XLIII (November 19, 1960), p. 24.

Muste, John M. "The Fractional Man as Hero: Bourjaily's *Confessions of a Spent Youth*," in *Critique: Studies in Modern Fiction.* XVII (1976), pp. 73–85.

————. "The Second Major Subwar: Four Novels by Vance Bourjaily," in *The Shaken Realist.* Edited by Melvin J. Friedman and John B. Vickery. Baton Rouge: Louisiana State University Press, 1970, pp. 323–326.

The End of My Life

Aldridge, John W. *After the Lost Generation.* New York: McGraw-Hill, 1951, pp. 121–132.

Bourjaily, Vance. "Vance Bourjaily," in *Talks with Authors.* Edited by Charles F. Madden. Carbondale: Southern Illinois University Press, 1968, pp. 201–214.

DeLancey, Robert W. "Man and Mankind in the Novels of Vance Bourjaily," in *English Record.* X (Winter, 1959), pp. 3–4.

Eisinger, Chester E.	*Fiction of the Forties.* Chicago: University of Chicago Press, 1963, pp. 28–29.

Miller, Merle.	"One for the Money," in *Saturday Review of Literature.* XXX (August 30, 1947), p. 17.

Muste, John M.	"The Second Major Subwar: Four Novels by Vance Bourjaily," in *The Shaken Realist.* Edited by Melvin J. Friedman and John B. Vickery. Baton Rouge: Louisiana State University Press, 1970, pp. 313–315.

The Violated

Adams, Phoebe.	"Neurotics Unlimited," in *Atlantic.* CCII (October, 1958), pp. 90–91.

Finn, James.	"A True Realist," in *Commonweal.* LXVIII (August 29, 1958), pp. 550–551.

Hicks, Granville.	"The Maturity of Vance Bourjaily," in *Saturday Review.* XLI (August 23, 1958), p. 13.

Howe, Irving.	"Novels of the Post-War World," in *New Republic.* CXXXIX (November 10, 1958), p. 17.

Muste, John M.	"The Second Major Subwar: Four Novels by Vance Bourjaily," in *The Shaken Realist.* Edited by Melvin J. Friedman and John B. Vickery. Baton Rouge: Louisiana State University Press, 1970, pp. 319–323.

ELIZABETH BOWEN
(1899–1973)

The Death of the Heart

Blodgett, Harriet. "The Great Hero: *The Death of the Heart*," in her *Patterns of Reality: Elizabeth Bowen's Novels*. The Hague: Mouton, 1975, pp. 114–153.

Bowen, Elizabeth. *Why Do I Write? An Exchange of Views*. London: Percival Marshall, 1948.

Brooke, Jocelyn. *Elizabeth Bowen*. London: Longmans, 1952.

Brown, Spencer Curtis. "Foreword," in Elizabeth Bowen's *Pictures and Conversations*. New York: Knopf, 1975, pp. vii–xlii.

Coles, Robert. "Youth: Elizabeth Bowen's *The Death of the Heart*," in his *Irony in the Mind's Life*. Charlottesville: University Press of Virginia, 1974, pp. 107–153.

Daiches, David. "The Novels of Elizabeth Bowen," in *English Journal*. XXXVIII (June, 1949), pp. 305–313.

Glendinning, Victoria. *Elizabeth Bowen: Portrait of a Writer*. New York: Knopf, 1978.

Hardwick, Elizabeth. "Elizabeth Bowen's Fiction," in *Partisan Review*. XVI (November, 1949), pp. 1114–1121.

Harkness, Bruce. "The Fiction of Elizabeth Bowen," in *English Journal*. XLIV (December, 1955), pp. 499–506.

Heath, William W. *Elizabeth Bowen: An Introduction to Her Novels*. Madison: University of Wisconsin Press, 1961.

Heinemann, Alison. "The Indoor Landscape in Bowen's *The Death of the Heart*," in *Critique*. X (Winter, 1968), pp. 5–12.

Kenney, Edwin J. *Elizabeth Bowen*. Lewisburg, Pa.: Bucknell University Press, 1975.

Parrish, Paul A. "Loss of Eden: Four Novels of Elizabeth Bowen," in *Critique*. XV (1973), pp. 86–100.

Sharp, Mary Corona. "The House as Setting and Symbol in Three Novels by Elizabeth Bowen," in *Xavier University Studies*. II (December, 1963), pp. 93–103.

Sullivan, W. "Sense of Place: Elizabeth Bowen and the Landscape of the Heart," in *Sewanee Review*. LXXXIV (Winter, 1976), pp. 142–149.

Van Duyn, Mona. "Pattern and Pilgrimage: A Reading of *The Death of the Heart*," in *Critique*. IV (Spring, 1961), pp. 52–66.

Wagner, Geoffrey. "Elizabeth Bowen and the Artificial Novel," in *Essays in Criticism.* XIII (April, 1963), pp. 155–163.

Williams, Raymond. "Realism and the Contemporary Novel," in *Partisan Review.* XXVI (Spring, 1959), pp. 200–213.

The Heat of the Day

Blodgett, Harriet. "Creatures of History: *The Heat of the Day,*" in her *Patterns of Reality: Elizabeth Bowen's Novels.* The Hague: Mouton, 1975, pp. 154–189.

Bowen, Elizabeth. *Why Do I Write? An Exchange of Views.* London: Percival Marshall, 1948.

Brooke, Jocelyn. *Elizabeth Bowen.* London: Longmans, 1952.

Brown, Spencer Curtis. "Foreword," in Elizabeth Bowen's *Pictures and Conversations.* New York: Knopf, 1975, pp. vii–xlii.

Daiches, David. "The Novels of Elizabeth Bowen," in *English Journal.* XXXVIII (June, 1949), pp. 305–313.

Dorenkamp, Angela G. "Fall or Leap: Bowen's *The Heat of the Day,*" in *Critique.* X (Winter, 1968), pp. 13–21.

Glendinning, Victoria. *Elizabeth Bowen: Portrait of a Writer.* New York: Knopf, 1978.

Hardwick, Elizabeth. "Elizabeth Bowen's Fiction," in *Partisan Review.* XVI (November, 1949), pp. 1114–1121.

Harkness, Bruce. "The Fiction of Elizabeth Bowen," in *English Journal.* XLIV (December, 1955), pp. 499–506.

Heath, William W. *Elizabeth Bowen: An Introduction to Her Novels.* Madison: University of Wisconsin Press, 1961.

Kenney, Edwin J. *Elizabeth Bowen.* Lewisburg, Pa.: Bucknell University Press, 1975.

Rupp, Richard H. "The Postwar Fiction of Elizabeth Bowen," in *Xavier University Studies.* IV (March, 1965), pp. 55–67.

Wagner, Geoffrey. "Elizabeth Bowen and the Artificial Novel," in *Essays in Criticism.* XIII (April, 1963), pp. 155–163.

Williams, Raymond. "Realism and the Contemporary Novel," in *Partisan Review.* XXVI (Spring, 1959), pp. 200–213.

The House in Paris

Blodgett, Harriet. "The Necessary Child: *The House in Paris,*" in her *Patterns of Reality: Elizabeth Bowen's Novels.* The Hague: Mouton, 1975, pp. 84–113.

Bowen, Elizabeth. *Why Do I Write? An Exchange of Views.* London: Percival Marshall, 1948.

Brooke, Jocelyn. *Elizabeth Bowen.* London: Longmans, 1952.

Brown, Spencer Curtis. "Foreword," in Elizabeth Bowen's *Pictures and Conversations.* New York: Knopf, 1975, pp. vii–xlii.

Daiches, David. "The Novels of Elizabeth Bowen," in *English Journal.* XXXVIII (June, 1949), pp. 305–313.

Glendinning, Victoria. *Elizabeth Bowen: Portrait of a Writer.* New York: Knopf, 1978.

Hardwick, Elizabeth. "Elizabeth Bowen's Fiction," in *Partisan Review.* XVI (November, 1949), pp. 1114–1121.

Harkness, Bruce. "The Fiction of Elizabeth Bowen," in *English Journal.* XLIV (December, 1955), pp. 499–506.

Heath, William W. *Elizabeth Bowen: An Introduction to Her Novels.* Madison: University of Wisconsin Press, 1961.

Kenney, Edwin J. *Elizabeth Bowen.* Lewisburg, Pa.: Bucknell University Press, 1975.

Parrish, Paul A. "Loss of Eden: Four Novels of Elizabeth Bowen," in *Critique.* XV (1973), pp. 86–100.

Sharp, Mary Corona. "The House as Setting and Symbol in Three Novels by Elizabeth Bowen," in *Xavier University Studies.* II (December, 1963), pp. 93–103.

Wagner, Geoffrey. "Elizabeth Bowen and the Artificial Novel," in *Essays in Criticism.* XIII (April, 1963), pp. 155–163.

Williams, Raymond. "Realism and the Contemporary Novel," in *Partisan Review.* XXVI (Spring, 1959), pp. 200–213.

PAUL BOWLES
(1911–   )

Let It Come Down

Eisinger, Chester E. "Paul Bowles and the Passionate Pursuit of Disengagement," in his *Fiction of the Forties*. Chicago: University of Chicago Press, 1963, pp. 283–288.

Evans, Oliver. "Paul Bowles and the 'Natural' Man," in *Critique*. III (1959), pp. 50–53. Reprinted in *Recent American Fiction*. Edited by Joseph J. Waldmeir. Boston: Houghton Mifflin, 1963, pp. 145–148.

Glicksberg, Charles I. "The Literary Struggle for Selfhood," in *Person*. XLII (January, 1961), pp. 62–63.

————. "Literature and the Meaning of Life," in *South Atlantic Quarterly*. LV (April, 1956), pp. 157–158.

Hassan, Ihab H. "The Pilgrim as Prey: A Note on Paul Bowles," in *Western Review*. XIX (Autumn, 1954), pp. 28–30. Reprinted in *Radical Innocence: Studies in the Contemporary American Novel*. Princeton, N.J.: Princeton University Press, 1961, pp. 87–88.

Lehan, Richard. "Existentialism in Recent American Fiction: The Demonic Quest," in *Texas Studies in Literature and Language*. I (Summer, 1959), pp. 185–186.

Stewart, Lawrence D. *Paul Bowles: The Illumination of North Africa*. Carbondale: Southern Illinois University Press, 1974, pp. 87–98.

Sheltering Sky

Aldridge, John W. "Paul Bowles: The Canceled Ship," in his *After the Lost Generation: A Critical Study of the Writers of Two Wars*. New York: McGraw-Hill, 1951, pp. 186–193.

Allen, Walter. *The Modern Novel in Britain and the United States*. New York: Dutton, 1964, pp. 300–301.

Eisinger, Chester E. "Paul Bowles and the Passionate Pursuit of Disengagement," in his *Fiction of the Forties*. Chicago: University of Chicago Press, 1963, pp. 283–288.

Evans, Oliver. "Paul Bowles and the 'Natural' Man," in *Critique*. III (1959), pp. 45–48. Reprinted in *Recent American Fiction*. Edited by Joseph J. Waldmeir. Boston: Houghton Mifflin, 1963, pp. 141–143.

Glicksberg, Charles L. *Literature and Religion: A Study in Conflict*. Dallas: Southern Methodist University Press, 1960, pp. 183–184.

Hassan, Ihab H. "The Pilgrim as Prey: A Note on Paul Bowles," in *Western Review*. XIX (Autumn, 1954), pp. 25–27. Reprinted in his *Radical Inno-

cence: Studies in the Contemporary American Novel. Princeton, N.J.: Princeton University Press, 1961, pp. 86–87.

Joost, Nicholas. "Was All for Naught? Robert Penn Warren and New Directions in the Novel," in *Fifty Years of the American Novel: A Christian Appraisal.* Edited by Harold C. Gardiner. New York: Scribner's, 1951, pp. 286–287.

Lehan, Richard. "Existentialism in Recent American Fiction: The Demonic Quest," in *Texas Studies in Literature and Language.* I (Summer, 1959), pp. 184–185.

Moffitt, Cecil L. "Paul Bowles' *Sheltering Sky* and Arabia," in *Research Studies.* XLII (1974), pp. 44–49.

Prescott, Orville. *In My Opinion: An Inquiry into the Contemporary Novel.* Indianapolis, Ind.: Bobbs-Merrill, 1952, pp. 116–117.

Solotaroff, Theodore. "Paul Bowles: The Desert Within," in *The Red Hot Vacuum, and Other Pieces on the Writing of the Sixties.* New York: Atheneum, 1970, pp. 254–260.

Stewart, Lawrence D. *Paul Bowles: The Illumination of North Africa.* Carbondale: Southern Illinois University Press, 1974, pp. 47–74.

Straumann, Heinrich. *American Literature in the Twentieth Century.* New York: Harper & Row, 1965, pp. 79–80.

HUGH HENRY BRACKENRIDGE
(1748–1816)

Modern Chivalry

Brennecke, Ernest. "Introduction," in *Modern Chivalry*. New York: Greenberg, 1926, p. xviii.

Cowie, Alexander. "Early Satire and Realism: Hugh Henry Brackenridge," in *The Rise of the American Novel*. New York: American Book Company, 1948, pp. 43–60.

Hemenway, Robert. "Fiction in the Age of Jefferson: The Early American Novel as Intellectual Document," in *Midcontinent American Studies Journal*. IX (Spring, 1968), pp. 91–102.

Marder, Daniel. *Hugh Henry Brackenridge*. New York: Twayne, 1967, pp. 83–98.

Nance, William L. "Satiric Elements in Brackenridge's *Modern Chivalry*," in *Texas Studies in Literature and Language*. IX (Autumn, 1967), pp. 381–389.

Newlin, Claude M. "Introduction," in *Modern Chivalry*. By Hugh Henry Brackenridge. New York: American Books, 1937, p. xiv.

Spiller, Robert. *Literary History of the United States*. New York: Macmillan, 1957, pp. 178–180.

Trent, William. *Cambridge History of American Literature*, Volume I. New York: G.P. Putnam, 1917, p. 186.

Van Doren, Carl. *The American Novel*. New York: Macmillan, 1922, pp. 4–6.

Wagenknecht, Edward. *Cavalcade of the American Novel*. New York: Holt, 1952, pp. 6–9.

WILLIAM BRADFORD
(1590–1657)

Of Plimouth Plantation

Bowden, Edwin T. *The Dungeon of the Heart: Human Isolation and the American Novel.* New York: Macmillan, 1961, pp. 1–19.

Bradford, E.F. "Conscious Art in Bradford's *History of Plymouth Plantation*," in *New England Quarterly.* I (1928), pp. 133–157.

Daly, Robert. "William Bradford's Vision of History," in *American Literature.* XLIV (1973), pp. 557–569.

Fritscher, John J. "The Sensibility and Conscious Style of William Bradford," in *Bucknell Review.* XVII (1969), pp. 80–89.

Gay, Peter. *A Loss of Mastery: Puritan Historians in Colonial America.* Berkeley: University of California Press, 1966, pp. 26–52.

Grabo, Norman S. "William Bradford: *Of Plymouth Plantation*," in *Landmarks of American Writing.* Edited by Hennig Cohen. New York: Basic Books, 1969, pp. 3–19.

Griffith, John. "*Of Plymouth Plantation* as a Mercantile Epic," in *Arizona Quarterly.* XXVIII (Autumn, 1972), pp. 231–242.

Hovey, Kenneth A. "The Theology of History in *Of Plymouth Plantation* and Its Predecessors," in *Early American Literature.* X (Spring, 1975), pp. 47–66.

Howard, Alan B. "Art and History in Bradford's *Of Plymouth Plantation*," in *William and Mary Quarterly.* XXVIII (1971), pp. 237–266.

Kraus, Michael. *The Writing of American History.* Norman: University of Oklahoma Press, 1953, pp. 14, 17–18, 20–24.

Levin, David. "William Bradford: The Value of Puritan Historiography," in *Major Writers of Early American Literature.* Edited by Everett Emerson. Madison: University of Wisconsin Press, 1972, pp. 11–32.

Major, Minor W. "William Bradford Versus Thomas Morton," in *Early American Literature.* V (1970), pp. 1–13.

Morison, Samuel E. "Introduction," in *Of Plymouth Plantation.* By William Bradford. New York: Knopf, 1952, pp. 3–11.

Murdock, Kenneth B. *Literature and Theology in Colonial New England.* Cambridge, Mass.: Harvard University Press, 1949, pp. 78–84.

Rosenmeier, Jesper. " 'With my owne eyes,' " in *The American Puritan Imagination.* Edited by Sacvan Bercovitch. New York: Cambridge University Press, 1974, pp. 77–106.

Scheick, William J. "The Theme of Necessity in Bradford's *Of Plymouth Plantation*," in *Seventeenth-Century News*. XXXII (Winter, 1974), pp. 88–90.

Seelye, John. *Prophetic Waters: The River in Early American Life and Literature*. New York: Oxford University Press, 1977, pp. 90–91, 107–108, 217–252.

Smith, Bradford E. *Bradford of Plymouth*. Philadelphia: Lippincott, 1951.

Westbrook, Perry D. *William Bradford*. Boston: Twayne, 1978.

JOHN BRAINE
(1922–   )

Room at the Top

Allsop, Kenneth. *The Angry Decade: A Survey of the Cultural Revolt of the Nineteen-fifties.* New York: British Book Centre, 1958, pp. 78–85.

Braine, John. "The Penalty of Being at the Top," in *John O'London's.* III (January, 1963), pp. 21, 23.

Fraser, G.S. *The Modern Writer and His World: Continuity and Innovation in Twentieth Century English Literature.* New York: Praeger, 1964, pp. 181–182.

Hurrell, John. "Class and Consciousness in John Braine and Kingsley Amis," in *Critique: Studies in Modern Fiction.* II (1958), pp. 39–53.

Karl, Frederick R. *The Contemporary English Novel.* New York: Farrar, Straus, 1962, pp. 229–230.

Lee, James W. *John Braine.* New York: Twayne, 1968, pp. 52–68.

Shestakov, Dmitri. "John Braine Facing His Fourth Novel," in *Soviet Literature.* VIII (1964), pp. 178–181.

Taylor, Archer. "John Braine's Proverbs," in *Western Folklore.* XXIII (1964), pp. 42–43.

Whannel, Paddy. "*Room at the Top,*" in *Universities and Left Review.* VI (Spring, 1959), pp. 21–24.

BERTOLT BRECHT
(1898–1956)

Baal

Bentley, Eric Russell. "Bertolt Brecht's First Play," in *Kenyon Review*. XXVI (Winter, 1964), pp. 83–92.

————. *Theatre of War: Comments on Thirty-two Occasions*. New York: Viking, 1972, pp. 123–130.

Blumberg, Phillip. "The Crisis of Association: Brecht's *Baal*," in *Yale/Theatre*. VI (1975), pp. 45–50.

Clurman, Harold. *The Naked Image; Observations on the Modern Theatre*. New York: Macmillan, 1966, pp. 181–184.

Epstein, Leslie. "Beyond the Baroque: The Role of the Audience in the Modern Theater," in *Tri-Quarterly*. XII (Spring, 1968), pp. 213–224.

Heller, P. "Nihilist into Activist: Two Phases in the Development of Bertolt Brecht," in *Germanic Review*. XXVIII (1953), pp. 144–155.

Hill, Claude. *Bertolt Brecht*. New York: Twayne, 1975, pp. 42–45.

Lyons, Charles R. *Bertolt Brecht; The Despair and the Polemic,* Carbondale: Southern Illinois University Press, 1968, pp. 3–24.

————. "Bertolt Brecht's *Baal*: The Structure of Images," in *Modern Drama*. VIII (December, 1965), pp. 311–323.

Matthews, Honor. *The Primal Curse: The Myth of Cain and Abel in the Theatre*. New York: Schocken, 1967, pp. 184–186.

Steer, W. "*Baal*: A Key to Brecht's Communism," in *German Life and Letters*. XIX (1965/1966), pp. 40–51.

Wealls, Gerald C. "Brecht and the Drama of Ideas," in *Ideas in the Drama*. Edited by John Gassner. New York: Columbia University Press, 1964, pp. 135–139.

The Caucasian Chalk Circle

Alter, M. "The Technique of Alienation in Bertolt Brecht's *Caucasian Chalk Circle*," in *College Language Association Journal*. VIII (September, 1964), pp. 60–65.

Bentley, Eric Russell. *Theatre of War: Comments on Thirty-two Occasions*. New York: Viking, 1972, pp. 172–182.

————. "Un-American Chalk Circle?," in *Tulane Drama Review*. X (1966), pp. 64–77.

Brustein, Robert Sanford. *The Theatre of Revolt; An Approach to the Modern Drama*. Boston: Little, Brown, 1964, pp. 255–276.

————. *The Third Theatre.* New York: Knopf, 1969, pp. 169–173.

Bunge, Hans. "The Dispute over the Valley," in *Tulane Drama Review.* IV (December, 1959), pp. 50–66.

Cohn, Ruby. *Currents of Contemporary Drama.* Bloomington: Indiana University Press, 1969, pp. 204–207.

Demetz, Peter, Editor. *Brecht; A Collection of Critical Essays.* Englewood Cliffs, N.J.: Prentice-Hall, 1962, pp. 151–156.

Fuegi, John. "Toward a Theory of Dramatic Literature for a Technological Age," in *Educational Theatre Journal.* XXVI (1974), pp. 433–440.

Gaskell, Ronald. *Drama and Reality: The European Theatre Since Ibsen.* London: Routledge and Kegan Paul, 1972, pp. 139–146.

————. "Form of *The Caucasian Chalk Circle,*" in *Modern Drama.* X (1967), pp. 195–201.

Kernodle, George R. *Invitation to the Theatre.* New York: Holt, Rinehart and Winston, 1967, pp. 48–53.

Kerr, Walter. *Thirty Plays Hath November; Pain and Pleasure in the Contemporary Theater.* New York: Simon and Schuster, 1969, pp. 277–283.

Ludowyk, E. "The Chalk Circle: A Legend in Four Centuries," in *Comparative Literature.* I (1960), pp. 249–256.

Lumley, Frederick. *New Trends in Twentieth Century Drama; A Survey Since Ibsen and Shaw.* New York: Oxford University Press, 1967, pp. 80–90.

Lyons, Charles R. *Bertolt Brecht; The Despair and the Polemic.* Carbondale: Southern Illinois University Press, 1968, pp. 132–154.

Marinello, L. "The Christian Side of Brecht? An Examination of the *Caucasian Chalk Circle,*" in *Drama Critique.* IV (May, 1961), pp. 77–86.

Mueller, G.H.S. "The Narrator in Brecht's *Der Kaukasische Kreidekreis,*" in *Furman Studies.* XXI (1974), pp. 41–46.

Politzer, H. "How Epic is Brecht's Epic Theater?," in *Modern Language Quarterly.* XXIII (1962), pp. 104–110.

Read, Malcolm. "Brecht, Klabund and the *Chalk Circle,*" in *Modern Languages.* LIII (1972), pp. 28–32.

Sagar, K.M. "Brecht in Neverneverland: *The Caucasian Chalk Circle,*" in *Modern Drama.* IX (1966), pp. 11–17.

Steer, W. "Brecht's Epic Theater," in *Modern Language Review.* LXIII (1968), pp. 636–649.

————. "The Thematic Unity of Brecht's *Der Kaukasische Kreidekreis,*" in *German Life and Letters.* XXI (1967), pp. 1–10.

Tynan, Kenneth. *Curtains; Selections from the Drama Criticism and Related Writings.* New York: Atheneum, 1961, pp. 452–454.

The Good Woman of Setzuan

Bentley, Eric Russell. "From Strindberg to Bertolt Brecht," in *Theatre and Drama in the Making*. Edited by John Gassner. Boston: Houghton Mifflin, 1964, pp. 774–775.

Cowell, Raymond. *Twelve Modern Dramatists*. London: Pergamon, 1967, pp. 79–81.

Esslin, M. "Brecht: Some Comments on Eleanor Hakim's Communication," in *Studies on the Left*. II (1961), pp. 77–78.

Freedman, Morris. *The Moral Impulse; Modern Drama from Ibsen to the Present*. Carbondale: Southern Illinois University Press, 1967, pp. 99–114.

Gassner, John. *Dramatic Soundings; Evaluations and Retractions Culled from Thirty Years of Dramatic Criticism*. New York: Crown, 1968, pp. 217–218.

_____. *Theatre at the Crossroads; Plays and Playwrights of the Midcentury American Stage*. New York: Holt, Rinehart and Winston, 1960, pp. 264–270.

Grossvogel, David I. *Four Playwrights and a Postscript: Brecht, Ionesco, Beckett and Genet*. Ithaca, N.Y.: Cornell University Press, 1962, pp. 22–25.

Hakim, Eleanor. "Brecht: A World Without Achilles," in *Studies on the Left*. II (1961), pp. 62–63.

Hill, Claude. *Bertolt Brecht*. New York: Twayne, 1975, pp. 121–126.

Lewis, Allan. *The Contemporary Theatre; The Significant Playwrights of Our Time*. New York: Crown, 1962, pp. 218–242.

Loomis, E.R. "A Re-interpretation of Bertolt Brecht," in *University of Kansas City Review*. XXVII (1960), pp. 51–56.

Lumley, Frederick. *New Trends in Twentieth Century Drama; A Survey Since Ibsen and Shaw*. New York: Oxford University Press, 1967, pp. 80–90.

Mews, Siegfried and Herbert Knust. *Essays on Brecht: Theater and Politics*. Chapel Hill: University of North Carolina Press, 1974, pp. 190–196.

Milnes, H. "The Concept of Man in Bertolt Brecht," in *Toronto Quarterly*. XXXII (April, 1963), pp. 222–223.

Nicol, Bernard de Bear. *Varieties of Dramatic Experience*. London: University of London Press, 1969, pp. 210–214.

Rippley, La Vern J. "Parody in Brecht's *Good Woman*," in *Germanic Notes*. I (1970), pp. 58–61.

Smiley, Sam. *Playwriting: The Structure of Action*. Englewood Cliffs, N.J.: Prentice-Hall, 1971, pp. 88–103.

Solem, D. "Brecht's Theatre," in *Hopkins Review*. III (Summer, 1949), pp. 74–76.

Sprinchorn, E.   "The Cruel World of Bertolt Brecht," in *Columbia University Forum*. IV (Fall, 1961), p. 46.

Tynan, Kenneth.   *Curtains; Selections from the Drama Criticism and Related Writings*. New York: Atheneum, 1961, pp. 146–148.

Williams, Raymond.   "The Achievement of Brecht," in *Critical Quarterly*. III (Summer, 1961), pp. 156–157.

————.   *Modern Tragedy*. Stanford, Calif.: Stanford University Press, 1966, pp. 196–198.

The Life of Galileo

Bentley, Eric Russell.   *Theatre of War: Comments on Thirty-two Occasions*. New York: Viking, 1972, pp. 146–164.

Berckman, Edward M.   "Brecht's *Galileo* and the Openness of History," in *Modernist Studies: Literature and Culture, 1920–1940*. I (1974), pp. 41–50.

Chiari, J.   *Landmarks of Contemporary Drama*. London: Herbert Jenkins, 1965, pp. 161–183.

Cohen, M.A.   "History and Moral in Brecht's *The Life of Galileo*," in *Contemporary Literature*. XI (1970), pp. 80–97.

Cohn, Ruby.   *Currents in Contemporary Drama*. Bloomington: Indiana University Press, (1969), pp. 117–120.

Demetz, Peter, Editor.   *Brecht; A Collection of Critical Essays*. Englewood Cliffs, N.J.: Prentice-Hall, 1962, pp. 117–126.

————.   "*Galileo* in East Berlin: Notes on Drama in the DDR," in *German Quarterly*. XXXVII (1964), pp. 239–245.

Fuegi, John.   "Toward a Theory of Dramatic Literature for a Technological Age," in *Educational Theatre Journal*. XXVI (1974), pp. 433–440.

Grossvogel, David I.   *Four Playwrights and a Postscript: Brecht, Ionesco, Beckett, and Genet*. Ithaca, N.Y.: Cornell University Press, 1962, pp. 39–42.

Hill, Claude.   *Bertolt Brecht*. New York: Twayne, 1975, pp. 112–121.

Losey, J.   "The Individual Eye," in *Encore*. VIII (March, 1961), pp. 5–15.

Lumley, Frederick.   *New Trends in Twentieth Century Drama; A Survey Since Ibsen and Shaw*. New York: Oxford University Press, 1967, pp. 80–90.

Lyons, Charles R.   *Bertolt Brecht; The Despair and the Polemic*. Carbondale: Southern Illinois University Press, 1968, pp. 110–131.

————.   "*The Life of Galileo*: The Focus of Ambiguity in the Villain Hero," in *Germanic Review*. XLI (1966), pp. 57–71.

Mews, Siegfried and Herbert Knust.   *Essays on Brecht: Theater and Politics*. Chapel Hill: University of North Carolina Press, 1974, pp. 174–189.

Milnes, H. "The Concept of Man in Bertolt Brecht," in *Toronto Quarterly.* XXXII (April, 1963), pp. 225–226.

Schumacher, Ernst. "The Dialectics of *Galileo*," in *Tulane Drama Review.* XII (1968), pp. 124–133.

Sorensen, Otto M. "Brecht's *Galileo*: Its Development from Ideotional into Ideological Theater," in *Modern Drama.* XI (1969), pp. 410–422.

Sprinchorn, E. "The Cruel World of Bertolt Brecht," in *Columbia University Forum.* IV (Fall, 1961), pp. 45–56.

Stern, Guy. "The Plight of the Exile: A Hidden Theme in Brecht's *Galileo Galilei*," in *Brecht Heute—Brecht Today.* I (1971), pp. 110–116.

White, Alfred D. "Brecht's *Leben des Galilei*: Armchair Theatre?," in *German Life and Letters.* XXVII (1974), pp. 124–132.

Williams, Raymond. "The Achievement of Brecht," in *Critical Quarterly.* III (Summer, 1961), pp. 159–161.

————. *Modern Tragedy.* Stanford, Calif.: Stanford University Press, 1966, pp. 199–202.

A Man's a Man

Baxandall, L. "*A Man's a Man*," in *Encore.* IX (November/December, 1962), pp. 17–21.

Bentley, Eric Russell. "On Brecht's *A Man's a Man*," in *Brecht; A Collection of Critical Essays.* Edited by Peter Demetz. Englewood Cliffs, N.J.: Prentice-Hall, 1961, pp. 53–57.

Brustein, Robert. *Seasons of Discontent: Dramatic Opinions 1959–1965.* New York: Simon and Schuster, 1965, pp. 71–74.

Clurman, Harold. *The Naked Image; Observations on the Modern Theatre.* New York: Macmillan, 1966, pp. 58–61.

Douglas, Mary. *Witchcraft, Confessions and Accusations.* New York: Barnes & Noble, 1970, pp. 18–199.

Gilman, Richard. *Common and Uncommon Masks: Writings on the Theatre, 1961–1970.* New York: Random House, 1971, pp. 49–53.

Grossvogel, David I. *Four Playwrights and a Postscript: Brecht, Ionesco, Beckett and Genet.* Ithaca, N.Y.: Cornell University Press, 1962, pp. 21–38.

Hakim, Eleanor. "Brecht: A World Without Achilles," in *Studies on the Left.* II (1961), pp. 69–70.

Hill, Claude. *Bertolt Brecht.* New York: Twayne, 1975, pp. 53–55.

Lyons, Charles R. *Bertolt Brecht; The Despair and the Polemic.* Carbondale: Southern Illinois University Press, 1968, pp. 45–67.

Mews, Siegfried and Herbert Knust. *Essays on Brecht: Theater and Politics.* Chapel Hill: University of North Carolina Press, 1974, pp. 99–113.

Shaw, Leroy Robert. *The Playwright and Historical Change; Dramatic Strategies in Brecht, Hauptmann, Kaiser, and Wedekind.* Madison: University of Wisconsin Press, 1970, pp. 117–168.

Thompson, L. "Bert Brecht," in *Kenyon Review.* II (Summer, 1940), pp. 322–323.

Weales, Gerald Clifford. "Brecht and the Drama of Ideas," in *Ideas in the Drama.* Edited by John Gassner. New York: Columbia University Press, 1964, pp. 125–135.

Mother Courage and Her Children

Bentley, Eric Russell. "The Songs in *Mother Courage*," in *Varieties of Literary Experience.* V (1963), pp. 45–74.

———. *Theatre of War: Comments on Thirty-two Occasions.* New York: Viking, 1972, pp. 165–171.

Blau, Herbert. "Brecht's *Mother Courage*: The Rite of War and the Rhythm of Epic," in *Educational Theatre Journal.* IX (1957), pp. 1–10.

Bostock, A. "*Mother Courage* in the Cold War," in *Encore.* VII (January/ February, 1960), pp. 35–38.

Brustein, Robert Sanford. "Brecht Against Brecht," in *Partisan Review.* XXX (Spring, 1963), pp. 45–53.

———. *The Theatre of Revolt; An Approach to the Modern Drama.* Boston: Little, Brown, 1964, pp. 267–276.

Burnshaw, Stanley. *Varieties of Literary Experience; Eighteen Essays in World Literature.* New York: New York University Press, 1962, pp. 45–62.

Chiari, J. *Landmarks of Contemporary Drama.* London: Herbert Jenkins, 1965, pp. 161–183.

Clurman, Harold. *The Divine Pastime; Theatre Essays.* New York: Macmillan, 1974, pp. 125–133.

Dickson, Keith. "Brecht: An Aristotelian 'Malgre Lui,' " in *Modern Drama.* XI (1968), pp. 111–121.

Dort, B. "Epic Form in Brecht's Theater," in *Yale/Theater.* I (Summer, 1968), pp. 29–32.

Fuegi, John. "Toward a Theory of Dramatic Literature for a Technological Age," in *Educational Theatre Journal.* XXVI (1974), pp. 433–440.

Glade, Henry. "The Death of Mother Courage," in *Tulane Drama Review.* XII (1967), pp. 137–148.

Gray, Ronald. "Brecht's *Mother Courage*," in *Oxford Review.* II (1966), pp. 44–45.

———. "*Mother Courage*," in *Cambridge Review.* LXXVIII (1956), pp. 43–45.

Hiller, R. "The Symbolism of Gestus in Brecht's Drama," in *Myth and Symbol; Critical Approaches and Applications.* Edited by Bernice Slote. Lincoln: University of Nebraska Press, 1963, pp. 97–100.

Himelstein, M. "The Pioneers of Bertolt Brecht in America," in *Modern Drama.* IX (1966/1967), pp. 182–189.

Lumley, Frederick. *New Trends in Twentieth Century Drama; A Survey Since Ibsen and Shaw.* New York: Oxford University Press, 1967, pp. 80–90.

Lyons, Charles R. *Bertolt Brecht; The Despair and the Polemic.* Carbondale: Southern Illinois University Press, 1968, pp. 89–109.

Mennemier, F. "Modern Courage," in *Brecht; A Collection of Critical Essays.* Edited by Peter Demetz. Englewood Cliffs, N.J.: Prentice-Hall, 1962, pp. 138–150.

Skelton, G. "Bertolt Brecht's *Mutter Courage*," in *World Review.* XXIII (January, 1951), pp. 65–67.

Speidel, E. "The Mute Person's Voice: Mutter Courage and Her Daughter," in *German Life and Letters.* XXIII (1970), pp. 332–339.

Steer, W. "Brecht's Epic Theater," in *Modern Language Review.* LXIII (1968), pp. 636–649.

Tynan, Kenneth. *Curtains; Selections from the Drama Criticism and Related Writings.* New York: Atheneum, 1961, pp. 99–101, 452–454.

Woodland, Ronald S. "The Danger of Empathy in *Mother Courage*," in *Modern Drama.* XV (1972), pp. 125–129.

Resistible Rise of Arturo Ui

Benn, M. "Bert Brecht's Hitler: The *Resistible Rise of Arturo Ui*," in *Journal of the Australasian Universities Language and Literature Association.* XI (September, 1959), pp. 48–55.

Beyerchen, Alan D. "The Basis for Political Dictatorship as Revealed in Three Works of Bertolt Brecht," in *German Life and Letters.* XXV (1971/1972), pp. 354–359.

Brustein, Robert. *The Third Theatre.* New York: Knopf, 1969, pp. 131–140.

Clurman, Harold. *The Naked Image; Observations on the Modern Theatre.* New York: Macmillan, 1966, pp. 64–66.

Gilman, Richard. *Common and Uncommon Masks: Writings on the Theatre, 1961–1970.* New York: Random House, 1971, pp. 46–48.

Hecht, W. "Remarks on Brecht," in *Theatre Research.* VIII (1967), pp. 173–174.

Kott, Jan. *Theatre Notebook; 1947–1967.* Garden City, N.Y.: Doubleday, 1968, pp. 108–110.

Ruland, R. "The American Plays of Bertolt Brecht," in *American Quarterly.* XV (Fall, 1963), pp. 386–389.

Saint Joan of the Stockyards

Barlow, D. "The Saint Joan Theme in Modern German Drama," in *German Life and Letters.* XVII (April, 1964), pp. 253–255.

Bentley, Eric Russell. *From the Modern Repertoire, Series Three.* Bloomington: Indiana University Press, 1956, pp. 522–524.

Cook, B. "Bertolt Brecht and the Dialectical Joans," in *Catholic World.* CXCVI (January, 1963), pp. 251–253.

Demetz, Peter, Editor. *Brecht; A Collection of Critical Essays.* Englewood Cliffs, N.J.: Prentice-Hall, 1962, pp. 51–58.

Dukore, Bernard F. and Daniel C. Gerould. "Explosions and Implosions; Avant-Garde Drama Between World Wars," in *Educational Theatre Journal.* XXI (March, 1969), pp. 1–16.

Eickhorst, W. "Recent German Treatments of the Joan of Arc Theme," in *Arizona Quarterly.* XVII (Winter, 1961), pp. 326–329.

Hakim, Eleanor. "A World Without Achilles Revisited," in *Studies on the Left.* II (1961), pp. 86–87.

Hill, Claude. *Bertolt Brecht.* New York: Twayne, 1975, pp. 70–76.

Mews, Siegfried and Herbert Knust. *Essays on Brecht: Theater and Politics.* Chapel Hill: University of North Carolina Press, 1974, pp. 114–140.

Ruland, R. "The American Plays of Bertolt Brecht," in *American Quarterly.* XV (Fall, 1963), pp. 381–384.

Sainer, Arthur. *The Sleepwalker and the Assassin.* New York: Bridgehead Books, 1964, pp. 111–113.

Taylor, J. "*St. Joan of the Stockyards,*" in *Encore.* XI (July/August, 1964), pp. 44–47.

Weintraub, S. "Bertolt Brecht's Barbara-Joan," in *Shaw Review.* IV (September, 1961), pp. 30–31.

The Three-penny Opera

Bauland, Peter. *The Hooded Eagle; Modern German Drama on the New York Stage.* Syracuse, N.Y.: Syracuse University Press, 1968, pp. 180–183.

Bentley, Eric Russell. *From the Modern Repertoire, Series One.* Bloomington: Indiana University Press, 1949, pp. 391–400.

Brustein, Robert Sanford. *The Theatre of Revolt; An Approach to the Modern Drama.* Boston: Little, Brown, 1964, pp. 259–267.

————. *The Third Theatre.* New York: Knopf, 1969, pp. 131–140.

Clurman, H. *Lies Like Truth.* New York: Macmillan, 1958, pp. 113–115.

Diller, E. "Human Dignity in Materialistic Society," in *Modern Language Quarterly.* XXII (1961), pp. 451–460.

Dort, B. "Epic Form in Brecht's Theater," in *Yale/Theater*. I (Summer, 1968), pp. 26–27.

Dukore, Bernard F. "The Averted Crucifixion of Macheath," in *Drama Survey*. IV (1965), pp. 51–56.

Grossvogel, David I. *Four Playwrights and a Postscript: Brecht, Ionesco, Beckett and Genet*. Ithaca, N.Y.: Cornell University Press, 1962, pp. 25–44.

Harper, A. "Brecht and Villon: Further Thoughts on Some *Dreigroschenoper* Songs," in *Forum for Modern Language Studies*. I (1965), pp. 191–194.

Hill, Claude. *Bertolt Brecht*. New York: Twayne, 1975, pp. 55–59.

Himelstein, M. "The Pioneers of Bertolt Brecht in America," in *Modern Drama*. IX (1966/1967), pp. 178–182.

Lumley, Frederick. *New Trends in Twentieth Century Drama; A Survey Since Ibsen and Shaw*. New York: Oxford University Press, 1967, pp. 80–90.

Marx, Robert. "The Operatic Brecht," in *American Scholar*. XLIV (1974/1975), pp. 283–290.

Milnes, H. "The Concept of Man in Bertolt Brecht," in *Toronto Quarterly*. XXXII (April, 1963), pp. 219–221.

Nicholson, H.A. *Voyage to Wonderland*. London: Heinemann, 1947, pp. 77–91.

Politzer, H. "How Epic is Brecht's Epic Theater?," in *Modern Language Quarterly*. XXIII (1962), pp. 103–104.

Salomon, G. "Happy Ending, Nice and Tidy," in *Kenyon Review*. XXIV (Summer, 1962), pp. 542–551.

Sherwin, Judith Johnson. " 'The World Is Mean and Man Uncouth,' " in *Virginia Quarterly Review*. XXXV (1959), pp. 258–270.

Sonnenfeld, A. "The Function of Brecht's Eclecticism," in *Books Abroad*. XXXVI (1962), pp. 134–138.

Swados, Harvey. *A Radical's America*. Boston: Little, Brown, 1962, pp. 184–190.

Thompson, L. "Bert Brecht," in *Kenyon Review*. II (Summer, 1940), pp. 324–326.

Weisstein, Ulrich. "Brecht's Victorian Version of Gay: Imitation and Originality in the *Dreigroschenoper*," in *Comparative Literature Studies*. VII (1970), pp. 314–335.

Williams, Raymond. "Achievement of Brecht," in *Critical Quarterly*. III (Summer, 1961), pp. 154–156.

————. *Modern Tragedy*. Stanford, Calif.: Stanford University Press, 1966, pp. 191–195.

ANNE BRONTË
(1820–1849)

Agnes Grey

Bentley, Phyllis. *The Brontës.* New York: Haskell House, 1975, pp. 104–107.

Calder, Jenni. *Women and Marriage in Victorian Fiction.* New York: Oxford University Press, 1976, pp. 30–31, 34, 57, 58.

Craik, W.A. *The Brontë Novels.* London: Methuen, 1968, pp. 202–227.

Gerin, Winifred. *Anne Brontë.* London: Thomas Nelson, 1959, pp. 125–127, 230–233.

Hale, Will T. *Anne Brontë: Her Life and Writings.* Folcraft, Pa.: Folcraft, 1929.

Halperin, John and Janet Kunert. *Plots and Characters in the Fiction of Jane Austen, the Brontës, and George Eliot.* Hamden, Conn.: Shoe String Press, 1976.

Harrison, Ada and Derek Stanford. *Anne Brontë: Her Life and Work.* London: Methuen, 1959, pp. 223–245.

Pinion, F.B. *A Brontë Companion: Literary Assessment, Background, and Reference.* London: Macmillan, 1975.

The Tenant of Wildfell Hall

Andrews, Sir Linton. "A Challenge by Anne Brontë," in *Brontë Society Transactions.* XIV (1965), pp. 25–30.

Bell, A. Craig. "Anne Brontë; A Re-Appraisal," in *Quarterly Review.* CCCIV (July, 1966), pp. 315–321.

Bentley, Phyllis. *The Brontës.* New York: Haskell House, 1975, pp. 107–109.

Ekeblad, Inga-Stina. "*The Tenant of Wildfell Hall* and *Women Beware Women,*" in *Notes and Queries.* X (1963), pp. 449–450.

Gerin, Winifred. *Anne Brontë.* London: Thomas Nelson, 1959, pp. 235–258.

Hale, Will T. *Anne Brontë: Her Life and Writings.* Folcraft, Pa.: Folcraft, 1929.

Halperin, John and Janet Kunert. *Plots and Characters in the Fiction of Jane Austen, the Brontës, and George Eliot.* Hamden, Conn.: Shoe String Press, 1976.

Hannah, Barbara. *Striving Towards Wholeness.* New York: Putnam's, 1971, pp. 177–189.

Harrison, Ada and Derek Stanford. *Anne Brontë: Her Life and Work.* London: Methuen, 1959, pp. 223–245.

Meier, T.K.   "*The Tenant of Wildfell Hall*: Morality as Art," in *Revue des Langues Vivantes*. XXXIX (1973), pp. 59–62.

Mews, Hazel.   *Frail Vessels: Woman's Role in Women's Novels from Fanny Burney to George Eliot*. London: Athlone, 1969, pp. 135–139.

Pinion, F.B.   *A Brontë Companion: Literary Assessment, Background, and Reference*. London: Macmillan, 1975.

CHARLOTTE BRONTË
(1816–1855)

Jane Eyre

Aldrich, John W., Margaret Webster and Lyman Bryson. *"Jane Eyre,"* in *Invitation to Learning: English and American Novels.* Edited by George D. Crothers. New York: Basic Books, 1966, pp. 109–117.

Beer, Patricia. *Reader, I Married Him: A Study of the Women Characters of Jane Austen, Charlotte Brontë, Elizabeth Gaskell and George Eliot.* London: Macmillan, 1974, pp. 86–126.

Benvenuto, Richard. "The Child of Nature, the Child of Grace, and the Unresolved Conflict of *Jane Eyre,"* in *Journal of English Literary History.* XXXIX (1972), pp. 620–638.

Blom, M.A. *"Jane Eyre:* Mind as Law unto Itself?," in *Criticism.* XV (1973), pp. 350–364.

Craik, W.A. *The Brontë Novels.* London: Methuen, 1968, pp. 70–122.

Day, Martin S. "Central Concepts of *Jane Eyre,"* in *Personalist.* XLI (Autumn, 1960), pp. 495–505.

Dunn, Richard J. Jane Eyre*: An Authoritative Text, Backgrounds, and Criticism.* New York: Norton, 1972.

Gribble, Jennifer. "Jane Eyre's Imagination," in *Nineteenth-Century Fiction.* XXIII (December, 1968), pp. 279–293.

Karl, Frederick R. *An Age of Fiction; The Nineteenth Century British Novel.* New York: Farrar, Straus and Giroux, 1964, pp. 77–103.

Knies, Earl A. *The Art of Charlotte Brontë.* Athens: Ohio University Press, 1969, pp. 171–184, 204–211.

Kramer, Dale. "Thematic Structure in *Jane Eyre,"* in *Papers on Language and Literature.* IV (1968), pp. 288–298.

Langford, Thomas A. "Prophetic Imagination and the Unity of *Jane Eyre,"* in *Studies in the Novel.* VI (1974), pp. 228–235.

Lodge, David. *Language of Fiction; Essays in Criticism and Verbal Analysis of the English Novel.* New York: Columbia University Press, 1966, pp. 114–143.

O'Neill, Judith. *Critics on Charlotte and Emily Brontë; Readings in Literary Criticism.* Coral Gables, Fla.: University of Miami Press, 1968, pp. 25–31.

Pell, Nancy. "Resistance, Rebellion and Marriage: The Economics of *Jane Eyre,"* in *Nineteenth-Century Fiction.* XXXI (March, 1977), pp. 397–430.

Pinion, F.B. *A Brontë Companion: Literary Assessment, Background, and Reference.* London: Macmillan, 1975.

Riley, Michael. "Gothic Melodrama and Spiritual Romance: Vision and Fidelity in Two Versions of *Jane Eyre,*" in *Literature/Film Quarterly.* III (1975), pp. 145–159.

Sherry, Norman. *Charlotte and Emily Brontë.* London: Evans, 1969, pp. 51–70.

Siebenschuh, William R. "The Image of the Child and the Plot of *Jane Eyre,*" in *Studies in the Novel.* VIII (1976), pp. 304–317.

Solomon, Eric. "*Jane Eyre*: Fire and Water," in *College English.* XXV (December, 1963), pp. 211–217.

Tillotson, Kathleen M. *Novels of the Eighteen-Forties.* London: Oxford University Press, 1961, pp. 257–313.

Williams, Raymond. *The English Novel: From Dickens to Lawrence.* London: Chatto and Windus, 1970, pp. 60–74.

Wilson, F.A.C. "The Primrose Wreath: The Heroes of the Brontë Novels," in *Nineteenth-Century Fiction.* XXIX (1974), pp. 42–46.

Yeazell, Ruth B. "More True Than Real: Jane Eyre's 'Mysterious Summons,' " in *Nineteenth-Century Fiction.* XXIX (1974), pp. 127–143.

Yuen, Maria. "Two Crises of Decision in *Jane Eyre,*" in *English Studies.* LVII (1976), pp. 215–226.

The Professor

Beer, Patricia. *Reader, I Married Him: A Study of the Women Characters of Jane Austen, Charlotte Brontë, Elizabeth Gaskell and George Eliot.* London: Macmillan, 1974, pp. 101–105.

Bentley, Phyllis. *The Brontës.* New York: Haskell House, 1975, pp. 60–64.

Burkhart, Charles. *Charlotte Brontë: A Psychosexual Study of Her Novels.* London: Gollancz, 1973, pp. 45–62.

Craik, W.A. *The Brontë Novels.* London: Methuen, 1968, pp. 48–69.

Gerin, Winifred. *Anne Brontë.* London: Thomas Nelson, 1959, pp. 224–227.

Halperin, John and Janet Kunert. *Plots and Characters in the Fiction of Jane Austen, the Brontës, and George Eliot.* Hamden, Conn.: Shoe String Press, 1976.

Knies, Earl A. *The Art of Charlotte Brontë.* Athens: Ohio University Press, 1969, pp. 88–98.

Kooiman-Van Middendorp, Gerarda M. *The Hero in the Feminine Novel.* New York: Haskell House, 1966, pp. 60–78.

Mews, Hazel. *Frail Vessels: Woman's Role in Women's Novels from Fanny Burney to George Eliot.* London: Athlone, 1969, pp. 73–75.

Pinion, F.B. *A Brontë Companion: Literary Assessment, Background, and Reference.* London: Macmillan, 1975.

Sherry, Norman. *Charlotte and Emily Brontë.* London: Evans, 1969, pp. 41–50.

Tillotson, Geoffrey. *A View of Victorian Literature.* Oxford: Clarendon Press, 1978, pp. 188, 196, 199–200.

Wheeler, Michael D. "Literary and Biblical Allusion in *The Professor*," in *Brontë Society Transactions.* XVII (1976), pp. 46–57.

Wilson, F.A.C. "The Primrose Wreath: The Heroes of the Brontë Novels," in *Nineteenth-Century Fiction.* XXIX (1974), pp. 46–47.

Shirley

Beer, Patricia. *Reader, I Married Him: A Study of the Women Characters of Jane Austen, Charlotte Brontë, Elizabeth Gaskell and George Eliot.* London: Macmillan, 1974, pp. 84–124.

Bentley, Phyllis. *The Brontës.* New York: Haskell House, 1975, pp. 69–75.

————. *The English Regional Novel.* New York: Haskell House, 1966, pp. 14–17.

Briggs, Asa. "Private and Social Themes in *Shirley*," in *Brontë Society Transactions.* XIII (1958), pp. 203–219.

Burkhart, Charles. *Charlotte Brontë: A Psychosexual Study of Her Novels.* London: Gollancz, 1973, pp. 78–95.

Cazamian, Louis. *The Social Novel in England, 1830–1850: Dickens, Mrs. Gaskell, Kingsley.* Translated by Martin Fido. London: Routledge and Kegan Paul, 1973, pp. 232–235.

Craik, W.A. *The Brontë Novels.* London: Methuen, 1968, pp. 123–157.

Eagleton, Terry. "Class, Power and Charlotte Brontë," in *Critical Quarterly.* XIV (1972), pp. 225–235.

Grayson, Laura. "*Shirley*: Charlotte Brontë's Own Evidence," in *Brontë Society Transactions.* XIV (1963), p. 31.

Holgate, Ivy. "The Structure of *Shirley*," in *Brontë Society Transactions.* XIV (1962), pp. 27–35.

Jeffares, A. Norman. "*Shirley*—A Yorkshire Novel," in *Brontë Society Transactions.* XV (1969), pp. 281–293.

Knies, Earl A. *The Art of Charlotte Brontë.* Athens: Ohio University Press, 1969, pp. 144–167.

Kooiman-Van Middendorp, Gerarda M. *The Hero in the Feminine Novel.* New York: Haskell House, 1966, pp. 60–78.

Korg, Jacob. "The Problem of Unity in *Shirley*," in *Nineteenth-Century Fiction.* XII (1957), pp. 125–136.

Kroeber, Karl. *Styles in Fictional Structure: The Art of Jane Austen, Charlotte Brontë, George Eliot.* Princeton, N.J.: Princeton University Press, 1971, pp. 89–94, 109–112, 151–180.

Mews, Hazel. *Frail Vessels: Woman's Role in Women's Novels from Fanny Burney to George Eliot.* London: Athlone, 1969, pp. 75–77, 184–185.

O'Neill, Judith. *Critics on Charlotte and Emily Brontë: Readings in Literary Criticism.* Coral Gables, Fla.: University of Miami Press, 1968, pp. 36–37.

Passel, Anne W. "The Three Voices in Charlotte Brontë's *Shirley,*" in *Brontë Society Transactions.* XV (1969), pp. 323–326.

Pinion, F.B. *A Brontë Companion: Literary Assessment, Background, and Reference.* London: Macmillan, 1975.

Rosengarten, Herbert J. "Charlotte Brontë's *Shirley* and the *Leeds Mercury,*" in *Studies in English Literature, 1500–1900.* XVI (1976), pp. 591–600.

Shapiro, Arnold. "Public Themes and Private Lives: Social Criticism in *Shirley,*" in *Papers on Language and Literature.* IV (1968), pp. 74–84.

Sherry, Norman. *Charlotte and Emily Brontë.* London: Evans, 1969, pp. 71–84.

Tillotson, Geoffrey. *A View of Victorian Literature.* Oxford: Clarendon Press, 1978.

Wilson, F.A.C. "The Primrose Wreath: The Heroes of the Brontë Novels," in *Nineteenth-Century Fiction.* XXIX (1974), pp. 47–48.

Villette

Beer, Patricia. *Reader, I Married Him: A Study of the Women Characters of Jane Austen, Charlotte Brontë, Elizabeth Gaskell and George Eliot.* London: Macmillan, 1974, pp. 87–126.

Bentley, Phyllis. *The Brontës.* New York: Haskell House, 1975, pp. 75–81.

Blackall, Jean F. "Point of View in *Villette,*" in *Journal of Narrative Technique.* VI (1976), pp. 14–28.

Burkhart, Charles. *Charlotte Brontë: A Psychosexual Study of Her Novels.* London: Gollancz, 1973, pp. 96–121.

———. "The Names of *Villette,*" in *Victorian Newsletter.* XLIV (1973), pp. 8–13.

Colby, Robert A. "*Villette* and the Life of the Mind," in *PMLA.* LXXV (1960), pp. 410–419.

Coursen, Herbert R., Jr. "Storm and Calm in *Villette,*" in *Discourse.* V (Summer, 1962), pp. 318–333.

Craik, W.A. *The Brontë Novels.* London: Methuen, 1968, pp. 158–201.

Dunbar, Georgia S. "Proper Names in *Villette,*" in *Nineteenth-Century Fiction.* XV (June, 1960), pp. 77–80.

Evans, Joan. *The Flowering of the Middle Ages.* New York: McGraw-Hill, 1966, pp. 11–40.

Goldfarb, Russell M. *Sexual Repression and Victorian Literature.* Lewisburg, Pa.: Bucknell University Press, 1970, pp. 139–157.

Hook, Andrew D. "Charlotte Brontë, the Imagination, and *Villette*," in *The Brontës: A Collection of Critical Essays.* Edited by Ian Gregor. Englewood Cliffs, N.J.: Prentice-Hall, 1970, pp. 137–156.

Johnson, E.D.H. " 'Daring the Dread Glance': Charlotte Brontë's Treatment of the Supernatural in *Villette*," in *Nineteenth-Century Fiction.* XX (March, 1966), pp. 325–336.

Knies, Earl A. *The Art of Charlotte Brontë.* Athens: Ohio University Press, 1969, pp. 171–200.

Kroeber, Karl. *Styles in Fictional Structure: The Art of Jane Austen, Charlotte Brontë, George Eliot.* Princeton, N.J.: Princeton University Press, 1971, pp. 89–94, 109–112, 151–180.

Mews, Hazel. *Frail Vessels: Woman's Role in Women's Novels from Fanny Burney to George Eliot.* London: Athlone, 1969, pp. 77–80.

Oldfield, Jennifer. " 'The Homely Web of Truth': Dress as the Mirror of Personality in *Jane Eyre* and *Villette*," in *Brontë Society Transactions.* XVI (1973), pp. 181–193.

O'Neill, Judith. *Critics on Charlotte and Emily Brontë: Readings in Literary Criticism.* Coral Gables, Fla.: University of Miami Press, 1968, pp. 38–47.

Pascal, Roy. "The Autobiographical Novel and the Autobiography," in *Essays in Criticism.* IX (April, 1959), pp. 134–150.

Pinion, F.B. *A Brontë Companion: Literary Assessment, Background, and Reference.* London: Macmillan, 1975.

Platt, Carolyn V. "How Feminist Is *Villette*?," in *Women and Literature.* III (1975), pp. 16–27.

Sherry, Norman. *Charlotte and Emily Brontë.* London: Evans, 1969, pp. 85–100.

Tillotson, Geoffrey. *A View of Victorian Literature.* Oxford: Clarendon Press, 1978.

Williams, Raymond. *The English Novel: From Dickens to Lawrence.* London: Chatto and Windus, 1970, pp. 70–74.

Wilson, F.A.C. "The Primrose Wreath: The Heroes of the Brontë Novels," in *Nineteenth-Century Fiction.* XXIX (1974), pp. 48–49.

EMILY BRONTË
(1818–1848)

The Poetry of Emily Brontë

Bentley, Phyllis. *The Brontës.* New York: Haskell House, 1975, pp. 83–89.

Brown, H. "The Influence of Byron on Emily Brontë," in *Modern Language Review.* XXXIV (July, 1939), pp. 374–381.

Donoghue, Denis. "The Other Emily," in *The Brontës: A Collection of Critical Essays.* Edited by Ian Gregor. Englewood Cliffs, N.J.: Prentice-Hall, 1970, pp. 157–172.

Drew, David P. "Emily Brontë and Emily Dickinson as Mystic Poets," in *Brontë Society Transactions.* XV (1968), pp. 227–232.

Grove, Robin. " 'It Would Not Do': Emily Brontë as Poet," in *The Art of Emily Brontë.* Edited by Anne Smith. New York: Barnes & Noble, 1976, pp. 33–67.

Hardy, Barbara. "The Lyricism of Emily Brontë," in *The Art of Emily Brontë.* Edited by Anne Smith. New York: Barnes & Noble, 1976, pp. 94–118.

Livermore, A.L. "Byron and Emily Brontë," in *Quarterly Review.* CCC (1962), pp. 337–344.

Maurer, K.W. "The Poetry of Emily Brontë," in *Anglia.* LXI (1937), pp. 442–448.

Miles, Rosalind. "A Baby God: The Creative Dynamism of Emily Brontë's Poetry," in *The Art of Emily Brontë.* Edited by Anne Smith. New York: Barnes & Noble, 1976, pp. 68–93.

Ratchford, F.E. "War in Gondal: Emily Brontë's Last Poem," in *Trollopian.* II (1947), pp. 137–155.

Starzyk, Lawrence J. "Emily Brontë: Poetry in a Mingled Tone," in *Criticism.* II (Spring, 1972), pp. 119–136.

Tinker, C.B. "The Poetry of the Brontës," in *Essays in Retrospect.* Edited by C.B. Tinker. Port Washington, N.Y.: Kennikat, 1948.

Visick, Mary. "Emily Brontë's Poetry," in *Critics on Charlotte and Emily Brontë.* Edited by Judith O'Neill. London: Unwin, 1968, pp. 108–113.

Willy, Margaret. "Emily Brontë: Poet and Mystic," in *English.* VI (Autumn, 1946), pp. 117–122.

Wordsworth, Jonathan. "Wordsworth and the Poetry of Emily Brontë," in *Brontë Society Transactions.* XVI (1972), pp. 85–100.

Wuthering Heights

Blondel, Jacques. "Imagery in *Wuthering Heights,*" in *Durham University Journal.* XXXVII (1976), pp. 1–7.

Brick, Allen R. "*Wuthering Heights*: Narrators, Audience and Message," in *College English*. XXI (November, 1959), pp. 80–86.

Burns, Wayne. "In Death They Were Not Divided: The Moral Magnificence of Unmoral Passion in *Wuthering Heights*," in *Hartford Studies in Literature*. V (1973), pp. 135–159.

Craik, W.A. *The Brontë Novels*. London: Methuen, 1968, pp. 5–47.

Davies, Cecil W. "A Reading of *Wuthering Heights*," in *Essays in Criticism*. XIX (July, 1969), pp. 254–272.

Drew, Elizabeth A. *The Novel; A Modern Guide to Fifteen English Master-pieces*. New York: Norton, 1963, pp. 173–190.

Fraser, John. "The Name of Action: Nelly Dean and *Wuthering Heights*," in *Nineteenth-Century Fiction*. XX (December, 1965), pp. 223–236.

Gose, Elliott B., Jr. "*Wuthering Heights*: The Heath and the Hearth," in *Nineteenth-Century Fiction*. XXI (June, 1966), pp. 1–19.

Grove, Robin. "*Wuthering Heights*," in *Critical Review*. VIII (1965), pp. 70–87.

Karl, Frederick R. *An Age of Fiction; The Nineteenth-Century British Novel*. New York: Farrar, Straus and Giroux, 1964, pp. 77–103.

Kooiman-Van Middendorp, Gerarda M. *The Hero in the Feminine Novel*. New York: Haskell House, 1966, pp. 78–81.

Langman, F.H. "*Wuthering Heights*," in *Essays in Criticism*. XV (July, 1965), pp. 294–312.

Lettis, Richard and William E. Morris. *A* Wuthering Heights *Handbook*. New York: Odyssey Press, 1961.

Madden, William A. "*Wuthering Heights*: The Binding of Passion," in *Nineteenth-Century Fiction*. XXVII (1972), pp. 127–154.

Moser, Thomas. "What Is the Matter with Emily Jane? Conflicting Impulses in *Wuthering Heights*," in *Nineteenth-Century Fiction*. XVII (June, 1962), pp. 1–19.

O'Neill, Judith. *Critics on Charlotte and Emily Brontë; Readings in Literary Criticism*. Coral Gables, Fla.: University of Miami Press, 1968, pp. 50–101.

Roberts, Mark. *The Tradition of Romantic Morality*. London: Macmillan, 1973, pp. 158–197.

Sagar, Keith. "The Originality of *Wuthering Heights*," in *The Art of Emily Brontë*. Edited by Anne Smith. New York: Barnes & Noble, 1976, pp. 121–159.

Shapiro, Arnold. "*Wuthering Heights* as a Victorian Novel," in *Studies in the Novel*. I (1969), pp. 284–296.

Shunami, Gideon. "The Unreliable Narrator in *Wuthering Heights*," in *Nineteenth-Century Fiction*. XXVII (1973), pp. 449–468.

Sucksmith, H.P. "The Theme of *Wuthering Heights* Reconsidered," in *Dalhousie Review*. LIV (1974), pp. 418–428.

Van de Laar, Elisabeth Th. M. *The Inner Structure of* Wuthering Heights*: A Study of an Imaginative Field*. The Hague: Mouton, 1969.

Vargish, Thomas. "Revenge and *Wuthering Heights*," in *Studies in the Novel*. III (1971), pp. 7–17.

Vogler, Thomas A. *Twentieth-Century Interpretations of* Wuthering Heights. Englewood Cliffs, N.J.: Prentice-Hall, 1968.

Wilson, F.A.C. "The Primrose Wreath: The Heroes of the Brontë Novels," in *Nineteenth-Century Fiction*. XXIX (1974), pp. 50–57.

RUPERT BROOKE
(1887–1915)

The Poetry of Brooke

Bergonzi, Bernard. *Heroes' Twilight: A Study of the Literature of the Great War.* New York: Coward-McCann, 1966, pp. 32–59.

De La Mare, Walter John. *Pleasures and Speculations.* London: Faber and Faber, 1940, pp. 172–199.

Hynes, Samuel Lynn. *Edwardian Occasions: Essays on English Writing in the Early Twentieth Century.* New York: Oxford, 1972, pp. 144–152.

Johnston, John H. *English Poetry of the First World War: A Study of the Evolution of Lyric and Narrative Form.* Princeton, N.J.: Princeton University Press, 1964, pp. 25–36.

Knight, G.W. "Rupert Brooke," in *Promise of Greatness: The War of 1914–1918.* Edited by George Andrew Panichas. New York: Day, 1968, pp. 488–502.

Pearsall, Robert Brainard. *Rupert Brooke: The Man and Poet.* Amsterdam: Rodopi, 1974.

Rogers, Timothy. "Rupert Brooke: Man and Monument," in *English.* XVII (1968), pp. 79–84.

————. *Rupert Brooke: A Reappraisal and Selection.* London: Routledge and Kegan Paul, 1971, pp. 180–190.

Ross, Robert H. *The Georgian Revolt, 1910–1922.* Carbondale: Southern Illinois Press, 1965, pp. 92–96.

Ward, Alfred Charles. "Rupert Brooke and the Soldier Poets," in *Twentieth Century Literature, 1901–1940.* London: Longmans, 1940, pp. 166–172.

Weygandt, Cornelius. *Time of Yeats: English Poetry of Today Against an American Background.* New York: Appleton, 1937, pp. 363–385.

Woodberry, George Edward. "Introduction," in *The Collected Poems of Rupert Brooke.* New York: Dodd, Mead, 1939, pp. 3–14.

CHARLES BROCKDEN BROWN
(1771–1810)

Arthur Mervyn

Bernard, Kenneth. "Arthur Mervyn: The Ordeal of Innocence," in *Texas Studies in Literature and Language.* VI (Winter, 1965), pp. 441–459.

————. "Charles Brockden Brown," in *Minor American Novelists.* Edited by Charles Hoyt. Carbondale: Southern Illinois University Press, 1970, pp. 1–9.

Btanaccio, P. "Studied Ambiguities: *Arthur Mervyn* and the Problem of the Unreliable Narrator," in *American Literature.* XLII (March, 1970), pp. 18–27.

Clark, David Lee. *Charles Brockden Brown: Pioneer Voice.* Durham, N.C.: Duke University Press, 1952, pp. 177–181.

Erskine, John. *Leading American Novelists.* New York: Holt, 1910, pp. 26–31.

Fiedler, Leslie A. *Love and Death in the American Novel.* New York: Stein and Day, 1960, pp. 148–161.

Justus, J.H. "Arthur Mervyn, American," in *American Literature.* XLII (November, 1970), pp. 304–324.

Kimball, Arthur. *Rational Fictions: A Study of Charles Brockden Brown.* McMinnville, Ore.: Linfield Research Institute, 1968, pp. 154–157, 171–185.

Marble, Annie Russell. *Heralds of American Literature.* Chicago: University of Chicago Press, 1907, pp. 297–301.

Ringe, Donald A. *Charles Brockden Brown.* New York: Twayne, 1966, pp. 65–85.

Spingemann, W.C. "The Poetics of Domesticity," in his *The Adventurous Muse.* New Haven, Conn.: Yale University Press, 1977, pp. 68–118.

Vilas, Martin S. *Charles Brockden Brown.* Burlington, Vt.: Free Press Association, 1904, pp. 31–33.

Warfel, Harry R. *Charles Brockden Brown.* Gainesville: University of Florida Press, 1949, pp. 141–148.

Wiley, Lulu Rumsey. *The Sources and Influence of the Novels of Charles Brockden Brown.* New York: Vantage, 1950, pp. 141–154.

Ormond

Bernard, Kenneth. "Charles Brockden Brown," in *Minor American Novelists.* Edited by Charles Hoyt. Carbondale: Southern Illinois University Press, 1970, pp. 1–9.

Clark, David Lee. *Charles Brockden Brown: Pioneer Voice of America.* Durham, N.C.: Duke University Press, 1952, pp. 171–174.

Davies, R.R. "Charles Brockden Brown's *Ormond*: A Possible Influence upon Shelley's Conduct," in *Philological Quarterly.* XLIII (January, 1964), pp. 133–137.

Erskine, John. *Leading American Novelists.* New York: Holt, 1910, pp. 22–24.

Fiedler, Leslie A. *Love and Death in the American Novel.* New York: Stein and Day, 1966, pp. 148–161.

Kimball, Arthur. *Rational Fictions: A Study of Charles Brockden Brown.* McMinnville, Ore.: Linfield Research Institute, 1968, pp. 115–124.

Krause, S.J. "Ormond: Seduction in a New Key," in *American Literature.* XLIV (January, 1973), pp. 570–584.

Marble, Annie Russell. *Heralds of American Literature.* Chicago: University of Chicago Press, 1907, p. 297.

Ringe, Donald A. *Charles Brockden Brown.* New York: Twayne, 1966, pp. 49–64.

Rodgers, P.C. "Brown's *Ormond*: The Fruits of Improvisation," in *American Quarterly.* XXVI (March, 1974), pp. 4–22.

Van Doren, Carl. *American Novel.* New York: Macmillan, 1922, p. 11.

Vilas, Martin S. *Charles Brockden Brown.* Burlington, Vt.: Free Press Association, 1904, pp. 27–30.

Warfel, Harry R. *Charles Brockden Brown.* Gainesville: University of Florida Press, 1949, pp. 125–140.

Wiley, Lulu Rumsey. *The Sources and Influence of the Novels of Charles Brockden Brown.* New York: Vantage, 1950, pp. 122–141, 279–282.

Wieland

Bernard, Kenneth. "Charles Brockden Brown," in *Minor American Novelists.* Edited by Charles Hoyt. Carbondale: Southern Illinois University Press, 1970, pp. 1–9.

Berthoff, W.B. "Lesson on Concealment: Brockden Brown's Method in Fiction," in *Philological Quarterly.* XXXVII (January, 1958), pp. 45–57.

Chase, Richard. *The American Novel and Its Tradition.* New York: Doubleday, 1957, pp. 29–35.

Clark, David Lee. *Charles Brockden Brown: Pioneer Voice of America.* Durham, N.C.: Duke University Press, 1952, pp. 162–169, 297–302.

Erskine, John. *Leading American Novelists.* New York: Holt, 1910, pp. 14–22.

Fiedler, Leslie A. *Love and Death in the American Novel.* New York: Stein and Day, 1966, pp. 148–161.

Frank, J.G. "The Wieland Family in Charles Brockden Brown," in *Monatshefte.* XLII (November, 1950), pp. 347–353.

Garrow, Scott. "Character Transformation in *Wieland,*" in *Southern Quarterly.* IV (April, 1966), pp. 308–318.

Gilmore, M.T. "Calvinism and Gothicism: The Example of Brown's *Wieland,*" in *Studies in the Novel.* IX (Summer, 1977), pp. 107–118.

Hendrickson, J.C. "Note on *Weiland,*" in *American Literature.* XIII (November, 1936), pp. 305–306.

Kerlin, R.T. "*Weiland* and the *Raven,*" in *Modern Language Notes.* XXXI (December, 1916), pp. 503–505.

Ketterer, David. "The Transformed World of Charles Brockden Brown's *Wieland,*" in *New Worlds for Old.* Bloomington: Indiana University Press, 1974, pp. 167–181.

Kimball, Arthur. *Rational Fictions: A Study of Charles Brockden Brown.* McMinnville, Ore.: Linfield Research Institute, 1968, pp. 44–74.

Krause, S.J. "Romanticism in *Wieland*: Brown and the Reconcilation of Opposites," in *Artful Thunder.* Edited by Robert J. DeMott. Kent, Oh.: Kent State University Press, 1975, pp. 13–24.

Manly, W.M. "Importance of Point of View in Brockden Brown's *Wieland,*" in *American Literature.* XXXV (November, 1963), pp. 311–321.

Marble, Annie Russell. *Heralds of American Literature.* Chicago: University of Chicago Press, 1907, pp. 294–296.

Prescott, F.C. "*Wieland* and *Frankenstein,*" in *American Literature.* II (May, 1930), pp. 172–173.

Ridgely, J.V. "The Empty World of *Wieland,*" in *Individual and Community.* Edited by Kenneth H. Baldwin. Durham, N.C.: Duke University Press, 1975, pp. 3–16.

Ringe, Donald A. *Charles Brockden Brown.* New York: Twayne, 1966, pp. 24–52.

Van Doren, Carl. *American Novel.* New York: Macmillan, 1922, pp. 13–14.

Wagenknecht, Edward C. "Brockden Brown and the Pioneers," in *Cavalcade of the American Novel.* New York: Holt, 1952, pp. 9–13.

Wiley, Lulu Rumsey. *The Sources and Influence of the Novels of Charles Brockden Brown.* New York: Vantage, 1950, pp. 84–87, 96–121.

Witherington, P. "Benevolence and the Utmost Stretch: Charles Brockden Brown's Narrative Dilemma," in *Criticism.* XIV (Spring, 1972), pp. 175–191.

Ziff, L. "Reading of *Wieland,*" in *PMLA.* LXXVII (March, 1962), pp. 51–57.

DEE ALEXANDER BROWN
(1908–   )

Bury My Heart at Wounded Knee

Adams, Phoebe. *"Bury My Heart at Wounded Knee,"* in *Atlantic.* CCVII (February, 1971), p. 130.

Eby, Cecil. *"Bury My Heart at Wounded Knee,"* in *Book World.* (February 28, 1971), p. 3.

Freilicher, L.P. *"Bury My Heart at Wounded Knee*: Story Behind the Book," in *Publisher's Weekly.* CXCIX (April 19, 1971), pp. 34–35.

Greenway, John. "Dee Brown's *Bury My Heart at Wounded Knee,"* in *National Review.* XXIII (March 9, 1971), p. 266.

McNeil, Helen. *"Bury My Heart at Wounded Knee,"* in *New Statesman.* LXXXII (October 1, 1971), p. 444.

Mohl, R.A. *"Bury My Heart at Wounded Knee,"* in *Best Sellers.* XXX (March 1, 1971), p. 513.

Momaday, N.S. "Dee Brown's *Bury My Heart at Wounded Knee,"* in *New York Times Book Review.* (March 7, 1971), p. 46.

WILLIAM HILL BROWN
(1765–1793)

The Power of Sympathy

Byers, J.R. "Further Verification of the Authorship of *Power of Sympathy*," XLIII (November, 1971), pp. 421–427.

Ellis, M. "Author of the First American Novel," in *American Literature*. IV (January, 1933), pp. 359–368.

McDowell, Tremaine. "The First American Novel," in *American Review*. II (November, 1933), pp. 73–81.

Marble, Annie Russell. *Heralds of American Literature*. Chicago: University of Chicago Press, 1907, p. 280.

Spiller, Robert. *Literary History of the United States*. New York: Macmillan Company, 1957, p. 177.

Wagenknecht, Edward. *Cavalcade of the American Novel*. New York: Holt, 1952, p. 2–5.

Walser, Richard. "More About the First American Novel," in *American Literature*. XXIV (November, 1952), pp. 352–357.

ELIZABETH BARRETT BROWNING
(1806–1861)

Aurora Leigh

Bevan, Bryan. "Poet's Novel," in *Poetry Review.* L (1959), pp. 29–31.

Lupton, Mary J. "The Printing Woman Who Lost Her Place: Elizabeth Barrett Browning," in *Woman: A Journal of Liberation.* II (1970), pp. 2–5.

Marshall, Edward H. "James Russell Lowell on *Aurora Leigh,*" in *Notes & Queries.* IV (July 29, 1899), p. 95.

Radley, Virginia L. *Elizabeth Barrett Browning.* New York: Twayne, 1972, pp. 120–125.

Rooney, Charles J., Jr. "A New Letter by Lowell," in *American Literature.* XXXVI (1964), pp. 214–215.

Shackford, Martha Hale. *E.B. Browning; R.H. Horne; Two Studies.* Wellesley, Mass.: Wellesley Press, 1935, pp. 5–27.

_____. *Studies of Certain Nineteenth Century Poets.* Natick, Mass.: Suburban Press, 1946, pp. 56–66.

_____. *Talks on Ten Poets: Wordsworth to Moody.* New York: Bookman Associates, 1958, pp. 81–97.

Thomson, Patricia. "Elizabeth Barrett and George Sand," in *Durham University Journal.* XXXIII (1972), pp. 205–219.

Turner, Paul. "Aurora Versus the Angel," in *Review of English Studies.* XXIV (July, 1948), pp. 227–235.

Wilsey, Mildred. "Elizabeth Barrett Browning's Heroine," in *College English.* VI (1944), pp. 75–81.

Woolf, Virginia. "*Aurora Leigh,*" in *Yale Review.* XX (June, 1931), pp. 677–690.

_____. *The Second Common Reader.* New York: Harcourt, Brace, 1932, pp. 218–231.

Sonnets from the Portuguese

Baker, Harry T. "Mrs. Browning's *Sonnets,*" in *Saturday Review of Literature.* V (April 13, 1929), p. 895.

Butler, Francis H. "*Sonnets from the Portuguese,*" in *Academy* (London). LXVI (March 5, 1904), p. 258.

Carter, John and Graham Pollard. *An Enquiry into the Nature of Certain Nineteenth Century Pamphlets.* London: Constable, 1934, pp. 8–37.

Cunnington, S. "*Sonnets from the Portuguese,*" in *Academy* (London). LXVI (February 13, 1904), p. 181.

Dodds, M.H. "*Sonnets from the Portuguese*," in *Notes & Queries.* CXCI (November 2, 1946), p. 193.

Fussell, Paul. *Poetic Meter and Poetic Form.* New York: Random House, 1965, pp. 124–128.

Gay, Robert. "Elizabeth Barrett Browning's *Sonnets from the Portuguese*," in *Explicator.* I (December, 1942), item 24.

Going, William T. "Elizabeth Barrett Browning's *Sonnets from the Portuguese,* XLIII," in *Explicator.* XI (June, 1953), item 58.

Gosse, Edmund. "The *Sonnets from the Portuguese*," in *Critical Kit-Kats.* London: Heinemann, 1913, pp. 1–17.

Hagedorn, Ralph. "Edmund Gosse and the *Sonnets from the Portuguese*," in *Papers of the Bibliographical Society of America.* XLVI (1952), pp. 67–70.

Heilman, Robert B. "Elizabeth Barrett Browning's *Sonnets from the Portuguese*," in *Explicator.* IV (October 14, 1945), item 3.

Kay, Carol M. "An Analysis of Sonnet 6 in *Sonnets from the Portuguese*," in *Concerning Poetry.* IV (1971), pp. 17–21.

O'Hagan, Thomas. *Studies in Poetry, Critical, Analytical, Interpretive.* Boston: Marlier, Callahan, 1900, pp. 38–50.

Phillipson, John S. " 'How Do I Love Thee?'—An Echo of St. Paul," in *Victorian Newsletter.* XXII (Fall, 1962), p. 22.

Radley, Virginia. *Elizabeth Barrett Browning.* New York: Twayne, 1972, pp. 90–106.

Smith, Grover. "Petronius Arbiter and Elizabeth Barrett," in *Notes & Queries.* CXCI (November 2, 1946), p. 190.

Taplin, Gardner. "Mrs. Browning's Poems in 1850," in *Boston Public Library Quarterly.* (October, 1957), pp. 181–194.

Zimmerman, Susan. "*Sonnets from the Portuguese*: A Negative and Positive Context," in *Mary Wollstonecraft Newsletter.* II (December, 1973), pp. 7–20.

ROBERT BROWNING
(1812–1889)

The Poetry of Browning

Armstrong, Isobel, Editor. *Robert Browning.* Athens: Ohio University Press, 1975.

Benvenuto, R. "Lippo and Andrea: The Pro and Contra of Browning's Realism," in *Studies in English Literature.* XIII (Autumn, 1973), pp. 643–652.

Blackburn, Thomas. *Robert Browning: A Study of His Poetry.* Totowa, N.J.: Rowman and Littlefield, 1974. Reprint of 1967 Edition.

Brooke, Stopford A. *The Poetry of Robert Browning.* New York: AMS Press, 1969. Reprint of 1902 Edition.

Bross, A.C. "Browning's Changing Concept of Faith," in *Victorian Poetry.* XIV (Spring, 1976), pp. 11–23.

Cook, Eleanor. *Browning's Lyrics: An Exploration.* Toronto: University of Toronto Press, 1974.

Drew, Philip. *The Poetry of Browning: A Critical Introduction.* London: Methuen, 1970.

Flowers, Betty S. *Browning and the Modern Tradition.* New York: Macmillan, 1976.

Hess, S.W. "Browning in Our Ear," in *Contemporary Review.* CCXVI (March, 1970), pp. 140–144.

Holmes, S.W. "Browning: Semantic Stutterer," in *ETC.* XXXI (March, 1974), pp. 73–99.

Irvine, William. *The Book, the Ring, and the Poet: A Biography of Robert Browning.* New York: McGraw-Hill, 1974.

Jack, Ian R. *Browning's Major Poetry.* Oxford: Clarendon Press, 1973.

Korg, J. "Browning's Art and 'By the Fireside,'" in *Victorian Poetry.* XV (Summer, 1977), pp. 147–158.

Langbaum, R. "Browning and the Quest of Myth," in *PMLA.* LXXXI (December, 1966), pp. 575–584.

Litzinger, Boyd, Editor. *Browning: The Critical Heritage.* New York: Barnes & Noble, 1970.

McComb, J.K. "Beyond the Dark Tower: Childe Roland's Painful Memories," in *ELH.* XLII (Fall, 1975), pp. 460–470.

Maynard, John. *Browning's Youth.* Cambridge, Mass.: Harvard University Press, 1977.

Melchiori, B. "Browning's Don Juan," in *Essays in Criticism.* XVI (October, 1966), pp. 416–440.

Mermin, D.M. "Speaker and Auditor in Browning's Dramatic Monologues," in *University of Toronto Quarterly*. XLV (Winter, 1976), pp. 139–157.

Pearsall, Robert B. *Robert Browning*. New York: Twayne, 1974.

Peterson, William S. *Robert and Elizabeth Barrett Browning: An Annotated Bibliography, 1951–1970*. New York: Browning Institute, 1974.

Poston, L. "Browning's Political Skepticism: Sordello and the Plays," in *PMLA*. LXXXVIII (March, 1973), pp. 260–270.

Preyer, R. "Two Styles in the Verse of Robert Browning," in *ELH*. XXXII (March, 1965), pp. 62–84.

Ryals, Clyde de L. *Browning's Later Poetry, 1871–1889*. Ithaca, N.Y.: Cornell University Press, 1975.

Siegchrist, M. "Thematic Coherence in Browning's Dramatic Idyls," in *Victorian Poetry*. XI (Autumn, 1977), pp. 229–239.

The Ring and the Book

Altick, Richard D. *Browning's Roman Murder Story: A Reading of* The Ring and the Book. Chicago: University of Chicago Press, 1968.

Armstrong, Isobel, Editor. *Robert Browning*. Athens: Ohio University Press, 1975.

Blackburn, Thomas. *Robert Browning: A Study of His Poetry*. Totowa, N.J.: Rowman and Littlefield, 1974. Reprint of 1967 Edition.

Brooke, Stopford A. *The Poetry of Robert Browning*. New York: AMS Press, 1969. Reprint of 1902 Edition.

Columbus, C.K. "*Ring and the Book*: A Masque for the Making of Meaning," in *Philological Quarterly*. LIII (Spring, 1974), pp. 237–255.

Cook, Eleanor. *Browning's Lyrics: An Exploration*. Toronto: University of Toronto Press, 1974.

Cundiff, Paul A. *Browning's Ring Metaphor and Truth*. Metuchen, N.J.: Scarecrow Press, 1972.

Drew, Philip. *The Poetry of Browning: A Critical Introduction*. London: Methuen, 1970.

Flowers, Betty S. *Browning and the Modern Tradition*. New York: Macmillan, 1976.

Gaylord, Harriet. *Pompilia and Her Poet*. New York: Literary Publishers, 1931.

Gross, D.H. "Browning's Positivist Count in Search of a Miracle: A Grim Parody in *The Ring and the Book*," in *Victorian Poetry*. XII (Summer, 1974), pp. 178–180.

Irvine, William. *The Book, the Ring, and the Poet: A Biography of Robert Browning*. New York: McGraw-Hill, 1974.

Jack, Ian R.   *Browning's Major Poetry*. Oxford: Clarendon Press, 1973.

James, Henry.   "The Novel in *The Ring and the Book*," in his *Notes on Novelists with Some Other Notes*. London: 1914, pp. 306–319.

Johnson, E.D.   "Robert Browning's Pluralistic Universe: A Reading of *The Ring and the Book*," in *University of Toronto Quarterly*. XXXI (1961), pp. 20–41.

Langbaum, Robert.   "The Importance of Fact in *The Ring and the Book*," in *Victorian Newsletter*. XVII (1960), pp. 11–17.

Litzinger, Boyd, Editor.   *Browning: The Critical Heritage*. New York: Barnes & Noble, 1970.

Maynard, John.   *Browning's Youth*. Cambridge, Mass.: Harvard University Press, 1977.

Pearsall, Robert B.   *Robert Browning*. New York: Twayne, 1974.

Peterson, William S.   *Robert and Elizabeth Barrett Browning: An Annotated Bibliography, 1951–1970*. New York: Browning Institute, 1974.

Ryals, Clyde de L.   *Browning's Later Poetry, 1871–1889*. Ithaca, N.Y.: Cornell University Press, 1975.

Thompson, George W.   "Authorial Detachment and Imagery in *The Ring and the Book*," in *Studies in English Literature*. X (Autumn, 1970), pp. 669–686.

Wasserman, George R.   "The Meaning of Browning's Ring Figure," in *Modern Language Notes*. LXXVI (May, 1961), pp. 420–426.

WILLIAM CULLEN BRYANT
(1794–1878)

The Poetry of Bryant

Arms, George. "William Cullen Bryant: A Respectable Station on Parnassus," in *University of Kansas City Review*. XV (1949), pp. 215–223.

Bailey, Elmer James. *Religious Thought in the Greater American Poets*. Freeport, N.Y.: Books for Libraries, 1968, pp. 10–31.

Bigelow, John. *William Cullen Bryant*. Boston: Houghton Mifflin, 1893, pp. 117–176.

Brenner, Rica. *Twelve American Poets Before 1900*. Freeport, N.Y.: Books for Libraries Press, 1968, pp. 23–47.

Brown, Charles H. *William Cullen Bryant*. New York: Scribner's, 1971.

Conner, Frederick William. *Cosmic Optimism: A Study of the Interpretation of Evolution by American Poets from Emerson to Robinson*. New York: Octagon Books, 1973, pp. 167–174.

Kreymborg, Alfred. *Our Singing Strength: An Outline of American Poetry (1620–1930)*. New York: Coward-McCann, 1929, pp. 27–40.

McDowell, Tremaine. "Bryant's Practice in Composition and Revision," in *PMLA*. LII (June, 1937), pp. 474–502.

McLean, Albert F., Jr. *William Cullen Bryant*. New York: Twayne, 1964.

Pearce, Roy Harvey. *The Continuity of American Poetry*. Princeton, N.J.: Princeton University Press, 1961, pp. 206–210.

Ringe, Donald A. "Kindred Spirits: Bryant and Cole," in *American Quarterly*. VI (Fall, 1954), pp. 233–244.

Sanford, Charles L. "The Concept of the Sublime in the Works of William Cullen Bryant," in *American Literature*. XXVIII (January, 1957), pp. 434–448.

Scheick, William J. "Bryant's River Imagery," in *College Language Association Journal*. XX (1976), pp. 205–209.

Strong, Augustus Hopkins. *American Poets and Their Theology*. Freeport, N.Y.: Books for Libraries Press, 1968, pp. 1–48.

Waggoner, Hyatt H. *American Poets from the Puritans to the Present*. Boston: Houghton Mifflin, 1968, pp. 34–42.

"The Prairies"

Arms, George. "William Cullen Bryant," in *University of Kansas City Review*. XV (Spring, 1949), p. 221.

Bradley, William Aspenwall. *William Cullen Bryant.* New York: Macmillan, 1905, pp. 140–143.

Brown, Charles H. *William Cullen Bryant.* New York: Scribner's, 1971, pp. 217–218.

McLean, Albert F., Jr. *William Cullen Bryant.* New York: Twayne, 1964, pp. 41–43.

Miller, Ralph N. "Nationalism in Bryant's 'The Prairies,' " in *American Literature.* XXI (May, 1949), pp. 227–232.

Pearce, Roy Harvey. *The Continuity of American Poetry.* Princeton, N.J.: Princeton University Press, 1961, pp. 207–208.

Waggoner, Hyatt H. *American Poets from the Puritans to the Present.* Boston: Houghton Mifflin, 1968, p. 42.

"Thanatopsis"

Arms, George. "William Cullen Bryant," in *University of Kansas City Review.* XV (Spring, 1949), p. 220.

Bradley, William Aspenwall. *William Cullen Bryant.* New York: Macmillan, 1905, pp. 28–33.

Brown, Charles H. *William Cullen Bryant.* New York: Scribner's, 1971, pp. 58–62, 78–80, 101–104.

Bryant, William Cullen II. "The Genesis of 'Thanatopsis,' " in *New England Quarterly.* XXI (June, 1948), pp. 163–184.

Budick, E. Miller. " 'Visible' Images and the 'Still Voice': Transcendental Vision in Bryant's 'Thanatopsis,' " in *ESQ: Journal of the American Renaissance.* XXII (1976), pp. 71–77.

Kreymborg, Alfred. *Our Singing Strength: An Outline of American Poetry (1620–1930).* New York: Coward-McCann, 1929, pp. 28–29.

McLean, Albert F., Jr. "Bryant's 'Thanatopsis': A Sermon in Stone," in *American Literature.* XXXI (January, 1960), pp. 474–479.

————. *William Cullen Bryant.* New York: Twayne, 1964, pp. 65–81.

Strong, Augustus Hopkins. *American Poets and Their Theology.* Freeport, N.Y.: Books for Libraries Press, 1968, pp. 9–11.

Van Doren, Carl. "The Growth of 'Thanatopsis,' " in *Nation.* CI (1915), pp. 432–433.

Waggoner, Hyatt H. *American Poets from the Puritans to the Present.* Boston: Houghton Mifflin, 1968, pp. 38–40.

Woodward, Robert H. " 'The Wings of Morning' in 'Thanatopsis,' " in *Emerson Society Quarterly.* LVIII (1970), p. 153.

"To a Waterfowl"

Arms, George. "William Cullen Bryant," in *University of Kansas City Review.* XV (Spring, 1949), pp. 221–222.

Bigelow, John. *William Cullen Bryant.* Boston: Houghton Mifflin, 1893, pp. 42–44.

Bradley, William Aspenwall. *William Cullen Bryant.* New York: Macmillan, 1905, pp. 48–49.

McLean, Albert F., Jr. *William Cullen Bryant.* New York: Twayne, 1964, pp. 31–33.

Rosenthal, M.L. *The New Poets: American and British Poetry Since World War II.* New York: Oxford University Press, 1967, pp. 10–11.

Waggoner, Hyatt H. *American Poets from the Puritans to the Present.* Boston: Houghton Mifflin, 1968, p. 41.

PEARL S. BUCK
(1892–1973)

Dragon Seed

Doàn-Cao-Lỳ. *Image of the Chinese Family in Pearl Buck's Novels.* Dùc-Sinh: Saigon, 1964, pp. 109–122.

Doyle, Paul A. *Pearl Buck.* New York: Twayne, 1965, pp. 117–121.

Henchoz, Ami. "A Permanent Element in Pearl Buck's Novels," in *English Studies.* XXV (1943), pp. 97–103.

The Good Earth

Canby, Henry S. "*The Good Earth*: Pearl Buck and the Nobel Prize," in *Saturday Review of Literature.* XIX (November 19, 1938), p. 8.

Cevasco, G.A. "Pearl Buck and the Chinese Novel," in *Asian Studies.* V (December, 1967), pp. 437–450.

Doyle, Paul A. *Pearl Buck.* New York: Twayne, 1965, pp. 36–54.

Gray, J. *On Second Thought.* Minneapolis: University of Minnesota Press, 1969, pp. 30–32.

Henchoz, Ami. "A Permanent Element in Pearl Buck's Novels," in *English Studies.* XXV (1943), pp. 97–103.

Langlois, Walter G. "*The Dream of the Red Chamber, The Good Earth,* and *Man's Fate*: Chronicles of Social Change in China," in *Literature East and West.* XI (March, 1967), pp. 1–10.

Shimizu, Mamoru. "On Some Stylistic Features, Chiefly Biblical, of *The Good Earth*," in *Studies in English Literature.* IV (1964), pp. 117–134.

Stuckey, W.J. *Pulitzer Prize Novels: A Critical Backward Look.* Norman: University of Oklahoma Press, 1966, pp. 90–93.

Thompson, Dody W. "Pearl Buck," in *American Winners of the Nobel Literary Prize.* Edited by Warren G. French and Walter E. Kidd. Norman: University of Oklahoma Press, 1968, pp. 85–110.

IVAN ALEXEYEVICH BUNIN
(1870–1953)

The Gentleman from San Francisco

Bedford, C.H. "The Fulfillment of Ivan Bunin," in *Canadian Slavonic Papers.* I (1956), pp. 31–44.

Brooks, Cleanth, John Purser and Robert P. Warren. *An Approach to Literature.* New York: Appleton-Century-Crofts, 1952, pp. 174–177.

Colin, Andrew G. "Ivan Bunin in Retrospect," in *Slavonic and East European Review.* XXXIV (1955), pp. 156–173.

Gardner, John and Lennis Dunlap. *The Forms of Fiction.* New York: Random House, 1962, pp. 179–187.

"The Gentleman from San Francisco," in *New York Times Book Review.* (January 28, 1923), p. 14.

"The Gentleman from San Francisco," in *Spectator.* CXXIX (July 15, 1922), p. 86.

Gross, Seymour. "Nature, Man, and God in Bunin's *The Gentleman from San Francisco,"* in *Modern Fiction Studies.* VI (1960), pp. 153–163.

Krutch, Joseph Wood. *"The Gentleman from San Francisco,"* in *Nation.* CXV (July 26, 1922), p. 100.

Kryzytski, Serge. *The Works of Ivan Bunin.* The Hague: Mouton, 1971, pp. 149–161.

McNamee, Maurice B. *Reading for Understanding.* New York: Rinehart, 1952, pp. 454–456.

Muir, Edwin. *"The Gentleman from San Francisco,"* in *Freeman.* VII (June 6, 1923), p. 309.

Murray, J.M. *"The Gentleman from San Francisco,"* in *Nation and Atheneaum.* CXXXI (June 24, 1922), p. 144.

Poggioli, Renato. *The Phoenix and the Spider.* Cambridge, Mass.: Harvard University Press, 1957, pp. 138–139.

Proffer, Carl R. *From Kazamin to Bunin.* Bloomington: Indiana University Press, 1969, pp. 44–49.

Struve, Gleb. "The Art of Ivan Bunin," in *Slavonic and East European Review.* XXXII (1933), pp. 423–436.

West, Ray B. and Robert W. Stallman. *The Art of Modern Fiction.* New York: Rinehart, 1949, pp. 117–120.

The Village

Bedford, C.H. "The Fulfillment of Ivan Bunin," in *Canadian Slavonic Papers.* I (1956), pp. 31–44.

Colin, Andrew G. "Ivan Bunin in Retrospect," in *Slavonic and East European Review*. XXXIV (1955), pp. 156–173.

Croise, Jacques. "Ivan Bunin," in *Russian Review*. XIII (1954), pp. 146–151.

Kryzytski, Serge. *The Works of Ivan Bunin*. The Hague: Mouton, 1971, pp. 66–84.

Lhevinne, Isadore. *"The Village,"* in *Literary Review of the New York Evening Post*. (August 4, 1923), p. 875.

Mirsky, D.S. "Ivan Bunin," in *Contemporary Movements in Literature*. Edited by William Rose and J. Isaacs. London: Routledge, 1928, pp. 153–154.

Pachmuss, Temira. "Ivan Bunin Through the Eyes of Zinaida Gippius," in *Slavonic and East European Review*. XLIV (July, 1966), pp. 338–340.

Poggioli, Renato. "The Art of Ivan Bunin," in *Harvard Slavic Studies*. I (1953), pp. 264–270.

————. *The Phoenix and the Spider*. Cambridge, Mass.: Harvard University Press, 1957, pp. 144–156.

Singleton, J.K. *"The Village,"* in *New Republic*. XXXVI (September 5, 1923), p. 52.

Smertenko, J. *"The Village,"* in *Nation*. CXVII (October 3, 1923), p. 358.

Struve, Gleb. "The Art of Ivan Bunin," in *Slavonic and East European Review*. XI (January, 1933), pp. 423–436.

"The Village," in *New York Times Book Review*. (June 3, 1923), p. 13.

"The Village," in *Times (London) Literary Supplement*. (October 25, 1923), p. 706.

JOHN BUNYAN
(1628–1688)

The Life and Death of Mr. Badman

Dobrée, Bonamy. *Variety of Ways.* Oxford: Clarendon Press, 1932, pp. 36–45.

Furlong, Monica. *Puritan's Progress.* New York: Coward, McCann and Geoghegan, 1975, pp. 126–133, 177, 196.

Garnett, R. *The Age of Dryden.* London: George Bell, 1922, pp. 242–243.

Griffith, Gwilym O. *John Bunyan.* London: Hodder, 1929, pp. 245–255.

Hussey, Maurice. "John Bunyan and the Books of God's Judgments," in *English.* VII (Spring, 1949), pp. 165–167.

Lindsay, Jack. *John Bunyan, Maker of Myths.* London: Methuen, 1937, pp. 203–211.

Sharrock, Roger. *John Bunyan.* London: Hutchinson's University Library, 1954, pp. 106–117.

Sutherland, James. *English Literature of the Late Seventeenth Century.* New York: Oxford University Press, 1969, pp. 333–335.

Talon, Henri A. *John Bunyan, the Man and His Works.* Translated by Barbara Wall. London: Rockliff, 1951, pp. 225–239.

Wharey, James B. "Bunyan's *Mr. Badman,*" in *Modern Language Notes.* XXXVI (1921), pp. 65–79.

————. "Bunyan's *Mr. Badman* and the Picaresque Novel," in *Studies in English.* (University of Texas). IV, (March 15, 1924), pp. 49–61.

Willcock, Mary P. *Bunyan Calling; a Voice from the Seventeenth Century.* London: Allen and Unwin, 1944, pp. 203–216.

The Pilgrim's Progress

Alpaugh, David J. "Emblem and Interpretation in *The Pilgrim's Progress,*" in *Journal of English Literary History.* XXXIII (September, 1966), pp. 299–314.

Baird, Charles W. *John Bunyan: A Study in Narrative Techniques.* Port Washington, N.Y.: Kennikat, 1977.

Downs, Robert B. *Molders of the Modern Mind; One Hundred Eleven Books That Shaped Western Civilization.* New York: Barnes & Noble, 1961, pp. 84–87.

Fish, Stanley E. "Progress in *The Pilgrim's Progress,*" in *English Literary Renaissance.* I (1971), pp. 261–293.

————. *Self-Consuming Artifacts: The Experience of Seventeenth-Century Literature.* Berkeley: University of California Press, 1972, pp. 224–264.

Forrest, James F.   "Bunyan's Ignorance and the Flatterer: A Study of the Literary Art of Damnation," in *Studies in Philology.* LX (January, 1963), pp. 12–22.

Furlong, Monica.   *Puritan's Progress.* New York: Coward, McCann and Geoghegan, 1975, pp. 92–125.

Gibson, Daniel, Jr.   "On the Genesis of *Pilgrim's Progress,*" in *Modern Philology.* XXXII (May, 1935), pp. 365–382.

Golder, Harold.   "Bunyan's Giant Despair," in *Journal of English and Germanic Philology.* XXX (1931), pp. 361–378.

————.   "Bunyan's Valley of the Shadow," in *Modern Philology.* XXVII (August, 1929), pp. 55–72.

Greaves, Richard L.   *John Bunyan.* Grand Rapids, Mich.: Eerdmans, 1969, pp. 27–160.

Hardin, Richard F.   "Bunyan, Mr. Ignorance, and the Quakers," in *Studies in Philology.* LXIX (1972), pp. 496–508.

Howell, Elmo.   "Bunyan's Two Valleys: A Note on the Ecumenic Element in *Pilgrim's Progress,*" in *Tennessee Studies in Literature.* XIX (1974), pp. 1–7.

Hussey, M.   "Bunyan's Mr. Ignorance," in *Modern Language Review.* XLIV (October, 1949), pp. 483–489.

Iser, Wolfgang.   *The Implied Reader: Patterns of Communication in Prose Fiction from Bunyan to Beckett.* Baltimore: Johns Hopkins Press, 1974, pp. 1–28.

Kaufmann, U.M.   The Pilgrim's Progress *and Traditions in Puritan Meditation.* New Haven, Conn.: Yale University Press, 1966.

Kelman, John.   *The Road; A Study of John Bunyan's* Pilgrim's Progress. Port Washington, N.Y.: Kennikat, 1912.

Knott, John R., Jr.   "Bunyan's Gospel Day: A Reading of *The Pilgrim's Progress,*" in *English Literary Renaissance.* III (1973), pp. 443–461.

Lewis, Clive S.   *Selected Literary Essays.* New York: Cambridge University Press, 1969, pp. 146–153.

————.   "The Vision of John Bunyan: *The Pilgrim's Progress,*" in *Listener.* LXVIII (December 13, 1962), pp. 1006–1008.

Lindsay, Jack.   *John Bunyan, Maker of Myths.* London: Methuen, 1937, pp. 165–196.

Rupp, Ernest G.   *Six Makers of English Religion, 1500–1700.* New York: Harper & Row, 1957, pp. 92–101.

Sharrock, Roger.   *John Bunyan.* London: Hutchinson's University Library, 1954, pp. 73–104.

Steeves, Harrison R.   *Before Jane Austen; The Shaping of the English Novel in the Eighteenth Century.* New York: Holt, Rinehart, and Winston, 1965, pp. 6–21.

White, Alison.   "*Pilgrim's Progress* as a Fairy-Tale," in *Children's Literature: The Great Excluded.* I (1972), pp. 42–45.

ANTHONY BURGESS
(1917–   )

Clockwork Orange

Aggeler, Geoffrey. "The Comic Art of Anthony Burgess," in *Arizona Quarterly*. XXV (1969), pp. 234–251.

Bergonzi, Bernard. *The Situation of the Novel*. Pittsburgh: University of Pittsburgh Press, 1970, pp. 178–187.

Carson, J. "Pronominalization in a *Clockwork Orange*," in *Papers on Language and Literature*. XII (Spring, 1976), pp. 200–205.

Davis, Robert Gorham. "The Perilous Balance," in *Hudson Review*. XVI (Summer, 1963), pp. 283–285.

De Vitis, A.A. "England, Education, and the Future," in *Anthony Burgess*. New York: Twayne, 1972, pp. 103–112.

Dix, Carol M. "The Philosophy," in *Anthony Burgess*. London: Longmans, 1971, pp. 13–16.

Le Clair, T. "Essential Opposition: The Novels of Anthony Burgess," in *Critique*. XII (1977), pp. 77–94.

Morris, Robert K. "The Bitter Fruits of Freedom," in *Consolations of Ambiguity*. Columbia: University of Missouri Press, 1971, pp. 55–74.

Pritchard, William H. "The Novels of Anthony Burgess," in *Massachusetts Review*. VII (Summer, 1966), pp. 525–539.

Tilton, John Wightman. "A *Clockwork Orange*: Awareness Is All," in *Cosmic Satire in the Contemporary Novel*. Lewisburg, Pa.: Bucknell University Press, 1977, pp. 21–42.

Wood, Michael. "A Dream of *Clockwork Oranges*," in *New Society*. (June 6, 1968), pp. 842–843.

Enderby

Aggeler, Geoffrey. "Mr. Enderby and Mr. Burgess," in *Malahat Review*. X (April, 1969), pp. 104–110.

De Vitis, A.A. "The Joseph Kell Books," in *Anthony Burgess*. New York: Twayne, 1972, pp. 124–133.

Dix, Carol M. "The Language," in *Anthony Burgess*. London: Longmans, 1971, pp. 22–25.

Hoffman, Charles G. "Mr. Kell and Mr. Burgess: Inside and Outside Mr. Enderby," in *The Shaken Realist*. Edited by Melvin Friedman. Baton Rouge: Louisiana State University Press, 1970, pp. 300–310.

Le Clair, T. "Essential Opposition: The Novels of Anthony Burgess," in *Critique*. XII (1977), pp. 77–94.

Morris, Robert K. "Inderby, Outerby, Enderby," in *Consolations of Ambiguity*. Columbia: University of Missouri Press, 1971, pp. 75–89.

Nicol, Charles. "A Poet for Posterity," in *National Review*. XXVII (May 9, 1975), p. 521.

O'Hara, J.D. "Enderby Reviewed," in *New York Times Book Review*. CXXIV (February 2, 1975), p. 4.

Prince, Peter. "Interamural," in *New Statesman*. XCI (June 21, 1974), p. 894.

Solotaroff, T. "Busy Hand of Burgess," in *The Red Hot Vacuum and Other Pieces on the Writing of the Sixties*. New York: Atheneum, 1970, pp. 269–275.

MF

Aggeler, Geoffrey. "Incest and the Artist: Anthony Burgess's *MF* as Summation," in *Modern Fiction Studies*. Lafayette, Ind.: Purdue University Research Foundation, 1973, pp. 529–543.

Dix, Carol M. "The Language," in *Anthony Burgess*. London: Longmans, 1971, pp. 28–29.

Foote, Audrey. "*MF* Reviewed," in *Book World*. VI (March 5, 1972), p. 7.

Gardner, John. "*MF*," in *Southern Review*. V (Winter, 1969), pp. 239–240.

Le Clair, T. "Essential Opposition: The Novels of Anthony Burgess," in *Critique*. XII (1977), pp. 77–94.

McInery, R. "*MF*," in *Commonweal*. XCIV (May 28, 1971), pp. 290–291.

Winter, Thomas. "A Protean Work," in *Prairie Schooner*. XLV (Spring, 1972), pp. 82–83.

Nothing Like the Sun

Aggeler, Geoffrey. "The Comic Art of Anthony Burgess," in *Arizona Quarterly*. XXV (1969), pp. 234–251.

———. "Prophetic Acrostic in Anthony Burgess's *Nothing Like the Sun*," in *Notes and Queries*. XXI (April, 1974), p. 136.

Burgess, Anthony. "Genesis and Headache," in *Afterwords: Novelists on Their Novels*. Edited by Thomas McCormack. New York: Harper, 1968, pp. 29–47.

De Vitis, A.A. "Back and Forth: East and West," in *Anthony Burgess*. New York: Twayne, 1972, pp. 141–148.

Dix, Carol M. "The Language," in *Anthony Burgess*. London: Longmans, 1971, p. 27.

Le Clair, T. "Essential Opposition: The Novels of Anthony Burgess," in *Critique*. XII (1977), pp. 77–94.

FANNY BURNEY
(1752–1840)

Cecilia

Adelstein, Michael E. *Fanny Burney*. New York: Twayne, 1968, pp. 64–73.

Baker, Ernest R. *The History of the English Novel*, Volume V. New York: Barnes & Noble, 1950, pp. 164–169.

Cecil, David. "Fanny Burney," in *Poets and Story-Tellers*. New York: Macmillan, 1949, pp. 77–96.

Dobson, Austin. *Fanny Burney*. New York: Macmillan, 1903, pp. 117–128.

Hemlow, Joyce. *The History of Fanny Burney*. Oxford: Clarendon Press, 1958, pp. 139–168.

Hinkley, Laura L. *Ladies of Literature*. New York: Hastings House, 1946, pp. 40–41.

Kooiman-Van Middendorp, Gerarda M. *The Hero in the Feminine Novel*. New York: Haskell House, 1966, pp. 24–30.

Lloyd, Christopher. *Fanny Burney*. London: Longmans, Green, 1937, pp. 115–131.

MacCarthy, Bridget G. *The Female Pen: The Later Women Novelists, 1744–1818*, Volume II. Oxford: B.H. Blackwell, 1947, pp. 115–120.

Masefield, Muriel. *Women Novelists from Fanny Burney to George Eliot*. London: Ivor Nicholson and Watson, 1934, pp. 29–30.

Mews, Hazel. *Frail Vessels: Woman's Role in Women's Novels from Fanny Burney to George Eliot*. London: Athlone, 1969, pp. 33–36.

Overman, Antoinette A. *An Investigation into the Character of Fanny Burney*. Amsterdam: H.J. Paris, 1933, pp. 48–56.

Steeves, Harrison R. *Before Jane Austen: The Shaping of the English Novel in the Eighteenth Century*. New York: Holt, Rinehart and Winston, 1965, pp. 218–220.

White, Eugene. *Fanny Burney, Novelist: A Study in Technique*. Hamden, Conn.: Shoe String Press, 1960.

Evelina

Adelstein, Michael E. *Fanny Burney*. New York: Twayne, 1968, pp. 28–44.

Baker, Ernest A. *The History of the English Novel*, Volume V. New York: Barnes & Noble, 1950, pp. 160–164.

Dobson, Austin. *Fanny Burney*. New York: Macmillan, 1903, pp. 61–87.

Glock, Waldo S. "Appearance and Reality: The Education of *Evelina*," in *Essays in Literature*. II (1975), pp. 32–41.

Hemlow, Joyce. *The History of Fanny Burney.* Oxford: Clarendon Press, 1958, pp. 78–104.

Hinkley, Laura L. *Ladies of Literature.* New York: Hastings House, 1946, pp. 21–34.

Kooiman-Van Middendorp, Gerarda M. *The Hero in the Feminine Novel.* New York: Haskell House, 1966, pp. 24–30.

Lloyd, Christopher. *Fanny Burney.* London: Longmans, Green, 1937, pp. 71–85.

MacCarthy, Bridget G. *The Female Pen: The Later Women Novelists, 1744–1818,* Volume II. Oxford: B.H. Blackwell, 1947, pp. 97–115.

Malone, Kemp. *"Evelina* Revisited," in *Papers on English Language and Literature.* I (Winter, 1965), pp. 3–19.

Masefield, Muriel. *Women Novelists from Fanny Burney to George Eliot.* London: Ivor Nicholson and Watson, 1934, pp. 24–29.

Mews, Hazel. *Frail Vessels: Woman's Role in Women's Novels from Fanny Burney to George Eliot.* London: Athlone, 1969, pp. 32–33.

Montague, Edwine and Louis L. Martz. "Fanny Burney's *Evelina,*" in *The Age of Johnson: Essays Presented to Chauncey Brewster Timker.* New Haven, Conn.: Yale University Press, 1949, pp. 170–181.

Newton, Judith. *"Evelina:* Or, the History of a Young Lady's Entrance into the Marriage Market," in *Modern Language Studies.* VI (1976), pp. 48–56.

Overman, Antoinette A. *An Investigation into the Character of Fanny Burney.* Amsterdam: H.J. Paris, 1933, pp. 38–48.

Rubenstein, Jill. "The Crisis of Identity in Fanny Burney's *Evelina,*" in *New Rambler.* CIX (Spring, 1972), pp. 45–50.

Scrutton, Mary. "Bourgeois Cinderellas," in *Twentieth Century.* CLV (April, 1954), pp. 355–360.

Staves, Susan. *"Evelina;* or, Female Difficulties," in *Modern Philology.* LXXIII (1976), pp. 368–381.

Steeves, Harrison R. *Before Jane Austen: The Shaping of the English Novel in the Eighteenth Century.* New York: Holt, Rinehart and Winston, 1965, pp. 204–218.

Swinnerton, Frank A. *A Galaxy of Fathers.* Garden City, N.Y.: Doubleday, 1966, pp. 103–108.

Vopat, James B. *"Evelina:* Life as Art—Notes Toward Becoming a Performer on the Stage of Life," in *Essays in Literature.* II (1975), pp. 42–52.

White, Eugene. "Fanny Burney," in *Minor British Novelists.* Edited by Charles Alva Hoyt. Carbondale: Southern Illinois University Press, 1967, pp. 3–12.

————. *Fanny Burney, Novelist: A Study in Technique.* Hamden, Conn.: Shoe String Press, 1960.

ROBERT BURNS
(1759–1796)

Tam O'Shanter

Campbell, Ian. "Burns's Poems and Their Audience," in *Critical Essays on Robert Burns*. Edited by Donald A. Low. London: Routledge & Kegan Paul, 1975, pp. 42–46.

Crawford, Thomas. *Burns: A Study of the Poems and Songs*. Stanford, Calif.: Stanford University Press, 1960, pp. 220–236, 358–361.

Daiches, David. *Robert Burns*. New York: Macmillan, 1966, pp. 249–260.

Kinsley, James. "A Note on *Tam O'Shanter*," in *English*. XX (1967), pp. 213–216.

Kroeber, Karl. *Romantic Narrative Art*. Madison: University of Wisconsin Press, 1960, pp. 3–11.

Mackensie, M.L. "A New Dimension for *Tam O'Shanter*," in *Studies in Scottish Literature*. I (1964), pp. 87–92.

MacLaine, Allan H. "Burns's Use of Parody in *Tam O'Shanter*," in *Criticism*. I (Fall, 1959), pp. 308–316.

Morton, Richard. "Narrative Irony in Robert Burns's *Tam O'Shanter*," in *Modern Language Quarterly*. XXII (1961), pp. 12–20.

Thomas, W.K. "Burns' *Tam O'Shanter*, 57–58," in *Explicator*. XXVIII (1969), item 33.

Troutner, Jack. "*Tam O'Shanter*'s Path of Glory: Tone in Robert Burns's Narrative," in *Massachusetts Studies in English*. I (1968), pp. 69–74.

Weston, John C. "The Narrator of *Tam O'Shanter*," in *Studies in English Literature, 1500–1900*. VIII (1968), pp. 537–550.

White, Gertrude M. "Don't Look Back: Something Might Be Gaining on You," in *Sewanee Review*. LXXXI (1973), pp. 870–874.

"To a Mouse"

Baird, John D. "Two Poets of the 1780's: Burns and Cowper," in *Critical Essays on Robert Burns*. Edited by Donald A. Low. London: Routledge & Kegan Paul, 1975, pp. 116–117.

Brooks, Cleanth and Robert P. Heilman. *Understanding Drama*. New York: Holt, 1945, pp. 19–22.

Bruce, George. "Burns: A Comparative View," in *Robert Burns, New Judgments; Essays by Six Contemporary Writers*. Edited by William Montgomerie. Glasgow, Scotland: W. MacLellan, 1947, pp. 19–20.

Crawford, Thomas. *Burns; A Study of the Poems and Songs*. Stanford, Calif.: Stanford University Press, 1960, pp. 164–168.

Daiches, David. *Robert Burns.* New York: Macmillan, 1966, pp. 151–154.

Highet, Gilbert. *Powers of Poetry.* New York: Oxford University Press, 1960, pp. 74–81.

WILLIAM BURROUGHS
(1914–   )

Naked Lunch

Bryant, Jerry H. *The Open Decision: The Contemporary American Novel and Its Intellectual Background.* New York: Free Press, 1970, pp. 199–228.

Hassan, Ihab. "The Novel of Outrage: A Minority Voice in Postwar American Fiction," in *The American Scholar.* XXXIV (Spring, 1965), pp. 250–252.

Hoffman, Frederick. *The Mortal No: Death and the Modern Imagination.* Princeton, N.J.: Princeton University Press, 1964, pp. 486–489.

Kazin, Alfred. *Bright Book of Life.* Boston: Little, Brown, 1973, pp. 262–271.

Kostelanetz, Richard. "The New American Fiction," in *Ramparts.* III (January–February, 1965), pp. 57–62.

————. "From Nightmare to Serendipity: A Retrospective Look at Burroughs," in *Twentieth Century Literature.* XI (October, 1965), pp. 123–130.

Lodge, David. "Objections to William Burroughs," in *Critical Quarterly.* VIII (Autumn, 1966), pp. 203–212.

————. *The Modes of Modern Writing.* Ithaca, N.Y.: Cornell University Press, 1977, pp. 35–38.

McCarthy, Mary. "Burroughs' *Naked Lunch*," in *Encounter.* XX (April, 1963), pp. 92–98.

————. *The Writing on the Wall.* New York: Harcourt, 1970, pp. 42–53.

McConnell, Frank D. "William Burroughs and the Literature of Addiction," in *Massachusetts Review.* VIII (Autumn, 1967), pp. 665–680.

Michelson, Peter. "Beardsley, Burroughs, Decadence, and the Poetics of Obscenity," in *Tri-Quarterly.* XII (1968), pp. 139–155.

Pearce, Richard. *Stages of the Clown.* Carbondale: Southern Illinois University Press, 1970, pp. 84–101.

Wain, John. "*Naked Lunch*," in *The Critic as Artist.* Edited by Gilbert A. Harrison. New York: Liveright, 1972, pp. 351–357.

SAMUEL BUTLER
(1612–1680)

Hudibras

Nelson, N.H. "Astrology, *Hudibras* and the Puritans," in *Journal of the History of Ideas.* XXXVII (July, 1976), pp. 521–536.

Richards, Edward. *Hudibras in the Burlesque Tradition.* New York: Octagon, 1972. Reprint of 1937 Edition.

Thorson, J.L. "Publication of *Hudibras,*" in *Papers of Bibliographical Society of America.* LX (October, 1966), pp. 418–438.

Wasserman, George R. "*Hudibras* and Male Chauvinism," in *Studies in English Literature.* XVI (Summer, 1976), pp. 351–361.

_____. *Samuel* Hudibras *Butler.* Boston: Twayne, 1976.

_____. "Strange Chimaera of Beasts and Men: The Argument and Imagery of *Hudibras,*" in *Studies in English Literature.* XIII (Summer, 1973), pp. 405–421.

Wilding, M. "Flecknoe's *Diarium*: A Source for *Hudibras,*" in *Notes and Queries.* XXII (July, 1975), pp. 310–312.

SAMUEL BUTLER
(1835–1902)

Erewhon

Bekker, Willem G. *An Historical and Critical Review of Samuel Butler's Literary Works.* New York: Haskell House, 1966. Reprint of 1925 Edition.

Breuer, H.P. "The Source of Morality in Butler's *Erewhon*," in *Victorian Studies.* XVI (March, 1973), pp. 317–328.

Cannan, Gilbert. *Samuel Butler, a Critical Study.* New York: Haskell House, 1970. Reprint of 1915 Edition.

Furbank, Philip H. *Samuel Butler, 1835–1902.* Hamden, Conn.: Archon Books, 1971. Reprint of 1948 Edition.

Garnett, Martha R. *Samuel Butler and His Family Relations.* Folcroft, Pa.: Folcroft Library Editions, 1976. Reprint of 1926 Edition.

Harris, John F. *Samuel Butler, Author of* Erewhon: *The Man and His Work.* Folcroft, Pa.: Folcroft Library Editions, 1973. Reprint of 1916 Edition.

Henderson, Philip. *Samuel Butler, the Incarnate Bachelor.* New York: Barnes & Noble, 1968. Reprint of 1953 Edition.

Holt, Lee E. *Samuel Butler.* New York: Twayne, 1964.

————. "Samuel Butler and His Victorian Critics," in *Journal of English Literary History.* VIII (June, 1941), pp. 146–159.

————. "Samuel Butler's Revisions of *Erewhon*," in *Papers of Bibliographical Society of America.* XXXVIII (1944), pp. 22–38.

Jones, Henry F. *Samuel Butler, Author of* Erewhon *(1835–1902): A Memoir.* New York: Octagon, 1968. Reprint of 1920 Edition.

Jones, Joseph J. *The Cradle of* Erewhon: *Samuel Butler in New Zealand.* Austin: University of Texas Press, 1959.

Knoepflmacher, Ulrich C. *Religious Humanism and the Victorian Novel: Eliot, Pater, and Butler.* Princeton, N.J.: Princeton University Press, 1965.

Muggeridge, Malcolm. *The Earnest Atheist: A Study of Samuel Butler.* New York: Haskell House, 1971. Reprint of 1937 Edition.

Rattray, Robert F. *Samuel Butler: A Chronicle and an Introduction.* New York: Haskell House, 1974. Reprint of 1935 Edition.

Salter, William H. *Essays on Two Moderns: Euripides and Samuel Butler.* Port Washington, N.Y.: Kennikat, 1970. Reprint of 1911 Edition.

Stillman, Clara G. *Samuel Butler, a Mid-Victorian Modern.* Port Washington, N.Y.: Kennikat, 1972. Reprint of 1932 Edition.

Willey, Basil. *Darwin and Butler: Two Versions of Evolution.* London: Chatto, 1960.

The Way of All Flesh

Bekker, Willem G. *An Historical and Critical Review of Samuel Butler's Literary Works.* New York: Haskell House, 1966. Reprint of 1925 Edition.

Bissell, Clyde T. "A Study of *The Way of All Flesh*," in *Nineteenth Century Studies.* Edited by Herbert Davis. Ithaca, N.Y.: Cornell University Press, pp. 277–303.

Cannan, Gilbert. *Samuel Butler, a Critical Study.* New York: Haskell House, 1970. Reprint of 1915 Edition.

Cole, George D. *Samuel Butler and* The Way of All Flesh. Norwood, Pa.: Norwood Editions, 1976. Reprint of 1947 Edition.

Furbank, Philip H. *Samuel Butler, 1835–1902.* Hamden, Conn.: Archon Books, 1971. Reprint of 1948 Edition.

Garnett, Martha R. *Samuel Butler and His Family Relations.* Folcroft, Pa.: Folcroft Library Editions, 1976. Reprint of 1926 Edition.

Henderson, Philip. *Samuel Butler, the Incarnate Bachelor.* New York: Barnes & Noble, 1968. Reprint of 1953 Edition.

Holt, Lee E. *Samuel Butler.* New York: Twayne, 1964.

————. "Samuel Butler and His Victorian Critics," in *Journal of English Literary History.* VIII (June, 1941), pp. 146–159.

————. Samuel Butler's Rise to Fame," in *PMLA.* LVII (September, 1942), pp. 867–878.

Howard, Daniel. "The Critical Significance of Autobiography in *The Way of All Flesh*," in *Victorian Newsletter.* XVII (Spring, 1960), pp. 12–18.

Jones, Henry F. *Samuel Butler, Author of* Erewhon *(1835–1902): A Memoir.* New York: Octagon, 1968. Reprint of 1920 Edition.

Knoepflmacher, Ulrich C. "Ishmael or Anti-Hero? The Division of Self in *The Way of All Flesh*," in *English Fiction in Transition.* IV (1961), pp. 28–35.

————. *Religious Humanism and the Victorian Novel: Eliot, Pater, and Butler.* Princeton, N.J.: Princeton University Press, 1965.

Linde, Ilse D. "*The Way of All Flesh* and *A Portrait of the Artist as a Young Man*: A Comparison," in *Victorian Newsletter.* IX (Spring, 1956), pp. 9–16.

Muggeridge, Malcolm. *The Earnest Atheist: A Study of Samuel Butler.* New York: Haskell House, 1971. Reprint of 1937 Edition.

Rattray, Robert F. *Samuel Butler: A Chronicle and an Introduction.* New York: Haskell House, 1974. Reprint of 1935 Edition.

Salter, William H. *Essays on Two Moderns: Euripides and Samuel Butler.* Port Washington, N.Y.: Kennikat, 1970. Reprint of 1911 Edition.

Stillman, Clara G. *Samuel Butler, a Mid-Victorian Modern.* Port Washington, N.Y.: Kennikat, 1972. Reprint of 1932 Edition.

Willey, Basil. *Darwin and Butler: Two Versions of Evolution.* London: Chatto, 1960.

GEORGE GORDON, LORD BYRON
(1788–1824)

Cain

Blackstone, Bernard. *Byron: A Survey*. London: Longmans, 1975, pp. 244–250.

Bostetter, Edward E. *The Romantic Ventriloquists: Wordsworth, Coleridge, Keats, Shelley, Byron*. Seattle: University of Washington Press, 1963, pp. 282–292.

Calvert, William J. *Byron: Romantic Paradox*. New York: Russell and Russell, 1962, pp. 174–196.

Chew, Samuel C., Jr. *The Dramas of Lord Byron: A Critical Study*. New York: Russell and Russell, 1964, pp. 118–134.

Cooke, Michael G. *The Blind Man Traces the Circle: On the Patterns and Philosophy of Byron's Poetry*. Princeton, N.J.: Princeton University Press, 1969, pp. 74–81.

Elledge, W. Paul. *Byron and the Dynamics of Metaphor*. Nashville, Tenn.: Vanderbilt University Press, 1968, pp. 139–151.

Gleckner, R.F. *Byron and the Ruins of Paradise*. Baltimore: Johns Hopkins University Press, 1967, pp. 323–327.

Joseph, M.K. *Byron the Poet*. London: Victor Gollancz, 1964, pp. 116–130.

Jump, John D. *Byron*. London: Routledge and Kegan Paul, 1972, pp. 166–182.

McGann, J.J. *Fiery Dust: Byron's Poetic Development*. Chicago: University of Chicago Press, 1968, pp. 245–273.

Marchand, Leslie A. *Byron's Poetry: A Critical Introduction*. Boston: Houghton Mifflin, 1965, pp. 84–91.

Marshall, William H. *The Structure of Byron's Major Poems*. Philadelphia: University of Pennsylvania Press, 1962, pp. 136–154.

Michaels, Leonard. "Byron's *Cain*," in *PMLA*. LXXXIV (January, 1969), pp. 71–78.

Thorslev, P.L. *The Byronic Hero: Types and Prototypes*. Minneapolis: University of Minnesota Press, 1962, pp. 176–184.

Trueblood, Paul G. *Lord Byron*. New York: Twayne, 1969, pp. 109–111.

Childe Harold's Pilgrimage

Berry, Francis. "The Poet of *Childe Harold*," in *Byron: A Symposium*. Edited by John D. Jump. New York: Barnes & Noble, 1975, pp. 35–51.

Blackstone, Bernard. *Byron: A Survey*. London: Longmans, 1975, pp. 79–105, 184–230.

Bostetter, Edward E. *The Romantic Ventriloquists: Wordsworth, Coleridge, Keats, Shelley, Byron.* Seattle: University of Washington Press, 1963, pp. 271–277.

Calvert, William J. *Byron: Romantic Paradox.* New York: Russell and Russell, 1962, pp. 111–113, 144–151.

Chew, Samuel C. "Introduction," in *Childe Harold's Pilgrimage and Other Romantic Poems.* New York: Odyssey, 1936, pp. ix–xxxiv.

Cooke, Michael G. *The Blind Man Traces the Circle: On the Patterns and Philosophy of Byron's Poetry.* Princeton, N.J.: Princeton University Press, 1969, pp. 38–60, 122–126.

————. *The Romantic Will.* New Haven, Conn.: Yale University Press, 1976, pp. 216–222.

Elledge, W. Paul. *Byron and the Dynamics of Metaphor.* Nashville, Tenn.: Vanderbilt University Press, 1968, pp. 54–81.

Gleckner, R.F. *Byron and the Ruins of Paradise.* Baltimore: Johns Hopkins University Press, 1967, pp. 53–90, 225–250, 271–297.

Joseph, M.K. *Byron the Poet.* London: Victor Gollancz, 1964, pp. 13–102.

Jump, John D. *Byron.* London: Routledge and Kegan Paul, 1972, pp. 75–84.

McGann, J.J. *Fiery Dust: Byron's Poetic Development.* Chicago: University of Chicago Press, 1968, pp. 31–138, 301–318.

Marchand, Leslie A. *Byron's Poetry: A Critical Introduction.* Boston: Houghton Mifflin, 1965, pp. 38–59.

Marshall, William H. *The Structure of Byron's Major Poems.* Philadelphia: University of Pennsylvania Press, 1962, pp. 36–39, 72–81.

Rutherford, Andrew. *Byron: A Critical Study.* London: Oliver and Boyd, 1962, pp. 26–35, 48–65, 93–102.

Thorslev, P.L. *The Byronic Hero: Types and Prototypes.* Minneapolis: University of Minnesota Press, 1962, pp. 127–145.

Trueblood, Paul G. *Lord Byron.* New York: Twayne, 1969, pp. 46–53, 76–80, 85–90.

Don Juan

Blackstone, Bernard. *Byron: A Survey.* London: Longmans, 1975, pp. 287–344.

Bostetter, Edward E. *The Romantic Ventriloquists: Wordsworth, Coleridge, Keats, Shelley, Byron.* Seattle: University of Washington Press, 1963, pp. 241–253.

Boyd, Elizabeth F. *Byron's* Don Juan: *A Critical Study.* New Brunswick, N.J.: Rutgers University Press, 1945. Partially reprinted in *Twentieth Century Interpretations of* Don Juan: *A Collection of Critical Essays.* Edited by Edward E. Bostetter. Englewood Cliffs, N.J.: Prentice-Hall, 1969, pp. 98–99.

Bredvold, Louis I.   "Introductory Essay," in *Lord Byron: Don Juan and Other Satirical Poems*. New York: Odyssey Press, 1935, pp. v–xxxv.

Calvert, William J.   *Byron: Romantic Paradox*. New York: Russell and Russell, 1962, pp. 182–210. Reprinted in *Byron: Childe Harold's Pilgrimage and Don Juan—A Casebook*. Edited by John D. Jump. London: Macmillan, 1973, pp. 111–131.

Cooke, Michael G.   *The Blind Man Traces the Circle: On the Patterns and Philosophy of Byron's Poetry*. Princeton, N.J.: Princeton University Press, 1969, pp. 128–174.

Gardner, Helen.   "Don Juan," in *London Magazine*. V (July, 1958), pp. 58–65. Reprinted in *Byron: A Collection of Critical Essays*. Edited by Paul West. Englewood Cliffs, N.J.: Prentice-Hall, 1963, pp. 113–121. Also reprinted in *English Romantic Poets: Modern Essays in Criticism*. Edited by M.H. Abrams. New York: Oxford University Press, 1975, pp. 303–312.

Gleckner, R.F.   *Byron and the Ruins of Paradise*. Baltimore: Johns Hopkins University Press, 1967, pp. 329–347. Reprinted in *Twentieth Century Interpretations of* Don Juan: *A Collection of Critical Essays*. Edited by Edward E. Bostetter. Englewood Cliffs, N.J.: Prentice-Hall, 1969, pp. 109–112.

Hirsch, E.D., Jr.   "Byron and the Terrestrial Paradise," in *From Sensibility to Romanticism*. New York: Oxford University Press, 1965, pp. 467–486. Reprinted in *Twentieth Century Interpretations of* Don Juan: *A Collection of Critical Essays*. Edited by Edward E. Bostetter. Englewood Cliffs, N.J.: Prentice-Hall, 1969, pp. 106–108.

Joseph, M.K.   *Byron the Poet*. London: Victor Gollancz, 1964, pp. 149–333. Partially reprinted in *Twentieth Century Interpretations of* Don Juan: *A Collection of Critical Essays*. Edited by Edward E. Bostetter. Englewood Cliffs, N.J.: Prentice-Hall, 1969, pp. 29–37.

Jump, John D.   *Byron*. London: Routledge and Kegan Paul, 1972, pp. 103–151.

Kernan, Alvin B.   *The Plot of Satire*. New Haven, Conn.: Yale University Press, 1965, pp. 171–222. Partially reprinted in *Twentieth Century Interpretations of* Don Juan: *A Collection of Critical Essays*. Edited by Edward E. Bostetter. Englewood Cliffs, N.J.: Prentice-Hall, 1969, pp. 85–93.

Kroeber, Karl.   *Romantic Narrative Art*. Madison: University of Wisconsin Press, 1960, pp. 135–167. Reprinted in *Twentieth Century Interpretations of* Don Juan: *A Collection of Critical Essays*. Edited by Edward E. Bostetter. Englewood Cliffs, N.J.: Prentice-Hall, 1969, pp. 103–105.

Lovell, Ernest J., Jr.   "Iron and Image in Byron's *Don Juan*," in *The Major English Romantic Poets: A Symposium in Reappraisal*. Edited by Clarence C. Thorpe, Carlos Baker and Bennett Weaver. Carbondale: Southern Illinois University Press, 1957, pp. 129–148. Reprinted in *Twentieth Century Interpretations of* Don Juan: *A Collection of Critical Essays*. Edited by Edward E. Bostetter. Englewood Cliffs, N.J.: Prentice-Hall, 1969, pp. 21–28.

McGann, J.J. *Fiery Dust: Byron's Poetic Development.* Chicago: University of Chicago Press, 1968, pp. 186–188, 199–201, 294–298.

Marchand, Leslie A. *Byron's Poetry: A Critical Introduction.* Boston: Houghton Mifflin, 1965, pp. 157–234.

Marshall, William H. *The Structure of Byron's Major Poems.* Philadelphia: University of Pennsylvania Press, 1962, pp. 174–177.

Ridenour, George M. *The Style of* Don Juan. New Haven, Conn.: Yale University Press, 1960. Partially reprinted in *Byron: A Collection of Critical Essays.* Edited by Paul West. Englewood Cliffs, N.J.: Prentice-Hall, 1963, pp. 122–137.

Robson, W.W. "Byron as Poet," in *Critical Essays.* London: Routledge and Kegan Paul, 1966, pp. 148–190. Reprinted in *Byron: A Collection of Critical Essays.* Edited by Paul West. Englewood Cliffs, N.J.: Prentice-Hall, 1963, pp. 88–95. Also reprinted in *Byron:* Childe Harold's Pilgrimage *and* Don Juan—*A Casebook.* Edited by John D. Jump. London: Macmillan, 1973, pp. 132–152.

Rutherford, Andrew. *Byron: A Critical Study.* London: Oliver and Boyd, 1962, pp. 125–217. Partially reprinted in *Twentieth Century Interpretations of* Don Juan: *A Collection of Critical Essays.* Edited by Edward E. Bostetter. Englewood Cliffs, N.J.: Prentice-Hall, 1969, pp. 51–62.

Steffan, Guy. *Byron's* Don Juan, *Volume I: The Making of a Masterpiece.* Austin: University of Texas Press, 1957, pp. 278–296. Reprinted in *Byron: A Collection of Critical Essays.* Edited by Paul West. Englewood Cliffs, N.J.: Prentice-Hall, 1963, pp. 96–112.

Trueblood, Paul G. *The Flowering of Byron's Genius: Studies in Byron's* Don Juan. New York: Russell and Russell, 1962.

————. *Lord Byron.* New York: Twayne, 1969, pp. 97–103, 135–161.

West, Paul. *Byron and the Spoiler's Art.* London: Chatto and Windus, 1960, pp. 66–73. Reprinted in *Twentieth Century Interpretations of* Don Juan: *A Collection of Critical Essays.* Edited by Edward E. Bostetter. Englewood Cliffs, N.J.: Prentice-Hall, 1969, pp. 100–102.

English Bards and Scotch Reviewers

Blackstone, Bernard. *Byron: A Survey.* London: Longmans, 1975, pp. 43–54.

Calvert, William J. *Byron: Romantic Paradox.* New York: Russell and Russell, 1962, pp. 42–45.

Gleckner, R.F. *Byron and the Ruins of Paradise.* Baltimore: Johns Hopkins University Press, 1967, pp. 27–31.

Joseph, M.K. *Byron the Poet.* London: Victor Gollancz, 1964, pp. 131–133.

Marchand, Leslie A. *Byron's Poetry: A Critical Introduction.* Boston: Houghton Mifflin, 1965, pp. 21–28.

Marshall, William H. *The Structure of Byron's Major Poems.* Philadelphia: University of Pennsylvania Press, 1962, pp. 27–36.

Mayne, Ethel C. *Byron.* New York: Scribner's, 1924, pp. 80–85.

Rutherford, Andrew. *Byron: A Critical Study.* London: Oliver and Boyd, 1962, pp. 20–24.

Trueblood, Paul G. *Lord Byron.* New York: Twayne, 1969, pp. 33–36.

Yarker, P.M. "Byron and the Satiric Temper," in *Byron: A Symposium.* Edited by John D. Jump. New York: Barnes & Noble, 1975, pp. 76–93.

Manfred

Blackstone, Bernard. *Byron: A Survey.* London: Longmans, 1975, pp. 152–154, 231–238.

Bostetter, Edward E. *The Romantic Ventriloquists: Wordsworth, Coleridge, Keats, Shelley, Byron.* Seattle: University of Washington Press, 1963, pp. 278–282.

Calvert, William J. *Byron: Romantic Paradox.* New York: Russell and Russell, 1962, pp. 139–144.

Chew, Samuel C., Jr. *The Dramas of Lord Byron: A Critical Study.* New York: Russell and Russell, 1964, pp. 59–84.

Cooke, Michael G. *The Blind Man Traces the Circle: On the Patterns and Philosophy of Byron's Poetry.* Princeton, N.J.: Princeton University Press, 1969, pp. 64–74.

Elledge, W. Paul. *Byron and the Dynamics of Metaphor.* Nashville, Tenn.: Vanderbilt University Press, 1968, pp. 81–94.

Gleckner, R.F. *Byron and the Ruins of Paradise.* Baltimore: Johns Hopkins University Press, 1967, pp. 256–265.

Joseph, M.K. *Byron the Poet.* London: Victor Gollancz, 1964, pp. 103–108.

Jump, John D. *Byron.* London: Routledge and Kegan Paul, 1972, pp. 84–87.

Marchand, Leslie A. *Byron's Poetry: A Critical Introduction.* Boston: Houghton Mifflin, 1965, pp. 75–84.

Marshall, William H. *The Structure of Byron's Major Poems.* Philadelphia: University of Pennsylvania Press, 1962, pp. 97–110.

Rutherford, Andrew. *Byron: A Critical Study.* London: Oliver and Boyd, 1962, pp. 76–92.

Thorslev, P.L. *The Byronic Hero: Types and Prototypes.* Minneapolis: University of Minnesota Press, 1962, pp. 165–176.

Trueblood, Paul G. *Lord Byron.* New York: Twayne, 1969, pp. 81–84.

West, Paul. *Byron and the Spoiler's Art.* London: Chatto and Windus, 1960, pp. 102–104.

The Prisoner of Chillon

Cooke, Michael G. *The Blind Man Traces the Circle: On the Patterns and Philosophy of Byron's Poetry.* Princeton, N.J.: Princeton University Press, 1969, pp. 87–88.

Elledge, W. Paul. *Byron and the Dynamics of Metaphor.* Nashville, Tenn.: Vanderbilt University Press, 1968, pp. 45–54.

Gleckner, R.F. *Byron and the Ruins of Paradise.* Baltimore: Johns Hopkins University Press, 1967, pp. 191–199.

McGann, J.J. *Fiery Dust: Byron's Poetic Development.* Chicago: University of Chicago Press, 1968, pp. 165–173.

Marchand, Leslie A. *Byron's Poetry: A Critical Introduction.* Boston: Houghton Mifflin, 1965, pp. 69–70.

Marshall, William H. *The Structure of Byron's Major Poems.* Philadelphia: University of Pennsylvania Press, 1962, pp. 82–96.

Rutherford, Andrew. *Byron: A Critical Study.* London: Oliver and Boyd, 1962, pp. 66–75.

Trueblood, Paul G. *Lord Byron.* New York: Twayne, 1969, pp. 72–75.

Wood, Gerald C. "Nature and Narrative in Byron's *The Prisoner of Chillon*," in *Keats-Shelley Journal.* XXIV (1975), pp. 108–117.

JAMES BRANCH CABELL
(1879–1958)

The Cream of the Jest

Davis, Joe Lee. *James Branch Cabell.* New York: Twayne, 1962, pp. 121–127.

Godshalk, William L. "Cabell's *Cream of the Jest* and Recent American Fiction," in *Southern Literary Journal.* V (1973), pp. 18–31.

Parks, Edd Winfield. "Cabell's *Cream of the Jest*," in *Modern Fiction Studies.* II (May, 1956), pp. 68–70.

Tarrant, Desmond. *James Branch Cabell: The Dream and the Reality.* Norman: University of Oklahoma Press, 1967, pp. 192–199.

Walpole, Hugh. *The Art of James Branch Cabell.* New York: Robert M. McBride, 1924, p. 32.

Wells, Arvin R. *Jesting Moses: A Study in Cabellian Comedy.* Gainesville: University of Florida Press, 1962, pp. 94–104.

Jurgen

Aiken, Conrad. *A Reviewer's A B C: Collected Criticism of Conrad Aiken from 1916 to the Present.* New York: Meridian Books, 1958, pp. 143–148.

Allen, Gay W. "*Jurgen* and Faust," in *Sewanee Review.* XXXIX (October–December, 1931), pp. 485–492.

Brewster, Paul G. "*Jurgen* and *Figures of Earth* and the Russian Shazki," in *American Literature.* XIII (January, 1942), pp. 305–318.

Brussel, I.R. "The First Fifty Years of *Jurgen*," in *Cabellian.* I (1969), p. 74.

Davis, Joe Lee. *James Branch Cabell.* New York: Twayne, 1962, pp. 88–94, 104–106.

Flora, Joseph M. "*Jurgen* in the Classroom," in *Cabellian.* I (1969), pp. 31–34.

Gabbard, G.N. "The Dance Version of *Jurgen*," in *Kalki.* VI (1975), pp. 115–117.

Hartman, Harry. " 'The Comstock Lewd': *Jurgen* and the Law—Updated," in *Kalki.* III (1969), pp. 16–19.

Loveman, Samuel. *A Round-Table in Poictesme.* Cleveland: Colophon Club, 1924, pp. 51–53.

Schley, Margaret A. "The Demiurge in *Jurgen*," in *Cabellian.* IV (1972), pp. 85–88.

Tarrant, Desmond. *James Branch Cabell: The Dream and the Reality.* Norman: University of Oklahoma Press, 1967, pp. 26–29, 86–89, 129–145.

Van Doren, Carl.   *James Branch Cabell.* New York: Robert M. McBride, 1925, pp. 41–51.

Walpole, Hugh.   *The Art of James Branch Cabell.* New York: Robert M. McBride, 1924, p. 23.

Wells, Arvin R.   *Jesting Moses: A Study in Cabellian Comedy.* Gainesville: University of Florida Press, 1962, pp. 108–118.

The Rivet in Grandfather's Neck

Davis, Joe Lee.   *James Branch Cabell.* New York: Twayne, 1962, pp. 83–87, 105–106.

Walpole, Hugh.   *The Art of James Branch Cabell.* New York: Robert M. McBride, 1924, p. 30.

Wells, Arvin R.   *Jesting Moses: A Study in Cabellian Comedy.* Gainesville: University of Florida Press, 1962, pp. 83–84, 92–94.

PEDRO CALDERÓN DE LA BARCA
(1600–1681)

The Constant Prince

Dunn, Peter N. "*El principe constante*: A Theatre of the World," in *Studies in Spanish Literature of the Golden Age Presented to Edward M. Wilson*. Edited by R.O. Jones. London: Tamesis, 1973, pp. 83–101.

Finch, Mary F. "*On Being and Essence* and *El principe constante*," in *Hispano*. XLIII (1971), pp. 17–24.

Gilman, Richard. *Common and Uncommon Masks: Writings on the Theatre, 1961–1970*. New York: Random House, 1971, pp. 308–310.

Hesse, Everett W. *Calderón de la Barca*. New York: Twayne, 1967, pp. 70–82.

Loftis, John. "*El principe constante* and *The Indian Emperour*: A Reconsideration," in *Modern Language Review*. LXV (October, 1970), pp. 761–767.

————. *The Spanish Plays of Neo-Classical England*. New Haven, Conn.: Yale University Press, 1973, pp. 178–208.

Norval, Maria. "Another Look at Calderón's *El principe constante*," in *Bulletin of the Comediantes*. XXV (1973), pp. 18–28.

Reichenberger, A.G. "Calderón's *El principe constante*: A Tragedy?," in *Modern Language Notes*. LXXV (1960), pp. 668–670.

Rivers, Elias L. "Fenix's Sonnet in Calderón's *Principe constante*," in *Hispanic Review*. XXXVII (1969), pp. 452–458.

Sears, H. "Minutes," in *Bulletin of the Comediantes*. IX (1959), pp. 6–7.

Sloane, Robert. "Action and Role in *El principe constante*," in *Modern Language Notes*. LXXXV (1970), pp. 167–183.

Spitzer, L. "The Figure of Fenix in Calderón's *El principe constante*," in *Critical Essays in the Theatre of Calderón*. Edited by Bruce Wardropper. New York: New York University Press, 1964, pp. 137–150.

Truman, R.W. "The Theme of Justice in *El principe constante*," in *Modern Language Review*. LIX (1964), pp. 43–52.

Wardropper, Bruce W. "Christian and Moor in Calderón's *El principe constante*," in *Modern Language Review*. LIII (1958), pp. 512–520.

Whitby, William M. "Calderón: *El principe constante*; Fenix's Role in the Ransom of Fernando's Body," in *Bulletin of the Comediantes*. VIII (1956), pp. 1–4.

Wilson, E.M. and W.J. Entwhistle. "Calderón's *Principe constante*: Two Appreciations," in *Modern Language Review*. XXXIV (1939), pp. 207–222.

————. "An Early Rehash of Calderón's *El principe constante*," in *Modern Language Notes.* LXXVI (1961), pp. 785–794.

The Devotion of the Cross

Honig, Edwin. *Calderón and the Seizures of Honor.* Cambridge, Mass.: Harvard University Press, 1972, pp. 53–80.

————. "Calderón's Strange Mercy Play," in *Massachusetts Review.* III (1961), pp. 80–107.

————. "Introduction," in *Calderón de la Barca: Four Plays.* New York: Hill and Wang, 1961, pp. xi–xxv.

————. "The Seizures of Honor in Calderón," in *Kenyon Review.* XXIII (Summer, 1961), pp. 439–441.

Horst, Robert ter. "Calderónian Cartesianism: The Iconography of the Mind in *La exaltacion de la cruz*," in *L'Ésprit Createur.* XV (1975), pp. 286–304.

Howe, Elizabeth Teresa. "Fate and Providence in Calderón de la Barca," in *Bulletin of the Comediantes.* XXIX (Fall, 1977), pp. 107–108.

Leech, Clifford. *Shakespeare's Tragedies, and Other Studies in Seventeenth Century Drama.* London: Chatto and Windus, 1961, pp. 209–211.

Neugaard, Edward J. "A New Possible Source for Calderón's *La devocion de la cruz*," in *Bulletin of the Comediantes.* XXV (1973), pp. 1–3.

Parker, A. "The Approach to the Spanish Drama of the Golden Age," in *Tulane Drama Review.* IV (September, 1959), pp. 42–55, 58–60.

————. "The Father-Son Conflict in the Drama of Calderón," in *Forum for Modern Language Studies.* II (1966), pp. 105–106, 112.

Smieja, Robert A. "Julia's Reasoning in Calderón's *La devocion de la cruz*," in *Bulletin of the Comediantes.* XXV (1973), pp. 37–39.

Wardropper, Bruce. *Critical Essays on the Theatre of Calderón.* New York: New York University Press, 1964, pp. 169–192.

Wilson, Margaret. *Spanish Drama of the Golden Age.* New York: Pergamon Press, 1969, pp. 168–169.

The Fairy Lady

Armes, Frederick A. de. "Cespedes y Meneses and Calderón's *La dama duende*," in *Romance Notes.* XI (1970), pp. 598–603.

Fucilla, Joseph G. "*La dama duende* and *La vinda valenciana*," in *Bulletin of the Comediantes.* XXII (1970), pp. 29–32.

Gerstinger, Heinz. *Pedro Calderón de la Barca.* New York: Frederick Ungar, 1973, pp. 51–64.

Honig, Edwin. *Calderón and the Seizures of Honor.* Cambridge, Mass.: Harvard University Press, 1972, pp. 110–157.

————. "Flickers of Incest on the Face of Honor: Calderón's *Phantom Lady*," in *Tulane Drama Review*. VI (1962), pp. 69–105.

————. "Introduction," in *Calderón de la Barca: Four Plays*. New York: Hill and Wang, 1961, pp. xi–xxv.

————. "The Seizures of Honor in Calderón," in *Kenyon Review*. XXIII (Summer, 1961), pp. 443–447.

Horst, Robert ter. "The Ruling Temper of Calderón's *La dama duende*," in *Bulletin of the Comediantes*. XXVII (1975), pp. 68–72.

Leavitt, S. "Humor in the 'Autos' of Calderón," in *Hispania*. XXXIX (1956), pp. 141–144.

Mujica, Barbara Kaminar. "Tragic Elements in Calderón's *La dama duende*," in *Kentucky Romance Quarterly*. XVI (1969), pp. 303–328.

Stroud, Matthew D. "Social-Comic Anagnorisis in *La dama duende*," in *Bulletin of the Comediantes*. XXIX (Fall, 1977), pp. 96–102.

Life Is a Dream

Brody, Ervin C. "Poland in Calderón's *Life Is a Dream*: Poetic Illusion or Historical Reality," in *Polish Review*. XIV (1969), pp. 21–62.

Bryans, J.V. "Rosaura Liberated, or a Woman's Rebellion: A New Reading of the Subplot of *La vida es sueño*," in *University of British Columbia Hispanic Studies*. Edited by Harold Livermore. London: Tamesis Books, 1976, pp. 19–32.

Buchanan, M.A. "Calderón's *Life Is a Dream*," in *PMLA*. XLVII (1933), pp. 1303–1321.

Connolly, Eileen M. "Further Testimony in the Rebel Soldier Case," in *Bulletin of the Comediantes*. XXIV (1972), pp. 11–15.

Dunn, P.N. "The Horoscope Motif in *La vida es sueño*," in *Atlante*. I (October, 1953), pp. 187–201.

Feal, Gisele and Carols Feal-Deibe. "Calderón's *Life Is a Dream*: From Psychology to Myth," in *Hartford Studies in Literature*. VI (1974), pp. 1–28.

Hall, H.B. "Poetic Justice in *La vida es sueño*," in *Bulletin of Hispanic Studies*. XLVI (1969), pp. 128–131.

————. "Segismundo and the Rebel Soldier," in *Bulletin of Hispanic Studies*. XLV (1968), pp. 189–200.

Heiple, Daniel L. "The Tradition Behind the Punishment of the Rebel Soldier in *La vida es sueño*," in *Bulletin of Hispanic Studies*. L (1973), pp. 1–17.

Hesse, Everett W. *Calderón de la Barca*. New York: Twayne, 1967, pp. 137–148.

————. "Calderón's Concept of the Perfect Prince in *La vida es sueño*," in *Critical Essays in the Theatre of Calderón*. Edited by Bruce Wardropper. New York: New York University Press, 1964, pp. 114–136.

————. "Some Observations on Imagery in *La vida es sueño*," in *Hispania*. XLIX (1966), pp. 241–249.

Honig, Edwin. *Calderón and the Seizures of Honor.* Cambridge, Mass.: Harvard University Press, 1972, pp. 158–177.

————. "Reading What's in *La vida es sueño*," in *Theatre Annual*. XX (1963), pp. 63–71.

Maurin, M. "The Monster, the Sepulchre and the Dark: Related Patterns of Imagery in *La vida es sueño*," in *Hispanic Review*. XXXV (1967), pp. 161–178.

May, T.E. "Brutes and Stars in *La vida es sueño*," in *Hispanic Studies in Honour of Joseph Manson*. Edited by Dorothy M. Atkinson and Anthony H. Clarke. Oxford: Dolphin, 1972, pp. 167–184.

Merrick, C.A. "Clotaldo's Role in *La vida es sueño*," in *Bulletin of Hispanic Studies*. L (1973), pp. 256–269.

Parker, Alexander A. *The Allegorical Drama of Calderón: An Introduction to the Autos Sacramentales*. London: Dolphin, 1943, pp. 197–226.

Sloman, Albert E. "The Structure of Calderón's *La vida es sueño*," in *Modern Language Review*. XLVIII (1953), pp. 293–300.

Sturm, Harlan G. "From Plato's Cave to Segismundo's Prison: The Four Levels of Reality and Experience," in *Modern Language Notes*. LXXXIX (March, 1974), pp. 280–289.

Weiger, John G. "Rebirth in *La vida es sueño*," in *Romance Notes*. X (1968), pp. 119–121.

Whitby, William M. "Rosaura's Role in the Structure of *La vida es sueño*," in *Hispanic Review*. XXVIII (1960), pp. 16–27.

Wilson, E. "On *La vida es sueño*," in *Critical Essays in the Theatre of Calderón*. Edited by Bruce Wardropper. New York: New York University Press, 1964, pp. 63–89.

Ziomek, Henry. "Historical Implications and Dramatic Influences in Calderón's *Life Is a Dream*," in *Polish Review*. XX (1975), pp. 111–128.

The Mayor of Zalamea

Beardsley, Theodore S., Jr. "Socrates, Shakespeare, and Calderón: Advice to a Young Man," in *Hispanic Review*. XLII (1974), pp. 185–198.

Colford, William E. "Introduction," in *The Mayor of Zalamea*. By Pedro Calderón de la Barca. Great Neck, N.Y.: Barron's Educational Series, 1959, pp. 5–17.

Davis, James H., Jr. and Ruth Lundelius. "Calderón's *El alcalde de Zalamea* in Eighteenth-Century France," in *Kentucky Romance Quarterly*. XXIII (1976), pp. 213–224.

Dunn, P.N.   "Honour and the Christian Background in Calderón," in *Critical Essays on the Theatre of Calderón*. Edited by Bruce Wardropper. New York: New York University Press, 1964, pp. 24–60.

Gerstinger, Heinz.   *Pedro Calderón de la Barca*. New York: Frederick Ungar, 1973, pp. 121–131.

Hayes, F.C.   "The Use of Proverbs as Titles and Motives in the Siglo de Oro Drama: Calderón," in *Hispanic Review*. XV (1947), pp. 453–463.

Hesse, Everett W.   *Calderón de la Barca*. New York: Twayne, 1967, pp. 57–63.

Honig, Edwin.   *Calderón and the Seizures of Honor*. Cambridge, Mass.: Harvard University Press, 1972, pp. 81–109.

————.   "Calderón's *Mayor*: Honor Humanized," in *Tulane Drama Review*. X (1966), pp. 134–155.

————.   "Introduction," in *Calderón de la Barca: Four Plays*. New York: Hill and Wang, 1961, pp. xi–xxv.

————.   "The Seizures of Honor in Calderón," in *Kenyon Review*. XXIII (Summer, 1961), pp. 441–443.

Jones, C.A.   "Honor in *El alcalde de Zalamea*," in *Modern Language Review*. L (October, 1955), pp. 444–449.

Leavitt, Sturgis E.   "Cracks in the Structure of Calderón's *El alcalde de Zalamea*," in *Hispanic Studies in Honor of N. Adams*. Chapel Hill: University of North Carolina Press, 1966, pp. 93–96.

Leech, C.   "Catholic and Protestant Drama," in *Durham University Journal*. XXXIII (June, 1941), pp. 180–181.

————.   *Shakespeare's Tragedies, and Other Studies in Seventeenth Century Drama*. London: Chatto and Windus, 1961, pp. 216–220.

Lowenthal, Leo.   *Literature and the Image of Man—Sociological Studies of the European Drama and Novel*. Boston: Beacon Press, 1957, pp. 12–14, 17–18.

Sloman, Albert E.   *The Dramatic Craftsmanship of Calderón*. Oxford: Dolphin, 1958, pp. 217–249.

————.   "Scene Division in Calderón's *El alcalde de Zalamea*," in *Hispanic Review*. XIX (1951), pp. 66–71.

Thompson, Francis.   *Literary Criticisms: Newly Discovered and Collected by Terence L. Connally*. New York: Dutton, 1948, pp. 530–533.

The Mock Astrologer

Oppenheimer, Max, Jr.   "The Burla in Calderón's *El Astrologo Fingido*," in *Philological Quarterly*. XXVII (1948), pp. 241–263.

————.   "Two Stones and One Bird: A Bird Lore Allusion in Calderón," in *Modern Language Notes*. LXVII (April, 1952), pp. 253–255.

Trench, Richard Chenevix. *An Essay on the Life and Genius of Calderón.* New York: Haskell House, 1970, pp. 138–139.

The Painter of His Own Dishonor

Dunn, P.N. "Honour and the Christian Background in Calderón," in *Critical Essays on the Theatre of Calderón.* Edited by Bruce Wardropper. New York: New York University Press, 1964, pp. 24–60.

Fisher, Susan L. "The Function and Significance of the Gracioso in Calderón's *El pintor de su deshonra*," in *Romance Notes.* XIV (1972), pp. 334–340.

Honig, Edwin. *Calderón and the Seizures of Honor.* Cambridge, Mass.: Harvard University Press, 1972, pp. 192–194.

Howe, Elizabeth Teresa. "Fate and Providence in Calderón de la Barca," in *Bulletin of the Comediantes.* XXIX (Fall, 1977), pp. 108–111.

Parker, A. "Toward a Definition of Calderónian Tragedy," in *Bulletin of Spanish Studies.* XXXIX (1962), pp. 230–237.

Paterson, Alan K. "Juan Roca's Northern Ancestry: A Study of Art Theory in Calderón's *El pintor de su deshonra*," in *Forum for Modern Language Studies.* VII (1971), pp. 195–210.

Sloane, Robert. "Diversion in Calderón's *El pintor de su deshonra*," in *Modern Language Notes.* XCI (1976), pp. 247–263.

————. "On Juanete's Final Story in Calderón's *El pintor de su deshonra*," in *Bulletin of the Comediantes.* XXVIII (1976), pp. 100–103.

Thompson, Francis. *Literary Criticisms: Newly Discovered and Collected by Terence L. Connolly.* New York: Dutton, 1948, pp. 530–533.

Wardropper, Bruce. "The Unconscious Mind in Calderón's *El pintor de su deshonra*," in *Hispanic Review.* XVIII (1950), pp. 285–301.

Watson, A. "*El pintor de su deshonra* and the Neo-Aristotelian Theory of Tragedy," in *Bulletin of Spanish Studies.* XL (1963), pp. 17–34.

Wilson, Margaret. *Spanish Drama of the Golden Age.* New York: Pergamon Press, 1969, pp. 157–163.

The Physician of His Own Honor

Dunn, P.N. "Honour and the Christian Background in Calderón," in *Critical Essays on the Theatre of Calderón.* Edited by Bruce Wardropper. New York: New York University Press, 1964, pp. 24–60.

Exum, Frances. " '¿Yo a un va sallo . . . ?' Prince Henry's Role in Calderón's *El medico de su honra*," in *Bulletin of the Comediantes.* XXIX (Spring, 1977), pp. 1–6.

Hesse, Everett W. *Calderón de la Barca.* New York: Twayne, 1967, pp. 110–122.

_____. "Gutierre's Personality in *El medico de su honra*," in *Bulletin of the Comediantes*. XXVIII (1976), pp. 11–16.

_____. "Introduction," in *The Surgeon of His Honor*. By Pedro Calderón de la Barca. Madison: University of Wisconsin Press, 1960, pp. vi–xxiv.

Howe, Elizabeth Teresa. "Fate and Providence in Calderón de la Barca," in *Bulletin of the Comediantes*. XXIX (Fall, 1977), pp. 108–111.

King, Lloyd. "The Role of King Pedro in Calderón's *El medico de su honra*," in *Bulletin of the Comediantes*. XXIII (1971), pp. 44–49.

Kossoff, A. "*El medico de su honra* and *La Amiga de Bernal Frances*," in *Hispanic Review*. XXIV (1956), pp. 66–70.

Lowenthal, Leo. *Literature and the Image of Man—Sociological Studies of the European Drama and Novel*. Boston: Beacon Press, 1957, pp. 16–19.

Reiter, Seymour. *World Theater: The Structure and Meaning of Drama*. New York: Horizon Press, 1973, pp. 170–194.

Rogers, D. "Tienen los celos pasos de ladrones: Silence in Calderón's *El medico de su honra*," in *Hispanic Review*. XXIII (1965), pp. 273–289.

Sloman, Albert E. "Calderón's *El Medico* and *La Amiga de Bernal Frances*," in *Bulletin of Hispanic Studies*. XXXIV (1957), pp. 168–169.

_____. *The Dramatic Craftsmanship of Calderón*. Oxford: Dolphin, 1958, pp. 18–58.

Thiher, Roberta J. "The Final Ambiguity of *El medico de su honra*," in *Studies in Philology*. LXVII (1970), pp. 237–244.

Touchard, P. "Calderón or Dramatic Action," in *Tulane Drama Review*. IV (December, 1959), pp. 108–109.

Wardropper, Bruce. "Poetry and Drama in Calderón's *El medico de su honra*," in *Romanic Review*. XLIX (1958), pp. 3–11.

Wilson, Margaret. *Spanish Drama of the Golden Age*. New York: Pergamon Press, 1969, pp. 157–163.

Secret Vengeance for a Secret Insult

Casa, Frank P. "Honor and the Wife-Killers of Calderón," in *Bulletin of the Comediantes*. XXIX (Spring, 1977), pp. 6–23.

Dunn, P.N. "Honour and the Christian Background in Calderón," in *Critical Essays on the Theatre of Calderón*. Edited by Bruce Wardropper. New York: New York University Press, 1964, pp. 24–60.

Honig, Edwin. *Calderón and the Seizures of Honor*. Cambridge, Mass.: Harvard University Press, 1972, pp. 37–52.

_____. "Calderón's Strange Mercy Play," in *Massachusetts Review*. III (Autumn, 1961), pp. 80–107.

————. "Introduction," in *Calderón de la Barca: Four Plays*. New York: Hill and Wang, 1961, pp. xi–xxv.

————. "The Seizures of Honor in Calderón," in *Kenyon Review*. XXIII (Summer, 1961), pp. 426–439.

Howe, Elizabeth Teresa. "Fate and Providence in Calderón de la Barca," in *Bulletin of the Comediantes*. XXIX (Fall, 1977), pp. 108–111.

May, T.E. "The Folly and the Wit of *Secret Vengeance*," in *Forum for Modern Language Studies*. II (1966), pp. 114–122.

Wardropper, Bruce. *Critical Essays on the Theatre of Calderón*. New York: New York University Press, 1964, p. 169.

Wilson, E. "Notes on the Text of *A Secreto Agravio*," in *Bulletin of Spanish Studies*. XXXV (1958), pp. 72–82.

Wilson, Margaret. *Spanish Drama of the Golden Age*. New York: Pergamon Press, 1969, pp. 157–163.

The Wonder-Working Magician

Edith, Sister M. "The Devil in Literature," in *Catholic World*. CLVII (January, 1944), p. 358.

Entwhistle, William J. "Justina's Temptation: An Approach to the Understanding of Calderón," in *Modern Language Review*. XL (1945), pp. 180–191.

Gerstinger, Heinz. *Pedro Calderón de la Barca*. New York: Frederick Ungar, 1973, pp. 65–72.

Heaton, Harry C. "Calderón and *El Magico Prodigioso*," in *Hispanic Review*. XIX (1951), pp. 11–36, 93–103.

————. "Passage in Calderón's *Magico Prodigioso*," in *Modern Language Notes*. XLVI (1931), pp. 31–33.

Hesse, Everett W. *Calderón de la Barca*. New York: Twayne, 1967, pp. 82–93.

————. "The Function of the Romantic Action in *El Magico Prodigioso*," in *Bulletin of the Comediantes*. XVII (1965), pp. 5–7.

Howe, Elizabeth Teresa. "Fate and Providence in Calderón de la Barca," in *Bulletin of the Comediantes*. XXIX (Fall, 1977), pp. 105–107.

Leech, C. "Catholic and Protestant Drama," in *Durham University Journal*. XXXIII (June, 1941), pp. 175–176.

May, T.E. "Symbolism of *El Magico Prodigioso*," in *Romanic Review*. LIV (1963), pp. 95–112.

Moon, H. "Calderón and Casona," in *Hispania*. XLIX (1966), pp. 37–38.

Moulton, Richard G. *World Literature and Its Place in General Culture*. New York: Macmillan, 1911, pp. 231–237.

Oppenheimer, Max, Jr. "The Baroque Impasse in Calderónian Drama," in *PMLA*. LXV (1950), pp. 1146–1165.

Parker, A. "The Approach to the Spanish Drama of the Golden Age," in *Tulane Drama Review*. IV (September, 1959), pp. 55–58.

————. "The Devil in the Drama of Calderón," in *Critical Essays on the Theatre of Calderón*. Edited by Bruce Wardropper. New York: New York University Press, 1964, pp. 14–23.

————. "Theology of the Devil in the Drama of Calderón," in *Aquinas Society Papers*. No. 32 (1958), pp. 12–20.

Rosenheim, R. *The Eternal Drama*. New York: Philosophical Library, 1952, pp. 133–138.

Sloman, A. "*El Magico Prodigioso*: Calderón Defended Against the Charge of Theft," in *Hispanic Review*. XX (1952), pp. 212–222.

Trench, Richard Chenevix. *An Essay on the Life and Genius of Calderón*. New York: Haskell House, 1970, pp. 36–37.

Wardropper, Bruce. "Interplay of Wisdom and Saintliness in *El Magico Prodigioso*," in *Hispanic Review*. XI (1943), pp. 116–124.

Wilson, Margaret. *Spanish Drama of the Golden Age*. New York: Pergamon Press, 1969, pp. 169–171.

ERSKINE CALDWELL
(1903–   )

God's Little Acre

Allen, Walter. *The Modern Novel in Britain and the United States.* New York: Dutton, 1964, pp. 119–120.

Beach, Joseph Warren. *American Fiction, 1920–1940.* New York: Russell and Russell, 1960, pp. 240–245.

Bradbury, John M. *Renaissance in the South: Critical History of the Literature 1920–1960.* Chapel Hill: University of North Carolina Press, 1963, pp. 100–101.

Burke, Kenneth. "Caldwell: Maker of Grotesques," in *Psychoanalysis and American Fiction.* Edited by Irving Malin. New York: Dutton, 1965, pp. 248–253.

Holman, Hugh. "Southern Social Issues and the Outer World," in *Southern Fiction Today.* Edited by George Gore. Athens: University of Georgia Press, 1969, pp. 21–28.

Itofuji, Horomi. "An Aspect of Erskine Caldwell in *God's Little Acre*," in *Kyusha American Literature.* II (May, 1959), pp. 17–22.

Korges, James. *Erskine Caldwell.* Minneapolis: University of Minnesota Press, 1968, pp. 25–32.

Kukie, Lawrence S. "*God's Little Acre*: An Analysis," in *Saturday Review of Literature.* XI (November 24, 1934), pp. 305–306, 312.

Wagenknecht, Edward. "Novelists of the Thirties: Erskine Caldwell," in *Cavalcade of the American Novel.* New York: Holt, 1952, pp. 415–417.

Tobacco Road

Beach, Joseph Warren. "Erskine Caldwell: The Comic Catharsis," in *American Fiction 1920–1940.* New York: Macmillan, 1941, pp. 225–231.

Bradbury, John M. *Renaissance in the South: Critical History of the Literature 1920–1960.* Chapel Hill: University of North Carolina Press, 1963, pp. 100–101.

Burke, Kenneth. "Caldwell: Maker of Grotesques," in *Psychoanalysis and American Fiction.* Edited by Irving Malin. New York: Dutton, 1965, pp. 248–253.

Couch, W.T. "*Tobacco Road*," in Virginia Quarterly Review. XIII (Spring 1938), p. 309.

Frohock, W.M. *The Novel of Violence in America.* Boston: Beacon Press, 1957, pp. 106–123.

Gossett, Louise Y.   *Violence in Recent Southern Fiction.* Durham, N.C.: Duke University Press, 1965, pp. 16–29.

Holman, Hugh.   "Southern Social Issues and the Outer World," in *Southern Fiction Today.* Edited by George Gore. Athens: University of Georgia Press, 1969, pp. 21–28.

Korges, James.   *Erskine Caldwell.* Minneapolis: University of Minnesota Press, 1969, pp. 22–24.

Krutch, Joseph Wood.   "Tragedy: Eugene O'Neill," in *American Drama Since 1918.* New York: Random House, 1939, pp. 122–126.

Marion, H.H.   "Star Dust Above *Tobacco Road*," in *Christian Century.* LX (February 16, 1938), pp. 204–206.

Sievers, W. David.   *Freud on Broadway.* New York: Hermitage House, 1955, pp. 237–238.

Snelling, Paula.   "Ground Itch, Art and Erskine Caldwell," in *From the Mountain.* Edited by Helen White. Memphis, Tenn.: Memphis State University Press, 1972, pp. 148–195.

Wagenknecht, Edward.   "Novelists of the Thirties: Erskine Caldwell," in *Cavalcade of the American Novel.* New York: Holt, 1952, pp. 415–417.

LUIS DE CAMOËNS
(1524–1580)

The Lusiad

Bacon, Leonard. "Introduction," in The Lusiad *of Luiz de Camoëns*. New York: Hispanic Society of America, 1950, pp. xi–xxx.

Bullough, Geoffrey. "Introduction," in *The Lusiad*. By Luis de Camoëns. London: Centaur Press, 1963, pp. 9–28.

De Sena, Jorge. "Camoëns: The Lyrical Poet," in *Camoëns: Some Poems.* Translated by Jonathan Griffin. London: Menard Press, 1976, pp. 5–14.

Freitas, William. *Camoëns and His Epic: A Historic, Geographic and Cultural Survey.* Stanford, Calif.: Stanford University Press, 1963.

Hart, Henry H. *Luis de Camoëns and the Epic of the* Lusiad. Norman: University of Oklahoma Press, 1962.

Hart, Thomas R. "The Author's Voice in *The Lusiads*," in *Hispanic Review.* XLIV (1976), pp. 45–55.

Jones, Roger S. "The Epic Similes of *Os Lusiadas*," in *Hispania.* LVII (1974), pp. 239–245.

Lucas-Gomes, Fabio. "A Note on Camoëns and *The Lusiads*," in *Texas Quarterly.* XV (1972), pp. 32–38.

Martins, Francisco. "The Significance of the Voyage to the Orient in *Os Lusiadas*," in *Journal of the American Portuguese Society.* VIII (1974), pp. 22–30.

Moser, Gerald M. "Camoëns 'Shipwreck,' " in *Hispania.* LVII (1974), pp. 213–219.

Parker, Alexander A. "The Age of Camoëns," in *Texas Quarterly.* XV (1972), pp. 7–18.

Pierce, Frank. "Ancient History in *Os Lusiadas*," in *Hispania.* LVII (1974), pp. 220–230.

―――――. "Introduction," in *Os Lusiadas*. By Luis de Camoëns. Oxford: Clarendon Press, 1973, pp. vii–xxxvii.

Piper, Anson C. "The Feminine Presence in *Os Lusiadas*," in *Hispania.* LVII (1974), pp. 231–238.

Rabassa, Clementine C. "Cynegetics and Irony in the Thematic Unity of *The Lusiad*," in *Luso-Brazilian Review.* X (1973), pp. 197–207.

Ramalho, Americo da C. "The Classical Tradition in *Os Lusiadas*," in *Journal of the American Portuguese Society.* VIII (1974), pp. 1–21.

Rogers, Francis M. "The Ninth Sphere of *Os Lusiadas*," in *Studies in Honor of Lloyd A. Kasten.* Madison, Wisc.: Hispanic Seminary of Medieval Studies, 1975, pp. 221–233.

Sims, James H.   "Camoëns, Milton, and Myth in the Christian Epic," in *Renaissance Papers*. (1972), pp. 79–87.

————.   "Christened Classicism in *Paradise Lost* and *The Lusiads*," in *Comparative Literature*. XXIV (1972), pp. 338–356.

Sousa, Ronald W.   "A Poet and His Nation: The Foreground Myth in *Os Lusiadas*," in *Texas Quarterly*. XV (1972), pp. 19–31.

ALBERT CAMUS
(1913–1960)

The Fall

Braun, Lev. *Witness of Decline—Albert Camus: Moralist of the Absurd.* Rutherford, N.J.: Fairleigh Dickinson University Press, 1974, pp. 208–212.

Bree, Germaine. *Camus.* New Brunswick, N.J.: Rutgers University Press, 1959, pp. 98–108, 128–131.

Brockmann, Charles B. "Metamorphoses of Hell: The Spiritual Quandary in *La Chute*," in *French Review*. XXXV (February, 1962), pp. 361–368.

Cruickshank, John. *Albert Camus and the Literature of Revolt.* New York: Oxford University Press, 1959, pp. 181–188.

Girard, Rene. "Camus' *Stranger* Retried," in *PMLA*. LXXIX (December, 1964), pp. 519–533.

Hanna, Thomas. *The Thought and Art of Albert Camus.* Chicago: Regnery, 1958, pp. 213–237.

Hartsock, Mildred. "Camus' *The Fall*: Dialogue of One," in *Modern Fiction Studies*. VII (Winter, 1961–1962), pp. 357–364.

King, Adele. *Albert Camus.* New York: Grove, 1964, pp. 81–94.

Lazere, Donald. *The Unique Creation of Albert Camus.* New Haven, Conn.: Yale University Press, 1973, pp. 183–198.

Lehan, Richard. "Levels of Reality in the Novels of Albert Camus," in *Modern Fiction Studies*. X (Autumn, 1964), pp. 240–244.

Lewis, R.W.B. *The Picaresque Saint.* New York: Lippincott, 1959, pp. 104–108.

Maquet, Albert. *Albert Camus: The Invincible Summer.* New York: George Braziller, 1958, pp. 150–167.

Matthews, J.H. "From *The Stranger* to *The Fall*: Confession and Complicity," in *Modern Fiction Studies*. X (Autumn, 1964), pp. 265–273.

Moore, Harry T. *Twentieth-Century French Literature Since World War II.* Carbondale: Southern Illinois University Press, 1966, pp. 68–72.

Mueller, William R. *The Prophetic Voice in Modern Fiction.* New York: Association Press, 1959, pp. 56–86.

O'Brien, Conor Cruise. *Albert Camus of Europe and Africa.* New York: Viking, 1970, pp. 61–108.

Quilliot, Roger. "An Ambiguous World," in *Camus: A Collection of Critical Essays*. Edited by Germaine Bree. Englewood Cliffs, N.J.: Prentice-Hall, 1962, pp. 157–169.

————. *The Sea and Prisons: A Commentary on the Life and Thought of Albert Camus.* University: University of Alabama Press, 1970, pp. 239–251.

Rhein, Phillip H.   *Albert Camus.* New York: Twayne, 1969, pp. 104–115.

Scott, Nathan A.   *Albert Camus.* London: Bowes and Bowes, 1962, pp. 82–88.

Starratt, Robert J.   "An Analysis of Albert Camus' *The Fall,*" in *Cithara.* I (November, 1961), pp. 27–38.

Stourzh, Gerald.   "The Unforgivable Sin: An Interpretation of *The Fall,*" in *Chicago Review.* XV (Summer, 1961), pp. 45–57.

Thody, Philip.   *Albert Camus: A Study of His Work.* New York: Grove, 1957, pp. 75–79.

Ullmann, Stephen.   *The Image in the Modern French Novel.* Cambridge: Cambridge University Press, 1960, pp. 274–287.

Yalom, Marilyn K.   "Albert Camus and the Myth of the Trial," in *Modern Literature Quarterly.* XXV (December, 1964), pp. 440–450.

The Myth of Sisyphus

Bree, Germaine.   *Camus.* New Brunswick, N.J.: Rutgers University Press, 1959, pp. 193–207.

————. *Camus and Sartre: Crisis and Commitment.* New York: Delacorte Press, 1972, pp. 133–137.

Cruickshank, John.   *Albert Camus and the Literature Revolt.* New York: Galaxy, 1960, pp. 41–88, 91–95.

Hanna, Thomas.   *The Thought and Art of Albert Camus.* Chicago: Regnery, 1958, pp. 13–43.

Hart, J.N.   "Beyond Existentialism," in *Yale Review.* XLV (March, 1956), pp. 444–451.

Henry, Patrick.   "*The Myth of Sisyphus* and *The Stranger* of Albert Camus," in *Philosophy Today.* XIX (Winter, 1975), pp. 358–368.

Lazere, Donald.   *The Unique Creation of Albert Camus.* New Haven, Conn.: Yale University Press, 1973, pp. 130–139.

Maquet, Albert.   *Albert Camus: The Invincible Summer.* New York: George Braziller, 1958, pp. 39–48.

Peterson, Carol.   *Albert Camus.* New York: Frederick Ungar, 1969, pp. 51–57.

Quilliot, Roger.   *The Sea and Prisons: A Commentary on the Life and Thought of Albert Camus.* University: University of Alabama Press, 1970, pp. 88–103.

Scott, Nathan A.   *Camus.* New York: Hillary House, 1963, pp. 20–29.

The Plague

Anderson, David.   *The Tragic Protest.* Atlanta: Knox, 1970, pp. 82–103.

Bertocci, Angelo P. "Camus' *La Peste* and the Absurd," in *Romanic Review*. XLIX (February, 1958), pp. 33–41.

Bespaloff, Rachel. "The World of the Man Condemned to Death," in *Camus: A Collection of Critical Essays*. Edited by Germaine Bree. Englewood Cliffs, N.J.: Prentice-Hall, 1962, pp. 98–101.

Braun, Lev. *Witness of Decline—Albert Camus: Moralist of the Absurd*. Rutherford, N.J.: Fairleigh Dickinson University Press, 1974, pp. 85–98.

Bree, Germaine. *Camus*. New Brunswick, N.J.: Rutgers University Press, 1961, pp. 118–130.

Clough, Wilson O. "Camus' *The Plague*," in *Colorado Quarterly*. VII (Spring, 1959), pp. 389–404.

Cruickshank, John. *Albert Camus and the Literature of Revolt*. New York: Oxford University Press, 1959, pp. 167–181.

Haggis, D.R. *Albert Camus:* La Peste. Woodbury, N.Y.: Barron's, 1962.

Hanna, Thomas. *The Thought and Art of Albert Camus*. Chicago: Henry Regnery, 1958, pp. 195–206.

Henninger, Francis J. "Plot Theme Fusion in *The Plague*," in *Modern Fiction Studies*. XIX (1973), pp. 216–221.

Kellog, Jean. *Dark Prophets of Hope*. Chicago: Loyola University Press, 1975, pp. 103–113.

King, Adele. *Albert Camus*. New York: Grove, 1964, pp. 64–80.

Lazere, Donald. *The Unique Creation of Albert Camus*. New Haven, Conn.: Yale University Press, 1973, pp. 173–182.

Lewis, R.W.B. *The Picaresque Saint*. New York: Lippincott, 1959, pp. 90–104.

Merton, Thomas. *Albert Camus'* The Plague*: Introduction and Commentary*. New York: Seabury Press, 1968.

Moses, Edwin. "Functional Complexity: The Narrative Techniques of *The Plague*," in *Modern Fiction Studies*. XX (Autumn, 1974), pp. 419–428.

O'Brien, Conor Cruise. *Albert Camus of Europe and Africa*. New York: Viking, 1970, pp. 35–60.

Parker, Emmett. *Albert Camus: The Artist in the Arena*. Madison: University of Wisconsin, 1965, pp. 112–114.

Peterson, Carol. *Albert Camus*. New York: Frederick Ungar, 1969, pp. 69–76.

Peyre, Henri. *The Contemporary French Novel*. New York: Oxford University Press, 1955, pp. 246–251.

Picon, Gaetan. "Notes on *The Plague*," in *Camus: A Collection of Critical Essays*. Edited by Germaine Bree. Englewood Cliffs, N.J.: Prentice-Hall, 1962, pp. 145–151.

Quilliot, Roger. *The Sea and Prisons: A Commentary on the Life and Thought of Albert Camus.* University: University of Alabama Press, 1970, pp. 136–157.

Scott, Nathan A. *Albert Camus.* London: Bowes and Bowes, 1962, pp. 52–62.

Thody, Philip. *Albert Camus: 1918–1960.* London: Hamish Hamilton, 1961, pp. 93–115.

The Stranger

Bespaloff, Rachel. "The World of the Man Condemned to Death," in *Camus: A Collection of Critical Essays.* Edited by Germaine Bree. Englewood Cliffs, N.J.: Prentice-Hall, 1962, pp. 92–98.

Braun, Lev. *Witness of Decline—Albert Camus: Moralist of the Absurd.* Rutherford, N.J.: Fairleigh Dickinson University Press, 1974, pp. 56–72.

Bree, Germaine. *Camus.* New Brunswick, N.J.: Rutgers University Press, 1961, pp. 112–117.

Champigny, Robert. "Ethics and Aesthetics in *The Stranger*," in *Camus: A Collection of Critical Essays.* Edited by Germaine Bree. Englewood Cliffs, N.J.: Prentice-Hall, 1962, pp. 122–131.

Cruickshank, John. *Albert Camus and the Literature of Revolt.* New York: Oxford University Press, 1959, pp. 151–164.

Feuerlicht, Ignace. "Camus's *L'Etranger* Reconsidered," in *PMLA.* LXXVIII (December, 1963), pp. 606–621.

Frohock, W.M. *Style and Temper: Studies in French Fiction, 1925–1960.* Cambridge, Mass.: Harvard University Press, 1966, pp. 107–113.

Girard, Rene. "Camus' *Stranger* Retried," in *PMLA.* LXXIX (December, 1964), pp. 519–533.

Hanna, Thomas. *The Thought and Art of Albert Camus.* Chicago: Regnery, 1958, pp. 46–64.

King, Adele. *Albert Camus.* New York: Grove, 1964, pp. 46–63.

Krieger, Murray. *The Tragic Vision.* New York: Holt, Rinehart and Winston, 1960, pp. 144–153.

Lazere, Donald. *The Unique Creation of Albert Camus.* New Haven, Conn.: Yale University Press, 1973, pp. 232–237.

Lehan, Richard. "Levels of Reality in the Novels of Albert Camus," in *Modern Fiction Studies.* X (Autumn, 1964), pp. 232–237.

Lewis, R.W.B. *The Picaresque Saint.* New York: Lippincott, 1959, pp. 65–79.

Maquet, Albert. *Albert Camus: The Invincible Summer.* New York: George Braziller, 1958, pp. 48–61.

Matthews, J.H. "From *The Stranger* to *The Fall*: Confession and Complicity," in *Modern Fiction Studies.* X (Autumn, 1964), pp. 265–273.

Moseley, Edwin M. *Pseudonyms of Christ in the Modern Novel.* Pittsburgh: University of Pittsburgh Press, 1962, pp. 195–204.

O'Brien, Conor Cruise. *Albert Camus of Europe and Africa.* New York: Viking, 1970, pp. 1–34.

Parker, Emmett. *Albert Camus: The Artist in the Arena.* Madison: University of Wisconsin Press, 1965, pp. 42–45.

Quilliot, Roger. *The Sea and Prisons: A Commentary on the Life and Thought of Albert Camus.* University: University of Alabama Press, 1970, pp. 69–83.

Rhein, Phillip H. *Albert Camus.* New York: Twayne, 1969, pp. 33–41.

Sartre, Jean-Paul. "An Explication of *The Stranger,*" in *Literary Essays.* New York: Philosophical Library, 1957, pp. 24–41. Reprinted in *Camus: A Collection of Critical Essays.* Edited by Germaine Bree. Englewood Cliffs, N.J.: Prentice-Hall, 1962, pp. 108–121.

Scott, Nathan A. *Albert Camus.* London: Bowes and Bowes, 1962, pp. 30–36.

Thody, Philip. *Albert Camus: A Study of His Work.* New York: Grove, 1959, pp. 1–9, 111–120.

Viggiani, Carl A. "Camus' *L'Etranger,*" in *PMLA.* LXXI (December, 1956), pp. 865–887.

KAREL ČAPEK
(1890–1938)

R.U.R.

Darlington, William A. *Literature in the Theatre, and Other Essays.* New York: Holt, 1933, pp. 137–144.

Haman, Ales and Paul I. Trensky. "Man Against the Absolute: The Art of Karel Čapek," in *Slavic and East European Journal.* XI (1967), pp. 168–184.

Harkins, William E. *Karel* Čapek. New York: Columbia University Press, 1962, pp. 84–95.

————. "Karel Čapek: From Relativism to Perspectivism," in *History of Ideas News Letter.* III (July, 1957), pp. 50–53.

————. "The Real Legacy of Karel Čapek," in *The Czechoslovak Contribution to World Culture.* The Hague: Mouton, 1964.

Matuska, Alexander. *Karel* Čapek, An Essay. London: Allen and Unwin, 1964, pp. 203–206.

Pletnev, R. "The Concept of Time and Space in *R.U.R.* by Karel Čapek," in *Etudes Slaves et Est-Europeenes.* XII (1967), pp. 17–24.

TRUMAN CAPOTE
(1924–   )

Breakfast at Tiffany's

Hassan, Ihab H. "Birth of a Heroine," in *Prairie Schooner*. XXXIV (Spring, 1960), pp. 78–83.

————. "The Daydream and Nightmare of Narcissus," in *Wisconsin Studies in Contemporary Literature*. I (Spring–Summer, 1960), pp. 16–21.

Hyman, S.E. "Fruitcake at Tiffany's," in *Standards: A Chronicle of Books for Our Time*. New York: Horizon, 1966, pp. 149–150.

Kazin, Alfred. *Contemporaries*. Boston: Little, Brown, 1962, pp. 250–254.

Ludwig, Jack. *Recent American Novelists*. Minneapolis: University of Minnesota Press, 1962, pp. 34–36.

Nance, William L. *The Worlds of Truman Capote*. New York: Stein and Day, 1970, pp. 107–124.

In Cold Blood

Creeger, George R. *Animals in Exile: Imagery and Theme in Capote's* In Cold Blood. Middletown, Conn.: Wesleyan University Press, 1967.

Enright, Dennis J. *Man Is an Onion; Reviews and Essays*. La Salle, Ill.: Library Press, 1973, pp. 44–51.

Friedman, Melvin J. "Towards an Aesthetic: Truman Capote's Other Voices," in *Truman Capote's* In Cold Blood: *A Critical Handbook*. Edited by Irving Malin. Belmont, Calif.: Wadsworth, 1968, pp. 163–176.

Galloway, David. "Why the Chickens Came Home to Roost in Holcomb, Kansas: Truman Capote's *In Cold Blood*," in *Truman Capote's* In Cold Blood: *A Critical Handbook*. Edited by Irving Malin. Belmont, Calif.: Wadsworth, 1968, pp. 154–163.

Garrett, George. "Crime and Punishment in Kansas: Truman Capote's *In Cold Blood*," in *Hollins Critic*. III (February, 1966), pp. 1–12.

Langbaum, Robert. "Capote's Nonfiction Novel," in *American Studies*. XXXV (Summer, 1966), pp. 570–580.

Levine, Paul. "Reality and Fiction," in *Hudson Review*. XIX (Spring, 1966), pp. 135–138.

Meacham, William S. "A Non-Fiction Study in Scarlet," in *Virginia Quarterly Review*. XLII (Spring, 1966), pp. 316–319.

Morris, Robert K. "Capote's Imagery," in *Truman Capote's* In Cold Blood: *A Critical Handbook*. Edited by Irving Malin. Belmont, Calif.: Wadsworth, 1968, pp. 176–186.

Nance, William L.   *The Worlds of Truman Capote.* New York: Stein and Day, 1970, pp. 155–185, 217–219, 225–229.

Plimpton, George.   "The Story Behind a Nonfiction Novel," in *Truman Capote's* In Cold Blood*: A Critical Handbook.* Edited by Irving Malin. Belmont, Calif.: Wadsworth, 1968, pp. 25–43.

Tanner, Tony.   "Death in Kansas," in *Truman Capote's* In Cold Blood*: A Critical Handbook.* Edited by Irving Malin. Belmont, Calif.: Wadsworth, 1968, pp. 98–102.

Tompkins, Phillip K.   "In Cold Fact," in *Truman Capote's* In Cold Blood*: A Critical Handbook.* Edited by Irving Malin. Belmont, Calif.: Wadsworth, 1968, pp. 44–58.

Trilling, Diana.   "Capote's Crime and Punishment," in *Partisan Review.* XXXIII (Spring, 1966), pp. 252–259.

Walcutt, Charles C.   *Man's Changing Mask: Modes and Methods of Characterization in Fiction.* Minneapolis: University of Minnesota Press, 1966, pp. 344–346.

West, Rebecca.   "A Grave and Reverend Book," in *Truman Capote's* In Cold Blood*: A Critical Handbook.* Edited by Irving Malin. Belmont, Calif.: Wadsworth, 1968, pp. 91–98.

Wiegand, William.   "The 'Non-Fiction' Novel," in *New Mexico Quarterly.* XXXVII (Autumn, 1967), pp. 243–257.

Other Voices, Other Rooms

Aldridge, John W.   *After the Lost Generation: A Critical Study of the Writers of the Wars.* New York: McGraw-Hill, 1951, pp. 194–230.

————.   "The Metaphorical World of Truman Capote," in *Western Review.* XV (Summer, 1951), pp. 250–260.

Eisinger, Chester E.   *Fiction of the Forties.* Chicago: University of Chicago Press, 1963, pp. 237–240.

Hassan, Ihab H.   *Radical Innocence: Studies in the Contemporary American Novel.* Princeton, N.J.: Princeton University Press, 1961, pp. 239–245.

Hoffman, Frederick J.   *Art of Southern Fiction: A Study of Some Modern Novelists.* Carbondale: Southern Illinois University Press, 1967, pp. 118–122.

Levine, Paul.   "Truman Capote: The Revelation of the Broken Image," in *Virginia Quarterly Review.* XXXIV (Autumn, 1958), pp. 600–617.

Malin, Irving.   *New American Gothic.* Carbondale: Southern Illinois University Press, 1962, pp. 50–52.

Mengeling, Marvin E.   "*Other Voices, Other Rooms*: Oedipus Between the Covers," in *American Imago.* XIX (Winter, 1962), pp. 361–374.

Nance, William L.   *The Worlds of Truman Capote.* New York: Stein and Day, 1970, pp. 40–63, 70–72, 219–226, 230–232.

Ruoff, Gene W.   "Truman Capote: The Novelist as a Commodity," in *The Forties: Fiction, Poetry, Drama.* Edited by Warren French. Deland, Fla.: Everett/Edwards, 1969, pp. 261–269.

Shrike, J.S.   "Recent Phenomena," in *Hudson Review.* I (Spring, 1948), pp. 136–144.

Young, Marguerite.   "Tiger Lilies," in *Kenyon Review.* X (Summer, 1948), pp. 516–518.

THOMAS CARLYLE
(1795–1881)

The French Revolution

Ben-Israel, Hedva. "Carlyle and the French Revolution," in *English Historians on the French Revolution*. Cambridge: Cambridge University Press, 1968, pp. 127–147.

Bentley, Eric R. *A Century of Hero Worship*. Philadelphia: Lippincott, 1944, pp. 42–44.

Cazamian, Louis. *Carlyle*. New York: Macmillan, 1932, pp. 153–167.

Cobban, Alfred. "Carlyle's *French Revolution*," in *History*. XLVIII (October, 1963), pp. 306–316.

Harrold, Charles F. "Carlyle's General Method in *The French Revolution*," in *PMLA*. XLIII (1928), pp. 1150–1169.

Holloway, John. *The Victorian Sage*. London: Macmillan, 1953, pp. 61–74.

Ikler, A. Abbott. *Puritan Temper and Transcendental Faith: Carlyle's Literary Vision*. Columbus: Ohio State University Press, 1972, pp. 43–46.

Kusch, Robert W. "The Eighteenth Century as 'Decaying Organism' in Carlyle's *The French Revolution*," in *Anglia*. LXXXIX (1971), pp. 456–470.

La Valley, Albert J. *Carlyle and the Idea of the Modern*. New Haven, Conn.: Yale University Press, 1968, pp. 121–186.

Lea, Frank A. "Carlyle and *The French Revolution*," in *Adelphi*. XVIII (November–December, 1941), pp. 20–24, 36–38.

Leicester, H.M., Jr. "The Dialectic of Romantic Historiography: Prospect and Retrospect in *The French Revolution*," in *Victorian Studies*. XV (1971), pp. 5–17.

Neff, Emery. *Carlyle*. New York: Norton, 1932, pp. 173–181.

Ralli, Augustus. *Guide to Carlyle*, Volume I. London: Allen and Unwin, 1920, pp. 210–226.

Rosenberg, Philip. *The Seventh Hero: Thomas Carlyle and the Theory of Radical Activism*. Cambridge, Mass.: Harvard University Press, 1974, pp. 79–107.

Symons, Julian. *Thomas Carlyle: The Life and Ideas of a Prophet*. New York: Oxford University Press, 1952, pp. 147–160.

History of Frederick II of Prussia

Adrian, Arthur A. and Vonna H. Adrian. "*Frederick the Great*: 'That Unutterable Horror of a Prussian Book,'" in *Carlyle Past and Present: A Collection of New Essays*. Edited by K.J. Fielding and Rodger L. Tarr. London: Vision, 1976, pp. 177–197.

Bentley, Eric R. *A Century of Hero Worship.* Philadelphia: Lippincott, 1944, pp. 45–55.

Cazamian, Louis. *Carlyle.* New York: Macmillan, 1932, pp. 232–239.

Clive, John. "Introduction," in *History of Friedrich II of Prussia, Called Frederick the Great.* Chicago: University of Chicago Press, 1969.

Holloway, John. *The Victorian Sage.* London: Macmillan, 1953, pp. 75–85.

La Valley, Albert J. *Carlyle and the Idea of the Modern.* New Haven, Conn.: Yale University Press, 1968, pp. 264–278.

Neff, Emery. *Carlyle.* New York: Norton, 1932, pp. 242–252.

Peckham, Morse. *"Frederick the Great,"* in *Carlyle Past and Present: A Collection of New Essays.* Edited by K.J. Fielding and Rodger L. Tarr. London: Vision, 1976, pp. 198–215.

Ralli, Augustus. *Guide to Carlyle,* Volume II. London: Allen and Unwin, 1920, pp. 330–350.

Symons, Julian. *Thomas Carlyle: The Life and Ideas of a Prophet.* New York: Oxford University Press, 1952, pp. 274–277.

On Heroes, Hero-Worship and the Heroic in History

Bentley, Eric R. *A Century of Hero Worship.* Philadelphia: Lippincott, 1944, pp. 31–42.

Cazamian, Louis. *Carlyle.* New York: Macmillan, 1932, pp. 167–181.

DeLaura, David J. "Ishmael as Prophet: *Heroes and Hero Worship* and the Self-expressive Basis of Carlyle's Art," in *Texas Studies in Language and Literature.* XI (1969), pp. 705–732.

Donovan, Robert A. "Carlyle and the Climate of *Hero-Worship*," in *University of Toronto Quarterly.* XLII (1973), pp. 122–141.

Holloway, John. *The Victorian Sage.* London: Macmillan, 1953, pp. 46–49.

Ikler, A. Abbott. *Puritan Temper and Transcendental Faith: Carlyle's Literary Vision.* Columbus: Ohio State University Press, 1972, pp. 22–24, 167–169.

Kusch, Robert E. "Pattern and Paradox in *Heroes and Hero Worship*," in *Studies in Scottish Literature.* VI (January, 1969), pp. 146–155.

La Valley, Albert J. *Carlyle and the Idea of the Modern.* New Haven, Conn.: Yale University Press, 1968, pp. 236–252.

Lehman, B.H. *Carlyle's Theory of the Hero: Its Sources, Development, History, and Influence on Carlyle's Work: A Study of a Nineteenth Century Idea.* Durham, N.C.: Duke University Press, 1928, pp. 40–60.

Ralli, Augustus. *Guide to Carlyle,* Volume I. London: Allen and Unwin, 1920, pp. 293–304.

Rosenberg, Philip. *The Seventh Hero: Thomas Carlyle and the Theory of Radical Activism.* Cambridge, Mass.: Harvard University Press, 1974, pp. 188–193.

Past and Present

Altick, Richard D. "Introduction," in *Past and Present.* Boston: Houghton Mifflin, 1965, pp. v–xviii.

————. *"Past and Present:* Topicality as Technique," in *Carlyle and His Contemporaries.* Edited by John Clubbe. Durham, N.C.: Duke University Press, 1976, pp. 112–128.

Calder, G.J. *The Writing of* Past and Present. New Haven, Conn.: Yale University Press, 1949.

Cazamian, Louis. *Carlyle.* New York: Macmillan, 1932, pp. 193–209.

Chandler, Alice K. *A Dream of Order: The Medieval Ideal in Nineteenth Century English Literature.* Lincoln: University of Nebraska Press, 1970, pp. 134–140.

Holloway, John. *The Victorian Sage.* London: Macmillan, 1953, pp. 44–46.

Ikler, A. Abbott. *Puritan Temper and Transcendental Faith: Carlyle's Literary Vision.* Columbus: Ohio State University Press, 1972, pp. 30–32.

La Valley, Albert J. *Carlyle and the Idea of the Modern.* New Haven, Conn.: Yale University Press, 1968, pp. 182–235.

Neff, Emery. *Carlyle.* New York: Norton, 1932, pp. 198–209.

Ralli, Augustus. *Guide to Carlyle,* Volume I. London: Allen and Unwin, 1920, pp. 339–351.

Rosenberg, Philip. *The Seventh Hero: Thomas Carlyle and the Theory of Radical Activism.* Cambridge, Mass.: Harvard University Press, 1974, pp. 146–175.

Rowse, A.L. "The Message of *Past and Present.*" in *New Statesman.* (June, 1943), pp. 5–12.

Stange, G. Robert. "Refractions of *Past and Present,*" in *Carlyle Past and Present: A Collection of New Essays.* Edited by K.J. Fielding and Rodger L. Tarr. London: Vision, 1976, pp. 96–111.

Symons, Julian. *Thomas Carlyle: The Life and Ideas of a Prophet.* New York: Oxford University Press, 1952, pp. 199–200.

Sartor Resartus

Brookes, Gerry H. *The Rhetorical Form of Carlyle's* Sartor Resartus. Berkeley: University of California Press, 1972.

Cazamian, Louis. *Carlyle.* New York: Macmillan, 1932, pp. 100–133.

Deen, Leonard W. "Irrational Form in *Sartor Resartus,*" in *Texas Studies in Literature and Language.* V (1963), pp. 438–451.

Deneau, Daniel P. "Relationship of Style and Device in *Sartor Resartus*," in *Victorian Newsletter*. XVII (1960), pp. 17–20.

Harrold, C.F. "Introduction," in *Sartor Resartus: The Life and Opinions of Herr Teufelsdröckh*. New York: Odyssey, 1937. Reprinted in *A Carlyle Reader*. Edited by G.B. Tennyson. New York: Modern Library, 1969.

Holloway, John. *The Victorian Sage*. London: Macmillan, 1953, pp. 24–26, 30.

La Valley, Albert J. *Carlyle and the Idea of the Modern*. New Haven, Conn.: Yale University Press, 1968, pp. 69–118.

Levine, George. *The Boundaries of Fiction: Carlyle, Macaulay, Newman*. Princeton, N.J.: Princeton University Press, 1968, pp. 19–78.

Metzger, Lore. "*Sartor Resartus*: A Victorian *Faust*," in *Comparative Literature*. XIII (1961), pp. 316–331.

Moore, Carlisle. "*Sartor Resartus* and the Problem of Carlyle's 'Conversion,' " in *PMLA*. LXX (1955), pp. 662–681.

Neff, Emery. *Carlyle*. New York: Norton, 1932, pp. 121–126.

Peckham, Morse. *Beyond the Tragic Vision: The Quest for Identity in the Nineteenth Century*. New York: George Braziller, 1962, pp. 177–180.

————. *Victorian Revolutionaries: Speculations on Some Heroes of a Culture Crisis*. New York: George Braziller, 1970, pp. 65–82.

Ralli, Augustus. *Guide to Carlyle*, Volume I. London: Allen and Unwin, 1920, pp. 140–150.

Reed, Walter J. "The Pattern of Conversion in *Sartor Resartus*," in *Journal of English Literary History*. XXXVIII (1971), pp. 411–431.

Rosenberg, Philip. *The Seventh Hero: Thomas Carlyle and the Theory of Radical Activism*. Cambridge, Mass.: Harvard University Press, 1974, pp. 45–62.

Sanders, Charles Richard. "The Byron Closed in *Sartor Resartus*," in *Studies in Romanticism*. III (1964), pp. 77–108.

Symons, Julian. *Thomas Carlyle: The Life and Ideas of a Prophet*. New York: Oxford University Press, 1952, pp. 127–146.

Tennyson, G.B. *"Sartor" Called "Resartus": The Genesis, Structure, and Style of Thomas Carlyle's First Major Work*. Princeton, N.J.: Princeton University Press, 1965.

LEWIS CARROLL
(1832–1898)

Alice's Adventures in Wonderland

Auerbach, Nina. "Alice and Wonderland: A Curious Child," in *Victorian Studies*. XVII (1973), pp. 31–47.

Ayres, H.M. *Carroll's Alice*. New York: Columbia University Press, 1936.

Baum, Alwin L. "Carroll's Alices: The Semiotics of Paradox," in *American Imago*. XXXIV (1977), pp. 86–108.

Blake, Kathleen. *Play, Games, and Sport: The Literary Works of Lewis Carroll*. Ithaca, N.Y.: Cornell University Press, 1974, pp. 108–136.

Boynton, Mary F. "An Oxford Don Quixote," in *Hispania*. XLIV (1964), pp. 738–750.

Egoff, Sheila, G.T. Stubbs and L.F. Ashley. *Only Connect; Readings on Children's Literature*. New York: Oxford University Press, 1969, pp. 150–155.

Empson, William. "*Alice in Wonderland*: The Child as Swain," in *English Pastoral Poetry*. New York: Norton, 1938, pp. 253–294.

Fadiman, Clifton. *Party of One; The Selected Writings of Clifton Fadiman*. New York: World, 1955, pp. 404–410.

Flescher, Jacqueline. "The Language of Nonsense in *Alice*," in *Yale French Studies*. XLIII (1969), pp. 128–144.

Graham, Neilson. "Sanity, Madness and Alice," in *Ariel*. IV (1973), pp. 80–89.

Henkle, Roger B. "The Mad Hatter's World," in *Virginia Quarterly Review*. XLIX (1973), pp. 100–106, 111–117.

Holmes, Roger W. "The Philosopher's *Alice in Wonderland*," in *Antioch Review*. XIX (Summer, 1959), pp. 133–149.

Johnson, Paula. "Alice Among the Analysts," in *Hartford Studies in Literature*. IV (1972), pp. 114–122.

Jorgens, Jack J. "Alice Our Contemporary," in *Children's Literature: The Great Excluded*. I (1972), pp. 152–161.

Kibel, Alvin C. "Logic and Satire in *Alice in Wonderland*," in *American Scholar*. XLIII (1974), pp. 605–629.

Kincaid, James R. "Alice's Invasion of Wonderland," in *PMLA*. LXXXVIII (1973), pp. 92–99.

Levin, Harry, "Wonderland Revisited," in *Kenyon Review*. XXVII (Autumn, 1965), pp. 591–616.

Matthews, Charles. "Satire in the Alice Books," in *Criticism*. XII (1971), pp. 105–119.

Pattison, Robert. *The Child Figure in English Literature.* Athens: University of Georgia Press, 1978, pp. 23, 120, 151–159.

Phillips, Robert. *Aspects of Alice: Lewis Carroll's Dreamchild as Seen Through the Critics' Looking Glasses, 1865–1971.* New York: Vanguard, 1971.

Phillips, William. *Art and Psychoanalysis.* New York: Criterion, 1957, pp. 185–217.

Rackin, Donald. Alice's Adventures in Wonderland*: A Critical Handbook.* Belmont, Calif.: Wadsworth, 1969.

_____. "Alice's Journey to the End of Night," in *PMLA.* LXXXI (1966), pp. 313–326.

_____. "Corrective Laughter; Carroll's *Alice* and Popular Children's Literature of the Nineteenth Century," in *Journal of Popular Culture.* I (1967), pp. 243–255.

Through the Looking-Glass

Arnoldi, Richard. "Parallels Between *Our Mutual Friend* and the Alice Books," in *Children's Literature: The Great Excluded.* I (1972), pp. 54–57.

Auerbach, Nina. "Alice and Wonderland: A Curious Child," in *Victorian Studies.* XVII (1973), pp. 31–47.

Baum, Alwin L. "Carroll's *Alices*: The Semiotics of Paradox," in *American Imago.* XXXIV (1977), pp. 86–108.

Blake, Kathleen. *Play, Games and Sport: The Literary Works of Lewis Carroll.* Ithaca, N.Y.: Cornell University Press, 1974, pp. 132–148.

Boynton, Mary F. "An Oxford Don Quixote," in *Hispania.* XLIV (1964), pp. 738–750.

Ettleson, A. *Carroll's* Through the Looking-Glass *Decoded.* New York: Philosophical Library, 1966.

Gardner, Martin. "Introduction," in *The Wasp in a Wig, a "Suppressed" Episode of* Through the Looking-Glass and What Alice Found There. By Lewis Carroll. New York: Clarkson N. Potter, 1977, pp. 1–11.

Henkle, Roger B. "The Mad Hatter's World," in *Virginia Quarterly Review.* XLIX (1973), pp. 107–111.

Johnson, Paula. "Alice Among the Analysts," in *Hartford Studies in Literature.* IV (1972), pp. 114–122.

Jorgens, Jack J. "Alice Our Contemporary," in *Children's Literature: The Great Excluded.* I (1972), pp. 152–161.

Matthews, Charles. "Satire in the Alice Books," in *Criticism.* XII (1971), pp. 105–119.

Otten, Terry. "Steppenwolf and Alice—In and Out of Wonderland," in *Studies in the Humanities.* IV (1974), pp. 28–34.

Pattison, Robert.   *The Child Figure in English Literature.* Athens: University of Georgia Press, 1978, pp. 152–154.

Priestley, J.B.   "Walrus and Carpenter; Political Symbolism in *Through the Looking-Glass*," in *New Statesman.* LIV (August 10, 1957), p. 168.

JOYCE CARY
(1888–1957)

The African Witch

Barba, Harry. "Cary's Image of the African in Transition," in *University of Kansas City Review*. XXIX (June, 1963), pp. 291–293.

Bloom, Robert. *The Indeterminate World: A Study of the Novels of Joyce Cary*. Philadelphia: University of Pennsylvania Press, 1962, pp. 52–54.

Collins, Harold R. "Joyce Cary's Troublesome Africans," in *Antioch Review*. XIII (September, 1953), pp. 397–406.

Echeruo, Michael J.C. *Joyce Cary and the Novel of Africa*. New York: Africana Publishing, 1973, pp. 74–113.

Foster, Malcolm. *Joyce Cary: A Biography*. Boston: Houghton Mifflin, 1968, pp. 321–324.

Hoffmann, Charles G. *Joyce Cary: The Comedy of Freedom*. Pittsburgh: University of Pittsburgh Press, 1964, pp. 25–34.

_____. "Joyce Cary's African Novels: There's a War On," in *South Atlantic Quarterly*. LXII (Spring, 1963), pp. 236–240.

Larsen, Golden L. *The Dark Descent: Social Change and Moral Responsibility in the Novels of Joyce Cary*. New York: Roy, 1966, pp. 36–45.

Mahood, M.M. *Joyce Cary's Africa*. Boston: Houghton Mifflin, 1965, pp. 145–166.

Noble, R.W. *Joyce Cary*. Edinburgh: Oliver and Boyd, 1973, pp. 18–24.

O'Connor, William Van. *Joyce Cary*. New York: Columbia University Press, 1966, pp. 19–21.

Steinbrecher, George. "Joyce Cary: Master Novelist," in *College English*. XVIII (May, 1957), pp. 387–395.

Tucker, Martin. *Africa in Modern Literature: A Study of Contemporary Writing in English*. New York: Frederick Ungar, 1967, pp. 40–42.

Wolkenfeld, Jack. *Joyce Cary: The Developing Style*. New York: New York University Press, 1968, pp. 3–20, 78–87, 116–120.

Wright, Andrew. *Joyce Cary: A Preface to His Novels*. New York: Harper, 1958, pp. 60–62, 80–82, 101–103.

Aissa Saved

Bloom, Robert. *The Indeterminate World: A Study of the Novels of Joyce Cary*. Philadelphia: University of Pennsylvania Press, 1962, pp. 46–48.

Cary, Joyce. "My First Novel," in *Listener*. XLIX (April 16, 1953), p. 637.

Collins, Harold R. "Joyce Cary's Troublesome Africans," in *Antioch Review.* XIII (September, 1953), pp. 397–406.

Echeruo, Michael J.C. *Joyce Cary and the Novel of Africa.* New York: Africana Publishing, 1973, pp. 28–43.

Foster, Malcolm. *Joyce Cary: A Biography.* Boston: Houghton Mifflin, 1968, pp. 315–318.

Hoffmann, Charles G. *Joyce Cary: The Comedy of Freedom.* Pittsburgh: University of Pittsburgh Press, 1964, pp. 8–18.

————. "Joyce Cary's African Novels: There's a War On," in *South Atlantic Quarterly.* LXII (Spring, 1963), pp. 229–233.

Larsen, Golden L. *The Dark Descent: Social Change and Moral Responsibility in the Novels of Joyce Cary.* New York: Roy, 1966, pp. 22–27.

Mahood, M.M. *Joyce Cary's Africa.* Boston: Houghton Mifflin, 1965, pp. 105–124.

Noble, R.W. *Joyce Cary.* Edinburgh: Oliver and Boyd, 1973, pp. 10–13.

O'Connor, William Van. *Joyce Cary.* New York: Columbia University Press, 1966, pp. 17–18.

Steinbrecher, George. "Joyce Cary: Master Novelist," in *College English.* XVIII (May, 1957), pp. 387–395.

Tucker, Martin. *Africa in Modern Literature: A Survey of Contemporary Writing in English.* New York: Ungar, 1967, pp. 37–39.

Wolkenfeld, Jack. *Joyce Cary: The Developing Style.* New York: New York University Press, 1968, pp. 56–69, 172–174.

Wright, Andrew. *Joyce Cary: A Preface to His Novels.* New York: Harper, 1958, pp. 84–87.

The American Visitor

Bloom, Robert. *The Indeterminate World: A Study of the Novels of Joyce Cary.* Philadelphia: University of Pennsylvania Press, 1962, pp. 48–52.

Collins, Harold R. "Joyce Cary's Troublesome Africans," in *Antioch Review.* XIII (September, 1953), pp. 397–406.

Echeruo, Michael J.C. *Joyce Cary and the Novel of Africa.* New York: Africana Publishing, 1973, pp. 44–73.

Foster, Malcolm. *Joyce Cary: A Biography.* Boston: Houghton Mifflin, 1968, pp. 318–321.

French, Warren. "Joyce Cary's American Rover Girl," in *Texas Studies in Literature and Language.* II (Autumn, 1960), pp. 281–291.

Hoffmann, Charles G. *Joyce Cary: The Comedy of Freedom.* Pittsburgh: University of Pittsburgh Press, 1964, pp. 18–25.

————. "Joyce Cary's African Novels: There's a War On," in *South Atlantic Quarterly*. LXII (Spring, 1963), pp. 233–236.

Larsen, Golden L. *The Dark Descent: Social Change and Moral Responsibility in the Novels of Joyce Cary*. New York: Roy, 1966, pp. 27–36.

Mahood, M.M. *Joyce Cary's Africa*. Boston: Houghton Mifflin, 1965, pp. 169–186.

Noble, R.W. *Joyce Cary*. Edinburgh: Oliver and Boyd, 1973, pp. 13–18.

O'Connor, William Van. *Joyce Cary*. New York: Columbia University Press, 1966, pp. 18–19.

Steinbrecher, George. "Joyce Cary: Master Novelist," in *College English*. XVIII (May, 1957), pp. 387–395.

Tucker, Martin. *Africa in Modern Literature: A Survey of Contemporary Writing in English*. New York: Frederick Ungar, 1967, pp. 39–40.

Wolkenfeld, Jack. *Joyce Cary: The Developing Style*. New York: New York University Press, 1968, pp. 69–78, 111–113.

Wright, Andrew. *Joyce Cary: A Preface to His Novels*. New York: Harper, 1958, pp. 59–60, 99–101.

Castle Corner

Bloom, Robert. *The Indeterminate World: A Study of the Novels of Joyce Cary*. Philadelphia: University of Pennsylvania Press, 1962, pp. 66–72.

Foster, Malcolm. *Joyce Cary: A Biography*. Boston: Houghton Mifflin, 1968, pp. 352–357.

Hoffmann, Charles G. *Joyce Cary: The Comedy of Freedom*. Pittsburgh: University of Pittsburgh Press, 1964, pp. 44–53.

————. " 'They Want to Be Happy': Joyce Cary's Unfinished *Castle Corner* Series," in *Modern Fiction Studies*. IX (Autumn, 1963), pp. 217–225.

Larsen, Golden L. *The Dark Descent: Social Change and Moral Responsibility in the Novels of Joyce Cary*. New York: Roy, 1966, pp. 45–48.

Noble, R.W. *Joyce Cary*. Edinburgh: Oliver & Boyd, 1973, pp. 24–28.

O'Connor, William Van. *Joyce Cary*. New York: Columbia University Press, 1966, pp. 30–31.

Stevenson, Lionel. "Joyce Cary and the Anglo-Irish Tradition," in *Modern Fiction Studies*. IX (Autumn, 1963), pp. 210–216.

Weintraub, Stanley. "*Castle Corner*: Joyce Cary's *Buddenbrooks*," in *Wisconsin Studies in Contemporary Literature*. V (Winter–Spring, 1964), pp. 54–63.

Wolkenfeld, Jack. *Joyce Cary: The Developing Style*. New York: New York University Press, 1968, pp. 87–89.

Woodcock, George. "Citizens of Babel: A Study of Joyce Cary," in *Queens Quarterly*. LXIII (Summer, 1956), pp. 237–240.

Wright, Andrew. *Joyce Cary: A Preface to His Novels*. New York: Harper, 1958, pp. 66–67, 82–84, 94–96.

Charley Is My Darling

Bloom, Robert. *The Indeterminate World: A Study of the Novels of Joyce Cary*. Philadelphia: University of Pennsylvania Press, 1962, pp. 59–63.

Echeruo, Michael J.C. *Joyce Cary and the Novel of Africa*. New York: Africana Publishing, 1973, pp. 123–130.

Foster, Malcolm. *Joyce Cary: A Biography*. Boston: Houghton Mifflin, 1968, pp. 346–351.

Hoffmann, Charles G. *Joyce Cary: The Comedy of Freedom*. Pittsburgh: University of Pittsburgh Press, 1964, pp. 54–66.

Kerr, Elizabeth M. "Joyce Cary: At the Beginning and in Mid-Career," in *Wisconsin Studies in Contemporary Literature*. II (Winter, 1961), pp. 102–106.

Larsen, Golden L. *The Dark Descent: Social Change and Moral Responsibility in the Novels of Joyce Cary*. New York: Roy, 1966, pp. 79–82.

Noble, R.W. *Joyce Cary*. Edinburgh: Oliver and Boyd, 1973, pp. 37–42.

O'Connor, William Van. *Joyce Cary*. New York: Columbia University Press, 1966, pp. 23–24.

Wolkenfeld, Jack. *Joyce Cary: The Developing Style*. New York: New York University Press, 1968, pp. 176–177.

Wright, Andrew. *Joyce Cary: A Preface to His Novels*. New York: Harper, 1958, pp. 69–70.

Except the Lord

Bettman, Elizabeth R. "Joyce Cary and the Problem of Political Morality," in *Antioch Review*. XVII (Summer, 1957), pp. 270–271.

Bloom, Robert. *The Indeterminate World: A Study of the Novels of Joyce Cary*. Philadelphia: University of Pennsylvania Press, 1962, pp. 139–169.

Foster, Malcolm. *Joyce Cary: A Biography*. Boston: Houghton Mifflin, 1968, pp. 483–487.

Gindin, James. *Harvest of a Quiet Eye; The Novel of Compassion*. Bloomington: Indiana University Press, 1971, pp. 265–270.

Hoffmann, Charles G. "Joyce Cary: Art and Reality," in *University of Kansas City Review*. XXVI (1960), pp. 273–282.

————. *Joyce Cary: The Comedy of Freedom*. Pittsburgh: University of Pittsburgh Press, 1964, pp. 139–147.

Kerr, Elizabeth M. "Joyce Cary's Second Trilogy," in *University of Toronto Quarterly*. XXIX (April, 1960), pp. 310–325.

King, Carlyle. "Joyce Cary and the Creative Imagination," in *Tamarack Review*. X (1959), pp. 39–51.

Mitchell, Giles. "Joyce Cary's *Except the Lord*," in *Arlington Quarterly*. II (Autumn, 1969), pp. 71–82.

Noble, R.W. *Joyce Cary*. Edinburgh: Oliver and Boyd, 1973, pp. 88–94.

Steinbrecher, George. "Joyce Cary: Master Novelist," in *College English*. XVIII (May, 1957), pp. 387–395.

Teeling, John. "Joyce Cary's Moral World," in *Modern Fiction Studies*. IX (Autumn, 1963), pp. 276–283.

Wright, Andrew. *Joyce Cary: A Preface to His Novels*. New York: Harper, 1958, pp. 142–148.

A Fearful Joy

Allen, Walter. *Joyce Cary*. London: Longmans, Green, 1954, pp. 16–19.

Bloom, Robert. *The Indeterminate World: A Study of the Novels of Joyce Cary*. Philadelphia: University of Pennsylvania Press, 1962, pp. 77–83.

Eastman, Richard M. "Historical Grace in Cary's *A Fearful Joy*," in *Novel*. I (Winter, 1968), pp. 150–157.

Foster, Malcolm. *Joyce Cary: A Biography*. Boston: Houghton Mifflin, 1968, pp. 428–434.

Gindin, James. *Harvest of a Quiet Eye: The Novel of Compassion*. Bloomington: Indiana University Press, 1971, pp. 273–275.

Hall, James. *The Tragic Comedians: Seven Modern British Novelists*. Bloomington: Indiana University Press, 1963, pp. 84–85.

Hoffmann, Charles G. *Joyce Cary: The Comedy of Freedom*. Pittsburgh: University of Pittsburgh Press, 1964, pp. 118–126.

McCormick, John. *Catastrophe and Imagination: An Interpretation of the Recent English and American Novel*. London: Longmans, Green, 1957, pp. 151–154.

Monas, Sidney. "What to Do with a Drunken Sailor," in *Hudson Review*. III (Autumn, 1950), pp. 466–474.

Noble, R.W. *Joyce Cary*. Edinburgh: Oliver and Boyd, 1973, pp. 76–80.

O'Connor, William Van. *Joyce Cary*. New York: Columbia University Press, 1966, pp. 33–36.

Pittock, Malcolm. "Joyce Cary: *A Fearful Joy*," in *Essays in Criticism*. XIII (October, 1963), pp. 428–432.

Prescott, Orville. *In My Opinion*. Indianapolis, Ind.: Bobbs-Merrill, 1952, pp. 180–199.

Wolkenfeld, Jack. *Joyce Cary: The Developing Style.* New York: New York University Press, 1968, pp. 135–139.

Wright, Andrew. *Joyce Cary: A Preface to His Novels.* New York: Harper, 1958, pp. 69–70.

Herself Surprised

Adams, Hazard. "Joyce Cary's Three Speakers," in *Modern Fiction Studies.* V (Summer, 1959), pp. 108–120.

Allen, Walter. *Joyce Cary.* London: Longmans, Green, 1954, pp. 19–27.

Bloom, Robert. *The Indeterminate World: A Study of the Novels of Joyce Cary.* Philadelphia: University of Pennsylvania Press, 1962, pp. 84–90.

Brawer, Judith. "The Triumph of Defeat: A Study of Joyce Cary's First Trilogy," in *Texas Studies in Literature and Language.* X (1969), pp. 629–634.

Cary, Joyce. "Three New Prefaces," in *Adam International Review.* XVIII (November–December, 1950), pp. 11–12.

Davies, William Robertson. *Voice from the Attic.* New York: Knopf, 1960, pp. 246–249.

Faber, Kathleen R. and M.D. Faber. "An Important Theme of Joyce Cary's Trilogy," in *Discourse.* XI (Winter, 1968), pp. 26–31.

Foster, Malcolm. *Joyce Cary: A Biography.* Boston: Houghton Mifflin, 1968, pp. 381–384.

Gindin, James. *Harvest of a Quiet Eye; The Novel of Compassion.* Bloomington: Indiana University Press, 1971, pp. 265–270.

Hall, James. *The Tragic Comedians: Seven Modern British Novelists.* Bloomington: Indiana University Press, 1963, pp. 86–87.

Hamilton, Kenneth. "Boon or Thorn? Joyce Cary and Samuel Beckett on Human Life," in *Dalhousie Review.* XXXVIII (Winter, 1959), pp. 433–442.

Hoffmann, Charles G. "The Genesis and Development of Joyce Cary's First Trilogy," in *PMLA.* LXXVIII (September, 1963), pp. 431–439.

————. "Joyce Cary and the Comic Mask," in *Western Humanities Review.* XIII (Spring, 1959), pp. 135–142.

————. "Joyce Cary: Art and Reality," in *University of Kansas City Review.* XXVI (June, 1960), pp. 275–277.

————. *Joyce Cary: The Comedy of Freedom.* Pittsburgh: University of Pittsburgh Press, 1964, pp. 70–77.

Larsen, Golden L. *The Dark Descent: Social Change and Moral Responsibility in the Novels of Joyce Cary.* New York: Roy, 1966, pp. 102–125.

Monas, Sidney. "What to Do with a Drunken Sailor," in *Hudson Review.* III (Autumn, 1950), pp. 466–474.

Noble, R.W. *Joyce Cary.* Edinburgh: Oliver and Boyd, 1973, pp. 48–69.

O'Connor, William Van. *Joyce Cary.* New York: Columbia University Press, 1966, pp. 26–29.

Prescott, Orville. *In My Opinion.* Indianapolis, Ind.: Bobbs-Merrill, 1952, pp. 180–199.

Reed, Peter J. " 'The Better the Heart': Joyce Cary's Sara Monday," in *Texas Studies in Literature and Language.* XV (1973), pp. 357–370.

Stockholder, Fred. "The Triple Vision in Joyce Cary's First Trilogy," in *Modern Fiction Studies.* IX (Autumn, 1963), pp. 276–283.

Wolkenfeld, Jack. *Joyce Cary: The Developing Style.* New York: New York University Press, 1968, pp. 22–23.

Wright, Andrew. *Joyce Cary: A Preface to His Novels.* New York: Harper, 1958, pp. 110–119.

The Horse's Mouth

Adams, Hazard. "Blake and Gulley Jimson: English Symbolists," in *Critique: Studies in Modern Fiction.* III (Spring–Fall, 1959), pp. 3–14.

————. "Joyce Cary's Three Speakers," in *Modern Fiction Studies.* V (Summer, 1959), pp. 108–120.

Adams, Robert H. "Freedom in *The Horse's Mouth,*" in *College English.* XXVI (March, 1965), pp. 451–454, 459–460.

Allen, Walter. *Joyce Cary.* London: Longmans, Green, 1954, pp. 19–27.

Alter, Robert. *Rogue's Progress: Studies in the Picaresque Novel.* Cambridge, Mass.: Harvard University Press, 1964, pp. 129–132.

Bloom, Robert. *The Indeterminate World: A Study of the Novels of Joyce Cary.* Philadelphia: University of Pennsylvania Press, 1962, pp. 96–105.

Brawer, Judith. "The Triumph of Defeat: A Study of Joyce Cary's First Trilogy," in *Texas Studies in Literature and Language.* X (1969), pp. 629–634.

Faber, Kathleen R. and M.D. Faber. "An Important Theme of Joyce Cary's Trilogy," in *Discourse.* XI (Winter, 1968), pp. 26–31.

Foster, Malcolm. *Joyce Cary: A Biography.* Boston: Houghton Mifflin, 1968, pp. 389–393.

Gindin, James. *Harvest of a Quiet Eye; The Novel of Compassion.* Bloomington: Indiana University Press, 1971, pp. 265–270.

Hall, James. *The Tragic Comedians: Seven Modern British Novelists.* Bloomington: Indiana University Press, 1963, pp. 87–97.

Hoffmann, Charles G. "Joyce Cary: Art and Reality," in *University of Kansas City Review.* XXVI (June, 1960), pp. 275–277.

————. *Joyce Cary: The Comedy of Freedom.* Pittsburgh: University of Pittsburgh Press, 1964, pp. 85–98.

Larsen, Golden L.   *The Dark Descent: Social Change and Moral Responsibility in the Novels of Joyce Cary.* New York: Roy, 1966, pp. 156–179.

Messenger, Ann P.   "A Painter's Prose: Similes in Joyce Cary's *The Horse's Mouth*," in *Re: Arts and Letters.* III (1970), pp. 16–28.

Monas, Sidney.   "What to Do with a Drunken Sailor," in *Hudson Review.* III (Autumn, 1950), pp. 466–474.

Noble, R.W.   *Joyce Cary.* Edinburgh: Oliver and Boyd, 1973, pp. 48–69.

Prescott, Orville.   *In My Opinion.* Indianapolis, Ind.: Bobbs-Merrill, 1952, pp. 180–199.

Ryan, Marjorie.   "An Interpretation of Joyce Cary's *The Horse's Mouth*," in *Critique: Studies in Modern Fiction.* II (Spring–Summer, 1958), pp. 29–38.

Seltzer, Alvin J.   "Speaking Out of Both Sides of *The Horse's Mouth*: Joyce Cary vs. Gulley Jimson," in *Contemporary Literature.* XV (1974), pp. 488–502.

Shapiro, Stephen A.   "Leopold Bloom and Gulley Jimson: The Economics of Survival," in *Twentieth Century Literature.* X (April, 1964), pp. 3–11.

Stockholder, Fred.   "The Triple Vision in Joyce Cary's First Trilogy," in *Modern Fiction Studies.* IX (Autumn, 1963), pp. 276–283.

Wolkenfeld, Jack.   *Joyce Cary: The Developing Style.* New York: New York University Press, 1968, pp. 23–41.

Wright, Andrew.   *Joyce Cary: A Preface to His Novels.* New York: Harper, 1958, pp. 124–137, 156–173.

Mister Johnson

Barba, Harry.   "Cary's Image of the African in Transition," in *University of Kansas City Review.* XXIX (June, 1963), pp. 293–296.

Bloom, Robert.   *The Indeterminate World: A Study of the Novels of Joyce Cary.* Philadelphia: University of Pennsylvania Press, 1962, pp. 54–59.

Collins, Harold R.   "Joyce Cary's Troublesome Africans," in *Antioch Review.* XIII (September, 1953), pp. 397–406.

Echeruo, Michael J.C.   *Joyce Cary and the Novel of Africa.* New York: Africana Publishing, 1973, pp. 121–139.

Foster, Malcolm.   *Joyce Cary: A Biography.* Boston: Houghton Mifflin, 1968, pp. 324–329.

Fyfe, Christopher.   "The Colonial Situation in *Mister Johnson*," in *Modern Fiction Studies.* IX (Autumn, 1963), pp. 226–230.

Gindin, James.   *Harvest of a Quiet Eye; the Novel of Compassion.* Bloomington: Indiana University Press, 1971, pp. 262–264.

Hoffmann, Charles G.   *Joyce Cary: The Comedy of Freedom.* Pittsburgh: University of Pittsburgh Press, 1964, pp. 34–43.

————. "Joyce Cary's African Novels: There's a War On," in *South Atlantic Quarterly*. LXII (Spring, 1963), pp. 240–243.

Kettle, Arnold. *An Introduction to the English Novel, Volume II: Henry James to the Present Day*. London: Hutchinson's, 1953, pp. 177–184.

Kronenfeld, J.Z. "In Search of Mister Johnson: Creation, Politics, and Culture in Cary's Africa," in *Ariel: A Review of International English Literature*. VII (1976), pp. 69–97.

Larsen, Golden L. *The Dark Descent: Social Change and Moral Responsibility in the Novels of Joyce Cary*. New York: Roy, 1966, pp. 49–79.

Mahood, M.M. *Joyce Cary's Africa*. Boston: Houghton Mifflin, 1965, pp. 169–186.

Moore, Gerald. "*Mister Johnson* Reconsidered," in *Black Orpheus*. IV (October, 1958), pp. 16–23.

Noble, R.W. *Joyce Cary*. Edinburgh: Oliver and Boyd, 1973, pp. 29–36.

O'Connor, William Van. *Joyce Cary*. New York: Columbia University Press, 1966, pp. 21–23.

Prescott, Orville. *In My Opinion; An Inquiry into the Contemporary Novel*. Indianapolis, Ind.: Bobbs-Merrill, 1952, pp. 192–194.

Raskin, Jonas. *The Mythology of Imperialism*. New York: Random House, 1971, pp. 294–309.

Sandison, Alan G. "Living Out the Lyric: *Mister Johnson* and the Present Day," in *English*. XX (1971), pp. 11–16.

Smith, B.R. "Moral Evaluation in *Mister Johnson*," in *Critique: Studies in Modern Fiction*. XI (1965), pp. 101–110.

Steinbrecher, George. "Joyce Cary: Master Novelist," in *College English*. XVIII (May, 1957), pp. 387–395.

Tucker, Martin. *Africa in Modern Literature: A Survey of Contemporary Writing in English*. New York: Frederick Ungar, 1967, pp. 43–47.

Wolkenfeld, Jack. *Joyce Cary: The Developing Style*. New York: New York University Press, 1968, pp. 94–103, 121–125.

Woodcock, George. "Citizens of Babel: A Study of Joyce Cary," in *Queens Quarterly*. LXIII (Summer, 1956), pp. 240–242.

Wright, Andrew. *Joyce Cary: A Preface to His Novels*. New York: Harper, 1958, pp. 84–87.

The Moonlight

Bloom, Robert. *The Indeterminate World: A Study of the Novels of Joyce Cary*. Philadelphia: University of Pennsylvania Press, 1962, pp. 72–77.

Foster, Malcolm. *Joyce Cary: A Biography*. Boston: Houghton Mifflin, 1968, pp. 425–428.

Hardy, Barbara. "Form in Joyce Cary's Novels," in *Essays in Criticism*. IV (April, 1954), pp. 180–190.

Hoffmann, Charles G. *Joyce Cary: The Comedy of Freedom.* Pittsburgh: University of Pittsburgh Press, 1964, pp. 107–118.

King, Carlyle. "Joyce Cary and the Creative Imagination," in *Tamarack Review*. X (1959), pp. 39–51.

Larsen, Golden L. *The Dark Descent: Social Change and Moral Responsibility in the Novels of Joyce Cary.* New York: Roy, 1966, pp. 183–185.

Noble, R.W. *Joyce Cary.* Edinburgh: Oliver and Boyd, 1973, pp. 70–76.

O'Connor, William Van. *Joyce Cary.* New York: Columbia University Press, 1966, pp. 31–33.

Wolkenfeld, Jack. *Joyce Cary: The Developing Style.* New York: New York University Press, 1968, pp. 129–135.

Wright, Andrew. *Joyce Cary: A Preface to His Novels.* New York: Harper, 1958, pp. 67–69.

Not Honour More

Battaglia, Francis J. "Spurious Armageddon: Joyce Cary's *Not Honour More*," in *Modern Fiction Studies*. XIII (Winter, 1967–1968), pp. 479–491.

Bettman, Elizabeth R. "Joyce Cary and the Problem of Political Morality," in *Antioch Review*. XVII (Summer, 1957), pp. 271–272.

Bloom, Robert. *The Indeterminate World: A Study of the Novels of Joyce Cary.* Philadelphia: University of Pennsylvania Press, 1962, pp. 170–200.

Foster, Malcolm. *Joyce Cary: A Biography.* Boston: Houghton Mifflin, 1968, pp. 148–156.

Gindin, James. *Harvest of a Quiet Eye; The Novel of Compassion.* Bloomington: Indiana University Press, 1971, pp. 265–270.

Kerr, Elizabeth M. "Joyce Cary's Second Trilogy," in *University of Toronto Quarterly*. XXIX (1959), pp. 39–51.

King, Carlyle. "Joyce Cary and the Creative Imagination," in *Tamarack Review*. X (1959), pp. 39–51.

Noble, R.W. *Joyce Cary.* Edinburgh: Oliver and Boyd, 1973, pp. 94–100.

Steinbrecher, George. "Joyce Cary: Master Novelist," in *College English*. XVIII (May, 1957), pp. 387–395.

Wolkenfeld, Jack. *Joyce Cary: The Developing Style.* New York: New York University Press, 1968, pp. 175–181.

Wright, Andrew. *Joyce Cary: A Preface to His Novels.* New York: Harper, 1958, pp. 148–153.

Prisoner of Grace

Bettman, Elizabeth R. "Joyce Cary and the Problem of Political Morality," in *Antioch Review*. XVII (Summer, 1957), pp. 267–270.

Bloom, Robert. *The Indeterminate World: A Study of the Novels of Joyce Cary*. Philadelphia: University of Pennsylvania Press, 1962, pp. 108–138.

Foster, Malcolm. *Joyce Cary: A Biography*. Boston: Houghton Mifflin, 1968, pp. 479–482.

Gindin, James. *Harvest of a Quiet Eye; The Novel of Compassion*. Bloomington: Indiana University Press, 1971, pp. 265–270.

Hoffmann, Charles G. "Joyce Cary: Art and Reality," in *University of Kansas City Review*. XXVI (1960), pp. 273–282.

————. *Joyce Cary: The Comedy of Freedom*. Pittsburgh: University of Pittsburgh Press, 1964, pp. 133–139.

Kerr, Elizabeth M. "Joyce Cary's Second Trilogy," in *University of Toronto Quarterly*. XXIX (April, 1960), pp. 310–325.

King, Carlyle. "Joyce Cary and the Creative Imagination," in *Tamarack Review*. X (1959), pp. 39–51.

Mitchell, Giles. "Joyce Cary's *Prisoner of Grace*," in *Modern Fiction Studies*. IX (Autumn, 1963), pp. 263–275.

Noble, R.W. *Joyce Cary*. Edinburgh: Oliver and Boyd, 1973, pp. 81–88.

Steinbrecher, George. "Joyce Cary: Master Novelist," in *College English*. XVIII (May, 1957), pp. 387–395.

Teeling, John. "Joyce Cary's Moral World," in *Modern Fiction Studies*. IX (Autumn, 1963), pp. 276–283.

Wolkenfeld, Jack. *Joyce Cary: The Developing Style*. New York: New York University Press, 1968, pp. 183–187.

Woodcock, George. "Citizens of Babel: A Study of Joyce Cary," in *Queens Quarterly*. LXIII (Summer, 1956), pp. 244–246.

Wright, Andrew. *Joyce Cary: A Preface to His Novels*. New York: Harper, 1958, pp. 137–142.

To Be a Pilgrim

Adams, Hazard. "Joyce Cary's Three Speakers," in *Modern Fiction Studies*. V (Summer, 1959), pp. 108–120.

Allen, Walter. *Joyce Cary*. London: Longmans, Green, 1954, pp. 19–27.

Bloom, Robert. *The Indeterminate World: A Study of the Novels of Joyce Cary*. Philadelphia: University of Pennsylvania Press, 1962, pp. 90–96.

Brawer, Judith. "The Triumph of Defeat: A Study of Joyce Cary's First Trilogy," in *Texas Studies in Literature and Language*. X (1969), pp. 629–634.

Cary, Joyce. "Three New Prefaces," in *Adam International Review*. XVIII (November–December, 1950), p. 12.

Davies, William Robertson. *Voice from the Attic*. New York: Knopf, 1960, pp. 246–249.

Faber, Kathleen R. and M.D. Faber. "An Important Theme of Joyce Cary's Trilogy," in *Discourse*. XI (Winter, 1968), pp. 26–31.

Foster, Malcolm. *Joyce Cary: A Biography*. Boston: Houghton Mifflin, 1968, pp. 384–389.

Gindin, James. *Harvest of a Quiet Eye; The Novel of Compassion*. Bloomington: Indiana University Press, 1971, pp. 265–270.

Hall, James. *The Tragic Comedians: Seven Modern British Novelists*. Bloomington: Indiana University Press, 1963, pp. 82–98.

Hamilton, Kenneth. "Boon or Thorn? Joyce Cary and Samuel Beckett on Human Life," in *Dalhousie Review*. XXXVIII (Winter, 1959), pp. 433–442.

Hoffmann, Charles G. "The Genesis and Development of Joyce Cary's First Trilogy," in *PMLA*. LXXVIII (September, 1963), pp. 431–439.

_____. "Joyce Cary and the Comic Mask," in *Western Humanities Review*. XIII (Spring, 1959), pp. 135–142.

_____. "Joyce Cary: Art and Reality," in *University of Kansas City Review*. XXVI (June, 1960), pp. 275–277.

_____. *Joyce Cary: The Comedy of Freedom*. Pittsburgh: University of Pittsburgh Press, 1964, pp. 77–85.

Larsen, Golden L. *The Dark Descent: Social Change and Moral Responsibility in the Novels of Joyce Cary*. New York: Roy, 1966, pp. 125–156.

Lyons, Richard S. "Narrative Method in Cary's *To Be a Pilgrim*," in *Texas Studies in Literature and Language*. VI (Summer, 1964), pp. 269–279.

Monas, Sidney. "What to Do with a Drunken Sailor," in *Hudson Review*. III (Autumn, 1950), pp. 466–474.

Noble, R.W. *Joyce Cary*. Edinburgh: Oliver and Boyd, 1973, pp. 48–69.

O'Connor, William Van. *Joyce Cary*. New York: Columbia University Press, 1966, pp. 26–29.

Prescott, Orville. *In My Opinion*. Indianapolis, Ind.: Bobbs-Merrill, 1952, pp. 180–199.

Shapiro, Stephen A. "Joyce Cary's *To Be a Pilgrim*: Mr. Facing-Both-Ways," in *Texas Studies in Literature and Language*. VIII (Spring, 1966), pp. 81–91.

Stockholder, Fred. "The Triple Vision in Joyce Cary's First Trilogy," in *Modern Fiction Studies*. IX (Autumn, 1963), pp. 276–283.

Wolkenfeld, Jack.   *Joyce Cary: The Developing Style.* New York: New York University Press, 1968, pp. 139–142.

Wright, Andrew.   *Joyce Cary: A Preface to His Novels.* New York: Harper, 1958, pp. 119–124.

BALDASSARE CASTIGLIONE
(1478–1529)

The Book of the Courtier

Bonadeo, Alfredo. "The Function and Purpose of the Courtier in *The Book of the Courtier* by Castiglione," in *Philological Quarterly.* L (1971), pp. 36–46.

Crane, Thomas Frederick. *Italian Social Customs of the Sixteenth Century and Their Influence on the Literature of Europe.* New Haven, Conn.: Yale University Press, 1920, pp. 174–207.

Cronin, Vincent. *The Flowering of the Renaissance.* New York: Dutton, 1969, pp. 97–101.

Durant, Will. *The Story of Civilization, Part V: The Renaissance.* New York: Simon and Schuster, 1953, pp. 345–348.

Fletcher, Jefferson Butler. *Literature of the Italian Renaissance.* New York: Macmillan, 1934, pp. 193–202.

Hallam, George W. "In Praise of Being a Gentleman: 1528–1976," in *Renaissance and Modern: Essays in Honor of Edwin M. Moseley.* Edited by Murray J. Levith. Syracuse, N.Y.: Syracuse University Press, 1976, pp. 3–10.

Hare, Christopher. *Life and Letters in the Italian Renaissance.* London: Stanley Paul, 1915, pp. 290–300.

Kemp, Walter H. "Some Notes on Music in Castiglione's *Il Libro del Cortegiano,*" in *Cultural Aspects of the Italian Renaissance: Essays in Honor of Paul Osklar Kristeller.* Edited by Cecil H. Clough. New York: Alfred F. Zambelli, 1976, pp. 354–369.

Lanham, Richard A. "The Self as Middle Style: *Cortegiano,*" in *The Motives of Eloquence: Literary Rhetoric in the Renaissance.* New Haven, Conn.: Yale University Press, 1976, pp. 144–164.

Martines, L. "The Gentleman in Renaissance Italy: Strains of Isolation in the Body Politic," in *The Darker Vision of the Renaissance: Beyond the Fields of Reason.* Edited by Robert S. Kinsman. Berkeley: University of California Press, 1974, pp. 77–93.

Mazzeo, Joseph Anthony. "Castiglione's *Courtier:* The Self as a Work of Art," in *Renaissance and Revolution: The Remaking of European Thought.* New York: Pantheon Books, 1966, pp. 131–160.

Ralph, Philip Lee. *The Renaissance in Perspective.* New York: St. Martin's Press, 1973, pp. 96–99.

Rebhorn, Wayne A. *Courtly Performances: Masking and Festivity in Castiglione's* Book of the Courtier. Detroit: Wayne State University Press, 1978.

Roeder, Ralph. "Castiglione," in *The Man of the Renaissance.* New York: Viking, 1933, pp. 313–482.

Ryan, L.V. "Book Four of Castiglione's *Courtier*: Climax or Afterthought?," in *Studies in the Renaissance*, Volume XIX. New York: Renaissance Society of America, 1972, pp. 156–179.

Sedgwick, Henry D. "At the Court of Urbino (1507)," in *In Praise of Gentlemen*. Boston: Little, Brown, 1935, pp. 91–99.

Shapiro, Marianne. "Mirror and Portrait: The Structure of *Il Libro del Cortegiano*," in *Journal of Medieval and Renaissance Studies*. V (1975), pp. 37–61.

Symonds, John Addington. *Renaissance in Italy*, Volume I. New York: Modern Library, 1935, pp. 93–96.

Taylor, Rachel Annand. *Invitation to Renaissance Italy*. New York: Harper, 1930, pp. 133–151.

Trafton, Dain A. "Structure and Meaning in *The Courtier*," in *English Literary Renaissance*. II (1972), pp. 283–297.

Whitfield, J.H. *A Short History of Italian Literature*. London: Cassell, 1962, pp. 166–169.

Wilkins, Ernest Hatch. "Castiglione and Other Prose Writers," in *History of Italian Literature*. Cambridge, Mass.: Harvard University Press, 1954, pp. 226–236.

Woodward, William Harrison. "The Doctrine of Courtesy," in *Studies in Education During the Age of the Renaissance, 1400–1600*. New York: Russell and Russell, 1965, pp. 244–267.

WILLA CATHER
(1873–1947)

Death Comes for the Archbishop

Bloom, Edward A. and Lillian D. Bloom. "The Genesis of *Death Comes for the Archbishop*," in *American Literature*. XXVI (January, 1955), pp. 479–506.

————. "On the Composition of a Novel," in *Willa Cather and Her Critics*. Edited by James Schroeter. Ithaca, N.Y.: Cornell University Press, 1967, pp. 323–355. Reprinted in *Willa Cather's Gift of Sympathy*. Carbondale: Southern Illinois University Press, 1962, pp. 19–21, 197–236.

Brown, Edward Killoran and Leon Edel. *Willa Cather: A Critical Biography*. New York: Knopf, 1953, pp. 251–265.

Charles, Sister Peter Damian, O.P. "*Death Comes for the Archbishop*: A Novel of Love and Death," in *New Mexico Quarterly*. XXXVI (Winter, 1966–1967), pp. 389–403.

Connolly, Francis X. "Willa Cather: Memory as Muse," in *Fifty Years of the American Novel: A Christian Appraisal*. Edited by Harold C. Gardiner. New York: Gordian Press, 1968, pp. 82–87.

Daiches, David. *Willa Cather: A Critical Introduction*. Ithaca, N.Y.: Cornell University Press, 1951, pp. 104–118.

Dinn, James M. "A Novelist's Miracle: Structure and Myth in *Death Comes for the Archbishop*," in *Western American Literature*. VII (Spring, 1972), pp. 39–46.

Fox, Maynard. "Proponents of Order: Tom Outland and Bishop Latour," in *Western American Literature*. IV (Summer, 1969), pp. 107–115.

Gale, Robert L. "Cather's *Death Comes for the Archbishop*," in *Explicator*. XXI (May, 1963), item 75.

Gerber, Philip L. *Willa Cather*. Boston: Twayne, 1975, pp. 120–127.

Giannone, Richard. "*Death Comes for the Archbishop*," in *Music in Willa Cather's Fiction*. Lincoln: University of Nebraska Press, 1968, pp. 185–200.

————. "The Southwest's Eternal Echo: Music in *Death Comes for the Archbishop*," in *Arizona Quarterly*. XXII (Spring, 1966), pp. 6–18.

Greene, George. "*Death Comes for the Archbishop*," in *New Mexico Quarterly*. XXVII (Spring–Summer, 1957), pp. 69–82.

McFarland, Dorothy Tuck. *Willa Cather*. New York: Frederick Ungar, 1972, pp. 95–110.

Powell, Lawrence Clark. "*Death Comes for the Archbishop*: Willa Cather," in *Southwest Classics: The Creative Literature of the Arid Lands. Essays on the Books and Their Writers.* Los Angeles: Ward Ritchie Press, 1974, pp. 121–135.

Randall, John H., III.   *The Landscape and the Looking Glass: Willa Cather's Search for Value.* Boston: Houghton Mifflin, 1960, pp. 257–310.

Rapin, René.   *Willa Cather.* New York: McBride, 1930, pp. 69–71.

Robinson, Cecil,   *With the Ears of Strangers: The Mexican in American Literature.* Tucson: University of Arizona Press, 1963, pp. 237–238, 265–267.

Stewart, D.H.   "Cather's Mortal Comedy," in *Queen's Quarterly.* LXXIII (Summer, 1966), pp. 244–259.

Stouck, David.   *Willa Cather's Imagination.* Lincoln: University of Nebraska Press, 1975, pp. 117–119, 129–149.

Stouck, Mary-Ann and David Stouck.   "Art and Religion in *Death Comes for the Archbishop*," in *Arizona Quarterly.* XXIX (1973), pp. 293–302.

Van Ghent, Dorothy.   *Willa Cather.* Minneapolis: University of Minnesota Press, 1964, pp. 35–38.

West, Rebecca.   "The Classic Artist," in *The Strange Necessity.* New York: Viking, 1928, pp. 233–248. Reprinted in *Willa Cather and Her Critics.* Edited by James Schroeter. Ithaca, N.Y.: Cornell University Press, 1967, pp. 62–71.

Whittington, Curtis, Jr.   "The Stream and the Broken Pottery: The Form of Willa Cather's *Death Comes for the Archbishop*," in *McNeese Review.* XVI (1965), pp. 16–24.

A Lost Lady

Bloom, Edward A. and Lillian D. Bloom.   *Willa Cather's Gift of Sympathy: A Lost Lady.* Carbondale: Southern Illinois University Press, 1962, pp. 67–74.

Brown, Edward Killoran and Leon Edel.   *Willa Cather: A Critical Biography.* New York: Knopf, 1953, pp. 228–235.

Brunauer, Dalma H.   "The Problem of Point of View in *A Lost Lady*," in *Renascence.* XXVIII (1975), pp. 47–52.

Daiches, David.   *Willa Cather: A Critical Introduction.* Ithaca, N.Y.: Cornell University Press, 1951, pp. 77–86.

Gerber, Philip L.   *Willa Cather.* Boston: Twayne, 1975, pp. 109–112.

Giannone, Richard.   "*A Lost Lady*," in *Music in Willa Cather's Fiction.* Lincoln: University of Nebraska Press, 1968, pp. 141–149.

Hamner, Eugenie Lambert.   "Affirmations in Willa Cather's *A Lost Lady*," in *Midwest Quarterly.* XVII (Spring, 1976), pp. 245–251.

Helmick, Evelyn Thomas.   "The Broken World: Medievalism in *A Lost Lady*," in *Renascence.* XXVIII (Autumn, 1975), pp. 39–48.

Hinz, John. "*A Lost Lady* and *The Professor's House*," in *Virginia Quarterly Review.* XXIX (Winter, 1953), pp. 70–85.

Krutch, Joseph Wood. "The Lady as Artist," in *Willa Cather and Her Critics.* Edited by James Schroeter. Ithaca, N.Y.: Cornell University Press, 1967, pp. 52–54.

Lasch, Robert N. "Willa Cather," in *Prairie Schooner.* I (April, 1927), pp. 166–169.

McFarland, Dorothy Tuck. *Willa Cather.* New York: Frederick Ungar, 1972, pp. 71–86.

Miller, Bruce E. "The Testing of Willa Cather's Humanism: *A Lost Lady* and other Cather Novels," in *Kansas Quarterly.* V (Fall, 1973), pp. 43–49.

Randall, John H., III. *The Landscape and the Looking Glass: Willa Cather's Search for Value.* Boston: Houghton Mifflin, 1960, pp. 174–202.

Rosowski, Susan J. "Willa Cather's *A Lost Lady*: The Paradoxes of Change," in *Novel.* XI (Fall, 1977), pp. 51–62.

Stouck, David. *Willa Cather's Imagination.* Lincoln: University of Nebraska Press, 1975, pp. 58–69.

Van Ghent, Dorothy. *Willa Cather.* Minneapolis: University of Minnesota Press, 1964, pp. 26–29.

Wilson, Edmund. "*A Lost Lady*," in *The Shores of Light: A Literary Chronicle of the Twenties and Thirties.* New York: Noonday, 1952, pp. 41–43. Reprinted in *Willa Cather and Her Critics.* Edited by James Schroeter. Ithaca, N.Y.: Cornell University Press, 1967, pp. 27–29.

Yongue, Patricia Lee. "*A Lost Lady*: The End of the First Cycle," in *Western American Literature.* VII (Spring, 1972), pp. 3–12.

My Ántonia

A., G.W. "Cather's *My Ántonia*," in *Explicator.* V (March, 1947), item 35.

Bowden, Edwin T. *The Dungeon of the Heart: Human Isolation and the American Novel.* New York: Macmillan, 1961, pp. 43–54.

Bridges, Jean B. "The Actress in Cather's Novel *My Ántonia*," in *Society for the Study of Midwestern Literature Newsletter.* VI (1976), pp. 10–11.

Brown, Edward Killoran and Leon Edel. *Willa Cather: A Critical Biography.* New York: Knopf, 1953, pp. 199–209.

Charles, Sister Peter Damian, O.P. "*My Ántonia*: A Dark Dimension," in *Western American Literature.* II (Summer, 1967), pp. 91–108.

Connolly, Francis X. "Willa Cather: Memory as Muse," in *Fifty Years of the American Novel: A Christian Appraisal.* Edited by Harold C. Gardiner. New York: Gordian Press, 1968, pp. 75–77.

Dahl, Curtis. "An American Georgic: Willa Cather's *My Ántonia*," in *Comparative Literature.* VII (Winter, 1955), pp. 43–51.

Daiches, David. *Willa Cather: A Critical Introduction.* Ithaca, N.Y.: Cornell University Press, 1951, pp. 43–61.

Gerber, Philip L. *Willa Cather.* Boston: Twayne, 1975, pp. 87–92.

Giannone, Richard. "*My Ántonia*," in *Music in Willa Cather's Fiction.* Lincoln: University of Nebraska Press, 1968, pp. 107–123.

Havighurst, Walter. "Introduction," in *My Ántonia.* Boston: Houghton Mifflin, 1949.

Helmick, Evelyn Thomas. "The Mysteries of Ántonia," in *Midwest Quarterly.* XVII (Winter, 1976), pp. 173–185.

McFarland, Dorothy Tuck. *Willa Cather.* New York: Frederick Ungar, 1972, pp. 39–50.

Mencken, H.L. "*My Ántonia*," in *Willa Cather and Her Critics.* Edited by James Schroeter. Ithaca, N.Y.: Cornell University Press, 1967, pp. 8–9.

Miller, James E., Jr. "*My Ántonia*: A Frontier Drama of Time," in *American Quarterly.* X (Winter, 1958), pp. 476–484. Reprinted in *Quests Surd and Absurd: Essays in American Literature.* Chicago: University of Chicago Press, 1967, pp. 66–75.

————. "*My Ántonia* and the American Dream," in *Prairie Schooner.* XLVIII (Summer, 1974), pp. 112–123.

Randall, John H., III. *The Landscape and the Looking Glass: Willa Cather's Search for Value.* Boston: Houghton Mifflin, 1960, pp. 105–149. Reprinted in *Willa Cather and Her Critics.* Edited by James Schroeter. Ithaca, N.Y.: Cornell University Press, 1967, pp. 272–322.

Rapin, René. *Willa Cather.* New York: McBride, 1930, pp. 47–51.

Rucker, Mary E. "Prospective Focus in *My Ántonia*," in *Arizona Quarterly.* XXIX (1973), pp. 303–316.

Scholes, Robert E. "Hope and Memory in *My Ántonia*," in *Shenandoah.* XIV (Autumn, 1962), pp. 24–29.

Stegner, Wallace. "Willa Cather: *My Antonia*," in *The American Novel from James Fenimore Cooper to William Faulkner.* New York: Basic Books, 1965, pp. 144–153.

Stouck, David. *Willa Cather's Imagination.* Lincoln: University of Nebraska Press, 1975, pp. 45–58.

Van Ghent, Dorothy. *Willa Cather.* Minneapolis: University of Minnesota Press, 1964, pp. 21–25.

O Pioneers!

Bohlke, L. Brent. "The Ecstasy of Alexandra Bergson," in *Colby Library Quarterly.* XI (1975), pp. 139–149.

Brown, Edward Killoran and Leon Edel. *Willa Cather: A Critical Biography.* New York: Knopf, 1953, pp. 173–179.

Charles, Sister Peter Damian, O.P. "Love and Death in Willa Cather's *O Pioneers!*" in *College Language Association Journal.* IX (December, 1965), pp. 140–150.

Daiches, David. *Willa Cather: A Critical Introduction.* Ithaca, N.Y.: Cornell University Press, 1951, pp. 15–29.

Fox, Maynard. "Symbolic Representation in Willa Cather's *O Pioneers!*" in *Western American Literature.* IX (Fall, 1974), pp. 187–196.

Gerber, Philip L. *Willa Cather.* Boston: Twayne, 1975, pp. 75–80.

Giannone, Richard. "*O Pioneers!*" in *Music in Willa Cather's Fiction.* Lincoln: University of Nebraska Press, 1968, pp. 69–81.

————. "*O Pioneers!*: Song of the Earth and Youth," in *South Dakota Review.* II (Spring, 1965), pp. 52–68.

McFarland, Dorothy Tuck. *Willa Cather.* New York: Frederick Ungar, 1972, pp. 19–28.

Rapin, René. *Willa Cather.* New York: McBride, 1930, pp. 21–26.

Randall, John H., III. *The Landscape and the Looking Glass: Willa Cather's Search for Value.* Boston: Houghton Mifflin, 1960, pp. 64–105.

Reaves, J. Russell. "Mythic Motivation in Willa Cather's *O Pioneers!*," in *Western Folklore.* XXVII (January, 1968), pp. 19–25.

Schneider, Sister Lucy, C.S.J. "*O Pioneers!* in the Light of Willa Cather's 'Land Philosophy,' " in *Colby Library Quarterly.* VIII (June, 1968), pp. 55–70.

Stouck, David. *Willa Cather's Imagination.* Lincoln: University of Nebraska Press, 1975, pp. 23–32.

Van Ghent, Dorothy. *Willa Cather.* Minneapolis: University of Minnesota Press, 1964, pp. 15–18.

The Professor's House

Arnold, Marilyn. "The Function of Structure in Cather's *The Professor's House*," in *Colby Library Quarterly.* XI (1975), pp. 169–178.

Brown, Edward Killoran. *Rhythm in the Novel.* Toronto: University of Toronto Press, 1950, pp. 71–78.

Brown, Edward Killoran and Leon Edel. *Willa Cather: A Critical Biography.* New York: Knopf, 1953, pp. 237–247.

Cecil, L. Moffitt. "Anti-Intellectualism as Theme in Willa Cather's *The Professor's House*," in *Research Studies.* XXXVII (September, 1969), pp. 235–241.

Charles, Sister Peter Damian, O.P. "*The Professor's House*: An Abode of Love and Death," in *Colby Library Quarterly.* VIII (June, 1968), pp. 70–82.

Connolly, Francis X. "Willa Cather: Memory as Muse," in *Fifty Years of the American Novel: A Christian Appraisal.* Edited by Harold C. Gardiner. New York: Gordian Press, 1968, pp. 79–82.

Daiches, David. *Willa Cather: A Critical Introduction.* Ithaca, N.Y.: Cornell University Press, 1951, pp. 87–101.

Edel, Leon. "Willa Cather's *The Professor's House*: An Inquiry Into the Use of Psychology in Literary Criticism," in *Literature and Psychology.* IV (1954), pp. 66–79. Reprinted in *Psychoanalysis and American Fiction.* Edited by Irving Malin. New York: Dutton, 1965, pp. 199–221.

Fox, Maynard. "Proponents of Order: Tom Outland and Bishop Latour," in *Western American Literature.* IV (Summer, 1969), pp. 107–115.

————. "Two Primitives: Huck Finn and Tom Outland," in *Western American Literature.* I (Spring, 1966), pp. 26–33.

Gerber, Philip L. *Willa Cather.* Boston: Twayne, 1975, pp. 112–117.

Giannone, Richard. "Music in *The Professor's House*," in *College English.* XXVI (March, 1965), pp. 464–469.

————. "*The Professor's House*: A Novel in Sonata-Form," in *Colby Library Quarterly.* VII (June, 1965), pp. 53–60.

————. "*The Professor's House*," in *Music in Willa Cather's Fiction.* Lincoln: University of Nebraska Press, 1968, pp. 151–168.

Hoffman, Frederick J. *The Twenties: American Writing in the Postwar Decade.* New York: Viking, 1955, pp. 157–162.

Jobes, Lavon Mattes. "Willa Cather's *The Professor's House*," in *University Review.* XXXIV (December, 1967), pp. 154–160.

Krutch, Joseph Wood. "Second Best," in *Willa Cather and Her Critics.* Edited by James Schroeter. Ithaca, N.Y.: Cornell University Press, 1967, pp. 54–56.

McFarland, Dorothy Tuck. *Willa Cather.* New York: Frederick Ungar, 1972, pp. 71–86.

Randall, John H., III. *The Landscape and the Looking Glass: Willa Cather's Search for Value.* Boston: Houghton Mifflin, 1960, pp. 203–234.

Rapin, René. *Willa Cather.* New York: McBride, 1930, pp. 72–77.

Schroeter, James. "Willa Cather and *The Professor's House*," in *Yale Review.* LIV (Summer, 1965), pp. 494–512. Reprinted in *Willa Cather and Her Critics.* Ithaca, N.Y.: Cornell University Press, 1967, pp. 363–381.

Stineback, David C. *Shifting World: Social Change and Nostalgia in the American Novel.* Lewisburg, Pa.: Bucknell University Press, 1976, pp. 101–114.

————. "Willa Cather's Ironic Masterpiece," in *Arizona Quarterly.* XXIX (1973), pp. 317–330.

Stouck, David. "Willa Cather and *The Professor's House*: Letting Go with the Heart," in *Western American Literature*. VII (Spring, 1972), pp. 13–24.

_____. *Willa Cather's Imagination*. Lincoln: University of Nebraska Press, 1975, pp. 96–109.

Van Ghent, Dorothy. *Willa Cather*. Minneapolis: University of Minnesota Press, 1964, pp. 29–32.

Wild, Barbara. " 'The Thing Not Named' in *The Professor's House*," in *Western American Literature*. XII (February, 1978), pp. 263–274.

Shadows on the Rock

Bloom, Edward A. and Lillian D. Bloom. "*Shadows on the Rock*: Notes on the Composition of a Novel," in *Twentieth Century Literature*. II (July, 1956), pp. 70–85.

Brown, Edward Killoran. "Willa Cather's Canada," in *University of Toronto Quarterly*. XXII (January, 1953), pp. 184–196.

Brown, Edward Killoran and Leon Edel. *Willa Cather: A Critical Biography*. New York: Knopf, 1953, pp. 266–286.

Daiches, David. *Willa Cather: A Critical Introduction*. Ithaca, N.Y.: Cornell University Press, 1951, pp. 119–128.

George, Benjamin. "The French-Canadian Connection: Willa Cather as a Canadian Writer," in *Western American Literature*. XI (Fall, 1976), pp. 249–261.

Gerber, Philip L. *Willa Cather*. Boston: Twayne, 1975, pp. 120–127.

Giannone, Richard. "The Shadow on the Rock," in *Music in Willa Cather's Fiction*. Lincoln: University of Nebraska Press, pp. 201–212.

McFarland, Dorothy Tuck. *Willa Cather*. New York: Frederick Ungar, 1972, pp. 111–116.

Murphy, John J. "The Art of *Shadows on the Rock*," in *Prairie Schooner*. L (Spring, 1976), pp. 37–51.

_____. "*Shadows on the Rock*: Cather's Medieval Refuge," in *Renascence*. XV (Winter, 1963), pp. 76–78.

Myers, Walter L. "The Novel Dedicate," in *Virginia Quarterly Review*. VIII (July, 1932), pp. 411–418.

Randall, John H., III. *The Landscape and the Looking Glass: Willa Cather's Search for Value*. Boston: Houghton Mifflin, 1960, pp. 310–341.

Stouck, David. *Willa Cather's Imagination*. Lincoln: University of Nebraska Press, 1975, pp. 119–120, 149–164.

Van Ghent, Dorothy. *Willa Cather*. Minneapolis: University of Minnesota Press, 1964, pp. 38–41.

The Song of the Lark

Brown, Edward Killoran and Leon Edel. *Willa Cather: A Critical Biography.* New York: Knopf, 1953, pp. 169–172, 187–194.

Daiches, David. *Willa Cather: A Critical Introduction.* Ithaca, N.Y.: Cornell University Press, 1951, pp. 29–42.

Gerber, Philip L. *Willa Cather.* Boston: Twayne, 1975, pp. 80–87.

Giannone, Richard. *Music in Willa Cather's Fiction.* Lincoln: University of Nebraska Press, 1968, pp. 85–99.

McFarland, Dorothy Tuck. *Willa Cather.* New York: Frederick Ungar, 1972, pp. 29–34.

Mencken, H.L. *"The Song of the Lark,"* in *Willa Cather and Her Critics.* Edited by James Schroeter. Ithaca, N.Y.: Cornell University Press, 1967, pp. 7–8.

Randall, John H., III. *The Landscape and the Looking Glass: Willa Cather's Search for Value.* Boston: Houghton Mifflin, 1960, pp. 42–51.

Rapin, René. *Willa Cather.* New York: McBride, 1930, pp. 27–46.

Roulston, Robert. "The Contrapuntal Complexity of Willa Cather's *The Song of the Lark,*" in *Midwest Quarterly.* XVII (Summer, 1976), pp. 350–368.

Stouck, David. *Willa Cather's Imagination.* Lincoln: University of Nebraska Press, 1975, pp. 183–198.

Van Ghent, Dorothy. *Willa Cather.* Minneapolis: University of Minnesota Press, 1964, pp. 18–21.

CATULLUS
(c.84 B.C.–c.54 B.C.)

Carmina

Copley, F.O. "Emotional Conflict and Its Significance in the Lesbia-Poems of Catullus," in *American Journal of Philology*. LXX (January, 1949), pp. 22–40.

Debatin, F.M. "Catullus—A Pivotal Personality," in *Classical Journal*. XXVI (December, 1930), pp. 207–222.

Ellis, Robinson. *A Commentary on Catullus*. Oxford: Clarendon Press, 1876.

Ferguson, J. "Catullus and Horace," in *American Journal of Philology*, LXXVII (January, 1956), pp. 1–18.

Frank, Tenny. *Catullus and Horace; Two Poets in Their Environment*. New York: Holt, 1928.

Hadas, Moses. "Lucretius and Catullus," in *History of Latin Literature*. New York: Columbia University Press, 1952, pp. 69–87.

Harrington, Karl Pomeroy. *Catullus and His Influence*. Boston: Marshall Jones, 1923.

Havelock, Eric Alfred. *The Lyric Genius of Catullus*. Oxford: Blackwell, 1939.

Highet, G. "Catullus: Life and Love," in *Poets in a Landscape*. New York: Knopf, 1957, pp. 3–44.

Quinn, Kenneth. *Approaches to Catullus*. New York: Barnes & Noble, 1972.

_____. *The Catullan Revolution*. Ann Arbor: University of Michigan Press, 1971.

_____. *Catullus; An Interpretation*. New York: Barnes & Noble, 1973.

_____. "Docte Catulle," in *Critical Essays on Roman Literature: Elegy and Lyric*. Edited by J.P. Sullivan. Cambridge, Mass.: Harvard University Press, 1962, pp. 31–63.

Reynolds, T. "Catullus," in *Arion*. VII (Autumn, 1968), pp. 453–465.

Ross, David O. *Style and Tradition in Catullus*. Cambridge, Mass.: Harvard University Press, 1969.

Wheeler, Arthur Leslie. *Catullus and the Traditions of Ancient Poetry*. Berkeley: University of California Press, 1934.

Wiseman, Timothy Peter. *Catullan Question*. Leicester, England: Leicester University Press, 1969.

Wright, Frederick Adam. *Three Roman Poets, Plautus, Catullus and Ovid; Their Lives, Times, and Works*. New York: Dutton, 1938.

CONSTANTINE P. CAVAFY
(1863–1933)

The Poetry of Cavafy

Auden, W.H. "C.P. Cavafy," in *Forewords and Afterwords*. Edited by Edward Mendelson. New York: Random House, 1973, pp. 333–344.

Bien, Peter. *Constantine Cavafy*. New York: Columbia University Press, 1964.

Bowra, C.M. *The Creative Experiment*. New York: Macmillan, 1949, pp. 29–60.

Enright, Dennis Joseph. "Too Many Ceasars: The Poems of C.P. Cavafy," in *Conspirators and Poets*. Chester Springs, Pa: Dufour, 1966, pp. 160–166.

Friar, Kimon. "One of the Great," in *New Republic*. CXXVIII (January 26, 1953), pp. 19–20.

Gregory, Horace. "A Twentieth Century Alexandrian," in *Poetry*. LXXXI (March, 1953), pp. 383–388.

Keeley, Edmund. *Cavafy's Alexandria: Study of a Myth in Progress*. Cambridge, Mass.: Harvard University Press, 1976.

———. "The 'New' Poems of Cavafy," in *Modern Greek Writers*. Edited by Edmund Keeley and Peter Bien. Princeton, N.J.: Princeton University Press, 1972, pp. 123–144.

Keeley, Edmund and Philip Sherrard. "Introduction," in *Six Poets of Modern Greece*. New York: Knopf, 1961.

Liddell, Robert. *Cavafy: A Biography*. New York: Schocken, 1976, pp. 132–205.

———. "Studies in Genius: Cavafy," in *Horizon*. XVIII (July–December, 1948), pp. 187–202.

Pinchin, Jane Lagoudis. *Alexandria Still: Forster, Durrell, and Cavafy*. Princeton, N.J.: Princeton University Press, 1977, pp. 34–81, 209–222.

Roditi, Edonard. "The Poetry of C.P. Cavafy," in *Poetry*. LXXXI (March, 1953), pp. 389–392.

Ruehlen, P.K. "Constantine Cavafy: A European Poet," in *Nine Essays in Modern Literature*. Edited by Donald E. Stanford. Baton Rouge: Louisiana State University Press, 1965, pp. 36–62.

Sepheriadēs, Georgios. "Cavafy and Eliot—A Comparison," in *On the Greek Style: Selected Essays in Poetry and Hellenism*. Boston: Little, Brown, 1966, pp. 121–161.

Sherrard, Philip. *The Marble Threshing Floor*. London: Vallentine, Mitchell, 1956, pp. 83–123.

Trypanis, C.A.   *Medieval and Modern Greek Poetry*. Oxford: Clarendon Press, 1951.

Warner, Rex.   "Introduction," in *The Poems of C.P. Cavafy*. New York: Grove, 1952.

CAMILO JOSÉ CELA
(1916–   )

The Novels of Cela

Donahue, Francis. "Cela and Spanish 'Tremendismo,' " in *Western Humanities Review*. XX (Autumn, 1966), pp. 301–306.

Eoff, Sherman. "Tragedy of the Unwanted Person in Three Versions: Pablos de Segovia, Pito Perez, Pascual Duarte," in *Hispania*. XXXIX (May, 1956), pp. 193–195.

Feldman, David M. "Camilo José Cela and *La Familia De Pascual Duarte*," in *Hispania*. XLIV (December, 1961), pp. 656–659.

Flasher, John J. "Aspects of Novelistic Technique in Cela's *La Colemena*," in *West Virginia University Philological Papers*. XII (November, 1959), pp. 30–43.

Kirsner, Robert. *The Novels and Travels of Camilo José Cela*. Chapel Hill: University of North Carolina Press, 1963, pp. 21–99.

Rand, Marguerite C. "Lazarillo de Tormes, Classic and Contemporary, in *Hispania*. XLIV (May, 1961), pp. 222–229.

Seator, Lynette Hubbard. "The Antisocial Humanism of Cela and Hemingway," in *Revista de Estudios Hispanicos*. (University of Alabama) IX (1975), pp. 425–439.

Thomas, Michael D. "Narrative Tension and Structural Unity in Cela's *La Familia de Pascual Duarte*," in *Symposium*. XXXI (1977), pp. 165–178.

Wade, Gerald E. "The Cult of Violence in the Contemporary Spanish Novel," in *Tennessee Studies in Literature*. I (1956), pp. 51–53.

Wicks, Ulrich. "Onlyman," in *Mosaic*. VIII (1975), pp. 21–47.

LOUIS-FERDINAND CÉLINE
(1894–1961)

Journey to the End of the Night

Brée, Germaine and Margaret Guiton. *An Age of Fiction: The French Novel from Gide to Camus.* New Brunswick, N.J.: Rutgers University Press, 1957, pp. 164–169.

Burgess, Anthony. "In Support of Céline," in *Harper's.* CCLIII (August, 1976), pp. 76, 80–82.

Frohock, W.M. "Céline's Quest for Love," in *Accent.* II (Winter, 1942), pp. 79–84.

Glicksberg, Charles. "The Novel and the Plague," in *University Review.* XXI (Autumn, 1954), p. 56.

Greenberg, Alvin. "The Novel of Disintegration: Paradoxical Impossibility in Contemporary Fiction," in *Wisconsin Studies in Contemporary Literature.* VII (Winter/Spring, 1966), pp. 103–108.

Hayman, David. *Louis-Ferdinand Céline.* New York: Columbia University Press, 1965.

Hindus, Milton. "Céline: A Reappraisal," in *Southern Review.* I (Winter, 1965), pp. 76–93.

_____. "The Recent Revival of Céline: A Consideration," in *Mosaic.* VI (Spring, 1973), pp. 57–66.

Howe, Irving. "Céline: The Sod Beneath the Skin," in *New Republic.* CXLIX (July 20, 1963), pp. 19–22.

Knapp, Bettina. *Céline: Man of Hate.* University: University of Alabama Press, 1974, pp. 22–51.

McCarthy, Patrick. *Céline.* New York: Viking, 1975, pp. 49–82.

Matthews, J.H. "Céline's *Journey to the End of the Night,*" in *Contemporary Review.* CXCI (March, 1957), pp. 157–161.

Nettelbeck, Colin W. "Journey to the End of Art: The Evolution of the Novels of Louis-Ferdinand Céline," in *PMLA.* LXXXVII (January, 1972), pp. 80–89.

O'Connell, David. *Louis-Ferdinand Céline.* Boston: Twayne, 1976, pp. 38–73.

Ostrovsky, Erika. *Céline and His Vision.* New York: New York University Press, 1967.

Peyre, Henri. *French Novelists Today.* New York: Oxford University Press, 1967, pp. 187–195.

Reck, Rima Dress. "Céline and the Aural Novel," in *Books Abroad.* XXXIX (Autumn, 1965), pp. 404–406.

Slochower, Harry. "Satanism in Céline," in *Books Abroad.* XVIII (Autumn, 1944), pp. 332–337.

Thiher, Allen. "Céline and Sartre," in *Philological Quarterly.* L (April, 1971), pp. 292–305.

————. *Céline: The Novels as Delirium.* New Brunswick, N.J.: Rutgers University Press, 1972, pp. 7–44.

Trotsky, Leon. "Novelist and Politician: Céline and Poincaré," in *Atlantic Monthly.* CLVI (October, 1935), pp. 413–420.

Wicks, Ulrich. "Onlyman," in *Mosaic.* VIII (Spring, 1975), pp. 24–28.

MIGUEL DE CERVANTES SAAVEDRA
(1547–1616)

Don Quixote de la Mancha

Allen, John J. *Don Quixote: Hero or Fool.* Gainesville: University of Florida Press, 1969.

————. "Narrators, the Reader and *Don Quixote*," in *Modern Language Notes.* XCI (March, 1976), pp. 201–212.

Baker, Armand F. "A New Look at the Structure of *Don Quijote*," in *Revista de Estudios Hispanicos.* VII (January, 1973), pp. 3–21.

Bates, Margaret J. *Discretion in the Works of Cervantes.* New York: AMS Press, 1945.

Benardete, Mair J. and Angel Flores, Editors. *Anatomy of* Don Quixote*: A Symposium.* Port Washington, N.Y.: Kennikat, 1969.

Close, Anthony J. *The Romantic Approach to* Don Quixote. New York: Cambridge University Press, 1978.

————. "Sancho Panza: Wise Fool," in *Modern Language Review.* LXVIII (April, 1973), pp. 344–357.

De Madariaga, Salvadore. *Don Quixote: An Introductory Essay in Psychology.* Oxford: Oxford University Press, 1961.

Dudley, E.J. "The Wild Man Goes Baroque," in *The Wild Man Within.* Edited by E.J. Dudley and M.E. Novak. Pittsburgh: University of Pittsburgh Press, 1973, pp. 115–139.

Duran, Manuel. *Cervantes.* New York: Twayne, 1974.

Efron, Arthur. Don Quixote *and the Dulcineated World.* Austin: University of Texas Press, 1971.

El Saffar, Ruth. *Distance and Control in* Don Quixote*: A Study in Narrative Technique.* Chapel Hill: University of North Carolina Press, 1975.

Girard, Rene. *Deceit, Desire, and the Novel.* Translated by Yvonne Freccero. Baltimore: Johns Hopkins University Press, 1975, pp. 1–52, 96–112.

Green, Otis H. *The Literary Mind of Medieval and Renaissance Spain.* Lexington: University Press of Kentucky, 1970, pp. 141–200.

Grossvogel, David I. *Limits of the Novel.* Ithaca, N.Y.: Cornell University Press, 1968, pp. 74–107.

Haley, George. "The Narrator in *Don Quixote*: Maese Pedro's Puppet Show," in *Modern Language Notes.* LXXX (1965), pp. 145–165.

Hatzfeld, H.A. "Why Is Don Quijote Baroque?," in *Philological Quarterly.* LI (January, 1972), pp. 158–176.

Immerwahr, R. "Structural Symmetry in the Episodic Narratives of *Don Quixote*, Part One," in *Comparative Literature*. X (1958), pp. 121–135.

Ledesman, Francisco N. *Cervantes: The Man and the Genius*. New York: McKay, 1972.

Levin, Harry. "The Quixotic Principle: Cervantes and Other Novelists," in *The Interpretation of Narrative: Theory and Practice*. Edited by Morton W. Bloomfield. Cambridge, Mass.: Harvard University Press, 1970, pp. 45–66.

Mackey, M. "Rhetoric and Characterization in *Don Quixote*," in *Hispanic Review*. XLII (Winter, 1974), pp. 51–66.

Mancing, Howard. "The Comic Function of Chivalric Names in *Don Quijote*," in *Names*. XXI (1973), pp. 220–235.

Nelson, Lowry, Editor. *Cervantes; A Collection of Critical Essays*. Englewood Cliffs, N.J.: Prentice-Hall, 1969.

Predmore, Richard L. *The World of Don Quixote*. Cambridge, Mass.: Harvard University Press, 1967.

Riley, Edward C. *Cervantes' Theory of the Novel*. Oxford: Oxford University Press, 1962.

Snodgrass, W.D. "Glorying in Failure: Cervantes and Don Quixote," in *Malahat Review*. XXVIII (October, 1973), pp. 17–45.

Sobre, J.M. "Don Quixote, the Hero Upside-Down," in *Hispanic Review*. XLIV (Spring, 1976), pp. 127–141.

Thorburn, David. "Fiction and Imagination in *Don Quixote*," in *Partisan Review*. XLII (1975), pp. 431–443.

Willey, F. "*Don Quixote* and the Theatre of Life and Art," in *Georgia Review*. XXXI (Winter, 1977), pp. 907–930.

Exemplary Novels

Atkinson, William C. "Cervantes, El Pinciano and the *Novelas Ejemplares*," in *Hispanic Review*. XVI (1948), pp. 189–208.

Avalle-Arce, Juan Bautista. *Cervantes: Three Exemplary Novels*. New York: Dell, 1964.

Casa, Frank P. "The Structural Unity of *El Licenciado Vidriera*," in *Bulletin of Hispanic Studies*. XLI (October, 1964), pp. 242–246.

Edwards, Gwynne. "Cervantes' *El Licenciado Vidriera*: Meaning and Structure," in *Modern Language Review*. LXVIII (July, 1973), pp. 559–568.

El Saffar, Ruth S. *Novel to Romance: A Study of Cervantes'* Novelas Ejemplares. Baltimore: Johns Hopkins University Press, 1974.

Entwistle, William J. "Cervantes, the Exemplary Novelist," in *Hispanic Review*. IX (1941), pp. 103–109.

Lewis, D.B. Wyndham. *The Shadow of Cervantes.* New York: Sheed and Ward, 1962, pp. 150–160.

Pierce, Frank. "Reality and Realism in the *Exemplary Novels*," in *Bulletin of Hispanic Studies.* XXX (July–September, 1953), pp. 134–142.

_____., **Editor.** *Two Cervantes Short Novels:* El Curioso Impertinente *and* El Celoso Extremeno. Oxford: Pergamon Press, 1970.

Randall, Dale B.J. *The Golden Tapestry.* Durham, N.C.: Duke University Press, 1963, pp. 136–151.

Riley, E.C. "Cervantes and the Cynics (*El Licenciado Vidriera* and *El Coloquio de Los Perros*)," in *Bulletin of Hispanic Studies.* LIII (1976), pp. 189–199.

Soons, Alan. "Three *Novelas Ejemplares* of Cervantes: Diptych Pattern and Spiritual Intention," in *Orbis Litterarum.* XXVI (1971), pp. 88–93.

Thompson, Jennifer. "The Structure of Cervantes' *Las Dos Doncellas*," in *Bulletin of Hispanic Studies.* XL (1963), pp. 144–150.

GEORGE CHAPMAN
(1559–1634)

All Fools

Bevington, David. *Tudor Drama and Politics: A Critical Approach to Topical Meaning.* Cambridge, Mass.: Harvard University Press, 1968, pp. 271–275.

E., S.Y. "Chapman's *All Fools*," in *Notes & Queries.* CXCIV (1949), p. 534.

Feldman, Sylvia. *The Morality-Patterned Comedy of the Renaissance.* The Hague: Mouton, 1970, pp. 26–30.

McPherson, David C. "Chapman's Adaptations of New Comedy," in *English Miscellany.* XIX (1968), pp. 51–64.

Spivack, Charlotte. *George Chapman.* New York: Twayne, 1967, pp. 68–74.

Woodbridge, Elizabeth. "An Unnoted Source of Chapman's *All Fools*," in *Journal of English and Germanic Philology.* I (1897), pp. 338–341.

Bussy d'Ambois

Adams, Robert. "Critical Myths and Chapman's Original *Bussy d'Ambois*," in *Renaissance Drama.* IX (1966), pp. 141–161.

————. "Transformations in the Late Elizabethan Tragic Sense of Life: New Critical Approaches," in *Modern Language Quarterly.* XXXV (1974), pp. 352–363.

Barber, C.L. "The Ambivalence of *Bussy d'Ambois*," in *Review of English Literature.* II (October, 1961), pp. 38–44.

Bement, Peter. "The Imagery of Darkness and Light in Chapman's *Bussy d'Ambois*," in *Studies in Philology.* LXIV (1967), pp. 187–198.

Burbridge, Roger T. "Speech and Action in Chapman's *Bussy d'Ambois*," in *Tennessee Studies in Literature.* XVII (1972), pp. 59–65.

Gilbert, A.H. "George Chapman's 'fortune with winged hands' in *Bussy d'Ambois*," in *Modern Language Notes.* LII (March, 1937), pp. 190–192.

Goldstein, Leonard. "George Chapman and the Decadence in Early Seventeenth Century Drama," in *Science and Society.* XXVII (Winter, 1963), pp. 33–37.

Graves, T.S. "The 'Third Man' in the Prologue to *Bussy d'Ambois*," in *Modern Philology.* XXIII (August, 1925), pp. 3–5.

Jacquot, Jean. "*Bussy d'Ambois* and Chapman's Conception of Tragedy," in *English Studies Today.* II (1959), pp. 129–141.

Lever, J.W. *The Tragedy of State.* London: Methuen, 1971, pp. 37–58.

McCollom, William G. "The Tragic Hero and Chapman's *Bussy d'Ambois*," in *University of Toronto Quarterly.* XVIII (April, 1949), pp. 227–233.

McDonald, Charles O. *The Rhetoric of Tragedy: Form in Stuart Drama.* Amherst: University of Massachusetts Press, 1966, pp. 179–224.

MacLure, Millar. *George Chapman; A Critical Study.* Toronto: University of Toronto Press, 1966, pp. 113–125.

Muir, Edwin. " 'Royal Man': Notes on the Tragedies of George Chapman," in *Orion.* II (1945), pp. 92–100.

Orange, Linwood E. "*Bussy d'Ambois*: The Web of Pretense," in *Southern Quarterly.* VIII (1969), pp. 37–56.

Ornstein, Robert. *The Moral Vision of Jacobean Tragedy.* Madison: University of Wisconsin Press, 1960, pp. 50–60.

Perkinson, Richard H. "Nature and the Tragic Hero in Chapman's Bussy Plays," in *Modern Language Quarterly.* III (1942), pp. 263–285.

Prior, Moody E. *The Language of Tragedy.* New York: Columbia University Press, 1947, pp. 104–111.

Ribner, Irving. "Character and Theme in Chapman's *Bussy d'Ambois*," in *Journal of English Literary History.* XXVI (December, 1959), pp. 482–496.

Simpson, Percy. *Studies in Elizabethan Drama.* Oxford: Clarendon Press, 1955, pp. 154–158.

Ure, Peter. "Chapman's Tragedies," in *Stratford-Upon-Avon Studies.* I (1960), pp. 227–237.

Weiss, Adrian B. "Chapman's *Bussy d'Ambois*, Act III, Scene iii," in *Explicator.* XXVII (1969), item 56.

Wieler, John William. *George Chapman—the Effect of Stoicism Upon His Tragedies.* New York: Octagon Books, 1969, pp. 21–51.

The Gentleman Usher

Cope, Jackson I. *The Theater and the Drama: From Metaphor to Form in Renaissance Drama.* Baltimore: Johns Hopkins University Press, 1973, pp. 29–76.

Lacy, Margaret. *The Jacobean Problem Play.* Ann Arbor: University of Michigan Press, 1956, pp. 114–135.

Mustard, W.P. "Hyprocrates' Twins," in *Modern Language Notes.* XLI (1927), p. 50.

Schoenbaum, Samuel. "The 'Deformed Mistress' Theme and Chapman's *Gentleman Usher*," in *Notes & Queries.* VII (1960), pp. 22–24.

Smith, John H. "The Genesis of the Strozza Subplot in George Chapman's *The Gentleman Usher*," in *PMLA.* LXXXIII (1968), pp. 1448–1453.

Spivack, Charlotte K. "The Comedy of Evil," in *Cresset.* XXVI (1963), pp. 8–15.

——. *George Chapman.* New York: Twayne, 1967, pp. 85–93.

Weidner, Henry Matthew. "The Dramatic Uses of Homeric Idealism: The Significance of Theme and Design in George Chapman's *The Gentleman Usher*," in *Journal of English Literary History.* XXVIII (June, 1961), pp. 121–136.

The Revenge of Bussy d'Ambois

Adams, Henry Hitch. "Cyril Tourneur on Revenge," in *Journal of English and Germanic Philology.* XLVIII (1949), pp. 71–87.

Aggeler, Geoffrey. "The Unity of Chapman's *The Revenge of Bussy d'Ambois*," in *Pacific Coast Philology.* IV (1969), pp. 5–18.

Bement, Peter. "Stoicism of Chapman's Clermont d'Ambois," in *Studies in English Literature, 1500–1900.* XII (Spring, 1972), pp. 345–357.

Bowers, Fredson T. *Elizabethan Revenge Tragedy.* Princeton: Princeton University Press, 1940, pp. 144–149.

Broude, Ronald. "George Chapman's Stoic-Christian Revenger," in *Studies in Philology.* LXX (1973), pp. 51–61.

——. "Revenge and Revenge Tragedy in Renaissance England," in *Renaissance Quarterly.* XXVIII (1975), pp. 38–58.

Chang, Joseph S.M.J. " 'Of Mighty Opposites': Stoicism and Machiavellianism," in *Renaissance Drama.* IX (1966), pp. 37–57.

Cohon, B.J. "A Catullian Echo in George Chapman's *The Revenge of Bussy d'Ambois*," in *Modern Language Notes.* LX (January, 1945), pp. 29–33.

Cook, A.S. "The Sources of Two Similes in *The Revenge of Bussy*," in *Journal of English and Germanic Philology.* I (1897), pp. 476–477.

Demers, Patricia. "Chapman's *The Revenge of Bussy d'Ambois*: Fixity and the Absolute Man," in *Renaissance and Reformation.* XII (1976), pp. 12–20.

Frost, David L. *The School of Shakespeare: The Influence of Shakespeare on English Drama, 1600–1642.* Cambridge: Cambridge University Press, 1968, pp. 191–194.

Goldstein, Leonard. "George Chapman and the Decadence in Early Seventeenth Century Drama," in *Science and Society.* XXVII (Winter, 1963), pp. 37–41.

Higgins, Michael H. "Chapman's 'Senecal Man': A Study in Elizabethan Psychology," in *Review of English Studies.* XLVII (July, 1945), pp. 186–191.

Leech, Clifford. *Shakespeare's Tragedies, and Other Studies in Seventeenth Century Drama.* London: Chatto and Windus, 1961, pp. 23–28, 195–196.

Ornstein, Robert. *The Moral Vision of Jacobean Tragedy.* Madison: University of Wisconsin Press, 1960, pp. 70–76.

Perkinson, R.H.   "Nature and the Tragic Hero in Chapman's Bussy Plays," in *Modern Language Quarterly*. III (1942), pp. 263–285.

Rees, Ennis.   *The Tragedies of George Chapman; Renaissance Ethics in Action*. Cambridge, Mass.: Harvard University Press, 1954, pp. 93–125.

Tomlinson, Thomas Brian.   *A Study of Elizabethan and Jacobean Tragedy*. Cambridge: Cambridge University Press, 1964, pp. 261–263.

Waggoner, G.R.   "An Elizabethan Attitude Toward Peace and War," in *Philological Quarterly*. XXXIII (1954), pp. 20–33.

Wilson, E.E.   "The Genesis of Chapman's *The Revenge of Bussy d'Ambois*," in *Modern Language Notes*. LXXI (December, 1956), pp. 567–569.

The Shadow of Night

Battenhouse, Roy W.   "Chapman's *The Shadow of Night*: An Interpretation," in *Studies in Philology*. XXXVIII (1941), pp. 584–608.

Cannon, Charles K.   "Chapman on the Unity of Style and Meaning," in *Journal of English and Germanic Philology*. LXVIII (1969), pp. 245–264.

MacLure, Millar.   *George Chapman: A Critical Study*. Toronto: University of Toronto Press, 1966, pp. 33–45.

Perkinson, R.H.   "The Body as a Triangular Structure in Spenser and Chapman," in *Modern Language Notes*. LXIV (1949), pp. 520–522.

Waddington, Raymond B.   *The Mind's Empire; Myth and Form in George Chapman's Narrative Poems*. Baltimore: Johns Hopkins University Press, 1974, pp. 45–112.

————.   "Prometheus and Hercules: The Dialectic of *Bussy d'Ambois*," in *Journal of English Literary History*. XXXIV (1967), pp. 21–48.

The Tragedy of Caesar and Pompey

Berger, Thomas L. and Dennis G. Donovan.   "A Note on the Text of Chapman's *Caesar and Pompey*," in *Papers of the Bibliographical Society of America*. LXV (1971), pp. 267–268.

Bergson, Allen.   "Stoicism Achieved: Cato in Chapman's *Tragedy of Caesar and Pompey*," in *Studies in English Literature, 1500–1900*. XVII (1977), pp. 295–302.

Crawley, Derek.   "Decision and Character in Chapman's *The Tragedy of Caesar and Pompey*," in *Studies in English Literature, 1500–1900*. VII (1967), pp. 277–297.

Goldstein, Leonard.   "George Chapman and the Decadence in Early Seventeenth Century Drama," in *Science and Society*. XXVII (Winter, 1963), pp. 41–48.

Hibbard, G.R.   "George Chapman: Tragedy and the Providential View of History," in *Shakespeare Survey*. XX (1967), pp. 27–31.

Ingledew, J.E. "Chapman's Use of Lucan in *Caesar and Pompey*," in *Review of English Studies.* XIII (August, 1962), pp. 283–288.

O'Callaghan, James F. "Chapman's Caesar," in *Studies in English Literature, 1500–1900.* XVI (1976), pp. 319–331.

Ornstein, Robert. *The Moral Vision of Jacobean Tragedy.* Madison: University of Wisconsin Press, 1960, pp. 79–83.

Schwartz, Elias. "A Neglected Play by Chapman," in *Studies in Philology.* LVIII (1956), pp. 140–159.

Spivack, Charlotte. *George Chapman.* New York: Twayne, 1967, pp. 144–151.

Sprott, S.E. "The Damned Crew," in *PMLA.* LXXXIV (1969), pp. 492–500.

Ure, Peter. "Chapman's Use of North's Plutarch in *Caesar and Pompey*," in *Review of English Studies.* IX (1958), pp. 281–284.

The Tragedy of Charles, Duke of Byron

Belsey, Catherine. "Senecan Vacillation and Elizabethan Deliberation: Influence or Confluence?" in *Renaissance Drama.* VI (1973), pp. 73–74.

Braunmuller, A.R. "Chapman's Use of Plutarck's 'De Fortuna Romanorum' in *The Tragedy of Charles, Duke of Byron*," in *Review of English Studies.* n.s. XXIII (May 1972), pp. 173–179.

Freije, George F. "Chapman's *Byron* and Batholomaeus Anglicus," in *English Language Notes.* XII (1975), pp. 168–171.

Gabel, John Butler. "The Original Version of Chapman's *Tragedy of Byron*," in *Journal of English and Germanic Philology.* LXIII (1964), pp. 433–440.

Halio, Jay L. "The Metaphor of Conception and Elizabethan Theories of the Imagination," in *Neophilologus.* L (1966), pp. 454–461.

Kennedy, Edward D. "James I and Chapman's Byron Plays," in *Journal of English and Germanic Philology.* LXIV (1965), pp. 677–690.

MacLure, Millar. *George Chapman; A Critical Study.* Toronto: University of Toronto Press, 1966, pp. 132–145.

Ornstein, Robert. *The Moral Vision of Jacobean Tragedy.* Madison: University of Wisconsin Press, 1960, pp. 60–64.

Parr, Johnstone. "The Duke of Byron's Malignant 'Caput Algol,' " in *Studies in Philology.* XLIII (1946), pp. 194–202.

Rees, Ennis. *The Tragedies of George Chapman; Renaissance Ethics in Action.* Cambridge, Mass.: Harvard University Press, 1954, pp. 51–92.

Schwartz, Elias. "Chapman's Renaissance Man: Byron Reconsidered," in *Journal of English and Germanic Philology.* LVIII (1959), pp. 613–626.

Spivack, Charlotte. *George Chapman.* New York: Twayne, 1967, pp. 119–131.

Ure, Peter. "Chapman's *Tragedy of Byron*, IV, ii, 291–5," in *Modern Language Review.* LIV (1959), pp. 557–558.

_____. *Elizabethan and Jacobean Drama; Critical Essays*. New York: Barnes & Noble, 1974, pp. 123–144.

_____. "The Main Outline of Chapman's *Byron*," in *Studies in Philology*. XLVII (1950), pp. 568–588.

Waith, Eugene M.   *Ideas of Greatness; Heroic Drama in England*. London: Routledge and Kegan Paul, 1971, pp. 113–138.

The Widow's Tears

Cope, Jackson I.   *The Theatre and the Drama: From Metaphor to Form in Renaissance Drama*. Baltimore: Johns Hopkins University Press, 1973, pp. 29–76.

Herring, Thelma.   "Chapman and an Aspect of Modern Criticism," in *Renaissance Drama*. VIII (1965), pp. 153–179.

Maxwell, J.C.   "Chapman, *The Widow's Tears*," in *Notes & Queries*. XXI (August, 1974), p. 290.

Pearson, Lu Emily.   "Elizabethan Widows," in *Stanford Studies in Language and Literature*. Stanford, Calif.: Stanford University Press, 1941, pp. 134–135.

Schoenbaum, Samuel.   "*The Widow's Tears* and the Other Chapman," in *Huntington Library Quarterly*. XXIII (August, 1960), pp. 321–338.

Tricomi, Albert H.   "The Social Disorder of Chapman's *The Widow's Tears*," in *Journal of English and Germanic Philology*. LXXII (1973), pp. 350–359.

Ure, Peter.   "The Widow of Ephesus: Some Reflections on an International Comic Theme," in *Durham University Journal*. XVIII (1956), pp. 1–9.

Weidner, Henry M.   "Homer and the Fallen World: Focus of Satire in George Chapman's *The Widow's Tears*," in *Journal of English and Germanic Philology*. LXII (July, 1963), pp. 518–532.

Williamson, Marilyn L.   "Matter of More Mirth," in *Renaissance Papers*. (1956), pp. 34–41.

GEOFFREY CHAUCER
(c. 1343–1400)

The Book of the Duchess

Boardman, P.C. "Courtly Language and the Strategy of Consolation in *The Book of the Duchess*," in *ELH*. XLIV (Winter, 1977), pp. 567–579.

Carson, M. Angela. "Easing of the 'Hert' in *The Book of the Duchess*," in *Chaucer Review*. I (1967), pp. 157–160.

Crampton, Georgia Ronan. "Transitions and Meaning in *The Book of the Duchess*," in *Journal of English and Germanic Philology*. LXII (1963), pp. 486–500.

Ebell, Julia G. "Chaucer's *The Book of the Duchess*: A Study of Medieval Iconography and Literary Structure," in *College English*. XXIX (1969), pp. 197–206.

Fyler, J.M. "Irony and The Age of Gold in *The Book of the Duchess*," in *Speculum*. LII (1977), pp. 314–328.

Grennen, Joseph E. "Hert-hunting in *The Book of the Duchess*," in *Modern Language Quarterly*. XXV (1964), pp. 131–139.

Hill, J.M. "*The Book of the Duchess*, Melancholy and That Eight-year Sickness," in *Chaucer Review*. IX (1974), pp. 35–50.

Jordan, R.M. "Compositional Structure of *The Book of the Duchess*," in *Chaucer Review*. IX (1974), pp. 99–117.

Palmer, J.J.N. "The Historical Context of *The Book of the Duchess*, a Revision," in *Chaucer Review*. VIII (1974), pp. 253–261.

Rowland, Beryl. "Chaucer as a Pawn in *The Book of the Duchess*," in *American Notes and Queries*. VI (1967), pp. 3–5.

Severs, J. Burke. "The Sources of *The Book of the Duchess*," in *Mediaeval Studies*. XXV (1963), pp. 355–362.

Stevens, Martin. "Narrative Focus in *The Book of the Duchess*," in *Annuale Medievale*. VII (1966), pp. 16–32.

Wilson, G.R., Jr. "The Anatomy of Compassion: Chaucer's *The Book of the Duchess*," in *Tulane Studies in Language and Literature*. XIV (1972), pp. 381–388.

Wimsatt, James I. "The Apotheosis of Blanche in *The Book of the Duchess*," in *Journal of English and Germanic Philology*. LXVI (1967), pp. 26–44.

————. *Chaucer and the French Love Poets: The Literary Background of The Book of the Duchess*. Chapel Hill: University of North Carolina Press, 1968.

The Canterbury Tales

Baum, P. "Chaucer's Puns," in *PMLA*. LXXI (1956), pp. 225–246, and LXXIII (1958), pp. 167–170.

Bennett, Henry Stanley. *Chaucer and the Fifteenth Century*. Oxford: Clarendon Press, 1970.

Bowden, Muriel Amanda. *A Reader's Guide to Geoffrey Chaucer*. New York: Farrar, Straus and Giroux, 1965.

Burrow, John Anthony, Editor. *Geoffrey Chaucer; A Critical Anthology*. Baltimore: Penguin, 1969.

Chesterton, Gilbert Keith. *Chaucer*. New York: Farrar and Rinehart, 1932.

Coulton, George Gordon. *Chaucer and His England*. London: Methuen, 1908.

Delasanto, Rodney. "The Theme of Judgement in *The Canterbury Tales*," in *Modern Language Quarterly*. XXXI (1970), pp. 298–307.

Economou, George D., Editor. *Geoffrey Chaucer: A Collection of Original Articles*. New York: McGraw-Hill, 1975.

French, Robert Dudley. *A Chaucer Handbook*. New York: F.S. Crofts, 1947.

Frost, W. "What Is a Canterbury Tale?," in *Western Humanities Review*. XXVII (1973), pp. 39–59.

Gardner, John Champlin. *The Life and Times of Chaucer*. New York: Knopf, 1976.

Gerould, Gordon Hall. *Chaucerian Essays*. Princeton, N.J.: Princeton University Press, 1952.

Harrington, N.T. "Experience, Art and the Framing of *The Canterbury Tales*," in *Chaucer Review*. X (Winter, 1976), pp. 187–200.

Hoffman, Richard L. *Ovid and* The Canterbury Tales. Philadelphia: University of Pennsylvania Press, 1966.

Howard, Donald R. "*The Canterbury Tales*: Memory and Form," in *Journal of English Literary History*. XXXVIII (1971), pp. 319–328.

————. *The Idea of* The Canterbury Tales. Berkeley: University of California Press, 1975.

Howard, Edwin J. *Geoffrey Chaucer*. New York: Twayne, 1964.

Huppe, Bernard F. *A Reading of* The Canterbury Tales. Albany: State University of New York Press, 1977.

Hussey, Maurice, et.al. *An Introduction to Chaucer*. Cambridge: Cambridge University Press, 1965.

Lawlor, John. *Chaucer*. London: Hutchinson's, 1968.

Leyerle, J. "Thematic Interlace in *The Canterbury Tales*," in *English Association Essays and Articles*. XXIX (1976), pp. 107–121.

Miller, Robert P. "Allegory in *The Canterbury Tales*," in *A Companion to Chaucer Studies*. Edited by Beryl Rowland. Toronto: Oxford University Press, 1968, pp. 268–290.

Miskimin, Alice. *The Renaissance Chaucer*. New Haven, Conn.: Yale University Press, 1975.

Ramsey, Vance. "Modes of Irony in *The Canterbury Tales*," in *A Companion to Chaucer Studies*. Edited by Beryl Rowland. Toronto: Oxford University Press, 1968, pp. 291–312.

Smyser, H. "How Shall the Undergraduate Read Chaucer?," in *College English*. X (1948–1949), pp. 375–379.

Whittock, Trevor. *A Reading of* The Canterbury Tales. London: Cambridge University Press, 1968.

Troilus and Criseyde

Adamson, Jane. "The Unity of *Troilus and Criseyde*," in *The Critical Review*. XIV (1971), pp. 17–37.

apRoberts, Robert P. "The Boethian God and the Audience of the *Troilus*," in *Journal of English and Germanic Philology*. LXIX (1969), pp. 425–436.

————. "Criseydes' Infidelity and the Moral of the *Troilus*," in *Speculum*. XLIV (1969), pp. 383–402.

Barney, Stephen A. "Troilus Bound," in *Speculum*. XLII (1972), pp. 445–458.

Baron, F.K. "Chaucer's Troilus and Self-renunciation in Love," in *Papers in Language and Literature*. X (Winter, 1974), pp. 5–14.

Berryman, Charles. "The Ironic Design of Fortune in *Troilus and Criseyde*," in *Chaucer Review*. II (1967), pp. 1–7.

Christmas, P. "*Troilus and Criseyde*: The Problem of Love and Necessity," in *Chaucer Review*. IX (1975), pp. 285–296.

Corsa, Helen S. "Dreams in *Troilus and Criseyde*," in *American Imago*. XXVII (1970), pp. 52–65.

Durham, Lonnie. "Love and Death in *Troilus and Criseyde*," in *Chaucer Review*. III (1968), pp. 1–11.

Farnham, Anthony E. "Chaucerian Irony and the Ending of the *Troilus*," in *Chaucer Review*. I (1967), pp. 207–216.

Fries, M. " 'Slydynge of Corage': Chaucer's Criseyde as Feminist and Victim," in *The Authority of Experience: Essays in Feminist Criticism*. Edited by Arlyn Diamond and Lee R. Edwards. Amherst: University of Massachusetts Press, 1977, pp. 45–69.

Gordon, Ida L. *The Double Sorrow of Troilus*. London: Oxford University Press, 1970.

Hanson, T.B. "The Center of *Troilus and Criseyde*," in *Chaucer Review*. IX (1975), pp. 297–302.

Hatcher, Elizabeth R. "Chaucer and the Psychology of Fear: Troilus in Book V," in *Journal of English Literary History*. XL (1973), pp. 307–324.

Heidtmann, Peter. "Sex and Salvation in *Troilus and Criseyde*," in *Chaucer Review*. II (1969), pp. 246–253.

Macey, Samuel L. "Dramatic Elements in Chaucer's *Troilus*," in *Texas Studies in Language and Literature*. XII (1970), pp. 301–323.

Meech, Sanford B. *Design in Chaucer's* Troilus. New York: Greenwood, 1969.

Moorman, Charles. " 'Once More Unto the Breach': The Meaning of *Troilus and Criseyde*," in *Studies in the Literary Imagination*. IV (1971), pp. 61–71.

Reiss, Edmund. "Troilus and the Failure of Understanding," in *Modern Language Quarterly*. XXIX (1968), pp. 131–144.

Rowe, Donald W. *O Love, O Charite! Contraries Harmonized in Chaucer's* Troilus. Carbondale: Southern Illinois University Press, 1976.

Schuman, S. "The Circle of Nature: Patterns of Imagery in Chaucer's *Troilus and Criseyde*," in *Chaucer Review*. X (1975), pp. 99–112.

Stanley, E.G. "About Troilus," in *English Association Essays and Articles*. XXIX (1976), pp. 84–106.

Steadman, John M. *Disembodied Laughter: Troilus and the Apotheosis Tradition; A Reexamination of Narrative and Thematic Contexts*. Berkeley: University of California Press, 1972.

Taylor, D. "Terms of Love: A Study of *Troilus'* Style," in *Speculum*. XLI (January, 1976), pp. 69–90.

Wimsatt, James I. "Medieval and Modern in Chaucer's *Troilus and Criseyde*," in *PMLA*. XCII (March, 1977), pp. 203–216.

JOHN CHEEVER
(1912–   )

The Wapshot Chronicle

Bracher, Frederick. "John Cheever and Comedy," in *Critique: Studies in Modern Fiction.* VI (Spring, 1963), pp. 66–77.

Coale, Samuel. *John Cheever.* New York: Frederick Ungar, 1977, pp. 65–80.

Hassan, Ihab. *Radical Innocence: Studies in the Contemporary American Novel.* Princeton, N.J.: Princeton University Press, 1961, pp. 187–194.

Hogan, William. "Mortal Men and Mermaids," in *New Yorker.* XXXIII (May 11, 1957), pp. 142–150.

Rupp, Richard H. *Celebration in Postwar American Fiction, 1945–1967.* Coral Gables, Fla.: University of Miami Press, 1970, pp. 28–33.

The Wapshot Scandal

Barratt, William. "New England Gothic," in *Atlantic.* CCXIII (1964), p. 140.

Coale, Samuel. *John Cheever.* New York: Frederick Ungar, 1977, pp. 81–94.

De Mott, Benjamin. "The Way We Feel Now," in *Harper's Magazine.* CCXXVIII (February, 1964), pp. 111–112.

Garrett, George. "John Cheever and the Charms of Innocence: The Craft of *The Wapshot Scandal*," in *The Sounder Few: Essays from The Hollins Critic.* Edited by R.H.W. Dillard, George Garrett, and John R. Moore. Athens: University of Georgia Press, 1971, pp. 19–41.

Greene, George. "From Christmas to Christmas—A Ramble with the Wapshots," in *Commonweal.* LXXIX (January 24, 1964), pp. 487–488.

Hardwick, Elizabeth. "The Family Way," in *New York Review of Books.* I (February 6, 1964), pp. 4–5.

Hicks, Granville. "Where Have All the Roses Gone," in *Saturday Review.* XLVII (January 4, 1964), pp. 75–76.

Hyman, Stanley Edgar. *Standards: A Chronicle of Books for Our Time.* New York: Horizon Press, 1966, pp. 199–203.

Ozick, Cynthia. "America Aglow," in *Commentary.* XXXVIII (July, 1964), pp. 66–67.

Rupp, Richard H. *Celebration in Postwar American Fiction, 1945–1967.* Coral Gables, Fla.: University of Miami Press, 1970, pp. 33–39.

ANTON CHEKHOV
(1860–1904)

The Cherry Orchard

Balukhaty, S.D. *"The Cherry Orchard*: A Formalist Approach," in *Chekhov: A Collection of Critical Essays.* Edited by Robert Louis Jackson. Englewood Cliffs, N.J.: Prentice-Hall, Inc., 1967, pp. 136–146.

Beckerman, Bernard. "Dramatic Analysis and Literary Interpretation: *The Cherry Orchard* as Exemplum," in *New Literary History.* II (1971), pp. 391–406.

Block, Anita. *Changing World in Plays and Theatre.* Boston: Little, Brown, 1939, pp. 70–73.

Brandon, J. "Toward a Middle View of Chekhov," in *Educational Theatre Journal.* XII (1960), pp. 270–275.

Bruford, Walter Horace. *Anton Chekhov.* London: Bowes and Bowes, 1957, pp. 54–58.

Brustein, Robert Sanford. *Theatre of Revolt.* Boston: Little, Brown, 1964, pp. 167–178.

Corbin, J. "Moscow and Broadway," in *American Theatre as Seen by Its Critics, 1752–1934.* Edited by M.J. Moses and J.M. Brown. New York: Norton, 1934, pp. 178–184.

Corrigan, Robert W. "The Plays of Chekhov," in *Context and Craft of Drama.* Edited by James Rosenberg. San Francisco: Chandler, 1964, pp. 137–167.

Deer, Irving. "Speech as Action in *The Cherry Orchard,*" in *Educational Theatre Journal.* X (March, 1958), pp. 30–34.

Fergusson, Francis. *"The Cherry Orchard*: A Theater-Poem of the Suffering of Change," in *Chekhov: A Collection of Critical Essays.* Edited by Robert Louis Jackson. Englewood Cliffs, N.J.: Prentice-Hall, 1967, pp. 147–160.

Ganz, A. "Arrivals and Departures: The Meaning of the Journey in the Major Plays of Chekhov," in *Drama Survey.* V (Spring, 1966), pp. 5–23.

Gerould, Daniel Charles. *"The Cherry Orchard* as a Comedy," in *Journal of General Education.* XI (April, 1958), pp. 109–122.

Gilman, Richard. *Common and Uncommon Masks.* New York: Random House, 1971, pp. 284–287.

Hahn, Beverly. *Chekhov: A Study of the Major Stories and Plays.* Cambridge: Cambridge University Press, 1977, pp. 12–36.

Kelson, John. "Allegory and Myth in *The Cherry Orchard,*" in *Western Humanities Review.* XIII (Summer, 1959), pp. 321–324.

Latham, Jacqueline. *"The Cherry Orchard* as Comedy," in *Educational Theatre Journal.* X (March, 1958), pp. 21–29.

Lewis, Allan. *Contemporary Theatre.* New York: Crown, 1962, pp. 66–70, 74–78.

Magarshack, David. *Chekhov the Dramatist.* London: John Lehmann, 1952, pp. 264–287.

Moravcevich, N. "The Obligatory Scenes in Chekhov's Drama," in *Drama Critique.* IX (Spring, 1966), pp. 97–104.

Remaley, Peter B. "Chekhov's *The Cherry Orchard,*" in *South Atlantic Bulletin.* XXXVIII (1973), pp. 16–20.

Silverstein, Norman. "Chekhov's Comic Spirit and *The Cherry Orchard,*" in *Modern Drama.* I (1958), pp. 91–100.

Smith, J. "Chekhov and the Theatre of the Absurd," in *Bucknell Review.* XIV (December, 1966), pp. 44–58.

Styan, John Louis. "Shifting Impressions," in *Elements of Drama.* Cambridge: Cambridge University Press, 1960, pp. 64–85.

Warner, P. "The Axe in Springtime (*Cherry Orchard*)," in *Theoria.* X (1958), pp. 41–57.

Young, Stark. "Heartbreak Houses," in *Immortal Shadows, a Book of Dramatic Criticism.* New York: Scribner's, 1948, pp. 206–210.

The Seagull

Brooks, Cleanth and Robert Heilman. *Understanding Drama.* New York: Holt, 1961, pp. 490–502.

Bruford, Walter Horace. *Anton Chekhov.* London: Bowes and Bowes, 1957, pp. 44–49.

Clurman, Harold. *Lies Like Truth.* New York: Macmillan, 1958, pp. 131–133.

Corrigan, Robert W. "The Plays of Chekhov," in *Context and Craft of Drama.* Edited by James Rosenberg. San Francisco: Chandler, 1964, pp. 137–167.

Croyden, M. "The Absurdity of Chekhov's Doctors," in *Texas Quarterly.* XI (1968), pp. 130–137.

Curtis, James M. "Spatial Form in Drama: *The Seagull,*" in *Canadian-American Slavic Studies.* VI (1972), pp. 13–37.

Erlich, V. "Chekhov and West European Drama," in *Yearbook of Comparative Literature.* XII (1963), pp. 56–60.

Ganz, A. "Arrivals and Departures: The Meaning of the Journey in the Major Plays of Chekhov," in *Drama Survey.* V (Spring, 1966), pp. 5–23.

Jackson, Robert Louis. *"The Seagull*: The Empty Well, the Dry Lake, and the Cold Cave," in *Chekhov: A Collection of Critical Essays.* Englewood Cliffs, N.J.: Prentice-Hall, 1967, pp. 99–111.

Kendle, B.   "Elusive Horses in *The Sea Gull*," in *Modern Drama*. XIII (May, 1970), pp. 63–66.

Krutch, Joseph Wood.   *Modernism in Modern Drama*. Ithaca, N.Y.: Cornell University Press, 1962, pp. 68–69, 74–75.

Magarshack, David.   *Chekhov the Dramatist*. London: John Lehmann, 1952, pp. 175–203.

Moravcevich, N.   "The Obligatory Scenes in Chekhov's Plays," in *Drama Critique*. IX (Spring, 1966), pp. 97–104.

Sagar, Keith.   "Chekhov's Magic Lake: A Reading of *The Seagull*," in *Modern Drama*. XV (1973), pp. 441–447.

Seyler, Dorothy.   "*The Sea Gull* and *The Wild Duck*: Birds of a Feather?," in *Modern Drama*. VIII (1965), pp. 167–173.

Styan, John Louis.   *Dark Comedy, the Development of Modern Comic Tragedy*. Cambridge: Cambridge University Press, 1962, pp. 89–91.

————.   *The Elements of Drama*. Cambridge: Cambridge University Press, 1960, pp. 103–105.

Valency, M.   *The Breaking String*. New York: Oxford University Press, 1966, pp. 117–178.

Williams, Raymond.   *Drama from Ibsen to Eliot*. London: Chatto and Windus, 1954, pp. 126–130.

Worsley, T.C.   *The Fugitive Art*. London: John Lehmann, 1952, pp. 99–103.

Young, Stark.   *Immortal Shadows*. New York: Scribner's, 1948, pp. 200–205.

The Three Sisters

Bennett, John L.   "An Examination of Chekhov's Presentation of Characters and Themes in Act I of *Three Sisters*," in *World Literature; General Education Journal*. XIII (1968), pp. 94–102.

Brandon, J.   "Toward a Middle View of Chekhov," in *Educational Theatre Journal*. XII (December, 1960), pp. 272–275.

Bruford, Walter Horace.   *Anton Chekhov*. London: Bowes and Bowes, 1957, pp. 51–54.

Brustein, Robert.   *Theater of Revolt*. Boston: Little, Brown, 1964, pp. 155–168.

Corrigan, Robert W.   "The Plays of Chekhov," in *Context and Craft of Drama*. Edited by James Rosenberg. San Francisco: Chandler, 1964, pp. 137–167.

Croyden, M.   "The Absurdity of Chekhov's Doctors," in *Texas Quarterly*. XI (1968), pp. 130–137.

Ganz, A.   "Arrivals and Departures: The Meaning of the Journey in the Major Plays of Chekhov," in *Drama Survey*. V (Spring, 1966), pp. 5–23.

Hahn, Beverly. *Chekhov: A Study of the Major Stories and Plays.* Cambridge: Cambridge University Press, 1977, pp. 284–309.

Hogan, Robert G. *Drama: The Major Genres—An Introductory Critical Anthology.* New York: Dodd, Mead, 1962, pp. 397–404.

Leaska, Mitchell. *The Voice of Tragedy.* New York: Speller, 1963, pp. 232–235.

Magarshack, David. *Chekhov the Dramatist.* London: John Lehmann, 1952, pp. 226–263.

Moravcevich, N. "The Obligatory Scenes in Chekhov's Plays," in *Drama Critique.* IX (Spring, 1966), pp. 97–104.

Paul, Barbara. "Chekhov's Five Sisters," in *Modern Drama.* XIV (February, 1972), pp. 436–440.

Purdon, Liam. "Time and Space in Chekhov's *The Three Sisters,*" in *Publications of the Arkansas Philological Association.* II (1976), pp. 47–53.

Smith, J. "Chekhov and the Theater of the Absurd," in *Bucknell Review.* XIV (December, 1966), pp. 44–58.

Styan, John Louis. *Dark Comedy, the Development of Modern Comic Tragedy.* Cambridge: Cambridge University Press, 1962, pp. 91–94.

————. *The Elements of Drama.* Cambridge: Cambridge University Press, 1960, pp. 206–212.

Tovstonogov, G. "*Three Sisters,*" in *Tulane Drama Review.* XIII (Winter, 1968), pp. 146–155.

Valency, M. *The Breaking String.* New York: Oxford University Press, 1966, pp. 206–250.

Walton, M. "If Only We Knew," in *New Theatre Magazine.* VIII (1967), pp. 29–35.

Worsley, T.C. *The Fugitive Art.* London: John Lehmann, 1952, pp. 220–223.

Young, V. "Social Drama and Big Daddy," in *Southwest Review.* XLI (Spring, 1956), pp. 194–197.

Uncle Vanya

Agate, J.E. *English Dramatic Critics; An Anthology, 1660–1932.* New York: Hill and Wang, 1958, pp. 300–306.

Bardinat, Philip. "Dramatic Structure in Cexov's [sic] *Uncle Vanya,*" in *Slavic and East European Journal.* XVI (1958), pp. 195–210.

Bentley, Eric. "Chekhov as Playwright," in *Kenyon Review.* XI (Spring, 1949), pp. 227–250.

————. "Craftsmanship in *Uncle Vanya,*" in *In Search of Theater.* New York: Knopf, 1959, pp. 322–343.

Bruford, Walter Horace. *Anton Chekhov.* London: Bowes and Bowes, 1957, pp. 49–51.

Corrigan, Robert W. "The Plays of Chekhov," in *Context and Craft of Drama.* Edited by James Rosenberg. San Francisco: Chandler, 1964, pp. 137–167.

Cowell, Raymond. *Twelve Modern Dramatists.* London: Pergamon Press, 1967, pp. 36–38.

Croyden, M. "The Absurdity of Chekhov's Doctors," in *Texas Quarterly.* XI (1968), pp. 130–137.

Ermilov, V.V. "*Uncle Vanya*: The Play's Movement," in *Chekhov; A Collection of Essays.* Edited by Robert Louis Jackson. Englewood Cliffs, N.J.: Prentice-Hall, 1967, pp. 112–120.

Freedman, M. *The Moral Impulse.* Carbondale: Southern Illinois University Press, 1967, pp. 37–40.

Ganz, A. "Arrivals and Departures: The Meaning of the Journey in the Major Plays of Chekhov," in *Drama Survey.* V (Spring, 1966), pp. 5–23.

Gassner, John. *Theatre at the Crossroads; Plays and Playwrights of the Midcentury American Stage.* New York: Holt, 1960, pp. 188–193.

Lewis, Allan. *The Contemporary Theatre.* New York: Crown, 1962, pp. 71–74, 79–80.

MacCarthy, Desmond. *Humanities.* London: MacGibbon and Kee, 1953, pp. 71–77.

Magarshack, David. *Chekhov the Dramatist.* London: John Lehmann, 1952, pp. 204–225.

———. *The Real Chekhov; An Introduction to Chekhov's Last Plays.* London: George Allen & Unwin, 1972, pp. 79–124.

Moravcevich, N. "The Obligatory Scenes in Chekhov's Plays," in *Drama Critique.* IX (Spring, 1966), pp. 97–104.

Oates, Joyce Carol. *The Edge of Impossibility; Tragic Forms in Literature.* New York: Vanguard Press, 1972, pp. 117–137.

Rayfield, Donald. *Chekhov; the Evolution of His Art.* New York: Barnes & Noble, 1975, pp. 211–215.

Tynan, Kenneth. *Curtains; Selections from the Drama Criticism and Related Writings.* New York: Antheneum, 1961, pp. 437–439.

Valency, M. *The Breaking String.* New York: Oxford University Press, 1966, pp. 179–205.

CHARLES WADDELL CHESNUTT
(1858–1932)

The Conjure Woman

Andrews, William L. "The Significance of Charles Waddell Chesnutt's 'Conjure Stories,' " in *Southern Literary Journal.* VII (1973), pp. 78–99.

Baldwin, Richard E. "The Art of *The Conjure Woman*," in *American Literature.* XLIII (1971), pp. 385–398.

Brawley, Benjamin. *The Negro in Literature and Art in the United States.* New York: Duffield, 1930, pp. 76–81.

Britt, David D. "Chesnutt's Conjure Tales: What You See Is What You Get," in *College Language Association Journal.* XV (1972), pp. 269–283.

Brown, Sterling. *The Negro in American Fiction.* Washington, D.C.: Associates in Negro Folk Education, 1937, pp. 78–82.

Dixon, Melvin. "The Teller as Folk Trickster in Chesnutt's *The Conjure Woman*," in *College Language Association Journal.* XVIII (1974), pp. 186–197.

Farnsworth, Robert M. "Charles Chesnutt and the Color Line," in *Minor American Novelists.* Edited by Charles A. Hoyt. Carbondale: Southern Illinois University Press, 1970, pp. 28–40.

————. "Introduction," in *The Conjure Woman.* By Charles Waddell Chesnutt. Ann Arbor: University of Michigan Press, 1969, pp. v–xix.

————. "Testing the Color Line—Dunbar and Chesnutt," in *The Black American Writer, Volume 1: Fiction.* Edited by C.W.E. Bigsby. Deland, Fla.: Everett/Edwards, 1969, pp. 118–120.

Gartner, Carol B. "Charles W. Chesnutt: Novelist of a Cause," in *Markham Review.* I (October, 1968), pp. 5–12.

Gloster, Hugh M. "Charles W. Chesnutt: Pioneer in the Fiction of Negro Life," in *Phylon.* II (1941), pp. 57–66.

Hemenway, Robert. "The Functions of Folklore in Charles Chesnutt's *The Conjure Woman*," in *Journal of the Folklore Institute.* XIII (1976), pp. 283–309.

Margolies, Edward. *Native Sons: A Critical Study of Twentieth Century Negro American Authors.* Philadelphia: Lippincott, 1968, pp. 24–25.

Redding, J. Saunders. *To Make a Poet Black.* Chapel Hill: University of North Carolina Press, 1939, pp. 68–77.

Render, Sylvia Lyons. "Tar Heelia in Chesnutt," in *College Language Journal.* IX (September, 1965), pp. 39–50.

Smith, Robert A. "A Note on the Folktales of Charles Waddell Chesnutt," in *College Language Association Journal.* V (March, 1962), pp. 229–232.

Whitlow, Roger. *Black American Literature: A Critical History.* Chicago: Nelson Hall, 1973, pp. 60–63.

The Marrow of Tradition

Barksdale, Richard and Keneth Kinnamon. *Black Writers of America: A Comprehensive Anthology.* New York: Macmillan, 1972, pp. 324–328.

Brown, Sterling. *The Negro in American Fiction.* Washington, D.C.: Associates in Negro Folk Education, 1937, pp. 78–82.

Chandler, G. Lewis. "Coming of Age: A Note on American Negro Novelists," in *Phylon.* IX (1948), pp. 25–29.

Farnsworth, Robert M. "Introduction," in *The Marrow of Tradition.* By Charles Waddell Chesnutt. Ann Arbor: University of Michigan Press, 1969, pp. v–xvii.

———. "Testing the Color Line—Dunbar and Chesnutt," in *The Black American Writer, Volume 1: Fiction.* Edited by C.W.E. Bigsby. Deland, Fla.: Everett/Edwards, 1969, pp. 121–124.

Gayle, Addison. *The Way of the New World: The Black Novel in America.* Garden City, N.Y.: Doubleday, 1975, pp. 47–58.

Gloster, Hugh M. "Charles W. Chesnutt: Pioneer in the Fiction of Negro Life," in *Phylon.* II (1941), pp. 57–66.

Jones, Le Roi. *Blues People.* New York: Morrow House, 1963, pp. 58–59.

Redding, J. Saunders. "American Negro Literature," in *American Scholar.* XVIII (1950), pp. 137–148.

———. *To Make a Poet Black.* Chapel Hill: University of North Carolina Press, 1939, pp. 68–77.

Reilly, John M. "The Dilemma of Chesnutt's *The Marrow of Tradition*," in *Phylon.* XXXII (1971), pp. 31–38.

Render, Sylvia Lyons. "Introduction," in *The Marrow of Tradition.* By Charles Waddell Chesnutt. New York: Arno Press, 1969, pp. i–vii.

Wideman, John. "Charles W. Chesnutt: *The Marrow of Tradition*," in *American Scholar.* XLII (1972), pp. 128–134.

PHILIP DORMER STANHOPE, LORD CHESTERFIELD
(1694–1773)

Letters to His Son

Collins, John Churton. *Essays and Studies.* London: Macmillan, 1895, pp. 193–262.

Coxon, Roger. *Chesterfield and His Critics.* London: Routledge, 1925.

Irving, W.H. *Providence of Wit in the English Letter Writers.* Durham, N.C.: Duke University Press, 1955, pp. 205–245.

Kelly, Richard M. "Chesterfield's *Letters to His Son*: The Victorian Judgment," in *Tennessee Studies in Literature.* XV (1974), pp. 109–123.

Krutch, J.W., et al. "Chesterfield: *Letters to His Son*," in *New Invitation to Learning.* Edited by Mark Van Doren. New York: Random House, 1942, pp. 269–282.

Lucas, F.L. *The Search for Good Sense: Four Eighteenth-Century Characters.* London: Cassell, 1958, pp. 131–176.

Schlesinger, A.M. *Learning How to Behave; A Historical Study of American Etiquette Book.* New York: Macmillan, 1946, pp. 8–14.

Shellabarger, Samuel. *Lord Chesterfield and His World.* Boston: Little, Brown, 1951.

Woolf, Virginia. *Collected Essays, III.* New York: Harcourt, 1966, pp. 80–85.

G.K. CHESTERTON
(1874–1936)

The Essays of G.K. Chesterton

Auden, W.H. "G.K. Chesterton's Non-Fictional Prose," in *Prose*. I (1970), pp. 17–28.

Barker, Dudley. *G.K. Chesterton: A Biography*. New York: Stein and Day, 1973, pp. 160–174.

Belloc, Hilaire. *On the Place of Gilbert Chesterton in English Letters*. Shepherdstown, W. Va.: Patmos, 1977.

Braybrooke, Patrick. *Gilbert Keith Chesterton*. Philadelphia: Lippincott, 1922, pp. 1–14.

Canovan, Margaret. *G.K. Chesterton: Radical Populist*. New York: Harcourt Brace Jovanovich, 1977, pp. 80–111.

Clipper, Lawrence J. *G.K. Chesterton*. New York: Twayne, 1974, pp. 101–119.

Derus, David L. "Chesterton as Literary Critic," in *Renascence*. XXV (1973), pp. 103–112.

————. "The Chesterton Style: Patterns and Paradox," in *Chesterton Review*. IV (Fall–Winter, 1977–1978), pp. 45–64.

Evans, Maurice. *G.K. Chesterton*. New York: Haskell House, 1972, pp. 40–70, 98–109.

Hall, J.A. "Chesterton's Contribution to English Sociology," in *Chesterton Review*. III (Spring–Summer, 1977), pp. 260–282.

Hollis, Christopher. *The Mind of Chesterton*. London: Hollis & Carter, 1970, pp. 228–271.

Kenner, Hugh. *Paradox in Chesterton*. New York: Sheed & Ward, 1947.

Lea, F.A. *The Wild Knight of Battersea: G.K. Chesterton*. London: James Clarke, 1945.

McLuhan, Marshall. "Formal Causality in Chesterton," in *Chesterton Review*. II (Spring–Summer, 1976), pp. 253–259.

Purnell, George. "The Humor of Chesterton," in *Chesterton Review*. II (Fall–Winter, 1975–1976), pp. 1–21.

West, Julius. *G.K. Chesterton: A Critical Study*. New York: Dodd, Mead, 1916, pp. 76–90.

Wills, Garry. *Chesterton: Man and Mask*. New York: Sheed & Ward, 1961, pp. 55–97.

The Everlasting Man

Clipper, Lawrence J. *G.K. Chesterton*. New York: Twayne, 1974, pp. 105–110.

Hollis, Christopher. *The Mind of Chesterton.* London: Hollis & Carter, 1970, pp. 262–271.

Mulloy, John J. "Chesterton and Mythology: A Reading of *The Everlasting Man*," in *Chesterton Review.* III (Fall–Winter, 1976–1977), pp. 129–140.

Ward, Masie. *Gilbert Keith Chesterton.* New York: Sheed & Ward, 1943, pp. 472–480.

Wills, Garry. *Chesterton: Man and Mask.* New York: Sheed & Ward, 1961, pp. 108–200.

Heretics

Barker, Dudley. *G.K. Chesterton: A Biography.* New York: Stein and Day, 1973, pp. 171–173.

Canovan, Margaret. *G.K. Chesterton: Radical Populist.* New York: Harcourt Brace Jovanovich, 1977, pp. 160–163.

Clipper, Lawrence J. *G.K. Chesterton.* New York: Twayne, 1974, pp. 39–43.

Evans, David. "The Making of G.K. Chesterton's *Heretics*," in *Yearbook of English Studies.* V (1975), pp. 207–213.

Hollis, Christopher. *The Mind of Chesterton.* London: Hollis & Carter, 1970, pp. 61–63, 66–67.

Ward, Masie. *Gilbert Keith Chesterton.* New York: Sheed & Ward, 1943, pp. 181–182.

Wills, Garry. *Chesterton: Man and Mask.* New York: Sheed & Ward, 1961, pp. 86–88.

The Man Who Was Thursday

Amis, Kingsley. "Four Fluent Fellows: An Essay on Chesterton's Fiction," in *G.K. Chesterton: A Centenary Appraisal.* Edited by John Sullivan. New York: Barnes & Noble, 1974, pp. 33–37.

Barker, Dudley. *G.K. Chesterton: A Biography.* New York: Stein and Day, 1973, pp. 175–179.

Batchelor, John. "Chesterton as an Edwardian Novelist," in *Chesterton Review.* I (Fall–Winter, 1974), pp. 27–30.

Boyd, Ian. *The Novels of G.K. Chesterton: A Study in Art and Propaganda.* New York: Barnes & Noble, 1975, pp. 40–51.

Braybrooke, Patrick. *Gilbert Keith Chesterton.* Philadelphia: Lippincott, 1922, pp. 87–89.

Clipper, Lawrence J. *G.K. Chesterton.* New York: Twayne, 1974, pp. 129–132.

Conlon, Denis. "Chesterton, Propaganda and the Gregorian Heresy," in *Chesterton Review.* II (Fall–Winter, 1975–1976), pp. 79–83.

Hollis, Christopher. *The Mind of Chesterton.* London: Hollis & Carter, 1970, pp. 54–60.

Ward, Masie. *Gilbert Keith Chesterton.* New York: Sheed & Ward, 1943, pp. 192–193.

West, Julius. *G.K. Chesterton: A Critical Study.* New York: Dodd, Mead, 1916, pp. 33–37.

Wills, Garry. *Chesterton: Man and Mask.* New York: Sheed & Ward, 1961, pp. 39–45.

Youngberg, Karen. "Job and the Gargoyles: A Study of *The Man Who Was Thursday*," in *Chesterton Review.* II (Spring–Summer, 1976), pp. 240–252.

The Napoleon of Notting Hill

Amis, Kingsley. "Four Fluent Fellows: An Essay on Chesterton's Fiction," in *G.K. Chesterton: A Centenary Appraisal.* Edited by John Sullivan. New York: Barnes & Noble, 1974, pp. 28–33.

Barker, Dudley. *G.K. Chesterton: A Biography.* New York: Stein and Day, 1973, pp. 140–144.

Batchelor, John. "Chesterton as an Edwardian Novelist," in *Chesterton Review.* I (Fall–Winter, 1974), pp. 24–27.

Boyd, Ian. *The Novels of G.K. Chesterton: A Study in Art and Propaganda.* New York: Barnes & Noble, 1975, pp. 9–30.

Braybrooke, Patrick. *Gilbert Keith Chesterton.* Philadelphia: Lippincott, 1922, pp. 80–82.

Canovan, Margaret. *G.K. Chesterton: Radical Populist.* New York: Harcourt Brace Jovanovich, 1977, pp. 99–107.

Clipper, Lawrence J. *G.K. Chesterton.* New York: Twayne, 1974, pp. 126–129.

Evans, Maurice. *G.K. Chesterton.* New York: Haskell House, 1972, pp. 76–78.

Hollis, Christopher. *The Mind of Chesterton.* London: Hollis & Carter, 1970, pp. 107–112.

Hunter, Lynette. "A Reading of *The Napoleon of Notting Hill*," in *Chesterton Review.* III (Fall–Winter, 1976–1977), pp. 118–128.

Lea, F.A. *The Wild Knight of Battersea: G.K. Chesterton.* London: James Clarke, 1945, pp. 27–30.

Quinn, Joseph A. "Eden and New Jerusalem: A Study of *The Napoleon of Notting Hill*," in *Chesterton Review.* III (Spring–Summer, 1977), pp. 230–239.

Ward, Masie. *Gilbert Keith Chesterton.* New York: Sheed & Ward, 1943, pp. 173–177.

West, Julius. *G.K. Chesterton: A Critical Study.* New York: Dodd, Mead, 1916, pp. 23–29.

Wills, Garry. *Chesterton: Man and Mask.* New York: Sheed & Ward, 1961, pp. 105–107.

Orthodoxy

Barker, Dudley. *G.K. Chesterton: A Biography.* New York: Stein and Day, 1973, pp. 178–180.

Braybrooke, Patrick. *Gilbert Keith Chesterton.* Philadelphia: Lippincott, 1922, pp. 5–11.

Canovan, Margaret. *G.K. Chesterton: Radical Populist.* New York: Harcourt Brace Jovanovich, 1977, pp. 20–29.

Clipper, Lawrence J. *G.K. Chesterton.* New York: Twayne, 1974, pp. 83–105.

Evans, Maurice. *G.K. Chesterton.* New York: Haskell House, 1972, pp. 20–33.

Hollis, Christopher. *The Mind of Chesterton.* London: Hollis & Carter, 1970, pp. 71–75.

Ward, Masie. *Gilbert Keith Chesterton.* New York: Sheed & Ward, 1943, pp. 215–218.

West, Julius. *G.K. Chesterton: A Critical Study.* New York: Dodd, Mead, 1916, pp. 115–129.

Wills, Garry. *Chesterton: Man and Mask.* New York: Sheed & Ward, 1961, pp. 89–97.

What's Wrong with the World

Amadeo, Mario. "Chesterton in South America: *What's Wrong with the World* Revisited," in *Chesterton Review.* II (Spring–Summer, 1976), pp. 260–266.

Canovan, Margaret. *G.K. Chesterton: Radical Populist.* New York: Harcourt Brace Jovanovich, 1977, pp. 47–58.

Clipper, Lawrence J. *G.K. Chesterton.* New York: Twayne, 1974, pp. 72–74.

Evans, Marice. *G.K. Chesterton.* New York: Haskell House, 1972, pp. 42–43, 62–66.

Hollis, Christopher. *The Mind of Chesterton.* London: Hollis & Carter, 1970, pp. 116–118.

Ward, Masie. *Gilbert Keith Chesterton.* New York: Sheed & Ward, 1943, pp. 299–306.

West, Julius. *G.K. Chesterton: A Critical Study.* New York: Dodd, Mead, 1916, pp. 149–162.

Wills, Garry. *Chesterton: Man and Mask.* New York: Sheed & Ward, 1961, pp. 107–110.

WINSTON CHURCHILL
(1871–1947)

Coniston

Blotner, Joseph. *The Modern American Political Novel, 1900–1960.* Austin: University of Texas Press, 1966, pp. 64–65.

Cooper, Frederic Taber. *Some American Story Tellers.* New York: Holt, 1911, pp. 48–67.

Johnson, Stanley. "The Novelist and His Novels in Politics," in *World's Work.* XVII (December, 1908), pp. 11,016–11,120.

Knight, Grant C. *The Strenuous Age in American Literature.* Chapel Hill: University of North Carolina Press, 1954, pp. 169–170.

Milne, Gordon. *The American Political Novel.* Norman: University of Oklahoma Press, 1966, pp. 87–95.

Noble, David W. "The Lost Generation: Winston Churchill, Ernest Hemingway, F. Scott Fitzgerald," in *The Eternal Adam and the New World.* New York: Braziller, 1968, pp. 140–144.

Pattee, Fred Lewis. *The New American Literature, 1890–1930.* New York: Century, 1930, pp. 93–98.

Pitt, William. "Who's Who in *Coniston*," in *Yankee.* (November, 1937), pp. 12–15.

Quinn, Arthur Hobson. *American Fiction: An Historical and Critical Survey.* New York: Appleton-Century, 1936, pp. 498–499.

Schneider, Robert W. *Novelist to a Generation: The Life and Thought of Winston Churchill.* Bowling Green, Oh.: Bowling Green University Popular Press, 1976, pp. 96–107.

————. "Winston Churchill: The Conservative Revolution," in *Five Novelists of the Progressive Era.* New York: Columbia University Press, 1965, pp. 205–251.

Speare, Morris Edmund. "Mr. Winston Churchill and the Novel of Political Reform," in *The Political Novel: Its Development in England and America.* New York: Oxford University Press, 1924, pp. 306–321.

Titus, Warren I. *Winston Churchill.* New York: Twayne, 1963, pp. 68–76.

Underwood, John. "Winston Churchill and Civic Righteousness," in *Literature and Insurgency.* New York: Mitchell Kennerley, 1914, pp. 322–331.

Van Doren, Carl. *Contemporary American Novelists, 1900–1920.* New York: Macmillan, 1923, pp. 47–56.

Walcutt, Charles C. *The Romantic Compromise in the Novels of Winston Churchill.* Ann Arbor: University of Michigan Press, 1951, pp. 11–13.

The Crisis

Hofstadter, Richard and Beatrice Hofstadter. "Winston Churchill: A Study in the Popular Novel," in *American Quarterly*. II (Spring, 1950), pp. 12–28. Reprinted in *The American Experience: Approaches to the Study of the United States*. Edited by Hennig Cohen. Boston: Houghton Mifflin, 1968, pp. 226–242.

Knight, Grant C. *The Strenuous Age in American Literature*. Chapel Hill: University of North Carolina Press, 1954, pp. 19–20.

Quinn, Arthur Hobson. *American Fiction: An Historical and Critical Survey*. New York: Appleton-Century, 1936, p. 497.

Schneider, Robert W. *Novelist to a Generation: The Life and Thought of Winston Churchill*. Bowling Green, Oh.: Bowling Green University Popular Press, 1976, pp. 45–55.

Titus, Warren I. *Winston Churchill*. New York: Twayne, 1963, pp. 46–52.

Underwood, John. "Winston Churchill and Civic Righteousness," in *Literature and Insurgency*. New York: Mitchell Kennerley, 1914, pp. 317–322.

Van Doren, Carl. *Contemporary American Novelists, 1900–1920*. New York: Macmillan, 1923, pp. 47–56.

The Crossing

Cooper, Frederic Taber. *Some American Story Tellers*. New York: Holt, 1911, pp. 59–61.

Hancock, Albert E. "The Historical Fiction of Winston Churchill," in *Outlook*. LXXVII (July 30, 1904), pp. 753–755.

Hofstadter, Richard and Beatrice Hofstadter. "Winston Churchill: A Study in the Popular Novel," in *American Quarterly*. II (Spring, 1950), pp. 12–28. Reprinted in *The American Experience: Approaches to the Study of the United States*. Edited by Hennig Cohen. Boston: Houghton Mifflin, 1968, pp. 226–242.

Quinn, Arthur Hobson. *American Fiction: An Historical and Critical Survey*. New York: Appleton-Century, 1936, pp. 497–498.

Schneider, Robert W. *Novelist to a Generation: The Life and Thought of Winston Churchill*. Bowling Green, Oh.: Bowling Green University Popular Press, 1976, pp. 67–81.

Titus, Warren I. *Winston Churchill*. New York: Twayne, 1963, pp. 53–59.

Underwood, John. "Winston Churchill and Civic Righteousness," in *Literature and Insurgency*. New York: Mitchell Kennerley, 1914, pp. 315–317.

Van Doren, Carl. *Contemporary American Novelists, 1900–1920*. New York: Macmillan, 1923, pp. 47–56.

Mr. Crewe's Career

Blotner, Joseph. *The Modern American Political Novel, 1900–1960.* Austin: University of Texas Press, 1966, pp. 32–33.

Hofstadter, Richard and Beatrice Hofstadter. "Winston Churchill: A Study in the Popular Novel," in *American Quarterly.* II (Spring, 1950), pp. 12–28. Reprinted in *The American Experience: Approaches to the Study of the United States.* Edited by Hennig Cohen. Boston: Houghton Mifflin, 1968, pp. 226–242.

Johnson, Stanley. "The Novelist and His Novels in Politics," in *World's Work.* XVII (December, 1908), pp. 11,016–11,120.

Knight, Grant C. *The Strenuous Age in American Literature.* Chapel Hill: University of North Carolina Press, 1954, pp. 170–171.

Milne, Gordon. *The American Political Novel.* Norman: University of Oklahoma Press, 1966, pp. 87–95.

Noble, David W. "The Lost Generation: Winston Churchill, Ernest Hemingway, F. Scott Fitzgerald," in *The Eternal Adam and the New World Garden.* New York: Braziller, 1968, pp. 140–144.

Quinn, Arthur Hobson. *American Fiction: An Historical and Critical Survey.* New York: Appleton-Century, 1936, p. 419.

Schneider, Robert W. *Novelist to a Generation: The Life and Thought of Winston Churchill.* Bowling Green, Oh.: Bowling Green University Popular Press, 1976, pp. 126–129.

————. "Winston Churchill: The Conservative Revolution," in *Five Novelists of the Progressive Era.* New York: Columbia University Press, 1965, pp. 205–251.

Speare, Morris Edmund. "Mr. Winston Churchill and the Novel of Political Reform," in *The Political Novel: Its Development in England and America.* New York: Oxford University Press, 1924, pp. 306–321.

Titus, Warren I. *Winston Churchill.* New York: Twayne, 1963, pp. 77–83.

Underwood, John. "Winston Churchill and Civic Righteousness," in *Literature and Insurgency.* New York: Mitchell Kennerley, 1914, pp. 331–340.

Walcutt, Charles C. *The Romantic Compromise in the Novels of Winston Churchill.* Ann Arbor: University of Michigan Press, 1951, pp. 14–20.

Richard Carvel

Cooper, Frederic Taber. *Some American Story Tellers.* New York: Holt, 1911, pp. 48–59.

Hofstadter, Richard and Beatrice Hofstadter. "Winston Churchill: A Study in the Popular Novel," in *American Quarterly.* II (Spring, 1950), pp. 12–28. Reprinted in *The American Experience: Approaches to the Study of the*

United States. Edited by Hennig Cohen. Boston: Houghton Mifflin, 1968, pp. 226–242.

Mott, Frank L. *Golden Multitudes: The Story of Best Sellers in the United States*. New York: Macmillan, 1947, pp. 212–213.

Pattee, Fred Lewis. *The New American Literature, 1890–1930*. New York: Century, 1930, pp. 93–98.

Quinn, Arthur Hobson. *American Fiction: An Historical and Critical Survey*. New York: Appleton-Century, 1936, pp. 496–497.

Schneider, Robert W. *Novelist to a Generation: The Life and Thought of Winston Churchill*. Bowling Green, Oh.: Bowling Green University Popular Press, 1976, pp. 31–37.

Titus, Warren I. *Winston Churchill*. New York: Twayne, 1963, pp. 36–44.

Underwood, John. "Winston Churchill and Civic Righteousness," in *Literature and Insurgency*. New York: Mitchell Kennerley, 1914, pp. 308–315.

COLLEY CIBBER
(1671–1757)

An Apology for the Life of Colley Cibber, Comedian

Ashley, Leonard R.N. *Colley Cibber.* New York: Twayne, 1965, pp. 130–139.

Barker, R.H. *Mr. Cibber of Drury Lane.* New York: Columbia University Press, 1939, pp. 194–203.

Britt, Albert. "Enter the Eighteenth Century," in his *Great Biographers.* New York: McGraw-Hill, 1936, pp. 63–64.

Dudden, F. Homes. *Henry Fielding: His Life, Works and Times,* Volume I. Oxford: Clarendon Press, 1952, pp. 257–259.

Eaton, Walter Prichard. "Colley Cibber as Critic," in his *The Actor's Heritage: Scenes from the Theatre of Yesterday and the Day Before.* Boston: Atlantic Monthly Press, 1924, pp. 155–198.

Fone, B.R.S. "Introduction," in *An Apology for the Life of Colley Cibber.* Ann Arbor: University of Michigan Press, 1968, pp. ix–xxvii.

Gosse, Edmund William. "Cibber's *Apology*," in his *Leaves and Fruit.* London: Heinemann, 1927, pp. 121–131.

Irving, H.B. "Colley Cibber's *Apology*," in *Nineteenth Century.* LVI (1904), pp. 451–468.

Johnson, Edgar. *One Mighty Torrent: The Drama of Biography.* New York: Macmillan, 1955, pp. 106–111, 118–119.

Spacks, Patricia Meyer. "The Sense of Audience: Samuel Richardson, Colley Cibber," in her *Imagining a Self: Autobiography and Novel in Eighteenth-Century England.* Cambridge: Harvard University Press, 1976, pp. 193–226.

The Careless Husband

Appleton, William W. "Introduction," in his *Colley Cibber: The Careless Husband.* Lincoln: University of Nebraska Press, 1966, pp. ix–xvi.

Ashley, Leonard R.N. *Colley Cibber.* New York: Twayne, 1965, pp. 55–59.

Barker, R.H. *Mr. Cibber of Drury Lane.* New York: Columbia University Press, 1939, pp. 47–53.

Bateson, F.W. *English Comic Drama, 1700–1750.* Oxford: Clarendon Press, 1929, pp. 26–31.

Boas, Frederick. *An Introduction to Eighteenth-Century Drama, 1700–1780.* Oxford: Clarendon Press, 1953, pp. 86–91.

Croissant, DeWitt C. "Studies in the Work of Colley Cibber," in *Bulletin of the University of Kansas Humanistic Studies.* I (October, 1912), pp. 49–52.

Habbema, D.M.E. *An Appreciation of Colley Cibber, Actor and Dramatist.* New York: Haskell House, 1967, pp. 63–78.

Hume, Robert D. *The Development of English Drama in the Late Seventeenth Century.* Oxford: Clarendon Press, 1976, pp. 469–470.

Nettleton, George H. *English Drama of the Restoration and Eighteenth Century* (1642–1780). New York: Macmillan, 1914, pp. 150–151.

Nicoll, Allardyce. *A History of Early Eighteenth Century Drama, 1700–1750.* Cambridge: Cambridge University Press, 1929, pp. 184–185.

Sullivan, Maurene. "Introduction," in *Colley Cibber: Three Sentimental Comedies.* New Haven, Conn.: Yale University Press, 1973, pp. xiii–li.

Thorndike, Ashley H. *English Comedy.* New York: Macmillan, 1929, pp. 354–356.

Tierney, James E. "Cibber's *The Careless Husband,*" in *Explicator.* XXXII (1973), item 17.

Ward, Adolphus William. *A History of English Dramatic Literature to the Death of Queen Anne,* Volume III. London: Macmillan, 1899, pp. 486–487.

WALTER VAN TILBURG CLARK
(1909–1971)

The City of Trembling Leaves

Barnett, Lincoln. "The Adventures of Timothy Hazard," in *New York Times Book Review*. L (May 27, 1945), p. 4.

Carpenter, Frederic I. "The West of Walter Van Tilburg Clark," in *College English*. XIII (February, 1952), pp. 243–248. Reprinted in *English Journal*. XLI (February, 1952), pp. 64–69.

Eisinger, Chester E. "The Fiction of Walter Van Tilburg Clark: Man and Nature in the West," in *Southwest Review*. XLIV (Summer, 1959), pp. 218–220. Reprinted in *Fiction of the Forties*. Chicago: University of Chicago Press, 1963, pp. 314–316.

Lee, L.L. *Walter Van Tilburg Clark*. Boise, Id.: Boise State University, 1973.

————. "Walter Van Tilburg Clark's Ambiguous American Dream," in *College English*. XXVI (February, 1965), pp. 382–387.

Milton, John R. "The Western Attitude: Walter Van Tilburg Clark," in *Critique*. II (Winter, 1959), pp. 62–64.

Portz, John. "Idea and Symbols in Walter Van Tilburg Clark," in *Accent*. XVII (Spring, 1957), pp. 112–128.

Stein, Paul. "Cowboys and Unicorns: The Novels of Walter Van Tilburg Clark," in *Western American Literature*. V (Winter, 1971), pp. 265–275.

Westbrook, Max. *Walter Van Tilburg Clark*. New York: Twayne, 1969, pp. 68–91.

Wilner, Herbert. "Walter Van Tilburg Clark," in *Western Review*. XX (Winter, 1956), pp. 103–122.

Wilson, Edmund. "White Peaks and Limpid Lakes: A Novel About Nevada," in *New Yorker*. XXI (May 26, 1945), pp. 75–77.

The Ox-Bow Incident

Andersen, Kenneth. "Character Portrayal in *The Ox-Bow Incident*," in *Western American Literature*. IV (Winter, 1970), pp. 287–298.

————. "Form in Walter Van Tilburg Clark's *The Ox-Bow Incident*," in *Western Review*. VI (Spring, 1969), pp. 19–25.

Banks, Loy Otis. "The Credible Literary West," in *Colorado Quarterly*. VIII (Summer, 1959), pp. 45–49.

Bates, Barclay W. "Clark's Man for All Seasons: The Achievement of Wholeness in *The Ox-Bow Incident*," in *Western American Literature*. III (Spring, 1968), pp. 37–49.

Carpenter, Frederic I. "The West of Walter Van Tilburg Clark," in *College English*. XIII (February, 1952), pp. 243–248. Reprinted in *English Journal*. XLI (February, 1952), pp. 64–69.

Cochran, Robert W. "Nature and the Nature of Man in *The Ox-Bow Incident*," in *Western American Literature*. V (Winter, 1971), pp. 253–264.

Eisinger, Chester E. "The Fiction of Walter Van Tilburg Clark: Man and Nature in the West," in *Southwest Review*. XLIV (Summer, 1959), pp. 215–218. Reprinted in *Fiction of the Forties*. Chicago: University of Chicago Press, 1963, pp. 311–314.

Gurian, Jay. "The Unwritten West," in *The American West*. II (Winter, 1965), pp. 61–62.

Houghton, Donald E. "The Failure of Speech in *The Ox-Bow Incident*," in *English Journal*. LIX (December, 1970), pp. 1245–1251.

Lee, L.L. *Walter Van Tilburg Clark*. Boise, Id.: Boise State University, 1973.

_____. "Walter Van Tilburg Clark's Ambiguous American Dream," in *College English*. XXVI (February, 1965), pp. 382–387.

Milton, John R. "The Western Attitude: Walter Van Tilburg Clark," in *Critique*. II (Winter, 1959), pp. 59–62.

Peterson, Levi S. "Tragedy and Western American Literature," in *Western American Literature*. VI (1972), pp. 243–249.

Portz, John. "Idea and Symbol in Walter Van Tilburg Clark," in *Accent*. XVII (Spring, 1957), pp. 112–128.

Redman, Ben Ray. "Magnificent Incident," in *Saturday Review of Literature*. XXIII (October 26, 1940), p. 6.

Stein, Paul. "Cowboys and Unicorns: The Novels of Walter Van Tilburg Clark," in *Western American Literature*. V (Winter, 1971), pp. 265–275.

Webb, Walter Prescott. "Afterword," in *The Ox-Bow Incident*. New York: Signet, 1960, pp. 219–224.

Westbrook, Max. "The Archetypal Ethic of *The Ox-Bow Incident*," in *Walter Van Tilburg Clark*. New York: Twayne, 1969, pp. 54–67.

Wilner, Herbert. "Walter Van Tilburg Clark," in *Western Review*. XX (Winter, 1956), pp. 103–122.

The Track of the Cat

Carpenter, Frederic I. "The West of Walter Van Tilburg Clark," in *College English*. XIII (February, 1952), pp. 243–248. Reprinted in *English Journal*. XLI (February, 1952), pp. 64–69.

Eisinger, Chester E. "The Fiction of Walter Van Tilburg Clark: Man and Nature in the West," in *Southwest Review*. XLIV (Summer, 1959), pp. 220–223. Reprinted in *Fiction of the Forties*. Chicago: University of Chicago Press, 1963, pp. 316–320.

Folsom, James K.   *The American Western Novel.* New Haven, Conn.: Yale University Press, 1966, pp. 172–176.

Fuller, Edmund.   "Man Against Relentless Evil," in *Saturday Review of Literature.* XXXII (June 4, 1949), pp. 9–10.

Hendricks, George D.   "Symbolism in Walter Van Tilburg Clark's *The Track of the Cat*," in *Southwestern American Literature.* III (1973), pp. 77–80.

Lee, L.L.   *Walter Van Tilburg Clark.* Boise, Id.: Boise State University, 1973.

————.   "Walter Van Tilburg Clark's Ambiguous American Dream," in *College English.* XXVI (February, 1965), pp. 382–387.

Milton, John.   "The American Novel: The Search for Home, Tradition, and Identity," in *Western Humanities Review.* XVI (Spring, 1962), pp. 179–180.

————.   "The Novel in the American West," in *South Dakota Review.* II (Autumn, 1964), pp. 68–70.

————.   "The Western Attitude: Walter Van Tilburg Clark," in *Critique.* II (Winter, 1959), pp. 64–69.

Portz, John.   "Idea and Symbol in Walter Van Tilburg Clark," in *Accent.* XVII (Spring, 1957), pp. 112–128.

Rogers, Douglas C.   "Man and Nature in Clark's *Track of the Cat*," in *South Dakota Review.* XII (1974), pp. 49–55.

Schorer, Mark.   "An Eloquent Novel of 'Place,' " in *New York Times Book Review.* LIV (June 5, 1949), pp. 1, 16.

Stein, Paul.   "Cowboys and Unicorns: The Novels of Walter Van Tilburg Clark," in *Western American Literature.* V (Winter, 1971), pp. 265–275.

Westbrook, Max.   *Walter Van Tilburg Clark.* New York: Twayne, 1969, pp. 92–110.

Wilner, Herbert.   "Walter Van Tilburg Clark," in *Western Review.* XX (Winter, 1956), pp. 103–122.

Young, Vernon.   "An American Dream and Its Parody," in *Arizona Quarterly.* VI (Summer, 1950), pp. 112–123.

The Watchful Gods

Brossard, Chandler.   "Noble Hawks and Neurotic Women," in *New American Mercury.* LXXII (February, 1951), pp. 230–234.

Carpenter, Frederic I.   "The West of Walter Van Tilburg Clark," in *College English.* XIII (February, 1952), pp. 243–248. Reprinted in *English Journal.* XLI (February, 1952), pp. 64–69.

DeVoto, Bernard.   "Tame Indian, Lone Sailor," in *New York Times Book Review.* LV (September 24, 1950), pp. 9, 18.

Eisinger, Chester E.   "The Fiction of Walter Van Tilburg Clark: Man and Nature in the West," in *Southwest Review.* XLIV (Summer, 1959), pp. 223–226.

Reprinted in his *Fiction of the Forties*. Chicago: University of Chicago Press, 1963, pp. 320–324.

Lee, L.L. *Walter Van Tilburg Clark*. Boise, Id.: Boise State University, 1973.

————. "Walter Van Tilburg Clark's Ambiguous American Dream," in *College English*. XXVI (February, 1965), pp. 382–387.

Milton, John. "The Western Attitude: Walter Van Tilburg Clark," in *Critique*. II (Winter, 1959), pp. 70–73.

Portz, John. "Idea and Symbol in Walter Van Tilburg Clark," in *Accent*. XVII (Spring, 1957), pp. 112–128.

West, Ray B. "The Nature Stage," in *Saturday Review of Literature*. XXXIII (September 30, 1950), pp. 17–18.

Westbrook, Max. *Walter Van Tilburg Clark*. New York: Twayne, 1969, pp. 112–124.

Wilner, Herbert. "Walter Van Tilburg Clark," in *Western Review*. XX (Winter, 1956), pp. 103–122.

Young, Vernon. "God's Without Heroes: The Tentative Myth of Walter Van Tilburg Clark," in *Arizona Quarterly*. VII (Summer, 1951), pp. 110–119.

ARTHUR HUGH CLOUGH
(1819–1861)

"Ambarvalia"

Armstrong, Isobel. *Arthur Hugh Clough.* London: Longmans, Green, 1962, pp. 17–20.

Chorley, Katherine. *Arthur Hugh Clough, the Uncommitted Mind: A Study of His Life and Poetry.* Oxford: Clarendon Press, 1962, pp. 174–181.

Hardy, Barbara. "Clough's Self-Consciousness," in *The Major Victorian Poets: Reconsiderations.* Edited by Isobel Armstrong. Lincoln: University of Nebraska Press, 1969, pp. 257–259.

Harris, Wendell V. *Arthur Hugh Clough.* New York: Twayne, 1970, pp. 52–65.

Houghton, Walter E. *The Poetry of Clough: An Essay in Revaluation.* New Haven, Conn.: Yale University Press, 1963, pp. 2–3.

Levy, Goldie. *Arthur Hugh Clough, 1819–1861.* London: Sidgwick & Jackson, 1938, pp. 87–93.

Osborne, James Insley. *Arthur Hugh Clough.* Boston: Houghton Mifflin, 1920, pp. 67–73.

Waddington, Samuel. *Arthur Hugh Clough: A Monograph.* London: George Bell, 1883, pp. 129–151.

Williams, David. *Too Quick Despairer: A Life of Arthur Hugh Clough.* London: Rupert Hart-Davis, 1969, pp. 59–65.

"Amours de Voyage"

Biswas, Robindra Kumar. *Arthur Hugh Clough: Towards a Reconsideration.* Oxford: Clarendon Press, 1972, pp. 298–321.

Brooke, Stopford A. *Four Victorian Poets.* New York: Putnam's, 1908, pp. 38–41.

Chorley, Katherine. *Arthur Hugh Clough, the Uncommitted Mind: A Study of His Life and Poetry.* Oxford: Clarendon Press, 1962, pp. 191–200.

Goode, John. " 'Amours de Voyage': *The Aqueous Poem,*" in *The Major Victorian Poets: Reconsiderations.* Edited by Isobel Armstrong. Lincoln: University of Nebraska Press, 1969, pp. 275–298.

Greenberger, Evelyn Barish. *Arthur Hugh Clough: The Growth of a Poet's Mind.* Cambridge, Mass.: Harvard University Press, 1970, pp. 172–173.

Harris, Wendell V. *Arthur Hugh Clough.* New York: Twayne, 1970, pp. 66–79.

Houghton, Walter E. *The Poetry of Clough: An Essay in Revaluation.* New Haven, Conn.: Yale University Press, 1963, pp. 119–125.

Levy, Goldie. *Arthur Hugh Clough, 1819–1861.* London: Sidgwick & Jackson, 1938, pp. 197–201.

Osborne, James Insley. *Arthur Hugh Clough.* Boston: Houghton Mifflin, 1920, pp. 114–128.

Parry, Graham. "The Unsentimental Traveler's 'Amours de Voyage,' " in *Caliban.* XIII (1976), pp. 55–67.

Sharp, Amy. *Victorian Poets.* Port Washington, N.Y.: Kennikat, 1970, pp. 128–130.

Timko, Michael. *Innocent Victorian: The Satiric Poetry of Arthur Hugh Clough.* Athens: Ohio University Press, 1966, pp. 137–152.

Waddington, Samuel. *Arthur Hugh Clough: A Monograph.* London: George Bell, 1883, pp. 252–275.

Williams, David. *Too Quick Despairer: A Life of Arthur Hugh Clough.* London: Rupert Hart-Davis, 1969, pp. 83–92.

"Blank Misgivings"

Biswas, Robindra Kumar. *Arthur Hugh Clough: Towards a Reconsideration.* Oxford: Clarendon Press, 1972, pp. 102–104.

Chorley, Katherine. *Arthur Hugh Clough, the Uncommitted Mind: A Study of His Life and Poetry.* Oxford: Clarendon Press, 1962, pp. 339–340, 344–345.

Harris, Wendell V. *Arthur Hugh Clough.* New York: Twayne, 1970, pp. 62–63.

Houghton, Walter E. *The Poetry of Clough: An Essay in Revaluation.* New Haven, Conn.: Yale University Press, 1963, pp. 31–32, 175–176.

Osborne, James Insley. *Arthur Hugh Clough.* Boston: Houghton Mifflin, 1920, pp. 52–55.

Timko, Michael. *Innocent Victorian: The Satiric Poetry of Arthur Hugh Clough.* Athens: Ohio University Press, 1966, pp. 26–27.

The Bothie of Tober-na-Vuolich

Biswas, Robindra Kumar. *Arthur Hugh Clough: Towards a Reconsideration.* Oxford: Clarendon Press, 1972, pp. 263–286.

Brooke, Stopford A. *Four Victorian Poets.* New York: Putnam's, 1908, pp. 45–48.

Chorley, Katherine. *Arthur Hugh Clough, The Uncommitted Mind: A Study of His Life and Poetry.* Oxford: Clarendon Press, 1962, pp. 147–169.

Greenberger, Evelyn Barish. *Arthur Hugh Clough: The Growth of a Poet's Mind.* Cambridge, Mass.: Harvard University Press, 1970, pp. 173–174.

Hardy, Barbara. "Clough's Self-Consciousness," in *The Major Victorian Poets: Reconsiderations*. Edited by Isobel Armstrong. Lincoln: University of Nebraska Press, 1969, pp. 268–269.

Harris, Wendell V. *Arthur Hugh Clough*. New York: Twayne, 1970, pp. 39–50.

Houghton, Walter C. *The Poetry of Clough: An Essay in Revaluation*. New Haven, Conn.: Yale University Press, 1963, pp. 92–118.

Levy, Goldie. *Arthur Hugh Clough, 1819–1861*. London: Sidgwick & Jackson, 1938, pp. 43–50, 78–87, 93–98.

McGrail, John P. "Three Image Motifs in Arthur Hugh Clough's *The Bothie of Tober-na-Vuolich*," in *Victorian Poetry*. XIII (1975), pp. 75–78.

Osborne, James Insley. *Arthur Hugh Clough*. Boston: Houghton Mifflin, 1920, pp. 94–111.

Rutland, R.B. "The Genesis of Clough's *Bothie*," in *Victorian Poetry*. XI (1973), pp. 277–284.

————. "Some Notes on the Highland Setting of Clough's *Bothie*," in *Victorian Poetry*. XIV (1976), pp. 125–133.

Sharp, Amy. *Victorian Poets*. Port Washington, N.Y.: Kennikat, 1970, pp. 125–128.

Timko, Michael. *Innocent Victorian: The Satiric Poetry of Arthur Hugh Clough*. Athens: Ohio University Press, 1966, pp. 126–137.

Waddington, Samuel. *Arthur Hugh Clough: A Monograph*. London: George Bell, 1883, pp. 152–194.

Williams, David. *Too Quick Despairer: A Life of Arthur Hugh Clough*. London: Rupert Hart-Davis, 1969, pp. 72–79.

Dipsychus

Armstrong, Isobel. *Arthur Hugh Clough*. London: Longmans, Green, 1962, pp. 27–32.

Biswas, Robindra Kumar. *Arthur Hugh Clough: Towards a Reconsideration*. Oxford: Clarendon Press, 1972, pp. 375–416.

Brooke, Stopford A. *Four Victorian Poets*. New York: Putnam's, 1908, pp. 48–49.

Chorley, Katherine. *Arthur Hugh Clough, the Uncommitted Mind: A Study of His Life and Poetry*. Oxford: Clarendon Press, 1962, pp. 251–261.

Greenberger, Evelyn Barish. *Arthur Hugh Clough: The Growth of a Poet's Mind*. Cambridge, Mass.: Harvard University Press, 1970, pp. 174–177.

Hardy, Barbara. "Clough's Self-Consciousness," in *The Major Victorian Poets: Reconsiderations*. Edited by Isobel Armstrong. Lincoln: University of Nebraska Press, 1969, pp. 256–257, 266–267.

Harris, Wendell V. *Arthur Hugh Clough*. New York: Twayne, 1970, pp. 80–92.

Houghton, Walter E. *The Poetry of Clough: An Essay in Revaluation*. New Haven, Conn.: Yale University Press, 1963, pp. 156–207.

Levy, Goldie. *Arthur Hugh Clough, 1819–1861*. London: Sidgwick & Jackson, 1938, pp. 125–127, 201–214.

Lewis, C. Day. *The Lyric Impulse*. Cambridge, Mass.: Harvard University Press, 1965, pp. 99–100.

Osborne, James Insley. *Arthur Hugh Clough*. Boston: Houghton Mifflin, 1920, pp. 129–154.

Ryals, Clyde de L. "An Interpretation of Clough's *Dipsychus*," in *Victorian Poetry*. I (August, 1963), pp. 182–188.

Sharp, Amy. *Victorian Poets*. Port Washington, N.Y.: Kennikat, 1970, pp. 130–133.

Timko, Michael. *Innocent Victorian: The Satiric Poetry of Arthur Hugh Clough*. Athens: Ohio University Press, 1966, pp. 152–168.

Waddington, Samuel. *Arthur Hugh Clough: A Monograph*. London: George Bell, 1883, pp. 214–251.

Williams, David. *Too Quick Despairer: A Life of Arthur Hugh Clough*. London: Rupert Hart-Davis, 1969, pp. 94–103.

"Epi-strauss-ium"

Castan, C. "Clough's 'Epi-strauss-ium' and Carlyle," in *Victorian Poetry*. IV (1966), pp. 54–56.

Forsyth, R.A. "Herbert, Clough and Their Church-Windows," in *Victorian Poetry*. VII (Spring, 1969), pp. 20–26.

Houghton, Walter E. *The Poetry of Clough: An Essay in Revaluation*. New Haven, Conn.: Yale University Press, 1963.

Timko, Michael. *Innocent Victorian: The Satiric Poetry of Arthur Hugh Clough*. Athens: Ohio University Press, 1966, p. 48.

"Mari Magno"

Armstrong, Isobel. *Arthur Hugh Clough*. London: Longmans, Green, 1962, pp. 37–39.

Biswas, Robindra Kumar. *Arthur Hugh Clough: Towards a Reconsideration*. Oxford: Clarendon Press, 1972, pp. 461–469.

Brooke, Stopford A. *Four Victorian Poets*. New York: Putnam's, 1908, pp. 42–45.

Chorley, Katherine. *Arthur Hugh Clough, the Uncommitted Mind: A Study of His Life and Poetry*. Oxford: Clarendon Press, 1962, pp. 261–263, 319–322.

Harris, Wendell V.   *Arthur Hugh Clough.* New York: Twayne, 1970, pp. 132–138.

Houghton, Walter E.   *The Poetry of Clough: An Essay in Revaluation.* New Haven, Conn.: Yale University Press, 1963, pp. 208–224.

Levy, Goldie.   *Arthur Hugh Clough, 1819–1861.* London: Sidgwick & Jackson, 1938, pp. 43–46, 182–192, 204–205.

Osborne, James Insley.   *Arthur Hugh Clough.* Boston: Houghton Mifflin, 1920, pp. 172–175.

Timko, Michael.   *Innocent Victorian: The Satiric Poetry of Arthur Hugh Clough.* Athens: Ohio University Press, 1966, pp. 54–55.

Waddington, Samuel.   *Arthur Hugh Clough: A Monograph.* London: George Bell, 1883, pp. 275–287.

Williams, David.   *Too Quick Despairer: A Life of Arthur Hugh Clough.* London: Rupert Hart-Davis, 1969, pp. 133–139.

The Poetry of Clough

Armstrong, Isobel.   *Arthur Hugh Clough.* London: Longmans, Green, 1962.

Biswas, Robindra Kumar.   *Arthur Hugh Clough: Towards a Reconsideration.* Oxford: Clarendon Press, 1972, pp. 196–416.

Brooke, Stopford A.   *Four Victorian Poets.* New York: Putnam's, 1908, pp. 30–55.

Castan, Constantine.   "The Marriage of Epithalamium and Elegy in a Poem by Clough," in *Victorian Poetry.* X (1972), pp. 145–160.

Chorley, Katherine.   *Arthur Hugh Clough, the Uncommitted Mind: A Study of His Life and Poetry.* Oxford: Clarendon Press, 1962.

Fairchild, Hoxie Neale.   *Religious Trends in English Poetry,* Volume IV, 1830–1880. New York: Colgate University Press, 1957, pp. 505–527.

Greenberger, Evelyn Barish.   *Arthur Hugh Clough: The Growth of a Poet's Mind.* Cambridge, Mass.: Harvard University Press, 1970, pp. 167–180.

Hardy, Barbara.   "Clough's Self-Consciousness," in *The Major Victorian Poets: Reconsiderations.* Edited by Isobel Armstrong. Lincoln: University of Nebraska Press, 1969, pp. 253–274.

Harris, Wendell V.   *Arthur Hugh Clough.* New York: Twayne, 1970.

Hopkins, Kenneth.   *English Poetry: A Short History.* Philadelphia: J.B. Lippincott, 1962, pp. 445–447, 450–451.

Houghton, Walter E.   *The Poetry of Clough: An Essay in Revaluation.* New Haven, Conn.: Yale University Press, 1963.

Levy, Goldie.   *Arthur Hugh Clough, 1819–1861.* London: Sidgwick & Jackson, 1938.

Miyoshi, Masao. "Clough's Poems of Self-Irony," in *Studies in English Literature, 1500–1900.* V (1965), pp. 691–704.

Osborne, James Insley. *Arthur Hugh Clough.* Boston: Houghton Mifflin, 1920.

Scott, Patrick Grieg. "The Victorianism of Clough," in *Victorian Poetry.* XVI (1978), pp. 32–42.

Sharp, Amy. *Victorian Poets.* Port Washington, N.Y.: Kennikat, 1970, pp. 121–136.

Timko, Michael. *Innocent Victorian: The Satiric Poetry of Arthur Hugh Clough.* Athens: Ohio University Press, 1966.

Williams, David. *Too Quick Despairer: A Life of Arthur Hugh Clough.* London: Rupert Hart-Davis, 1969.

"Say Not the Struggle Nought Availeth"

Armstrong, Isobel. *Arthur Hugh Clough.* London: Longmans, Green, 1962, pp. 15–17.

Chorley, Katherine. *Arthur Hugh Clough, the Uncommitted Mind: A Study of His Life and Poetry.* Oxford: Clarendon Press, 1962, p. 248.

Cooper, Charles W. and John Holmes. *Preface to Poetry.* New York: Harcourt, Brace, 1946, pp. 177–181.

Harris, Wendell V. *Arthur Hugh Clough.* New York: Twayne, 1970, pp. 146–148.

Houghton, Walter E. *The Poetry of Clough: An Essay in Revaluation.* New Haven, Conn.: Yale University Press, 1963, pp. 47–48.

Howard, William. " 'Say Not the Struggle Nought Availeth,' " in *Explicator.* XV (March, 1957), item 39.

Levy, Goldie. *Arthur Hugh Clough, 1819–1861.* London: Sidgwick & Jackson, 1938, pp. 110–111, 204–217.

Millett, Fred R. *Reading Poetry: A Method of Analysis with Selections for Study.* New York: Harper, 1950, pp. 17–18.

Williams, David. *Too Quick Despairer: A Life of Arthur Hugh Clough.* London: Rupert Hart-Davis, 1969, pp. 145–147.

JEAN COCTEAU
(1889–1963)

The Holy Terrors

Brown, Frederick. *An Impersonation of Angels.* New York: Viking, 1968, pp. 284–285, 296–300, 330–332.

Fifield, William. *Jean Cocteau.* New York: Columbia University Press, 1974, pp. 19–20.

Fowlie, Wallace. *Jean Cocteau; The History of a Poet's Age.* Bloomington: Indiana University Press, 1966, pp. 106–110.

Furbank, P.N. "Maugham and Cocteau," in *Listener.* LXXI (January 30, 1964), pp. 209–210.

Kaplan, Jane P. "Complexity of Character and the Overlapping of a Single Personality in Cocteau's *Les Enfants Terribles*," in *Australian Journal of French Studies.* XII (1975), pp. 89–104.

Knapp, Bettina Leibowitz. *Jean Cocteau.* New York: Twayne, 1970, pp. 119–124.

Knowles, Dorothy. *French Drama of the Inter-War Years, 1918–39.* London: George G. Harrap, 1967, pp. 60–61.

Maclean, Mary. "The Artificial Paradise and the Lost Paradise: Baudelarian Themes in Cocteau's *Les Enfants Terribles*," in *Australian Journal of French Studies.* XII (1975), pp. 57–88.

McNab, James P. "Mythical Space in *Les Enfants Terribles*," in *French Studies.* VI (1974), pp. 162–170.

Mudrick, Marvin. "Cocteau's Poem of Childhood," in *Spectrum.* I (Fall, 1957), pp. 25–33.

Oxenhandler, Neal. *Scandal and Parade: The Theater of Jean Cocteau.* New Brunswick, N.J.: Rutgers University Press, 1957, pp. 200–211.

Roudiez, Leon S. "Cocteau's *Les Enfants Terribles* as a Blind Text," in *Mosaic.* V (1972), pp. 159–166.

Steegmuller, Francis. *Cocteau; A Biography.* Boston: Little, Brown, 1970, pp. 395–399.

The Infernal Machine

Aylen, Leo. *Greek Tragedy and the Modern World.* London: Methuen, 1964, pp. 260, 263–265.

Belli, Angela. *Ancient Greek Myths and Modern Drama; A Study in Continuity.* New York: New York University Press, 1971, pp. 3–19.

Bentley, Eric Russell. *The Playwright as Thinker.* Cleveland: World, 1964, pp. 193, 202.

Bishop, Thomas. *Pirandello and the French Theater.* New York: New York University Press, 1960, pp. 106–107.

Brown, Frederick. *An Impersonation of Angels.* New York: Viking, 1968, pp. 306, 309–311.

Chiari, Joseph. *The Contemporary French Theatre; The Flight from Naturalism.* New York: Macmillan, 1959, pp. 102–106.

————. *Landmarks of Contemporary Drama.* London: Herbert Jenkins, 1965, pp. 50–51, 53.

Dickinson, Hugh. *Myth on the Modern Stage.* Urbana: University of Illinois Press, 1969, pp. 96–112.

Fergusson, Francis. *Idea of a Theater, a Study of Ten Plays; The Art of Drama in Changing Perspective.* Princeton, N.J.: Princeton University Press, 1949, pp. 194–228.

————. *"The Infernal Machine*: The Myth Behind the Modern City," in *Oedipus, Myth and Dramatic Form.* Edited by James L. Sanderson. Boston: Houghton Mifflin, 1968, pp. 330–335.

Feynman, Alberta E. *"The Infernal Machine,* Hamlet and Ernest Jones," in *Modern Drama.* VI (May, 1963), pp. 72–83.

Fifield, William. *Jean Cocteau.* New York: Columbia University Press, 1974, pp. 42–46.

Fowlie, Wallace. *Dionysus in Paris; A Guide to Contemporary French Theater.* New York: Meridian Books, 1960, pp. 82–85.

————. *Jean Cocteau; The History of a Poet's Age.* Bloomington, Ind.: Indiana University Press, 1966, pp. 64–70.

Gassner, John. *The Theatre in Our Times.* New York: Crown, 1954, pp. 184–194.

Grossvogel, David I. *The Self-Conscious Stage in Modern French Drama.* New York: Columbia University Press, 1958, pp. 59–62.

Knapp, Bettina Liebowitz. *Jean Cocteau.* New York: Twayne, 1970, pp. 102–104, 126–127, 159–160.

Knowles, Dorothy. *French Drama of the Inter-War Years, 1918–39.* London: George G. Harrap, 1967, pp. 53–57.

Lumley, Frederick. *New Trends in Twentieth Century Drama: A Survey Since Ibsen and Shaw.* London: Oxford University Press, 1967, pp. 108–109, 111.

MacCarthy, Desmond. *"The Infernal Machine,"* in *New Statesman and Nation.* XX (September 21, 1940), pp. 281–282.

Moore, Marianne. *Predilections.* New York: Viking, 1955, pp. 126–129.

Oxenhandler, Neal. *Scandal and Parade: The Theatre of Jean Cocteau.* New Brunswick, N.J.: Rutgers University Press, 1957, pp. 129–148, 216–220.

Steegmuller, Francis. *Cocteau; A Biography.* Boston: Little, Brown, 1970, pp. 430–431.

Wimsatt, William Kurtz. *Literary Criticism; Idea and Act.* Berkeley: University of California Press, 1974, pp. 590–601.

Wyatt, Euphemia. *"The Infernal Machine,"* in *Catholic World.* CLXXXVII (April, 1958), p. 69.

Orpheus

Aylen, Leo. *Greek Tragedy and the Modern World.* London: Methuen, 1964, pp. 260–263.

Bentley, Eric Russell. *The Playwright as Thinker.* Cleveland: World, 1964, pp. 193, 195.

Brown, Frederick. *An Impersonation of Angels.* New York: Viking, 1968, pp. 263–266.

Chiari, Joseph. *The Contemporary French Theatre; The Flight From Naturalism.* New York: Macmillan, 1959, pp. 109–111.

Dickinson, Hugh. *Myth on the Modern Stage.* Urbana: University of Illinois Press, 1969, pp. 85–91.

Fifield, William. *Jean Cocteau.* New York: Columbia University Press, 1974, pp. 29–33.

Fowlie, Wallace. *Age of Surrealism.* New York: Swallow Press, 1950, pp. 125–129.

_____. *Dionysus in Paris; A Guide to Contemporary French Theater.* New York: Meridian Books, 1960, pp. 78–82.

_____. *Jean Cocteau; The History of a Poet's Age.* Bloomington, Ind.: Indiana University Press, 1966, pp. 61–64, 110–114.

Grossvogel, David I. *The Self-Conscious Stage in Modern French Drama.* New York: Columbia University Press, 1958, pp. 54–59.

Ingham, Patricia. "The Renaissance of Hell," in *Listener.* LXII (September 3, 1959), pp. 349–351.

Kauffmann, Stanley. "The Truth and Where to Find It," in *New Republic.* CXLVI (May 14, 1962), pp. 34, 36–37.

Knapp, Bettina Liebowitz. *Jean Cocteau.* New York: Twayne, 1970, pp. 78–79, 81–83.

Knowles, Dorothy. *French Drama of the Inter-War Years, 1918–39.* London: George G. Harrap, 1967, pp. 52–53.

Lee, M. Owen. "Orpheus and Eurydice: Some Modern Versions," in *Classical Journal.* LVI (1960/1961), pp. 307–313.

Long, Chester Clayton. "Cocteau's *Orphee*: From Myth to Drama to Film," in *Quarterly Journal of Speech.* LI (1965), pp. 311–325.

Lumley, Frederick. *New Trends in the Twentieth Century Drama: A Survey Since Ibsen and Shaw.* London: Oxford University Press, 1967, pp. 105–114.

MacCarthy, Desmond. *Drama.* London: Putnam's, 1940, pp. 184–189.

————. *Humanities.* London: Oxford University Press, 1954, pp. 105–109.

Moore, Harry T. *Twentieth Century French Literature to World War II,* Volume 1. Carbondale: Southern Illinois University Press, 1966, pp. 120–125.

Nathan, George Jean. *Theatre Book of the Year, 1946–1947; A Record and an Interpretation.* New York: Knopf, 1947, pp. 41–42.

Oxenhandler, Neal. *Scandal and Parade: The Theater of Jean Cocteau.* New Brunswick, N.J.: Rutgers University Press, 1957, pp. 79–103.

Porter, David H. "Ancient Myth and Modern Play; A Significant Counterpoint," in *Classical Bulletin.* XLVIII (November, 1971), pp. 1–9.

Sainer, Arthur. *The Sleepwalker and the Assassin, a View of the Contemporary Theatre.* New York: Bridgehead Books, 1964, pp. 54–55.

Steegmuller, Francis. *Cocteau; A Biography.* Boston: Little, Brown, 1970, pp. 353–356, 363–364, 368–371.

SAMUEL TAYLOR COLERIDGE
(1772–1834)

Biographia Literaria

Abrams, M.H. "Coleridge and the Romantic Vision of the World," in *Coleridge's Variety: Bicentenary Studies.* Edited by John Beer. Pittsburgh: University of Pittsburgh Press, 1974, pp. 102–133.

Appleyard, J.A. "Coleridge and Criticism: I. Critical Theory," in *Writers and Their Background: S.T. Coleridge.* Edited by R.L. Brett. London: Bell, 1971, pp. 135–140.

Barth, J. Robert. *The Symbolic Imagination: Coleridge and the Romantic Tradition.* Princeton, N.J.: Princeton University Press, 1977, pp. 22–23, 44–49.

Bate, Walter Jackson. *Coleridge.* New York: Macmillan, 1968, pp. 130–131.

Brett, R.L. *Fancy & Imagination.* London: Methuen, 1969, pp. 31–53.

Cooke, Michael G. "Quisque Sui Faber: Coleridge in the *Biographia Literaria*," in *Philological Quarterly.* L (1971), pp. 208–229.

Fields, Beverly. *Reality's Dark Dream: Dejection in Coleridge.* Kent, Oh.: Kent State University Press, 1967, pp. 104–108.

Fruman, Norman. *Coleridge, the Damaged Archangel.* New York: George Braziller, 1971, pp. 69–107.

Gilpin, George H. "Coleridge and the Spiral of Poetic Thought," in *Studies in English Literature, 1500–1900.* XII (1972), pp. 639–652.

————. "Coleridge: The Pleasure of Truth," in *South Central Bulletin.* XXX (1970), pp. 191–194.

Harding, Anthony John. *Coleridge and the Idea of Love: Aspects of Relationship in Coleridge's Thought and Writing.* London: Cambridge University Press, 1974, pp. 36–37, 84–85, 179–180, 200–201.

McFarland, Thomas. *Coleridge and the Pantheist Tradition.* Oxford: Clarendon Press, 1969, pp. 40–44.

————. "The Origin and Significance of Coleridge's Theory of Secondary Imagination," in *New Perspectives on Coleridge and Wordsworth: Selected Papers from the English Institute.* Edited by Geoffrey H. Hartman. New York: Columbia University Press, 1972, pp. 195–226.

Mallette, Richard. "Narrative Technique in the *Biographia Literaria*," in *Modern Language Review.* LXX (1975), pp. 32–40.

Prickett, Stephen. *Coleridge and Wordsworth: The Poetry of Growth.* Cambridge: University Press, 1970, pp. 70–81.

Read, Herbert. "Coleridge as Critic," in *Coleridge: A Collection of Critical Essays*. Edited by Kathleen Coburn. Englewood Cliffs, N.J.: Prentice-Hall, 1967, pp. 94–111.

Shaffer, Elinor S. "The 'Postulates in Philosophy' in the *Biographia Literaria*," in *Comparative Literature Studies*. VII (1970), pp. 297–313.

Teich, Nathaniel. "Coleridge's *Biographia* and the Contemporary Controversy About Style," in *The Wordsworth Circle*. III (1971), pp. 61–70.

Whalley, George. "On Reading Coleridge," in *Writers and Their Background: S.T. Coleridge*. Edited by R.L. Brett. London: Bell, 1971, pp. 32–35.

Willey, Basil. *Samuel Taylor Coleridge*. New York: Norton, 1972, pp. 188–205.

Yarlott, Geoffrey. *Coleridge & the Abyssinian Maid*. London: Methuen, 1967, pp. 280–282.

Christabel

Adair, Patricia M. *The Waking Dream: A Study of Coleridge's Poetry*. New York: Barnes & Noble: 1967, pp. 144–171.

Adlard, John. "The Quantock *Christabel*," in *Philological Quarterly*. L (1971), pp. 230–238.

Alley, Alvin D. "Coleridge and Existentialism," in *Southern Humanities Review*. II (Fall, 1968), pp. 459–460.

Angus, Douglas. "The Theme of Love and Guilt in Coleridge's Three Major Poems," in *Journal of English and Germanic Philology*. LIX (October, 1960), pp. 655–668.

Basler, Roy P. "Christabel," in *Sewanee Review*. LI (Winter, 1943), pp. 73–95.

————. *Sex, Symbolism, and Psychology in Literature*. New Brunswick, N.J.: Rutgers University Press, 1948, pp. 25–51.

Bate, Walter Jackson. *Coleridge*. New York: Macmillan, 1968, pp. 65–74.

Beer, J.B. *Coleridge the Visionary*. New York: Collier, 1962, pp. 185–208.

Cornwell, John. *Coleridge: Poet and Revolutionary, 1772–1804; A Critical Biography*. London: Allen Lane, 1973, pp. 287–291.

Farrison, W. Edward. "Coleridge's *Christabel*, 'The Conclusion to Part II,' " in *College Language Association Journal*. V (December, 1961), pp. 83–94.

Fields, Beverly. *Reality's Dark Dream: Dejection in Coleridge*. Kent, Oh.: Kent State University Press, 1967, pp. 56–86.

Flory, Wendell Stallard. "Fathers and Daughters: Coleridge and *Christabel*," in *Women & Literature: A Journal of Women Writers and the Literary Treatment of Women up to 1900*. III (1975), pp. 5–15.

Harding, Anthony John. *Coleridge and the Idea of Love: Aspects of Relationship in Coleridge's Thought and Writing.* London: Cambridge University Press, 1974, pp. 66–74.

Holstein, Michael E. "Coleridge's *Christabel* as Psychodrama: Five Perspectives on the Intruder," in *Wordsworth Circle.* VII (1976), pp. 119–128.

Hunting, Constance. "Another Look at 'The Conclusion of Part II' of *Christabel,"* in *English Language Notes.* XII (1975), pp. 171–176.

Radley, Virginia L. "*Christabel*: Directions Old and New," in *Studies in English Literature, 1500–1900.* IV (Autumn, 1964), pp. 531–541.

Spatz, Jonas. "The Mystery of Eros: Sexual Initiation in Coleridge's *Christabel,"* in *PMLA.* XC (1975), pp. 107–116.

Tomlinson, Charles. "*Christabel,"* in *Interpretations: Essays on Twelve English Poems.* Edited by John Wain. London: Routledge and Kegan Paul, 1955, pp. 103–112.

Twitchell, James. "Coleridge's *Christabel,"* in *Explicator.* XXXV (1976), pp. 28–29.

Walsh, William. *Coleridge: The Work and the Relevance.* New York: Barnes & Noble, 1967, pp. 109–112.

Wormhoudt, Arthur. *The Demon Lover: A Psychoanalytic Approach to Literature.* New York: Exposition, 1949, pp. 29–42.

Yarlott, Geoffrey. *Coleridge & the Abyssinian Maid.* London: Methuen, 1967, pp. 176–202.

"Dejection: An Ode"

Bate, Walter Jackson. *Coleridge.* New York: Macmillan, 1968, pp. 106–110.

Bowra, C.M. *The Romantic Imagination.* Cambridge, Mass.: Harvard University Press, 1949, pp. 85–92.

Brett, R.L. "Coleridge and Wordsworth," in *Writers and Their Background: S.T. Coleridge.* Edited by R.L. Brett. London: Bell, 1971, pp. 186–188.

Fields, Beverly. *Reality's Dark Dream: Dejection in Coleridge.* Kent, Oh.: Kent State University Press, 1967, pp. 105–167.

Fogle, Richard H. "The Dejection of Coleridge's Ode," in *Journal of English Literary History.* XVII (March, 1950), pp. 71–77.

Fruman, Norman. *Coleridge, the Damaged Archangel.* New York: George Braziller, 1971, pp. 422–429.

Gay, R.M. " 'Dejection: An Ode,' " in *Explicator.* II (November, 1943), item 14.

Harding, Anthony John. *Coleridge and the Idea of Love: Aspects of Relationship in Coleridge's Thought and Writing.* London: Cambridge University Press, 1974, pp. 74–78.

Jones, A.R. "Coleridge and Poetry: I. The Conversational and Other Poems," in *Writers and Their Background: S.T. Coleridge.* Edited by R.L. Brett. London: Bell, 1971, pp. 116–122.

Knight, G. Wilson. *The Starlit Dome: Essays in the Poetry of Vision.* New York: Oxford University Press, 1941, pp. 105–107.

Lefebure, Molly. *Samuel Taylor Coleridge: A Bondage of Opium.* New York: Stein and Day, 1974, pp. 355–358.

Mays, Morley J. " 'Dejection: An Ode,' " in *Explicator.* II (February, 1943), item 27.

Parker, Reeve. *Coleridge's Meditative Art.* Ithaca, N.Y.: Cornell University Press, 1975, pp. 180–209.

Prickett, Stephen. *Coleridge and Wordsworth: The Poetry of Growth.* Cambridge: Cambridge University Press, 1970, pp. 110–113.

Smith, James. "The Poetry of Coleridge," in *Scrutiny.* VIII (March, 1940), pp. 416–420.

Stallknecht, Newton Phelps. "The Doctrine of Coleridge's *Dejection* and Its Relation to Wordsworth's Philosophy," in *PMLA.* XLIX (March, 1934), pp. 196–207.

Thompson, William I. "Collapsed Universe and Structured Poem: Essay in Whiteheadian Criticism," in *College English.* XXVIII (October, 1966), pp. 27–29.

Walsh, William. *Coleridge: The Work and the Relevance.* New York: Barnes & Noble, 1967, pp. 131–136.

Yarlott, Geoffrey. *Coleridge & the Abyssianian Maid.* London: Methuen, 1967, pp. 248–274.

"Kubla Khan"

Adair, Patricia M. *The Waking Dream: A Study of Coleridge's Poetry.* New York: Barnes & Noble, 1967, pp. 108–143.

Angus, Douglas. "The Theme of Love and Guilt in Coleridge's Three Major Poems," in *Journal of English and Germanic Philology.* LIX (October, 1960), pp. 655–668.

Bate, Walter Jackson. *Coleridge.* New York: Macmillan, 1968, pp. 75–84.

Beer, John. "Coleridge and Poetry: I. Poems of the Supernatural," in *Writers and Their Background: S.T. Coleridge.* Edited by R.L. Brett. London: Bell, 1971, pp. 60–70.

————. *Coleridge the Visionary.* New York: Collier, 1962, pp. 209–240.

Bodkin, Maud. *Archetypal Patterns in Poetry.* London: Oxford University Press, 1934, pp. 90–116.

Cornwell, John. *Coleridge: Poet and Revolutionary, 1772–1804; A Critical Biography.* London: Allen Lane, 1973, pp. 181–190.

England, A.B. " 'Kubla Khan' Again: The Ocean, the Caverns, and the Ancestral Voices," in *Ariel: A Review of International English Literature*. IV (1973), pp. 63–72.

Fleissner, Robert F. "Shakespeare Again in Xanadu," in *Research Studies*. XLIII (1975), pp. 193–196.

Fogle, Richard Harter. "The Romantic Unity of 'Kubla Khan,' " in *College English*. XIII (October, 1951), pp. 13–18.

Gerber, Richard. "Keys to 'Kubla Khan,' " in *English Studies*. XLIV (October, 1963), pp. 321–341.

Hoffpauir, Richard A. " 'Kubla Khan' and the Critics: Romantic Madness as Poetic Theme and Critical Response," in *English Studies in Canada*. II (1976), pp. 402–422.

Meier, Hans Heinreich. "Ancient Lights on Kubla's Lines," in *English Studies*. XLVI (February, 1965), pp. 15–29.

Mercer, Dorothy F. "The Symbolism of 'Kubla Khan,' " in *Journal of Aesthetics and Art Criticism*. XII (September, 1953), pp. 784–801.

Patterson, Charles I., Jr. "The Daemonic in 'Kubla Khan': Toward Interpretation," in *PMLA*. LXXXIX (1974), pp. 1033–1042.

Piper, H.W. "Two Paradises in 'Kubla Khan,' " in *Review of English Studies*. XXVII (1976), pp. 148–158.

Raine, Kathleen. "Traditional Symbolism in 'Kubla Khan,' " in *Sewanee Review*. LXXII (Autumn, 1964), pp. 626–642.

Sloane, Eugene H. "Coleridge's 'Kubla Khan': The Living Catacombs of the Mind," in *American Imago*. XXIX (1972), pp. 97–122.

Smith, James. "The Poetry of Coleridge," in *Scrutiny*. VII (March, 1940), pp. 411–414.

Starr, Nathan Comfort. "Coleridge's Sacred River," in *Papers on Language and Literature*. II (Spring, 1966), pp. 117–125.

Stevenson, Warren. " 'Kubla Khan' as Symbol," in *Texas Studies in Literature and Language*. XIV (1972), pp. 605–630.

Walsh, William. *Coleridge: The Work and the Relevance*. New York: Barnes & Noble, 1967, pp. 111–122.

Woodring, Carl R. "Coleridge and the Khan," in *Essays in Criticism*. IX (October, 1959), pp. 361–368.

Yarlott, Geoffrey. *Coleridge & the Abyssinian Maid*. London: Methuen, 1967, pp. 126–154.

The Rime of the Ancient Mariner

Alley, Alvin D. "Coleridge and Existentialism," in *Southern Humanities Review*. II (Fall, 1968), pp. 456–458.

Angus, Douglas. "The Theme of Love and Guilt in Coleridge's Three Major Poems," in *Journal of English and Germanic Philology.* LIX (October, 1960), pp. 655–668.

Bosletter, Edward E. "The Nightmare World of *The Ancient Mariner,*" in *Coleridge: A Collection of Critical Essays.* Edited by Kathleen Coburn. Englewood Cliffs, N.J.: Prentice-Hall, 1967, pp. 65–77.

Brett, R.L. *Reason and Imagination: A Study of Form and Meaning in Four Poems.* London: Oxford University Press, 1960, pp. 78–107.

Buchan, A.M. "The Sad Wisdom of the Mariner," in *Studies in Philology.* LXI (October, 1964), pp. 669–688.

Creed, Howard. "*The Rime of the Ancient Mariner*: A Rereading," in *English Journal.* XLIX (April, 1960), pp. 215–222.

Delson, Abe. "The Symbolism of the Sun and Moon in *The Rime of the Ancient Mariner,*" in *Texas Studies in Literature and Language.* XV (1974), pp. 707–720.

Dyck, Sarah. "Perspective in *The Rime of the Ancient Mariner,*" in *Studies in English Literature, 1500–1900.* XIII (1973), pp. 591–604.

Ebbatson, J.R. "Coleridge's Mariner and the Rights of Man," in *Studies in Romanticism.* XI (1972), pp. 171–206.

Empson, William. "The Ancient Mariner," in *Critical Quarterly.* VI (Winter, 1964), pp. 298–319.

Fulmer, O. Bryan. "The Ancient Mariner and the Wandering Jew," in *Studies in Philology.* LXVI (October, 1969), pp. 797–815.

Gibbons, Edward E. "Point of View and Moral: *The Ancient Mariner,*" in *University Review.* XXXV (June, 1969), pp. 257–261.

Gose, Elliot B., Jr. "Coleridge and the Luminous Gloom: An Analysis of the 'Symbolic Language' in *The Rime of the Ancient Mariner,*" in *PMLA.* LXXV (June, 1960), pp. 238–244.

Harding, D.W. "The Theme of *The Ancient Mariner,*" in *Coleridge: A Collection of Critical Essays.* Edited by Kathleen Coburn. Englewood Cliffs, N.J.: Prentice-Hall, 1967, pp. 51–64.

Littman, Mark. "*The Ancient Mariner* and Initiation Rites," in *Papers on Language and Literature.* IV (Fall, 1968), pp. 370–389.

Lupton, Mary Jane H. "*The Rime of the Ancient Mariner*: The Agony of Thirst," in *American Imago.* XXVII (1970), pp. 140–159.

McDonald, Daniel. "Too Much Reality: A Discussion of *The Rime of the Ancient Mariner,*" in *Studies in English Literature.* IV (Autumn, 1964), pp. 543–554.

May, Charles E. "Objectifying the Nightmare: Cain and the Mariner," in *Ball State University Forum.* XIV (1973), pp. 45–48.

Owen, Charles A. "Structure in *The Ancient Mariner*," in *College English*. XXIII (January, 1962), pp. 261–267.

Pafford, Ward. "Coleridge's Wedding-Guest," in *Studies in Philology*. LX (October, 1963), pp. 618–626.

Piper, H.W. "*The Ancient Mariner*: Biblical Allegory, Poetic Symbolism and Religious Crisis," in *Southern Review*. X (1977), pp. 232–242.

Rowell, Charles H. "Coleridge's Symbolic Albatross," in *College Language Association Journal*. VI (December, 1962), pp. 133–135.

Stevenson, Warren. "*The Rime of the Ancient Mariner* as Epic Symbol," in *Dalhousie Review*. LVI (1976), pp. 542–547.

Ware, Malcolm. "*The Rime of the Ancient Mariner*: A Discourse on Prayer?," in *Review of English Studies*. XI (August, 1960), pp. 303–304.

COLETTE
(1873–1954)

Chéri

Benet, Mary Kathleen. "Colette," in her *Writers in Love*. New York: Macmillan, 1977, pp. 224–225, 229–232, 237–251.

Bogan, Louise. "Colette," in her *Selected Criticism: Prose, Poetry*. New York: Noonday, 1955, pp. 28–32.

Cottrell, Robert D. *Colette*. New York: Ungar, 1974, pp. 88–93.

Crosland, Margaret. *Colette: The Difficulty of Loving*. Indianapolis: Bobbs-Merrill, 1973, pp. 173–178.

Davies, Margaret. *Colette*. Edinburgh: Oliver and Boyd, 1961, pp. 55–63.

Hayes, Richard. "Wisdom of Colette," in *Commonweal*. LVI (September 5, 1952), pp. 536–538.

Lesser, Simon O. "The Wages of Adjustment: *Chéri* and *The Last of Chéri*," in *Minnesota Review*. IV (Winter, 1964), pp. 212–225.

Marks, Elaine. *Colette*. New Brunswick, N.J.: Rutgers University Press, 1960, pp. 124–138, 148–150.

Mitchell, Yvonne. *Colette: A Taste for Life*. New York: Harcourt Brace Jovanovich, 1975, pp. 143–145, 161–162.

Moore, Harry T. *Twentieth Century French Literature to World War II*. Carbondale: Southern Illinois University Press, 1966, pp. 51–56.

Olken, I.T. "Aspects of Imagery in Colette: Color and Light," in *PMLA*. LXXVII (March, 1962), pp. 140–148.

————. "Imagery in *Chéri* and *La Fin de Chéri*," in *French Studies*. XVI (July, 1962), pp. 245–261. Also in *Studies in Philology*. LX (January, 1963), pp. 96–115.

Peyre, Henri. "Contemporary Feminine Literature in France," in *Yale French Studies*. XXVII (Spring–Summer, 1961), pp. 48–51. Reprinted in his *French Novelists of Today*. New York: Oxford University Press, 1967, pp. 276–278.

Stansbury, Milton H. *French Novelists of Today*. Philadelphia: University of Pennsylvania Press, 1935, pp. 101–119.

Wescott, Glenway. "Introduction," in *Short Novels of Colette*. New York: Dial, 1951, pp. xxiii–xxxiii. Reprinted in his *Images of Truth: Remembrances and Criticism*. New York: Harper, 1962, pp. 101–113.

The End of Chéri

Bogan, Louise. "Colette," in her *Selected Criticism: Prose, Poetry*. New York: Noonday, 1955, pp. 28–32.

Crosland, Margaret. *Colette: The Difficulty of Loving.* Indianapolis: Bobbs-Merrill, 1973, pp. 173–178.

Cottrell, Robert D. *Colette.* New York: Ungar, 1974, pp. 93–97.

Davies, Margaret. *Colette.* Edinburgh: Oliver and Boyd, 1961, pp. 55–63.

Hayes, Richard. "Wisdom of Colette," in *Commonweal.* LVI (September 5, 1952), pp. 536–538.

Lesser, Simon O. "The Wages of Adjustment: *Chéri* and *The Last of Chéri*," in *Minnesota Review.* IV (Winter, 1964), pp. 212–225.

Marks, Elaine. *Colette.* New Brunswick, N.J.: Rutgers University Press, 1960, pp. 100–108, 131–133, 138–143, 148–150.

Mitchell, Yvonne. *Colette: A Taste for Life.* New York: Harcourt Brace Jovanovich, 1975, pp. 161–162.

Moore, Harry T. *Twentieth Century French Literature to World War II.* Carbondale: Southern Illinois University Press, 1966, pp. 51–56.

Olken, I.T. "Aspects of Imagery in Colette: Color and Light," in *PMLA.* LXXVII (March, 1962), pp. 140–148.

————. "Imagery in *Chéri* and *La Fin de Chéri*," in *French Studies.* XVI (July, 1962), pp. 245–261. Also in *Studies in Philology.* LX (January, 1963), pp. 96–115.

Stansbury, Milton H. *French Novelists of Today.* Philadelphia: University of Pennsylvania Press, 1935, pp. 101–119.

Wescott, Glenway. "Introduction," in *Short Novels of Colette.* New York: Dial, 1951, pp. xxiii–xxxiii. Reprinted in his *Images of Truth: Remembrances and Criticism.* New York: Harper, 1962, pp. 101–113.

The Pure and the Impure

Benet, Mary Kathleen. "Colette," in her *Writers in Love.* New York: Macmillan, 1977, pp. 237–251.

Crosland, Margaret. *Colette: The Difficulty of Loving.* Indianapolis: Bobbs-Merrill, 1973, pp. 195–197.

Davies, Margaret. *Colette.* Edinburgh: Oliver and Boyd, 1961, pp. 79–81.

Flanner, Janet. "Introduction," in *The Pure and the Impure.* By Colette. New York: Farrar, Straus and Giroux, 1967.

Marks, Elaine. *Colette.* New Brunswick, N.J.: Rutgers University Press, 1960, pp. 216–219.

WILKIE COLLINS
(1824–1889)

The Moonstone

Ashley, Robert P. "Wilkie Collins and the Detective Story," in *Nineteenth-Century Fiction*. VI (1951), pp. 47–60.

Hutter, Albert D. "Dreams, Transformations, and Literature: The Implications of Detective Fiction," in *Victorian Studies*. XIX (1975), pp. 181–209.

Laidlaw, R.P. " 'Awful Images and Associations': A Study of Wilkie Collins' *The Moonstone*," in *Southern Review*. IX (1976), pp. 211–227.

Lawson, Lewis A. "Wilkie Collins and *The Moonstone*," in *American Imago*. XX (1963), pp. 61–79.

McCleary, G.F. "A Victorian Classic," in *Fortnightly Review*. CLX (1946), pp. 137–141.

Marshall, William H. *Wilkie Collins*. New York: Twayne, 1970, pp. 77–85.

Milley, Henry James Wye. "*The Eustace Diamonds* and *The Moonstone*," in *Studies in Philology*. XXXVI (1939), pp. 651–663.

Murch, A.E. *The Development of the Detective Novel*. New York: Philosophical Library, 1958, pp. 108–113.

Ousby, Ian. *Bloodhounds of Heaven; The Detective in English Fiction from Godwin to Doyle*. Cambridge, Mass.: Harvard University Press, 1976, pp. 117–128.

————. "Wilkie Collins's *The Moonstone* and the Constance Kent Case," in *Notes & Queries*. XXI (1974), p. 25.

Phillips, Walter Clarke. *Dickens, Reade, and Collins, Sensation Novelists: A Study in the Conditions and Theories of Novel Writing in Victorian England*. New York: Columbia University Press, 1919.

Reed, John R. "English Imperialism and the Unacknowledged Crime of *The Moonstone*," in *Clio*. II (1973), pp. 281–290.

Robinson, Kenneth. *Wilkie Collins, a Biography*. Westport, Conn.: Greenwood, 1972, pp. 212–224, 226–227.

Rycroft, Charles. "A Detective Story: Psychoanalytic Observations," in *Psychoanalytic Quarterly*. XXVI (1957), pp. 229–245.

Sayers, Dorothy L. *The Omnibus of Crime*. New York: Harcourt, Brace, 1929, pp. 22–25.

Symons, Julian. *Mortal Consequences; A History—From the Detective Story to the Crime Novel*. New York: Harper & Row, 1972, pp. 45–49.

Wolfe, Peter. "Point of View and Characterization in Wilkie Collins's *The Moonstone*," in *Forum* (Houston). IV (Summer, 1965), pp. 27–29.

The Woman in White

Caracciolo, Peter. "Wilkie Collins's 'Divine Comedy': The Use of Dante in *The Woman in White*," in *Nineteenth-Century Fiction*. XXV (1971), pp. 383–404.

Hyder, Clyde K. "Wilkie Collins and *The Woman in White*," in *PMLA*. LIV (1939), pp. 297–303.

Kendrick, Walter M. "The Sensationalism of *The Woman in White*," in *Nineteenth-Century Fiction*. XXXII (June, 1977), pp. 18–35.

Marshall, William H. *Wilkie Collins*. New York: Twayne, 1970, pp. 56–66.

Muller, C.H. "Incident and Characterization in *The Woman in White*," in *Unisa English Studies*. XI (1973), pp. 33–50.

Robinson, Kenneth. *Wilkie Collins, a Biography*. Westport, Conn.: Greenwood, 1972, pp. 137–154, 159–162.

Wright, Austin. *Victorian Literature; Modern Essays in Criticism*. London: Oxford University Press, 1961, pp. 128–135.

IVY COMPTON-BURNETT
(1892–1969)

Brothers and Sisters

Baldanza, Frank. *Ivy Compton-Burnett.* New York: Twayne, 1964, pp. 43–46.

Burkhart, Charles. *Ivy Compton-Burnett.* London: Gollancz, 1965, pp. 101–103.

Grylls, Rosalie G. *Ivy Compton-Burnett.* Harlow, England: Longmans, 1971.

Johnson, Pamela H. *Ivy Compton-Burnett.* London: Longmans, Green, 1951, p. 27.

Liddell, Robert. *The Novels of Ivy Compton-Burnett.* London: Gollancz, 1955, pp. 37–39.

————. *A Treatise on the Novel.* London: Jonathan Cape, 1947, pp. 146–163.

May, James B. "Ivy Compton-Burnett: A Time Exposure," in *Trace.* XLIX (Summer, 1963), pp. 92–99.

Nevius, Blake. *Ivy Compton-Burnett.* New York: Columbia University Press, 1970, pp. 9–10.

Powell, Violet. *A Compton-Burnett Compendium.* London: Heinemann, 1973, pp. 12–17.

Darkness and Day

Baldanza, Frank. *Ivy Compton-Burnett.* New York: Twayne, 1964, pp. 83–86.

Burkhart, Charles. *Ivy Compton-Burnett.* London: Gollancz, 1965, pp. 47–48, 54–55, 119–122.

Curtis, Mary M. "The Moral Comedy of Miss Compton-Burnett," in *Wisconsin Studies in Contemporary Literature.* V (Autumn, 1964), pp. 213–221.

Grylls, Rosalie G. *Ivy Compton-Burnett.* Harlow, England: Longmans, 1971.

Johnson, Pamela H. *Ivy Compton-Burnett.* London: Longmans, Green, 1951, pp. 34–35.

Nevius, Blake. *Ivy Compton-Burnett.* New York: Columbia University Press, 1970, p. 40.

Powell, Violet. *A Compton-Burnett Compendium.* London: Heinemann, 1973, pp. 148–161.

Daughters and Sons

Baldanza, Frank. *Ivy Compton-Burnett.* New York: Twayne, 1964, pp. 58–61.

Burkhart, Charles. *Ivy Compton-Burnett.* London: Gollancz, 1965, pp. 52–53, 58–62, 108–110.

Grylls, Rosalie G. *Ivy Compton-Burnett.* Harlow, England: Longmans, 1971.

Johnson, Pamela H. *Ivy Compton-Burnett.* London: Longmans, Green, 1951, pp. 30–31.

Liddell, Robert. *The Novels of Ivy Compton-Burnett.* London: Gollancz, 1955, pp. 26–28, 30–31, 42.

————. *A Treatise on the Novel.* London: Jonathan Cape, 1947, pp. 146–163.

Nevius, Blake. *Ivy Compton-Burnett.* New York: Columbia University Press, 1970, pp. 29–31.

Powell, Violet. *A Compton-Burnett Compendium.* London: Heinemann, 1973, pp. 65–76.

Dolores

Baldanza, Frank. *Ivy Compton-Burnett.* New York: Twayne, 1964, pp. 39–41.

Burkhart, Charles. *Ivy Compton-Burnett.* London: Gollancz, 1965, pp. 98–100.

Grylls, Rosalie G. *Ivy Compton-Burnett.* Harlow, England: Longmans, 1971.

Johnson, Pamela H. *Ivy Compton-Burnett.* London: Longmans, Green, 1951, pp. 24–25.

Liddell, Robert. *The Novels of Ivy Compton-Burnett.* London: Gollancz, 1955, pp. 15–17, 24.

————. *A Treatise on the Novel.* London: Jonathan Cape, 1947, pp. 146–163.

Nevius, Blake. *Ivy Compton-Burnett.* New York: Columbia University Press, 1970, pp. 4–6.

Powell, Violet. *A Compton-Burnett Compendium.* London: Heinemann, 1973, pp. 1–4.

Elders and Betters

Baldanza, Frank. *Ivy Compton-Burnett.* New York: Twayne, 1964, pp. 69–72.

Bowan, E. *Collected Impressions.* New York: Knopf, 1950, pp. 85–91.

Burkhart, Charles. *Ivy Compton-Burnett.* London: Gollancz, 1965, pp. 89–90, 113–115.

Grylls, Rosalie G. *Ivy Compton-Burnett.* Harlow, England: Longmans, 1971.

Johnson, Pamela H. *Ivy Compton-Burnett.* London: Longmans, Green, 1951, pp. 11–13.

Liddell, Robert. *The Novels of Ivy Compton-Burnett.* London: Gollancz, 1955, pp. 44–45, 59–61.

————. *A Treatise on the Novel.* London: Jonathan Cape, 1947, pp. 146–163.

Nevius, Blake. *Ivy Compton-Burnett.* New York: Columbia University Press, 1970, pp. 34–37.

Powell, Violet. *A Compton-Burnett Compendium.* London: Heinemann, 1973, pp. 99–113.

A Family and a Fortune

Baldanza, Frank. *Ivy Compton-Burnett.* New York: Twayne, 1964, pp. 61–65.

Burkhart, Charles. *Ivy Compton-Burnett.* London: Gollancz, 1965, pp. 91–92, 110–111.

Gold, Joseph. "Exit Everybody; The Novels of Ivy Compton-Burnett," in *Dalhousie Review.* XLII (Summer, 1962), pp. 227–238.

Grylls, Rosalie G. *Ivy Compton-Burnett.* Harlow, England: Longmans, 1971.

Johnson, Pamela H. *Ivy Compton-Burnett.* London: Longmans, Green, 1951, pp. 14–17.

Kettle, Arnold. *An Introduction to the English Novel. Volume II.* London: Hutchinson's, 1953, pp. 184–190.

Liddell, Robert. *The Novels of Ivy Compton-Burnett.* London: Gollancz, 1955, pp. 31–34.

————. *A Treatise on the Novel.* London: Jonathan Cape, 1947, pp. 146–163.

McCarthy, Mary T. *The Writing on the Wall, and Other Literary Essays.* New York: Harcourt Brace Jovanovich, 1970, pp. 145–152.

Nevius, Blake. *Ivy Compton-Burnett.* New York: Columbia University Press, 1970, pp. 31–33.

Powell, Violet. *A Compton-Burnett Compendium.* London: Heinemann, 1973, pp. 77–87.

A Father and His Fate

Baldanza, Frank. *Ivy Compton-Burnett.* New York: Twayne, 1964, pp. 93–96.

Burkhart, Charles. *Ivy Compton-Burnett.* London: Gollancz, 1965, pp. 55–56, 60–61, 93–94, 124–125.

Grylls, Rosalie G. *Ivy Compton-Burnett.* Harlow, England: Longmans, 1971.

Powell, Violet. *A Compton-Burnett Compendium.* London: Heinemann, 1973, pp. 186–197.

A God and His Gifts

Baldanza, Frank. *Ivy Compton-Burnett.* New York: Twayne, 1964, pp. 102–105.

Brophy, Brigid I. *Don't Never Forget; Collected Views and Re-views.* New York: Holt, Rinehart, 1966, pp. 167–170.

Burkhart, Charles. *Ivy Compton-Burnett.* London: Gollancz, 1965, pp. 56–57, 94–96, 128–129.

Grylls, Rosalie G. *Ivy Compton-Burnett.* Harlow, England: Longmans, 1971.

McCarthy, Mary T. "The Inventions of Ivy Compton-Burnett," in *Encounter.* XXVII (November, 1966), pp. 19–31.

Nevius, Blake. *Ivy Compton-Burnett.* New York: Columbia University Press, 1970, pp. 44–45.

Powell, Violet. *A Compton-Burnett Compendium.* London: Heinemann, 1973, pp. 218–229.

Prescott, Orville. *In My Opinion; An Inquiry into the Contemporary Novel.* Indianapolis, Ind.: Bobbs-Merrill, 1952, pp. 98–100.

A Heritage and Its History

Baldanza, Frank. *Ivy Compton-Burnett.* New York: Twayne, 1964, pp. 96–99.

Burkhart, Charles. *Ivy Compton-Burnett.* London: Gollancz, 1965, pp. 125–127.

Grylls, Rosalie G. *Ivy Compton-Burnett.* Harlow, England: Longmans, 1971.

Iser, Wolfgang. *The Implied Reader; Patterns of Communication in Prose Fiction from Bunyan to Beckett.* Baltimore: Johns Hopkins University Press, 1974, pp. 152–163, 234–256.

Powell, Violet. *A Compton-Burnett Compendium.* London: Heinemann, 1973, pp. 45–64.

Preston, John. " 'The Matter in a Word,' " in *Essays in Criticism.* X (July, 1960), pp. 348–356.

A House and Its Head

Baldanza, Frank. *Ivy Compton-Burnett.* New York: Twayne, 1964, pp. 102–105.

Burkhart, Charles. *Ivy Compton-Burnett.* London: Gollancz, 1965, pp. 26–27, 107–108.

Grylls, Rosalie G. *Ivy Compton-Burnett.* Harlow, England: Longmans, 1971.

Johnson, Pamela H. *Ivy Compton-Burnett.* London: Longmans, Green, 1951, p. 30.

Liddell, Robert. *The Novels of Ivy Compton-Burnett.* London: Gollancz, 1955, pp. 25–26, 43–44, 77–78.

―――――. *A Treatise on the Novel.* London: Jonathan Cape, 1947, pp. 146–163.

Nevius, Blake. *Ivy Compton-Burnett.* New York: Columbia University Press, 1970, pp. 28–29.

Powell, Violet. *A Compton-Burnett Compendium.* London: Heinemann, 1973, pp. 45–64.

The Last and the First

Davenport, Guy. *"The Last and the First,"* in *New York Times Book Review.* (August 15, 1971), pp. 2–3.

Grylls, Rosalie G. *Ivy Compton-Burnett.* Harlow, England: Longmans, 1971.

Powell, Violet. *A Compton-Burnett Compendium.* London: Heinemann, 1973, pp. 230–233.

Ricks, Christopher. "Death of the Family," in *New York Review of Books.* XVII (October 21, 1971), pp. 33–35.

Weales, Gerald. "Fiction Chronicle," in *Hudson Review.* XXIV (Winter, 1971–1972), pp. 716–718.

West, Paul. *"The Last and the First,"* in *Saturday Review of Literature.* LIV (September 4, 1971), p. 33.

Men and Wives

Baldanza, Frank. *Ivy Compton-Burnett.* New York: Twayne, 1964, pp. 46–49.

Burkhart, Charles. *Ivy Compton-Burnett.* London: Gollancz, 1965, pp. 57–58, 103–106.

Grylls, Rosalie G. *Ivy Compton-Burnett.* Harlow, England: Longmans, 1971.

Johnson, Pamela H. *Ivy Compton-Burnett.* London: Longmans, Green, 1951, pp. 27–28.

Liddell, Robert. *The Novels of Ivy Compton-Burnett.* London: Gollancz, 1955, pp. 28–29, 39–42, 74–77.

————. *A Treatise on the Novel.* London: Jonathan Cape, 1974, pp. 146–163.

Nevius, Blake. *Ivy Compton-Burnett.* New York: Columbia University Press, 1970, pp. 23–25.

Powell, Violet. *A Compton-Burnett Compendium.* London: Heinemann, 1973, pp. 25–34.

The Mighty and Their Fall

Baldanza, Frank. *Ivy Compton-Burnett.* New York: Twayne, 1964, pp. 99–102.

Burkhart, Charles. *Ivy Compton-Burnett.* London: Gollancz, 1965, pp. 72–74, 127–128.

Curtis, Mary M. "The Moral Comedy of Miss Compton-Burnett," in *Wisconsin Studies in Contemporary Literature.* V (Autumn, 1964), pp. 213–221.

Grylls, Rosalie G. *Ivy Compton-Burnett.* Harlow, England: Longmans, 1971.

Powell, Violet. *A Compton-Burnett Compendium.* London: Heinemann, 1973, pp. 210–217.

Mr. Bullivant and His Lambs

Baldanza, Frank. *Ivy Compton-Burnett.* New York: Twayne, 1964, pp. 72–76.

Burkhart, Charles. *Ivy Compton-Burnett.* London: Gollancz, 1965, pp. 36–39, 115–117.

Grylls, Rosalie G. *Ivy Compton-Burnett.* Harlow, England: Longmans, 1971.

Johnson, Pamela H. *Ivy Compton-Burneet.* London: Longmans, Green, 1951, pp. 32–33.

Karl, Frederick R. *The Contemporary English Novel.* New York: Farrar, Straus, 1962, pp. 212–215.

Liddell, Robert. *The Novels of Ivy Compton-Burnett.* London: Gollancz, 1955, pp. 40–42, 61–62.

———. *A Treatise on the Novel.* London: Jonathan Cape, 1947, pp. 146–163.

Nevius, Blake. *Ivy Compton-Burnett.* New York: Columbia University Press, 1970, pp. 37–38.

Powell, Violet. *A Compton-Burnett Compendium.* London: Heinemann, 1973, pp. 114–134.

More Women Than Men

Baldanza, Frank. *Ivy Compton-Burnett.* New York: Twayne, 1964, pp. 50–53.

Burkhart, Charles. *Ivy Compton-Burnett.* London: Gollancz, 1965, pp. 84–86, 104–106.

Grylls, Rosalie G. *Ivy Compton-Burnett.* Harlow, England: Longmans, 1971.

Johnson, Pamela H. *Ivy Compton-Burnett.* London: Longmans, Green, 1951, pp. 28–29.

Liddell, Robert. *The Novels of Ivy Compton-Burnett.* London: Gollancz, 1955, pp. 29–30, 42.

———. *A Treatise on the Novel.* London: Jonathan Cape, 1947, pp. 146–163.

Nevius, Blake. *Ivy Compton-Burnett.* New York: Columbia University Press, 1970, pp. 27–28.

Powell, Violet. *A Compton-Burnett Compendium.* London: Heinemann, 1973, pp. 35–44.

Mother and Son

Amis, Kingsley, "One World and Its Way," in *Twentieth Century.* CLVIII (August, 1955), pp. 168–175.

Baldanza, Frank. *Ivy Compton-Burnett.* New York: Twayne, 1964, pp. 89–92.

Burkhart, Charles. *Ivy Compton-Burnett.* London: Gollancz, 1965, pp. 122–124.

Gold, Joseph. "Exit Everybody: The Novels of Ivy Compton-Burnett," in *Dalhousie Review.* XLII (Summer, 1962), pp. 227–238.

Grylls, Rosalie G. *Ivy Compton-Burnett.* Harlow, England: Longmans, 1971.

Nevius, Blake. *Ivy Compton-Burnett.* New York: Columbia University Press, 1970, pp. 42–43.

Powell, Violet. *A Compton-Burnett Compendium.* London: Heinemann, 1973, pp. 173–185.

West, Anthony. *Principles and Persuasions: The Literary Essays of Anthony West.* Harcourt Brace Jovanovich, 1957, pp. 225–232.

Parents and Children

Baldanza, Frank. *Ivy Compton-Burnett.* New York: Twayne, 1964, pp. 65–69.

Bowan, E. *Collected Impressions.* New York: Knopf, 1950, pp. 82–85.

Burkhart, Charles. *Ivy Compton-Burnett.* London: Gollancz, 1965, pp. 111–113.

Grylls, Rosalie G. *Ivy Compton-Burnett.* Harlow, England: Longmans, 1971.

Liddell, Robert. *A Treatise on the Novel.* London: Jonathan Cape, 1947, pp. 146–163.

Nevius, Blake. *Ivy Compton-Burnett.* New York: Columbia University Press, 1970, pp. 33–34.

Powell, Violet. *A Compton-Burnett Compendium.* London: Heinemann, 1973, pp. 88–98.

Pastors and Masters

Baldanza, Frank. *Ivy Compton-Burnett.* New York: Twayne, 1964, pp. 41–43, 56–57.

Burkhart, Charles. *Ivy Compton-Burnett.* London: Gollancz, 1965, pp. 87–88, 100–101.

Gold, Joseph. "Exit Everybody: The Novels of Ivy Compton-Burnett," in *Dalhousie Review.* XLII (Summer, 1962), pp. 227–238.

Greenfield, Stanley B. "*Pastors and Masters*: The Spoils of Genius," in *Criticism.* II (1960), pp. 66–80.

Grylls, Rosalie G. *Ivy Compton-Burnett.* Harlow, England: Longmans, 1971.

Johnson, Pamela H. *Ivy Compton-Burnett.* London: Longmans, Green, 1951, p. 26.

Liddell, Robert. *The Novels of Ivy Compton-Burnett.* London: Gollancz, 1955, pp. 24–25, 37, 72–73.

————. *A Treatise on the Novel*. London: Jonathan Cape, 1947, pp. 146–163.

Nevius, Blake. *Ivy Compton-Burnett*. New York: Columbia University Press, 1970, pp. 7–9.

Powell, Violet. *A Compton-Burnett Compendium*. London: Heinemann, 1973, pp. 5–11.

The Present and the Past

Baldanza, Frank. *Ivy Compton-Burnett*. New York: Twayne, 1964, pp. 86–89.

Burkhart, Charles. *Ivy Compton-Burnett*. London: Gollancz, 1965, pp. 46–47, 121–122.

Grylls, Rosalie G. *Ivy Compton-Burnett*. Harlow, England: Longmans, 1971.

Liddell, Robert. *The Novels of Ivy Compton-Burnett*. London: Gollancz, 1955, pp. 42–43, 46–47.

Nevius, Blake. *Ivy Compton-Burnett*. New York: Columbia University Press, 1970, pp. 40–42.

Powell, Violet. *A Compton-Burnett Compendium*. London: Heinemann, 1973, pp. 162–172.

Two Worlds and Their Ways

Baldanza, Frank. *Ivy Compton-Burnett*. New York: Twayne, 1964, pp. 76–79.

Burkhart, Charles. *Ivy Compton-Burnett*. London: Gollancz, 1965, pp. 118–119.

Grylls, Rosalie G. *Ivy Compton-Burnett*. Harlow, England: Longmans, 1971.

Johnson, Pamela H. *Ivy Compton-Burnett*. London: Longmans, Green, 1951, pp. 33–34.

Karl, Frederick R. *The Contemporary English Novel*. New York: Farrar, Straus, 1962, pp. 215–218.

Nevius, Blake. *Ivy Compton-Burnett*. New York: Columbia University Press, 1970, pp. 39–40.

Powell, Violet. *A Compton-Burnett Compendium*. London: Heinemann, 1973, pp. 135–147.

WILLIAM CONGREVE
(1670–1729)

The Double Dealer

Corman, B. "Mixed Way of Comedy: Congreve's *The Double Dealer*," in *Modern Philology*. LXXI (May, 1974), pp. 356–365.

Dobrée, Bonamy. *William Congreve*. London: British Council, 1963.

Fujimura, Thomas H. *The Restoration Comedy of Wit*. Princeton, N.J.: Princeton University Press, 1952.

Gosse, Edmund William. *The Life of William Congreve*. Port Washington, N.Y.: Kennikat, 1972. Reprint of 1924 Edition.

Holland, Norman. *The First Modern Comedies*. Cambridge, Mass.: Harvard University Press, 1959.

Knights, L.C. "Restoration Comedy: The Reality and the Myth," in his *Explorations*. London: Chatto and Windus, 1946, pp. 58–72.

Krutch, Joseph Wood. *Comedy and Conscience After the Restoration*. New York: Columbia University Press, 1961. Reprint of 1924 Edition.

Leech, Clifford. "Congreve and the Century's End," in *Philological Quarterly*. XLI (1962), pp. 275–293.

Loftis, John. *Comedy and Society from Congreve to Fielding*. Palo Alto, Calif.: Stanford University Press, 1958.

Lynch, Kathleen. *A Congreve Gallery*. Cambridge, Mass.: Harvard University Press, 1951.

McIntosh, C. "Matter of Style: Static and Dynamic Predicates," in *PMLA*. XCII (January, 1977), pp. 110–121.

Morris, Brian, Editor. *William Congreve*. Totowa, N.J.: Rowman and Littlefield, 1972.

Novak, Maximillian E. *William Congreve*. New York: Twayne, 1971.

Noyes, Robert Gale. "Congreve and His Comedies in the Eighteenth Century Novel," in *Philological Quarterly*. XXXIX (1960), pp. 464–480.

Rosowski, S.J. "Thematic Development in the Comedies of William Congreve: The Individual in Society," in *Studies in English Literature*. XVI (Summer, 1976), pp. 387–406.

Taylor, Daniel C. *William Congreve*. Folcroft, Pa.: Folcroft Press, 1969. Reprint of 1931 Edition.

Turner, Darwin. "The Servant in the Comedies of William Congreve," in *College Language Association Journal*. I (1958), pp. 68–74.

Voris, William van. "Congreve's Gilded Carousel," in *Educational Theater Journal*. X (1957), pp. 211–217.

Wain, John. "Restoration Comedy and Its Modern Critics," in *Essays in Criticism*. VI (1965), pp. 367–385.

Williams, Aubrey. "Poetical Justice, the Contrivances of Providence, and the Works of William Congreve," in *English Literary History*. XXXV (1968), pp. 540–565.

Love for Love

Cooke, Arthur L. "Two Parallels Between Dryden's *Wild Gallant* and Congreve's *Love for Love*," in *Notes and Queries*. I (1954), pp. 27–28.

Dobrée, Bonamy. *William Congreve*. London: British Council, 1963.

Fujimura, Thomas H. *The Restoration Comedy of Wit*. Princeton, N.J.: Princeton University Press, 1952.

Gosse, Anthony C. "The Omitted Scene in Congreve's *Love for Love*," in *Modern Philology*. LXI (1963), pp. 40–42.

Gosse, Edmund William. *The Life of William Congreve*. Port Washington, N.Y.: Kennikat, 1972. Reprint of 1924 Edition.

Hodges, John C. "The Ballad in Congreve's *Love for Love*," in *PMLA*. XLVIII (1933), pp. 953–954.

Holland, Norman. *The First Modern Comedies*. Cambridge, Mass.: Harvard University Press, 1959.

Knights, L.C. "Restoration Comedy: The Reality and the Myth," in his *Explorations*. London: Chatto and Windus, 1946, pp. 58–72.

Krutch, Joseph Wood. *Comedy and Conscience After the Restoration*. New York: Columbia University Press, 1961. Reprint of 1924 Edition.

Leech, Clifford. "Congreve and the Century's End," in *Philological Quarterly*. XLI (1962), pp. 275–293.

Loftis, John. *Comedy and Society from Congreve to Fielding*. Palo Alto, Calif.: Stanford University Press, 1958.

Lynch, Kathleen. *A Congreve Gallery*. Cambridge, Mass.: Harvard University Press, 1951.

Lyons, Charles. "Congreve's Miracle of Love," in *Criticism*. VI (1964), pp. 331–348.

Morris, Brian, Editor. *William Congreve*. Totowa, N.J.: Rowman and Littlefield, 1972.

Novak, Maximillian E. *William Congreve*. New York: Twayne, 1971.

Noyes, Robert Gale. "Congreve and His Comedies in the Eighteenth Century Novel," in *Philological Quarterly*. XXXIX (1960), pp. 464–480.

Rosowski, S.J. "Thematic Development in the Comedies of William Congreve," in *Studies in English Literature*. XVI (Summer, 1976), pp. 387–406.

Taylor, Daniel C. *William Congreve.* Folcroft, Pa.: Folcroft Press, 1969. Reprint of 1931 Edition.

Turner, Darwin. "The Servant in the Comedies of William Congreve," in *College Language Association Journal.* I (1958), pp. 68–74.

Voris, William van. "Congreve's Gilded Carousel," in *Educational Theater Journal.* X (1957), pp. 211–217.

Williams, Aubrey. "Poetical Justice, the Contrivances of Providence, and the Works of William Congreve," in *English Literary History.* XXXV (1968), pp. 540–565.

The Old Bachelor

Dobrée, Bonamy. *William Congreve.* London: British Council, 1963.

Fujimura, Thomas H. *The Restoration Comedy of Wit.* Princeton, N.J.: Princeton University Press, 1952.

Gosse, Edmund William. *The Life of William Congreve.* Port Washington, N.Y.: Kennikat, 1972. Reprint of 1924 Edition.

Hodges, John C. "The Composition of Congreve's First Play," in *PMLA.* LVIII (1943), pp. 971–976.

Holland, Norman. *The First Modern Comedies.* Cambridge, Mass.: Harvard University Press, 1959.

Knights, L.C. "Restoration Comedy: The Reality and the Myth," in his *Explorations.* London: Chatto and Windus, 1946, pp. 58–72.

Krutch, Joseph Wood. *Comedy and Conscience After the Restoration.* New York: Columbia University Press, 1961. Reprint of 1924 Edition.

Leech, Clifford. "Congreve and the Century's End," in *Philological Quarterly.* XLI (1962), pp. 275–293.

Loftis, John. *Comedy and Society from Congreve to Fielding.* Palo Alto, Calif.: Stanford University Press, 1958.

Lynch, Kathleen. *A Congreve Gallery.* Cambridge, Mass.: Harvard University Press, 1951.

McComb, J.F. "Congreve's *The Old Bachelor*: A Satiric Anatomy," in *Studies in English Literature.* XVII (Summer, 1977), pp. 361–372.

Morris, Brian, Editor. *William Congreve.* Totowa, N.J.: Rowman and Littlefield, 1972.

Novak, Maximillian E. "Congreve's *The Old Bachelor*: From Formula to Art," in *Essays in Criticism.* XX (April, 1970), pp. 182–199.

————. *William Congreve.* New York: Twayne, 1971.

Noyes, Robert Gale. "Congreve and His Comedies in the Eighteenth Century Novel," in *Philological Quarterly.* XXXIX (1960), pp. 464–480.

Rosowski, S.J.   "Thematic Development in the Comedies of William Congreve: The Individual in Society," in *Studies in English Literature.* XVI (Summer, 1976), pp. 387–406.

Taylor, Daniel C.   *William Congreve.* Folcroft, Pa.: Folcroft Press, 1969. Reprint of 1931 Edition.

Turner, Darwin.   "The Servant in the Comedies of William Congreve," in *College Language Association Journal.* I (1958), pp. 68–74.

Voris, William van.   "Congreve's Gilded Carousel," in *Educational Theater Journal.* X (1957), pp. 211–217.

Williams, Aubrey.   "Poetical Justice, the Contrivances of Providence, and the Works of William Congreve," in *English Literary History.* XXXV (1968), pp. 540–565.

The Way of the World

Corman, B.   "*The Way of the World* and Morally Serious Comedy," in *University of Toronto Quarterly.* XLIV (Spring, 1975), pp. 199–212.

Dobrée, Bonamy.   *William Congreve.* London: British Council, 1963.

Fujimura, Thomas H.   *The Restoration Comedy of Wit.* Princeton, N.J.: Princeton University Press, 1952.

Gosse, Edmund William.   *The Life of William Congreve.* Port Washington, N.Y.: Kennikat, 1972. Reprint of 1924 Edition.

Hinnant, C.H.   "Wit, Propriety and Style in *The Way of the World*," in *Studies in English Literature.* XVII (Summer, 1977), pp. 373–386.

Holland, Norman.   *The First Modern Comedies.* Cambridge, Mass.: Harvard University Press, 1959.

Hurley, P.J.   "Law and the Dramatic Rhetoric of *The Way of the World*," in *South Atlantic Quarterly.* LXX (Spring, 1971), pp. 191–202.

Knights, L.C.   "Restoration Comedy: The Reality and the Myth," in his *Explorations.* London: Chatto and Windus, 1946, pp. 58–72.

Krutch, Joseph Wood.   *Comedy and Conscience After the Restoration.* New York: Columbia University Press, 1961. Reprint of 1924 Edition.

Lambert, J.W.   "*The Way of the World*," in *Drama.* CXIII (Summer, 1974), pp. 53–54.

Leech, Clifford.   "Congreve and the Century's End," in *Philological Quarterly.* XLI (1962), pp. 275–293.

Loftis, John.   *Comedy and Society from Congreve to Fielding.* Palo Alto, Calif.: Stanford University Press, 1958.

Lynch, Kathleen.   *A Congreve Gallery.* Cambridge, Mass.: Harvard University Press, 1951.

Morris, Brian, Editor. *William Congreve.* Totowa, N.J.: Rowman and Littlefield, 1972.

Mueschke, Paul. *A New View of Congreve's* The Way of the World. Folcroft, Pa.: Folcroft Library Editions, 1973. Reprint of 1958 Edition.

Novak, Maximillian E. *William Congreve.* New York: Twayne, 1971.

Noyes, Robert Gale. "Congreve and His Comedies in the Eighteenth Century Novel," in *Philological Quarterly.* XXXIX (1960), pp. 464–480.

Roper, A. "Language and Action in *The Way of the World*, Love's Last Shift, and the Relapse," in *ELH*. XL (Spring, 1973), pp. 44–69.

Rosowski, S.J. "Thematic Development in the Comedies of William Congreve: The Individual in Society," in *Studies in English Literature*. XVI (Summer, 1976), pp. 387–406.

Taylor, Daniel C. *William Congreve.* Folcroft, Pa.: Folcroft Press, 1969. Reprint of 1931 Edition.

Teyssandier, H. "Congreve's *The Way of the World:* Decorum and Morality," in *English Studies*. LII (April, 1971), pp. 124–131.

Turner, Darwin. "The Servant in the Comedies of William Congreve," in *College Language Association Journal*. I (1958), pp. 68–74.

Voris, William van. "Congreve's Gilded Carousel," in *Educational Theater Journal*. X (1957), pp. 211–217.

Williams, Aubrey. "Poetical Justice, the Contrivances of Providence, and the Works of William Congreve," in *English Literary History*. XXXV (1968), pp. 540–565.

EVAN S. CONNELL, JR.
(1924–   )

Mr. Bridge

Davenport, Guy. *"Mr. Bridge,"* in *New York Times Book Review.* (April 20, 1969), p. 1.

Gross, John. *"Mr. Bridge,"* in *New York Review of Books.* XII (April 24, 1969), p. 41.

Samuels, Charles Thomas. "Dead Center," in *New Republic.* CLX (June 7, 1969), pp. 21–23.

Sandberg, P.L. "He Who Had It All," in *Saturday Review.* LII (May 3, 1969), p. 32.

Shapiro, Charles. "This Familiar and Lifeless Scene," in *Nation.* CCVIII (June 30, 1969), pp. 836–837.

Thompson, John. "Way Past the Hudson," in *Commentary.* XLVIII (July, 1969), pp. 63–65.

Mrs. Bridge

Blaisdell, Gus. "After Ground Zero: The Writings of Evan S. Connell, Jr.," in *New Mexico Quarterly.* XXXVI (Summer, 1966), pp. 186–188.

Chamberlain, Anne. *"Mrs. Bridge,"* in *New York Herald Tribune Book Review.* (January 18, 1959), p. 3.

Gutwillig, Robert. "Ruthless Selection," in *Commonweal.* LXIX (February 13, 1959), pp. 525–526.

Robbins, Michael. "In the Eye of the Tornado," in *CCC: The Journal of the Conference on College Composition and Communications.* XIII (May, 1962), pp. 9–13.

Summers, Hollis. "Kansas City Lady," in *Saturday Review.* XLII (January 31, 1959), p. 18.

Van Bark, Bella S. "The Alienated Person in Literature," in *American Journal of Psychoanalysis.* XXI (1961), pp. 189–191.

Waterhouse, Keith. "New Novels," in *New Statesman.* LIX (February 13, 1960), p. 229.

Notes from a Bottle Found on the Beach at Carmel

Carruth, Hayden. "Last Initiation," in *Nation.* CXCVI (June 15, 1963), pp. 512–513.

Eberhart, Richard. *"Notes from a Bottle Found on the Beach at Carmel,"* in *New York Times Book Beview.* (November 10, 1963), p. 18.

Kostelanetz, R.K.   "Scope and Craft," in *Commonweal*. LXXVIII (August 23, 1963), pp. 516–518.

Phelps, Robert.   "*Notes from a Bottle Found on the Beach at Carmel*," in *New York Herald Tribune Books*. (May 26, 1963), p. 7.

Scott, W.T.   "Listening for the Different Voice," in *Saturday Review*. XLVI (October 26, 1963), p. 36.

JOSEPH CONRAD
(1857–1924)

Almayer's Folly

Allen, Jerry. "Conrad's River," in *Columbia University Forum*. V (Winter, 1962), pp. 29–35.

Altick, Richard. *The Scholar Adventurers*. New York: Macmillan, 1950, pp. 289–297.

Andreas, Osborn. *Joseph Conrad: A Study in Non-Conformity*. New York: Philosophical Library, 1959, pp. 5–9.

Baines, Jocelyn. *Joseph Conrad: A Critical Biography*. New York: McGraw-Hill, 1960, pp. 142–155.

Boyle, Ted Eugene. *Symbol and Meaning in the Fiction of Joseph Conrad*. New York: Humanities Press, 1965, pp. 16–37.

Crankshaw, Edward. *Joseph Conrad: Some Aspects of the Art of the Novel*. London: John Lane, 1936, pp. 63–87.

Dowden, Wilfred S. *Joseph Conrad: The Imaged Style*. Nashville, Tenn.: Vanderbilt University Press, 1970, pp. 15–21.

Friedman, Alan. *The Turn of the Novel*. New York: Oxford University Press, 1966, pp. 75–105.

Gordan, John D. *Joseph Conrad: The Making of a Novelist*. Cambridge, Mass.: Harvard University Press, 1940, pp. 112–129.

Guerard, Albert J. *Conrad the Novelist*. Cambridge, Mass.: Harvard University Press, 1958, pp. 70–78, 81–85.

Guetti, James L., Jr. *The Rhetoric of Joseph Conrad*. Amherst, Mass.: Amherst College Press, 1960, pp. 9–16.

Gurko, Leo. *Joseph Conrad: Giant in Exile*. New York: Macmillan, 1962, pp. 50–57.

Hicks, John H. "Conrad's *Almayer's Folly*: Structure, Theme and Critics," in *Nineteenth-Century Fiction*. XIX (June, 1964), pp. 17–31.

Johnson, Bruce. *Conrad's Models of Mind*. Minneapolis: University of Minnesota Press, 1971, pp. 8–23.

Karl, Frederick R. *A Reader's Guide to Joseph Conrad*. New York: Noonday, 1960, pp. 91–100.

Kirschner, Paul. *Conrad: The Psychologist as Artist*. Edinburgh: Oliver and Boyd, 1968, pp. 27–34.

Kreisel, Henry. "Joseph Conrad and the Dilemma of the Uprooted Man," in *Tamarack Review*. VII (Spring, 1958), pp. 78–85.

Morf, Gustav. *The Polish Shades and Ghosts of Joseph Conrad.* New York: Twayne, 1976, pp. 114–117.

O'Connor, Peter D. "The Function of Nina in *Almayer's Folly*," in *Conradiana.* VII (1975), pp. 225–232.

Roussel, Royal. *The Metaphysics of Darkness: A Study in the Unity and Development of Conrad's Fiction.* Baltimore: Johns Hopkins University Press, 1971, pp. 28–50.

Stawell, F. Melian. "Joseph Conrad," in *Essays and Studies by Members of the English Association.* VI (1920), pp. 88–111.

Stein, William B. "*Almayer's Folly*: The Terror Time," in *Conradiana.* I (Summer, 1968), pp. 27–34.

Visiak, E.H. *The Mirror of Conrad.* New York: Philosophical Library, 1956, pp. 176–181.

Watt, Ian. "*Almayer's Folly*: Memories and Models," in *Mosaic.* VIII (Fall, 1974), pp. 171–182.

Wiley, Paul L. *Conrad's Measure of Man.* Madison: University of Wisconsin Press, 1954, pp. 34–38.

Heart of Darkness

Andreas, Osborn. *Joseph Conrad: A Study in Non-Conformity.* New York: Philosophical Library, 1959, pp. 46–54.

Baines, Jocelyn. *Joseph Conrad: A Critical Biography.* New York: McGraw-Hill, 1960, pp. 223–230.

Berthoud, Jacques. *Joseph Conrad: The Major Phase.* New York: Cambridge University Press, 1978, pp. 41–63.

Collins, Harold R. "Kurtz, the Cannibals, and the Second-Rate Helmsman," in *Western Humanities Review.* VIII (1954), pp. 299–310. Reprinted in *Joseph Conrad's* Heart of Darkness: *Backgrounds and Criticisms.* Edited by Leonard Dean. Englewood Cliffs, N.J.: Prentice-Hall, 1960, pp. 149–159.

Crews, Frederick C. "Conrad's Uneasiness—and Ours," in *Out of My System: Psychoanalysis, Ideology, and Critical Method.* New York: Oxford University Press, 1975, pp. 41–62.

Daleski, Herman M. *Joseph Conrad, The Way of Dispossession.* New York: Holmes and Meier, 1977, pp. 51–76.

Dowden, Wilfred S. "The Light and the Dark: Imagery and Thematic Development in Conrad's *Heart of Darkness*," in *Rice Institute Pamphlet.* XLIV (1958), pp. 33–51. Reprinted in *Conrad's* Heart of Darkness *and the Critics.* Edited by Bruce Harkness. San Francisco: Wadsworth, 1960, pp. 137–145.

Evans, Robert O. "Conrad's Underworld," in *Modern Fiction Studies.* II (1956), pp. 56–62. Reprinted in *The Art of Joseph Conrad: A Critical Symposium.* Edited by Robert W. Stallman. East Lansing: Michigan State University Press, 1960, pp. 171–178. Also reprinted in *Conrad's* Heart of Darkness *and the Critics*. Edited by Bruce Harkness. San Francisco: Wadsworth, 1960, pp. 137–145.

Feder, Lillian. "Marlow's Descent into Hell," in *Nineteenth-Century Fiction*. IX (1955), pp. 280–292. Reprinted in *The Art of Joseph Conrad: A Critical Symposium*. Edited by Robert W. Stallman. East Lansing: Michigan State University Press, 1960, pp. 162–170. Also reprinted in *Heart of Darkness*. Edited by Robert Kimbrough. New York: Norton, 1963, pp. 186–189.

Guerard, Albert J. *Conrad the Novelist*. Cambridge, Mass.: Harvard University Press, 1958, pp. 33–48. Reprinted in *Joseph Conrad's* Heart of Darkness: *Backgrounds and Criticisms*. Englewood Cliffs, N.J.: Prentice-Hall, 1960, pp. 166–177. Also reprinted in *Conrad's* Heart of Darkness *and the Critics*. Edited by Bruce Harkness. San Francisco: Wadsworth, 1960, pp. 111–119. Also reprinted in *Modern British Fiction: Essays in Criticism*. Edited by Mark Schorer. New York: Oxford University Press, 1961, pp. 110–118. Also reprinted in *Heart of Darkness*. Edited by Robert Kimbrough. New York: Norton, 1963, pp. 168–176. Also reprinted in *The Personal Voice*. Edited by Albert J. Guerard. Philadelphia: Lippincott, 1964, pp. 464–474.

Gurko, Leo. *Joseph Conrad: Giant in Exile*. New York: Macmillan, 1962, pp. 148–163. Reprinted in *Heart of Darkness*. Edited by Robert Kimbrough. New York: Norton, 1963, pp. 218–223.

Haugh, Robert F. *Joseph Conrad: Discovery in Design*. Norman: University of Oklahoma Press, 1957, pp. 35–55. Reprinted in *Heart of Darkness*. Edited by Robert Kimbrough. New York: Norton, 1963, pp. 163–167.

Hewitt, Douglas. *Conrad: A Reassessment*. Cambridge: Bowes and Bowes, 1952, pp. 31–39. Reprinted in *Conrad's* Heart of Darkness *and the Critics*. Edited by Bruce Harkness. San Francisco: Wadsworth, 1960, pp. 103–111.

Karl, Frederick R. *A Reader's Guide to Joseph Conrad*. New York: Noonday, 1960, pp. 133–140.

Krieger, Murray. *The Tragic Vision*. New York: Holt, Rinehart and Winston, 1960, pp. 154–165.

Leavis, F.R. "Joseph Conrad," in *Scrutiny*. X (June, 1941), pp 23–32. Reprinted in *The Great Tradition: George Eliot, Henry James, Joseph Conrad*. London: Chatto and Windus, 1948, pp. 174–182. Reprinted in *Critiques and Essays on Modern Fiction*. Edited by John W. Aldridge. New York: Ronald, 1952, pp. 107–113. Also reprinted in *Modern British Fiction: Essays in Criticism*. Edited by Mark Schorer. New York: Oxford University Press, 1961, pp. 88–92.

McClure, John A. "The Rhetoric of Restraint in *Heart of Darkness*," in *Nineteenth-Century Fiction*. XXXII (December, 1977), pp. 310–326.

Mudrick, Marvin. "The Originality of Conrad," in *Hudson Review*. XI (1958), pp. 545–553. Reprinted in *Conrad's* Heart of Darkness *and the Crit-*

ics. Edited by Bruce Harkness. San Francisco: Wadsworth, 1960, pp. 135–136. Also reprinted in *Heart of Darkness*. Edited by Robert Kimbrough. New York: Norton, 1963, pp. 207–211. Also reprinted in *Conrad: A Collection of Critical Essays*. Edited by Marvin Mudrick. Englewood Cliffs, N.J.: Prentice-Hall, 1966, pp. 37–44.

Reid, Stephen A. "The 'Unspeakable Rites' in *Heart of Darkness*," in *Modern Fiction Studies*. IX (Winter, 1963–1964), pp. 347–356. Reprinted in *Conrad: A Collection of Critical Essays*. Edited by Marvin Mudrick. Englewood Cliffs, N.J.: Prentice-Hall, 1966, pp. 45–54.

Ridley, Florence H. "The Ultimate Meaning of *Heart of Darkness*," in *Nineteenth-Century Fiction*. XVIII (1963), pp. 43–53.

Ryf, Robert S. "Joseph Conrad," in *Six Modern British Novelists*. Edited by George Stade. New York: Columbia University Press, 1974, pp. 145–149.

Singh, Frances B. "The Colonialistic Bias of *Heart of Darkness*," in *Conradiana*. X (1978), pp. 41–54.

Thale, Jerome. "Marlow's Quest," in *University of Toronto Quarterly*. XXIV (1955), pp. 351–358. Reprinted in *The Art of Joseph Conrad: A Critical Symposium*. Edited by Robert W. Stallman. East Lansing: Michigan State University Press, 1960, pp. 154–161. Also reprinted in *Joseph Conrad's* Heart of Darkness: *Backgrounds and Criticisms*. Edited by Leonard Dean. Englewood Cliffs, N.J.: Prentice-Hall, 1960, pp. 159–166. Also reprinted in *Heart of Darkness*. Edited by Robert Kimbrough. New York: Norton, 1963, pp. 180–186.

Watt, Ian Pierre. "Impressionism and Symbolism in *Heart of Darkness*," in *Joseph Conrad: A Commemoration*. Edited by Norman Sherry. New York: Barnes & Noble, 1977, pp. 37–53.

Watts, C.T. "*Heart of Darkness*: The Covert Murder-Plot and the Darwinian Theme," in *Conradiana*. VII (1975), pp. 137–143.

Lord Jim

Allen, Walter E. *Six Great Novelists*. London: H. Hamilton, 1955, pp. 165–172.

Andreach, Robert J. *The Slain and Resurrected God: Conrad, Ford, and the Christian Myth*. New York: New York University Press, 1970, pp. 58–66.

Baines, Jocelyn. *Joseph Conrad: A Critical Biography*. New York: McGraw-Hill, 1960, pp. 241–252. Reprinted in *Twentieth Century Interpretations of Lord Jim: A Collection of Critical Essays*. Edited by Robert E. Kuehn. Englewood Cliffs, N.J.: Prentice-Hall, 1969, pp. 35–45.

Berthoud, Jacques. *Joseph Conrad: The Major Phase*. New York: Cambridge University Press, 1978, pp. 64–93.

Cox, C.B. "The Metamorphosis of Lord Jim," in *Critical Quarterly*. XV (1973), pp. 9–31.

Curle, Richard. *Joseph Conrad and His Characters*. London: Heinemann, 1957, pp. 29–65.

Daleski, Herman M. *Joseph Conrad, The Way of Dispossession*. New York: Holmes and Meier, 1977, pp. 77–103.

Drew, Elizabeth A. *The Novel: A Modern Guide to Fifteen English Masterpieces*. New York: Norton, 1963, pp. 156–172.

Epstein, Harry S. "*Lord Jim* as a Tragic Action," in *Studies in the Novel*. V (1973), pp. 229–247.

Guerard, Albert J. *Conrad the Novelist*. Cambridge, Mass.: Harvard University Press, 1958, pp. 126–178. Reprinted in *Twentieth Century Interpretations of* Lord Jim: *A Collection of Critical Essays*. Edited by Robert E. Kuehn. Englewood Cliffs, N.J.: Prentice-Hall, 1969, pp. 82–99.

Haugh, Robert F. *Joseph Conrad: Discovery in Design*. Norman: University of Oklahoma Press, 1957, pp. 56–77.

Hewitt, Douglas. *Conrad: A Reassessment*. Cambridge: Bowes and Bowes, 1952, pp. 31–49. Reprinted in *Conrad: A Collection of Critical Essays*. Edited by Marvin Mudrick. New York: Prentice-Hall, 1966, pp. 55–62.

Karl, Frederick. *A Reader's Guide to Joseph Conrad*. New York: Noonday, 1960, pp. 120–131.

Krieger, Murray. *The Tragic Vision: Variations on a Theme in Literary Interpretation*. New York: Holt, Rinehart and Winston, 1960, pp. 165–179.

Madden, William A. "The Search for Forgiveness in Some Nineteenth Century English Novels," in *Comparative Literature Studies*. III (1966), pp. 139–153.

Marković, Vida E. *The Changing Face: Disintegration of Personality in the Twentieth Century British Novel, 1900–1950*. Carbondale: Southern Illinois University Press, 1970, pp. 3–17.

Miller, Joseph H. "The Interpretation of *Lord Jim*," in *The Interpretation of Narrative: Theory and Practice*. Edited by Morton W. Bloomfield. Cambridge, Mass.: Harvard University Press, 1970, pp. 211–228.

Morf, Gustav. *The Polish Shades and Ghosts of Joseph Conrad*. New York: Twayne, 1976, pp. 143–158.

Perry, John Oliver. "Action, Vision or Voice: The Moral Dilemmas in Conrad's Tale-Telling," in *Modern Fiction Studies*. X (Spring, 1964), pp. 3–14.

Roussel, Royal. *The Metaphysics of Darkness: A Study in the Unity and Development of Conrad's Fiction*. Baltimore: Johns Hopkins University Press, 1971, pp. 80–108.

Saveson, John E. *Joseph Conrad: The Making of a Moralist*. Amsterdam: Rodopi, 1972, pp. 37–53, 65–83, 89–107, 137–161, 165–178.

Tanner, Tony. "Butterflies and Beetles—Conrad's Two Truths," in *Chicago Review*. XVI (Winter–Spring, 1963), pp. 123–140. Reprinted in *Twentieth Century Interpretations of* Lord Jim: *A Collection of Critical Essays*. Edited by Robert E. Kuehn. Englewood Cliffs, N.J.: Prentice-Hall, 1969, pp. 53–67.

Van Ghent, Dorothy. "On *Lord Jim*," in *The English Novel: Form and Function*. New York: Holt, Rinehart and Winston, 1953, pp. 229–244. Reprinted in *Twentieth Century Interpretations of* Lord Jim: *A Collection of Critical Essays*. Edited by Robert E. Kuehn. Englewood Cliffs, N.J.: Prentice-Hall, 1969, pp. 68–81.

Wiley, Paul L. *Conrad's Measure of Man*. Madison: University of Wisconsin Press, 1954, pp. 5–63. Reprinted in *Twentieth Century Interpretations of* Lord Jim: *A Collection of Critical Essays*. Edited by Robert E. Kuehn. Englewood Cliffs, N.J.: Prentice-Hall, 1969, pp. 46–52.

Wright, Walter F. *Romance and Tragedy in Joseph Conrad*. Lincoln: University of Nebraska Press, 1949, pp. 107–123.

The Nigger of the "Narcissus"

Andreas, Osborn. *Joseph Conrad: A Study in Non-Conformity*. New York: Philosophical Library, 1959, pp. 16–22.

Baines, Jocelyn. *Joseph Conrad: A Critical Biography*. New York: McGraw-Hill, 1960, pp. 180–187.

Beach, Joseph Warren. *The Twentieth Century Novel: Studies in Technique*. New York: Appleton-Century-Crofts, 1932, pp. 348–352.

Berthoud, Jacques. *Joseph Conrad: The Major Phase*. New York: Cambridge University Press, 1978, pp. 23–40.

Boyle, Ted Eugene. *Symbol and Meaning in the Fiction of Joseph Conrad*. New York: Humanities Press, 1965, pp. 38–59.

Daleski, Herman M. *Joseph Conrad, The Way of Dispossession*. New York: Holmes and Meier, 1977, pp. 26–50.

Dowden, Wilfred. *Joseph Conrad: The Imaged Style*. Nashville, Tenn.: Vanderbilt University Press, 1970, pp. 48–56.

Follett, Wilson. *Joseph Conrad: A Short Study of His Intellectual and Emotional Attitude Toward His Work and of the Chief Characteristics of His Novels*. Garden City, N.Y.: Doubleday and Page, 1915, pp. 40–48.

Gordan, John D. *Joseph Conrad: The Making of a Novelist*. Cambridge, Mass.: Harvard University Press, 1940, pp. 130–150.

Guerard, Albert J. *Conrad the Novelist*. Cambridge, Mass.: Harvard University Press, 1958, pp. 100–125. Reprinted in *Conrad: A Collection of Critical Essays*. Edited by Marvin Mudrick. New York: Prentice-Hall, 1966, pp. 17–36. Also reprinted in *Twentieth Century Interpretations of* The Nigger of the "Narcissus": *A Collection of Critical Essays.* Edited by John A. Palmer. Englewood Cliffs, N.J.: Prentice-Hall, 1969, pp. 56–68. Also reprinted in *The Art of Joseph Conrad: A Critical Symposium.* Edited by Robert W. Stallman. East Lansing: Michigan State University Press, 1960, pp. 121–139.

Gurko, Leo. *Joseph Conrad: Giant in Exile.* New York: Macmillan, 1962, pp. 68–79.

Haugh, Robert F. *Joseph Conrad: Discovery in Design.* Norman: University of Oklahoma Press, 1957, pp. 3–24.

Johnson, Bruce. *Conrad's Models of Mind.* Minneapolis: University of Minnesota Press, 1971, pp. 24–40.

Karl, Frederick R. *A Reader's Guide to Joseph Conrad.* New York: Noonday, 1960, pp. 108–117.

Mayne, Ernest J. "Waimbo in Conrad's *The Nigger of the 'Narcissus,'*" in *Conradiana.* X (1978), pp. 55–61.

Miller, James E., Jr. "*The Nigger of the 'Narcissus'*: A Re-Examination," in *PMLA.* LXVI (December, 1951), pp. 911–918. Reprinted in *Twentieth Century Interpretations of* The Nigger of the "Narcissus": *A Collection of Critical Essays.* Edited by John A. Palmer. Englewood Cliffs, N.J.: Prentice-Hall, 1969, pp. 18–24.

Moorthy, P. Rama. "*The Nigger of the 'Narcissus,'*" in *Literary Criterion.* VII (1965), pp. 49–58.

Morf, Gustav. *The Polish Shades and Ghosts of Joseph Conrad.* New York: Twayne, 1976, pp. 160–177.

Mudrick, Marvin. "The Artist's Conscience and *The Nigger of the 'Narcissus,'*" in *Nineteenth-Century Fiction.* XI (1957), pp. 288–297. Reprinted in *Twentieth Century Interpretations of* The Nigger of the "Narcissus": *A Collection of Critical Essays.* Edited by John A. Palmer. Englewood Cliffs, N.J.: Prentice-Hall, 1969, pp. 69–77.

Scrimgeour, Cecil. "Jimmy Wait and the Dance of Death: Conrad's *Nigger of the 'Narcissus,'*" in *Critical Quarterly.* VII (Winter, 1965), pp. 339–352. Reprinted in *Twentieth Century Interpretations of* The Nigger of the "Narcissus": *A Collection of Critical Essays.* Edited by John A. Palmer. Englewood Cliffs, N.J.: Prentice-Hall, 1969, pp. 40–55.

Smith, David R. " 'One Word More' About *The Nigger of the 'Narcissus,'* " in *Nineteenth-Century Fiction.* XXIII (1968), pp. 201–216.

Watt, Ian. "Conrad Criticism and *The Nigger of the 'Narcissus,'*" in *Nineteenth-Century Fiction.* XII (1958), pp. 257–283. Reprinted in *Twentieth Century Interpretations of* The Nigger of the "Narcissus": *A Collection of Critical Essays.* Edited by John A. Palmer. Englewood Cliffs, N.J.: Prentice-Hall, 1969, pp. 78–99.

Wiley, Paul L. *Conrad's Measure of Man.* Madison: University of Wisconsin Press, 1954, pp. 44–50. Reprinted in *Twentieth Century Interpretations of* The Nigger of the "Narcissus": *A Collection of Critical Essays.* Edited by John A. Palmer. Englewood Cliffs, N.J.: Prentice-Hall, 1969, pp. 108–112.

Young, Vernon. "Trial by Water: Joseph Conrad's *The Nigger of the 'Narcissus,'* " in *Accent.* XII (Spring, 1952), pp. 67–81. Reprinted in *The Art of Joseph Conrad: A Critical Symposium.* Edited by Robert W. Stallman. East Lansing: Michigan State University Press, 1960, pp. 108–120. Also reprinted in *Twentieth Century Interpretations of* The Nigger of the "Narcissus": *A Collection of Critical Essays.* Edited by John A. Palmer. Englewood Cliffs, N.J.: Prentice-Hall, 1969, pp. 25–39.

Zabel, Morton Dauwen. *Craft and Character in Modern Fiction: Texts, Methods, and Vocation in Modern Fiction.* New York: Viking, 1957, pp. 168–186.

Nostromo

Allen, Walter Ernest. *Six Great Novelists.* London: H. Hamilton, 1955, pp. 175–181.

Andreach, Robert J. *The Slain and Resurrected God: Conrad, Ford, and the Christian Myth.* New York: New York University Press, 1970, pp. 66–76.

Baines, Jocelyn. *Joseph Conrad: A Critical Biography.* New York: McGraw-Hill, 1960, pp. 297–315. Reprinted in *Conrad: A Collection of Critical Essays.* Edited by Marvin Mudrick. Englewood Cliffs, N.J.: Prentice-Hall, 1966, pp. 83–101.

Berthoud, Jacques. *Joseph Conrad: The Major Phase.* New York: Cambridge University Press, 1978, pp. 94–130.

Bevan, Ernest, Jr. "*Nostromo*: The Permanence of the Past," in *Conradiana.* X (1978), pp. 63–71.

Cooper, Christopher. *Conrad and the Human Dilemma.* New York: Barnes & Noble, 1970, pp. 105–148.

Cox, C.B. *Joseph Conrad: The Modern Imagination.* Totowa, N.J.: Rowman and Littlefield, 1974, pp. 60–82.

Curle, Richard. *Joseph Conrad and His Characters.* London: Heinemann, 1957, pp. 67–107.

Daiches, David. *The Novel and the Modern World.* Chicago: University of Chicago Press, 1960, pp. 42–54.

Daleski, Herman M. *Joseph Conrad, The Way of Dispossession.* New York: Holmes and Meier, 1977, pp. 113–143.

Friedman, Alan. *The Turn of the Novel.* New York: Oxford University Press, 1966, pp. 75–105.

Guerard, Albert J. *Conrad the Novelist.* Cambridge, Mass.: Harvard University Press, 1958, pp. 175–217.

Gurko, Leo. *Joseph Conrad: Giant in Exile.* New York: Macmillan, 1962, pp. 122–143.

Hay, Eloise Knapp. *The Political Novels of Joseph Conrad.* Chicago: University of Chicago Press, 1963, pp. 161–216.

Hewitt, Douglas J. *Conrad: A Reassessment.* Cambridge: Bowes and Bowes, 1952, pp. 46–69.

Johnson, Bruce. *Conrad's Models of Mind.* Minneapolis: University of Minnesota Press, 1971, pp. 106–125.

Karl, Frederick R. *A Reader's Guide to Joseph Conrad.* New York: Noonday, 1960, pp. 145–188.

Leavis, F.R. *The Great Tradition: George Eliot, Henry James, Joseph Conrad.* London: Chatto and Windus, 1948, pp. 191–201. Reprinted in *Critiques and Essays on Modern Fiction, 1920–1951.* Edited by John W. Aldridge. New York: Ronald Press, 1952, pp. 120–128.

Morf, Gustav. *The Polish Shades and Ghosts of Joseph Conrad.* New York: Twayne, 1976, pp. 160–177.

Muller, Herbert J. *In Pursuit of Relevance.* Bloomington: Indiana University Press, 1971, pp. 164–176.

Oates, Joyce Carol. " 'The Immense Indifference of Things': The Tragedy of Conrad's *Nostromo*," in *Novel.* IX (1975), pp. 5–22.

Rosenfield, Claire. *Paradise of Snakes: An Archetypal Analysis of Conrad's Political Novels.* Chicago: University of Chicago Press, 1967, pp. 43–78.

Tillyard, Eustace M.W. *The Epic Strain in the English Novel.* Fair Lawn, N.J.: Essential Books, 1958, pp. 126–167.

Warren, Robert Penn. "*Nostromo*," in *Sewanee Review.* LIX (Summer, 1951), pp. 363–391. Reprinted as "Introduction" to *Nostromo.* New York: Modern Library Edition, 1951. Also reprinted in *Selected Essays.* New York: Random House, 1958, pp. 31–58. Also reprinted in *Joseph Conrad: A Critical Symposium.* Edited by Robert W. Stallman. East Lansing: Michigan State University Press, 1960, pp. 209–227.

Wiley, Paul L. *Conrad's Measure of Man.* Madison: University of Wisconsin Press, 1954, pp. 98–106.

The Secret Agent

Baines, Jocelyn. *Joseph Conrad: A Critical Biography.* New York: McGraw-Hill, 1960, pp. 329–340.

Berthoud, Jacques. *Joseph Conrad: The Major Phase.* New York: Cambridge University Press, 1978, pp. 131–159.

Boyle, Ted Eugene. *Symbol and Meaning in the Fiction of Joseph Conrad.* New York: Humanities Press, 1965, pp. 38–59.

Cooper, Christopher. *Conrad and the Human Dilemma.* New York: Barnes & Noble, 1970, pp. 18–61.

Cox, C.B. *Joseph Conrad: The Modern Imagination.* Totowa, N.J.: Rowman and Littlefield, 1974, pp. 83–101.

Curle, Richard. *Joseph Conrad and His Characters.* London: Heinemann, 1957, pp. 109–144.

Daleski, Herman M. *Joseph Conrad, The Way of Dispossession.* Holmes and Meier, 1977, pp. 144–170.

Dowden, Wilfred S. *Joseph Conrad: The Imaged Style.* Nashville, Tenn.: Vanderbilt University Press, 1970, pp. 112–123.

Guerard, Albert J. *Conrad the Novelist.* Cambridge, Mass.: Harvard University Press, 1958, pp. 218–231. Reprinted in *Conrad:* The Secret Agent, *A Casebook.* Edited by Ian Watt. London: Macmillan, 1973, pp. 150–165.

Gurko, Leo. *Joseph Conrad: Giant in Exile.* New York: Macmillan, 1962, pp. 164–178.

Haugh, Robert F. *Joseph Conrad: Discovery in Design.* Norman: University of Oklahoma Press, 1957, pp. 136–146.

Hewitt, Douglas. *Conrad: A Reassessment.* Cambridge: Bowes and Bowes, 1952, pp. 85–88.

Holland, Norman. "Style as Character: *The Secret Agent,*" in *Modern Fiction Studies.* XII (1966), pp. 221–231.

Howe, Irving. *Politics and the Novel.* New York: Horizon Press, 1957, pp. 93–100. Reprinted in *Conrad:* The Secret Agent, *A Casebook.* Edited by Ian Watt. London: Macmillan, 1973, pp. 140–149.

Knoepflmacher, Ulrich Camillus. *Laughter and Despair: Readings in Ten Novels of the Victorian Era.* Berkeley: University of California Press, 1971, pp. 240–273.

Leavis, F.R. *The Great Tradition: George Eliot, Henry James, Joseph Conrad.* London: Chatto and Windus, 1948, pp. 209–221. Reprinted in *Conrad:* The Secret Agent, *A Casebook.* Edited by Ian Watt. London: Macmillan, 1973, pp. 118–132.

Mann, Thomas. *Past Masters and Other Papers.* London: Secker and Warburg, 1933, pp. 231–247. Reprinted in *Conrad:* The Secret Agent, *A Casebook.* Edited by Ian Watt. London: Macmillan, 1973, pp. 99–112.

Miller, Joseph H. *Poets of Reality: Six Twentieth-Century Writers.* Cambridge, Mass.: Harvard University Press, 1966, pp. 39–67.

Morf, Gustav. *The Polish Shades and Ghosts of Joseph Conrad.* New York: Twayne, 1976, pp. 178–184.

O'Grady, Walter. "On Plot in Modern Fiction: Hardy, James and Conrad," in *Modern Fiction Studies*. XI (Summer, 1965), pp. 107–115.

Spector, Robert D. "Irony as Theme: Conrad's *The Secret Agent*," in *Nineteenth-Century Fiction*. XIII (1958), pp. 69–71. Reprinted in *Conrad: The Secret Agent, A Casebook*. Edited by Ian Watt. London: Macmillan, 1973, pp. 166–169.

Tillyard, Eustace M.W. "*The Secret Agent* Reconsidered," in *Essays in Criticism*. XI (July, 1961), pp. 309–318. Reprinted in *Conrad: A Collection of Critical Essays*. Edited by Marvin Mudrick. Englewood Cliffs, N.J.: Prentice-Hall, 1966, pp. 103–110.

Warner, Oliver. *Joseph Conrad*. London: Longmans, 1951, pp. 104–113.

Wiley, Paul L. *Conrad's Measure of Man*. Madison: University of Wisconsin Press, 1954, pp. 107–121.

Wright, Walter F. *Romance and Tragedy in Joseph Conrad*. Lincoln: University of Nebraska Press, 1949, pp. 175–197.

"The Secret Sharer"

Andreas, Osborn. *Joseph Conrad: A Study in Non-Conformity*. New York: Philosophical Library, 1959, pp. 135–138.

Baines, Jocelyn. *Joseph Conrad: A Critical Biography*. New York: McGraw-Hill, 1960, pp. 355–359. Reprinted in *Conrad's "The Secret Sharer" and the Critics*. Edited by Bruce Harkness. Belmont, Calif.: Wadsworth, 1962, pp. 116–121.

Benson, Carl. "Conrad's Two Stories of Initiations," in *PMLA*. LXIX (1954), pp. 46–56. Reprinted in *Conrad's "The Secret Sharer" and the Critics*. Edited by Bruce Harkness. Belmont, Calif.: Wadsworth, 1962, pp. 83–93.

Curley, Daniel. "Legate of the Ideal," in *Conrad's "The Secret Sharer" and the Critics*. Edited by Bruce Harkness. Belmont, Calif.: Wadsworth, 1962, pp. 75–82. Reprinted in *Conrad: A Collection of Critical Essays*. Edited by Marvin Mudrick. Englewood Cliffs, N.J.: Prentice-Hall, 1966, pp. 75–82.

Daleski, Herman M. *Joseph Conrad, The Way of Dispossession*. New York: Holmes and Meier, 1977, pp. 171–183.

Day, Robert A. "The Rebirth of Leggatt," in *Literature and Psychology*. XIII (Summer, 1963), pp. 74–81.

Gettman, Royal and Bruce Harkness. "Morality and Psychology in 'The Secret Sharer,' " in *Conrad's "The Secret Sharer" and the Critics*. Edited by Bruce Harkness. Belmont, Calif.: Wadsworth, 1962, pp. 125–132.

Guerard, Albert J. *Conrad the Novelist*. Cambridge, Mass.: Harvard University Press, 1958, pp. 21–29. Reprinted in *Conrad's "The Secret Sharer" and the Critics*. Edited by Bruce Harkness. Belmont, Calif.: Wadsworth, 1962, pp. 59–74. Also reprinted in *The Personal Voice*. Edited by Albert J. Guerard, et. al. Philadelphia: Lippincott, 1964, pp. 458–464.

Haugh, Robert F. *Joseph Conrad: Discovery in Design.* Norman: University of Oklahoma Press, 1957, pp. 78–82.

Hewitt, Douglas. *Conrad: A Reassessment.* Cambridge: Bowes and Bowes, 1952, pp. 70–79. Reprinted in *The Art of Joseph Conrad: A Critical Symposium.* Edited by Robert W. Stallman. East Lansing: Michigan State University Press, 1960, pp. 289–295.

Hoffmann, Charles G. "Point of View in 'The Secret Sharer,' " in *College English.* XXIII (1962), pp. 651–654.

Karl, Frederick R. *A Reader's Guide to Joseph Conrad.* New York: Noonday, 1960, pp. 230–236.

Leiter, Louis H. "Echo Structures: Conrad's 'The Secret Sharer,' " in *Twentieth-Century Literature.* V (January, 1960), pp. 159–175. Reprinted in *Conrad's "The Secret Sharer" and the Critics.* Edited by Bruce Harkness. Belmont, Calif.: Wadsworth, 1962, pp. 133–150. Also reprinted in *Approaches to the Short Story.* Edited by Neil D. Isaacs and Louis H. Leiter. San Francisco: Chandler, 1963, pp. 185–207.

Morf, Gustav. *The Polish Shades and Ghosts of Joseph Conrad.* New York: Twayne, 1976, pp. 205–207.

Moser, Thomas. *Joseph Conrad: Achievement and Decline.* Cambridge, Mass.: Harvard University Press, 1957, pp. 138–141.

Robinson, E. Arthur. "Conrad's 'The Secret Sharer,' " in *Explicator.* XVIII (February, 1960), item 28.

Stallman, Robert W. "Conrad and 'The Secret Sharer,' " in *Accent.* IX (1949), pp. 131–143. Reprinted in *The Art of Modern Fiction.* Edited by Ray B. West and Robert W. Stallman. New York: Rinehart, 1949, pp. 490–498. Also reprinted in *The Art of Joseph Conrad: A Critical Symposium.* Edited by Robert W. Stallman. East Lansing: Michigan State University Press, 1960, pp. 275–288. Also reprinted in *Conrad's "The Secret Sharer" and the Critics.* Edited by Bruce Harkness. Belmont, Calif.: Wadsworth, 1962, pp. 94–109.

Wiley, Paul L. *Conrad's Measure of Man.* Madison: University of Wisconsin Press, 1954, pp. 94–97.

Williams, Porter, Jr. "The Brand of Cain in 'The Secret Sharer,' " in *Modern Fiction Studies.* X (Spring, 1964), pp. 27–30.

————. "The Matter of Conscience in Conrad's 'The Secret Sharer,' " in *PMLA.* LXXIX (December, 1964), pp. 626–630.

Wills, John H. "Conrad's 'The Secret Sharer,' " in *University of Kansas City Review.* XXVIII (Winter, 1961), pp. 115–126.

Wright, Walter F. *Romance and Tragedy in Joseph Conrad.* Lincoln: University of Nebraska Press, 1949, pp. 48–50. Reprinted in *Conrad's "The Secret Sharer" and the Critics.* Edited by Bruce Harkness. Belmont, Calif.: Wadsworth, 1962, pp. 122–124.

Zabel, Morton Dauwen. "Conrad: 'The Secret Sharer,' " in *New Republic.* CIV (April 21, 1941), pp. 567–568, 570–574.

Under Western Eyes

Andreach, Robert J. *The Slain and Resurrected God: Conrad, Ford, and the Christian Myth.* New York: New York University Press, 1970, pp. 86–96.

Baines, Jocelyn. *Joseph Conrad: A Critical Biography.* New York: McGraw-Hill, 1960, pp. 360–373.

Berthoud, Jacques. *Joseph Conrad: The Major Phase.* New York: Cambridge University Press, 1978, pp. 160–185.

Boyle, Ted Eugene. *Symbol and Meaning in the Fiction of Joseph Conrad.* New York: Humanities Press, 1965, pp. 195–217.

Canby, Henry Seidel. *"Under Western Eyes,"* in *A Conrad Memorial Library.* Edited by George T. Keating. Garden City, N.Y.: Doubleday, 1929, pp. 187–193.

Cooper, Christopher. *Conrad and the Human Dilemma.* New York: Barnes & Noble, 1970, pp. 62–104.

Cox, C.B. *Joseph Conrad: The Modern Imagination.* Totowa, N.J.: Rowman and Littlefield, 1974, pp. 102–117.

Curle, Richard. *Joseph Conrad and His Characters.* London: Heinemann, 1957, pp. 145–183.

Daleski, Herman M. *Joseph Conrad, The Way of Dispossession.* New York: Holmes and Meier, 1977, pp. 184–209.

Eagleton, Terence. *Exiles and Émigrés: Studies in Modern Literature.* New York: Schocken, 1970, pp. 21–32.

Gilliam, Harriet. "Time in Conrad's *Under Western Eyes,*" in *Nineteenth-Century Fiction.* XXXI (March, 1977), pp. 421–439.

Guerard, Albert J. *Conrad the Novelist.* Cambridge, Mass.: Harvard University Press, 1958, pp. 218–221, 231–253.

Gurko, Leo. *Joseph Conrad: Giant in Exile.* New York: Macmillan, 1962, pp. 182–196.

Haugh, Robert F. *Joseph Conrad: Discovery in Design.* Norman: University of Oklahoma Press, 1957, pp. 119–135.

Hay, Eloise Knapp. *The Political Novels of Joseph Conrad.* Chicago: University of Chicago Press, 1963, pp. 265–313.

Hewitt, Douglas. *Conrad: A Reassessment.* Cambridge: Bowes and Bowes, 1952, pp. 80–84.

Johnson, Bruce. *Conrad's Models of Mind.* Minneapolis: University of Minnesota Press, 1971, pp. 140–158.

Karl, Frederick R. *A Reader's Guide to Joseph Conrad.* New York: Noonday, 1960, pp. 211–228.

Leavis, F.R. *The Great Tradition: George Eliot, Henry James, Joseph Conrad.* London: Chatto and Windus, 1948, pp. 219–222.

Martin, W.R. "Compassionate Realism in Conrad and *Under Western Eyes*," in *English Studies in Africa* (Johannesburg). XVII (1974), pp. 89–100.

Morf, Gustav. *The Polish Shades and Ghosts of Joseph Conrad.* New York: Twayne, 1976, pp. 184–193.

Rosenfield, Claire. *Paradise of Snakes: An Archetypal Analysis of Conrad's Political Novels.* Chicago: University of Chicago Press, 1967, pp. 123–172.

Warner, Oliver. *Joseph Conrad.* London: Longmans, 1951, pp. 113–120.

Wiley, Paul L. *Conrad's Measure of Man.* Madison: University of Wisconsin Press, 1954, pp. 122–126.

Zabel, Morton Dauwen. "Introduction," in *Under Western Eyes.* New York: Doubleday, 1963. Reprinted in *Craft and Character: Texts, Methods, and Vocation in Modern Fiction.* New York: Viking, 1957, pp. 187–207. Also reprinted in *Conrad: A Collection of Critical Essays.* Edited by Marvin Mudrick. Englewood Cliffs, N.J.: Prentice-Hall, 1966, pp. 111–144.

Victory

Andreach, Robert J. *The Slain and Resurrected God: Conrad, Ford, and the Christian Myth.* New York: New York University Press, 1970, pp. 96–107.

Baines, Jocelyn. *Joseph Conrad: A Critical Biography.* New York: McGraw-Hill, 1960, pp. 394–400.

Beebe, Maurice. *Ivory Towers and Sacred Founts: The Artist as Hero in Fiction from Goethe to Joyce.* New York: New York University Press, 1964, pp. 114–171.

Bonney, William W. "Narrative Perspective in *Victory*: The Thematic Relevance," in *Journal of Narrative Technique.* V (1975), pp. 24–39.

Boyle, Ted Eugene. *Symbol and Meaning in the Fiction of Joseph Conrad.* New York: Humanities Press, 1965, pp. 218–238.

Cox, C.B. *Joseph Conrad: The Modern Imagination.* Totowa, N.J.: Rowman and Littlefield, 1974, pp. 125–136.

Curle, Richard. *Joseph Conrad and His Characters.* London: Heinemann, 1957, pp. 219–254.

Follett, Wilson. *Joseph Conrad: A Short Study of His Intellectual and Emotional Attitude Toward His Work and of the Chief Characteristics of His Novels.* Garden City, N.Y.: Doubleday and Page, 1915, pp. 14–28.

Guerard, Albert J. *Conrad the Novelist.* Cambridge, Mass.: Harvard University Press, 1958, pp. 254–261.

Gurko, Leo. *Joseph Conrad: Giant in Exile.* New York: Macmillan, 1962, pp. 212–221.

Haugh, Robert F. *Joseph Conrad: Discovery in Design.* Norman: University of Oklahoma Press, 1957, pp. 102–116.

Hewitt, Douglas. *Conrad: A Reassessment.* Cambridge: Bowes and Bowes, 1952, pp. 103–111.

Johnson, Bruce. *Conrad's Models of Mind.* Minneapolis: University of Minnesota Press, 1971, pp. 159–176.

Kaehéle, Sharon and Howard German. "Conrad's *Victory*: A Reassessment," in *Modern Fiction Studies.* X (Spring, 1964), pp. 55–72.

Karl, Frederick R. *A Reader's Guide to Joseph Conrad.* New York: Noonday, 1960, pp. 246–267.

Krieger, Murray. *The Tragic Vision: Variations on a Theme in Literary Interpretation.* New York: Holt, 1960, pp. 154–194.

Leavis, F.R. *The Great Tradition: George Eliot, Henry James, Joseph Conrad.* London: Chatto and Windus, 1948, pp. 201–209.

Lewis, R.W.B. "The Current of Conrad's *Victory*," in *Twelve Original Essays on Great English Novels.* Edited by Charles Shapiro. Detroit: Wayne State University Press, 1960, pp. 203–231. Reprinted in *Trials of the Word.* New Haven, Conn.: Yale University Press, 1965, pp. 148–169.

Meyers, Jeffrey. *Homosexuality and Literature, 1890–1930.* Montreal: McGill-Queens University Press, 1977, pp. 76–89.

Morf, Gustav. *The Polish Shades and Ghosts of Joseph Conrad.* New York: Twayne, 1976, pp. 215–221.

Palmer, John A. *Joseph Conrad's Fiction: A Study in Literary Growth.* Ithaca, N.Y.: Cornell University Press, 1968, pp. 166–197.

Park, Douglas B. "Conrad's *Victory*: The Anatomy of a Pose," in *Nineteenth-Century Fiction.* XXXI (September, 1976), pp. 150–169.

Warner, Oliver. *Joseph Conrad.* London: Longmans, 1951, pp. 120–126.

Webster, H.T. "Joseph Conrad: A Reinterpretation of Five Novels," in *College English.* VII (December, 1945), pp. 125–134.

Wiley, Paul L. *Conrad's Measure of Man.* Madison: University of Wisconsin Press, 1954, pp. 151–157.

BENJAMIN CONSTANT
(1767–1830)

Adolphe

Alexander, Ian W. *Benjamin Constant:* Adolphe. London: Edward Arnold, 1973.

Baguley, David. "The Role of Letters in Constant's *Adolphe*," in *Forum for Modern Language Studies.* XI (1975), pp. 29–35.

Blanchot, Maurice. "*Adolphe*, or, the Curse of Real Feelings," in *Yale French Studies.* XIII (Spring–Summer, 1954), pp. 62–75.

————. "*Adolphe*; or, the Misfortunes of Sincerity," in *Horizon.* XX (August, 1949), pp. 94–110.

Cruickshank, John. *Benjamin Constant.* New York: Twayne, 1974, pp. 135–140.

Fairlie, Alison. "The Art of Constant's *Adolphe*: Creation of Character," in *Forum for Modern Language Studies.* II (July, 1966), pp. 253–263.

————. "The Art of Constant's *Adolphe*: Structure and Style," in *French Studies.* XX (July, 1966), pp. 226–240.

George, Albert J. *Short Fiction in France: 1800–1850.* Syracuse, N.Y.: Syracuse University Press, 1964, pp. 47–52.

Greshoff, C.J. "Adolphe *and the Romantic Delusion*," in *Forum for Modern Language Studies.* I (January, 1965), pp. 30–36.

Hobson, Marian. "Theme and Structure in *Adolphe*," in *Modern Language Review.* LXVI (1971), pp. 306–314.

Holdheim, William W. *Benjamin Constant.* London: Bowes and Bowes, 1961, pp. 41–48.

Merken-Spaas, Godelieve. "Ecriture in Constant's *Adolphe*," in *French Review.* Special Issue VI (1974), pp. 57–62.

Murry, John Middleton. *The Conquest of Death.* London: Peter Nevill, 1951, pp. 125–306.

Nicolson, Harold. *Benjamin Constant.* Garden City, N.Y.: Doubleday and Company, 1949, pp. 201–207.

Shapiro, Norman R. "The Symmetry of Benjamin Constant's *Adolphe*," in *French Review.* XXXIV (December, 1960), pp. 186–188.

Sullivan, Edward D. "Constraint and Expansion in Benjamin Constant's *Adolphe*," in *French Review.* XXXII (February, 1959), pp. 293–299.

Thomas, Ruth P. "The Ambiguous Narrator of *Adolphe*," in *Romance Notes.* XIV (1973), pp. 486–495.

Turnell, Martin. *The Novel in France.* New York: New Directions, 1951, pp. 91–122.

JOHN ESTEN COOKE
(1830–1886)

The Works of Cooke

Beaty, John O. *John Esten Cooke, Virginian.* New York: Columbia University Press, 1922.

Cowie, Alexander. *The Rise of the American Novel.* New York: American Book, 1948, pp. 463–472.

Holliday, Carl. "John Esten Cooke as a Novelist," in *Sewanee Review.* XIII (April, 1905), pp. 216–220.

Hubbell, Jay B. *The South in American Literature, 1607–1900.* Durham, N.C.: Duke University Press, 1954, pp. 511–521.

O'Brien, Matthew C. "John Esten Cooke, George Washington, and the Virginia Cavaliers," in *Virginia Magazine of History and Biography.* LXXXIV (1976), pp. 259–265.

Patten, Irene M. "The Civil War as Romance: Of Noble Warriors and Maidens Chaste," in *American Heritage.* XXII (1971), pp. 48–53.

Starnes, Lucy G. "Scribe of the Old Dominion," in *Virginia Cavalcade.* XIII (1963), pp. 32–37.

JAMES FENIMORE COOPER
(1789–1851)

The Chainbearer

Cosgrove, William E. "Family Lineage and Narrative Pattern in Cooper's Littlepage Trilogy," in *Forum* (Houston). XII (1974), pp. 2–8.

Dekker, George. *James Fenimore Cooper: The American Scott.* New York: Barnes & Noble, 1967, pp. 229–232, 234–235.

Dryden, Edgar A. "History and Progress: Some Implications of Form in Cooper's Littlepage Novels," in *Nineteenth-Century Fiction.* XXVI (1971), pp. 49–64.

Ellis, David M. "*The Chainbearer,*" in *James Fenimore Cooper: A Re-appraisal.* Edited by Mary Cunningham. New York: New York State Historical Association, 1954, pp. 412–422.

McWilliams, John P., Jr. *Political Justice in a Republic: James Fenimore Cooper's America.* Berkeley: University of California Press, 1972, pp. 315–325.

Ringe, Donald A. "Cooper's Littlepage Novels: Change and Stability in American Society," in *American Literature.* XXXII (November, 1960), pp. 280–290.

Walker, Warren S. *James Fenimore Cooper; an Introduction and Interpretation.* New York: Holt, Rinehart and Winston, 1962, pp. 94–97.

————. *Plots and Characters in the Works of James Fenimore Cooper.* Hamden, Conn.: Shoe String Press, 1978.

The Deerslayer

Baym, Nina. "The Women of Cooper's Leatherstocking Tales," in *American Quarterly.* XXIII (1971), pp. 696–709.

Bowden, Edwin T. *The Dungeon of the Heart: Human Isolation and the American Novel.* New York: Macmillan, 1961, pp. 20–23.

Davis, David B. "The Deerslayer, a Democratic Knight of the Wilderness," in *Twelve Original Essays on Great American Novels.* Edited by Charles Shapiro. Detroit: Wayne State University Press, 1958, pp. 1–22.

Dekker, George. *James Fenimore Cooper: The American Scott.* New York: Barnes & Noble, 1967, pp. 170–191.

Frederick, John T. "Cooper's Eloquent Indians," in *PMLA.* LXXXI (1956), pp. 1004–1017.

House, Kay S. *Cooper's Americans.* Columbus: Ohio State University Press, 1965, pp. 315–326.

Lawrence, D.H.   "Fenimore Cooper's Leatherstocking Novels," in *Studies in Classic American Literature*. New York: Doubleday, 1955, pp. 55–73.

McAleer, John J.   "Biblical Analogy in the Leatherstocking Tales," in *Nineteenth-Century Fiction*. XVII (1962), pp. 217–235.

McWilliams, John P., Jr.   *Political Justice in a Republic: James Fenimore Cooper's America*. Berkeley: University of California Press, 1972, pp. 238–246, 276–291.

Mizener, Arthur.   *Twelve Great American Novels*. New York: World, 1969, pp. 1–8.

Noble, David W.   "Cooper, Leatherstocking and the Death of the American Adam," in *American Quarterly*. XVI (1964), pp. 419–431.

Paine, Gregory L.   "The Indians of the Leatherstocking Tales," in *Studies in Philology*. XXIII (1926), pp. 16–39.

Pearce, Roy H.   "The Leatherstocking Tales Re-examined," in *South Atlantic Quarterly*. XLVI (1947), pp. 524–536.

Pound, Louise.   "The Dialect of Cooper's Leatherstocking," in *American Speech*. II (1927), pp. 479–488.

Ringe, Donald A.   *James Fenimore Cooper*. New York: Twayne, 1962, pp. 84–90.

Sandy, Alan F., Jr.   "The Voices of Cooper's *The Deerslayer*," in *Emerson Society Quarterly*. LX (1970), pp. 5–9.

Smith, Henry N.   "Consciousness and Social Order: The Theme of Transcendence in the Leatherstocking Tales," in *Western American Literature*. V (1970), pp. 177–194.

VanDerBeets, Richard.   "Cooper and the 'Semblance of Reality': A Source for *The Deerslayer*," in *American Literature*. XLII (1971), pp. 544–546.

Vlach, John M.   "Fenimore Cooper's Leatherstocking as Folk Hero," in *New York Folklore Quarterly*. XXVII (1971), pp. 323–338.

Walker, Warren S.   *James Fenimore Cooper; An Introduction and Interpretation*. New York: Holt, Rinehart and Winston, 1962, pp. 32–36, 49–53.

————.   *Plots and Characters in the Works of James Fenimore Cooper*. Hamden, Conn.: Shoe String Press, 1978.

Zoellner, Robert H.   "Conceptual Ambivalence in Cooper's Leatherstocking," in *American Literature*. XXXI (January, 1960), pp. 397–420.

The Last of the Mohicans

Baym, Nina.   "The Women of Cooper's Leatherstocking Tales," in *American Quarterly*. XXIII (1971), pp. 696–709.

Butler, M.D.   "Narrative Structure and Historical Process in *The Last of the Mohicans*," in *American Literature*. XLVIII (May, 1976), pp. 117–139.

Darnell, Donald. "Uncas as Hero: The Ubi Sunt Formula in *The Last of the Mohicans*," in *American Literature.* XXXVII (November, 1965), pp. 259–266.

Fiedler, Leslie A. *Love and Death in the American Novel.* New York: Criterion, 1960, pp. 197–206.

Frederick, John T. "Cooper's Eloquent Indians," in *PMLA.* LXXXI (1956), pp. 1004–1017.

French, David P. "James Fenimore Cooper and Fort William Henry," in *American Literature.* XXXII (March, 1960), pp. 28–38.

Haberly, D.T. "Women and Indians: *The Last of the Mohicans* and the Captivity Traditions," in *American Quarterly.* XXVIII (Fall, 1976), pp. 431–443.

House, Kay S. *Cooper's Americans.* Columbus: Ohio State University Press, 1965, pp. 277–293.

McAleer, John J. "Biblical Analogy in the Leatherstocking Tales," in *Nineteenth-Century Fiction.* XVII (1962), pp. 217–235.

McWilliams, John P., Jr. *Political Justice in a Republic: James Fenimore Cooper's America.* Berkeley: University of California Press, 1972, pp. 238–246, 287–291.

Martin, Terence. "From the Ruins of History: *The Last of the Mohicans*," in *Novel: A Forum on Fiction.* II (1969), pp. 221–229.

Maxwell, Desmond E.S. *American Fiction: The Intellectual Background.* New York: Columbia University Press, 1963, pp. 97–140.

Noble, David W. "Cooper, Leatherstocking and the Death of the American Adam," in *American Quarterly.* XVI (1964), pp. 419–431.

Paine, Gregory L. "The Indians of the Leatherstocking Tales," in *Studies in Philology.* XXIII (1926), pp. 16–39.

Pearce, Roy H. "The Leatherstocking Tales Re-examined," in *South Atlantic Quarterly.* XLVI (1947), pp. 524–536.

Philbrick, Thomas. "*The Last of the Mohicans* and the Sounds of Discord," in *American Literature.* XLIII (1971), pp. 25–41.

Pound, Louise. "The Dialect of Cooper's Leatherstocking," in *American Speech.* II (1927), pp. 479–488.

Smith, Henry N. "Consciousness and Social Order: The Theme of Transcendence in the Leatherstocking Tales," in *Western American Literature.* V (1970), pp. 177–194.

Vlach, John M. "Fenimore Cooper's Leatherstocking as Folk Hero," in *New York Folklore Quarterly.* XXVII (1971), pp. 323–338.

Walker, Warren S. *James Fenimore Cooper; An Introduction and Interpretation.* New York: Holt, Rinehart and Winston, 1962, pp. 53–57, 105–106.

————. *Plots and Characters in the Works of James Fenimore Cooper.* Hamden, Conn.: Shoe String Press, 1978.

Zoellner, Robert H.   "Conceptual Ambivalence in Cooper's Leatherstocking," in *American Literature.* XXXI (January, 1960), pp. 397–420.

The Pathfinder

Baym, Nina.   "The Women of Cooper's Leatherstocking Tales," in *American Quarterly.* XXIII (1971), pp. 696–709.

Bush, Sargent, Jr.   "Charles Cap of *The Pathfinder:* A Foil to Cooper's Views on the American Character in the 1840's," in *Nineteenth-Century Fiction.* XX (December, 1965), pp. 267–273.

Dekker, George.   *James Fenimore Cooper: The American Scott.* New York: Barnes & Noble, 1967, pp. 161–169.

Frederick, John T.   "Cooper's Eloquent Indians," in *PMLA.* LXXXI (1956), pp. 1004–1017.

House, Kay S.   *Cooper's Americans.* Columbus: Ohio State University Press, 1965, pp. 306–315.

McAleer, John J.   "Biblical Analogy in the Leatherstocking Tales," in *Nineteenth-Century Fiction.* XVII (1962), pp. 217–235.

McWilliams, John P., Jr.   *Political Justice in a Republic: James Fenimore Cooper's America.* Berkeley: University of California Press, 1972, pp. 238–246, 261, 288–291.

Noble, David W.   "Cooper, Leatherstocking and the Death of the American Adam," in *American Quarterly.* XVI (1964), pp. 419–431.

Paine, Gregory L.   "The Indians of the Leatherstocking Tales," in *Studies in Philology.* XXIII (1926), pp. 16–39.

Pearce, Roy H.   "The Leatherstocking Tales Re-examined," in *South Atlantic Quarterly.* XLVI (1947), pp. 524–536.

Pound, Louise.   "The Dialect of Cooper's Leatherstocking," in *American Speech.* II (1927), pp. 479–488.

Smith, Henry N.   "Consciousness and Social Order: The Theme of Transcendence in the Leatherstocking Tales," in *Western American Literature.* V (1970), pp. 177–194.

Vlach, John M.   "Fenimore Cooper's Leatherstocking as Folk Hero," in *New York Folklore Quarterly.* XXVII (1971), pp. 323–338.

Walker, Warren S.   *James Fenimore Cooper; An Introduction and Interpretation.* New York: Holt, Rinehart and Winston, 1962, pp. 41–44, 57–58.

————. *Plots and Characters in the Works of James Fenimore Cooper.* Hamden, Conn.: Shoe String Press, 1978.

Zoellner, Robert H.   "Conceptual Ambivalence in Cooper's Leatherstocking," in *American Literature.* XXXI (January, 1960), pp. 397–420.

The Pilot

Anderson, Charles. "Cooper's Sea Novels Spurned in the Maintop," in *Modern Language Notes.* LXVI (June, 1951), pp. 388–391.

Dekker, George. *James Fenimore Cooper: The American Scott.* New York: Barnes & Noble, 1967, pp. 37, 64, 113–118.

McWilliams, John P., Jr. *Political Justice in a Republic: James Fenimore Cooper's America.* Berkeley: University of California Press, 1972, pp. 64–73.

Peck, H. Daniel. "A Repossession of America: The Revolution in Cooper's Trilogy of Nautical Romances," in *Studies in Romanticism.* XV (Fall, 1976), pp. 589–605.

Philbrick, Thomas. *James Fenimore Cooper and the Development of American Sea Fiction.* Cambridge, Mass.: Harvard University Press, 1961, pp. 52–54, 81–83, 127–128.

Walker, Warren S. *James Fenimore Cooper; An Introduction and Interpretation.* New York: Holt, Rinehart and Winston, 1962, pp. 25–26, 71–82, 117–118.

_____. *Plots and Characters in the Works of James Fenimore Cooper.* Hamden, Conn.: Shoe String Press, 1978.

The Pioneers

Baym, Nina. "The Women of Cooper's Leatherstocking Tales," in *American Quarterly.* XXIII (1971), pp. 696–709.

Bercovitch, Sacvan. "Huckleberry Bumppo: A Comparison of *Tom Sawyer* and *The Pioneers,*" in *Mark Twain Journal.* XIV (Summer, 1968), pp. 1–4.

Dekker, George. *James Fenimore Cooper: The American Scott.* New York: Barnes & Noble, 1967, pp. 43–63.

Frederick, John T. "Cooper's Eloquent Indians," in *PMLA.* LXXXI (1956), pp. 1004–1017.

House, Kay S. *Cooper's Americans.* Columbus: Ohio State University Press, 1965, pp. 303–317.

_____. "*The Pioneers,*" in *The American Novel from James Fenimore Cooper to William Faulkner.* Edited by Wallace Stegner. New York: Basic Books, 1965.

Kasson, J.S. "Templeton Revisited: Social Criticism in *The Pioneers* and *Home as Found,*" in *Studies in the Novel.* IX (Spring, 1977), pp. 54–64.

Kehler, J.R. "Architectural Dialecticism in Cooper's *The Pioneers,*" in *Texas Studies in Literature and Language.* XVIII (Spring, 1976), pp. 124–134.

Kraus, Sister Mary Conrad. "Civilized Law vs. Primitive Law in *The Pioneers,*" in *CEA Critic.* XXXIX (March, 1977), pp. 9–10.

McAleer, John J. "Biblical Analogy in the Leatherstocking Tales," in *Nineteenth-Century Fiction.* XVII (1962), pp. 217–235.

McWilliams, John P., Jr. *Political Justice in a Republic: James Fenimore Cooper's America.* Berkeley: University of California Press, 1972.

Noble, David W. "Cooper, Leatherstocking and the Death of the American Adam," in *American Quarterly.* XVI (1964), pp. 419–431.

Otten, Kurt. "Cooper: *The Pioneers,*" in *Nathanael West: The Cheaters and the Cheated.* Edited by David Madden. Deland, Fla.: Everett/Edwards, 1973, pp. 21–50.

Paine, Gregory L. "The Indians of the Leatherstocking Tales," in *Studies in Philology.* XXIII (1926), pp. 16–39.

Pearce, Roy H. "The Leatherstocking Tales Re-examined," in *South Atlantic Quarterly.* XLVI (1947), pp. 524–536.

Philbrick, Thomas. "Cooper's *The Pioneers*: Origins and Structure," in *PMLA.* LXXIX (1964), pp. 579–593.

Pound, Louise. "The Dialect of Cooper's Leatherstocking," in *American Speech.* II (1927), pp. 479–488.

Ringe, Donald A. *James Fenimore Cooper.* New York: Twayne, 1962, pp. 32–37.

Robinson, E. Arthur. "Conservation in Cooper's *The Pioneers,*" in *PMLA.* LXXXII (December, 1967), pp. 564–578.

Smith, Henry N. "Consciousness and Social Order: The Theme of Transcendence in the Leatherstocking Tales," in *Western American Literature.* V (1970), pp. 177–194.

Stineback, David C. *Shifting World; Social Change and Nostalgia in the American Novel.* Cranbury, N.J.: Bucknell University Press, 1976, pp. 23–42.

Vlach, John M. "Fenimore Cooper's Leatherstocking as Folk Hero," in *New York Folklore Quarterly.* XXVII (1971), pp. 323–338.

Walker, Warren S. *James Fenimore Cooper; An Introduction and Interpretation.* New York: Holt, Rinehart and Winston, 1962, pp. 36–38, 62–63, 74, 88.

———. *Plots and Characters in the Works of James Fenimore Cooper.* Hamden, Conn.: Shoe String Press, 1978.

The Prairie

Baym, Nina. "The Women of Cooper's Leatherstocking Tales," in *American Quarterly.* XXIII (1971), pp. 696–709.

Bewley, Marius. "*The Cage* and *The Prairie*: Two Notes on Symbolism," in *Hudson Review.* X (Autumn, 1957), pp. 408–413.

Bier, Jesse. "Lapsarians on *The Prairie*: Cooper's Novel," in *Texas Studies in Literature and Language.* IV (Spring, 1962), pp. 49–57.

Chase, Richard. *The American Novel and Its Tradition.* New York: Doubleday, 1957, pp. 52–65.

Dekker, George. *James Fenimore Cooper: The American Scott.* New York: Barnes & Noble, 1967, pp. 89–103, 169–174.

Frederick, John T. "Cooper's Eloquent Indians," in *PMLA.* LXXXI (1956), pp. 1004–1017.

Hirsch, David H. *Reality and Idea in the Early American Novel.* The Hague: Mouton, 1971, pp. 106–121.

House, Kay S. "James Fenimore Cooper: *The Prairie,*" in *The American Novel from James Fenimore Cooper to William Faulkner.* Edited by Wallace Stegner. New York: Basic Books, 1965, pp. 1–12.

Lewis, Merrill. "Lost—and Found—In the Wilderness: The Desert Metaphor in Cooper's *The Prairie,*" in *Western American Literature.* V (1970), pp. 195–204.

McAleer, John J. "Biblical Analogy in the Leatherstocking Tales," in *Nineteenth-Century Fiction.* XVII (1962), pp. 217–235.

McWilliams, John P., Jr. *Political Justice in a Republic: James Fenimore Cooper's America.* Berkeley: University of California Press, 1972, pp. 238–246, 259–291, 321–322.

Noble, David W. "Cooper, Leatherstocking and the Death of the American Adam," in *American Quarterly.* XVI (1964), pp. 419–431.

Paine, Gregory L. "The Indians of the Leatherstocking Tales," in *Studies in Philology.* XXIII (1926), pp. 16–39.

Pearce, Roy H. "The Leatherstocking Tales Re-examined," in *South Atlantic Quarterly.* XLVI (1947), pp. 524–536.

Pound, Louise. "The Dialect of Cooper's Leatherstocking," in *American Speech.* II (1927), pp. 479–488.

Ringe, Donald A. "Man and Nature in Cooper's *The Prairie,*" in *Nineteenth-Century Fiction.* XV (1961), pp. 312–323.

Smith, Henry N. "Consciousness and Social Order: The Theme of Transcendence in the Leatherstocking Tales," in *Western American Literature.* V (1970), pp. 177–194.

Stein, William B. "*The Prairie*: The Scenario of the Wise Old Man," in *Bucknell Review.* XIX (1971), pp. 15–36.

Vance, W.L. " 'Man and Beast': The Meaning of Cooper's *The Prairie,*" in *PMLA.* LXXXIX (March, 1974), pp. 323–331.

Vlach, John M. "Fenimore Cooper's Leatherstocking as Folk Hero," in *New York Folklore Quarterly.* XXVII (1971), pp. 323–338.

Walker, Warren S. *James Fenimore Cooper; An Introduction and Interpretation.* New York: Holt, Rinehart and Winston, 1962, pp. 38–40, 58–63.

————. *Plots and Characters in the Works of James Fenimore Cooper.* Hamden, Conn.: Shoe String Press, 1978.

The Red Rover

Anderson, Charles. "Cooper's Sea Novels Spurned in the Maintop," in *Modern Language Notes*. LXVI (June, 1951), pp. 388–391.

Dekker, George. *James Fenimore Cooper: The American Scott*. New York: Barnes & Noble, 1967.

House, Kay S. *Cooper's Americans*. Columbus: Ohio State University Press, 1965, pp. 192–200.

McWilliams, John P., Jr. *Political Justice in a Republic: James Fenimore Cooper's America*. Berkeley: University of California Press, 1972, pp. 65–66, 103.

Peck, H. Daniel. "A Repossession of America: The Revolution in Cooper's Trilogy of Nautical Romances," in *Studies in Romanticism*. XV (Fall, 1976), pp. 589–605.

Philbrick, Thomas. *James Fenimore Cooper and the Development of American Sea Fiction*. Cambridge, Mass.: Harvard University Press, 1961, pp. 51–75.

Walker, Warren S. *James Fenimore Cooper; An Introduction and Interpretation*. New York: Holt, Rinehart and Winston, 1962.

————. *Plots and Characters in the Works of James Fenimore Cooper*. Hamden, Conn.: Shoe String Press, 1978.

The Redskins

Cosgrove, William E. "Family Lineage and Narrative Pattern in Cooper's Littlepage Trilogy," in *Forum* (Houston). XII (1974), pp. 2–8.

Dekker, George. *James Fenimore Cooper: The American Scott*. New York: Barnes & Noble, 1967.

Dryden, Edgar A. "History and Progress: Some Implications of Form in Cooper's Littlepage Novels," in *Nineteenth-Century Fiction*. XXVI (1971), pp. 49–64.

Ellis, David M. "*The Redskins*," in *James Fenimore Cooper: A Re-appraisal*. Edited by Mary Cunningham. New York: New York State Historical Association, 1954, pp. 412–422.

McWilliams, John P., Jr. *Political Justice in a Republic: James Fenimore Cooper's America*. Berkeley: University of California Press, 1972.

Ringe, Donald A. "Cooper's Littlepage Novels: Change and Stability in American Society," in *American Literature*. XXXII (November, 1960), pp. 280–290.

Walker, Warren S. *James Fenimore Cooper; An Introduction and Interpretation*. New York: Holt, Rinehart and Winston, 1962, pp. 26–27, 94, 96–100.

———. *Plots and Characters in the Works of James Fenimore Cooper.* Hamden, Conn.: Shoe String Press, 1978.

Satanstoe

Bier, Jesse. "The Bisection of Cooper: *Satanstoe* as Prime Example," in *Texas Studies in Literature and Language.* IX, (Winter, 1968), pp. 511–521.

Chase, Richard. *The American Novel and Its Tradition.* New York: Doubleday, 1957, pp. 47–52.

Cosgrove, William E. "Family Lineage and Narrative Pattern in Cooper's Littlepage Trilogy," in *Forum* (Houston). XII (1974), pp. 2–8.

Dekker, George. *James Fenimore Cooper: The American Scott.* New York: Barnes & Noble, 1967, pp. 218–227.

Dryden, Edgar A. "History and Progress: Some Implications of Form in Cooper's Littlepage Novels," in *Nineteenth-Century Fiction.* XXVI (1971), pp. 49–64.

Hicks, Granville. "Landlord Cooper and the Anti-Renters," in *Antioch Review.* V (1945), pp. 95–109.

McWilliams, John P., Jr. *Political Justice in a Republic: James Fenimore Cooper's America.* Berkeley: University of California Press, 1972, pp. 311–315.

Pickering, James H. "*Satanstoe*: Cooper's Debt to William Dunlap," in *American Literature.* XXXVIII (January, 1967), pp. 468–477.

Ringe, Donald A. "Cooper's Littlepage Novels: Change and Stability in American Society," in *American Literature.* XXXII (November, 1960), pp. 280–290.

Walker, Warren S. *James Fenimore Cooper; An Introduction and Interpretation.* New York: Holt, Rinehart and Winston, 1962, pp. 95, 112.

———. *Plots and Characters in the Works of James Fenimore Cooper.* Hamden, Conn.: Shoe String Press, 1978.

The Spy

Beard, James F. "Cooper and the Revolutionary Mythos," in *Early American Literature.* XI (Spring, 1976), pp. 84–104.

Dekker, George. *James Fenimore Cooper: The American Scott.* New York: Barnes & Noble, 1967, pp. 33–37, 41–42, 113–114.

Diemer, James S. "A Model for Harvey Birch," in *American Literature.* XXVI (May, 1954), pp. 242–247.

Fink, Robert A. "Harvey Birch: The Yankee Peddler as an American Hero," in *New York Folklore Quarterly.* XXX (1974), pp. 137–152.

House, Kay S. *Cooper's Americans.* Columbus: Ohio State University Press, 1965, pp. 206–216.

Hubbell, Jay B.   *Southern Life in Fiction.* Athens: University of Georgia Press, 1960, pp. 47–48.

McDowell, Tremaine.   "The Identity of Harvey Birch," in *American Literature.* II (1930), pp. 111–120.

McWilliams, John P., Jr.   *Political Justice in a Republic: James Fenimore Cooper's Americans.* Berkeley: University of California Press, 1972, pp. 8, 48–64, 159, 397–398.

Walker, Warren S.   *James Fenimore Cooper; An Introduction and Interpretation.* New York: Holt, Rinehart and Winston, 1962, pp. 12–13, 22–29.

————.   *Plots and Characters in the Works of James Fenimore Cooper.* Hamden, Conn.: Shoe String Press, 1978.

————.   "The Prototype of Harvey Birch," in *New York History.* XXXVII (1956), pp. 399–413.

PIERRE CORNEILLE
(1606–1684)

Le Cid

Abraham, Claude. *Pierre Corneille.* New York: Twayne, 1972, pp. 54–60.

Ault, Harold C. "The Tragic Genius of Corneille," in *Modern Language Review.* XLV (1950), pp. 164–176.

Brereton, Geoffrey. *French Tragic Drama in the Sixteenth and Seventeenth Centuries.* London: Methuen, 1973, pp. 133–139.

Daniel, G.B. "Some Aspects of Age and Time in *Le Cid*," in *Studies in Honor of Alfred G. Engstrom.* Edited by Robert T. Cargo and Emanuel J. Mickel, Jr. Chapel Hill: University of North Carolina Press, 1972, pp. 45–51.

Fowlie, Wallace. *Love in Literature: Studies in Symbolic Expression.* Freeport, N.Y.: Books for Libraries Press, 1972, pp. 37–57.

Goode, William O. "Hand, Heart and Mind: The Complexity of the Heroic Quest in *Le Cid*," in *PMLA.* XCI (1976), pp. 44–53.

Jones, L.E. "The Position of the King in *Le Cid*," in *French Review.* XL (1967), pp. 643–646.

Lancaster, H.C. *A History of French Dramatic Literature in the Seventeenth Century*, Volume I, Part II. Baltimore: Johns Hopkins University Press, 1932, pp. 118–151.

Lockert, Lacy. "The Amazing Career of Pierre Corneille," in *Studies in French Classical Tragedy.* Nashville, Tenn.: Vanderbilt University Press, 1958, pp. 29–37.

────────. "Introduction," in *The Chief Plays of Corneille.* Princeton, N.J.: Princeton University Press, 1957, pp. 4–10.

Nelson, Robert J. *Corneille: His Heroes and Their Worlds.* Philadelphia: University of Pennsylvania Press, 1963, pp. 68–87.

────────. "The Dénouement of *Le Cid*," in *French Studies.* XIV (1960), pp. 141–147.

Pocock, Gordon. *Corneille and Racine: Problems of Tragic Form.* Cambridge: Cambridge University Press, 1973, pp. 28–39.

Riddle, Lawrence Melville. *The Genesis and Sources of Pierre Corneille's Tragedies from* Médée *to* Pertharite. Baltimore: Johns Hopkins University Press, 1926, pp. 11–17.

Sainte-Beuve, Charles Augustin. *Selected Essays.* Edited by Francis Steigmuller and Norbert Guterman. Garden City, N.Y.: Doubleday, 1963, pp. 29–61.

Segall, J.B. *Corneille and the Spanish Drama.* New York: Columbia University Press, 1902, pp. 31–93.

Sellestrom, A.D. "The Structure of Corneille's Masterpieces," in *Romanic Review*. XLIX (1958), pp. 269–277.

Turnell, Martin. *The Classical Moment: Studies of Corneille, Molière and Racine*. London: Hamish Hamilton, 1951, pp. 27–30.

Valency, Maurice. *The Flower and the Castle: Introduction to Modern Drama*. New York: Macmillan, 1963, pp. 31–40.

Vincent, Leon H. *Corneille*. Boston: Houghton Mifflin, 1901, pp. 45–62.

Wang, Leonard. "The 'Tragic' Theatre of Corneille," in *French Review*. XXV (1951–1952), pp. 182–191.

Yarrow, P.J. *Corneille*. New York: St. Martin's Press, 1963, pp. 107–109, 181–184.

————. "The Dénouement of *Le Cid*," in *Modern Language Review*. L (1955), pp. 270–273.

Yost, C.A. "Historical Truth in the Dramas of Corneille," in *South Atlantic Quarterly*. XVI (1917), pp. 56–59.

Cinna

Abraham, Claude. *Pierre Corneille*. New York: Twayne, 1972, pp. 67–73.

Allentuch, Harriet R. "The Problem of *Cinna*," in *French Review*. XLVIII (1975), pp. 878–886.

Ault, H.C. "Reflections on *Cinna*," in *Modern Languages*. XXXIV (1952–1953), pp. 22–26.

————. "The Tragic Genius of Corneille," in *Modern Language Review*. XLV (1950), pp. 164–176.

Brereton, Geoffrey. *French Tragic Drama in the Sixteenth and Seventeenth Centuries*. London: Methuen, 1973, pp. 142–143.

Clarke, D.R. "Heroic Prudence and Reason in the 17th Century—Auguste's Pardon of *Cinna*," in *Forum for Modern Language Studies*. I (1965), pp. 328–338.

Garrity, Henry A. "Le commun bonheur: Limits of Personal Freedom in Corneille's Later Plays," in *French Review*. XLVIII (1974), pp. 65–73.

Lancaster, H.C. *A History of French Dramatic Literature in the Seventeenth Century*, Volume I, Part II. Baltimore: Johns Hopkins University Press, 1932, pp. 312–319.

Lockert, Lacy. "The Amazing Career of Pierre Corneille," in *Studies in French-Classical Tragedy*. Nashville, Tenn.: Vanderbilt University Press, 1958, pp. 44–49.

————. "Introduction," in *The Chief Plays of Corneille*. Princeton, N.J.: Princeton University Press, 1957, pp. 16–20.

Nelson, Robert J. *Corneille: His Heroes and Their Worlds*. Philadelphia: University of Pennsylvania Press, 1963, pp. 97–99.

————. "Kinship and Kingship in *Cinna*," in *Forum for Modern Language Studies*. I (1965), pp. 311–327.

Pocock, Gordon. *Corneille and Racine: Problems of Tragic Form*. Cambridge: Cambridge University Press, 1973, pp. 40–63.

Riddle, Lawrence Melville. *The Genesis and Sources of Pierre Corneille's Tragedies from* Médée *to* Pertharite. Baltimore: Johns Hopkins University Press, 1926, pp. 41–56.

Turnell, Martin. *The Classical Moment: Studies of Corneille, Molière and Racine*. London: Hamish Hamilton, 1951, pp. 35–37.

Vincent, Leon H. *Corneille*. Boston: Houghton Mifflin, 1901, pp. 117–121.

Yarrow, P.J. *Corneille*. New York: St. Martin's Press, 1963, pp. 186–190, 236–237, 250–251.

Yost, C.A. "Historical Truth in the Dramas of Corneille," in *South Atlantic Quarterly*. XVI (1917), pp. 56–59.

Horace

Abraham, Claude. *Pierre Corneille*. New York: Twayne, 1972, pp. 60–66.

Ault, Harold C. "The Tragic Genius of Corneille," in *Modern Language Review*. XLV (1950), pp. 164–176.

Barber, W.H. "Patriotism and Gloire in Corneille's *Horace*," in *Modern Language Review*. XLVI (1951), pp. 368–378.

Brereton, Geoffrey. *French Tragic Drama in the Sixteenth and Seventeenth Centuries*. London: Methuen, 1973, pp. 139–142.

Cloonan, William. "Women in *Horace*," in *Romance Notes*. XVI (1975), pp. 647–652.

Goodman, Paul. "Critique of Corneille's *Horace*: Combination of Critical Methods," in *The Structure of Literature*. Chicago: University of Chicago Press, 1954, pp. 257–266.

Gossip, Christopher J. "Tragedy and Moral Order in Corneille's *Horace*," in *Forum for Modern Language Studies*. XI (1975), pp. 15–28.

Grant, Elliott M. "Reflections on Corneille's *Horace*," in *French Review*. XXXVII (1964), pp. 537–541.

Harvey, Lawrence E. "Corneille's *Horace*: A Study in Tragic and Artistic Ambivalence," in *Studies in 17th Century French Literature Presented to Morris Bishop*. Edited by Jean-Jacques Demorest. Ithaca, N.Y.: Cornell University Press, 1962, pp. 65–97.

Lancaster, H.C. *A History of French Dramatic Literature in the Seventeenth Century*, Volume I, Part II. Baltimore: Johns Hopkins University Press, 1932, pp. 303–312.

Lockert, Lacy. "The Amazing Career of Pierre Corneille," in *Studies in French-Classical Tragedy.* Nashville, Tenn.: Vanderbilt University Press, 1958, pp. 37–44.

————. "Introduction," in *The Chief Plays of Corneille.* Princeton, N.J.: Princeton University Press, 1957, pp. 10–16.

Mazzara, Richard A. "More on Unity of Character of Action in *Horace,*" in *French Review.* XXXVI (1963), pp. 588–594.

Moore, W.G. "Corneille's *Horace* and the Interpretation of French Classical Drama," in *Modern Language Review.* XXXIV (1939), pp. 382–395.

Nelson, Robert J. *Corneille: His Heroes and Their Worlds.* Philadelphia: University of Pennsylvania Press, 1963, pp. 87–96.

Newmark, Peter. "A New View of *Horace,*" in *French Studies.* X (1956), pp. 1–10.

Nurse, Peter H. *Classical Voices: Studies of Corneille, Racine, Molière, Mme. de Lafayette.* London: George G. Harrap, 1971, pp. 27–60.

Riddle, Lawrence Melville. *The Genesis and Sources of Pierre Corneille's Tragedies from Médée to Pertharite.* Baltimore: Johns Hopkins University Press, 1926, pp. 19–39.

Scott, J.W. "The 'Irony' of *Horace,*" in *French Studies.* XII (1959), pp. 11–17.

Sellestrom, A.D. "The Structure of Corneille's Masterpieces," in *Romanic Review.* XLIX (1958), pp. 269–277.

Trafton, Dain A. "On Corneille's *Horace,*" in *Interpretation: A Journal of Political Philosophy.* II (1972), pp. 183–193.

Vincent, Leon H. *Corneille.* Boston: Houghton Mifflin, 1901, pp. 104–117.

Whiting, Charles G. "The Ambiguity of the Hero in Corneille's *Horace,*" in *Symposium.* XXIII (1969), pp. 163–170.

Yarrow, P.J. *Corneille.* New York: St. Martin's Press, 1963, pp. 109–110, 184–186.

Yost, C.A. "Historical Truth in the Dramas of Corneille," in *South Atlantic Quarterly.* XVI (1917), pp. 56–59.

L'Illusion Comique

Abraham, Claude. *Pierre Corneille.* New York: Twayne, 1972, pp. 44–47.

Brereton, Geoffrey. *French Comic Drama from the Sixteenth to the Eighteenth Century.* London: Methuen, 1977, pp. 24–26.

————. *French Tragic Drama in the Sixteenth and Seventeenth Centuries.* London: Methuen, 1973, pp. 131–132.

Buffum, Imbrie. "A Baroque Dramatist Repents His Youth: Three Early Comedies of Corneille," in his *Studies in the Baroque from Montaigne to Rotrou.* New Haven, Conn.: Yale University Press, 1957, pp. 163–211.

Koch, Philip. "Cornelian Illusion," in *Symposium*. XIV (1960), pp. 85–99.

Lancaster, H.C. *A History of French Dramatic Literature in the Seventeenth Century*, Volume I, Part II. Baltimore: Johns Hopkins University Press, 1932, pp. 107–110.

Nelson, Robert J. *Corneille: His Heroes and Their Worlds*. Philadelphia: University of Pennsylvania Press, 1963, pp. 66–67.

————. "Pierre Corneille's *L'Illusion Comique*: The Play as Magic," in *PMLA*. LXXI (December, 1956), pp. 1127–1140. Reprinted in *Play Within a Play: The Dramatist's Conception of His Art—Shakespeare to Anouilh*. New Haven, Conn.: Yale University Press, 1958, pp. 47–61.

Segal, J.B. *Corneille and the Spanish Drama*. New York: Columbia University Press, 1902, pp. 20–29.

Sellestrom, A.D. "*L'Illusion Comique* of Corneille: The Tragic Scenes of Act V," in *Modern Language Notes*. LXXIII (1958), pp. 421–427.

Walters, Gordon, Jr. "Society and the Theatre in Corneille's *L'Illusion Comique*," in *Romance Notes*. X (1969), pp. 325–331.

Wang, Leonard. "The 'Tragic' Theatre of Corneille," in *French Review*. XXV (1951–1952), pp. 182–191.

Yarrow, P.J. *Corneille*. New York: St. Martin's Press, 1963, pp. 81–83.

Le Menteur

Abraham, Claude. *Pierre Corneille*. New York: Twayne, 1972, pp. 81–85.

Brereton, Geoffrey. *French Comic Drama from the Sixteenth to the Eighteenth Century*. London: Methuen, 1927, pp. 26–28.

Nelson, Robert J. *Corneille: His Heroes and Their Worlds*. Philadelphia: University of Pennsylvania Press, 1963, pp. 130–138.

Segall, J.B. *Corneille and the Spanish Drama*. New York: Columbia University Press, 1902, pp. 94–130.

Yarrow, P.J. *Corneille*. New York: St. Martin's Press, 1963, pp. 83–84, 100–102.

Polyeucte

Abraham, Claude. *Pierre Corneille*. New York: Twayne, 1972, pp. 71–76.

Ault, Harold C. "The Tragic Genius of Corneille," in *Modern Language Review*. XLV (1950), pp. 164–176.

Brereton, Geoffrey. *French Tragic Drama in the Sixteenth and Seventeenth Centuries*. London: Methuen, 1973, pp. 143–144.

Currie, Peter. *Corneille:* Polyeucte. London: Edward Arnold, 1960.

Doolittle, J. "Heroism and Passion in *Polyeucte*," in *Symposium*. VIII (1954), pp. 217–241.

Falk, Eugene H. *Renunciation as a Tragic Focus: A Study of Five Plays.* Minneapolis: University of Minnesota Press, 1954, pp. 34–72.

Harvey, L.E. "The Role of Emulation in Corneille's *Polyeucte*," in *PMLA.* LXXXII (1967), pp. 314–324.

Lancaster, H.C. *A History of French Dramatic Literature in the Seventeenth Century,* Volume I, Part II. Baltimore: Johns Hopkins University Press, 1932, pp. 319–331.

Lockert, Lacy. "The Amazing Career of Pierre Corneille," in his *Studies in French-Classical Tragedy.* Nashville, Tenn.: Vanderbilt University Press, 1958, pp. 49–58.

————. "Introduction," in *The Chief Plays of Corneille.* Princeton, N.J.: Princeton University Press, 1957, pp. 20–27.

Nelson, Robert J. *Corneille: His Heroes and Their Worlds.* Philadelphia: University of Pennsylvania Press, 1963, pp. 99–128.

Pocock, Gordon. *Corneille and Racine: Problems of Tragic Form.* Cambridge: Cambridge University Press, 1973, pp. 64–77.

Riddle, Lawrence Melville. *The Genesis and Sources of Pierre Corneille's Tragedies from* Médée *to* Pertharite. Baltimore: Johns Hopkins University Press, 1926, pp. 57–77.

Spiers, A.G.H. "Corneille's *Polyeucte* Technically Considered," in *Modern Language Review.* XIV (1919), pp. 44–56.

Turnell, Martin. *The Classical Moment: Studies of Corneille, Molière and Racine.* London: Hamish Hamilton, 1951, pp. 31–35.

Vincent, Leon H. *Corneille.* Boston: Houghton Mifflin, 1901, pp. 121–129.

Woodbridge, B.M. "A New Interpretation of Corneille's *Polyeucte*," in *Romanic Review.* XXVI (1935), pp. 57–59.

Yarrow, P.J. *Corneille.* New York: St. Martin's Press, 1963, pp. 111–112, 190–194, 239–240.

Yost, C.A. "Historical Truth in the Dramas of Corneille," in *South Atlantic Quarterly.* XVI (1917), pp. 56–59.

NOEL COWARD
(1899–1973)

Design for Living

Brown, John Mason. *Two on the Aisle; Ten Years of the American Theatre in Performance.* New York: Norton, 1938, pp. 114–116.

Levin, Milton. *Noel Coward.* New York: Twayne, 1968, pp. 105–110, 118–119.

Marx, Milton. *Enjoyment of Drama.* New York: Appleton-Century-Crofts, 1947, pp. 166–170.

Morse, Clarence R. "Mad Dogs and Englishmen: A Study of Noel Coward," in *Emporia State Research Studies.* XXXI (1973), pp. 15–44.

Nathan, George Jean. *Passing Judgments.* New York: Knopf, 1935, pp. 140–176.

O'Casey, Sean. *The Green Crow.* New York: George Braziller, 1956, pp. 99–107.

Sievers, W. David. *Freud on Broadway.* New York: Hermitage House, 1955, pp. 217–218.

Wilson, S. *"Design for Living,"* in *Plays and Players.* XXI (1974), pp. 45–47.

Private Lives

Jennings, R. *"Private Lives,"* in *Spectator.* CXLV (October 11, 1930), pp. 488–489.

Levin, Milton. *Noel Coward.* New York: Twayne, 1968, pp. 101–105, 119–120.

MacCarthy, Desmond. *Drama.* London: Putnam's, 1940, pp. 243–246.

————. *Humanities.* London: MacGibbon and Kee, 1953, pp. 94–96.

————. *"Private Lives,"* in *New Statesman.* XXXVI (October 11, 1930), pp. 14–15.

Macdonell, A.G. "The Plays of Noel Coward," in *Living Age.* CCCXLI (1932), pp. 439–446.

Morse, Clarence R. "Mad Dogs and Englishmen: A Study of Noel Coward," in *Emporia State Research Studies.* XXXI (1973), pp. 15–44.

Taylor, John Russell. *The Rise and Fall of the Well-Made Play.* London: Methuen, 1967, pp. 103–131.

Wakefield, G. *"Private Lives,"* in *Saturday Review.* CL (September 27, 1930), p. 370.

MALCOLM COWLEY
(1898–   )

Blue Juniata

Burke, Kenneth. " 'I Dipped My Finger in the Lake and Wrote,' " *in New York Times Book Review*. (November 17, 1968), pp. 8, 76.

Tate, Allen. "A Regional Poet," in *New Republic*. LX (August 28, 1928), pp. 51–52.

Winters, Yvor. "The Poetry of Malcolm Cowley," in *Yvor Winters: Uncollected Essays and Reviews*. Chicago: Swallow, 1973, pp. 60–63.

Young, Philip. "For Malcolm Cowley: Critic, Poet, 1898–   ," in *Southern Review*. IX (1973), pp. 783–785.

Zabel, Morton. *"Blue Juniata,"* in *Nation*. CXXIX (August 21, 1929), pp. 200–201.

Exile's Return

Aldridge, John W. *In Search of Heresy*. New York: McGraw-Hill, 1956, pp. 166–176.

De Voto, Bernard. *Forays and Rebuttals*. Boston: Little, Brown, 1936, pp. 315–323.

Farrell, James T. *A Note on Literary Criticism*. New York: Vanguard, 1936, pp. 157–174.

Mizzener, Arthur. "The Long Debauch," in *New Statesman*. LXII (September 29, 1961), pp. 433–434.

Young, Philip. "For Malcolm Cowley: Critic, Poet, 1898–   ," in *Southern Review*. IX (1973), pp. 780–787.

WILLIAM COWPER
(1731–1800)

The Poetry of Cowper

Boyd, D. "Satire and Pastoral in *The Task*," in *Papers in Language and Literature*. X (Fall, 1974), pp. 363–377.

Danchin, P. "William Cowper's Poetic Purpose as Seen in His Letters," in *English Studies*. XLVI (June, 1965), pp. 235–244.

Davie, Donald. "The Critical Principles of William Cowper," in *The Cambridge Journal*. VII (1953), pp. 182–188.

Free, William N. *William Cowper*. New York: Twayne, 1970.

Gregory, H.K. "Cowper's Love of Subhuman Nature: A Psycho-Analytic Approach," in *Philological Quarterly*. XLVI (January, 1967), pp. 42–57.

Hartley, Lodwick. *William Cowper, Humanitarian*. Chapel Hill: Unversity of North Carolina Press, 1938.

————. *William Cowper, the Continuing Revaluation: An Essay and a Bibliography of Cowperian Studies, from 1895 to 1960*. Chapel Hill: University of North Carolina Press, 1960.

Jones, M. "Wordsworth and Cowper: The Eye Made Quiet," in *Essays in Criticism*. XXI (July, 1971), pp. 236–247.

Kroitor, H.P. "Cowper, Deism and the Divinization of Nature," in *Journal of the History of Ideas*. XXI (October, 1960), pp. 511–526.

————. "The Influence of Popular Science on William Cowper," in *Modern Philology*. LXI (May, 1964), pp. 281–287.

Memes, John S. *The Life of William Cowper*. Port Washington, N.Y.: Kennikat, 1972.

Nicholson, Norman. *William Cowper*. London: John Lehmann, 1951.

Price, Warwick J. "Cowper's *Task*: A Literary Milestone," in *Sewanee Review*. XXIV (1916), pp. 155–164.

Quinlan, Maurice J. *William Cowper: A Critical Life*. Westport, Conn.: Greenwood, 1970. Reprint of 1953 Edition.

Roy, James A. *Cowper and His Poetry*. New York: AMS Press, 1972. Reprint of 1914 Edition.

Spacks, P.H. "Soul's Imaginings: Daniel Defoe, William Cowper," in *PMLA*. XCI (May, 1976), pp. 420–435.

Waugh, Arthur. "William Cowper," in *Fortnightly Review*. CXXXVI (1931), pp. 590–603.

Wright, Thomas. *The Life of William Cowper*. New York: Haskell House, 1971. Reprint of 1892 Edition.

JAMES GOULD COZZENS
(1903–1978)

By Love Possessed

Bracher, Frederick. *The Novels of James Gould Cozzens.* New York: Harcourt, 1959, pp. 49–51, 106–108, 155–158.

Burns, Wayne. "Cozzens vs. Life and Art," in *Northwest Review.* I (Summer, 1958), pp. 7–18.

_____. "Reiterations," in *Northwest Review.* II (Fall–Winter, 1958), pp. 38–43.

Cass, Colin S. "Two Stylistic Analyses of the Narrative Prose in Cozzen's *By Love Possessed*," in *Style.* IV (Winter, 1970), pp. 213–238.

Garett, George. "*By Love Possessed*: The Pattern and the Hero," in *Critique: Studies in Modern Fiction.* I (Winter, 1958), pp. 41–47.

Hicks, Granville. *James Gould Cozzens.* Minneapolis: University of Minnesota Press, 1966, pp. 31–35.

Howe, Irving. "*By Love Possessed*," in *The Critic as Artist: Essays on Books, 1920–1970.* New York: Liveright, 1972, pp. 167–180.

Mizener, Arthur. "The Undistorting Mirror," in *Kenyon Review.* XXVIII (November, 1966), pp. 595–601.

Mooney, Harry J. Jr. *James Gould Cozzens: Novelist of Intellect.* Pittsburgh: University of Pittsburgh Press, 1963, pp. 125–156.

Noble, David W. *The Eternal Adam and the New World Garden: The Central Myth in the American Novel Since 1830.* New York: Braziller, 1968, pp. 186–193.

Watts, Harold H. "James Gould Cozzens and the Genteel Tradition," *Colorado Quarterly.* VI (Winter, 1958), pp. 263–273.

Guard of Honor

Bracher, Frederick. *The Novels of James Gould Cozzens.* New York: Harcourt, 1959, pp. 69–76, 87–88, 130–135, 165–168.

Eisinger, Chester E. *Fiction of the Forties.* Chicago: University of Chicago Press, 1963, pp. 164–170.

_____. "The Voice of Aggressive Aristocracy," in *Midway.* XVIII (Spring, 1964), pp. 117–127.

Fergusson, Francis. "Three Novels," in *Perspectives U.S.A.* VI (Winter, 1954), pp. 30–44.

French, Warren. *The Forties: Fiction, Poetry, Drama.* Deland, Fla.: Everett/Edwards, 1969, pp. 9–15.

Hicks, Granville. *James Gould Cozzens.* Minneapolis: University of Minnesota Press, 1966, pp. 28–31.

Maxwell, D.E.S. *American Fiction: The Intellectual Background.* New York: Columbia University Press, 1963, pp. 284–287.

————. *Cozzens.* Edinburgh: Oliver and Boyd, 1964, pp. 92–102.

Millgate, Michael. *American Social Fiction: James to Cozzens.* New York: Barnes & Noble, 1965, pp. 188–194.

Mizener, Arthur. *Twelve Great American Novels.* New York: New American Library, 1967, pp. 166–176.

Mooney, Harry J., Jr. *James Gould Cozzens: Novelist of Intellect.* Pittsburgh: University of Pittsburgh Press, 1963, pp. 99–124.

Parrish, James A., Jr. "James Gould Cozzens Fights a War," in *Arizona Quarterly.* XVIII (Winter, 1962), pp. 335–340.

Scholes, Robert E. "The Commitment of James Gould Cozzens," in *Arizona Quarterly.* XVI (Summer, 1960), pp. 138–141.

Stuckey, W.J. *The Pulitzer Prize Novels: A Critical Backward Look.* Norman: University of Oklahoma Press, 1966, pp. 143–151.

Waldmeir, Joseph J. *American Novels of the Second World War.* The Hague: Mouton, 1968, pp. 130–137.

HART CRANE
(1899–1932)

Atlantis

Butterfield, R.W. *The Broken Arc: A Study of Hart Crane.* Edinburgh: Oliver and Boyd, 1969, pp. 206–212.

Clark, David R. "Hart Crane's Technique," in *Texas Studies in Language and Literature.* V (Autumn, 1963), pp. 389–397.

Dembo, L.S. *Hart Crane's Sanskrit Charge: A Study of* The Bridge. Ithaca, N.Y.: Cornell University Press, 1960, pp. 127–130.

Friar, Kimon and John Malcolm Brinnin. *Modern Poetry, American and British.* New York: Appleton-Century-Crofts, 1951, pp. 453–455.

Hazo, Samuel. *Hart Crane: An Introduction and Interpretation.* New York: Holt, Rinehart and Winston, 1963, pp. 113–117.

Leibowitz, Herbert A. *Hart Crane: An Introduction to the Poetry.* New York: Columbia University Press, 1968, pp. 137–143.

Lewis, R.W.B. *The Poetry of Hart Crane: A Critical Study.* Princeton, N.J.: Princeton University Press, 1967, pp. 365–373.

Paul, Sherman. *Hart's* Bridge. Urbana: University of Illinois Press, 1972, pp. 273–283.

Quinn, Vincent. *Hart Crane.* New York: Twayne, 1963, pp. 100–102.

Rupp, Richard H. "Hart Crane: Vitality as *Credo* in *Atlantis*," in *Midwest Quarterly.* III (1962), pp. 265–275.

Sugg, Richard P. *Hart Crane's* The Bridge*: A Description of Its Life.* University: University of Alabama Press, 1976, pp. 108–118.

Uroff, M.D. *Hart Crane: The Patterns of His Poetry.* Urbana: University of Illinois Press, 1974, pp. 145–150, 214–216.

Weber, Brom. *Hart Crane: A Biographical and Critical Study.* New York: Bodley Press, 1948, pp. 375–378.

Ave Maria

Butterfield, R.W. *The Broken Arc: A Study of Hart Crane.* Edinburgh: Oliver and Boyd, 1969, pp. 154–157.

Dembo, L.S. *Hart Crane's Sanskrit Charge: A Study of* The Bridge. Ithaca, N.Y.: Cornell University Press, 1960, pp. 53–62.

Friar, Kimon and John Malcolm Brinnin. *Modern Poetry, American and British.* New York: Appleton-Century-Crofts, 1951, pp. 451–452.

Hazo, Samuel. *Hart Crane: An Introduction and Interpretation.* New York: Holt, Rinehart and Winston, 1963, pp. 76–81.

Lewis, R.W.B. *The Poetry of Hart Crane: A Critical Study.* Princeton, N.J.: Princeton University Press, 1967, pp. 256–267.

Quinn, Vincent. *Hart Crane.* New York: Twayne, 1963, pp. 81–83.

Sugg, Richard P. *Hart Crane's* The Bridge*: A Description of Its Life.* University: University of Alabama Press, 1976, pp. 30–39.

Uroff, M.D. *Hart Crane: The Patterns of His Poetry.* Urbana: University of Illinois Press, 1974, pp. 207–210.

Weber, Brom. *Hart Crane: A Biographical and Critical Study.* New York: Bodley Press, 1948, pp. 341–346, 350–352.

The Bridge

Alvarez, A. "The Lyric of Hart Crane," in *Twentieth Century.* CLX (December, 1956), pp. 506–517. Reprinted in *Stewards of Excellence.* New York: Scribner's, 1958, pp. 107–123.

Arpad, Joseph J. "Hart Crane's Platonic Myth: The Brooklyn Bridge," in *American Literature.* XXXIX (1967), pp. 75–86.

Bewley, Marius. *Masks and Mirrors: Essays in Criticism.* New York: Atheneum, 1970, pp. 325–328, 330–334.

Butterfield, R.W. *The Broken Arc: A Study of Hart Crane.* Edinburgh: Oliver and Boyd, 1969, pp. 121–214.

Cambon, Glauco. *The Inclusive Flame: Studies in American Poetry.* Bloomington: Indiana University Press, 1963, pp. 120–183.

Coffman, Stanley K., Jr. "Symbolism in *The Bridge*," in *PMLA.* LXVI (March, 1951), pp. 65–77. Reprinted in *The Merrill Studies in* The Bridge. Edited by David R. Clark. Columbus, Oh.: Merrill, 1970, pp. 52–66.

Dembo, L.S. *Hart Crane's Sanskrit Charge: A Study of* The Bridge. Ithaca, N.Y.: Cornell University Press, 1960. Partially reprinted in *The Merrill Studies in* The Bridge. Edited by David R. Clark. Columbus, Oh.: Merrill, 1970, pp. 74–86.

Deutsch, Babette. *This Modern Poetry.* New York: Norton, 1935, pp. 141–148.

Friedman, Paul. "*The Bridge*: A Study in Symbolism," in *Psychoanalytical Quarterly.* XXI (1952), pp. 49–80.

Hazo, Samuel. *Hart Crane: An Introduction and Interpretation.* New York: Holt, Rinehart and Winston, 1963, pp. 68–73.

Hoffman, Frederick J. *The Twenties: American Writing in the Postwar Decade.* New York: Free Press, 1962, pp. 257–274.

Lewis, R.W.B. *The Poetry of Hart Crane: A Critical Study.* Princeton, N.J.: Princeton University Press, 1967, pp. 219–382.

Metzger, Deena Posy. "Hart Crane's *Bridge*: The Myth Active," in *Arizona Quarterly.* XX (Spring, 1964), pp. 36–46.

Moss, Howard. "Disorder as Myth: Hart Crane's *The Bridge*," in *Poetry*. LXII (April, 1943), pp. 32–45.

Paul, Sherman. *Hart's* Bridge. Urbana: University of Illinois Press, 1972, pp. 166–283.

Pease, Donald. "*The Bridge*: Emotional Dynamics of an Epic of Consciousness," in *The Twenties: Fiction, Poetry, Drama*. Edited by Warren French. Deland, Fla.: Everett/Edwards, 1975, pp. 387–403.

Quinn, Vincent. *Hart Crane*. New York: Twayne, 1963, pp. 71–103.

Shapiro, Karl. "The Meaning of the Discarded Poem," in *Poets at Work*. Edited by Charles D. Abbott. New York: Harcourt, 1948, pp. 111–118. Reprinted in *The Merrill Studies in* The Bridge. Edited by David R. Clark. Columbus, Oh.: Merrill, 1970, pp. 37–43.

Spears, Monroe K. *Hart Crane*. Minneapolis: University of Minnesota Press, 1965, pp. 33–40.

Sugg, Richard P. *Hart Crane's* The Bridge: *A Description of Its Life*. University: University of Alabama Press, 1976.

Trachtenberg, Allan. *Brooklyn Bridge: Fact and Symbol*. New York: Oxford University Press, 1965, pp. 142–165. Reprinted in *The Merrill Studies in* The Bridge. Edited by David R. Clark. Columbus, Oh.: Merrill, 1970, pp. 113–131.

Uroff, M.D. *Hart Crane: The Patterns of His Poetry*. Urbana: University of Illinois Press, 1974, pp. 114–152.

Van Nostrand, Albert. "*The Bridge* and Hart Crane's 'Span of Consciousness,' " in *Aspects of American Poetry*. Edited by R.M. Ludwig. Columbus: Ohio State University Press, 1962, pp. 171–203.

Vogler, Thomas. "A New View of Hart Crane's *Bridge*," in *Sewanee Review*. LXXIII (July–September, 1965), pp. 381–408.

Weber, Brom. *Hart Crane: A Biographical and Critical Study*. New York: Bodley Press, 1948, pp. 317–378.

"The Broken Tower"

Bewley, Marius. *Masks and Mirrors: Essays in Criticism*. New York: Atheneum, 1970, pp. 324–326, 328–330.

Butterfield, R.W. *The Broken Arc: A Study of Hart Crane*. Edinburgh: Oliver and Boyd, 1969, pp. 239–243.

Hazo, Samuel. *Hart Crane: An Introduction and Interpretation*. New York: Holt, Rinehart and Winston, 1963, pp. 129–132.

Lewis, R.W.B. *The Poetry of Hart Crane: A Critical Study*. Princeton, N.J.: Princeton University Press, 1967, pp. 410–420.

Lyon, Melvin E. *The Centrality of Hart Crane's "The Broken Tower."* Lincoln: University of Nebraska Press, 1972.

Martey, Herbert. "Hart Crane's 'The Broken Tower': A Study in Technique," in *University of Kansas City Review.* XVIII (Spring, 1952), pp. 199–205.

Quinn, Vincent. *Hart Crane.* New York: Twayne, 1963, pp. 55–56.

Rukeyser, Muriel. *The Life of Poetry.* New York: A.A. Wyn, 1949, pp. 32–33.

Spears, Monroe K. *Hart Crane.* Minneapolis: University of Minnesota Press, 1965, pp. 43–44.

Uroff, M.D. *Hart Crane: The Patterns of His Poetry.* Urbana: University of Illinois Press, 1974, pp. 38–41, 192–196.

Cape Hatteras

Butterfield, R.W. *The Broken Arc: A Study of Hart Crane.* Edinburgh: Oliver and Boyd, 1969, pp. 180–189.

Dembo, L.S. *Hart Crane's Sanskrit Charge: A Study of* The Bridge. Ithaca, N.Y.: Cornell University Press, 1960, pp. 93–106.

Hazo, Samuel. *Hart Crane: An Introduction and Interpretation.* New York: Holt, Rinehart and Winston, 1963, pp. 99–104.

Lewis, R.W.B. *The Poetry of Hart Crane: A Critical Study.* Princeton, N.J.: Princeton University Press, 1967, pp. 323–337.

Paul, Sherman. *Hart's* Bridge. Urbana: University of Illinois Press, 1972, pp. 231–242.

Quinn, Vincent. *Hart Crane.* New York: Twayne, 1963, pp. 92–94.

Sugg, Richard P. *Hart Crane's* The Bridge: *A Description of Its Life.* University: University of Alabama Press, 1976, pp. 71–82.

Uroff, M.D. *Hart Crane: The Patterns of His Poetry.* Urbana: University of Illinois Press, 1974, pp. 131–141.

"The Dance"

Butterfield, R.W. *The Broken Arc: A Study of Hart Crane.* Edinburgh: Oliver and Boyd, 1969, pp. 166–171.

Dembo, L.S. *Hart Crane's Sanskrit Charge: A Study of* The Bridge. Ithaca, N.Y.: Cornell University Press, 1960, pp. 73–80.

Hazo, Samuel. *Hart Crane: An Introduction and Interpretation.* New York: Holt, Rinehart and Winston, 1963, pp. 90–94.

Lewis, R.W.B. *The Poetry of Hart Crane: A Critical Study.* Princeton, N.J.: Princeton University Press, 1967, pp. 307–316.

Paul, Sherman. *Hart's* Bridge. Urbana: University of Illinois Press, 1972, pp. 216–222.

Quinn, Vincent. *Hart Crane.* New York: Twayne, 1963, pp. 88–90.

Sugg, Richard P. *Hart Crane's* The Bridge: *A Description of Its Life.* University: University of Alabama Press, 1976, pp. 54–61.

Uroff, M.D.   *Hart Crane: The Patterns of His Poetry*. Urbana: University of Illinois Press, 1974, pp. 98–105.

Weber, Brom.   *Hart Crane: A Biographical and Critical Study*. New York: Bodley Press, 1948, pp. 356–362.

Winters, Yvor.   *Primitivism and Decadence*. New York: Arrow, 1933, pp. 30–32.

"The Harbor Dawn"

Butterfield, R.W.   *The Broken Arc: A Study of Hart Crane*. Edinburgh: Oliver and Boyd, 1969, pp. 158–159.

Dembo, L.S.   *Hart Crane's Sanskrit Charge: A Study of* The Bridge. Ithaca, N.Y.: Cornell University Press, 1960, pp. 63–65.

Friar, Kimon and John Malcolm Brinnin.   *Modern Poetry, American and British*. New York: Appleton-Century-Crofts, 1951, pp. 452–453.

Hazo, Samuel.   *Hart Crane: An Introduction and Interpretation*. New York: Holt, Rinehart and Winston, 1963, pp. 82–85.

Lewis, R.W.B.   *The Poetry of Hart Crane: A Critical Study*. Princeton, N.J.: Princeton University Press, 1967, pp. 290–292.

Paul, Sherman.   *Hart's* Bridge. Urbana: University of Illinois Press, 1972, pp. 197–201.

Quinn, Vincent.   *Hart Crane*. New York: Twayne, 1963, pp. 83–84.

Sugg, Richard P.   *Hart Crane's* The Bridge: *A Description of Its Life*. University: University of Alabama Press, 1976, pp. 40–43.

Uroff, M.D.   *Hart Crane: The Patterns of His Poetry*. Urbana: University of Illinois Press, 1974, pp. 87–89.

The Poetry of Crane

Alvarez, A.   "The Lyric of Hart Crane," in *Twentieth Century*. CLX (December, 1956), pp. 506–517. Reprinted in his *Stewards of Excellence*. New York: Scribner's, 1958, pp. 107–123.

Andreach, Robert J.   *Studies in Structure*. New York: Fordham University Press, 1964, pp. 102–129.

Blackmur, R.P.   *Form and Value in Modern Poetry*. Garden City, N.Y.: Doubleday, 1957, pp. 269–285.

Cargill, Oscar.   *Intellectual America: Ideas on the March*. New York: Macmillan, 1941, pp. 274–281.

Clark, David R.   "Hart Crane's Technique," in *Texas Studies in Language and Literature*. V (Autumn, 1963), pp. 389–397.

Davidson, Eugene.   "The Symbol and the Poets," in *Yale Review*. XXIII (September 1933), pp. 178–182.

Deutsch, Babette.   *Poetry in Our Time.* New York: Holt, 1952, pp. 312–330.

Fitzell, Lincoln.   "The Sword and the Dragon," in *South Atlantic Quarterly.* L (April, 1951), pp. 214–232.

Frank, Waldo.   "Introduction," in *The Collected Poems of Hart Crane.* New York: Liveright, 1933. Reprinted in *Critics of Culture.* Edited by Alan Trachtenberg. New York: John Wiley, 1976, pp. 257–271.

Hazo, Samuel.   *Hart Crane: An Introduction and Interpretation.* New York: Holt, Rinehart and Winston, 1963.

Herman, Barbara.   "The Language of Hart Crane," in *Sewanee Review.* LVIII (January–March, 1950), pp. 52–67.

Jennings, Elizabeth.   *Every Changing Shape.* London: Deutsch, 1961, pp. 223–233.

Landry, Hilton.   "Of Prayer and Praise: The Poetry of Hart Crane," in *The Twenties: Poetry and Prose.* Edited by Richard E. Langford and William E. Taylor. Deland, Fla.: Everett/Edwards Press, 1966, pp. 18–24.

Leibowitz, Herbert A.   *Hart Crane: An Introduction to the Poetry.* New York: Columbia University Press, 1968, pp. 23–256.

Lutyens, David Bulwer.   *The Creative Encounter.* London: Secker and Warburg, 1960, pp. 98–127.

McMichael, James.   "Hart Crane," in *Southern Review.* VIII (1972), pp. 290–309.

McMillan, Douglas.   *Transition: The History of a Literary Era, 1927–1938.* New York: Braziller, 1975, pp. 125–147.

Quinn, Vincent.   *Hart Crane.* New York: Twayne, 1963.

Rosenthal, M.L.   *The Modern Poets: A Critical Introduction.* New York: Oxford University Press, 1960, pp. 168–182.

Spears, Monroe K.   *Hart Crane.* Minneapolis: University of Minnesota Press, 1965.

Tate, Allen.   *Collected Essays.* Denver: Swallow, 1959, pp. 225–237, 528–532.

Winters, Yvor.   *In Defense of Reason.* New York: Swallow and Morrow, 1947, pp. 575–603.

Powhatan's Daughter

Dembo, L.S.   *Hart Crane's Sanskrit Charge: A Study of* The Bridge. Ithaca, N.Y.: Cornell University Press, 1960, pp. 63–86.

Hazo, Samuel.   *Hart Crane: An Introduction and Interpretation.* New York: Holt, Rinehart and Winston, 1963, pp. 81–95.

Lewis, R.W.B.   *The Poetry of Hart Crane: A Critical Study.* Princeton, N.J.: Princeton University Press, 1967, pp. 287–319.

Quinn, Vincent.   *Hart Crane.* New York: Twayne, 1963, pp. 83–91.

Rosenthal, M.L.   *The Modern Poets: A Critical Introduction.* New York: Oxford University Press, 1960, pp. 173–175.

Sugg, Richard P.   *Hart Crane's* The Bridge*: A Description of Its Life.* University: University of Alabama Press, 1976, pp. 40–65.

Uroff, M.D.   *Hart Crane: The Patterns of His Poetry.* Urbana: University of Illinois Press, 1974, pp. 79–113.

Weber, Brom.   *Hart Crane: A Biographical and Critical Study.* New York: Bodley Press, 1948, pp. 352–362.

"The River"

Butterfield, R.W.   *The Broken Arc: A Study of Hart Crane.* Edinburgh: Oliver and Boyd, 1969, pp. 161–166.

Dembo, L.S.   *Hart Crane's Sanskrit Charge: A Study of* The Bridge. Ithaca, N.Y.: Cornell University Press, 1960, pp. 69–72.

Ghiselin, Brewster.   "Bridge into the Sea," in *Partisan Review.* XVI (July, 1949), pp. 679–686.

Hazo, Samuel.   *Hart Crane: An Introduction and Interpretation.* New York: Holt, Rinehart and Winston, 1963, pp. 86–90.

Lewis, R.W.B.   *The Poetry of Hart Crane: A Critical Study.* Princeton, N.J.: Princeton University Press, 1967, pp. 296–307.

Paul, Sherman.   *Hart's* Bridge. Urbana: University of Illinois Press, 1972, pp. 206–216.

Quinn, Vincent.   *Hart Crane.* New York: Twayne, 1963, pp. 85–88.

Sugg, Richard P.   *Hart Crane's* The Bridge*: A Description of Its Life.* University: University of Alabama Press, 1976, pp. 46–54.

Uroff, M.D.   *Hart Crane: The Patterns of His Poetry.* Urbana: University of Illinois Press, 1974, pp. 92–98.

Weber, Brom.   *Hart Crane: A Biographical and Critical Study.* New York: Bodley Press, 1948, pp. 353–357.

"Voyages"

Alvarez, A.   "The Lyric of Hart Crane," in *Twentieth Century.* CLX (December, 1956), pp. 506–517. Reprinted in *Stewards of Excellence.* New York: Scribner's, 1958, pp. 107–123.

Beach, Joseph Warren.   "Hart Crane and Moby Dick," in *Western Review.* XX (Spring, 1956), pp. 183–196.

Butterfield, R.W.   *The Broken Arc: A Study of Hart Crane.* Edinburgh: Oliver and Boyd, 1969, pp. 94–105.

Day, Robert A. "Image and Idea in 'Voyages II,' " in *Criticism.* VII (Summer, 1965), pp. 224–234.

Drew, Elizabeth. *Directions in Modern Poetry.* New York: Norton, 1940, pp. 212–217.

Friar, Kimon and John Malcolm Brinnin. *Modern Poetry, American and British.* New York: Appleton-Century-Crofts, 1951, pp. 455–456.

Hazo, Samuel. *Hart Crane: An Introduction and Interpretation.* New York: Holt, Rinehart and Winston, 1963, pp. 55–67.

Hinz, Evelyn J. "Hart Crane's 'Voyages' Reconsidered," in *Contemporary Literature.* XIII (1972), pp. 315–333.

Kramer, Maurice. "Six Voyages of a Derelict Seer," in *Sewanee Review.* LXXIII (July–September, 1965), pp. 410–423.

Leibowitz, Herbert A. *Hart Crane: An Introduction to the Poetry.* New York: Columbia University Press, 1968, pp. 80–102.

Lewis, R.W.B. *The Poetry of Hart Crane: A Critical Study.* Princeton, N.J.: Princeton University Press, 1967, pp. 149–179.

Morris, H.C. "Crane's 'Voyages' as a Single Poem," in *Accent.* XIV (Autumn, 1954), pp. 291–299.

Paul, Sherman. *Hart's* Bridge. Urbana: University of Illinois Press, 1972, pp. 133–165.

Quinn, Vincent. *Hart Crane.* New York: Twayne, 1963, pp. 105–115.

Richman, Sidney. "Hart Crane's 'Voyages II': An Experiment in Redemption," in *Wisconsin Studies in Contemporary Literature.* III (Spring–Summer, 1962), pp. 65–78.

Rosenthal, M.L. *The Modern Poets: A Critical Introduction.* New York: Oxford University Press, 1960, pp. 179–182.

Uroff, M.D. *Hart Crane: The Patterns of His Poetry.* Urbana: University of Illinois Press, 1974, pp. 58–79.

Spears, Monroe K. *Hart Crane.* Minneapolis: University of Minnesota Press, 1965, pp. 27–32.

Walcutt, Charles C. "Crane's 'Voyages,' " in *Explicator.* IV (1946), item 53.

STEPHEN CRANE
(1871–1900)

"The Blue Hotel"

Bergon, Frank. *Stephen Crane's Artistry*. New York: Columbia University Press, 1965, pp. 124–131.

Cox, James T. "Stephen Crane as Symbolic Naturalist: An Analysis of 'The Blue Hotel,' " in *Modern Fiction Studies*. III (1957), pp. 147–158.

Davison, Richard A. "Crane's 'Blue Hotel' Revisited: The Illusion of Fate," in *Modern Fiction Studies*. XV (1969), pp. 537–539.

Gibson, Donald B. *The Fiction of Stephen Crane*. Carbondale: Southern Illinois University Press, 1968, pp. 106–118.

Greenfield, Stanley B. "The Unmistakable Stephen Crane," in *PMLA*. LXXIII (1958), pp. 565–568.

Klotz, Marvin. "Stephen Crane: Tragedian or Comedian: 'The Blue Hotel,' " in *University of Kansas City Review*. XXVII (1961), pp. 170–174.

Maclean, Hugh. "The Two Worlds of 'The Blue Hotel,' " in *Modern Fiction Studies*. V (1959), pp. 260–270.

Pierce, J.F. "Stephen Crane's Use of Figurative Language in 'The Blue Hotel,' " in *South Central Bulletin*. XXXIV (1974), pp. 160–164.

Solomon, Eric. *Stephen Crane: From Parody to Realism*. Cambridge, Mass.: Harvard University Press, 1966, pp. 257–274.

Sutton, Walter. "Pity and Fear in 'The Blue Hotel,' " in *American Quarterly*. IV (1952), pp. 73–76.

Van Der Beets, Richard. "Character as Structure: Ironic Parallel and Transformation in 'The Blue Hotel,' " in *Studies in Short Fiction*. V (1968), pp. 294–295.

West, Ray B. "Stephen Crane: Author in Transition," in *American Literature*. XXXIV (1962), pp. 223–227.

"The Bride Comes to Yellow Sky"

Bernard, Kenneth. " 'The Bride Comes to Yellow Sky': History as Elegy," in *English Record*. XVII (April, 1967), pp. 17–20.

Bloom, Edward A. *The Order of Fiction*. New York: Odyssey, 1969, pp. 100–104.

Cook, Robert G. "Stephen Crane's 'The Bride Comes to Yellow Sky,' " in *Studies in Short Fiction*. II (1965), pp. 368–369.

Folsom, James K. *The American Western Novel*. New Haven, Conn.: Yale College and University Press, 1966, pp. 91–94.

Holton, Milne. *Cylinders of Vision: The Fiction and Journalistic Writing of Stephen Crane.* Baton Rouge: Louisiana State University Press, 1972, pp. 226–233.

James, Overton P. "The 'Game' in 'The Bride Comes to Yellow Sky,' " in *Xavier University Studies.* IV (1965), pp. 3–11.

Solomon, Eric. *Stephen Crane: From Parody to Realism.* Cambridge, Mass.: Harvard University Press, 1966, pp. 252–257.

Tibbetts, A.M. "Stephen Crane's 'The Bride Comes to Yellow Sky,' " in *English Journal.* LIV (1965), pp. 314–316.

Vorpahl, Ben M. "Murder by the Minute: Old and New in 'The Bride Comes to Yellow Sky,' " in *Nineteenth-Century Fiction.* XXVI (1971), pp. 196–218.

West, Ray B. *The Art of Writing Fiction.* New York: Crowell, 1968, pp. 134–140.

"George's Mother"

Berryman, John. *Stephen Crane.* New York: William Sloane, 1950, pp. 318–320.

Brennan, Joseph X. "The Imagery and Art of 'George's Mother,' " in *College Language Association Journal.* IV (1960), pp. 106–115.

Geismar, Maxwell. *Rebels and Ancestors: The American Novel, 1890–1915.* Boston: Houghton Mifflin, 1953, pp. 92–94.

Gibson, Donald B. *The Fiction of Stephen Crane.* Carbondale: Southern Illinois University Press, 1968, pp. 40–52.

Gullason, Thomas A. "Thematic Patterns in Stephen Crane's Early Novels," in *Nineteenth-Century Fiction.* XVI (1961), pp. 59–67.

Holton, Milne. *Cylinders of Vision: The Fiction and Journalistic Writing of Stephen Crane.* Baton Rouge: Louisiana State University Press, 1972, pp. 55–63.

Jackson, Agnes M. "Stephen Crane's Imagery of Conflict in 'George's Mother,' " in *Arizona Quarterly.* XXV (1969), pp. 313–318.

LaFrance, Marston. *A Reading of Stephen Crane.* New York: Oxford University Press, 1971, pp. 84–93.

Simoneaux, Katherine G. "Color Imagery in Crane's 'George's Mother,' " in *College Language Association Journal.* XIV (1971), pp. 410–419.

Smith, Leverett T. "Stephen Crane's Calvinism," in *Canadian Review of American Studies.* II (Spring, 1971), pp. 18–21.

Solomon, Eric. *Stephen Crane: From Parody to Realism.* Cambridge, Mass.: Harvard University Press, 1966, pp. 49–67.

Maggie: A Girl of the Streets

Brennan, Joseph. "Irony and Symbolic Structure in Crane's *Maggie*," in *Nineteenth-Century Fiction*. XVI (March, 1962), pp. 303–315.

Brooks, Van Wyck. *Maggie: A Girl of the Streets and George's Mother*. Greenwich, Conn.: Fawcett, 1960, pp. 5–8.

Bruccoli, Matthew J. "Maggie's Last Night," in *Stephen Crane Newsletter*. II (Fall, 1967), pp. 10–11.

Cady, Edwin Harrison. "Stephen Crane's *Maggie: A Girl of the Streets*," in *Landmarks of American Writing*. Edited by Hennig Cohen. New York: Basic Books, 1969, pp. 172–181.

Colvert, James B. "Structure and Theme in Stephen Crane's Fiction," in *Modern Fiction Studies*. V (Autumn, 1959), pp. 199–208.

Cunliffe, Marcus. *The Literature of the United States*. Baltimore: Penguin, 1954, pp. 204–207.

————. "Stephen Crane and the American Background of *Maggie*," in *American Quarterly*. VII (Spring, 1955), pp. 31–44.

Fitelson, David. "Stephen Crane's *Maggie* and Darwinism," in *American Quarterly*. XVI (Summer, 1964), pp. 182–194.

Fox, Austin M. *Maggie and Other Stories*. New York: Washington Square Press, 1960, pp. v–xviii.

Gullason, Thomas A. "The Sources of Stephen Crane's *Maggie*," in *Philological Quarterly*. XXXVIII (Oct., 1959), pp. 497–502.

————. "Thematic Patterns in Stephen Crane's Early Novels," in *Nineteenth-Century Fiction*. XVI (June, 1961), pp. 59–67.

Kahn, Sholom J. "Stephen Crane and Whitman: A Possible Source for *Maggie*," in *Walt Whitman Review*. VII (Dec., 1961), pp. 71–77.

Katz, Joseph. "The *Maggie* Nobody Knows," in *Modern Fiction Studies*. XII (Summer, 1966), pp. 200–212.

La France, M. "George's Mother and the Other Half of Maggie," in *Stephen Crane in Transition*. Edited by Joseph Katz. De Kalb: Northern Illinois University Press, 1972, pp. 35–53.

Martin, John. "Childhood in Stephen Crane's *Maggie*, 'The Monster' and *Whilomville Stories*," in *Midwestern University Quarterly*. II (1967), pp. 40–46.

Overmyer, Janet. "The Structure of Crane's *Maggie*," in *University of Kansas City Review*. XXIX (October, 1962), pp. 71–72.

Pizer, Donald. "Stephen Crane's *Maggie* and American Naturalism," in *Criticism*. VII (Spring, 1965), pp. 168–175.

Seymour-Smith, Martin. *Fallen Women*. London: Nelson, 1969, pp. 182–185.

Simoneaux, Katherine G. "Color Imagery in Crane's *Maggie: A Girl of the Streets*," in *College Language Association Journal.* XVIII (1974), pp. 91–100.

Stallman, Robert Wooster. "Crane's *Maggie*: A Reassessment," in *Modern Fiction Studies.* V (Autumn, 1959), pp. 251–259.

————. *The Houses That James Built and Other Literary Studies.* East Lansing: Michigan State University Press, 1961, pp. 63–72.

————. "Stephen Crane's Revision of *Maggie: A Girl of the Streets*," in *American Literature.* XXVI (January, 1955), pp. 528–536.

Stein, William Bysshe. "New Testament Inversions in Crane's *Maggie*," in *Modern Language Notes.* LXXIII (April, 1958), pp. 268–272.

Wertheim, Stanley. "The Saga of March 23rd: Garland, Gilder, and Crane," in *Stephen Crane Newsletter.* III (Winter, 1968), pp. 1–3.

"The Monster"

Ahmebrink, Lars. *The Beginnings of Naturalism in American Fiction: A Study of the Works of Hamlin Garland, Stephen Crane and Frank Norris.* Uppsala, Sweden: Lundequistska, 1950, pp. 378–381.

Beer, Thomas. *Stephen Crane: A Study in American Letters.* Garden City, N.Y.: Garden City Publishing, 1927.

Bergon, Frank. *Stephen Crane's Artistry.* New York: Columbia University Press, 1965, pp. 35–36.

Berryman, John. *Stephen Crane.* New York: William Sloane, 1950, pp. 191–196.

Cody, Edwin H. *Stephen Crane.* New York: Twayne, 1962, pp. 159–160.

Cooley, John R. " 'The Monster'—Stephen Crane's 'Invisible Man,' " in *Markham Review.* V (Fall, 1975), pp. 10–14.

Geismar, Maxwell. *Rebels and Ancestors: The American Novel, 1890–1915.* Boston: Houghton Mifflin, 1953, pp. 116–120.

Gibson, Donald B. *The Fiction of Stephen Crane.* Carbondale: Southern Illinois University Press, 1968, pp. 136–140.

Gullason, Thomas A. "The Symbolic Unity of 'The Monster,' " in *Modern Language Notes.* LXXV (1960), pp. 663–668.

Hafley, James. " 'The Monster' and the Art of Stephen Crane," in *Accent.* XIX (1959), pp. 159–165.

Holton, Milne. *Cylinders of Vision: The Fiction and Journalistic Writing of Stephen Crane.* Baton Rouge: Louisiana State University Press, 1972, pp. 204–213.

Kahn, Sy. "Stephen Crane and the Great Voice in the Night: An Explication of 'The Monster,' " in *Essays in Modern American Literature.* Edited by Richard E. Langford. DeLand, Fla.: Stetson University Press, 1963, pp. 35–45.

Knight, Grant C.   *The Critical Period in American Literature.* Chapel Hill: University of North Carolina Press, 1951, pp. 154–155.

LaFrance, Marston.   *A Reading of Stephen Crane.* New York: Oxford University Press, 1971, pp. 205–210.

Mayer, Charles W.   "Social Forms Versus Human Brotherhood in Crane's 'The Monster,' " in *Ball State University Forum.* XIV (1973), pp. 29–37.

Solomon, Eric.   *Stephen Crane: From Parody to Realism.* Cambridge, Mass.: Harvard University Press, 1966, pp. 180–200.

"The Open Boat"

Adams, Richard P.   "Naturalistic Fiction: 'The Open Boat,' " in *Tulane Studies in English.* IV (1954), pp. 137–145.

Autrey, Max L.   "The Word Out of the Sea: A View of Crane's 'The Open Boat,' " in *Arizona Quarterly.* XXX (1974), pp. 101–110.

Beer, Thomas.   *Stephen Crane: A Study in American Letters.* Garden City, N.Y.: Garden City Publishing, 1927, pp. 143–146.

Bergon, Frank.   *Stephen Crane's Artistry.* New York: Columbia University Press, 1975, pp. 86–93.

Buitenhuis, Peter.   "The Essentials of Life: 'The Open Boat' as Existentialist Fiction," in *Modern Fiction Studies.* V (1959), pp. 243–250.

Burns, Landon C.   "On 'The Open Boat,' " in *Studies in Short Fiction.* III (1966), pp. 455–457.

Colvert, James B.   "Style and Meaning in Stephen Crane's 'The Open Boat,' " in *University of Texas Studies in English.* XXXVII (1958), pp. 34–45.

Day, Cyrus.   "Stephen Crane and the Ten-Foot Dinghy," in *Boston University Studies in English.* III (1957), pp. 193–213.

Gerstenberger, Donna.   " 'The Open Boat': Additional Perspective," in *Modern Fiction Studies.* XVII (1972), pp. 557–561.

Gordon, Caroline.   "Stephen Crane," in *Accent.* IX (1949), pp. 153–157.

Holton, Milne.   *Cylinders of Vision: The Fiction and Journalistic Writing of Stephen Crane.* Baton Rouge: Louisiana State University Press, 1972, pp. 150–168.

Kissane, Leedice.   "Interpretation Through Language: A Study of the Metaphors in Stephen Crane's 'The Open Boat,' " in *Rendezvous.* I (Spring, 1966), pp. 18–22.

Lytle, Andrew.   *The Hero with the Private Parts.* Baton Rouge: Louisiana State University Press, 1966, pp. 60–75.

Marcus, Mordecai.   "The Three-Fold View of Nature in 'The Open Boat,' " in *Philological Quarterly.* XLI (1962), pp. 511–515.

Metzger, Charles R. "Realistic Devices in Stephen Crane's 'The Open Boat,' " in *Midwest Quarterly*. IV (1962), pp. 47–54.

Munson, Gorham. *Style and Form in American Prose*. New York: Doubleday, 1929, pp. 159–170.

Napier, James J. "Land Imagery in 'The Open Boat,' " in *College English Association Critic*. XXIX (April, 1967), p. 15.

Parks, Edd W. "Crane's 'The Open Boat,' " in *Nineteenth-Century Fiction*. VIII (1953), p. 77.

Solomon, Eric. *Stephen Crane: From Parody to Realism*. Cambridge, Mass.: Harvard University Press, 1966, pp. 157–176.

Stallman, Robert W. "The Land-Sea Irony in 'The Open Boat,' " in *College English Association Critic*. XXX (May, 1968), p. 15.

Stewart, Randall. "Dreiser and the Naturalist Heresy," in *Virginia Quarterly Review*. XXXIV (1958), pp. 102–103.

West, Ray B. "Stephen Crane: Author in Transition," in *American Literature*. XXXIV (1962), pp. 219–221.

White, W.M. "The Crane-Hemingway Code: A Reevaluation," in *Ball State University Forum*. X (Spring, 1969), pp. 15–20.

The Red Badge of Courage

Albrecht, Robert C. "Content and Style in *The Red Badge of Courage*," in *College English*. XXVII (March, 1966), pp. 487–492.

Berryman, John. *The Freedom of the Poet*. New York: Farrar, Straus and Giroux, 1976, pp. 176–184.

Breslin, Paul. "Courage and Convention: *The Red Badge of Courage*," in *Yale Review*. LXVI (1976), pp. 209–222.

Burhans, Clinton S., Jr. "Judging Henry Judging: Point of View in *The Red Badge of Courage*," in *Ball State University Forum*. XV (1974), pp. 38–48.

————. "Twin Lights on Henry Fleming: Structural Parallels in *The Red Badge of Courage*," in *Arizona Quarterly*. XXX (1974), pp. 149–159.

Cazemajou, J. "*The Red Badge of Courage*: The 'Religion of Peace' and the War Archetype," in *Stephen Crane in Transition*. Edited by Joseph Katz. De Kalb: Northern Illinois University Press, 1972, pp. 54–65.

Cox, James T. "The Imagery of *The Red Badge of Courage*," in *Modern Fiction Studies*. V (Autumn, 1959), pp. 209–219.

Gollin, Rita K. " 'Little Souls Who Thirst for Fight' in *The Red Badge of Courage*," in *Arizona Quarterly*. XXX (1974), pp. 111–118.

Greenfield, Stanley B. "The Unmistakable Stephen Crane," in *PMLA*. LXXIII (December, 1958), pp. 562–572.

Hart, John E.   "*The Red Badge of Courage* as Myth and Symbol," in *University of Kansas City Review*. XIX (Summer, 1953), pp. 249–256.

Hoffman, Michael J.   *The Subversive Vision; American Romanticism in Literature*. Port Washington, N.Y.: Kennikat, 1973, pp. 129–139.

Hungerford, Harold R.   "That Was at Chancellorsville: The Factual Framework of *The Red Badge of Courage*," in *American Literature*. XXXIV (January, 1963), pp. 520–531.

Klotz, Marvin.   "Romance or Realism?: Plot, Theme, and Character in *The Red Badge of Courage*," in *College Language Association Journal*. VI (December, 1962), pp. 98–106.

Lorch, Thomas M.   "The Cyclical Structure of *The Red Badge of Courage*," in *College Language Association Journal*. X (March, 1967), pp. 229–238.

Mangum, Bryant.   "Crane's Red Badge and Zola's," in *American Literary Realism, 1870–1910*. IX (1976), pp. 279–280.

Marcus, Mordecai.   "The Unity of *The Red Badge of Courage*," in The Red Badge of Courage: *Text and Criticism*. Edited by Richard Lettis. New York: Harcourt, Brace, 1960, pp. 189–195.

Maynard, Reid.   "Red as Leitmotiv in *The Red Badge of Courage*," in *Arizona Quarterly*. XXX (1974), pp. 135–141.

Morace, Robert A.   "A 'New' Review of *The Red Badge of Courage*," in *American Literary Realism, 1870–1910*. VIII (1975), pp. 163–165.

Rathbun, John W.   "Structure and Meaning in *The Red Badge of Courage*," in *Ball State University Forum*. X (Winter, 1969), pp. 8–16.

Rechnitz, Robert M.   "Depersonalization and the Dream in *The Red Badge of Courage*," in *Studies in the Novel* (North Texas State University). VI (1974), pp. 76–87.

Solomon, Eric.   "The Structure of *The Red Badge of Courage*," in *Modern Fiction Studies*. V (Autumn, 1959), pp. 220–234.

Van Meter, Jan.   "Sex and War in *The Red Badge of Courage*: Cultural Themes and Literary Criticism," in *Genre*. VII (1974), pp. 71–90.

Vanderbilt, Kermit and Daniel Weiss.   "From Rifleman to Flagbearer: Henry Fleming's Separate Peace in *The Red Badge of Courage*," in *Modern Fiction Studies*. XI (Winter, 1965/66), pp. 371–380.

Weiss, Daniel.   "*The Red Badge of Courage*," in *Psychoanalytic Review*. LII (Summer, 1965), pp. 35–52 and LII (Fall, 1965), pp. 130–154.

Zambrano, Ana Laura.   "The Role of Nature in *The Red Badge of Courage*," in *Arizona Quarterly*. XXX (1974), pp. 164–166.

RICHARD CRASHAW
(1612–1649)

"Blessed Be the Paps Which Thou Hast Sucked"

Adams, Robert M.   *Strains of Discord: Studies in Literary Openness.* Ithaca, N.Y.: Cornell University Press, 1958, p. 136.

————.   "Taste and Bad Taste in Metaphysical Poetry: Richard Crashaw and Dylan Thomas," in *Hudson Review.* VIII (Spring, 1955), pp. 68–69.

Bertonasco, Marc F.   *Crashaw and the Baroque.* University: University of Alabama Press, 1971, pp. 9–11.

Goldfarb, Russell M.   "Crashaw's 'Suppose He Had Been Tabled at Thy Teates,' " in *Explicator.* XIX (1961), item 35.

"Hymn to Saint Teresa"

Bertonasco, Marc F.   *Crashaw and the Baroque.* University: University of Alabama Press, 1971, pp. 26–27.

Foy, Rev. Thomas.   *Richard Crashaw: Poet and Saint.* Folcroft, Pa: Folcroft Library Editions, 1971, pp. 54–56.

Martz, Louis L.   *The Wit of Love: Donne, Carew, Crashaw, Marvell.* Notre Dame, Ind.: University of Notre Dame Press, 1969, pp. 131–135.

Miner, Earl.   *The Metaphysical Mode from Donne to Cowley.* Princeton, N.J.: Princeton University Press, 1969, pp. 186–187.

Rickey, Mary Ellen.   *Rhyme and Meaning in Richard Crashaw.* Lexington: University of Kentucky Press, 1961, pp. 57–60.

Unger, Leonard and William Van O'Connor.   *Poems for Study.* New York: Rinehart, 1953, pp. 171–175.

Warren, Austin.   *Richard Crashaw: A Study in Baroque Sensibility.* London: Faber and Faber, 1939, pp. 139–146.

Williamson, George.   *Six Metaphysical Poets: A Reader's Guide.* New York: Farrar, Straus and Giroux, 1967, pp. 138–141.

The Poetry of Crashaw

Adams, Robert Martin.   "Taste and Bad Taste in Metaphysical Poetry: Richard Crashaw and Dylan Thomas," in *The Hudson Review.* VIII (1955), pp. 60–77.

Bertonasco, Marc F.   *Crashaw and the Baroque.* University: University of Alabama Press, 1971.

Ditsky, John M.   "Symbol-Patterns in Crashaw's *Carmen Deo Nostro,*' " in *North Dakota Quarterly.* XL (1972), pp. 31–36.

Geha, Richard, Jr. "Richard Crashaw: (1613?–1650?): The Ego's Soft Fall," in *American Imago.* XXIII (1966), pp. 158–168.

Gilman, Harvey. "Crashaw's Reflexive Recoil," in *Seventeenth Century News.* XXII (1964), pp. 2–4.

Larsen, Kenneth J. "Richard Crashaw's *Epigrammata Sacra,*" in *The Latin Poetry of English Poets.* Edited by J.W. Binns. London: Routledge and Kegan Paul, 1974, pp. 93–120.

LeClerq, R.V. "Crashaw's Epithalamium: Pattern and Vision," in *Literary Monographs.* VI (1975), pp. 71–108.

McCanles, Michael. "The Rhetoric of the Sublime in Richard Crashaw's Poetry," in *The Rhetoric of Renaissance Poetry from Wyatt to Milton.* Edited by Thomas O. Sloan and Raymond B. Waddington. Berkeley: University of California Press, 1974, pp. 189–211.

Martz, Louis L. *The Wit of Love: Donne, Carew, Crashaw, Marvell.* Notre Dame, Ind.: University of Notre Dame Press, 1969, pp. 124–147.

Raspa, Anthony. "Crashaw and the Jesuit Poetic," in *University of Toronto Quarterly.* XXXVI (1966), pp. 37–54.

Rickey, Mary Ellen. *Rhyme and Meaning in Richard Crashaw.* Lexington: University of Kentucky Press, 1961.

Schwenger, Peter. "Crashaw's Perspectivist Metaphor," in *Comparative Literature.* XXVIII (1976), pp. 65–74.

Spender, Constance. "Richard Crashaw, 1613–1648," in *Contemporary Review.* CXVI (1919), pp. 210–215.

Steele, Thomas J. "The Tactile Sensorium of Richard Crashaw," in *Seventeenth Century News.* XXX (1972), pp. 9–10.

Summers, Joseph H. *The Heirs of Donne and Jonson.* New York: Oxford University Press, 1970, pp. 102–115.

Tytell, John. "Sexual Imagery in the Secular and Sacred Poems of Richard Crashaw," in *Literature and Psychology.* XXI (1971), pp. 21–27.

Warren, Austin. "Crashaw's Epigrammata Sacra," in *Journal of English and Germanic Philology.* XXXIII (1934), pp. 233–239.

————. "The Mysticism of Richard Crashaw," in *Symposium.* IV (1933), pp. 135–155.

————. *Richard Crashaw: A Study in Baroque Sensibility.* London: Faber and Faber, 1939.

Watkin, E.I. "Richard Crashaw (1612–1649)," in *The English Way.* Edited by Maisie Ward. New York: Books for Libraries Press, 1968, pp. 268–296.

White, Helen C. *The Metaphysical Poets: A Study in Religious Experience.* New York: Collier Books, 1962, pp. 214–239.

Williams, George Walton. *Image and Symbol in the Sacred Poetry of Richard Crashaw.* Columbia: University of South Carolina Press, 1963.

————. "Introduction," in *The Complete Poetry of Richard Crashaw.* New York: New York University Press, 1972, pp. xv–xxii.

Williamson, George. *Six Metaphysical Poets: A Reader's Guide.* New York: Farrar, Straus and Giroux, 1967, pp. 119–145.

"The Weeper"

Adams, Robert M. *Strains of Discord: Studies in Literary Openness.* Ithaca, N.Y.: Cornell University Press, 1958, pp. 131–133, 136–137.

————. "Taste and Bad Taste in Metaphysical Poetry: Richard Crashaw and Dylan Thomas," in *Hudson Review.* VIII (Spring, 1955), pp. 66–67, 69–71.

Beachcroft, T.O. "Crashaw and the Baroque Style," in *Criterion.* XIII (1934), pp. 407–425.

Bertonasco, Marc. *Crashaw and the Baroque.* University: University of Alabama Press, 1971, pp. 94–117.

————. "A New Look at Crashaw and 'The Weeper,' " in *Texas Studies in Literature and Language.* X (Summer, 1968), pp. 177–188.

Chambers, Leland H. "In Defense of 'The Weeper,' " in *Papers on Language and Literature.* III (Spring, 1967), pp. 111–121.

Foy, Rev. Thomas. *Richard Crashaw: Poet and Saint.* Folcroft, Pa.: Folcroft Library Editions, 1971, pp. 77–83.

Manning, Stephen. "The Meaning of 'The Weeper,' " in *Journal of English Literary History.* XXII (March, 1955), pp. 34–47.

Martz, Louis L. *The Wit of Love: Donne, Carew, Crashaw, Marvell.* Notre Dame, Ind.: University of Notre Dame Press, 1969, pp. 201–202.

Peter, John. "Crashaw and 'The Weeper,' " in *Scrutiny.* XIX (October, 1953), pp. 259–273.

Rickey, Mary Ellen. *Rhyme and Meaning in Richard Crashaw.* Lexington: University of Kentucky Press, 1961, pp. 64–67.

Summers, Joseph H. *The Heirs of Donne and Jonson.* New York: Oxford University Press, 1970, pp. 104–105.

Warren, Austin. *Richard Crashaw: A Study in Baroque Sensibility.* London: Faber and Faber, 1939, pp. 126–132.

White, Helen C. *The Metaphysical Poets: A Study in Religious Experience.* New York: Collier Books, 1962, pp. 236–237.

Williams, George Walton. *Image and Symbol in the Sacred Poetry of Richard Crashaw.* Columbia: University of South Carolina Press, 1963, pp. 98–104.

Williamson, George.   *Six Metaphysical Poets: A Reader's Guide.* New York: Farrar, Straus and Giroux, 1967, pp. 122–123.

Winters, Yvor.   *The Anatomy of Nonsense.* Norfolk, Conn.: New Directions, 1943, pp. 209–210.

E.E. CUMMINGS
(1894–1962)

The Enormous Room

Burke, Kenneth. "A Decade of American Fiction," in *Bookman*, LXIX, (August, 1929), pp. 561–567.

Dos Passos, John. "Off the Shoals," in *Dral.* LXXIII (July, 1922), pp. 97–102. Reprinted in *EΣTI: E.E. Cummings and the Critics*. Edited by S.V. Baum. East Lansing: Michigan State University Press, 1962, pp. 4–9.

Dougherty, James P. "E.E. Cummings: *The Enormous Room*," in *Landmarks of American Writing*. Edited by Henning Cohen. New York: Basic Books, 1969, pp. 288–302.

Dumas, Bethany K. *E.E. Cummings: A Remembrance of Miracles*. New York: Barnes & Noble, 1974, pp. 110–120.

Eckley, Wilton. *The Merrill Guide to e.e. cummings*. Columbus: Merrill, 1970, pp. 6–12.

Friedman, Norman. *e.e. cummings: The Growth of a Writer*. Carbondale: Southern Illinois University Press, 1964, pp. 22–35.

Gaull, Marilyn. "Language and Identity: A Study of E.E. Cummings' *The Enormous Room*," in *American Quarterly*. XIX (1967), pp. 645–662.

Graves, Robert. "Introduction," in *The Enormous Room*. London: Jonathan Cape, 1928, pp. 7–15.

Hoffman, Frederick J. *The Twenties: American Writing in the Post-War Decade*. New York: Viking, 1955, pp. 62–66.

Kingsley, Widmer. "Timeless Prose," in *Twentieth Century Literature*. IV, (April–July, 1958), pp. 3–8.

Lawrence, Floyd B. "Two Novelists of the Great War: Dos Passos and Cummings," in *University Review*. XXXVI (1969), pp. 35–41.

Norman, Charles. *The Magic Maker: E.E. Cummings*. New York: Macmillan, 1958, pp. 108–127.

Rosenfeld, Paul. "The Enormous Cummings." in *Twice a Year*. II–IV (Fall–Winter, 1939; Spring-Summer, 1940), pp. 271–280. Reprinted in *EΣTI: E.E. Cummings and the Critics*. East Lansing: Michigan State University Press, 1962, pp. 72–80.

Smith, David E. "*The Enormous Room* and *The Pilgrim's Progress*," in *Twentieth Century Literature*. XI (July, 1965), pp. 67–75. Reprinted in *E.E. Cummings: A Collection of Critical Essays*. Edited by Norman Friedman. Englewood Cliffs, N.J.: Prentice-Hall, 1972, pp. 121–132.

Walsh, J. "The Painful Process of Unthinking: E.E. Cummings' Social Vision in *The Enormous Room*," in *The First World War in Fiction*. Edited by Holger Michael Klein. New York: Barnes & Noble, 1977, pp. 32–42.

Wegner, Robert E. *The Poetry and Prose of E.E. Cummings*. New York: Harcourt, 1965, pp. 24–25, 68–70, 76–77.

Wickes, George. "E.E. Cummings at War," in *Columbia Forum*. XII (Fall, 1969), pp. 31–33.

Widmer, Kinglsey. "Timeless Prose," in *Twentieth Century Literature*. IV (April–July, 1958), pp. 3–8.

The Poetry of Cummings

Baum, S.V. "E.E. Cummings: The Technique of Immediacy," in *South Atlantic Quarterly*. LIII (January, 1954), pp. 70–88. Reprinted in *E.E. Cummings: A Collection of Critical Essays*. Edited by Norman Friedman. Englewood Cliffs, N.J.: Prentice-Hall, 1972, pp. 104–120.

Bode, Carl. "E.E. Cummings and Exploded Verse," in *The Great Experiment in American Literature*. New York: Praeger, 1961, pp. 79–100.

Cline, Patrician Buchanan Tal-Mason. "The Whole E.E. Cummings," in *Twentieth Century Literature*. XIV (July, 1968), pp. 90–97. Reprinted in *E.E. Cummings: A Collection of Critical Essays*. Edited by Norman Friedman. Englewood, Cliffs, N.J.: Prentice-Hall, 1972, pp. 60–70.

Dickey, James. "E.E. Cummings," in *Babel to Byzantium: Poets and Poetry Now*. New York: Farrar, Straus and Giroux, 1968, pp. 100–106.

Dumas, Bethany K. *E.E. Cummings: A Remembrance of Miracles*. New York: Barnes & Noble, 1974, pp. 51–106, 143–148.

Eckley, Wilton. *The Merrill Guide to e.e. cummings*. Columbus: Merrill, 1970.

Fairley, Irene R. *E.E. Cummings and Ungrammar*. New York: Watermill, 1975.

Friedman, Norman. *e.e. cummings: The Art of His Poetry*. Baltimore: Johns Hopkins University Press, 1960.

————. *e.e. cummings: The Growth of a Writer*. Carbondale: Southern Illinois University Press, 1964, pp. 3–21, 36–108, 125–173. Part reprinted in *E.E. Cummings: A Collection of Critical Essays*. Edited by Norman Friedman. Englewood Cliffs, N.J.: Prentice-Hall, 1972, pp. 46–59.

Haines, George, IV. "::2:1—The World and E.E. Cummings," in *Sewanee Review*. LIX (Spring, 1951), pp. 206–227. Reprinted in *E.E. Cummings: A Collection of Critical Essays*. Edited by Norman Friedman. Englewood Cliffs, N.J.: Prentice-Hall, 1972, pp. 15–30.

Hayakawa, S.I. "Is Indeed 5," in *Poetry*. LII (August, 1938), pp. 284–292. Printed in *EΣTI: E.E. Cummings and the Critics*. East Lansing: Michigan State University Press, 1962, pp. 92–98.

Honig, Edwin. " 'Proud of His Scientific Attitude,' " in *Kenyon Review*. XVII (Summer, 1955), pp. 484–490.

Lane, Gary. *I Am: A Study of E.E. Cummings's Poems*. Lawrence: University Press of Kansas, 1976.

Logan, John. "The Organ Grinder and the Cockatoo: An Introduction to E.E. Cummings," in *Modern American Poetry: Essays in Criticism*. Edited by Jerome Mazzaro. New York: David McKay, 1970, pp. 249–271.

Marks, Barry A. *E.E. Cummings*. New York: Twayne, 1964.

Maurer, Robert E. "Latter-Day Notes on E.E. Cummings' Language," in *Bucknell Review*. V (May, 1955), pp. 1–23. Reprinted in *E.E. Cummings: A Collection of Critical Essays*. Edited by Norman Friedman. Englewood Cliffs, N.J.: Prentice-Hall, 1972, pp. 79–99.

Norman, Charles. *E.E. Cummings: The Magic Maker*. Indianapolis: Bobbs-Merrill, 1972.

Pearce, Roy Harvey. *The Continuity of American Poetry*. Princeton, N.J.: Princeton University Press, 1961, pp. 359–366.

Tate, Allen. *Reactionary Essays on Poetry and Ideas*. New York: Scribner's, 1936, pp. 228–233. Reprinted in *E.E. Cummings: A Collection of Critical Essays*. Edited by Norman Friedman. Englewood Cliffs, N.J.: Prentice-Hall, 1972, pp. 71–74.

Triem, Eve. *E.E. Cummings*. Minneapolis: University of Minnesota Press, 1969.

Von Abele, Rudolph. " 'Only to Grow': Change in the Poetry of E.E. Cummings," in *PMLA*. LXX, (December, 1955), pp. 913–933.

Watson, Barbara. "The Dangers of Security: E.E. Cummings' Revolt Against the Future," in *Kenyon Review*. XVIII (1956), pp. 519–537. Reprinted in *E.E. Cummings: A Collection of Critical Essays*. Edited by Norman Friedman. Englewood Cliffs, N.J.: Prentice-Hall, 1972, pp. 31–45.

Wegner, Robert E. *The Poetry and Prose of E.E. Cummings*. New York: Harcourt, Brace and World, 1965.

RICHARD HENRY DANA, JR.
(1815–1882)

Two Years Before the Mast

Bennett, James O'Donnell. *Much Loved Books: Best Sellers of the Ages.* New York: Liveright, 1938, pp. 386–392.

Bode, Carl. *The Half-world of American Culture: A Miscellany.* Carbondale: Southern Illinois University Press, 1965, pp. 33–53.

Cline, Walter. "Dana at the Point, Discrepancies in the Narrative," in *Historical Society of Southern California Quarterly.* XXXII (June, 1950), pp. 127–132.

Downs, Robert Bingham. *Famous American Books.* New York: McGraw-Hill, 1972, pp. 94–99.

Gallery, Daniel V. "Too Far Before the Mast," in *Colophon.* II (Autumn, 1936), pp. 60–64.

Hart, James D. "An Eyewitness of Eight Years Before the Mast," in *New Colophon.* III (1950), pp. 128–131.

Hill, Douglas B., Jr. "Richard Henry Dana, Jr., and *Two Years Before the Mast*," in *Criticism.* IX (1967), pp. 312–325.

Lawrence, D.H. "Dana's *Two Years Before the Mast*," in *Studies in Classic American Literature.* New York: Viking, 1923, pp. 163–192.

Lucid, Robert F. "*Two Years Before the Mast* as Propaganda," in *American Quarterly.* XII (Fall, 1960), pp. 392–403.

McWilliams, John. "Rounding Cape Horn: Melville, Dana and Literary Tradition," in *Extracts.* XXV (1976), p. 3.

Metzdorf, Robert F. "The Publishing History of Richard Henry Dana's *Two Years Before the Mast*," in *Harvard Library Bulletin.* VII (Autumn, 1953), pp. 312–332.

Powell, Lawrence Clark. *California Classics: the Creative Literature of the Golden State.* Los Angeles: Ward Ritchie Press, 1971, pp. 151–162.

Shapiro, Samuel. *Richard Henry Dana, Jr., 1815–1882.* East Lansing: Michigan State University Press, 1961, pp. 187–198.

————. "With Dana Before the Mast," in *American Heritage.* XI (October, 1960), pp. 26–37, 94–97.

Spengemann, W.C. *The Adventurous Muse: The Poetics of American Fiction, 1789–1900.* New Haven, Conn.: Yale University Press, 1977, pp. 6–67.

Winterich, John T. "*Two Years Before the Mast* by Richard Henry Dana, Jr.," in *Georgia Review.* IX (Winter, 1955), pp. 459–461.

GABRIELE D'ANNUNZIO
(1863–1938)

The Triumph of Death

Gullace, Giovanni. *Gabriele d'Annunzio in France; A Study in Cultural Relations.* Syracuse, N.Y.: Syracuse University Press, 1966, pp. 15–19.

Jullian, Philippe. *D'Annunzio.* New York: Viking, 1971, pp. 74–77, 95–96.

Rhodes, Anthony. *The Poet as Superman; A Life of Gabriele d'Annunzio.* London: Weidenfield and Nicolson, 1956, pp. 44–46.

Winwar, Frances. *Wings of Fire; A Biography of Gabriele d'Annunzio and Eleonora Duse.* London: Alvin Redman, 1956, pp. 82–85, 94–97.

DANTE ALIGHIERI
(1265–1321)

The Divine Comedy

Auerbach, Eric. *Dante: Poet of the Secular World.* Translated by Ralph Manheim. Chicago: University of Chicago Press, 1974.

Bergin, Thomas G. "Dante's *Comedy*—Letter and Spirit," in *Virginia Quarterly Review.* XLI (Autumn, 1965), pp. 525–541.

————. *Perspectives on* The Divine Comedy. New Brunswick, N.J.: Rutgers University Press, 1967.

Bernardo, Aldo S. "Flesh, Spirit and Re-Birth at the Center of Dante's *Comedy*," in *Symposium.* XIX (Winter, 1965), pp. 335–351.

Ciardi, John. "How to Read Dante," in *Varieties of Literary Experience.* Edited by S. Burnshaw. New York: New York University Press, 1962.

Clements, Robert J., Editor. *American Critical Essays on* The Divine Comedy. New York: New York University Press, 1966.

Cosmo, Umberto. *A Handbook to Dante Studies.* Folcroft, Pa.: Folcroft Library Editions, 1899, pp. 133–188.

Demaray, John C. *The Invention of Dante's* Commedia. New Haven, Conn.: Yale University Press, 1974.

Fergusson, Francis. *Dante.* New York: Macmillan, 1966.

————. *Trope and Allegory: Themes Common to Dante and Shakespeare.* Athens: University of Georgia Press, 1977.

Gilbert, Allan H. *Dante and His* Comedy. New York: New York University Press, 1963.

Grandgent, C.H. and Charles S. Singleton, Editors. *A Companion to* The Divine Comedy. Cambridge, Mass.: Harvard University Press, 1975.

Hollander, Robert. *Allegory in Dante's* Comedy. Princeton, N.J.: Princeton University Press, 1969.

Mazzeo, Joseph Anthony. *Medieval Cultural Tradition in Dante's* Comedy. Ithaca, N.Y.: Cornell University Press, 1960.

Mazzotta, G. "Dante's Literary Typology," in *Modern Language Notes.* LXXXVII (January, 1972), pp. 1–19.

Moore, Edward. *Studies in Dante.* Series 1–3. Oxford: Clarendon Press, 1899–1903.

Musa, Mark. *Advent at the Gates: Dante's* Comedy. Bloomington: Indiana University Press, 1974.

Page, Thomas Nelson. *Dante and His Influence; Studies.* Port Washington, N.Y.: Kennikat, 1969.

Sayers, Dorothy. *Introductory Papers on Dante.* London: Methuen, 1954.

Scott, J.A. "Dante's Allegory: Review Article," in *Romance Philology.* XXVI (February, 1973), pp. 558–591.

Shapiro, Marianne. *Woman Earthly and Divine in the* Comedy *of Dante.* Lexington: University Press of Kentucky, 1975.

Singleton, Charles S. *Dante Studies,* Volume I. Cambridge, Mass.: Harvard University Press, 1965.

Symonds, John A. *Introduction to the Study of Dante.* New York: AMS Press, 1899.

Toynbee, Page. *Dictionary of Proper Names and Notable Matters in the Works of Dante.* Revised by Charles S. Singleton. Oxford: Clarendon Press, 1968.

Wicksteed, Philip Henry. *From* Vita Nuova *to* Paradiso. Manchester, England: Manchester University Press, 1922.

Vita Nuova

Aronoff, Marcia. "Dream and Non-Dream in Dante's *Vita Nuova,*" in *Cithara.* XVI (1976), pp. 18–32.

Boyde, Patrick. *Dante's Style and His Lyric Poetry.* Cambridge: Cambridge University Press, 1971.

Eliot, T.S. "The *Vita Nuova,*" in *Dante; A Collection of Critical Essays.* Edited by John Freccero. Englewood Cliffs, N.J.: Prentice-Hall, 1965, pp. 23–27.

Fergusson, F. "Romantic Love in Dante and Shakespeare," in *Sewanee Review.* LXXXIII (Spring, 1975), pp. 253–266.

Glickman, Enrica J. "Courtly Love: A Background to Dante's *New Life,*" in *Revista de Letras.* III (1971), pp. 68–91.

Hollander, Robert. "*Vita Nuova*: Dante's Perception of Beatrice," in *Dante Studies with the Annual Report of the Dante Society.* XCII (1974), pp. 1–18.

Levy, Bernard S. "Beatrice's Greeting and Dante's 'Sigh' in the *Vita Nuova,*" in *Dante Studies with the Annual Report of the Dante Society.* XCII (1974), pp. 53–62.

Maurino, F. "Originality in the *Vita Nuova,*" in *Forum Italicum.* (1967), pp. 62–66.

Mazzaro, Jerome. "The Fact of Beatrice in the *Vita Nuova,*" in *The Literature of Fact: Selected Papers of the English Institute.* Edited by Angus Fletcher. New York: Columbia University Press, 1976, pp. 83–108.

Montgomery, Marion. *The Reflective Journey Toward Order: Essays on Dante, Wordsworth, Eliot and Others.* Athens: University of Georgia Press, 1973, pp. 33–39, 142–161, 198–206.

Musa, Mark.   "Introduction," in *The Vita Nuova*. Edited and translated by Mark Musa. Bloomington: Indiana University Press, 1973.

Singleton, Charles S.   *An Essay on the* Vita Nuova. Cambridge, Mass.: Published for the Dante Society by Harvard University Press, 1949.

Strauch, E.H.   "Dante's *Vita Nuova* as Riddle," in *Symposium.* XXI (Winter, 1967), pp. 324–330.

Wheelock, J.T.S.   "The Function of the Amore Figure in the *Vita Nuova*," in *Romanic Review.* LXVIII (November, 1977), pp. 276–286.

Wicksteed, Philip Henry.   *From* Vita Nuova *to* Paradiso. Manchester, England: Manchester University Press, 1922.

RUBÉN DARÍO
(1867–1916)

Azul . . .

Franco, Jean. *A Literary History of Spain: Spanish American Literature Since Independence.* London: Ernest Benn, 1973, pp. 113–114.

Fraser, Howard M. "Irony in the Fantastic Stories of *Azul,*" in *Latin American Literary Review.* I (1973), pp. 37–41.

Goldberg, Isaac. *Studies in Spanish-American Literature.* New York: Brentano's, 1920, pp. 130–138.

Skyrme, Raymond. "Darío's *Azul . . .*: A Note on the Derivation of the Title," in *Romance Notes.* X (1968), pp. 73–76.

————. *Rubén Darío and the Pythagorean Tradition.* Gainesville: University Presses of Florida, 1975, pp. 81–83.

The Poetry of Darío

Anderson-Imbert, Enrique. "Rubén Darío and the Fantastic Element in Literature," in *Rubén Darío: Centennial Studies.* Edited by Miguel Gonzalez-Gerth and George D. Schade. Austin: Department of Spanish and Portuguese, University of Texas at Austin, 1970, pp. 97–117.

Ballew, Hal L. "Rubén Darío's Literary Personality," in *South Central Bulletin.* XXVII (1967), pp. 58–63.

Cardwell, Richard A. "Darío and el arto puro: The Enigma of Life and the Beguilement of Art," in *Bulletin of Hispanic Studies.* XLVII (1970), pp. 37–51.

Carrera Andrade, Jorge. *Reflections on Spanish-American Poetry.* Albany: State University of New York Press, 1973, pp. 8–10.

Ellis, Keith. "Concerning the Question of Influence," in *Hispania.* LV (1972), pp. 340–342.

Enguidanos, Miguel. "Inner Tensions in the Work of Rubén Darío," in *Rubén Darío: Centennial Studies.* Edited by Miguel Gonzalez-Gerth and George D. Schade. Austin: Department of Spanish and Portuguese, University of Texas at Austin, 1970, pp. 13–29.

Fiber, L.A. "Rubén Darío's Debt to Paul Verlaine in 'El reino interior,' " in *Romance Notes.* XIV (1972), pp. 92–95.

Florit, Eugenio. "The Modernist Prefigurement in the Early Work of Rubén Darío," in *Rubén Darío: Centennial Studies.* Edited by Miguel Gonzalez-Gerth and George D. Schade. Austin: Department of Spanish and Portuguese, University of Texas at Austin, 1970, pp. 31–47.

Franco, Jean. *A Literary History of Spain: Spanish American Literature Since Independence.* London: Ernest Benn, 1973, pp. 111–120.

Goldberg, Isaac.   *Studies in Spanish-American Literature.* New York: Brentano's, 1920, pp. 101–183.

Imbert, Enrique Anderson.   *Spanish-American Literature: A History.* Detroit: Wayne State University Press, 1963, pp. 266–271.

Paz, Octavio.   "Prologue," in *Selected Poems of Rubén Dario.* Austin: University of Texas Press, 1965, pp. 7–18.

Predmore, Michael P.   "A Stylistic Analysis of 'Lo Fatal,' " in *Hispanic Review.* XXXIX (1971), pp. 433–438.

Skyrme, Raymond.   *Rubén Dario and the Pythagorean Tradition.* Gainesville: University Presses of Florida, 1975.

Torres-Rioseco, Arturo.   "Rubén Dario: Classic Poet," in *Rubén Dario: Centennial Studies.* Edited by Miguel Gonzalez-Gerth and George D. Schade. Austin: Department of Spanish and Portuguese, University of Texas at Austin, 1970, pp. 85–94.

Trueblood, Alan S.   "Rubén Dario: The Sea and the Jungle," in *Comparative Literature Studies.* IV (1967), pp. 425–456.

CHARLES DARWIN
(1809–1882)

The Voyage of the "Beagle"

Barlow, Nora.   *Charles Darwin and* The Voyage of the "Beagle." New York: Philosophical Library, 1946.

Burstyn, Harold L.   "If Darwin Wasn't the *'Beagle's'* Naturalist, Why Was He on Board?," in *British Journal for the History of Science.* VIII (March, 1975), pp. 62–69.

Gruber, H.E. and V. Gruber.   "The Eye of Reason: Darwin's Development During the *'Beagle'* Voyage," in *Isis.* LIII (June, 1962), pp. 186–200.

Gruber, Jacob W.   "Who Was the *'Beagle's'* Naturalist?," in *British Journal for the History of Science.* IV (June,1969), pp. 266–282.

Hopkins, Robert S.   *Darwin's South America.* New York: Day, 1969.

Moorehead, Alan.   *Darwin and the "Beagle."* New York: Harper & Row, 1969.

ALPHONSE DAUDET
(1840–1897)

Kings in Exile

Dobie, G.V. *Alphonse Daudet.* London: Thomas Nelson, 1949, pp. 199–203.

Roche, Alphonse V. *Alphonse Daudet.* Boston: Twayne, 1976, pp. 53–54, 63–66.

Sachs, Murray. *The Career of Alphonse Daudet: A Critical Study.* Cambridge, Mass.: Harvard University Press, 1965, pp. 111–118.

Sappho

Dobie, G.V. *Alphonse Daudet.* London: Thomas Nelson, 1949, pp. 232–234.

Pritchett, V.S. *Books in General.* London: Chatto and Windus, 1953, pp. 104–109.

Roche, Alphonse V. *Alphonse Daudet.* Boston: Twayne, 1976, pp. 75–82.

Sachs, Murray. *The Career of Alphonse Daudet: A Critical Study.* Cambridge, Mass.: Harvard University Press, 1965, pp. 130–135.

Tartarin of Tarascon

Cohen, J.M. "Introduction," in *Tartarin of Tarascon.* By Alphonse Daudet. London: Folio Society, 1968, pp. 7–10.

Dobie, G.V. *Alphonse Daudet.* London: Thomas Nelson, 1949, pp. 117–121.

Favreau, Alphonse R. "The Background of *Tartarin of Tarascon*," in *American Society of Legion of Honor Magazine.* XVII (Spring, 1946), pp. 282–292.

Roche, Alphonse V. *Alphonse Daudet.* Boston: Twayne, 1976, pp. 46–50,147–150.

Sachs, Murray. "Alphonse Daudet's Tartarin Trilogy," in *Modern Language Review.* LXI (April, 1966), pp. 210–213.

————. *The Career of Alphonse Daudet: A Critical Study.* Cambridge, Mass.: Harvard University Press, 1965, pp. 65–73.

DANIEL DEFOE
(1660–1731)

Captain Singleton

Brooks, Douglas. *Number and Pattern in the Eighteenth-Century Novel.* London: Routledge, 1973, pp. 30–37.

Hahn, H.G. "An Approach to Character Development in Defoe's Narrative Prose," in *Philological Quarterly.* LI (1972), pp. 848–851.

Richetti, John J. *Defoe's Narratives; Situations and Structures.* Oxford: Clarendon Press, 1975, pp. 63–93.

Schonhorn, Manuel. "Defoe's *Captain Singleton*: A Reassessment with Observations," in *Papers on Language and Literature.* VII (1971), pp. 38–51.

Scrimgeour, Gary J. "The Problem of Realism in Defoe's *Captain Singleton*," in *Huntington Library Quarterly.* XXVII (1963), pp. 21–37.

Secord, Arthur Wellesley. *Studies in the Narrative Method of Defoe.* (University of Illinois Studies in Language and Literature, v.9). Urbana: University of Illinois, 1924, pp. 112–164.

Shinagel, Michael. *Daniel Defoe and Middle-Class Gentility.* Cambridge, Mass.: Harvard University Press, 1968, pp. 134–137.

Sutherland, James. *Daniel Defoe.* Cambridge, Mass.: Harvard University Press, 1971, pp. 144–150.

Walton, James. "The Romance of Gentility: Defoe's Heroes and Heroines," in *Literary Monographs.* IV (1971), pp. 95–98.

The History of Colonel Jacque

Brooks, Douglas. *Number and Pattern in the Eighteenth-Century Novel.* London: Routledge, 1973, pp. 30–37.

Hahn, H.G. "An Approach to Character Development in Defoe's Narrative Prose," in *Philological Quarterly.* LI (1972), pp. 854–858.

McBurney, William H. "*Colonel Jack*: Defoe's Definition of the Complete Gentleman," in *Studies in English Literature, 1500–1900.* II (Summer, 1962), pp. 321–336.

Moore, John Robert. "Defoe's Use of Personal Experience in *Colonel Jack*," in *Modern Language Notes.* LIV (1939), pp. 362–363.

Novak, Maximillian E. "Colonel Jack's Thieving Roguing Trade to Mexico and Defoe's Attack on Economic Individualism," in *Huntington Library Quarterly.* XXIV (1961), pp. 349–353.

Richetti, John J. *Defoe's Narrative; Situations and Structures.* Oxford: Clarendon Press, 1975, pp. 145–191.

Shinagel, Michael. *Daniel Defoe and Middle-Class Gentility.* Cambridge, Mass.: Harvard University Press, 1968, pp. 161–177.

Sutherland, James. *Daniel Defoe.* Cambridge, Mass.: Harvard University Press, 1971, pp. 195–205.

Walton, James K. "The Romance of Gentility: Defoe's Heroes and Heroines," in *Literary Monographs.* IV (1971), pp. 98–110.

A Journal of the Plague Year

Bastian, F. "Defoe's *Journal of the Plague Year* Reconsidered," in *Review of English Studies.* XVI (1965), pp. 151–173.

Blair, Joel. "Defoe's Art in *A Journal of the Plague Year*," in *South Atlantic Quarterly.* LXXII (1973), pp. 243–254.

Flanders, W. Austin. "Defoe's *Journal of the Plague Year* and the Modern Urban Experience," in *Centennial Review.* XVI (1972), pp. 328–348.

Hahn, H.G. "An Approach to Character Development in Defoe's Narrative Prose," in *Philological Quarterly.* LI (1972), pp. 851–854.

James, E. Anthony. *Daniel Defoe's Many Voices: A Rhetorical Study of Prose Style and Literary Methods.* Amsterdam: Rodopi Nv, 1972, pp. 135–153, 156–158.

Johnson, Clifford. "Defoe's Reaction to Enlightened Secularism: *A Journal of the Plague Year*," in *Enlightenment Essays.* III (1973), pp. 169–177.

Kay, Donald. "Defoe's Sense of History in *A Journal of the Plague Year*," in *Xavier University Studies.* IX (1970), pp. 1–8.

Nicholson, Watson. *Historical Sources of Defoe's Journal of the Plague Year.* Port Washington, N.Y.: Kennikat, 1966.

Richetti, John J. *Defoe's Narratives: Situation and Structure.* Oxford: Clarendon Press, 1975, pp. 233–240.

Rynell, Alarik. "Defoe's *A Journal of the Plague Year*," in *English Studies.* L (1969), pp. 452–464.

Schonhorn, Manuel. "Defoe's *Journal of the Plague Year*: Topography and Intention," in *Review of English Studies.* n.s., XIX (1968), pp. 387–402.

Sutherland, James. *Daniel Defoe.* Cambridge, Mass.: Harvard University Press, 1971, pp. 163–172.

Vickers, Brian. "Daniel Defoe's *Journal of the Plague Year*: Notes for a Critical Analysis," in *Filologia Moderna.* XIII (1973), pp. 161–170.

Walton, James. "The Romance of Gentility: Defoe's Heroes and Heroines," in *Literary Monographs.* IV (1971), pp. 110–122.

Zimmerman, Everett. "H.F.'s Meditations: *A Journal of the Plague Year*," in *PMLA.* LXXXVII (1972), pp. 417–423.

Moll Flanders

Alter, Robert. "A Bourgeois Picaroon," in *Rogue's Progress: Studies in the Picaresque Novel*. Cambridge, Mass.: Harvard University Press, 1962, pp. 35–57.

Brooks, Douglas. "Defoe: *Moll Flanders* and *Roxana*," in *Number and Pattern in the Eighteenth-Century Novel*. London: Routledge, 1973, pp. 41–64.

————. "*Moll Flanders*: An Interpretation," in *Essays in Criticism*. XIX (January, 1969), pp. 46–59.

Columbus, Robert R. "Conscious Artistry in *Moll Flanders*," in *Studies in English Literature, 1500–1900*. III (Summer, 1963), pp. 415–432.

Donoghue, Denis. "The Values of *Moll Flanders*," in *Sewanee Review*. LXXI (Spring, 1963), pp. 287–303.

Donovan, Robert Alan. "The Two Heroines of *Moll Flanders*," in *The Shaping Vision: Imagination in the English Novel from Defoe to Dickens*. Ithaca, N.Y.: Cornell University Press, 1966, pp. 21–46.

Goldberg, M.A. "*Moll Flanders*: Christian Allegory in a Hobbesian Mode," in *University Review*. XXXIII (June, 1967), pp. 267–278.

Hahn, H.G. "An Approach to Character Development in Defoe's Narrative Prose," in *Philological Quarterly*. LI (1972), pp. 854–858.

Hartog, Curt. "Aggression, Fear and Irony in *Moll Flanders*," in *Literature and Psychology*. XXII (1972), pp. 121–138.

Karl, Frederick. "Moll's Many-Colored Coat: Veil and Disguise in the Fiction of Defoe," in *Studies in the Novel*. V (1973), pp. 89–95.

Koonce, Howard L. "Moll's Muddle: Defoe's Use of Irony in *Moll Flanders*," in *Journal of English Literary History*. XXX (1963), pp. 377–394.

Krier, William J. "A Courtesy Which Grants Integrity: A Literal Reading of *Moll Flanders*," in *Journal of English Literary History*. XXXVIII (1971), pp. 397–410.

McMaster, Juliet. "The Equation of Love and Money in *Moll Flanders*," in *Studies in the Novel*. II (1970), pp. 131–144.

Martin, Terence. "The Unity of *Moll Flanders*," in *Modern Language Quarterly*. XXII (July, 1961), pp. 115–124.

Novak, Maximillian E. "Conscious Irony in *Moll Flanders*: Facts and Problems," in *College English*. XXVI (1964), pp. 198–204.

————. "Defoe's 'Indifferent Monitor': The Complexity of *Moll Flanders*," in *Eighteenth Century Studies*. III (1970), pp. 351–365.

Piper, William B. "*Moll Flanders* as a Structure of Topics," in *Studies in English Literature, 1500–1900*. IX (Summer, 1969), pp. 489–502.

Rogal, Samuel J. "The Profit and Loss of *Moll Flanders*," in *Studies in the Novel*. V (1973), pp. 98–103.

Schorer, Mark. "A Study in Defoe: Moral Vision and Structural Form," in *Thought.* XXV (1950), pp. 275–287.

Shinagel, Michael. "The Maternal Theme in *Moll Flanders*: Craft and Character," in *Cornell Literary Journal.* VII (1969), pp. 3–23.

Smith, LeRoy W. "Daniel Defoe: Incipient Pornographer," in *Literature and Psychology.* XXII (1972), pp. 165–178.

Sutherland, James. *Daniel Defoe.* Cambridge, Mass.: Harvard University Press, 1971, pp. 175–194.

Watson, Tommy G. "Defoe's Attitude Toward Marriage and the Position of Women as Revealed in *Moll Flanders*," in *Southern Quarterly.* III (October, 1964), pp. 1–8.

Robinson Crusoe

Ayers, Robert W. "*Robinson Crusoe*: Allusive Allegorick History," in *PMLA.* LXXXII (1967), pp. 399–407.

Benjamin, Edwin R. "Symbolic Elements in *Robinson Crusoe*," in *Philological Quarterly.* XXX (1951), pp. 206–211.

Egan, James. "Crusoe's Monarchy and the Puritan Concept of the Self," in *Studies in English Literature, 1500–1900.* XIII (1973), pp. 451–461.

Gerber, Richard. "The English Island Myth: Remarks on the Englishness of Utopian Fiction," in *Critical Quarterly.* I (1959), pp. 36–43.

Grief, M.J. "The Conversion of Robinson Crusoe," in *Studies in English Literature, 1500–1900.* VI (Summer, 1966), pp. 551–574.

Halewood, William H. "Religion and Invention in *Robinson Crusoe*," in *Essays in Criticism.* XIV (October, 1964), pp. 339–351.

Hartog, Curt. "Authority and Autonomy in *Robinson Crusoe*," in *Enlightenment Essays.* V (1974), pp. 33–43.

Hearne, John. "Naked Footprint: An Enquiry into Crusoe's Island," in *Review of English Literature.* VIII (October, 1967), pp. 97–107.

James, E. Anthony. "Defoe's Narrative Artistry: Naming and Describing in *Robinson Crusoe*," in *Costerus.* V (1972), pp. 52–66.

MacDonald, Robert H. "The Creation of an Ordered World in *Robinson Crusoe*," in *Dalhousie Review.* LVI (1976), pp. 23–34.

Novak, Maximillian E. "Crusoe the King and the Political Evolution of His Island," in *Studies in English Literature, 1500–1900.* II (Summer, 1962), pp. 337–350.

————. "Imaginary Islands and Real Beasts: The Imaginative Genesis of *Robinson Crusoe*," in *Tennessee Studies in Literature.* XIX (1974), pp. 57–78.

————. "The Problem of Necessity in Defoe's Fiction," in *Philological Quarterly.* XL (1961), pp. 513–524.

————. "Robinson Crusoe's Fear and the Search for Natural Man," in *Modern Philology*. LVIII (1961), pp. 238–245.

Parker, George. "The Allegory of Robinson Crusoe," in *History*. X (1925), pp. 11–25.

Peck, Daniel H. "*Robinson Crusoe*: The Moral Geography of Limitation," in *Journal of Narrative Technique*. III (1973), pp. 20–31.

Robins, Harry. "How Smart Was Robinson Crusoe?," in *PMLA*. LXVII (1952), pp. 782–789.

Rogers, Pat. "Crusoe's Home," in *Essays in Criticism*. XXIV (1974), pp. 375–390.

Swados, Harvey. "Robinson Crusoe—The Man Alone," in *Antioch Review*. XVIII (1958), pp. 25–40.

Thornburg, Thomas R. "*Robinson Crusoe*," in *Ball State University Forum*. XV (1974), pp. 11–18.

Watson, Francis. "*Robinson Crusoe*: An Englishman of the Age," in *History Today*. IX (November, 1959), pp. 760–766.

————. "*Robinson Crusoe*: Fact and Fiction," in *Listener*. LXII (1959), pp. 617–619.

Watt, Ian. "*Robinson Crusoe* as a Myth," in *Essays in Criticism*. I (1951), pp. 95–119.

Zimmerman, Everett. "Defoe and Crusoe," in *Journal of English Literary History*. XXXVIII (1971), pp. 377–396.

Roxana

Bordner, Marsha. "Defoe's Androgynous Vision in *Moll Flanders* and *Roxana*," in *Gypsy Scholar*. II (1972), pp. 76–93.

Brooks, Douglas. *Number and Pattern in the Eighteenth-Century Novel*. London: Routledge, 1973, pp. 53–60.

Cather, Willa. "Defoe's *The Fortunate Mistress*," in *On Writing; Critical Studies on Writing as an Art*. New York: Knopf, 1949, pp. 75–88.

Hahn, H.G. "An Approach to Character Development in Defoe's Narrative Prose," in *Philological Quarterly*. LI (1972), pp. 854–858.

Higdon, David Leon. "The Critical Fortunes and Misfortune of Defoe's *Roxana*," in *Bucknell Review*. XX (1972), pp. 67–82.

Hume, Robert D. "The Conclusion of Defoe's *Roxana*: Fiasco or Tour de Force?," in *Eighteenth-Century Criticism*. III (1970), pp. 475–490.

Jackson, Wallace. "*Roxana* and the Development of Defoe's Fiction," in *Studies in the Novel*. VII (1975), pp. 181–194.

James, E. Anthony. *Daniel Defoe's Many Voices; A Rhetorical Study of Prose Style and Literary Method*. Amsterdam: Rodopi Nv., 1972, pp. 231–253.

Jenkins, Ralph E. "The Structure of *Roxana*," in *Studies in the Novel*. II (1970), pp. 145–158.

Kropf, C.R. "Theme and Structure in Defoe's *Roxana*," in *Studies in English Literature, 1500–1900*. XII (1972), pp. 467–480.

McKillop, Alan Dugald. *The Early Masters of English Fiction*. Lawrence: University of Kansas Press, 1956, pp. 35–38.

Novak, Maximillian E. "Crime and Punishment in Defoe's *Roxana*," in *Journal of English and Germanic Philology*. LXV (July, 1966), pp. 445–465.

Olshin, Toby A. " 'Thoughtful of the Main Chance': Defoe and the Cycle of Anxiety," in *Hartford Studies in Literature*. VI (1974), pp. 121–122.

Peterson, Spiro. "The Matrimonial Theme of Defoe's *Roxana*," in *PMLA*. LXX (1955), pp. 166–191.

Raleigh, John Henry. "Style and Structure and Their Import in Defoe's *Roxana*," in *University of Kansas City Review*. XX (Winter, 1953), pp. 128–135.

Richetti, John J. *Defoe's Narratives; Situations and Structures*. Oxford: Clarendon Press, 1975, pp. 192–232.

Smith, LeRoy W. "Daniel Defoe: Incipient Pornographer," in *Literature and Psychology*. XXII (1972), pp. 165–177.

Snow, Malinda. "Diabolic Intervention in Defoe's *Roxana*," in *Essays in Literature* (Western Illinois University). III (1976), pp. 52–60.

Starr, George A. "Sympathy vs. Judgment in Roxana's First Liaison," in *The Augustan Milieu: Essays Presented to Louis A. Landa*. Edited by Henry Knight Miller. Oxford: Clarendon Press, 1970, pp. 59–76.

Walton, James. "The Romance of Gentility: Defoe's Heroes and Heroines," in *Literary Monographs*. IV (1971), pp. 122–135.

Zimmerman, Everett. "Language and Character in Defoe's *Roxana*," in *Essays in Criticism*. XXI (1971), pp. 227–235.

A Tour Thro' the Whole Island of Great Britain

Barringer, George Martyn. "Defoe's *A Tour Thro' the Whole Island of Great Britain*," in *Thoth*. IX (1968), pp. 3–13.

Bastian, F. "Defoe's *Tour* and the Historian," in *History Today*. XVII (1967), pp. 845–851.

Cole, George Douglas Howard. *Persons & Periods; Studies*. Toronto: Macmillian, 1938, pp. 20–41.

Davies, Godfrey. "Daniel Defoe: *A Tour Thro' the Whole Island of Great Britain*," in *Modern Philology*. XLVIII (1950), pp. 21–36.

Rogers, Pat. "Defoe and Virgil: The Georgic Element in *A Tour Thro' Great Britain*," in *English Miscellany*. XXII (1971), pp. 93–106.

————. "Defoe as Plagiarist: Camden's *Britannia* and *A Tour Thro' the Whole Island of Great Britain*," in *Philological Quarterly*. LII (1973), pp. 771–774.

————. "Defoe at Work: The Making of *A Tour Thro' Great Britain, Volume I*," in *Bulletin of the New York Public Library*. LXXVIII (1975), pp. 431–450.

————. "Literary Art in Defoe's *Tour*: The Rhetoric of Growth and Decay," in *Eighteenth-Century Studies*. VI (1973), pp. 153–185.

Sill, Geoffrey M. "Defoe's *Tour*: Literary Art or Moral Imperative?," in *Eighteenth-Century Studies*. XI (Fall, 1977), pp. 79–83.

Sutherland, James. *Daniel Defoe*. Cambridge, Mass.: Harvard University Press, 1971, pp. 221–227.

THOMAS DEKKER
(1572–1632?)

The Gull's Hornbook

Armstrong, William A. "The Audience of the Elizabethan Private Theaters," in *The Seventeenth-Century Stage: A Collection of Critical Essays*. Edited by Gerald Eades Bentley. Chicago: University of Chicago Press, 1968, pp. 224–227.

Gurr, Andrew. *The Shakespearean Stage, 1574–1642*. Cambridge: Cambridge University Press, 1970, pp. 153–154.

Hunt, Mary Leonard. *Thomas Dekker: A Study*. New York: Russell and Russell, 1964, pp. 121–123, 142–144.

Price, George R. *Thomas Dekker*. New York: Twayne, 1969, pp. 121–123.

Thornton, George E. "The Social and Moral Philosophy of Thomas Dekker," in *Emporia State Research Studies*. IV (December, 1955), pp. 19–20.

The Honest Whore

Berlin, Normand. "Thomas Dekker: A Partial Reappraisal," in *Studies in English Literature, 1500–1900*. V (1966), pp. 263–277.

Bradbrooke, M.C. *The Growth and Structure of Elizabethan Comedy*. Berkeley and Los Angeles: University of California Press, 1956, pp. 228–232.

Brown, Arthur. "Citizen Comedy and Domestic Drama," in *Stratford-Upon-Avon Studies*. I (1960), pp. 69–73.

Champion, Larry S. "From Melodrama to Comedy: A Study of the Dramatic Perspective in Dekker's *The Honest Whore*, Parts I and II," in *Studies in Philology*. LXIX (1972), pp. 192–209.

Hunt, Mary Leland. *Thomas Dekker: A Study*. New York: Russell and Russell, 1964, pp. 91–101.

Keyishian, Harry. "Dekker's *Whore* and Marston's *Courtesan*," in *English Language Notes*. IV (1967), pp. 261–266.

Kistner, A.L. and M.K. Kistner. "*The Honest Whore*: A Comedy of Blood," in *Humanities Association Bulletin*. XXIII (1972), pp. 23–27.

Lacy, Margaret S. *The Jacobean Problem Play*. Ann Arbor: University of Michigan Press, 1956, pp. 60–84.

Price, George R. *Thomas Dekker*. New York: Twayne, 1969, pp. 60–69.

Reed, Robert Rentoul, Jr. *Bedlam on the Jacobean Stage*. Cambridge, Mass.: Harvard University Press, 1952, pp. 29–30, 40–43.

Ribner, Irving. *The English History Play in the Age of Shakespeare*. Princeton, N.J.: Princeton University Press, 1957, pp. 284–288.

Silvette, Herbert. *The Doctor on the Stage: Medicine and Medical Men in Seventeenth-Century England.* Knoxville: University of Tennessee Press, 1967, pp. 50–51, 139–140.

Spivack, Charlotte. "Bedlam and Bridewell: Ironic Design in *The Honest Whore*," in *Komos: A Quarterly of Drama and Arts of the Theater.* III (1973), pp. 10–16.

Thornton, George E. "The Social and Moral Philosophy of Thomas Dekker," in *Emporia State Research Studies.* IV (December, 1955), pp. 21–33.

Turner, Robert K., Jr. "Dekker's 'Black-Door'd Italian': One Honest Whore," in *Notes and Queries.* CCV (January, 1960), pp. 25–26.

Ure, Peter. "Patient Madman and Honest Whore: The Middleton-Dekker Oxymoron," in *Essays and Studies.* XIX (1966), pp. 18–40.

———. *Elizabethan and Jacobean Drama: Critical Essays.* New York: Barnes & Noble, 1974, pp. 187–208.

Old Fortunatus

Adams, H. *English Domestic or Homiletic Tragedies, 1575–1642.* New York: Columbia University Press, 1943, pp. 80–82.

Ashton, J.W. "Dekker's Use of Folklore in *Old Fortunatus, If This Be Not a Good Play*, and *The Witch of Edmonton*," in *Philological Quarterly.* XLI (January, 1962), pp. 240–243.

Boas, Frederick S. *An Introduction to Stuart Drama.* London: Oxford University Press, 1946, pp. 150–152.

Bowers, Fredson. "Essex's Rebellion and Dekker's *Old Fortunatus*," in *Review of English Studies.* III (October, 1952), pp. 365–366.

Bradbrooke, M.C. *The Growth and Structure of Elizabethan Comedy.* Berkeley and Los Angeles: University of California Press, 1956, pp. 228–229.

Homan, S.R. "*Dr. Faustus*, Dekker's *Old Fortunatus*, and the Morality Plays," in *Modern Language Quarterly.* XXVI (1965), pp. 497–505.

Hunt, Mary Leland. *Thomas Dekker: A Study.* New York: Russell and Russell, 1964, pp. 29–35.

Lacy, Margaret S. *The Jacobean Problem Play.* Ann Arbor: University of Michigan Press, 1956, pp. 48–60.

Price, George R. *Thomas Dekker.* New York: Twayne, 1969, pp. 40–49.

Reed, Robert Rentoul, Jr. *The Occult on the Tudor and Stuart Stage.* Boston: Christopher, 1965, pp. 93–97.

Satiromastix

Bevington, David. *Tudor Drama and Politics: A Critical Approach to Topical Meaning.* Cambridge, Mass.: Harvard University Press, 1968, pp. 282–285.

Boas, Frederick S.   *An Introduction to Stuart Drama.* London: Oxford University Press, 1946, pp. 71–72, 152–153.

Bradbrooke, M.C.   *The Growth and Structure of Elizabethan Comedy.* Berkeley and Los Angeles: University of California Press, 1956, pp. 99–102.

Harrison, G.B.   *Elizabethan Plays and Players.* Ann Arbor: University of Michigan Press, 1956, pp. 272–277.

Hunt, Mary Leland.   *Thomas Dekker: A Study.* New York: Russell and Russell, 1964, pp. 64–75.

Price, George R.   *Thomas Dekker.* New York: Twayne, 1969, pp. 53–60.

The Shoemaker's Holiday

Berlin, Normand.   "Thomas Dekker: A Partial Reappraisal," in *Studies in English Literature, 1500–1900.* VI (1966), pp. 263–277.

Bevington, David.   *Tudor Drama and Politics: A Critical Approach to Topical Meaning.* Cambridge, Mass.: Harvard University Press, 1968, pp. 291–292.

Boas, Frederick S.   *An Introduction to Stuart Drama.* London: Oxford University Press, 1946, pp. 148–150.

Bradbrooke, Muriel C.   *The Growth and Structure of Elizabethan Comedy.* London: Chatto and Windus, 1955, pp. 119–132.

Brown, Arthur.   "Citizen Comedy and Domestic Drama," in *Stratford-Upon-Avon Studies.* I (1960), pp. 63–69.

Burelbach, Frederick M., Jr.   "War and Peace in *The Shoemaker's Holiday,*" in *Tennessee Studies in Literature.* XIII (1968), pp. 99–107.

Gayley, Charles Mills.   *Representative English Comedies.* Volume 3. New York: Macmillan, 1912–1914, pp. 3–17.

Halstead, W.L.   "New Source Influence on *The Shoemaker's Holiday,*" in *Modern Language Notes.* CVI (February, 1941), pp. 127–129.

Hidden, Norman.   "*The Shoemaker's Holiday,*" in *The Use of English.* XIII (Summer, 1962), pp. 249–252.

Hunt, Mary Leland.   *Thomas Dekker: A Study.* New York: Russell and Russell, 1964, pp. 56–59, 200–201.

Kaplan, Joel H.   "Virtue's Holiday: Thomas Dekker and Simon Eyre," in *Renaissance Drama.* II (1969), pp. 103–122.

Knights, Lionel Charles.   *Drama and Society in the Age of Jonson.* London: Chatto and Windus, 1962, pp. 236–240.

McClure, Donald S.   "Versification and Master Hammond in *The Shoemaker's Holiday,*" in *Studies in the Humanities.* I (1969), pp. 50–54.

Manheim, Michael.   "The Construction of *The Shoemaker's Holiday,*" in *Studies in English Literature, 1500–1900.* X (1970), pp. 15–23.

Mortenson, Peter. "The Economics of Joy in *The Shoemaker's Holiday*," in *Studies in English Literature, 1500–1900.* XVI (1976), pp. 241–252.

Nathan, Norman. "*Julius Caesar* and *The Shoemaker's Holiday*," in *Modern Language Review.* XLVII (April, 1953), pp. 178–179.

Novarr, David. "Dekker's Gentle Craft and the Lord Mayor of London," in *Modern Philology.* LVII (1960), pp. 233–239.

Palmer, D.J. "Introduction," in *The Shoemaker's Holiday.* By Thomas Dekker. London: Ernest Benn, 1975, pp. ix–xx.

Popcock, Guy Noel. *Little Room.* New York: Dutton, 1926, pp. 218–229.

Price, George R. *Thomas Dekker.* New York: Twayne, 1969, pp. 49–53.

Spender, Constance. "The Plays of Thomas Dekker," in *Contemporary Review.* CXXX (1926), pp. 332–339.

Steane, J.B. "Introduction," in *The Shoemaker's Holiday.* By Thomas Dekker. Cambridge: Cambridge University Press, 1965, pp. 1–23.

Thomas, Patricia. "The Old Way and the New Way: Dekker and Massinger," in *Modern Language Review.* LI (April, 1956), pp. 168–178.

Toliver, Harold E. "*The Shoemaker's Holiday*: Theme and Image," in *Boston University Studies in English.* V (Winter, 1961), pp. 208–218.

Wells, Henry W. *Elizabethan and Jacobean Playwrights.* New York: Columbia University Press, 1964, pp. 219–221.

WALTER DE LA MARE
(1873–1956)

"The Listeners"

Dyson, A.E. "Walter de la Mare's 'The Listeners,' " in *Critical Quarterly*. II (Summer, 1960), pp. 150–154.

Ferguson, DeLancey. " 'The Listeners,' " in *Explicator*. IV (November, 1945), item 15.

Frankenberg, Lloyd. *Invitation to Poetry*. New York: Doubleday, 1956, p. 139.

Gwynn, Frederick and Ralph W. Condee. " 'The Listeners,' " in *Explicator*. XII (February, 1954), item 26.

Pierson, Robert M. "The Meter of 'The Listeners,' " in *English Studies*. XLV (October, 1964), pp. 373–381.

Purcell, J.M. " 'The Listeners,' " in *Explicator*. III (March, 1945), item 42.

————. " 'The Listeners,' " in *Explicator*. IV (February, 1946), item 31.

The Poetry of de la Mare

Brenner, Rica. *Ten Modern Poets*. New York: Harcourt, Brace and World, 1930, pp. 151–172.

Brown, E.K. "The Epilogue to Mr. de la Mare's Poetry," in *Poetry*. LXVIII (May, 1946), pp. 90–92.

Daniels, Earl. *The Art of Reading Poetry*. New York: Farrar & Rinehart, 1941, pp. 57–59.

Leavis, F.R. *New Bearings in English Poetry*. London: Chatto and Windus, 1932, pp. 53–54.

Press, John. *A Map of Modern English Verse*. London: Oxford University Press, 1969, pp. 120–121.

————. "The Poetry of Walter de la Mare," in *Ariel: A Review of International English Literature*. I (1970), pp. 29–38.

Robson, W.W. *Modern English Literature*. London: Oxford University Press, 1970, pp. 64–66.

Schneider, Elisabeth. " 'Maerchen,' " in *Explicator*. IV (February, 1946), item 29.

Scott-James, R.A. *Fifty Years of English Literature, 1900–1950, with a Postscript, 1951–1955*. London: Longmans, 1956, pp. 117–118.

Simon, Myron. *The Georgian Poetic*. Berkeley and Los Angeles: University of California Press, 1975, pp. 92–95.

Sisson, C.H.   *English Poetry, 1900–1950: An Assessment.* London: Rupert Hart-Davis, 1971, pp. 47–50.

Sturgeon, Mary C.   *Studies of Contemporary Poets.* London: George C. Harrap, 1920, pp. 72–86.

Swinnerton, Frank.   *The Georgian Literary Scene, 1910–1935.* London: Hutchinson, 1969, pp. 206–208.

Untermeyer, Louis.   *Lives of the Poets.* New York: Simon and Schuster, 1959, pp. 653–655.

Ward, A.C.   *Twentieth-Century Literature, 1901–1940.* London: Methuen, 1940, pp. 179–181.

The Short Stories of de la Mare

Beachcroft, T.O.   *The Modest Art: A Survey of the Short Story in English.* London: Oxford University Press, 1968, pp. 210–211.

Irwin, W.R.   *The Game of the Impossible: A Rhetoric of Fantasy.* Urbana: University of Illinois Press, 1976, pp. 105–107.

McCrossen, Doris R.   *Walter de la Mare.* New York: Twayne, 1966, pp. 27–45.

Pedden, William.   *Twenty-Nine Stories.* Boston: Houghton Mifflin, 1960, p. 150.

Penzoldt, Peter.   *The Supernatural in Fiction.* New York: Humanities Press, 1965, pp. 206–223.

GRAZIA DELEDDA
(1875–1936)

The Mother

McCormick, E. Allen. "Grazia Deledda's *La madre* and the Problems of Tragedy," in *Symposium.* XXII (1968), pp. 62–71.

Pacifici, Sergio. *The Modern Italian Novel: From Capuana to Tozzi.* Carbondale: Southern Illinois University Press, 1973, pp. 86–97.

Vittorini, Domenico. *The Modern Italian Novel.* New York: Russell and Russell, 1967, pp. 68–70.

THOMAS DELONEY
(c.1543–1600)

The Novels of Deloney

Cazanian, L.F. "Deloney," in *The Development of English Humor*. Durham, N.C.: Duke University Press, 1952, pp. 175–179.

Davis, Walter R. *Idea and Act in Elizabethan Fiction*. Princeton, N.J.: Princeton University Press, 1969, pp. 238–252.

Dorinsville, Max. "Design in Deloney's *Jack of Newby*," in *PMLA*.LXXXVIII (1973), pp. 233–239.

Kuehn, G.W. "Thomas Deloney: Two Notes," in *Modern Language Notes*. LII (February, 1937), pp. 103–105.

Lawlis, Merritt E. *Apology for the Middle Class: The Dramatic Novels of Thomas Deloney*. Bloomington: Indiana University Press, 1961.

Parker, David. "*Jack of Newby*: A New Source," in *English Language Notes*. X (1973), pp. 173–180.

Patzold, Kurt-Michael. "Thomas Deloney and the English Jest-Book Tradition," in *English Studies*. LIII (1972), pp. 313–328.

Pourys, Llewellyn. "Thomas Deloney," in *Virginia Quarterly Review*. IX (1933), pp. 578–594.

Roberts, Warren E. "Folklore in the Novels of Thomas Deloney," in *Studies in Folklore*. X (1958), pp. 119–129.

Rollins, H.E. "Deloney's Sources for Euphuistic Learning," in *PMLA*. LI (June, 1936), pp. 399–406.

————. "Thomas Deloney's Euphuistic Learning and the Forest," in *PMLA*. L (September, 1935), pp. 679–686.

THOMAS DE QUINCEY
(1785–1859)

Confessions of an English Opium Eater

Abrams, M.H. *The Milk of Paradise: The Effect of Opium Visions on the Works of De Quincey, Crabbe, Francis Thompson, and Coleridge.* Cambridge, Mass.: Harvard University Press, 1934, pp. 6–13.

Bett, Walter R. *The Infirmities of Genius.* London: Christopher Johnson, 1952, pp. 91–102.

Bilsland, John W. "De Quincey's Opium Experiences," in *Dalhousie Review.* LV (1975), pp. 419–430.

Blake, Kathleen. "The Whispering Gallery and Structural Coherence in De Quincey's Revised *Confessions of an English Opium Eater*," in *Studies in English Literature.* XIII (1973), pp. 13, 632–642.

Bolitho, William. "Introduction," in *Confessions of an English Opium Eater.* Oxford: Shakespeare Head Press, 1930, pp. i–vii.

Cooke, Michael G. "De Quincey, Coleridge, and the Formal Uses of Intoxication," in *Yale French Studies.* L (1974), pp. 26–40.

Davies, Hugh Sykes. *Thomas De Quincey.* London: Longmans, Green, 1964, pp. 5–35.

Elton, Oliver. "Thomas De Quincey," in his *A Survey of English Literature, 1780–1830*, Volume II. London: Edward Arnold, 1912, pp. 312–333.

Elwin, Malcolm. "Introduction," in *Confessions of an English Opium Eater.* London: MacDonald, 1956, pp. vii–xx.

Grant, Douglas. "Thomas De Quincey," in *Some British Romantics: A Collection of Essays.* Edited by James V. Logan, John E. Jordan and Northrop Frye. Columbus: Ohio State University Press, 1966, pp. 143–166.

Hayter, Althea. "Introduction," in *Confessions of an English Opium Eater.* Harmondsworth, England: Penguin, 1971, pp. 7–24.

Jack, Ian. *English Literature, 1815–1832.* Oxford: Clarendon Press, 1963, pp. 292–311.

Lyon, Judson S. *Thomas De Quincey.* New York: Twayne, 1969, pp. 91–97, 177–179.

Mayoux, Jean-Jacques. "De Quincey: Humor and the Drugs," in *Veins of Humor.* Edited by Harry Levin. Cambridge, Mass.: Harvard University Press, 1972, pp. 109–129.

Miller, J. Hillis. *The Disappearance of God: Five Nineteenth-Century Writers.* Cambridge, Mass.: Harvard University Press, 1963, pp. 17–80.

Porte, Joel. "In the Hands of an Angry God: Religious Terror in Gothic Fiction," in *The Gothic Imagination: Essays in Dark Romanticism.* Edited by G.R. Thompson. Pullman: Washington State University Press, 1974, pp. 45–50.

Rubenstein, Jill. "The Curse of Subjectivity: De Quincey's *Confessions of an English Opium Eater* and Baudelaire's *Paradis Artificiels*," in *Romance Notes.* XV (Autumn, 1973), pp. 68–73.

Sackville West, Edward. *Thomas De Quincey: His Life and Work.* New Haven, Conn.: Yale University Press, 1936.

Woolf, Virginia. *The Common Reader.* New York: Harcourt, Brace, 1948, pp. 141–149.

PETER DE VRIES
(1910–   )

The Blood of the Lamb

Davies, Robertson. *The Voice from the Attic.* New York: Knopf, 1960.

Hamblen, Abigail A. "Peter De Vries: Calvinist Gone Underground," in *Trace.* XLVIII (Spring, 1963), pp. 20–24.

Jellema, Roderick. *Peter De Vries: A Critical Essay.* Grand Rapids, Mich.: Eerdmans, 1966, pp. 36–40.

————. "Peter De Vries: The Decline and Fall of the Moot Point," in *The Reformed Journal.* XIII (April, 1963), pp. 9–15.

Kort, Wesley A. *Shriven Selves; Religious Problems in Recent American Fiction.* Philadelphia: Fortress, 1972, pp. 36–63.

Comfort Me with Apples

Davies, Robertson. *The Voice from the Attic.* New York: Knopf, 1960.

Hamblen, Abigail A. "Peter De Vries: Calvinist Gone Underground," in *Trace.* XLVIII (Spring, 1963), pp. 20–24.

Jellema, Roderick. *Peter De Vries: A Critical Essay.* Grand Rapids, Mich.: Eerdmans, 1966, pp. 18–20.

————. "Peter De Vries: The Decline and Fall of the Moot Point," in *The Reformed Journal.* XIII (April, 1963), pp. 9–15.

Let Me Count the Ways

Davies, Robertson. *The Voice from the Attic.* New York: Knopf, 1960.

Hamblen, Abigail A. "Peter De Vries: Calvinist Gone Underground," in *Trace.* XLVIII (Spring, 1963), pp. 20–24.

Jellema, Roderick. *Peter De Vries: A Critical Essay.* Grand Rapids, Mich.: Eerdmans, 1966, pp. 40–43.

————. "Peter De Vries: The Decline and Fall of the Moot Point," in *The Reformed Journal.* XIII (April, 1963), pp. 9–15.

The Mackerel Plaza

Byrd, Max. "*The Mackerel Plaza* by Peter De Vries," in *New Republic.* CLXXIV (October 23, 1976), pp. 29–31.

Davies, Horton. *A Mirror of the Ministry in Modern Novels.* New York: Oxford University Press, 1959.

Davies, Robertson. *The Voice from the Attic.* New York: Knopf, 1960.

Hamblen, Abigail A.   "Peter De Vries: Calvinist Gone Underground," in *Trace*. XLVIII (Spring, 1963), pp. 20–24.

Jellema, Roderick.   *Peter De Vries: A Critical Essay*. Grand Rapids, Mich.: Eerdmans, 1966, pp. 32–35.

————.   "Peter De Vries: The Decline and Fall of the Moot Point," in *The Reformed Journal*. XIII (April, 1963), pp. 9–15.

Reuben, Reuben

Davies, Robertson.   *The Voice from the Attic*. New York: Knopf, 1960.

Hamblen, Abigail A.   "Peter De Vries: Calvinist Gone Underground," in *Trace*. XLVIII (Spring, 1963), pp. 20–24.

Jellema, Roderick.   *Peter De Vries: A Critical Essay*. Grand Rapids, Mich.: Eerdmans, 1966, pp. 15–18.

————.   "Peter De Vries: The Decline and Fall of the Moot Point," in *The Reformed Journal*. XIII (April, 1963), pp. 9–15.

The Tents of Wickedness

Davies, Robertson.   *The Voice from the Attic*. New York: Knopf, 1960.

Hamblen, Abigail A.   "Peter De Vries: Calvinist Gone Underground," in *Trace*. XLVIII (Spring, 1963), pp. 20–24.

Jellema, Roderick.   *Peter De Vries: A Critical Essay*. Grand Rapids, Mich.: Eerdmans, 1966, pp. 20–23.

————.   "Peter De Vries: The Decline and Fall of the Moot Point," in *The Reformed Journal*. XIII (April, 1963), pp. 9–15.

Walcutt, Charles C.   *Man's Changing Mask: Modes and Methods of Characterization in Fiction*. Minneapolis: University of Minnesota Press, 1966, pp. 247–251.

Through the Fields of Clover

Davies, Robertson.   *The Voice from the Attic*. New York: Knopf, 1960.

Hamblen, Abigail A.   "Peter De Vries: Calvinist Gone Underground," in *Trace*. XLVIII (Spring, 1963), pp. 20–24.

Jellema, Roderick.   *Peter De Vries: A Critical Essay*. Grand Rapids, Mich.: Eerdmans, 1966, pp. 24–27.

————.   "Peter De Vries: The Decline and Fall of the Moot Point," in *The Reformed Journal*. XIII (April, 1963), pp. 9–15.

Wain, John.   "Home Truths," in *New Yorker*. XXXVIII (February 25, 1961), pp. 130–133.

The Tunnel of Love

Davies, Robertson.   *The Voice from the Attic*. New York: Knopf, 1960.

Hamblen, Abigail A. "Peter De Vries: Calvinist Gone Underground," in *Trace*. XLVIII (Spring, 1963), pp. 20–24.

Jellema, Roderick. *Peter De Vries: A Critical Essay*. Grand Rapids, Mich.: Eerdmans, 1966, pp. 15–18.

————. "Peter De Vries: The Decline and Fall of the Moot Point," in *The Reformed Journal*. XIII (April, 1963), pp. 9–15.

The Vale of Laughter

Davies, Robertson. *The Voice from the Attic*. New York: Knopf, 1960.

Hamblen, Abigail A. "Peter De Vries: Calvinist Gone Underground," in *Trace*. XLVIII (Spring, 1963), pp. 20–24.

Jellema, Roderick. "Peter De Vries: The Decline and Fall of the Moot Point," in *The Reformed Journal*. XIII (April, 1963), pp. 9–15.

CHARLES DICKENS
(1812–1870)

Barnaby Rudge

Brantlinger, Patrick. "The Case Against Trade Unions in Early Victorian Fiction," in *Victorian Studies*. XIII (September, 1969), pp. 37–52.

Chesterton, Gilbert K. *Criticisms and Appreciations of the Works of Charles Dickens*. London: Dent, 1933, pp. 65–75.

Dabney, Ross H. *Love and Property in the Novels of Dickens*. Berkeley: University of California Press, 1967, pp. 22–30.

Davis, Earle. *The Flint and the Flame: The Artistry of Charles Dickens*. Columbia: University of Missouri Press, 1963, pp. 140–143.

Dyson, A.E. *"Barnaby Rudge*: The Genesis of Violence," in *Critical Quarterly*. IX (Summer, 1967), pp. 142–160.

————. *The Inimitable Dickens; A Reading of the Novels*. London: Macmillan, 1970, pp. 47–70.

Fleishman, Avrom. *The English Historical Novel; Walter Scott to Virginia Woolf*. Baltimore: Johns Hopkins University Press, 1971, pp. 102–114.

Folland, Harold F. "The Doer and the Deed; Theme and Pattern in *Barnaby Rudge*," in *PMLA*. LXXIV (September, 1959), pp. 406–417.

Gibson, Frank A. "The Love Interest in *Barnaby Rudge*," in *The Dickensian*. LIV (Winter, 1958), pp. 21–23.

————. "A Note on George Gordon," in *The Dickensian*. LVII (May, 1961), pp. 81–85.

Gissing, George R. *Critical Studies of the Works of Charles Dickens*. New York: Greenberg, 1924, pp. 103–118.

Gold, Joseph. *Charles Dickens: Radical Moralist*. Minneapolis: University of Minnesota Press, 1972, pp. 116–129.

Gottshall, James K. "Devils Abroad: The Unity and Significance of *Barnaby Rudge*," in *Nineteenth-Century Fiction*. XVI (September, 1961), pp. 133–146.

Greaves, John. *Who's Who in Dickens*. New York: Taplinger, 1972.

Hollingsworth, Keith. "The Newgate Theme of *Barnaby Rudge*," in *The Newgate Novel (1830–1847): Bulwer, Ainsworth, Dickens, and Thackeray*. Detroit: Wayne State University Press, 1963, pp. 177–182.

Hornback, Bert G. *"Noah's Arkitecture": A Study of Dickens' Mythology*. Athens: Ohio University Press, 1972, pp. 35–41.

Johnson, Edgar. *Charles Dickens, His Tragedy and Triumph*. New York: Simon and Schuster, 1952, pp. 329–337.

Kincaid, James R. *Dickens and the Rhetoric of Laughter.* Oxford: Clarendon, 1971, pp. 105–131.

Lary, N.M. *Dostoevsky and Dickens: A Study of Literary Influence.* London: Routledge and Kegan Paul, 1973, pp. 126–134.

Lindsay, Jack. "*Barnaby Rudge,*" in *Dickens and the Twentieth Century.* Edited by J. Gross and G. Pearson. London: Routledge and Kegan Paul, 1962, pp. 91–106.

Lucas, John. *The Melancholy Man: A Study of Dickens' Novels.* London: Methuen, 1970, pp. 92–112.

Manning, Sylvia B. *Dickens as Satirist.* New Haven, Conn.: Yale University Press, 1971, pp. 63–69.

Monod, Sylvère. "Rebel with a Cause; Hugh of the Maypole," in *Dickens Studies.* V (January, 1969), pp. 4–26.

O'Brien, Anthony. "Benevolence and Insurrection: The Conflicts of Form and Purpose in *Barnaby Rudge,*" in *Dickens Studies.* V (January, 1969), pp. 26–44.

Rice, Thomas J. "Dickens, Poe and the Time Scheme of *Barnaby Rudge,*" in *Dickens Studies Newsletter.* VII (1976), pp. 34–38.

Bleak House

Axton, William F. "Religious and Scientific Imagery in *Bleak House,*" in *Nineteenth-Century Fiction.* XXII (March, 1968), pp. 349–359.

————. "The Trouble with Esther," in *Modern Language Quarterly.* XXVI (1965), pp. 545–557.

Barnard, Robert. *Imagery and Theme in the Novels of Dickens.* New York: Humanities Press, 1974, pp. 62–76.

Blount, Trevor. "Dickens' Slum Satire in *Bleak House,*" in *Modern Language Review.* LX (July, 1965), pp. 340–351.

Burke, Alan R. "The Strategy and Theme of Urban Observation in *Bleak House,*" in *Studies in English Literature, 1500–1900.* IX (Autumn, 1969), pp. 659–676.

Cohan, Steven. " 'They Are All Secret': The Fantasy Content of *Bleak House,*" in *Literature and Psychology.* XXVI (1976), pp. 79–91.

Coolidge, Archibald. "Dickens' Complex Plots," in *The Dickensian.* LVII (Autumn, 1961), pp. 174–182.

Crompton, Louis. "Satire and Symbolism in *Bleak House,*" in *Nineteenth-Century Fiction.* XII (March, 1958), pp. 284–303.

Daleski, Herman M. *Dickens and the Art of Analogy.* New York: Schocken, 1970, pp. 156–190.

Donovan, R.A. "Structure and Idea in *Bleak House,*" in *Journal of English Literary History.* XXIX (June, 1962), pp. 175–201.

Dunn, Richard J. "Esther's Role in *Bleak House*," in *The Dickensian*. LXII (September, 1966), pp. 163–166.

Dyson, A.E. *The Inimitable Dickens; A Reading of the Novels*. London: Macmillan, 1970, pp. 154–182.

Johnson, Edgar. "*Bleak House*, The Anatomy of Society," in *Nineteenth-Century Fiction*. VII (September, 1952), pp. 73–89.

Korg, Jacob. *Twentieth Century Interpretations of* Bleak House. Englewood Cliffs, N.J.: Prentice-Hall, 1968.

Manning, Sylvia B. *Dickens as Satirist*. New Haven, Conn.: Yale University Press, 1971, pp. 101–131.

Moers, Ellen. "*Bleak House*: The Agitating Women," in *The Dickensian*. LXIX (1973), pp. 13–24.

Ousby, Ian. "The Broken Glass: Vision and Comprehension in *Bleak House*," in *Nineteenth-Century Fiction*. XXIX (1975), pp. 381–392.

Partlow, Robert B., Jr. *Dickens the Craftsman; Strategies of Presentation*. Carbondale: Southern Illinois University Press, 1970, pp. 115–139.

Pederson, Winifred J. "Jo in *Bleak House*," in *The Dickensian*. LX (Autumn, 1964), pp. 162–167.

Serlin, Ellen. "The Two Worlds of *Bleak House*," in *Journal of English Literary History*. XLIII (Winter, 1976), pp. 551–566.

Stoehr, Taylor. *Dickens: The Dreamer's Stance*. Ithaca, N.Y.: Cornell University Press, 1965, pp. 137–170.

Wilkinson, Ann Y. "*Bleak House*: From Faraday to Judgement Day," in *Journal of English Literary History*. XXXIV (1967), pp. 225–247.

Winslow, Joan D. "Esther Summerson: The Betrayal of the Imagination," in *Journal of Narrative Technique*. VI (1976), pp. 1–13.

Zabel, Morton D. *Craft and Character: Texts, Methods and Vocation in Modern Fiction*. New York: Viking, 1957, pp. 15–49.

Zwerdling, Alex. "Esther Summerson Rehabilitated," in *PMLA*. LXXXVIII (1973), pp. 429–439.

A Christmas Carol

Brown, John M. "Ghouls and Holly," in *Seeing More Things*. New York: McGraw-Hill, 1948, pp. 161–167.

Butt, John. "*A Christmas Carol*: Its Origin and Design," in *The Dickensian*. LI (December, 1954), pp. 15–18.

_____. *Pope, Dickens and Others: Essays and Addresses*. Edinburgh: Edinburgh University Press, 1969, pp. 130–139.

Dickens, Charles and Michael P. Hearn. *Annotated* Christmas Carol. New York: Avon, 1978.

Donovan, Frank. *Dickens and Youth.* New York: Dodd, Mead, 1968, pp. 223–226.

Gilbert, Elliot L. "The Ceremony of Innocence: Charles Dickens' *A Christmas Carol,*" in *PMLA.* XC (1975), pp. 22–31.

Gold, Joseph. *Charles Dickens: Radical Moralist.* Minneapolis: University of Minnesota Press, 1972, pp. 147–154.

Goldberg, Michael. *Carlyle and Dickens.* Athens: University of Georgia Press, 1972, pp. 32–34, 39–41.

Greaves, John. *Who's Who in Dickens.* New York: Taplinger, 1972.

Hewett, Edward W. "Christmas Spirits in Dickens," in *Dickens Studies Newsletter.* VII (1976), pp. 99–106.

Lucas, John. *The Melancholy Man: A Study of Dickens' Novels.* London: Methuen, 1970, pp. 137–141.

McNulty, J.H. "The Two Spirits of Fun and Beauty," in *The Dickensian.* XXXVIII (June, 1942), pp. 143–146.

Morris, William E. "The Conversion of Scrooge: A Defense of That Good Man's Motivation," in *Studies in Short Fiction.* III (Fall, 1965), pp. 46–55.

Patten, Robert L. "Dickens Time and Again," in *Dickens Studies Annual.* II (1972), pp. 163–196.

David Copperfield

Bandelin, Carl. "*David Copperfield*: A Third Interesting Penitent," in *Studies in English Literature, 1500–1900.* XVI (1976), pp. 601–611.

Bell, Vereen M. "The Emotional Matrix of *David Copperfield,*" in *Studies in English Literature, 1500–1900.* VIII (1968), pp. 633–649.

Brown, Janet H. "The Narrator's Role in *David Copperfield,*" in *Dickens Studies Annual.* II (1972), pp. 197–207.

Davis, Earle. *The Flint and the Flame: The Artistry of Charles Dickens.* Columbia: University of Missouri Press, 1963, pp. 157–182.

Donovan, Frank. *Dickens and Youth.* New York: Dodd, Mead, 1968, pp. 24–60.

Dunn, Richard J. "*David Copperfield*: All Dickens Is There," in *English Journal.* LIV (1965), pp. 789–794.

Dyson, A.E. *The Inimitable Dickens; A Reading of the Novels.* London: Macmillan, 1970, pp. 119–153.

Gard, Roger. "*David Copperfield,*" in *Essays in Criticism.* XV (July, 1965), pp. 313–325.

Hardy, Barbara. *The Moral Art of Dickens.* New York: Oxford University Press, 1970, pp. 122–138.

Hornback, Bert G. "Frustration and Resolution in *David Copperfield*," in *Studies in English Literature, 1500–1900*. VIII (1969), pp. 651–667.

Hughes, Felicity. "Narrative Complexity in *David Copperfield*," in *Journal of English Literary History*. XLI (1974), pp. 89–105.

Kincaid, James R. "Dickens' Subversive Humor: *David Copperfield*," in *Nineteenth-Century Fiction*. XXII (March, 1968), pp. 313–329.

————. "The Structure of *David Copperfield*," in *Dickens Studies*. II (1966), pp. 74–95.

————. "Symbol and Subversion in *David Copperfield*," in *Studies in the Novel*. I (1969), pp. 196–206.

Kraus, W. Keith. *Charles Dickens*: David Copperfield. New York: Barnes & Noble, 1966.

Lucas, John. *The Melancholy Man: A Study of Dickens' Novels*. London: Methuen, 1970, pp. 166–201.

Manning, Sylvia B. *Dickens as Satirist*. New Haven, Conn.: Yale University Press, 1971, pp. 96–98.

Maugham, William S. *Art of Fiction; An Introduction to Ten Novels and Their Authors*. Garden City N.Y.: Doubleday, 1955, pp. 135–161.

Reed, John R. "Confinement and Character in Dickens' Novels," in *Dickens Studies Annual*. I (1970), pp. 51–54.

Robison, Roselee. "Time, Death and the River in Dickens' Novels," in *English Studies*. LIII (1972), pp. 436–454.

Schilling, Bernard N. *The Comic Spirit; Boccaccio to Thomas Mann*. Detroit: Wayne State University Press, 1965, pp. 98–144.

Spilka, Mark. "*David Copperfield* as Psychological Fiction," in *Critical Quarterly*. I (Winter, 1959), pp. 292–301.

Stone, Harry. "Fairy Tales and Ogres; Dickens' Imagination and *David Copperfield*," in *Criticism*. VI (1964), pp. 324–330.

Tick, Stanley. "The Memorializing of Mr. Dick," in *Nineteenth-Century Fiction*. XXIV (September, 1969), pp. 142–153.

Worth, George J. "The Control of Emotional Response in *David Copperfield*," in his *The English Novel in the Nineteenth Century: Essays on the Literary Mediation of Human Values*. Urbana: University of Illinois Press, 1972, pp. 97–108.

Dombey and Son

Adamowski, Thomas H. "Dombey and Son and Sutpan and Son," in *Studies in the Novel*. IV (1972), pp. 378–384.

Axton, William. "*Dombey and Son*: From Stereotype to Archetype," in *Journal of English Literary History*. XXXI (September, 1964), pp. 301–317.

Barnard, Robert. *Imagery and Theme in the Novels of Dickens.* New York: Humanities Press, 1974, pp. 49–61.

Chesterton, Gilbert K. *Criticisms and Interpretations of the Works of Charles Dickens.* London: Dent, 1933, pp. 114–128.

Davis, Earle. *The Flint and the Flame: The Artistry of Charles Dickens.* Columbia: University of Missouri Press, 1963, pp. 150–156.

Donoghue, Denis. "The English Dickens and *Dombey and Son*," in *Dickens Centennial Essays.* Edited by Ada Nisbet and Blake Nevius. Berkeley: University of California Press, 1971, pp. 1–21.

Donovan, Frank. *Dickens and Youth.* New York: Dodd, Mead, 1968, pp. 115–125.

Dyson, A.E. *The Inimitable Dickens; A Reading of the Novels.* London: Macmillan, 1970, pp. 96–118.

Halperin, John. *Egoism and Self-Discovery in the Victorian Novel: Studies in the Ordeal of Knowledge in the Nineteenth Century.* New York: Burt Franklin, 1974, pp. 81–103.

Howard, David, et al. *Tradition and Tolerance in Nineteenth Century Fiction; Critical Essays on Some English and American Novels.* New York: Barnes & Noble, 1967, pp. 99–140.

Kennedy, G.W. "The Two Worlds of *Dombey and Son*," in *English Studies Colloquium.* IV (1976), pp. 1–11.

Leavis, F.R. "*Dombey and Son*," in *Sewanee Review.* LXX (Spring, 1962), pp. 177–201.

Lucas, John. *The Melancholy Man: A Study of Dickens' Novels.* London: Methuen, 1970, pp. 141–165.

McDonald, Andrew. "The Preservation of Innocence in *Dombey and Son*: Florence's Identity and the Role of Walter Gay," in *Texas Studies in Literature and Language.* XVIII (1976), pp. 1–19.

Mack, Maynard and Ian Gregor. *Imagined Worlds; Essays on Some English Novels and Novelists in Honour of John Butt.* London: Methuen, 1968, pp. 173–182.

Manning, Sylvia B. *Dickens as Satirist.* New Haven, Conn.: Yale University Press, 1971, pp. 87–95.

Milner, Ian. "The Dickens Drama: Mr. Dombey," in *Dickens Centennial Essays.* Edited by Ada Nisbet and Blake Nevius. Berkeley: University of California Press, 1971, pp. 155–165.

Pattison, Robert. *The Child Figure in English Literature.* Athens: University of Georgia Press, 1978, pp. 76–80, 82–84, 86–87, 99.

Pearson, Gabriel. "Towards a Reading of *Dombey and Son*," in his *The Modern English Novel: The Reader, the Writer, and the Work.* New York: Barnes & Noble, 1976, pp. 54–76.

Robison, Roselee. "Time, Death and the River in Dickens' Novels," in *English Studies*. LIII (1972), pp. 436–454.

Stone, Harry. "The Novel as Fairy Tale; Dickens' *Dombey and Son*," in *English Studies*. XLVII (February, 1966), pp. 1–27.

Tillotson, Kathleen M. *Novels of the Eighteen-Forties*. London: Oxford University Press, 1961, pp. 157–199.

Williams, Raymond. *The English Novel; From Dickens to Lawrence*. London: Chatto and Windus, 1970, pp. 37–47.

Wright, Austin. *Victorian Literature; Modern Essays in Criticism*. London: Oxford University Press, 1961, pp. 136–153.

Great Expectations

Barnard, Robert. "Imagery and Theme in *Great Expectations*," in *Dickens Studies Annual*. I (1970), pp. 238–251.

Bodelson, C.A. "Some Notes on Dickens' Symbolism," in *English Studies*. XL (December, 1959), pp. 420–431.

Crouch, W. George. *Critical Study Guide to Dickens'* Great Expectations. Totowa, N.J.: Littlefield, Adams, 1968.

Dessner, Lawrence J. "*Great Expectations*: 'the ghost of a man's own father,' " in *PMLA*. XCI (1976), pp. 436–449.

Donovan, Frank. *Dickens and Youth*. New York: Dodd, Mead, 1968, pp. 185–196.

Drew, Elizabeth A. *The Novel; A Modern Guide to Fifteen English Masterpieces*. New York: Norton, 1963, pp. 191–207.

Dyson, A.E. *The Inimitable Dickens; A Reading of the Novels*. London: Macmillan, 1970, pp. 228–247.

Hagan, John H., Jr. "The Poor Labyrinth: The Theme of Social Injustice in Dickens' *Great Expectations*," in *Nineteenth-Century Fiction*. IX (December, 1954), pp. 169–178.

Hynes, Joseph A. "Image and Symbol in *Great Expectations*," in *Journal of English Literary History*. XXX (1963), pp. 258–292.

Lelchuk, Alan. "Self, Family, and Society in *Great Expectations*," LXXVIII (1970), pp. 407–426.

Levine, George. "Communication in *Great Expectations*," in *Nineteenth-Century Fiction*. XVIII (September, 1963), pp. 175–181.

Lucas, John. *The Melancholy Man: A Study of Dickens' Novels*. London: Methuen, 1970, pp. 287–314.

Marcus, Phillip L. "Theme and Suspense in the Plot of *Great Expectations*," in *Dickens Studies*. II (Spring, 1966), pp. 57–73.

Marshall, William H. "The Conclusion of *Great Expectations* as the Fulfillment of Myth," in *Personalist*. XLIV (Summer, 1963), pp. 337–347.

Milhauser, Milton. "*Great Expectations*: The Three Endings," in *Dickens
Studies Annual*. II (1972), pp. 267–277.

Moynahan, Julian. "The Hero's Guilt; The Case of *Great Expectations*," in
Essays in Criticism. X (January, 1960), pp. 60–79.

New, William H. "The Four Elements in *Great Expectations*," in *Dickens
Studies*. III (1967), pp. 111–121.

Pearce, Richard A. *Stages of the Clown; Perspectives on Modern Fiction
from Dostoyevsky to Beckett*. Carbondale: Southern Illinois University Press,
1970, pp. 26–46.

Ricks, Christopher. "*Great Expectations*," in *Dickens and the Twentieth
Century*. Edited by J. Gross and G. Pearson. London: Routledge and Kegan
Paul, 1962, pp. 199–211.

Shapiro, Charles. *Twelve Original Essays on Great English Novels*. Detroit:
Wayne State University Press, 1960, pp. 103–124.

Shores, Lucille P. "The Character of Estella in *Great Expectations*," in *Massachusetts Studies in English*. III (1972), pp. 91–99.

Stone, Harry. "Fire, Hand, and Gate: Dickens' *Great Expectations*," in *Kenyon Review*. XXIV (Autumn, 1962), pp. 662–691.

Tomlin, E.W.F. *Charles Dickens, 1812–1870; A Centennial Volume*. New
York: Simon and Schuster, 1969, pp. 109–131, 237–263.

Van Ghent, Dorothy. *The English Novel*. New York: Rinehart, 1953,
pp. 125–138.

Winner, Anthony. "Character and Knowledge in Dickens: The Enigma of Jag-
gers," in *Dickens Studies Annual*. III (1974), pp. 100–121.

Hard Times

Atkinson, F.G. "*Hard Times*: Motifs and Meanings," in *Use of English*. XIV
(Spring, 1963), pp. 165–169.

Barnard, Robert. *Imagery and Theme in the Novels of Dickens*. New York:
Humanities Press, 1974, pp. 77–90.

Batwin, Joseph. "*Hard Times*: The News and the Novel," in *Nineteenth-
Century Fiction*. XXXII (September, 1977), pp. 166–187.

Benn, J. Miriam. "A Landscape with Figures: Characterization and Expression
in *Hard Times*," in *Dickens Studies Annual*. I (1970), pp. 168–182.

Berman, Ronald. "Human Scale: A Note on *Hard Times*," in *Nineteenth-
Century Fiction*. XXII (December, 1967), pp. 288–293.

Brantlinger, Patrick. "The Case Against Trade Unions in Early Victorian Fiction," in *Victorian Studies*. XIII (September, 1969), pp. 37–52.

Cazamian, Louis. *The Social Novel in England, 1830–1850: Dickens, Disraeli, Mrs. Gaskell, Kingsley.* Translated by Martin Fido. London: Routledge and Kegan Paul, 1973, pp. 162–173.

Cooperman, Stanley. "Dickens and the Secular Blasphemy; Social Criticism in *Hard Times, Little Dorrit,* and *Bleak House,*" in *College English.* XXII (1960), pp. 156–160.

Crockett, Judith. "Theme and Metaphor in *Hard Times,*" in *Spectrum.* VI (Fall, 1962), pp. 80–81.

Deneau, Daniel P. "The Brother–Sister Relationship in *Hard Times,*" in *The Dickensian.* LX (Autumn, 1964), pp. 173–177.

Donovan, Frank. *Dickens and Youth.* New York: Dodd, Mead, 1968, pp. 152–159.

Dyson, A.E. "*Hard Times*: The Robber Fancy," in *The Dickensian.* LXV (May, 1963), pp. 67–79.

————. *The Inimitable Dickens; A Reading of the Novels.* London: Macmillan, 1970, pp. 183–202.

Ford, George H. and Sylvère Monod. Hard Times: *An Authoritative Text, Backgrounds, Sources and Contemporary Reactions.* New York: Norton, 1966.

Gray, Paul E. *Twentieth Century Interpretations of* Hard Times. Englewood Cliffs, N.J.: Prentice-Hall, 1969.

Heck, Edwin J. "*Hard Times*: The Handwriting on the Factory Wall," in *English Journal.* LXI (1972), pp. 23–27.

Johnson, Alan P. "*Hard Times*: 'Performance' or 'Poetry,' " in *Dickens Studies.* V (1969), pp. 62–80.

Lodge, David. *Language of Fiction; Essays in Criticism and Verbal Analysis of the English Novel.* New York: Columbia University Press, 1966, pp. 144–163.

Lougy, Robert E. "Dickens' *Hard Times*: The Romance as Radical Literature," in *Dickens Studies Annual.* II (1972), pp. 237–254.

Manning, Sylvia B. *Dickens as Satirist.* New Haven, Conn.: Yale University Press, 1971, pp. 132–154.

Melada, Ivan. *The Captain of Industry in English Fiction, 1821–1871.* Albuquerque: University of New Mexico Press, 1970, pp. 110–115.

Palmer, William J. "*Hard Times*: A Dickens Fable of Personal Salvation," in *Dalhousie Review.* LII (1972), pp. 67–77.

Sonstroem, David. "Fettered Fancy in *Hard Times,*" in *PMLA.* LXXXIV (1969), pp. 520–529.

Voss, A.E. "A Note on Theme and Structure in *Hard Times,*" in *Theoria.* XXIII (1964), pp. 35–42.

Winters, Warrington. "Dickens' *Hard Times*: The Lost Childhood," in *Dickens Studies Annual*. II (1972), pp. 217–236.

Little Dorrit

Barnard, Robert. *Imagery and Theme in the Novels of Dickens*. New York: Humanities Press, 1974, pp. 91–105.

Burgan, William. "People in the Setting of *Little Dorrit*," in *Texas Studies in Literature and Language*. XV (1973), pp. 111–128.

Carlisle, Janice M. "*Little Dorrit*: Necessary Fictions," in *Studies in the Novel*. VII (1975), pp. 195–214.

Coolidge, Archibald. "Dickens' Complex Plots," in *The Dickensian*. LVII (Autumn, 1961), pp. 174–182.

Cooperman, Stanley. "Dickens and the Secular Blasphemy: Social Criticism in *Hard Times*, *Little Dorrit*, and *Bleak House*," in *College English*. XXII (December, 1960), pp. 156–160.

Donovan, Frank. *Dickens and Youth*. New York: Dodd, Mead, 1968, pp. 103–109.

Easson, Angus. "Marshalsea Prisoners: Mr. Dorrit and Mr. Hemens," in *Dickens Studies Annual*. III (1974), pp. 77–86.

Fleishman, Avrom. "Master and Servant in *Little Dorrit*," in *Studies in English Literature, 1500–1900*. XIV (1974), pp. 575–586.

Grove, T.N. "The Psychological Prison of Arthur Clennam in Dickens's *Little Dorrit*," in *Modern Language Review*. LXVIII (1973), pp. 750–755.

Jefferson, D.W. "The Moral Centre of *Little Dorrit*," in *Essays in Criticism*. XXVI (1976), pp. 300–317.

Kincaid, James R. *Dickens and the Rhetoric of Laughter*. Oxford: Clarendon Press, 1971, pp. 192–222.

Lineham, Tom. "The Importance of Plot in *Little Dorrit*," in *Journal of Narrative Technique*. VI (1976), pp. 116–131.

Lucas, John. *The Melancholy Man: A Study of Dickens' Novels*. London: Methuen, 1970, pp. 244–286.

Manning, Sylvia B. *Dickens as Satirist*. New Haven, Conn.: Yale University Press, 1971, pp. 155–180.

Myers, William. "The Radicalism of *Little Dorrit*," in *Literature and Politics in the Nineteenth Century*. Edited by John Lucas. London: Methuen, 1971, pp. 77–104.

Partlow, Robert B., Jr. *Dickens the Craftsman; Strategies of Presentation*. Carbondale: Southern Illinois University Press, 1970, pp. 140–164.

Pearce, Roy H. *Experience in the Novel; Selected Papers from the English Institute*. New York: Columbia University Press, 1968, pp. 107–131.

Reed, John R. "Confinement and Character in Dickens' Novels," in *Dickens Studies Annual.* I (1970), pp. 45–48.

Roopnaraine, R. Rupert. "Time and the Circle in *Little Dorrit*," in *Dickens Studies Annual.* III (1974), pp. 54–76.

Slater, Michael. *Dickens 1970; Centenary Essays.* New York: Stein and Day, 1970, pp. 125–149.

Sucksmith, Harvey P. "The Melodramatic Villain in *Little Dorrit*," in *The Dickensian.* LXXI (1975), pp. 76–83.

Tick, Stanley. "The Sad Case of Mr. Meagles," in *Dickens Studies Annual.* III (1974), pp. 87–99.

Wain, John. "*Little Dorrit*," in *Dickens and the Twentieth Century.* Edited by J. Gross and G. Pearson. London: Routledge and Kegan Paul, 1962, pp. 175–186.

Wall, Stephen. "Dickens' Plot of Fortune," in *Review of English Literature.* VI (January, 1965), pp. 56–67.

Wilde, Alan. "Mr. F's Aunt and the Analogical Structure of *Little Dorrit*," in *Nineteenth-Century Fiction.* XIX (June, 1964), pp. 33–44.

Martin Chuzzlewit

Barnard, Robert. *Imagery and Theme in the Novels of Dickens.* New York: Humanities Press, 1974, pp. 37–48.

Beasley, Jerry C. "The Role of Tom Pinch in *Martin Chuzzlewit*," in *Ariel.* V (1974), pp. 77–89.

Benjamin, Edwin B. "The Structure of *Martin Chuzzlewit*," in *Philological Quarterly.* XXXIV (January, 1955), pp. 39–47.

Brogunier, Joseph. "The Dreams of Montague Tigg and Jonas Chuzzlewit," in *The Dickensian.* LVIII (Autumn, 1962), pp. 165–170.

Burke, Alan R. "The House of Chuzzlewit and the Architectural City," in *Dickens Studies Annual.* III (1974), pp. 14–40.

Carolan, Katherine. "Dickens' American Secretary and *Martin Chuzzlewit*," in *Dickens Studies Newsletter.* VII (1976), pp. 109–110.

Coolidge, Archibald. "Dickens' Complex Plots," in *The Dickensian.* LVII (Autumn, 1961), pp. 174–182.

Daleski, Herman M. *Dickens and the Art of Analogy.* New York: Schocken, 1970, pp. 79–115.

Dyson, A.E. *The Inimitable Dickens; A Reading of the Novels.* London: Macmillan, 1970, pp. 71–95.

————. "*Martin Chuzzlewit*: Howls the Sublime," in *Critical Quarterly.* IX (Autumn, 1967), pp. 234–253.

Gold, Joseph.   *Charles Dickens: Radical Moralist.* Minneapolis: University of Minnesota Press, 1972, pp. 130–146.

————.   " 'Living in a Wale': *Martin Chuzzlewit,*" in *Dickens Studies Annual.* II (1972), pp. 150–162.

Greaves, John.   *Who's Who in Dickens.* New York: Taplinger, 1972.

Guerard, Albert J.   "*Martin Chuzzlewit*: The Novel as Comic Entertainment," in *Mosaic.* IX (1976), pp. 107–129.

Hannaford, Richard.   "Irony and Sentimentality: Conflicting Modes in *Martin Chuzzlewit,*" in *Victorian Newsletter.* XLVI (1974), pp. 26–28.

Hardy, Barbara.   "The Change in Heart in Dickens' Novels," in *Victorian Studies.* V (September, 1961), pp. 49–67.

————.   "*Martin Chuzzlewit,*" in *Dickens and the Twentieth Century.* Edited by J. Gross and G. Pearson. London: Routledge and Kegan Paul, 1962, pp. 107–120.

————.   *The Moral Art of Dickens.* New York: Oxford University Press, 1970, pp. 100–121.

Kincaid, James R.   *Dickens and the Rhetoric of Laughter.* Oxford: Clarendon Press, 1971, pp. 105–131.

Lucas, John.   *The Melancholy Man: A Study of Dickens' Novels.* London: Methuen, 1970, pp. 113–137.

Manning, Sylvia B.   *Dickens as Satirist.* New Haven, Conn.: Yale University Press, 1971, pp. 71–86.

Phillips, George L.   "Dickens and the Chimney-Sweepers," in *The Dickensian.* LIX (Winter, 1963), pp. 28–44.

Shereikes, Robert.   "Selves at the Center: The Theme of Isolation in Dickens' *Martin Chuzzlewit,*" in *Dickens Studies Newsletter.* VII (1976), pp. 38–42.

Steig, Michael.   "*Martin Chuzzlewit*: Pinch and Pecksniff," in *Studies in the Novel.* I (Summer, 1969), pp. 181–188.

Wall, Stephen.   "Dickens' Plot of Fortune," in *Review of English Literature.* VI (January, 1965), pp. 56–67.

The Mystery of Edwin Drood

Aylmer, Felix.   *The Drood Case.* New York: Barnes & Noble, 1965.

Baker, Richard M.   *The Drood Murder Case; Five Studies in Dickens' Edwin Drood.* Berkeley: University of California Press, 1951.

————.   "Who Was Dick Datchery?," in *Nineteenth-Century Fiction.* II (March, 1948), pp. 201–222, and III (June, 1948), pp. 35–53.

Barnard, Robert.   *Imagery and Theme in the Novels of Dickens.* New York: Humanities Press, 1974, pp. 134–144.

Bilham, D.M. "*Edwin Drood*: To Resolve a Mystery," in *The Dickensian*. LXII (September, 1966), pp. 181–193.

Cohen, Jane R. "Dickens' Artists and Artistry in *The Mystery of Edwin Drood*," in *Dickens Studies*. III (1967), pp. 126–145.

Coolidge, Archibald C. "Dickens' Complex Plots," in *The Dickensian*. LIX (Winter, 1963), pp. 57–60.

Cox, Arthur J. "The 'Drood' Remains," in *Dickens Studies*. II (1966), pp. 33–44.

————. "The Morals of Edwin Drood," in *The Dickensian*. LVIII (January, 1962), pp. 32–43.

Davis, Earle. *The Flint and the Flame: The Artistry of Charles Dickens*. Columbia: University of Missouri Press, 1963, pp. 150–156.

Dyson, A.E. "*Edwin Drood*: A Horrible Wonder Apart," in *Critical Quarterly*. XI (Summer, 1969), pp. 138–157.

————. *The Inimitable Dickens; A Reading of His Novels*. London: Macmillan, 1970, pp. 267–293.

Gottschalk, Paul. "Time in *Edwin Drood*," in *Dickens Studies Annual*. I (1970), pp. 265–272.

Greenhalgh, Mollie. "*Edwin Drood*: The Twilight of a God," in *The Dickensian*. LV (May, 1959), pp. 68–75.

Johnson, Edgar. *Charles Dickens, His Tragedy and Triumph*. New York: Simon and Schuster, 1952, pp. 1115–1126.

Mitchell, Charles. "*Mystery of Edwin Drood*: The Interior and Exterior of Self," in *Journal of English Literary History*. XXXIII (June, 1966), pp. 228–246.

Pritchett, V.S. *The Living Novel and Later Appreciations*. New York: Random House, 1964, pp. 81–87.

Robison, Roselee. "Time, Death and the River in Dickens' Novels," in *English Studies*. LIII (1972), pp. 436–454.

Saunders, Montagu. *The Mystery in the Drood Family*. New York: Haskell, 1974.

Stone, Harry. "Dickens and the Interior Monologue," in *Philological Quarterly*. XXXVIII (January, 1959), pp. 52–65.

Walter, J.C. *Clues to Dickens'* Mystery of Edwin Drood. New York: Haskell, 1905.

Whipple, Edwin P. *Charles Dickens; The Man and His Work*. Boston: Houghton Mifflin, 1912, pp. 300–354.

Wilson, Edmund. *The Wound and the Bow*. New York: Oxford University Press, 1947, pp. 83–104.

Wing, George.   "*Edwin Drood* and *Desperate Remedies*: Prototypes of Detective Fiction in 1870," in *Studies in English Literature, 1500–1900*. XIII (1973), pp. 677–680, 684–686.

Nicholas Nickleby

Adrian, Arthur A.   "*Nicholas Nickleby* and Educational Reform," in *Nineteenth-Century Fiction*. IV (December, 1949), pp. 237–241.

Barnard, Robert.   *Imagery and Theme in the Novels of Dickens*. New York: Humanities Press, 1974, pp. 25–36.

Bergonzi, Bernard.   "*Nicholas Nickleby*," in *Dickens and the Twentieth Century*. Edited by J. Gross and G. Pearson. London: Routledge and Kegan Paul, 1962, pp. 65–76.

Chesterton, Gilbert K.   *Criticisms and Appreciations of the Works of Charles Dickens*. London: Dent, 1933, pp. 26–37.

Donovan, Frank.   *Dickens and Youth*. New York: Dodd, Mead, 1968, pp. 110–115, 137–148.

Ganz, Margaret.   "*Nicholas Nickleby*: The Victories of Humor," in *Mosaic*. IX (1976), pp. 131–148.

Gissing, George R.   *Critical Studies of the Works of Charles Dickens*. New York: Greenberg, 1924, pp. 58–71.

Gold, Joseph.   *Charles Dickens: Radical Moralist*. Minneapolis: University of Minnesota Press, 1972, pp. 66–92.

Greaves, John.   *Who's Who in Dickens*. New York: Taplinger, 1972.

Grillo, Virgil.   *Charles Dickens' "Sketches by Boz": End in the Beginning*. Boulder: Colorado Associated University Press, 1974, pp. 129–167.

Hannaford, Richard.   "Fairy-Tale Fantasy in *Nicholas Nickleby*," in *Criticism*. XVI (1974), pp. 247–259.

Johnson, Edgar.   *Charles Dickens, His Tragedy and Triumph*. New York: Simon and Schuster, 1952, pp. 283–291.

Kelty, Jean M.   "The Modern Tones of Charles Dickens," in *The Dickensian*. LVII (Autumn, 1961), pp. 160–165.

Lucas, John.   *The Melancholy Man: A Study of Dickens' Novels*. London: Methuen, 1970, pp. 55–73.

Manning, Sylvia B.   *Dickens as Satirist*. New Haven, Conn.: Yale University Press, 1971, pp. 54–57.

Meckier, Jerome.   "The Faint Image of Eden: The Many Worlds of *Nicholas Nickleby*," in *Dickens Studies Annual*. I (1970), pp. 129–146.

Melada, Ivan.   *The Captain of Industry in English Fiction, 1821–1871*. Albuquerque: University of New Mexico Press, 1970, pp. 103–110.

Noffsinger, John W. "The Complexity of Ralph Nickleby," in *Dickens Studies Newsletter.* V (1974), pp. 112–114.

Reed, John R. "Some Indefinable Resemblance: Moral Form in Dickens' *Nicholas Nickleby*," in *Papers on Language and Literature.* III (1967), pp. 134–147.

Roulet, Ann. "A Comparative Study of *Nicholas Nickleby* and *Bleak House*," in *The Dickensian.* LX (Spring, 1964), pp. 117–124.

Thompson, Leslie M. "Mrs. Nickleby's Monologue: The Dichotomy of Pessimism and Optimism in *Nicholas Nickleby*," in *Studies in the Novel.* I (Summer, 1969), pp. 222–229.

Whipple, Edwin P. *Charles Dickens; The Man and His Work,* Volume I. Boston: Houghton Mifflin, 1912, pp. 72–99.

Williams, Raymond. *The English Novel; From Dickens to Lawrence.* London: Chatto and Windus, 1970, pp. 50–52.

Wing, G.D. "A Part to Tear a Cat in," in *The Dickensian.* LXIV (January, 1968), pp. 10–19.

The Old Curiosity Shop

Chesterton, Gilbert K. *Criticisms and Appreciations of the Works of Charles Dickens.* London: Dent, 1933, pp. 50–64.

Donovan, Frank. *Dickens and Youth.* New York: Dodd, Mead, 1968, pp. 88–103, 160–162, 167–176.

Dyson, A.E. *The Inimitable Dickens; A Reading of the Novels.* London: Macmillan, 1970, pp. 21–46.

————. "*The Old Curiosity Shop*: Innocence and the Grotesque," in *Critical Quarterly.* VIII (Summer, 1966), pp. 111–130.

Engle, Monroe. " 'A Kind of Allegory'; *The Old Curiosity Shop*," in *The Interpretation of Narrative: Theory and Practice.* Edited by Morton W. Bloomfield. Cambridge, Mass.: Harvard University Press, 1970, pp. 138–147.

Gibson, John W. "*The Old Curiosity Shop*: The Critical Allegory," in *The Dickensian.* LX (Autumn, 1964), pp. 178–183.

Gissing, George R. *Critical Studies of the Works of Charles Dickens.* New York: Greenberg, 1924, pp. 119–135.

Gold, Joseph. *Charles Dickens: Radical Moralist.* Minneapolis: University of Minnesota Press, 1972, pp. 93–115.

Johnson, Edgar. *Charles Dickens, His Tragedy and Triumph.* New York: Simon and Schuster, 1952, pp. 319–329.

Kincaid, James R. *Dickens and the Rhetoric of Laughter.* Oxford: Clarendon Press, 1971, pp. 41–75.

Lucas, John. *The Melancholy Man: A Study of Dickens' Novels.* London: Methuen, 1970, pp. 73–92.

McLean, Robert S. "Putting Quilp to Rest," in *Victorian Newsletter.* XXXIV (Fall, 1968), pp. 29–33.

Manning, Sylvia B. *Dickens as Satirist.* New Haven, Conn.: Yale University Press, 1971, pp. 57–63.

Partlow, Robert B., Jr. *Dickens the Craftsman; Strategies of Presentation.* Carbondale: Southern Illinois University Press, 1970, pp. 44–94.

Pattison, Robert. *The Child Figure in English Literature.* Athens: University of Georgia Press, 1978, pp. 76–80, 82–84, 86–87, 99.

Pratt, Branwen. "Sympathy for the Devil: A Dissenting View of Quilp," in *Hartford Studies in Literature.* VI (1974), pp. 129–146.

Priestley, J.B. *The English Comic Characters.* London: J. Lane, 1928, pp. 224–240.

Rogers, Philip. "The Dynamics of Time in *The Old Curiosity Shop*," in *Nineteenth-Century Fiction.* XXVIII (1973), pp. 127–144.

Senelick, Laurence. "Little Nell and the Prurience of Sentimentality," in *Dickens Studies.* III (1967), pp. 146–159.

Steig, Michael. "The Central Action of *Old Curiosity Shop* or Little Nell Revisited Again," in *Literature and Psychology.* XV (Summer, 1965), pp. 163–170.

Whipple, Edwin P. *Charles Dickens; The Man and His Work,* Volume I. Boston: Houghton Mifflin, 1912, pp. 100–127.

Winters, Warrington. "*The Old Curiosity Shop*: A Consummation Devoutly to Be Wished," in *The Dickensian.* XLIII (September, 1967), pp. 176–180.

Oliver Twist

Austen, Zelda. "*Oliver Twist*: A Divided View," in *Dickens Studies Newsletter.* VII (1976), pp. 8–12.

Bishop, Jonathan. "The Hero-Villain of *Oliver Twist*," in *Victorian Newsletter.* XV (Spring, 1959), pp. 14–16.

Cazamian, Louis. *The Social Novel in England, 1830–1850: Dickens, Disraeli, Mrs. Gaskell, Kingsley.* Translated by Martin Fido. London: Routledge and Kegan Paul, 1973, pp. 141–143.

Chesterton, Gilbert K. *Criticisms and Appreciations of the Works of Charles Dickens.* London: Dent, 1933, pp. 38–49.

Colby, Robert A. *Fiction with a Purpose; Major and Minor Nineteenth Century Novels.* Bloomington: Indiana University Press, 1967, pp. 105–137.

Daleski, Herman M. *Dickens and the Art of Analogy.* New York: Schocken, 1970, pp. 49–78.

Donovan, Frank. *Dickens and Youth.* New York: Dodd, Mead, 1968, pp. 61–87.

Duffy, Joseph M. "Another Version of Pastoral: *Oliver Twist*," in *Journal of English Literary History.* XXXV (1968), pp. 403–421.

Frederick, Kenneth C. "The Cold, Cold Hearth: Domestic Strife in *Oliver Twist*," in *College English.* XXVII (1966), pp. 465–470.

Gissing, George R. *Critical Studies of the Works of Charles Dickens.* New York: Greenberg, 1924, pp. 43–57.

Gold, Joseph. *Charles Dickens: Radical Moralist.* Minneapolis: University of Minnesota Press, 1972, pp. 25–65.

————. "Dickens' Exemplary Aliens: Bumble the Beadle and Fagin the Fence," in *Mosaic.* II (1968), pp. 77–89.

Greaves, John. *Who's Who in Dickens.* New York: Taplinger, 1972.

Hollingsworth, Keith. *The Newgate Novel (1830–1847): Bulwer, Ainsworth, Dickens, and Thackeray.* Detroit: Wayne State University Press, 1963, pp. 111–131.

Johnson, Edgar, George Shuster and Lyman Bryson. "*Oliver Twist*," in *Invitation to Learning: English and American Novels.* Edited by George D. Crothers. New York: Basic Books, 1966, pp. 99–107.

Kincaid, James R. *Dickens and the Rhetoric of Laughter.* Oxford: Clarendon Press, 1971, pp. 41–75.

Lucas, Alec. "*Oliver Twist* and the Newgate Novel," in *Dalhousie Review.* XXXIV (Spring, 1954), pp. 381–387.

Lucas, John. *The Melancholy Man: A Study of Dickens' Novels.* London: Methuen, 1970, pp. 21–54.

Manning, Sylvia B. *Dickens as Satirist.* New Haven, Conn.: Yale University Press, 1971, pp. 51–54.

Marcus, Steven. "Who Is Fagin?," in *Commentary.* XXXIII (June, 1962), pp. 48–59.

Patten, Robert L. "Capitalism and Compassion in *Oliver Twist*," in *Studies in the Novel.* I (Summer, 1969), pp. 207–221.

Slater, Michael. "On Reading *Oliver Twist*," in *The Dickensian.* LXX (1974), pp. 75–81.

Tillotson, Kathleen. "*Oliver Twist*," in *Essays and Studies by Members of the English Society.* XII (1959), pp. 87–105.

Westburg, Barry. " 'His Allegorical Way of Expressing It': Civil War and Psychic Conflict in *Oliver Twist* and *A Child's History*," in *Studies in the Novel.* VI (1974), pp. 27–37.

Our Mutual Friend

Baker, Robert S. "Imagination and Literacy in Dickens' *Our Mutual Friend*," in *Criticism.* XVIII (1976), pp. 57–72.

Barnard, Robert. "The Choral Symphony: *Our Mutual Friend*," in *Review of English Literature.* II (July, 1961), pp. 89–99.

————. *Imagery and Theme in the Novels of Dickens.* New York: Humanities Press, 1974, pp. 120–133.

Chesterton, Gilbert K. *Criticisms and Appreciations of the Works of Charles Dickens.* London: Dent, 1933, pp. 207–217.

Daleski, Herman M. *Dickens and the Art of Analogy.* New York: Schocken, 1970, pp. 270–336.

Davis, Earle. *The Flint and the Flame: The Artistry of Charles Dickens.* Columbia: University of Missouri Press, 1963, pp. 264–282.

Donovan, Frank. *Dickens and Youth.* New York: Dodd, Mead, 1968, pp. 176–180.

Dunn, Richard J. "Dickens and the Tragi-Comic Grotesque," in *Studies in the Novel.* I (Summer, 1969), pp. 147–156.

Dyson, A.E. *The Inimitable Dickens; A Reading of the Novels.* London: Macmillan, 1970, pp. 248–266.

Friedman, Stanley. "The Motif of Reading in *Our Mutual Friend*," in *Nineteenth-Century Fiction.* XXVIII (1973), pp. 38–61.

Hardy, Barbara. "The Change of Heart in Dickens' Novels," in *Victorian Studies.* V (September, 1961), pp. 49–67.

Kennedy, G.W. "Naming and Language in *Our Mutual Friend*," in *Nineteenth-Century Fiction.* XXVIII (1973), pp. 165–178.

Knoepflmacher, Ulrich C. *Laughter and Despair; Readings in Ten Novels of the Victorian Age.* Berkeley: University of California Press, 1971, pp. 137–167.

Lanham, Richard A. "*Our Mutual Friend*: The Birds of Prey," in *Victorian Newsletter.* XXIV (Fall, 1963), pp. 6–12.

McMaster, R.D. "Birds of Prey: A Study of *Our Mutual Friend*," in *Dalhousie Review.* XL (Summer, 1960), pp. 372–381.

Manning, Sylvia B. *Dickens as Satirist.* New Haven, Conn.: Yale University Press, 1971, pp. 199–227.

Miyoshi, Masao. "Resolution of Identity in *Our Mutual Friend*," *Victorian Newsletter.* XXVI (Fall, 1964), pp. 5–9.

Morse, R. "*Our Mutual Friend*," in *Partisan Review.* XVI (March, 1949), pp. 277–289.

Muir, Kenneth, "Image and Structure in *Our Mutual Friend*," in *Essays and Studies.* XIX (1966), pp. 92–105.

Robison, Roselee. "Time, Death and the River in Dickens' Novels," in *English Studies.* LIII (1972), pp. 436–454.

Shea, F.X. "Mr. Venus Observed: The Plot Change in *Our Mutual Friend*," in *Papers in Language and Literature.* IV (1968), pp. 170–181.

————. "No Change of Intension in *Our Mutual Friend*," in *The Dickensian.* LXIII (January, 1967), pp. 37–40.

Stewart, Garrett. "The 'Golden Bower' of *Our Mutual Friend*," in *Journal of English Literary History.* XL (1973), pp. 105–130.

Thompson, Leslie M. "The Marks of Pride in *Our Mutual Friend*," in *The Dickensian.* LX (Spring, 1964), pp. 124–128.

Wall, Stephen. "Dickens' Plot of Fortune," in *Review of English Literature.* VI (January, 1965), pp. 56–67.

The Pickwick Papers

Axton, William. "Unity and Coherence in *The Pickwick Papers*," in *Studies in English Literature, 1500–1900.* V (1965), pp. 633–676.

Bevington, David M. "Seasonal Relevance in *The Pickwick Papers*," in *Nineteenth-Century Fiction.* XVI (1961), pp. 219–230.

Chesterton, Gilbert K. *Charles Dickens.* London: Methuen, 1936, pp. 51–71.

————. *Criticisms and Appreciations of the Works of Charles Dickens.* London: Dent, 1933, pp. 13–25.

Daleski, Herman M. *Dickens and the Art of Analogy.* New York: Schocken, 1970, pp. 17–48.

Easson, Angus. "Imprisonment for Debt in *Pickwick Papers*," in *The Dickensian.* LXIV (May, 1968), pp. 105–112.

Fadiman, Clifton. *Party of One; The Selected Writings of Clifton Fadiman.* New York: World, 1955, pp. 203–225.

Gold, Joseph. *Charles Dickens: Radical Moralist.* Minneapolis: University of Minnesota Press, 1972, pp. 12–24.

Greaves, John. *Who's Who in Dickens.* New York: Taplinger, 1972.

Hardy, Barbara. *The Moral Art of Dickens.* New York: Oxford University Press, 1970, pp. 81–99.

Herbert, Christopher. "Converging Worlds in *Pickwick Papers*," in *Nineteenth-Century Fiction.* XXVII (1972), pp. 1–20.

Killham, John. "*Pickwick*, Dickens and the Art of Fiction," in *Dickens and the Twentieth Century.* Edited by J. Gross and G. Pearson. London: Routledge and Kegan Paul, 1962, pp. 35–47.

Kincaid, James R. *Dickens and the Rhetoric of Laughter.* Oxford: Clarendon Press, 1971, pp. 20–40.

Lucas, John. *The Melancholy Man: A Study of Dickens' Novels.* London: Methuen, 1970, pp. 1–20.

Maclean, H.N. "Mr. Pickwick and the Seven Deadly Sins," in *Nineteenth-Century Fiction.* VIII (December, 1953), pp. 198–212.

Manheim, Leonard. "Dickens' Fools and Madmen," in *Dickens Studies Annual.* II (1972), pp. 74–77.

Manning, Sylvia B. *Dickens as Satirist.* New Haven, Conn.: Yale University Press, 1971, pp. 41–51.

Marcus, Steven. "Language into Structure: Pickwick Revisited," in *Daedalus.* CI (1972), pp. 183–202.

Patten, Robert L. "The Art of *Pickwick's* Interpolated Tales," in *Journal of English Literary History.* XXXIV (1967), pp. 349–366.

————. "Boz, Phiz, and Pickwick in the Pound," in *Journal of English Literary History.* XXXVI (1969), pp. 575–591.

Priestley, J.B. *The English Comic Characters.* London: J. Lane, 1928, pp. 198–223.

Rogers, Philip. "Mr. Pickwick's Innocence," in *Nineteenth-Century Fiction.* XXVII (1972), pp. 21–37.

Rubin, Stan S. "Spectator and Spectacle: Narrative Evasion and Narrative Voice in *Pickwick Papers*," in *Journal of Narrative Technique.* VI (1976), pp. 188–203.

A Tale of Two Cities

Davis, Earle. *The Flint and the Flame: The Artistry of Charles Dickens.* Columbia: University of Missouri Press, 1963, pp. 238–254.

Dyson, A.E. *The Inimitable Dickens; A Reading of the Novels.* London: Macmillan, 1970, pp. 212–227.

Elliot, Ralph. *A Critical Commentary on Dickens'* A Tale of Two Cities. London: Macmillan, 1966.

Fleishman, Avrom. *The English Historical Novel; Walter Scott to Virginia Woolf.* Baltimore: Johns Hopkins University Press, 1971, pp. 114–126.

Gold, Joseph. *Charles Dickens: Radical Moralist.* Minneapolis: University of Minnesota Press, 1972, pp. 231–240.

Goldberg, Michael. *Carlyle and Dickens.* Athens: University of Georgia, 1972, pp. 100–128.

Greaves, John. *Who's Who in Dickens.* New York: Taplinger, 1972.

Gregory, Michael. "Old Bailey Speech in *A Tale of Two Cities*," in *Review of English Literature.* VI (April, 1965), pp. 42–55.

Gross, John. "*A Tale of Two Cities*," in *Dickens and the Twentieth Century*. Edited by J. Gross and G. Pearson. London: Routledge and Kegan Paul, 1962, pp. 187–197.

Halperin, John. *Egoism and Self-Discovery in the Victorian Novel: Studies in the Ordeal of Knowledge in the Nineteenth Century*. New York: Burt Franklin, 1974, pp. 103–109.

Lindsay, Jack. "*A Tale of Two Cities*," in *Life and Letters*. LXII (1949), pp. 191–204.

Manheim, Leonard. "A Tale of Two Characters: A Study in Multiple Projection," in *Dickens Studies Annual*. I (1970), pp. 229–237.

————. "*A Tale of Two Cities*: A Study in Psychoanalytic Criticism," in *English Review*. (Spring, 1959), pp. 13–28.

Manning, Sylvia B. *Dickens as Satirist*. New Haven, Conn.: Yale University Press, 1971, pp. 183–192.

Marcus, David D. "The Carlylean Vision of *A Tale of Two Cities*," in *Studies in the Novel*. VIII (1976), pp. 56–68.

Marshall, William H. "The Method of *A Tale of Two Cities*," in *The Dickensian*. LVII (Autumn, 1961), pp. 183–189.

Monod, Sylvère. "Dickens's Attitudes in *A Tale of Two Cities*," in *Dickens Centennial Essays*. Edited by Ada Nisbet and Blake Nevius. Berkeley: University of California Press, 1971, pp. 166–183.

Partlow, Robert B., Jr. *Dickens the Craftsman; Strategies of Presentation*. Carbondale: Southern Illinois University Press, 1970, pp. 165–186.

Rance, Nicholas. *The Historical Novel and Popular Politics in Nineteenth-Century England*. London: Vision, 1975, pp. 83–101.

Stange, G. Robert. "Dickens and the Fiery Past: *A Tale of Two Cities* Reconsidered," in *English Journal*. XLIV (1957), pp. 381–390.

Stoehr, Taylor. *Dickens: The Dreamer's Stance*. Ithaca, N.Y.: Cornell University Press, 1965, pp. 195–203.

Wagenknecht, Edward C. *Dickens and the Scandalmongers; Essays in Criticism*. Norman: University of Oklahoma Press, 1965, pp. 121–131.

Zabel, Morton D. *Craft and Character; Texts, Methods and Vocation in Modern Fiction*. New York: Viking, 1957, pp. 49–69.

Zambrano, Ana L. "The Styles of Dickens and Griffith: *A Tale of Two Cities* and *Orphans of the Storm*," in *Language and Style*. VII (1974), pp. 53–60.

JAMES DICKEY
(1923–   )

Buckdancer's Choice

Bly, Robert. "The Collapse of James Dickey," in *The Sixties*. IX (Spring, 1967), pp. 70–79.

Dickey, William. "The Thing Itself," in *Hudson Review*. XIX (Spring, 1966), pp. 146–155.

Huff, Robert. "The Lamb, the Clocks, the Blue Light," in *Poetry*. CIX (October, 1966), pp. 46–48.

Ignatow, David. "The Permanent Hell," in *Nation*. CCII (June 20, 1966), pp. 752–753.

Strange, W.C. "To Dream, To Remember: James Dickey's *Buckdancer's Choice*," in *Northwest Review*. VII (Fall–Winter, 1965–1966), pp. 33–34.

Deliverance

Beidler, Peter G. " 'The Pride of Thine Heart Hath Deceived Thee': Narrative Distortion in Dickey's *Deliverance*," in *South Carolina Review*. V (1972), pp. 29–40.

Davis, Charles E. "The Wilderness Revisited: Irony in James Dickey's *Deliverance*," in *Studies in American Fiction*. IV (1976), pp. 223–230.

Edwards, C. Hines, Jr. "Dickey's *Deliverance*: The Owl and the Eye," in *Critique: Studies in Modern Fiction*. XV (1973), pp. 95–101.

Finholt, Richard. *American Visionary Fiction: Mad Metaphysics as Salvation Psychology*. Port Washington, N.Y.: Kennikat, 1978, pp. 128–143.

Greiner, Donald J. "The Harmony of Bestiality in James Dickey's *Deliverance*," in *South Carolina Review*. V (1972), pp. 43–49.

Guillory, Daniel L. "Myth and Meaning in James Dickey's *Deliverance*," in *College Literature*. XV (1976), pp. 56–62.

Italia, Paul G. "Love and Lust in James Dickey's *Deliverance*," in *Modern Fiction Studies*. XXI (1975), pp. 203–213.

Lindborg, Henry J. "James Dickey's *Deliverance*: The Ritual of Art," in *Southern Literary Journal*. VI (1974), pp. 83–90.

Marin, D.B. "James Dickey's *Deliverance*: Darkness Visible," in *South Carolina Review*. III (1970), pp. 49–59.

Markos, Donald W. "Art and Immediacy: James Dickey's *Deliverance*," in *Southern Review*. VII (1971), pp. 947–953.

Stephenson, William. "*Deliverance* from What?," in *Georgia Review*. XXVIII (1974), pp. 114–120.

Verburg, T. Larry. "Water Imagery in James Dickey's *Deliverance*," in *Notes on Contemporary Literature.* IV (1974), pp. 11–13.

Drowning with Others

Gunn, Thomas. "Things, Voices, Minds," in *Yale Review.* LII (Autumn, 1962), pp. 129–138.

Korges, James. "James Dickey and Other Good Poets," in *Minnesota Review.* III (Summer, 1963), pp. 473–491.

Nemerov, Howard. "Poems of Darkness and a Specialized Light," in *Sewanee Review.* LXXI (Winter, 1963), pp. 99–104.

————. *Reflections on Poetry and Poetics.* New Brunswick, N.J.: Rutgers University Press, 1972, pp. 71–76.

Simon, John. "More Brass Than Enduring," in *Hudson Review.* XV (Autumn, 1962), pp. 455–468.

The Eye-Beaters, Blood, Victory, Madness, Buckhead and Mercy

Calhoun, Richard J. " 'His Reason Argues with His Invention': James Dickey's *Self-Interviews* and *The Eye-Beaters*," in *South Carolina Review.* III 1971), pp. 9–16.

DeMott, Benjamin. " 'The More Life School' of James Dickey," in *Saturday Review of Literature.* LIII (March 28, 1970), p. 25.

Howard, Richard. "Resurrection for a Little While," in *The Nation.* CCX (March 23, 1970), pp. 341–342.

Helmets

Berry, Wendell. "James Dickey's New New Book," in *Poetry.* CV (November, 1964), pp. 130–131.

Bornhauser, Fred. "Poetry by Poem," in *Virginia Quarterly Review.* XLI (Winter, 1965), pp. 146–152.

Martz, Louis L. "Recent Poetry: The Elegaic Mode," in *Yale Review.* LIV (December, 1964), pp. 285–298.

Meredith, William. "James Dickey's Poems," in *Partisan Review.* XXXII (Summer, 1965), pp. 456–457.

Poems: 1957–1967

Corrington, John W. "James Dickey's *Poems: 1957–1967*: A Personal Appraisal," in *Georgia Review.* XXII (Spring, 1968), pp. 12–23.

Glancy, Eileen. *James Dickey: The Critic as Poet.* Troy, N.Y.: Whitston, 1971, pp. 1–33.

Guillory, Daniel L. "Water Magic in the Poetry of James Dickey," in *English Language Notes.* VIII (1970), pp. 131–137.

Lieberman, Lawrence. "The Expansional Poet: A Return to Personality," in *Yale Review.* LVII (Winter, 1968), pp. 258–272.

————. *Unassigned Frequencies; American Poetry in Review. 1964–1977.* Urbana: University of Illinois Press, 1977, pp. 74–106, 263–271.

————. "The Wordly Mystic," in *Hudson Review.* XX (August, 1967), pp. 513–517.

Mills, Ralph J., Jr. "The Poetry of James Dickey," in *Triquarterly.* XI (Winter, 1968), pp. 231–242.

Tillinghast, Richard. "Pilot into Poet," in *New Republic.* CLVII (September 9, 1967), pp. 28–29.

Untermeyer, Louis. "A Way of Seeing and Saying," in *Saturday Review of Literature.* L (May 6, 1967), p. 31.

EMILY DICKINSON
(1830–1886)

The Poetry of Dickinson

Anderson, Charles R. *Emily Dickinson's Poetry: Stairway of Surprise.* New York: Holt, Rinehart and Winston, 1960.

Blake, Caesar R., Editor. *The Recognition of Emily Dickinson: Selected Criticism Since 1890.* Ann Arbor: University of Michigan Press, 1964.

Buckingham, Willis J., Editor. *Emily Dickinson, an Annotated Bibliography: Writings, Criticism, 1850–1968.* Bloomington: Indiana University Press, 1970.

Cambon, G. "Emily Dickinson's Circumference," in *Sewanee Review.* LXXXIV (Spring, 1976), pp. 342–350.

Cuddy, L.A. "The Influence of Latin Poetics on Emily Dickinson's Style," in *Comparative Literature Studies.* XIII (Spring, 1976), pp. 214–229.

Diehl, J.F. "Emerson, Dickinson, and the Abyss," in *ELH.* XLIV (Winter, 1977), pp. 683–690.

Folsom, L.E. "Souls That Snow: Winter in the Poetry of Emily Dickinson," in *American Literature.* XLVII (November, 1975), pp. 361–376.

Ford, Thomas W. *Heaven Beguiles the Tired: Death in the Poetry of Emily Dickinson.* University: University of Alabama Press, 1966.

Francis, R. "Emily Dickinson," in *Critical Quarterly.* XIX (Spring, 1977), pp. 65–69.

Gelpi, Albert J. *Emily Dickinson, the Mind of the Poet.* Cambridge, Mass.: Harvard University Press, 1965.

Griffith, Clark. *The Long Shadow: Emily Dickinson's Tragic Poetry.* Princeton, N.J.: Princeton University Press, 1964.

Higgins, David. *Portrait of Emily Dickinson: The Poet and Her Prose.* New Brunswick, N.J.: Rutgers University Press, 1967.

Johnson, Thomas H. *Emily Dickinson, an Interpretative Biography.* Cambridge, Mass.: Harvard University Press, 1955.

Lindberg-Seyersted, Brita. *The Voice of the Poet: Aspects of Style in the Poetry of Emily Dickinson.* Cambridge, Mass.: Harvard University Press, 1968.

Miller, Ruth. *The Poetry of Emily Dickinson.* Middletown, Conn.: Wesleyan University Press, 1968.

Porter, David T. *The Art of Emily Dickinson's Early Poetry.* Cambridge, Mass.: Harvard University Press, 1966.

Sherwood, William Robert.   *Circumference and Circumstance: Stages in the Mind and Art of Emily Dickinson.* New York: Columbia University Press, 1968.

Taggard, Genevieve.   *The Life and Mind of Emily Dickinson.* New York: Knopf, 1930.

Ward, Theodora.   *The Capsule of the Mind, Chapters in the Life of Emily Dickinson.* Cambridge, Mass.: Harvard University Press, 1961.

Whicher, George Frisbie.   *This Was a Poet, a Critical Biography of Emily Dickinson.* New York: Scribner's, 1938.

JOAN DIDION
(1934–   )

Play It as It Lays

Davenport, Guy. "On the Edge of Being," in *National Review.* XXII (August 25, 1970), p. 903.

Geherin, David J. "Nothingness and Beyond: Joan Didion's *Play It as It Lays*," in *Critique: Studies in Modern Fiction.* XVI (1974), pp. 64–78.

Jones, D.A.N. "Divided Selves," in *New York Review of Books.* XV (October 22, 1970), pp. 38–42.

Samstag, Nicholas A. "*Play It as It Lays*," in *Saturday Review.* LIII (August 15, 1970), p. 27.

Schorer, Mark. "Novels and Nothingness," in *American Scholar.* XL (Winter, 1970–1971), pp. 168–174.

ISAK DINESEN
(1885–1962)

Anecdotes of Destiny

Arendt, Hannah. "Isak Dinesen: 1885–1962," in *New Yorker*. XLIV (November 9, 1968), pp. 223–236.

Howes, Barbara. "The Baroness Entertains," in *New Republic*. CXXXIX (November 24, 1958), p. 15.

Kennebeck, Edwin. "Destiny Refined," in *Commonweal*. LXIX (December 5, 1958), pp. 270–273.

Langbaum, Robert. *The Gayety of Vision: A Study of Isak Dinesen's Art.* London: Chatto and Windus, 1964, pp. 245–274.

Martin, Jean. "Have You Got a Story?," in *Nation*. CLXXXVII (November 8, 1958), pp. 345–346.

Migel, Parmenia. *Titania: The Biography of Isak Dinesen.* New York: Random House, 1967, pp. 216–218.

Redman, Ben Ray. "A Fabulist's Fine," in *Saturday Review*. XLI (October 25, 1958), pp. 28–29.

Whissen, Thomas R. *Isak Dinesen's Aesthetics.* Port Washington, N.Y.: Kennikat, 1973.

Last Tales

Arendt, Hannah. "Isak Dinesen: 1885–1962," in *New Yorker*. XLIV (November 9, 1968), pp. 223–236.

Gossman, Ann. "Sacramental Imagery in Two Stories by Isak Dinesen," in *Wisconsin Studies in Contemporary Literature*. IV (1963), pp. 319–326.

Green, Howard. "Isak Dinesen," in *Hudson Review*. XVII (Winter, 1965), pp. 517–530.

Johannesson, Eric O. *The World of Isak Dinesen.* Seattle: University of Washington Press, 1961, pp. 11–19, 42–44, 104–106, 120–125.

Langbaum, Robert. *The Gayety of Vision: A Study of Isak Dinesen's Art.* London: Chatto and Windus, 1964, pp. 197–244.

Lange, Victor. "Deceptive Cadenza," in *New Republic*. CXXXVII (November 18, 1957), pp. 17–18.

Migel, Parmenia. *Titania: The Biography of Isak Dinesen.* New York: Random House, 1967, pp. 204–205.

Sansom, William. "In the Heroic Tradition," in *Saturday Review*. XL (November 2, 1957), pp. 14–15.

Trilling, Lionel. "The Story and the Novel," in *Griffin*. VII (January, 1958), pp. 4–12.

Wescott, Glenway. "Isak Dinesen, the Storyteller," in *Images of Truth: Remembrances and Criticism*. New York: Harper & Row, 1962, pp. 156–159.

Whissen, Thomas R. "The Bow of the Lord: Isak Dinesen's 'Portrait of the Artist,' " in *Scandinavian Studies*. XLVI (Winter, 1974), pp. 47–58.

_____. *Isak Dinesen's Aesthetics*. Port Washington, N.Y.: Kennikat, 1973.

Out of Africa

Davenport, John. "A Noble Pride: The Art of Karen Blixen," in *Twentieth Century*. CLIX (March, 1956), pp. 264–274.

Davis, Hassoldt. "African Earth," in *Saturday Review of Literature*. XVII (March 5, 1938), p. 5.

Green, Howard. "Isak Dinesen," in *Hudson Review*. XVII (Winter, 1965), pp. 517–530.

Hannah, Donald. "In Memoriam Karen Blixen: Some Aspects of Her Attitude to Life," in *Sewanee Review*. LXXI (Autumn, 1963), pp. 585–604.

Johannesson, Eric O. *The World of Isak Dinesen*. Seattle: University of Washington Press, 1961, pp. 126–145.

Langbaum, Robert. *The Gayety of Vision: A Study of Isak Dinesen's Art*. London: Chatto and Windus, 1964, pp. 119–148.

Lessing, Doris. "A Deep Darkness: A Review of *Out of Africa* by Karen Blixen," in *A Small Personal Voice: Essays, Reviews, Interviews*. Edited by Paul Schlueter. New York: Knopf, 1974, pp. 147–152.

Lewis, Janet. "Isak Dinesen: An Appreciation," in *Southern Review*. II (April, 1966), pp. 297–314.

McCullers, Carson. "Isak Dinesen: In Praise of Radiance," in *The Mortgaged Heart*. Edited by Margarita G. Smith. Boston: Houghton Mifflin, 1971, pp. 269–273.

Migel, Parmenia. *Titania: The Biography of Isak Dinesen*. New York: Random House, 1967, pp. 106–113.

Mitchell, Philip M. *A History of Danish Literature*. Copenhagen, Denmark: Gyldendal, 1957, pp. 275–278.

Spacks, Patricia Meyer. *The Female Imagination*. New York: Knopf, 1975, pp. 299–304.

Van Doren, Mark. "The Eighth Gothic Tale," in *Nation*. CXLVI (March 12, 1938), p. 306. Reprinted in *The Private Reader*. New York: Holt, 1942, pp. 277–281.

Wescott, Glenway. "Isak Dinesen, the Storyteller," in *Images of Truth: Remembrances and Criticism*. New York: Harper & Row, 1962, pp. 152–155.

Seven Gothic Tales

Arendt, Hannah. "Isak Dinesen," in her *Men in Dark Times*. New York: Harcourt, Brace and World, 1968, pp. 106–109.

Benét, William Rose. "A Danish Genius," in *Saturday Review of Literature*. X (April 14, 1934), p. 627.

Bogan, Louise. "Isak Dinesen," in her *Selected Criticism: Prose, Poetry*. New York: Noonday, 1955, pp. 231–234.

Canfield, Dorothy. "Introduction," in *Seven Gothic Tales*. New York: Harrison Smith and Robert Haas, 1934, pp. v–x.

Cate, Curtis. "Isak Dinesen: The Scheherazade of Our Times," in *Cornhill Magazine*. CLXXI (Winter, 1959–1960), pp. 120–137.

Davenport, John. "A Noble Pride: The Art of Karen Blixen," in *Twentieth Century*. CLIX (March, 1956), pp. 264–274.

Green, Howard. "Isak Dinesen," in *Hudson Review*. XVII (Winter, 1965), pp. 517–530.

Johannesson, Eric O. *The World of Isak Dinesen*. Seattle: University of Washington Press, 1961.

Langbaum, Robert. *The Gayety of Vision: A Study of Isak Dinesen's Art*. London: Chatto and Windus, 1964, pp. 73–118.

Lewis, Janet. "Isak Dinesen: An Appreciation," in *Southern Review*. II (April, 1966), pp. 297–314.

Madsen, Børge G. "Isak Dinesen, A Modern Aristocrat," in *American-Scandinavian Review*. XLI (Winter, 1953), pp. 328–332.

Migel, Parmenia. *Titania: The Biography of Isak Dinesen*. New York: Random House, 1967, pp. 93–100.

Mitchell, Philip M. *A History of Danish Literature*. Copenhagen: Gyldendal, 1957, pp. 275–278.

Saul, George Brandon. "Daughter of Vikings: An Essay on Isak Dinesen," in *Arizona Quarterly*. XV (Autumn, 1959), pp. 240–245. Reprinted in his *Withdrawn in Gold: Three Commentaries on Genius*. The Hague: Mouton, 1970, pp. 42–48.

Whissen, Thomas R. "The Bow of the Lord: Isak Dinesen's 'Portrait of the Artist,' " in *Scandinavian Studies*. XLVI (Winter, 1974), pp. 47–58.

————. *Isak Dinesen's Aesthetics*. Port Washington, N.Y.: Kennikat, 1973.

Winter's Tales

Bogan, Louise. "Isak Dinesen," in *Nation*. CLXI (June 26, 1943), pp. 894–895.

Burt, Struthers. "The Fine Wine of Isak Dinesen," in *Saturday Review of Literature*. XXVI (May 15, 1943), pp. 5, 34.

Davenport, John. "A Noble Pride: The Art of Karen Blixen," in *Twentieth Century*. CLIX (March, 1956), pp. 264–274.

Green, Howard. "Isak Dinesen," in *Hudson Review*. XVII (Winter, 1965), pp. 517–530.

Hannah, Donald. "In Memoriam Karen Blixen: Some Aspects of Her Attitude to Life," in *Sewanee Review*. LXXI (Autumn, 1963), pp. 585–604.

Harrington, David V. "Isak Dinesen's 'Alkmene,' " in *Discourse*. IX (1966), pp. 471–480.

Johannesson, Eric O. *The World of Isak Dinesen*. Seattle: University of Washington Press, 1961.

Langbaum, Robert. *The Gayety of Vision: A Study of Isak Dinesen's Art*. London: Chatto and Windus, 1964, pp. 155–196.

McCullers, Carson. "Isak Dinesen, Denmark: *Winter's Tales*," in *New Republic*. CVIII (June 7, 1943), p. 768. Reprinted in *The Mortgaged Heart*. Edited by Margarita G. Smith. Boston: Houghton Mifflin, 1971, pp. 266–268.

Migel, Parmenia. *Titania: The Biography of Isak Dinesen*. N.Y.: Random House, 1967, pp. 122–126.

Mitchell, Philip M. *A History of Danish Literature*. Copenhagen, Denmark: Gyldendal, 1957, pp. 275–278.

Trilling, Lionel. "On 'The Sailor-Boys' Tale,' " in *The Experience of Literature*. New York: Holt, Rinehart and Winston, 1967, pp. 723–725.

Whissen, Thomas R. *Isak Dinesen's Aesthetics*. Port Washington, N.Y.: Kennikat, 1973.

J.P. DONLEAVY
(1926–   )

The Beastly Beatitudes of Balthazar B.

Deedy, John. *"The Beastly Beatitudes of Balthazar B.,"* in *Commonweal.* LXXXIX (March 7, 1969), p. 710.

Kaye, Howard. "The Old and the New," in *New Republic.* CLX (March 1, 1969), pp. 22–25.

LeClair, Thomas. "A Case of Death: The Fiction of J.P. Donleavy," in *Contemporary Literature.* XII (Summer, 1971), pp. 329–344.

Masinton, Charles G. *J.P. Donleavy: The Style of His Sadness and Humor.* Bowling Green, Oh.: Bowling Green University Popular Press, 1975, pp. 54–59.

O'Connell, Shaun. "Joey and Sebastian Grow Up," in *Nation.* CCVIII (January 20, 1969), pp. 85–86.

Scholes, Robert. "Of Life and Laughter, Death and Loneliness," in *Saturday Review.* LI (November 23, 1968), pp. 64–65.

The Ginger Man

Allsop, Kenneth. *The Angry Decade: A Survey of the Cultural Revolt of the Nineteen-fifties.* New York: British Book Centre, 1958, pp. 73–75.

Corrigan, Robert A. "The Artist as Censor: J.P. Donleavy and *The Ginger Man*," in *Midcontinent American Studies Journal.* VIII (Spring, 1967), pp. 60–72.

Curley, Thomas F. "Fool, Rogue, Philosopher," in *Commonweal.* LXVIII (August 15, 1958), pp. 500–502.

Hassan, Ihab. *Radical Innocence: Studies in the Contemporary American Novel.* Princeton, N.J.: Princeton University Press, 1961, pp. 194–200.

Hicks, Granville. *"The Ginger Man,"* in *Saturday Review.* XLI (May 10, 1958), pp. 10, 31–32.

LeClair, Thomas. "A Case of Death: The Fiction of J.P. Donleavy," in *Contemporary Literature.* XII (Summer, 1971), pp. 329–344.

Malcolm, Donald. "The Lout's Progress," in *New Yorker.* XXXIV (October 25, 1958), pp. 194–198.

Masinton, Charles G. *J.P. Donleavy: The Style of His Sadness and Humor.* Bowling Green, Oh.: Bowling Green University Popular Press, 1975, pp. 5–25.

Mercier, Vivian. "The Fool-Rogue," in *Nation.* CLXXXVI (May 24, 1958), p. 480.

Morris, William E. "J.P. Donleavy's Wild Gingerbread Man: Antichrist and Crazy Cookie," in *USF Language Quarterly*. VI (Spring–Summer, 1968), pp. 41–42.

Morse, Donald E. " 'The Skull Beneath the Skin': J.P. Donleavy's *The Ginger Man*," in *Michigan Academician*. VI (1974), pp. 273–280.

Podhoretz, Norman. *Doings and Undoings: The Fifties and After in American Writing.* New York: Farrar, Straus and Giroux, 1964, pp. 168–170.

Sherman, William D. "J.P. Donleavy: Anarchic Man as Dying Dionysian," in *Twentieth Century Literature*. XIII (January, 1968), pp. 216–221.

Widmer, Kingsley. *The Literary Rebel.* Carbondale: Southern Illinois University Press, 1965, pp. 136–139.

A Singular Man

Adler, Renata. "Conversation," in *New Yorker*. XL (May 16, 1964), pp. 203–204.

Algren, Nelson. "What Happened?," in *Nation*. CXCVII (December 14, 1963), pp. 422–423.

Allan, Donald A. "The Nuts That Bolt," in *Reporter*. XXX (January 30, 1964), p. 56.

Corke, Hilary. "A Singular Author," in *New Republic*. CXLIX (December 14, 1963), pp. 22–25.

Hicks, Granville. "Plenty of Room at the Tomb," in *Saturday Review*. XLVI (November 23, 1963), pp. 37–38.

LeClair, Thomas. "A Case of Death: The Fiction of J.P. Donleavy," in *Contemporary Literature*. XII (Summer, 1971), pp. 329–344.

Masinton, Charles G. *J.P. Donleavy: The Style of His Sadness and Humor.* Bowling Green, Oh.: Bowling Green University Popular Press, 1975, pp. 26–44.

Moore, John R. "Hard Times and the Noble Savage: J.P. Donleavy's *A Singular Man*," in *The Sounder Few: Essays from The Hollins Critic*. Edited by R.H.W. Dillard, George Garrett, and John R. Moore. Athens: University of Georgia Press, 1971, pp. 3–17.

Sherman, William D. "J.P. Donleavy: Anarchic Man as Dying Dionysian," in *Twentieth Century Literature*. XIII (January, 1968), pp. 221–224.

Weales, Gerald. "J.P. Donleavy," in *Contemporary American Novelists*. Carbondale: Southern Illinois University Press, 1964, pp. 153–154.

JOHN DONNE
(1572–1631)

"Batter My Heart"

Clements, Arthur L. "Donne's 'Holy Sonnet XIV,' " in *Modern Language Notes*. LXXVI (June, 1961), pp. 484–489.

Cornelius, David K. "Donne's 'Holy Sonnet XIV,' " in *Explicator*. XXIV (1965), item 25.

Drew, Elizabeth. *Poetry: A Modern Guide to Its Understanding and Enjoyment*. New York: Norton, 1959, pp. 58–60.

Leishman, J.B. *The Monarch of Wit: An Analytical and Comparative Study of the Poetry of John Donne*. London: Hutchinson, 1965, pp. 266–268.

Louthan, Doniphan. *The Poetry of John Donne: A Study in Explication*. New York: Bookman, 1951, pp. 123–125.

Mueller, William R. "Donne's Adulterous Female Town," in *Modern Language Notes*. LXXVI (April, 1961), pp. 312–314.

Parish, John E. "No. 14 of Donne's *Holy Sonnets*," in *College English*. XXIV (January, 1963), pp. 299–302.

Roston, Murray. *The Soul of Wit: A Study of John Donne*. Oxford: Clarendon Press, 1974, pp. 172–175.

Sanders, Wilbur. *John Donne's Poetry*. Cambridge: Cambridge University Press, 1971, pp. 129–131.

Schwartz, Elias. "Donne's *Holy Sonnets*, XIV," in *Explicator*. XXVI (1967), item 27.

Stauffer, Donald A. *The Nature of Poetry*. New York: Norton, 1946, pp. 135–136.

Untermeyer, Louis. *Play in Poetry*. New York: Harcourt, Brace, 1938, pp. 15–18.

Winny, James. *A Preface to Donne*. London: Longmans, 1970, pp. 140–143.

"The Canonization"

Andreasen, N.J.C. *John Donne: Conservative Revolutionary*. Princeton, N.J.: Princeton University Press, 1967, pp. 160–168.

Brooks, Cleanth. *The Well Wrought Urn*. New York: Harcourt, Brace and World, 1947, pp. 10–17. Reprinted in *John Donne: A Collection of Critical Essays*. Edited by Helen Gardner. Englewood Cliffs, N.J.: Prentice-Hall, 1962, pp. 100–108.

Chambers, A.B. "The Fly in Donne's 'Canonization,' " in *Journal of English and Germanic Philology*. LXV (April, 1966), pp. 252–259.

Clair, John A. Donne's 'The Canonization,' " in *PMLA*. LXXX (June, 1965), pp. 300–302.

Collins, Carvel. "Canonization," in *Explicator*. XII (October, 1953), item 3.

Corin, Fernand. "A Note on Donne's 'Canonization,' " in *English Studies*. L (February, 1969), pp. 89–93.

Daiches, David and William Charvat. *Poems in English, 1530–1940*. New York: Ronald Press, 1950, pp. 657–658.

Duncan, Edgar Hill. "Donne's Alchemical Figures," in *English Literary History*. IX (1942), pp. 257–285. Reprinted in *Discussion of John Donne*. Edited by Frank Kermode. Boston: D.C. Heath, 1962, pp. 73–89.

Guss, Donald L. "Donne's Petrarchism," in *Journal of English and Germanic Philology*. LXIV (1965), pp. 17–28.

Hunt, Clay. *Donne's Poetry: Essays in Literary Analysis*. Hamden, Conn.: Archon, 1969, pp. 72–95.

Krieger, Murray. *The New Apologists for Poetry*. Minneapolis: University of Minnesota Press, 1956, pp. 13–18.

Legouis, Pierre. *Donne the Craftsman*. Paris: Henry Didier, 1928, pp. 55–61.

Leishman, J.E. *The Monarch of Wit: An Analytical and Comparative Study of the Poetry of John Donne*. London: Hutchinson's, 1965, pp. 214–216.

Rooney, William J. " 'The Canonization'—the Language of Paradox Reconsidered," in *English Literary History*. XXIII (March, 1956), pp. 36–47.

Sanders, Wilbur. *John Donne's Poetry*. Cambridge: Cambridge University Press, 1971, pp. 21–25, 50–56.

Stampfer, Judah. *John Donne and the Metaphysical Gesture*. New York: Funk and Wagnalls, 1970, pp. 153–156.

Unger, Leonard. *The Man in the Name: Essays on the Experience of Poetry*. Minneapolis: University of Minnesota Press, 1956, pp. 49–53.

Williamson, George. *Six Metaphysical Poets: A Reader's Guide*. New York: Noonday, 1967, pp. 60–61.

Wilson, G.R., Jr. "The Interplay of Perception and Reflection: Mirror Imagery in Donne's Poetry," in *Studies in English Literature*. IX (Winter, 1969), pp. 113–115.

"The Extasie"

Adams, Robert M. *Strains of Discord: Studies in Literary Openness*. Ithaca, N.Y.: Cornell University Press, 1958, pp. 108–109.

Andreasen, N.J.C. *John Donne: Conservative Revolutionary*. Princeton, N.J.: Princeton University Press, 1967, pp. 168–178.

Brower, Reuben Arthur. *The Fields of Light: An Experiment in Critical Reading.* New York: Oxford University Press, 1951, pp. 79–83.

Doggett, Frank A. "Donne's Platonism," in *Sewanee Review.* XLII (July–September, 1934), pp. 284–290.

Empson, William. "Donne the Space Man," in *Kenyon Review.* XIX (Summer, 1957), pp. 368–369.

_____. *English Pastoral Poetry.* New York: Norton, 1938, pp. 132–136.

Gransden, K.W. *John Donne.* Hamden, Conn.: Archon Books, 1969, pp. 74–76.

Graziani, Rene. "John Donne's 'The Extasie' and Ecstacy," in *Review of English Studies.* XIX (May, 1968), pp. 121–136.

Louthan, Doniphan. *The Poetry of John Donne: A Study in Explication.* New York: Bookman, 1951, pp. 84–94.

McCanles, Michael. "Distinguish in Order to Unite: Donne's 'The Extasie,' " in *Studies in English Literature.* VI (Winter, 1966), pp. 59–65.

Marshall, John. "The Extasie," in *Hound and Horn.* III (October–December, 1929), pp. 121–124.

Mitchell, Charles. "Donne's 'The Extasie': Love's Sublime Knot," in *Studies in English Literature.* VIII (Winter, 1968), pp. 91–101.

Sanders, Wilbur. *John Donne's Poetry.* Cambridge: Cambridge University Press, 1971, pp. 96–104.

Spitzer, Leo. *A Method of Interpreting Literature.* Northampton, Mass.: Smith College Press, 1949, pp. 5–21.

Stampfer, Judah. *John Donne and the Metaphysical Gesture.* New York: Funk and Wagnalls, 1970, pp. 127–136.

Stauffer, Donald A. *The Nature of Poetry.* New York: Norton, 1947, pp. 219–221.

Tillyard, E.M.W. *The Metaphysicals and Milton.* London: Chatto and Windus, 1956, pp. 79–84.

Turnell, Martin. "John Donne and the Quest for Unity," in *Nineteenth Century.* CXLVII (April, 1950), pp. 267–268.

Wheelwright, Philip. *The Burning Fountain: A Study in the Language of Symbolism.* Bloomington: Indiana University Press, 1954, pp. 72–73.

Williamson, George. *Six Metaphysical Poets: A Reader's Guide.* New York: Noonday, 1967, pp. 73–74.

Wilson, G.R., Jr. "The Interplay of Perception and Reflection: Mirror Imagery in Donne's Poetry," in *Studies in English Literature.* IX (Winter, 1969), pp. 111–113.

Winny, James. *A Preface to Donne.* London: Longmans, 1970, pp. 88–89.

"The Flea"

Gransden, K.W. *John Donne.* Hamden, Conn: Archon Books, 1969, pp. 64–65.

Legouis, Pierre. *Donne the Craftsman: An Essay Upon the Structure of the Songs and Sonnets.* Paris: Henri Didier, 1928, pp. 71–79. Reprinted in *John Donne: A Collection of Critical Essays.* Edited by Helen Gardner. Englewood Cliffs, N.J.: Prentice-Hall, 1962, pp. 47–48.

Leishman, J.B. *The Monarch of Wit: An Analytical and Comparative Study of the Poetry of John Donne.* London: Hutchinson's, 1965, pp. 164–166.

Louthan, Doniphan. *The Poetry of John Donne: A Study in Explication.* New York: Bookman, 1951, pp. 81–84.

Madison, Arthur L. "Explication of John Donne's 'The Flea,' " in *Notes and Queries.* IV (1957), pp. 60–61.

O'Connor, William Van. "Nature and the Anti-Poetic in Modern Poetry," in *Journal of Aesthetics and Art Criticism.* V (1946), pp. 35–44.

Richmond, H.M. *The School of Love: The Evolution of the Stuart Love Lyric.* Princeton, N.J.: Princeton University Press, 1964, pp. 16–17.

Roston, Murray. *The Soul of Wit: A Study of John Donne.* Oxford: Clarendon Press, 1974, pp. 108–112.

Stauffer, Donald A. *The Nature of Poetry.* New York: Norton, 1947, pp. 151–153.

Tuve, Rosemond. *Elizabethan and Metaphysical Imagery.* Chicago: University of Chicago Press, 1947, pp. 172–173.

Unger, Leonard. *The Man in the Name: Essays on the Experience of Poetry.* Minneapolis: University of Minnesota Press, 1956, pp. 79–80.

Untermeyer, Louis. *Play in Poetry.* New York: Harcourt, Brace, 1938, pp. 13–15.

Winny, James. *A Preface to Donne.* London: Longmans, 1970, pp. 126–128.

"Good Friday, 1613, Riding Westward"

Barnes, T.R. *English Verse: Voice and Movement from Wyatt to Yeats.* Cambridge: Cambridge University Press, 1967, pp. 70–72.

Beck, Rosalie. "A Precedent for Donne's Imagery in 'Good Friday, 1613, Riding Westward,' " in *Review of English Studies.* XIX (May, 1968), pp. 166–169.

Bellette, Antony F. " 'Little Worlds Made Cunningly': Significant Form in Donne's *Holy Sonnets* and 'Good Friday, 1613,' " in *Studies in Philology.* LXXII (1975), pp. 322–347.

Chambers, A.B. " 'Good Friday, 1613, Riding Westward': The Poem and the Tradition," in *English Literary History.* XXVIII (1961), pp. 31–53. Reprinted in *Essential Articles for the Study of John Donne's Poetry*. Edited by John R. Roberts. Hamden, Conn.: Archon Books, 1975, pp. 333–348.

Francis, W. Nelson. "Good Friday, 1613," in *Explicator*. XIII (February, 1955), item 21.

Herman, George. "Good Friday, 1613," in *Explicator*. XIV (June, 1956), item 60.

Martz, Louis L. *The Poetry of Meditation: A Study in English Religious Literature*. New Haven, Conn.: Yale University Press, 1954, pp. 54–56.

Rosenthal, M.L. and A.J.M. Smith. *Exploring Poetry*. New York: Macmillan, 1955, pp. 479–483.

Roston, Murray. *The Soul of Wit: A Study of John Donne*. Oxford: Clarendon Press, 1974, pp. 205–209.

Stampfer, Judah. *John Donne and the Metaphysical Gesture*. New York: Funk and Wagnalls, 1970, pp. 278–283.

Williamson, George. *Six Metaphysical Poets: A Reader's Guide*. New York: Noonday, 1967, pp. 88–90.

"The Good-Morrow"

Andreasen, N.J.C. *John Donne: Conservative Revolutionary*. Princeton, N.J.: Princeton University Press, 1967, pp. 215–218.

Brooks, Cleanth, John T. Purser and Robert Penn Warren. *An Approach to Literature*. New York: Crofts, 1952, pp. 374–376.

Daiches, David and William Charvat. *Poems in English, 1530–1940*. New York: Ronald Press, 1950, pp. 656–657.

Empson, William. "Donne the Space Man," in *Kenyon Review*. XIX (Summer, 1957), pp. 358–362.

Hunt, Clay. *Donne's Poetry: Essays in Literary Analysis*. Hamden, Conn.: Archon Books, 1969, pp. 53–71.

Leishman, J.B. *The Monarch of Wit: An Analytical and Comparative Study of the Poetry of John Donne*. London: Hutchinson's, 1965, pp. 200–201, 204.

Sanders, Wilbur. *John Donne's Poetry*. Cambridge: Cambridge University Press, 1971, pp. 58–59, 64–68.

Smith, James. "On Metaphysical Poetry," in *Scrutiny*. II (December, 1933), pp. 229–230.

Stampfer, Judah. *John Donne and the Metaphysical Gesture*. New York: Funk and Wagnalls, 1970, pp. 141–151.

Stein, Arnold. *John Donne's Lyrics: The Eloquence of Action*. Minneapolis: University of Minnesota Press, 1962, pp. 65–77.

Unger, Leonard. *The Man in the Name: Essays on the Experience of Poetry.* Minneapolis: University of Minnesota Press, 1956, pp. 46–49.

Williamson, George. *Six Metaphysical Poets: A Reader's Guide.* New York: Noonday, 1967, pp. 58–59.

Wilson, G.R., Jr. "The Interplay of Perception and Reflection: Mirror Imagery in Donne's Poetry," in *Studies in English Literature.* IX (Winter, 1969), pp. 109–111.

"A Valediction: Forbidding Mourning"

Adams, Robert M. *Strains of Discord: Studies in Literary Openness.* Ithaca, N.Y.: Cornell University Press, 1958, pp. 109–111.

Andreasen, N.J.C. *John Donne: Conservative Revolutionary.* Princeton, N.J.: Princeton University Press, 1967, pp. 223–229.

Barnes, T.R. *English Verse: Voice and Movement from Wyatt to Yeats.* Cambridge: Cambridge University Press, 1967, pp. 61–64.

Brooks, Cleanth. *The Well Wrought Urn.* New York: Reynal and Hitchcock, 1947, pp. 222–223.

Ciardi, John. *How Does a Poem Mean?* Boston: Houghton Mifflin, 1959, pp. 873–875.

Daniels, Earl. *The Art of Reading Poetry.* New York: Farrar and Rinehart, 1941, pp. 213–216.

Duncan, Edgar H. "Valediction," in *Explicator.* I (June, 1943), item 63.

Empson, William. "Donne the Space Man," in *Kenyon Review.* XIX (Summer, 1957), pp. 391–394.

Foxell, Nigel. *Ten Poems Analyzed.* Oxford: Pergamon, 1966, pp. 1–12.

Freccero, John. "Donne's 'Valediction: Forbidding Mourning,' " in *English Literary History.* XXX (1963), pp. 335–376. Reprinted in *Essential Articles for the Study of John Donne's Poetry.* Edited by John R. Roberts. Hamden, Conn.: Archon Books, 1975, pp. 279–304.

Gransden, K.W. *John Donne.* Hamden, Conn.: Archon Books, 1969, pp. 34–36.

Kreuzer, James R. *Elements of Poetry.* New York: Macmillan, 1955, pp. 84–86.

Louthan, Donophan. *The Poetry of John Donne: A Study in Explication.* New York: Bookman, 1951, pp. 46–50.

Millett, Fred B. *Reading Poetry.* New York: Harper, 1950, pp. 62–63.

Roston, Murray. *The Soul of Wit: A Study of John Donne.* Oxford: Clarendon Press, 1974, pp. 122–125.

Sanders, Wilbur. *John Donne's Poetry.* Cambridge: Cambridge University Press, 1971, pp. 83–89.

Smith, James. "On Metaphysical Poetry," in *Scrutiny.* II (December, 1933), pp. 230–231.

Stampfer, Judah. *John Donne and the Metaphysical Gesture.* New York: Funk and Wagnalls, 1970, pp. 162–165.

Stein, Arnold. "Structures of Sound in Donne's Verse," in *Kenyon Review.* XII (Spring, 1951), pp. 267–268.

Tate, Allen. "The Point of Dying: Donne's 'Virtuous Men,'" in *Sewanee Review.* LXI (Winter, 1953), pp. 76–81.

————. "Tension in Poetry," in *Southern Review.* IV (Summer, 1938), pp. 109–111. Reprinted in *Reason in Madness.* New York: Putnams, 1941, pp. 73–75, 90–91.

Unger, Leonard. *The Man in the Name: Essays on the Experience of Poetry.* Minneapolis: University of Minnesota Press, 1956, pp. 73–74.

Wheelwright, Philip. *The Burning Fountain: A Study in the Language of Symbolism.* Bloomington: Indiana University Press, 1954, pp. 103–104.

Williamson, George. *Six Metaphysical Poets: A Reader's Guide.* New York: Noonday, 1967, pp. 72–73.

Winny, James. *A Preface to Donne.* London: Longmans, 1970, pp. 136–140.

JOHN DOS PASSOS
(1896–1970)

Manhattan Transfer

Arden, Eugene. "*Manhattan Transfer*: An Experiment in Technique," in *University of Kansas City Review*. XXII (Winter, 1955), pp. 153–158.

Beach, Joseph Warren. *American Fiction, 1920–1940*. New York: Russell and Russell, 1960, pp. 35–44, 47–52.

Brantley, John D. *The Fiction of John Dos Passos*. The Hague: Mouton, 1968, pp. 45–54.

Canby, Henry Seidel. "Thunder in Manhattan," in *Saturday Review*. II (January 16, 1926), pp. 489, 495.

Diggins, John P. "Dos Passos and Veblen's Villains," in *Antioch Review*. XXIII (Winter, 1963–1964), pp. 492–496.

Frohock, Wilbur M. *The Novel of Violence in America*. Second Edition, Revised and Enlarged. Dallas: Southern Methodist University Press, 1957, pp. 36–43.

Gelfant, Blanche Housman. "Technique as Social Commentary in *Manhattan Transfer*," in *The American City Novel*. Norman: University of Oklahoma Press, 1954, pp. 138–166.

Henderson, Philip. *The Novel Today: Studies in Contemporary Attitudes*. London: John Lane, 1936, pp. 130–136.

Hughson, Lois. "Narration in the Making of *Manhattan Transfer*," in *Studies in the Novel*. VIII (1976), pp. 185–198.

Lane, James B. "*Manhattan Transfer* as a Gateway to the Twenties," in *Centennial Review*. XVI (1972), pp. 293–311.

Lewis, Sinclair. "Manhattan at Last!," in *Saturday Review*. II (December 5, 1925), p. 361.

Lowry, E.A. "*Manhattan Transfer*: Dos Passos' Wasteland," in *University Review*. XXX (1963), pp. 47–52.

Lowry, Edward D. "The Lively Art of *Manhattan Transfer*," in *PMLA*. LXXXIV (1969), pp. 1628–1638.

Ruoff, Gene W. "Social Mobility and the Artist in *Manhattan Transfer* and *The Music of Time*," in *Wisconsin Studies in Contemporary Literature*. V (Winter–Spring, 1964), pp. 64–76.

Wrenn, John H. *John Dos Passos*. New York: Twayne, 1961, pp. 121–131.

Midcentury

Brantley, John D. *The Fiction of John Dos Passos*. The Hague: Mouton, 1968, pp. 122–126.

Chase, Richard. "The Chronicles of Dos Passos," in *Commentary*. XXXI (May, 1961), pp. 396–398.

Davis, Robert G. *John Dos Passos*. Minneapolis: University of Minnesota Press, 1962, pp. 39–44.

Hicks, Granville. "*Midcentury*," in *Saturday Review*. XLIV (February 25, 1961), p. 2.

Moore, H.T. "Dos Passos' *Midcentury*," in *New York Times Book Review*. (February 26, 1961), p. 1.

Rolo, Charles. "Dos Passos' *Midcentury*," in *Atlantic*. CCVII (March, 1961), p. 112.

Rowland, S.J. "Dos Passos' *Midcentury*," in *Christian Century*. LXXVIII (May 24, 1961), p. 653.

Vidal, Gore. *Homage to Daniel Shays: Collected Essays, 1952–1972*. New York: Random House, 1972, pp. 96–102.

Three Soldiers

Brantley, John D. *The Fiction of John Dos Passos*. The Hague: Mouton, 1968, pp. 21–36.

Canby, Henry Seidel. "*Three Soldiers*," in *Literary Review*. (October 8, 1921), p. 67.

Cooperman, Stanley. *World War I and the American Novel*. Baltimore: Johns Hopkins Press, 1967, pp. 152–155, 175–181.

Dawson, Coningsby. "Dos Passos' *Three Soldiers*," in the *New York Times Book Review*. (October 2, 1921), p. 1.

Frohock, Wilbur M. *The Novel of Violence in America*. Second Edition, Revised and Enlarged. Dallas: Southern Methodist University Press, 1957, pp. 31–36.

Hackett, Francis. "Dos Passos' *Three Soldiers*," in *New Republic*. XXVIII (October 5, 1921), p. 162.

Hoffman, Frederick J. "I Had Seen Nothing Sacred," in *The Twenties: American Writing in the Post War Decade*. New York: Viking, 1955, pp. 57–61.

Howard, Sidney. "*Three Soldiers*," in *Survey*. XLVII (November 5, 1921), p. 221.

West, Thomas Reed. *Flesh of Steel: Literature and the Machine in American Culture*. Nashville, Tenn.: Vanderbilt University Press, 1967, pp. 59–62.

Wrenn, John H. *John Dos Passos*. New York: Twayne, 1961, pp. 108–117.

U.S.A.

Aldridge, John W. *After the Lost Generation*. New York: McGraw-Hill, 1951, pp. 71–77.

Allen, Walter. *The Modern Novel in Britain and the United States.* New York: Dutton, 1964, pp. 144–148.

Beach, Joseph Warren. *American Fiction, 1920–1940.* New York: Russell and Russell, 1960, pp. 52–66.

Blake, Nelson Manfred. *Novelist's America: Fiction as History, 1910–1940.* Syracuse, N.Y.: Syracuse University Press, 1969, pp. 168–183.

Brantley, John D. *The Fiction of John Dos Passos.* The Hague: Mouton, 1968, pp. 55–78.

Cowley, Malcolm. "The Poet Against the World," in *After the Genteel Tradition: American Writers, 1910–1930.* Carbondale: Southern Illinois University Press, 1964, pp. 134–146.

Davis, Robert G. *John Dos Passos.* Minneapolis: University of Minnesota Press, 1962, pp. 21–31.

Feied, Frederick. *No Pie in the Sky: The Hobo as American Cultural Hero in the Works of Jack London, John Dos Passos and Jack Kerouac.* New York: Citadel, 1964, pp. 41–56.

Geismar, Maxwell. *Writers in Crisis: The American Novel, 1925–1940.* Revised Edition. Boston: Houghton Mifflin, 1961, pp. 109–120, 123–130.

Gelfant, Blanche Housman. *The American City Novel.* Norman: University of Oklahoma Press, 1954, pp. 166–174.

Goldman, Arnold. "Dos Passos and His U.S.A.," in *New Literary History.* I (1970), pp. 471–483.

Gurko, Leo. "John Dos Passos' *U.S.A.*: A 1930's Spectacular," in *Proletarian Writers of the Thirties.* Edited by David Madden. Carbondale: Southern Illinois University Press, 1968, pp. 46–63.

Hoffman, Arnold R. "An Element of Structure in *U.S.A.*," in *CEA Critic.* XXXI (October, 1968), pp. 12–13.

Knox, George. "Voice in the *U.S.A.* Biographies," in *Texas Studies in Literature and Language.* IV (1962), pp. 109–116.

Lydenberg, John. "Dos Passos' *U.S.A.*: The Words of Hollow Men," in *Essays on Determinism in American Literature.* Edited by Sydney J. Frause. Kent, Oh.: Kent State University Press, 1964, pp. 97–107.

Magney, Claude-Edmonde. "Dos Passos' *U.S.A.*, or the Impersonal Novel," in *The Age of the American Novel: The Film Aesthetic of Fiction Between the Two Wars.* Translated by Eleanor Hochman. New York: Frederick Ungar, 1972, pp. 105–123.

Maynard, Reid. "John Dos Passos' One-Sided Panorama," in *Discourse.* XI (Autumn, 1968), pp. 468–474.

Millgate, Michael. *American Social Fiction: James to Cozzens.* New York: Barnes & Noble, 1965, pp. 130–135.

Sanders, David, Editor.   *Studies in* U.S.A. Columbus, Oh.: Charles E. Merrill, 1971.

Schwartz, Delmore.   "John Dos Passos and the Whole Truth," in *Southern Review*. IV (Autumn, 1938), pp. 351–365.

Smith, James S.   "The Novelist of Discomfort: A Reconsideration of John Dos Passos," in *College English*. XIX (May, 1958), pp. 332–338.

Walcutt, Charles Child.   *American Literary Naturalism, A Divided Stream.* Minneapolis: University of Minnesota Press, 1956, pp. 283–289.

Widmer, Eleanor.   "The Lost Girls of *U.S.A.*: Dos Passos' Thirties Movie," in *The Thirties: Fiction, Poetry, Drama.* Edited by Warren French. Deland, Fla.: Everett/Edwards, 1967, pp. 11–19.

Wrenn, John H.   *John Dos Passos.* New York: Twayne, 1961, pp. 154–166.

FYODOR MIKHAILOVICH DOSTOEVSKI
(1821–1881)

The Brothers Karamazov

Amend, Victor E. "Theme and Form in *The Brothers Karamazov*," in *Modern Fiction Studies*. IV (Autumn, 1958), pp. 240–252.

Baring, Maurice. *Landmarks in Russian Literature*. London: Methuen, 1910, pp. 240–250.

Calder, Angus. "Revolt and the Golden Age: Dostoevsky's Later Fiction," in *Russia Discovered: Nineteenth-Century Fiction from Pushkin to Chekhov*. New York: Barnes & Noble, 1976, pp. 173–208.

Carr, Edward Hallett. *Dostoevsky: A New Biography*. New York: Houghton Mifflin, 1931, pp. 281–301.

Gifford, Henry. *The Novel in Russia: From Pushkin to Pasternak*. New York: Harper & Row, 1964, pp. 106–117.

Hesse, Hermann. "*The Brothers Karamazov*, or, The Decline of Europe," in *My Belief: Essays on Life and Art*. Edited by Theodore Ziolkowski. New York: Farrar, Straus and Giroux, 1974, pp. 70–85.

Hingley, Ronald. *The Undiscovered Dostoyevsky*. London: Hamish Hamilton, 1962, pp. 195–228.

Holquist, Michael. *Dostoevsky and the Novel*. Princeton, N.J.: Princeton University Press, 1977, pp. 165–192.

Jones, Malcolm V. *Dostoyevsky: The Novel of Discord*. New York: Barnes & Noble, 1976, pp. 166–193.

Jones, Peter. "The Self and Others in *The Brothers Karamazov*," in *Philosophy and the Novel: Philosophical Aspects of* Middlemarch, Anna Karenina, The Brothers Karamazov, A la Recherche du Temps Perdu, *and of the Methods of Criticism*. New York: Oxford University Press, 1975, pp. 112–146.

Kellogg, Bene. *Dark Prophets of Hope: Dostoevsky, Sartre, Camus, Faulkner*. Chicago: Loyola University Press, 1975, pp. 16–53.

Lavrin, Janko. *Dostoevsky: A Study*. New York: Macmillan, 1947, pp. 119–146.

Maugham, W. Somerset. *Great Novelists and Their Novels*. Philadelphia: Winston, 1948, pp. 185–208.

Muchnic, Helen. *An Introduction to Russian Literature*. New York: Doubleday, 1947, pp. 165–172.

Murry, J. Middleton. *Fyodor Dostoevsky: A Critical Study*. New York: Dodd, Mead, 1916, pp. 203–259.

Oates, Joyce Carol. "Tragic and Comic Visions in _The Brothers Karamazov_," in _The Edge of Impossiblity: Tragic Forms in Literature_. New York: Vanguard, 1972, pp. 85–113.

Peace, Richard. _Dostoyevsky: An Examination of the Major Novels_. New York: Cambridge University Press, 1971, pp. 218–296.

Rahv, Philip. "The Legend of the Grand Inquisitor," in _Partisan Review_. XXI (June, 1954), pp. 249–271.

Spilka, Mark. "Human Worth in _The Brothers Karamazov_," in _Minnesota Review_. V (January–April, 1965), pp. 38–49.

Thurneysen, Eduard. _Dostoevsky_. Richmond, Va.: John Knox Press, 1963, pp. 51–67.

Troyat, Henry. _Firebrand: The Life of Dostoevsky_. New York: Roy, 1946, pp. 395–416.

Vivas, Eliseo. _Creation and Discovery_. New York: Noonday, 1955, pp. 47–70. Reprinted in _Dostoevsky: A Collection of Critical Essays_. Edited by Rene Wellek. Englewood Cliffs, N.J.: Prentice-Hall, 1962, pp. 71–89.

Wasiolek, Edward. _Dostoevsky: The Major Fiction_. Cambridge: MIT Press, 1964, pp. 149–187.

Yarmolinsky, Avrahm. _Dostoevsky: His Life and Art_. New York: Criterion Books, 1957, pp. 355–361; 372–390.

Yermilov, V. _Fyodor Dostoyevsky_. Moscow: Foreign Languages Publishing, N.D., pp. 250–294.

Crime and Punishment

Baring, Maurice. _Landmarks in Russian Literature_. London: Methuen, 1910, pp. 191–201.

Beebe, Maurice. "The Three Motives of Raskolnikov: A Reinterpretation of _Crime and Punishment_,' in _College English_. XVII (December, 1955), pp. 151–158.

Blackmur, R.P. _Eleven Essays in the European Novel_. New York: Harcourt, 1964, pp. 119–140.

Chirkov, Nicholas M. "A Great Philosophical Novel," in _Twentieth Century Interpretations of_ Crime and Punishment. Edited by Robert Louis Jackson. Englewood Cliffs, N.J.: Prentice-Hall, 1974, pp. 49–70.

Dauner, Louise. "Raskolnikov in Search of a Soul," in _Modern Fiction Studies_. IV (Autumn, 1958), pp. 199–210.

Fanger, Donald. _Dostoevsky and Romantic Realism_. Cambridge, Mass.: Harvard University Press, 1965, pp. 184–213.

Frank, Joseph. "The World of Raskolnikov," in _Encounter_. XXVI (June, 1966), pp. 30–35. Reprinted in _Twentieth Century Interpretations of_ Crime

Lavrin, Janko. *Dostoevsky: A Study.* New York: Macmillan, 1947, pp. 87–94.

Magarshack, David. *Dostoevsky.* New York: Harcourt, Brace and World, 1961, pp. 296–302, 307–309, 327–328.

Maurina, Zenta. *A Prophet of the Soul: Fyodor Dostoievsky.* London: James Clarke, 1940, pp. 132–135, 142–147.

Muchnic, Helen. *An Introduction to Russian Literature.* New York: Doubleday, 1947, pp. 161–163.

Murry, J. Middleton. *Fyodor Dostoevsky: A Critical Study.* New York: Dodd, Mead, 1916, pp. 129–156.

Pachmuss, Temira. *F.M. Dostoevsky: Dualism and Synthesis of the Human Soul.* Carbondale: Southern Illinois University Press, 1963, pp. 75–84, 142–150.

Pascal, Roy. *The Dual Voice: Free Indirect Speech and Its Functioning in the Nineteenth Century European Novel.* Totowa, N.J.: Rowman and Littlefield, 1977, pp. 123–134.

Peace, Richard. *Dostoyevsky: An Examination of the Major Novels.* New York: Cambridge University Press, 1971, pp. 59–139.

Phelps, William L. *Essays on Russian Novelists.* New York: Macmillan, 1917, pp. 157–162.

Rosenberg, Harold. *Act and the Actor: Making the Self.* Cleveland: World, 1970, pp. 104–125.

Simmons, Ernest J. *Dostoevsky: The Making of a Novelist.* New York: Vintage Books, 1940, pp. 183–218.

Wasiolek, Edward. *Dostoevsky: The Major Fiction.* Cambridge: Massachusetts Institute of Technology Press, 1964, pp. 85–109.

Yarmolinsky, Avrahm. *Dostoevsky: His Life and Art.* New York: Criterion, 1957, pp. 246–261.

Letters from the Underworld

Beardsley, Monroe C. "Dostoyevsky's Metaphor of the 'Underground,' " in *Journal of the History of Ideas.* III (June, 1942), pp. 266–269.

Berdyaev, Nicholas. *Dostoevsky.* New York: Meridian Books, 1957, pp. 50–54.

Carrier, Warren. "Artistic Form and Unity in *Notes from Underground,*" in *Renascence.* XVI (Spring, 1964), pp. 142–145.

Fagin, N. Bryllion. "Dostoevsky's Underground Man Takes Over," in *Antioch Review.* XIII (March, 1953), pp. 25–32.

Fanger, Donald. *Dostoevsky and Romantic Realism.* Cambridge, Mass.: Harvard University Press, 1965, pp. 177–183.

Frank, Joseph. "Nihilism and *Notes from Underground*," in *Sewanee Review*. LXIX (Winter, 1961), pp. 1–33.

Harper, Ralph. *The Seventh Solitude: Man's Isolation in Kierkegaard, Dostoevsky, and Nietzsche.* Baltimore: Johns Hopkins Press, 1965, pp. 41–46.

Hingley, Ronald. *The Undiscovered Dostoyevsky.* London: Hamish Hamilton, 1962, pp. 69–79.

Holquist, Michael. *Dostoevsky and the Novel.* Princeton, N.J.: Princeton University Press, 1977, pp. 54–74.

Ivanov, Vyacheslav. *Freedom and the Tragic Life: A Study in Dostoevsky.* New York: Noonday, 1952, pp. 134–140.

Jones, Malcolm V. *Dostoyevsky: The Novel of Discord.* New York: Barnes & Noble, 1976, pp. 55–66.

Meier-Graefe, Julius. *Dostoevsky: The Man and His Work.* New York: Harcourt, 1928, pp. 98–110.

Peace, Richard. *Dostoyevsky: An Examination of the Major Novels.* New York: Cambridge University Press, 1971, pp. 1–18.

Pfleger, Karl. *Wrestlers with Christ.* London: Sheed and Ward, 1936, pp. 191–202.

Phillips, Williams. "Dostoevsky's Underground Man," in *Partisan Review.* XII (1946), pp. 551–561. Rreprinted in *The Short Stories of Dostoevsky.* New York: Dial, 1946, pp. vii–xx.

Powys, John Cowper. *Dostoievsky.* London: John Lane, 1946, pp. 82–87.

Rodoyce, L. "Writer in Hell: Notes on Dostoevsky's Letters," in *California Slavic Studies.* IX (1976), pp. 71–122.

Simmons, Ernest J. *Dostoevsky: The Making of a Novelist.* New York: Vintage Books, 1940, pp. 109–126.

Spilka, Mark. "Playing Crazy in the Underground," in *Minnesota Review.* VI (1966), pp. 233–243.

Steiner, George. *Tolstoy or Dostoevsky.* New York: Knopf, 1959, pp. 220–230.

Traschen, Isadore. "Dostoyevsky's *Notes from Underground*," in *Accent.* XVI (Autumn, 1956), pp. 255–264.

Troyat, Henry. *Firebrand: A Life of Dostoevsky.* New York: Roy, 1946, pp. 248–290.

Wasiolek, Edward. *Dostoevsky: The Major Fiction.* Cambridge: Massachusetts Institute of Technology Press, 1964, pp. 39–59.

Wilson, Colin. *The Outsider.* London: Golancz, 1956, pp. 157–162.

Yarmolinsky, Avrahm. *Dostoevsky: His Life and Art.* New York: Criterion Books, 1957, pp. 177–178, 187–192.

Poor People

Baring, Maurice. *Landmarks in Russian Literature.* London: Methuen, 1910, pp. 165–191.

Carr, Edward H. *Dostoevsky, 1821–1881: A New Biography.* Boston: Houghton Mifflin, 1931, pp. 40–44.

Fanger, Donald. *Dostoevsky and Romantic Realism.* Cambridge, Mass.: Harvard University Press, 1965, pp. 153–159.

Hingley, Ronald. *The Undiscovered Dostoyevsky.* London: Hamish Hamilton, 1962, pp. 3–8.

Jackson, Robert Louis. *Dostoevsky's Quest for Form: A Study of His Philosophy of Art.* New Haven, Conn.: Yale University Press, 1966, pp. 18–26.

Magarshack, David. *Dostoevsky.* New York: Harcourt, Brace and World, 1961, pp. 24–25, 78–85, 94–98.

Meier-Graefe, Julius. *Dostoevsky: The Man and His Work.* New York: Harcourt, 1928, pp. 64–69.

Payne, Robert. *Dostoyevsky: A Human Portrait.* New York: Knopf, 1961, pp. 38–55.

Phelps, William L. *Essays on Russian Novelists.* New York: Macmillan, 1917, pp. 139–142.

Simmons, Ernest J. *Dostoevsky: The Making of a Novelist.* New York: Vintage Books, 1940, pp. 12–24.

Vogue, E. Melchior de. *The Russian Novel.* New York: Knopf, 1916, pp. 208–216.

Yarmolinsky, Avrahm. *Dostoevsky: His Life and Art.* New York: Criterion Books, 1957, pp. 39–41, 91–92.

The Possessed

Baring, Maurice. *Landmarks in Russian Literature.* London: Methuen, 1910, pp. 215–240.

Blackmur, R.P. "In the Birdcage: Notes on *The Possessed* of Dostoevsky," in *Hudson Review.* I (Spring, 1948), pp. 7–28.

Carr, Edward H. *Dostoevsky: A New Biography.* New York: Houghton Mifflin, 1931, pp. 218–232.

Cook, Albert. *The Meaning of Fiction.* Detroit: Wayne State University Press, 1960, pp. 218–223.

Dolan, Paul J. *Of War and War's Alarms: Fiction and Politics in the Modern World.* New York: Free Press, 1976, pp. 36–39.

Glicksberg, Charles I. "To Be or not to Be: The Literature of Suicide," in *Queen's Quarterly.* LXVII (Autumn, 1960), pp. 386–390.

Harper, Ralph. *The Seventh Solitude: Man's Isolation in Kierkegaard, Dostoevsky, and Nietzsche.* Baltimore: Johns Hopkins Press, 1965, pp. 52–54, 65–70.

Hingley, Ronald. *The Undiscovered Dostoyevsky.* London: Hamish Hamilton, 1962, pp. 133–161.

Holquist, Michael. *Dostoevsky and the Novel.* Princeton, N.J.: Princeton University Press, 1977, pp. 124–147.

Howe, Irving. *Politics and the Novel.* New York: Horizon Press, 1957, pp. 57–75. Reprinted in *Dostoevsky: A Collection of Critical Essays.* Edited by Rene Wellek. Englewood Cliffs. N.J.: Prentice-Hall, 1962, pp. 58–70.

Jones, Malcolm V. *Dostoyevsky: The Novel of Discord.* New York: Barnes & Noble, 1976, pp. 128–153.

Lavrin, Janko. *Dostoevsky: A Study.* New York: Macmillan, 1947, pp. 94–109.

Magarshack, David. *Dostoevsky.* New York: Harcourt, Brace and World, 1961, pp. 314–315, 319–322, 338–343.

Maurina, Zenta. *A Prophet of the Soul: Fyodor Dostoievsky.* London: James Clarke, 1940, pp. 135–141.

Murry, J. Middleton. *Fyodor Dostoevsky: A Critical Study.* New York: Dodd, Mead, 1916, pp. 157–202.

Pachmuss, Temira. *F.M. Dostoevsky: Dualism and Synthesis of the Human Soul.* Carbondale: Southern Illinois University Press, 1963, pp. 8–14, 39–41, 49–55.

Peace, Richard. *Dostoyevsky: An Examination of the Major Novels.* New York: Cambridge University Press, 1971, pp. 140–217.

Rahv, Philip. *Image and Idea.* Norfolk, Conn.: Laughlin, 1949, pp. 86–110.

Richards, Ivor Armstrong. *Complementaries: Uncollected Essays.* Edited by John Paul Russo. Cambridge, Mass.: Harvard University Press, 1976, pp. 148–158.

Simmons, Ernest J. *Dostoevsky: The Making of a Novelist.* New York: Vintage Books, 1940, pp. 232–283.

Steiner, George. *Tolstoy or Dostoevsky.* New York: Knopf, 1959, pp. 182–190, 211–213, 308–319.

Wasiolek, Edward. *Dostoevsky: The Major Fiction.* Cambridge: Massachusetts Institute of Technology Press, 1964, pp. 110–136.

Wilson, Colin. *The Outsider.* London: Golancz, 1956, pp. 168–177.

Woolf, Virginia. *Granite and Rainbow.* London: Hogarth Press, 1958, pp. 126–130.

Yarmolinsky, Avrahm. *Dostoevsky: His Life and Art.* New York: Criterion Books, 1957, pp. 285–298, 304–307.

ARTHUR CONAN DOYLE
(1859–1930)

The Sign of Four

Boyd, Andrew. "Dr. Watson's Dupe," in *Encounter*. XIV (March, 1960), pp. 64–66.

Dakin, D. Martin. *A Sherlock Holmes Commentary*. New York: Drake, 1972, pp. 23–27.

Higham, Charles. *The Adventures of Conan Doyle*. New York: Norton, 1976, pp. 80–84.

Jaffee, Irving L. *Elementary My Dear Watson*. Brooklyn, N.Y.: Gaus' Sons, 1965, pp. 57–67.

Knox, Ronald A. "The Mathematics of Mrs. Watson," in *New Statesman and Nation*. IV (November 12, 1932), pp. 588, 590.

McCleary, George F. "The Apotheosis of Sherlock Holmes," in *National Review*. CXXVII (December, 1946), pp. 504–508.

Nordon, Pierre. *Conan Doyle*. London: John Murray, 1966, pp. 228–233, 262–263.

Pearsall, Ronald. *Conan Doyle; A Biographical Solution*. New York: St. Martin's Press, 1977, pp. 34–35, 57–58.

Symons, Julian. *Mortal Consequences; A History—From the Detective Story to the Crime Novel*. New York: Harper & Row, 1972, pp. 64–65.

Watson, Harold F. "An Old Sea Dog in Baker Street," in *Baker Street Journal*. XVIII (March, 1968), pp. 32–38.

A Study in Scarlet

Christ, Jay Finley. "Sherlock and the Canons," in *Baker Street Journal*. III (January, 1953), pp. 5–12.

Dakin, D. Martin. *A Sherlock Holmes Commentary*. New York: Drake, 1972, pp. 9–22.

Donegall, Lord. " ' "I Should Like to Meet Him," I Said'—Dr. J. H. Watson," in *The New Strand*. I (April, 1962), pp. 548–550.

Harrison, Michael. "A Study in Surmise," in *Ellery Queen's Mystery Magazine*. LVII (February, 1971), pp. 58–79.

Higham, Charles. *The Adventures of Conan Doyle*. New York: Norton, 1976, pp. 71–77.

Marshall, Margaret. "Alkali Dust in Your Eyes," in *American Scholar*. XXXVII (Autumn, 1968), pp. 650–654.

Nordon, Pierre. *Conan Doyle.* London: John Murray, 1966, pp. 221–230, 244–245, 269–270.

Ousby, Ian. *Bloodhounds of Heaven; The Detective in English Fiction from Godwin to Doyle.* Cambridge, Mass.: Harvard University Press, 1976, pp. 141–144, 151–161.

Pearsall, Ronald. *Conan Doyle; A Biographical Solution.* New York: St. Martin's Press, 1977, pp. 28–31, 34–37.

Ritunnano, Jeanne. "Mark Twain vs. Arthur Conan Doyle on Detective Fiction," in *Mark Twain Journal.* XVI (Winter, 1971/1972), pp. 10–14.

Symons, Julian. *Mortal Consequences; A History—From the Detective Story to the Crime Novel.* New York: Harper & Row, 1972, pp. 63–64, 66.

THEODORE DREISER
(1871–1945)

An American Tragedy

Campbell, Charles L. "*An American Tragedy*; or Death in the Woods," in *Modern Fiction Studies*. XV (Summer, 1969), pp. 251–259.

Coursen, Herbert R. "Clyde Griffiths and the American Dream," in *New Republic*. CXLV (September 4, 1961), pp. 21–22.

Davidson, Donald. "Theodore Dreiser," in his *The Spyglass*. Nashville, Tenn: Vanderbilt University Press, 1963, pp. 67–70.

Farrell, James T. "Dreiser's *Tragedy*: The Distortion of American Values," in *Prospects: Annual of American Cultural Studies*. I (1975), pp. 19–27.

Frohock, W.M. "Theodore Dreiser," in *Seven Novelists in the American Naturalist Tradition*. Edited by Charles Walcutt. Minneapolis: University of Minnesota, 1974, pp. 92–130.

Gerber, Philip L. *Theodore Dreiser*. New York: Twayne, 1964, pp. 127–153.

Grebstein, Sheldon N. "*An American Tragedy*: Theme and Structure," in *The Twenties*. Edited by R.E. Langford and W.E. Taylor. Deland, Fla.: Edwards, 1966, pp. 62–66.

Harter, Carol C. "Strange Bedfellows: *The Wasteland* and *An American Tragedy*," in *The Twenties*. Edited by W.G. French. Deland, Fla.: Everett/ Edwards, 1975, pp. 51–64.

Hoffman, Frederick J. "The Scene of Violence: Dostoevsky and Dreiser," in *Modern Fiction Studies*. VI (Summer, 1960), pp. 91–105.

Howe, Irving. "Dreiser: The Springs of Desire," in his *Decline of the New*. New York: Harcourt, Brace and World, 1970, pp. 137–150.

————. "Dreiser and Tragedy," in *Dreiser: A Collection of Critical Essays*. Edited by John Lydenberg. Englewood Cliffs, N.J.: Prentice-Hall, 1971, pp. 141–152.

Lane, Lauriat, Jr. "The Double in *An American Tragedy*," in *Modern Fiction Studies*. XII (Summer, 1966), pp. 213–220.

Lehan, Richard. "Dreiser's *An American Tragedy*: A Critical Study," in *College English*. XXV (December, 1963), pp. 187–193. Also in *The Modern American Novel*. Edited by Max R. Westbrook. New York: Random House, 1967, pp. 21–32.

McAleer, John J. *Theodore Dreiser*. New York: Holt, Rinehart and Winston, 1968, pp. 127–146.

Matthiessen, F.O. "Of Crime and Punishment," in *The Stature of Theodore Dreiser*. Edited by Alfred Kazin. Bloomington: Indiana University Press, 1955, pp. 204–218.

Mencken, H.L. "Dreiser," in *Mencken Christomathy*. New York: A.A. Knopf, 1949, pp. 501–505.

Moers, Ellen. *Two Dreisers*. New York: Viking, 1969, pp. 209–306.

Morgan, W. Wayne. "Theodore Dreiser: The Naturalist as Humanist," in his *American Writers in Rebellion*. New York: Hill and Wang, 1965, pp. 175–180.

Pizer, Donald. *The Novels of Theodore Dreiser*. Minneapolis: University of Minnesota, 1976, pp. 203–289.

Salzman, Jack, Editor. *Theodore Dreiser: The Critical Reception*. New York: David Lewis, 1972, pp. 439–502.

Samuels, Charles Thomas. "Mr. Trilling, Mr. Warren, and *An American Tragedy*," in *Yale Review*. LIII (June, 1964), pp. 629–640. Also in *Dreiser: A Collection of Critical Essays*. Edited by John Lydenberg. Englewood Cliffs, N.J.: Prentice-Hall, 1971, pp. 163–173.

Shafer, Robert. "*An American Tragedy*: A Humanistic Demurer," in *The Stature of Theodore Dreiser*. Edited by Alfred Kazin. Bloomington: Indiana University, 1955, pp. 113–126.

Shapiro, Charles. "*An American Tragedy*: The Dream, the Failure, and the Hope," in his *Theodore Dreiser*. Carbondale: Southern Illinois University Press, 1962, pp. 81–113.

Walcutt, Charles Child. "The Divided Stream," in *Dreiser: A Collection of Critical Essays*. Edited by John Lydenberg. Englewood Cliffs, N.J.: Prentice-Hall, 1971, pp. 120–122.

Warren, Robert Penn. "*An American Tragedy*," in *Yale Review*. LII (Autumn, 1962), pp. 1–15. Also in *Dreiser: A Collection of Critical Essays*. Edited by John Lydenberg. Englewood Cliffs, N.J.: Prentice-Hall, 1971, pp. 129–140.

The Bulwark

Freidrich, Gerhard. "A Major Influence on Theodore Dreiser's *The Bulwark*," in *American Literature*. XXIX (May, 1957), pp. 180–193.

Gerber, Philip L. *Theodore Dreiser*. New York: Twayne, 1964, pp. 154–171.

Hicks, Granville. "Theodore Dreiser and *The Bulwark*," in *The Stature of Theodore Dreiser*. Edited by Alfred Kazin. Bloomington: Indiana University Press, 1955, pp. 219–224. Also in *American Mercury*. LXII (June, 1946), pp. 751–756.

McAleer, John J. *Theodore Dreiser*. New York: Holt, Rinehart and Winston, 1968, pp. 147–161.

Pizer, Donald. *The Novels of Theodore Dreiser*. Minneapolis: University of Minnesota, 1976, pp. 299–331.

Richman, Sidney. "Theodore Dreiser's *The Bulwark*; a Final Resolution," in *American Literature.* XXXIV (May, 1962), pp. 229–245.

Salzman, Jack, Editor. *Theodore Dreiser: The Critical Reception.* New York: David Lewis, 1972, pp. 661–716.

Shapiro, Charles. "*The Bulwark*: American Religion and the American Dream," in his *Theodore Dreiser.* Carbondale: Southern Illinois University Press, 1962, pp. 65–80.

Spatz, J. "Dreiser's *Bulwark*: An Archaic Masterpiece," in *The Forties: Fiction, Poetry, Drama.* Edited by Warren French. Deland, Fla.: Everett/Edwards, 1969, pp. 155–162.

Walcutt, Charles Child. "The Divided Stream," in *Dreiser: A Collection of Critical Essays.* Edited by John Lydenberg. Englewood Cliffs, N.J.: Prentice-Hall, 1971, pp. 126–128.

Willen, Gerald. "Dreiser's Moral Seriousness," in *Dreiser: A Collection of Critical Essays.* Edited by John Lydenberg. Englewood Cliffs, N.J.: Prentice-Hall, 1971, pp. 96–103.

The Financier

Elias, Robert H. *Theodore Dreiser: Apostle of Nature.* Ithaca, N.Y.: Cornell University Press, 1970, pp. 164–165.

Gerber, Philip L. "Frank Cowperwood: Boy Financier," in *Studies in American Fiction.* II (1974), pp. 165–174.

————. *Theodore Dreiser.* New York: Twayne, 1964, pp. 87–110.

Howe, Irving. "Dreiser: The Springs of Desire," in *Decline of the New.* New York: Harcourt, Brace and World, 1970, pp. 139–142.

Mookerjee, R.N. *Theodore Dreiser: His Thought and Social Criticism.* Delhi, India: National Publishing House, 1974, pp. 49–56.

Pizer, Donald. *The Novels of Theodore Dreiser.* Minneapolis: University of Minnesota, 1976, pp. 160–182.

Rosenthal, T.G. "Introduction," in *The Financier.* By Theodore Dreiser. London: Panther, 1968.

Salzman, Jack, Editor. *Theodore Dreiser: The Critical Reception.* New York: David Lewis, 1972, pp. 97–140.

Shapiro, Charles. *Theodore Dreiser.* Carbondale: Southern Illinois University Press, 1962, pp. 25–42.

Sherman, Stuart P. "The Barbaric Nature of Mr. Dreiser," in *Dreiser: A Collection of Critical Essays.* Edited by John Lydenberg. Englewood Cliffs, N.J.: Prentice-Hall, 1971, pp. 63–72.

Walcutt, Charles Child. "The Divided Stream," in *Dreiser: A Collection of Critical Essays.* Edited by John Lydenberg. Englewood Cliffs, N.J.: Prentice-

Hall, 1971, pp. 116–122. Reprinted in *The Stature of Theodore Dreiser*. Edited by Alfred Kazin. Bloomington: Indiana University Press, 1976, pp. 246–269.

The "Genius"

Auerbach, Joseph S. "Oral Argument Against the Suppression of *The 'Genius,'*" in his *Essays and Miscellanies III*. New York: Harper, 1922, pp. 130–168. Also extracted as "Authorship and Liberty," in *North American Review*. CCVII (June, 1918), pp. 902–917.

Blackstone, Walter. "The Fall and Rise of Eugene Witla: Dramatic Vision of Artistic Integrity in *The 'Genius,'*" in *Language Quarterly*. V (Fall–Winter, 1966), pp. 15–18.

Durham, Frank. "Mencken as Missionary," in *American Literature*. XXIX (January, 1958), pp. 478–483.

Elias, Robert H. *Theodore Dreiser: Apostle of Nature*. Ithaca, N.Y.: Cornell University Press, 1970, pp. 155–157, 177–179.

Kwait, Joseph J. "Dreiser's *The 'Genius'* and Everett Shinn, the 'Ash-Can' Painter," in *PMLA*. LXVII (March, 1952), pp. 15–31.

McAleer, John J. *Theodore Dreiser*. New York: Holt, Rinehart and Winston, 1968, pp. 120–126.

Matthiessen, F.O. *Theodore Dreiser*. New York: William Sloane, 1951, pp. 159–173.

Mookerjee, R.N. *Theodore Dreiser: His Thought and Social Criticism*. Delhi, India: National Publishing House, 1974, pp. 56–60.

Morgan, W. Wayne. "Theodore Dreiser: The Naturalist as Humanist," in his *American Writers in Rebellion*. New York: Hill and Wang, 1965, pp. 171–174.

Pizer, Donald. *The Novels of Theodore Dreiser*. Minneapolis: University of Minnesota, 1976, pp. 133–152.

Salzman, Jack, Editor. *Theodore Dreiser: The Critical Reception*. New York: David Lewis, 1972, pp. 209–254.

Shapiro, Charles. "*The 'Genius'*: The American Artist and the American Dream," in his *Theodore Dreiser*. Carbondale: Southern Illinois University Press, 1962, pp. 45–64.

Jennie Gerhardt

Elias, Robert H. *Theodore Dreiser: Apostle of Nature*. Ithaca, N.Y.: Cornell University Press, 1970, pp. 152–176.

Fiedler, Leslie. "Dreiser and the Sentimental Novel," in *Dreiser: A Collection of Critical Essays*. Edited by John Lydenberg. Englewood Cliffs, N.J.: Prentice-Hall, 1971, pp. 45–51.

Howe, Irving. "Dreiser: The Springs of Desire," in his *Decline of the New.* New York: Harcourt, Brace and World, 1970, pp. 139–142.

McAleer, John J. *Theodore Dreiser.* New York: Holt, Rinehart and Winston, 1968, pp. 93–102.

Mookerjee, R.N. *Theodore Dreiser: His Thought and Social Criticism.* Delhi, India: National Publishing House, 1974, pp. 45–49.

Morgan, W. Wayne. "Theodore Dreiser: The Naturalist as Humanist," in his *American Writers in Rebellion.* New York: Hill and Wang, 1965, pp. 171–174.

Pizer, Donald. *The Novels of Theodore Dreiser.* Minneapolis: University of Minnesota, 1976, pp. 96–130.

Salzman, Jack, Editor. *Theodore Dreiser: The Critical Reception.* New York: David Lewis, 1972, pp. 56–96.

Shapiro, Charles. "*Jennie Gerhardt*: The American Family and the American Dream," in his *Twelve Original Essays on Great American Novels.* Detroit: Wayne State University Press, 1960, pp. 177–195. Also in his *Theodore Dreiser.* Carbondale: Southern Illinois University Press, 1962, pp. 14–24.

Sherman, Stuart. "The Barbaric Naturalism of Mr. Dreiser," in *Dreiser: A Collection of Critical Essays.* Edited by John Lydenberg. Englewood Cliffs, N.J.: Prentice-Hall, 1971, pp. 63–72.

Walcutt, Charles Child. "The Divided Stream," in *Dreiser: A Collection of Critical Essays.* Edited by John Lydenberg. Englewood Cliffs, N.J.: Prentice-Hall, 1971, pp. 109–115.

Sister Carrie

Auchincloss, Louis. *Louis Auchincloss on* Sister Carrie. New York: Merrill, 1968.

Cowley, Malcolm. "Sister Carrie's Brother," in *The Stature of Theodore Dreiser.* Edited by Alfred Kazin. Bloomington: Indiana University Press, 1955, pp. 171–181. Also in his *A Many Windowed House.* Carbondale: Southern Illinois University Press, 1970, pp. 153–165.

Elias, Robert H. *Theodore Dreiser: Apostle of Nature.* Ithaca, N.Y.: Cornell University Press, 1970, pp. 103–117.

Farrell, James T. "Dreiser's *Sister Carrie*," in his *The League of Frightened Philistines.* New York: Vanguard, 1945, pp. 12–19.

Gerber, Philip L. *Theodore Dreiser.* New York: Twayne, 1964, pp. 51–70.

Griffin, R.J. "Carrie and Music: A Note on Dreiser's Technique," in *From Irving to Steinbeck.* Edited by Motley Deakin and Peter Lisca. Gainesville: University Presses of Florida, 1972, pp. 73–81.

Griffith, Clark. "*Sister Carrie*: Dreiser's Wasteland," in *American Studies.* XVI, pp. 41–47.

Hakutani, Yoshinobu. "*Sister Carrie* and the Problem of Literary Naturalism," in *Twentieth Century Literature.* XIII (April, 1967), pp. 3–17.

Hoffman, Michael J. "From Realism to Naturalism: *Sister Carrie* and the Sentimentality of Nihilism," in his *The Subversive Vision: American Romanticism in Literature.* Port Washington, N.Y.: Kennikat, 1972, pp. 139–153.

Hussman, Lawrence E., Jr. "Thomas Edison and *Sister Carrie*: A Source for Character and Theme," in *American Literary Realism.* VIII (Spring, 1975), pp. 155–158.

Kazin, Alfred. "The Stature of Theodore Dreiser," in *Dreiser: A Collection of Critical Essays.* Edited by John Lydenberg. Englewood Cliffs, N.J.: Prentice-Hall, 1971, pp. 11–15. Also in his *The Stature of Theodore Dreiser.* Bloomington: Indiana University Press, 1955, pp. 3–12.

Lynn, Kenneth S. "*Sister Carrie*," in *Visions of America.* Compiled by David Kherdian. New York: Macmillan, 1973, pp. 137–148.

McAleer, John J. *Theodore Dreiser.* New York: Holt, Rinehart and Winston, 1968, pp. 76–92.

Martin, Jay. *Harvests of Change, American Literature 1865–1914.* Englewood Cliffs, N.J.: Prentice-Hall, 1964, pp. 252–253, 256–258.

Matthiessen, F.O. *Theodore Dreiser.* New York: William Sloane, 1951, pp. 55–108.

Moers, Ellen. "The Finesse of Dreiser," in *American Scholar.* XXXIII (Winter, 1963–1964), pp. 109–114. Also in *Dreiser: A Collection of Critical Essays.* Edited by John Lydenberg. Englewood Cliffs, N.J.: Prentice-Hall, 1971, pp. 153–162.

————. *Two Dreisers.* New York: Viking, 1969, pp. 73–154.

Mookerjee, R.N. *Theodore Dreiser: His Thought and Social Criticism.* Delhi, India: National Publishing House, 1974, pp. 38–41.

Noble, D.W. "Progress vs. Tragedy: Veblin and Dreiser," in *Intellectual History in America*, Volume II. Edited by Cushing Strout. New York: Harper & Row, 1968, pp. 70–72.

Pizer, Donald. "Nineteenth-Century American Naturalism: An Essay in Definition," in *Bucknell Review.* XIII (December, 1965), pp. 1–18. Also in his *Realism and Naturalism in Nineteenth Century American Literature.* Carbondale: Southern Illinois University Press, 1966, pp. 11–32.

————. *The Novels of Theodore Dreiser.* New York: Holt, Rinehart and Winston, 1976, pp. 31–95.

Salzman, Jack, Editor. *Theodore Dreiser: The Critical Reception.* New York: David Lewis, 1972, pp. 1–55.

Seltzer, Leon F. "*Sister Carrie* and the Hidden Longing for Love: Sublimation or Subterfuge?," in *Twentieth Century Literature*. XXII (1976), pp. 192–209.

Shapiro, Charles. *Theodore Dreiser*. Carbondale: Southern Illinois University Press, 1962, pp. 1–14.

Simpson, Claude. "*Sister Carrie* Reconsidered," in *Southwest Review*. XLIV (Winter, 1959), pp. 44–53.

_____. "Theodore Dreiser: *Sister Carrie*," in *The American Novel*. Edited by Wallace Stegner. New York: Basic Books, 1965, pp. 106–116.

Taylor, Gordon O. "The Voice of Want: Frank Norris and Theodore Dreiser," in his *The Passages of Thought*. New York: Oxford University Press, 1969, pp. 136–157.

Walcutt, Charles Child. "The Divided Stream," in *Dreiser: A Collection of Critical Essays*. Edited by John Lydenberg. Englewood Cliffs, N.J.: Prentice-Hall, 1971, pp. 109–115. Also in *The Stature of Theodore Dreiser*. Edited by Alfred Kazin. Bloomington: Indiana University Press, 1976, pp. 246–269.

The Stoic

Gerber, Philip L. "Dreiser's *Stoic*: A Study in Literary Frustration," in *Literary Monographs*. VII (1975), pp. 85–144.

_____. *Theodore Dreiser*. New York: Twayne, 1964, pp. 87–110.

McAleer, John J. *Theodore Dreiser*. New York: Holt, Rinehart and Winston, 1968, pp. 113–119.

Mookerjee, R.N. *Theodore Dreiser: His Thought and Social Criticism*. Delhi, India: National Publishing House, 1974, pp. 215–222.

Pizer, Donald. *The Novels of Theodore Dreiser*. Minneapolis: University of Minnesota, 1976, pp. 332–346.

Salzman, Jack, Editor. *Theodore Dreiser: The Critical Reception*. New York: David Lewis, 1972, pp. 717–738.

Walcutt, Charles Child. "The Divided Stream," in *Dreiser: A Collection of Critical Essays*. Edited by John Lydenberg. Englewood Cliffs, N.J.: Prentice-Hall, 1971, pp. 122–126.

The Titan

Berryman, John. "Enslavement: Three American Cases: Dreiser's *The Titan*," in his *The Freedom of the Poet*. New York: Farrar, Straus, and Giroux, 1976, pp. 190–197.

Elias, Robert H. *Theodore Dreiser: Apostle of Nature*. Ithaca, N.Y.: Cornell University, 1970, pp. 171–174.

Gerber, Philip L. *Theodore Dreiser*. New York: Twayne, 1964, pp. 87–110.

Matthiessen, F.O.   *Theodore Dreiser.* New York: William Sloane, 1951, pp. 127–158.

Mookerjee, R.N.   *Theodore Dreiser: His Thought and Social Criticism.* Delhi, India: National Publishing House, 1974, pp. 49–56.

Pizer, Donald.   *The Novels of Theodore Dreiser.* Minneapolis: University of Minnesota, 1976, pp. 183–200.

Rosenthal, T.G.   "Introduction," in *The Titan.* By Theodore Dreiser. London: Panther, 1968.

Sherman, Stuart.   "The Barbaric Naturalism of Mr. Dreiser," in *Dreiser: A Collection of Critical Essays.* Edited by John Lydenberg. Englewood Cliffs, N.J.: Prentice-Hall, 1971, pp. 63–72.

Walcutt, Charles Child.   "The Divided Stream," in *Dreiser: A Collection of Critical Essays.* Edited by John Lydenberg. Englewood Cliffs, N.J.: Prentice-Hall, 1971, pp. 116–122.

Willen, Gerald.   "Dreiser's Moral Seriousness," in *Dreiser: A Collection of Critical Essays.* Edited by John Lydenberg. Englewood Cliffs, N.J.: Prentice-Hall, 1971, pp. 96–103.

Wilson, William E.   "The Titan and the Gentleman," in *Antioch Review.* XXIII (Spring, 1963), pp. 25–34.

JOHN DRYDEN
(1631–1700)

Absalom and Achitophel

Ball, Albert. "Charles II: Dryden's Christian Hero," in *Modern Philology*. IX (August, 1961), pp. 25–35.

Brodwin, Leonora L. "Miltonic Allusion in *Absalom and Achitophel*: Its Function in the Political Satire," in *Journal of English and Germanic Philology*. LXVIII (January, 1969), pp. 24–44.

Dyson, A.E. and J. Lovelock. "Beyond the Polemics: A Dialogue on the Opening of *Absalom and Achitophel*," in *Critical Survey*. V (1971), pp. 133–145.

Farley-Hills, D. "John Dryden," in *The Benevolence of Laughter: Comic Poetry of the Commonwealth and Restoration*. Totowa, N.J.: Rowman and Littlefield, 1974, pp. 99–131.

French, A.L. "Dryden, Marvell and Political Poetry," in *Studies in English Literature, 1500–1900*. VIII (Summer, 1968), pp. 397–413.

Guilhamet, Leon M. "Dryden's Debasement of Scripture in *Absalom and Achitophel*," in *Studies in English Literature, 1500–1900*. IX (Summer, 1969), pp. 395–413.

Harth, Phillip. "Legends. No Histories: The Case of *Absalom and Achitophel*," in *Studies in Eighteenth Century Culture*, Volume IV. Edited by Harold E. Pagliaro. Madison: University of Wisconsin Press, 1975, pp. 13–29.

Hogg, James. *Dryden as Propagandist:* Absalom and Achitophel *and Its Background*. Atlantic Highlands, N.J.: Humanities Press, 1978.

Jones, Richard F. "The Originality of *Absalom and Achitophel*," in *Modern Language Notes*. XLVI (1931), pp. 211–218.

Kinsley, James. "Historical Allusions in *Absalom and Achitophel*," in *Review of English Studies*. VI (1955), pp. 291–297.

Lewalski, Barbara K. "The Scope and Function of Biblical Allusion in *Absalom and Achitophel*," in *English Language Notes*. III (1965), pp. 29–35.

Lord, George. "*Absalom and Achitophel* and Dryden's Political Cosmos," in *John Dryden*. Edited by Earl Miner. Athens: Ohio University Press, 1972, pp. 156–190.

McFadden, George. *Dryden the Public Writer, 1660–1685*. Princeton, N.J.: Princeton University Press, 1978, pp. 227–264.

Maresca, Thomas E. "The Context of Dryden's *Absalom and Achitophel*," in *Journal of English Literary History*. XLI (1974), pp. 340–358.

————. *Epic to Novel*. Columbus: Ohio State University Press, 1974, pp. 3–75.

Miner, Earl. *Dryden's Poetry.* Bloomington: Indiana University Press, 1967, pp. 106–143.

————. "Some Characteristics of Dryden's Use of Metaphor," in *Studies in English Literature, 1500–1900.* II (Summer, 1962), pp. 312–316.

Peterson, R.G. "Larger Manners and Events: Sallust and Virgil in *Absalom and Achitophel,*" in *PMLA.* LXXXII (May, 1967), pp. 236–244.

Previte-Orton, Charles W. *Political Satire in English Poetry.* New York: Haskell House, 1966, pp. 97–100.

Ricks, Christopher. "Dryden's *Absalom,*" in *Essays in Criticism.* XI (1961), pp. 273–289.

Robinson, K.E. "A Reading of *Absalom and Achitophel,*" in *Yearbook of English Studies.* VI (1976), pp. 53–62.

Schilling, Bernard. *Dryden and the Conservative Myth: A Reading of* Absalom and Achitophel. New Haven, Conn.: Yale University Press, 1961.

Sutherland, W.O.S., Jr. *The Art of the Satirist: Essays on the Satire of Augustan England.* Austin: University of Texas Press, 1965, pp. 38–53.

Thomas, W.K. "The Matrix of *Absalom and Achitophel,*" in *Philological Quarterly.* XLIX (January, 1970), pp. 92–99.

Zwicker, Steven N. *Dryden's Political Poetry, the Typology of King and Nation.* Providence, R.I.: Brown University Press, 1972, pp. 83–101.

All for Love

Armstrong, R. "The Great Chain of Being in Dryden's *All for Love,*" in *A Provision of Human Nature; Essays on Fielding and others.* Edited by Donald Kay. University: University of Alabama Press, 1977, pp. 133–143.

Canfield, J. Douglas. "The Jewel of Great Price: Mutability and Constancy in Dryden's *All For Love,*" in *Journal of English Literary History.* XLII (1975), pp. 36–61.

Dobrèe, Bonamy. *Restoration Tragedy 1660–1720.* Oxford: Clarendon Press, 1929.

Emerson, Everett H., Harold E. Davis and Ira Johnson. "Intention and Achievement in *All for Love,*" in *College English.* XVII (1955), pp. 84–87.

Goggin, L.P. "This Bow of Ulysses," in *Essays and Studies in Language and Literature.* XXII (1963), pp. 49–86.

Griffith, Benjamin W., Jr. All for Love, *or the World Well Lost.* Woodbury, N.Y.: Barron's, 1961, pp. 5–40.

Hughes, Derek W. "The Significance of *All for Love,*" in *Journal of English Literary History.* XXXVII (1970), pp. 540–563.

Hughes, R.E. "Dryden's *All for Love*: The Sensual Dilemma," in *Drama Critique.* III (1960), pp. 68–72.

Hyman, Stanley E. *Poetry and Criticism; Four Revaluations in Literary Taste.* New York: Atheneum, 1961, pp. 39–84.

Kearful, Frank J. " 'Tis Past Recovery': Tragic Consciousness in *All for Love*," in *Modern Language Quarterly.* XXXIV (1973), pp. 227–246.

King, Bruce. "Dryden's Intent in *All for Love*," in *College English.* XXIV (1963), pp. 267–271.

————. *Dryden's Major Plays.* New York: Barnes & Noble, 1966, pp. 133–147.

————. *Twentieth Century Interpretations of* All for Love. Englewood Cliffs, N.J.: Prentice-Hall, 1968.

Martin, Leslie H. "*All for Love* and the Millenarian Tradition," in *Comparative Literature.* XXVII (1975), pp. 289–306.

Miner, Earl. *Dryden's Poetry.* Bloomington: Indiana University Press, 1967, pp. 36–73.

Nazareth, Peter. "*All for Love*: Dryden's Hybrid Play," in *English Studies in Africa.* VI (1963), pp. 154–163.

Ramsey, Paul. *The Art of John Dryden.* Lexington: University of Kentucky Press, 1969, pp. 142–166.

Starnes, D.T. "Imitation of Shakespeare in Dryden's *All for Love*," in *Texas Studies in Literature and Language.* VI (1964), pp. 39–46.

————. "More About Dryden as an Adapter of Shakespeare," in *Studies in English.* VIII (1928), pp. 100–106.

Tracy, Clarence. "The Tragedy of *All for Love*," in *University of Toronto Quarterly.* XLV (1976), pp. 186–199.

Waith, Eugene M. "*All for Love*," in *Restoration Dramatists: A Collection of Critical Essays.* Edited by Earl Miner. Englewood Cliffs, N.J.: Prentice-Hall, 1966, pp. 51–62.

————. *Ideas of Greatness; Heroic Drama in England.* New York: Barnes & Noble, 1971, pp. 231–235.

Wasserman, George R. *John Dryden.* New York: Twayne, 1964, pp. 91–95.

Weinbrot, Howard D. "Alexas in *All for Love*: His Genealogy and Function," in *Studies in Philology.* LXIV (1967), pp. 625–639.

An Essay of Dramatic Poesy

Aden, John. "Dryden, Corneille, and the *Essay of Dramatic Poesy*," in *Review of English Studies.* VI (1955), pp. 147–156.

Archer, Stanley. "The Persons in *An Essay of Dramatic Poesy*," in *Papers on Language and Literature.* II (1966), pp. 305–314.

Davie, Donald A. "Dramatic Poetry: Dryden's Conversation-Piece," in *Cambridge Journal.* V (1951–1952), pp. 553–561.

Ellis, Amanda M. "Horace's Influence on Dryden," in *Philological Quarterly.* IV (1925), pp. 39–60.

Grace, Joan C. *Tragic Theory in the Critical Works of Thomas Rymer, John Dennis, and John Dryden.* Rutherford, N.J.: Fairleigh Dickinson University Press, 1975, pp. 98–100, 103–110.

Huntley, Frank L. *On Dryden's Essay of Dramatic Poesy.* Ann Arbor: University of Michigan Press, 1951.

————. "On the Persons in Dryden's *Essay of Dramatic Poesy*," in *Modern Language Notes.* LXIII (1948), pp. 88–95.

LeClercq, Richard V. "The Academic Nature of the Whole Discourse of *An Essay of Dramatic Poesy*," in *Papers on Language and Literature.* VIII (1972), pp. 27–38.

————. "Corneille and *An Essay of Dramatic Poesy*," in *Comparative Literature.* XXII (1970), pp. 319–327.

Moore, Frank H. *The Nobler Pleasure: Dryden's Comedy in Theory and Practice.* Chapel Hill: University of North Carolina Press, 1963, pp. 28–36.

Noyes, George R. " 'Crites' in Dryden's *Essay of Dramatic Poesy*," in *Modern Language Notes.* XXXVIII (1923), pp. 333–337.

Pechter, Edward. *Dryden's Classical Theory of Literature.* New York: Cambridge University Press, 1975, pp. 36–61.

Pendlebury, B.J. *Dryden's Heroic Plays, a Study of the Origins.* New York: Russell and Russell, 1923, pp. 51–65.

Thale, Mary. "The Framework of *An Essay of Dramatic Poesy*," in *Papers on Language and Literature.* VIII (1972), pp. 362–369.

Trowbridge, Frederick H. *From Dryden to Jane Austen; Essays on English Critics and Writers, 1660–1818.* Albuquerque: University of New Mexico Press, 1977, pp. 13–31.

Tyson, Gerald P. "Dryden's Dramatic Essay," in *Ariel.* IV (1973), pp. 72–86.

Wasserman, George R. *John Dryden.* New York: Twayne, 1964, pp. 55–69.

Williamson, George. "The Occasion of *An Essay of Dramatic Poesy*," in *Modern Philology.* XLIV (1946), pp. 1–9.

Marriage à la Mode

Alleman, Gilbert S. *Matrimonial Law and the Materials of Restoration Comedy.* Philadelphia: University of Pennsylvania Press, 1942.

Bruce, Donald. *Topics of Restoration Comedy.* New York: St. Martin's Press, 1974, pp. 152–154.

Gagen, Jean E. *The New Woman: Her Emergence in English Drama, 1600–1730.* New York: Twayne, 1954.

King, Bruce. *Dryden's Major Plays*. New York: Barnes & Noble, 1966, pp. 82–94.

———. "Dryden's *Marriage à la Mode*," in *Drama Survey*. IV (1965), pp. 28–37.

Kronenberger, Louis. *The Thread of Laughter: Chapters on English Stage Comedy from Jonson to Maugham*. New York: Knopf, 1952, pp. 81–92.

Martin, Leslie H. "The Source and Originality of Dryden's Melantha," in *Philological Quarterly*. LII (1973), pp. 746–753.

Moore, Frank H. *The Nobler Pleasure: Dryden's Comedy in Theory and Practice*. Chapel Hill: University of North Carolina Press, 1963, pp. 101–111.

Okerlund, A.N. "Dryden's Joke on the Courtiers: *Marriage à la Mode*," in *Seventeenth-Century News*. XXXIV (1976), pp. 5–7.

Ristine, Frank H. *English Tragicomedy: Its Origin and History*. New York: Columbia University Press, 1910, pp. 170–173.

Schneider, Ben R., Jr. *The Ethos of Restoration Comedy*. Urbana: University of Illinois Press, 1971, pp. 11–12, 119–120.

Traugott, John. "The Rake's Comedy: A Study in Comic Form," in *Studies in English Literature, 1500–1900*. VI (1966), pp. 381–407.

Wasserman, George R. *John Dryden*. New York: Twayne, 1964, pp. 75–79.

The Poetry of Dryden

Blair, Joe. "Dryden's Ceremonial Hero," in *Studies in English Literature, 1500–1900*. IX (Summer, 1969), pp. 379–393.

Budick, Sanford. *Poetry of Civilization: Mythopoeic Displacement in the Verse of Milton, Dryden, Pope, and Johnson*. New Haven, Conn.: Yale University Press, 1974, pp. 81–110.

Davison, Dennis. *Dryden*. London: Evans, 1968.

Emslie, M. "Dryden's Couplets: Imagery Vowed to Poverty," in *Critical Quarterly*. II (Spring, 1960), pp. 51–57.

Fujimura, Thomas H. "The Personal Element in Dryden's Poetry," in *PMLA*. LXXXIX (1974), pp. 1007–1123.

Hamilton, K.G. *John Dryden and the Poetry of Statement*. East Lansing: Michigan State University Press, 1969.

Hughes, R.E. "John Dryden's Greatest Compromise," in *Texas Studies in Literature and Language*. II (Winter, 1961), pp. 458–463.

Korshin, Paul J. *From Concord to Dissent; Major Themes in English Poetic Theory, 1640–1700*. Menston, England: Scholar Press, 1973, pp. 105–144, 175–215.

McFadden, George. *Dryden the Public Writer, 1660–1685*. Princeton, N.J.: Princeton University Press, 1978, pp. 23–182.

Miner, Earl. "Dryden and the Issue of Human Progress," in *Philological Quarterly*. XL (1961), pp. 120–129.

―――――. *Dryden's Poetry*. Bloomington: Indiana University Press, 1967.

Nicoll, Allardyce. *Dryden and His Poetry*. New York: Russell and Russell, 1967.

Ramsey, Paul. *The Art of John Dryden*. Lexington: University of Kentucky Press, 1969.

Roper, Alan. *Dryden's Poetic Kingdoms*. New York: Barnes & Noble, 1965.

Sherbo, Arthur. *English Poetic Diction from Chaucer to Wordsworth*. East Lansing: Michigan State University Press, 1975, pp. 105–131.

Van Doren, Mark. *The Poetry of John Dryden*. Bloomington: Indiana University Press, 1960.

Zwicker, Steven N. *Dryden's Political Poetry, the Topology of King and Nation*. Providence, R.I.: Brown University Press, 1972.

The Spanish Friar

Alleman, Gilbert S. *Matrimonial Law and the Materials of Restoration Comedy*. Philadelphia: University of Pennsylvania Press, 1942.

Bredvold, Louis I. "Political Aspects of Dryden's *Amboyna* and *The Spanish Friar*," in *University of Michigan Publications, Language and Literature*. VIII (1932), pp. 119–132.

King, Bruce. "Dryden's Ark: The Influence of Filmer," in *Studies in English Literature, 1500–1900*. VII (1967), pp. 403–414.

―――――. *Dryden's Major Plays*. New York: Barnes & Noble, 1966, pp. 148–164.

Kronenberger, Louis. *The Thread of Laughter: Chapters on English Stage Comedy from Jonson to Maugham*. New York: Knopf, 1952, pp. 81–92.

Moore, Frank H. *The Nobler Pleasure: Dryden's Comedy in Theory and Practice*. Chapel Hill: University of North Carolina Press, 1963, pp. 154–166.

Nicoll, Allardyce. "Political Plays of the Restoration," in *Modern Language Review*. XVI (1921), pp. 224–242.

Osborn, Scott C. "Heroical Love in Dryden's Heroic Drama," in *PMLA*. LXXIII (1958), pp. 480–490.

Ristine, Frank H. *English Tragicomedy: Its Origin and History*. New York: Russell and Russell, 1963, pp. 170–174, 186–189, 199.

Schneider, Ben R., Jr. *The Ethos of Restoration Comedy*. Urbana: University of Illinois Press, 1971, pp. 62–63.

Whiting, George W. "Political Satire in London Stage Plays, 1680–83," in *Modern Philology*. XXVIII (1930), pp. 29–43.

Winterbottom, John A. "The Place of Hobbesian Ideas in Dryden's

Tragedies," in *Journal of English and Germanic Philology*. LVII (1958), pp. 665–683.

Zebouni, Selma A. *Dryden: A Study in Heroic Characterization*. Baton Rouge: Louisiana State University Press, 1965, pp. 59–63.

ALEXANDRE DUMAS, PÈRE
(1802–1870)

The Black Tulip

Bell, A. Craig. *Alexandre Dumas: A Biography and Study.* London: Cassell, 1950.

Stowe, Richard S. *Alexandre Dumas Père.* Boston: Twayne, 1976.

The Chevalier of the Maison Rouge

Stowe, Richard S. *Alexandre Dumas Père.* Boston: Twayne, 1976.

Thompson, John A. *Alexandre Dumas and the Romantic Drama in Spain, 1830–1850.* Ann Arbor: University Microfilms, 1937.

The Corsican Brothers

Stowe, Richard S. *Alexandre Dumas Père.* Boston: Twayne, 1976.

Thompson, John A. *Alexandre Dumas and the Romantic Drama in Spain, 1830–1850.* Ann Arbor: University Microfilms, 1937.

The Count of Monte-Cristo

Bell, A. Craig. *Alexandre Dumas: A Biography and Study.* London: Cassell, 1950, pp. 158–165.

Marinetti, A. "Death, Resurrection and Fall in Dumas' *Comte Monte-Cristo*," in *French Review.* L (1976), pp. 260–269.

Maurois, André. *Alexandre Dumas: A Great Life in Brief.* New York: Knopf, 1955, pp. 124–126.

———. *The Titans.* New York: Harper, 1957, pp. 219–227.

Stowe, Richard S. *Alexandre Dumas Père.* Boston: Twayne, 1976, pp. 116–126.

The Countess de Charny

Stowe, Richard S. *Alexandre Dumas Père.* Boston: Twayne, 1976, pp. 106–108.

Thompson, John A. *Alexandre Dumas in the Romantic Drama in Spain, 1830–1850.* Ann Arbor: University Microfilms, 1937.

Memoirs of a Physician

Stowe, Richard S. *Alexandre Dumas Père.* Boston: Twayne, 1976, pp. 100–111.

Thompson, John A. *Alexandre Dumas and the Romantic Drama in Spain, 1830–1850.* Ann Arbor: University Microfilms, 1937.

The Queen's Necklace

Stowe, Richard S. *Alexandre Dumas Père.* Boston: Twayne, 1976, pp. 102–106.

Thompson, John A. *Alexandre Dumas and the Romantic Drama in Spain, 1830–1850.* Ann Arbor: University Microfilms, 1937.

The Three Musketeers

Bell, A. Craig. *Alexandre Dumas: A Biography and Study.* London: Cassell, 1950, pp. 150–164.

Garnett, R.S. "The Genius and the Ghost," in *Blackwood's Magazine.* CCXXVI (July, 1929), pp. 129–142.

Maurois, André. *The Titans.* New York: Harper, 1957, pp. 176–181.

Packer, Richard. "Some Additional Sources of *Les Trois Mousquetaires*," in *Modern Philology.* XLII (August, 1944), pp. 34–39.

Stowe, Richard S. *Andexandre Dumas Père.* Boston: Twayne, 1976, pp. 66–75.

Twenty Years After

Stowe, Richard S. *Alexandre Dumas Père.* Boston: Twayne, 1976, pp. 75–81.

Thompson, John A. *Alexandre Dumas and the Romantic Drama in Spain, 1830–1850.* Ann Arbor: University Microfilms, 1937.

The Vicomte de Bragelonne

Stowe, Richard S. *Alexandre Dumas Père.* Boston: Twayne, 1976.

Thompson, John A. *Alexandre Dumas and the Romantic Drama in Spain, 1830–1850.* Ann Arbor: University Microfilms, 1937.

ALEXANDRE DUMAS, FILS
(1824–1895)

Camille

Finn, Michael R. "Provost and Dumas Fils: *Odette* and *La Dame Aux Camelias*," in *French Review*. XLVII (1974), pp. 528–542.

Lamm, Martin. *Modern Drama*. Translated by Karin Elliott. Oxford: Blackwell, 1952, pp. 18–22.

Marek, George R. *Front Seat at the Opera*. New York: Allen, Towne and Heath, 1948, pp. 80–86.

Perkins, M. "Matilda Heron's Camielle," in *Comparative Literature*. VII (1955), pp. 338–343.

Saunders, E. "The Patron Saint of Courtesans," in *Twentieth Century*. CLVIII (1955), pp. 140–147.

Schwarz, Henry S. *Alexandre Dumas, Fils, Dramatist*. Ann Arbor: University Microfilms, 1927.

Seidlin, O. "Greatness and Decline of the Bourgeois: Dramas by Schiller and Dumas," in *Comparative Literature*. VI (1954), pp. 123–129.

Tynan, Kenneth. *Curtains; Selections from the Drama Criticism and Related Writings*. New York: Atheneum, 1961.

Young, Stark. *Immortal Shadows: A Book of Dramatic Criticism*. New York: Scribner's, 1948, pp. 67–71.

Zucker, A.E. and P. de F. Henderson. "*Camille* as the Translation of *La Dame Aux Camelias*," in *Modern Language Notes*. XLIX (November, 1934), pp. 472–476.

The Demi-Monde

James, Henry. *The Scenic Art: Notes on Acting and the Drama, 1872–1901*. New Brunswick, N.J.: Rutgers University Press, 1948.

Lamm, Martin. *Modern Drama*. Translated by Karin Elliott. Oxford: Blackwell, 1952, pp. 22–25.

Lancaster, C. "Dumas the Younger and French Dramatic Forms Existing in 1850," in *Poet Lore*. LI (Winter, 1945), pp. 347–348.

The Question of Money

Lancaster, C. "Dumas the Younger and French Dramatic Forms Existing in 1850," in *Poet Lore*. LI (Winter, 1945), pp. 349–350.

Yedlicka, J. "Speculation in the 2nd Empire: *La Question d'Argent* of Dumas Fils," in French Review. XXXVI (1962–1963), pp. 606–616.

PETRU DUMITRIU
(1924–   )

The Extreme Occident

Davenport, Guy. "Once More, a Little Louder," in *National Review*. XVIII (October 4, 1966), pp. 1001–1003.

Grossman, Edward. "Price Tags on Prosperity," in *New Republic*. CLV (November 12, 1966), pp. 33–35.

Stilwell, Robert L. "Ideological Framework for Fiction," in *Saturday Review*. XLIX (September 10, 1966), pp. 61–63.

Incognito

Courtines, Pierre. "*Incognito*," in *America*. CXI (October 17, 1964), pp. 459–460.

Clinton, F. "*Incognito*," in *National Review*. XVI (December 15, 1964), p. 1121.

Elman, Richard M. "Alibi for Rumania," in *New Republic*. CLI (September 12, 1964), pp. 21–24.

Howe, Irving. "Dangerous Acquaintances," in *New York Review of Books*. III (September 24, 1964), pp. 17–18.

Stilwell, Robert L. "Trials of the Disenchanted," in *Saturday Review*. XLVII (September 19, 1964), p. 48.

LAWRENCE DURRELL
(1912–   )

Balthazar

Bode, Carl. "Durrell's Way to Alexandria," in *College English.* XXII (May, 1961), pp. 531–538.

Card, James. " 'Tell Me, Tell Me': The Writer as Spellbinder in Lawrence Durrell's *Alexandria Quartet*," in *Modern British Literature.* I (1976), pp. 74–83.

Decancq, Roland. "What Lies Beyond? An Analysis of Darley's 'Quest' in Lawrence Durrell's *Alexandria Quartet*," in *Revue des Langues Vivantes.* XXXIV (1968), pp. 134–150.

DeMott, Benjamin. "Grading the Emanglons," in *Hudson Review.* XIII (Autumn, 1960), pp. 456–464.

Dobrée, Bonamy. "Durrell's Alexandrian Series," in *Sewanee Review.* LXIX (Winter, 1961), pp. 61–79.

Eskin, Stanley G. "Durrell's Themes in the *Alexandria Quartet*," in *Texas Quarterly.* V (Winter, 1962), pp. 43–60.

Friedman, Alan W. *Lawrence Durrell and* The Alexandria Quartet: *Art for Love's Sake.* Norman: University of Oklahoma Press, 1970, pp. 87–110.

Gossman, Ann. "Love's Alchemy in the *Alexandria Quartet*," in *Critique: Studies in Modern Fiction.* XIII (1971), pp. 83–96.

Hagopian, John V. "The Resolution of the *Alexandria Quartet*," in *Critique: Studies in Modern Fiction.* VII (Spring, 1964), pp. 97–106.

Kelly, John C. "Lawrence Durrell: *The Alexandria Quartet*," in *Studies.* LII (Spring, 1963), pp. 52–68.

Kruppa, Joseph E. "Durrell's *Alexandria Quartet* and the Implosion of the Modern Consciousness," in *Modern Fiction Studies.* XIII (Autumn, 1967), pp. 401–416.

Lemon, Lee T. "*The Alexandria Quartet*: Form and Fiction," in *Wisconsin Studies in Contemporary Literature.* IV (Autumn, 1963), pp. 327–338.

Mackworth, Cecily. "Lawrence Durrell and the New Romanticism," in *Twentieth Century.* CLXVII (March, 1960), pp. 203–213.

Morcos, Mona L. "Elements of the Autobiography in *The Alexandria Quartet*," in *Modern Fiction Studies.* XIII (1967), pp. 343–359.

Proser, Matthew N. "Darley's Dilemma: The Problem of Structure in Durrell's *Alexandria Quartet*," in *Critique: Studies in Modern Fiction.* IV (Spring–Summer, 1961), pp. 18–28.

Read, Phyllis J. "The Illusion of Personality: Cyclical Time in Durrell's *Alexandria Quartet*," in *Modern Fiction Studies.* XIII (Autumn, 1967), pp. 389–399.

Weatherhead, A.K. "Romantic Anachronism in *The Alexandria Quartet*," in *Modern Fiction Studies.* X (Summer, 1964), pp. 128–136.

Bitter Lemons

Friedman, Alan W. *Lawrence Durrell and* The Alexandria Quartet*: Art for Love's Sake.* Norman: University of Oklahoma Press, 1970, pp. 51–61.

Merrick, Gordon. "Will Lawrence Durrell Spoil America?," in *New Republic.* CXXXVIII (May 26, 1958), pp. 20–21.

Rolo, Charles. "Troubled Island," in *Atlantic Monthly.* CCI (April, 1958), pp. 93–94.

Stark, Freva. "An Idyll Broken by Shrill Voices and Flashes of Hate," in *New York Times Book Review.* (March 2, 1958), p. 6.

Steiner, George. "On the Scene," in *Yale Review.* XLVII (June, 1958), pp. 600–602.

Stolle, Jane. "An Englishman on Cyprus," in *Nation.* CLXXXVI (April 26, 1958), p. 366.

Wakin, Jeanette. "A Paradise Lost," in *Saturday Review of Literature.* XLI (April 12, 1958), pp. 62–63.

Weigel, John A. *Lawrence Durrell.* New York: Twayne, 1965, pp. 122–126.

The Black Book

Allen, Walter. *The Modern Novel in Britain and the United States.* New York: Dutton, 1964, pp. 284–288.

Brown, Sharon L. "*The Black Book*: A Search for Method," in *Modern Fiction Studies.* XIII (Autumn, 1967), pp. 319–328.

Frazer, George S. *Lawrence Durrell: A Study.* Revised Edition. London: Faber and Faber, 1973, pp. 46–68.

Friedman, Alan W. *Lawrence Durrell and* The Alexandria Quartet*: Art for Love's Sake.* Norman: University of Oklahoma Press, 1970, pp. 4–6.

Glicksburg, Charles I. "The Fictional World of Lawrence Durrell," in *Bucknell Review.* XI (March, 1963), pp. 118–122.

Moore, Harry T. *The World of Lawrence Durrell.* Carbondale: Southern Illinois University Press, 1962, pp. 100–102.

Pritchett, Victor S. *The Living Novel and Later Appreciations.* New York: Random House, 1964, pp. 303–309.

Rexroth, Kenneth. *Assays.* New York: New Directions, 1962, pp. 118–130.

Unterecker, John. *Lawrence Durrell.* New York: Columbia University Press, 1964, pp. 11–12, 24–31.

Weigel, John A. *Lawrence Durrell.* New York: Twayne, 1965, pp. 43–48.

Clea

Bode, Carl. "Durrell's Way to Alexandria," in *College English.* XXII (May, 1961), pp. 531–538.

Card, James. " 'Tell Me, Tell Me': The Writer as Spellbinder in Lawrence Durrell's *Alexandria Quartet,*" in *Modern British Literature.* I (1976), pp. 74–83.

Corke, Hilary. "Mr. Durrell and Brother Criticus," in *Encounter.* XIV (May, 1960), pp. 65–70.

Decancq, Roland. "What Lies Beyond? An Analysis of Darley's 'Quest' in Lawrence Durrell's *Alexandria Quartet,*" in *Revue des Langues Vivantes.* XXXIV (1968), pp. 134–150.

DeMott, Benjamin. "Grading the Emanglons," in *Hudson Review.* XIII (Autumn, 1960), pp. 456–464.

Dobrée, Bonamy. "Durrell's Alexandrian Series," in *Sewanee Review.* LXIX (Winter, 1961), pp. 61–79.

Eskin, Stanley G. "Durrell's Themes in the *Alexandria Quartet,*" in *Texas Quarterly.* V (Winter, 1962), pp. 43–60.

Fraiberg, Louis. "Durrell's Dissonant Quartet," in *Contemporary British Novelists.* Carbondale: Southern Illinois University Press, 1965, pp. 16–35.

Friedman, Alan W. *Lawrence Durrell and* The Alexandria Quartet: *Art for Love's Sake.* Norman: University of Oklahoma Press, 1970, pp. 136–165.

Gossman, Ann. "Love's Alchemy in the *Alexandria Quartet,*" in *Critique: Studies in Modern Fiction.* XIII (1971), pp. 83–96.

Hagopian, John V. "The Resolution of the *Alexandria Quartet,*" in *Critique: Studies in Modern Fiction.* VII (Spring, 1964), pp. 97–106.

Inglis, Fred. *An Essential Discipline: An Introduction to Literary Criticism.* London: Methuen, 1968, pp. 197–199.

Kelly, John C. "Lawrence Durrell: *The Alexandria Quartet,*" in *Studies.* LII (Spring, 1963), pp. 52–68.

Kermode, Frank. "Fourth Dimension," in *Review of English Literature.* I (April, 1960), pp. 73–77.

Kruppa, Joseph E. "Durrell's *Alexandria Quartet* and the Implosion of the Modern Consciousness," in *Modern Fiction Studies.* XIII (Autumn, 1967), pp. 401–416.

Lemon, Lee T. "*The Alexandria Quartet*: Form and Fiction," in *Wisconsin Studies in Contemporary Literature.* IV (Autumn, 1963), pp. 327–338.

Mackworth, Cecily. "Lawrence Durrell and the New Romanticism," in *Twentieth Century.* CLXVII (March, 1960), pp. 203–213.

Morcos, Mona L. "Elements of the Autobiography in *The Alexandria Quartet,*" in *Modern Fiction Studies.* XIII (1967), pp. 343–359.

Proser, Matthew N. "Darley's Dilemma: The Problem of Structure in Durrell's *Alexandria Quartet,*" in *Critique: Studies in Modern Fiction.* IV (Spring–Summer, 1961), pp. 18–28.

Read, Phyllis J. "The Illusion of Personality: Cyclical Time in Durrell's *Alexandria Quartet,*" in *Modern Fiction Studies.* XIII (Autumn, 1967), pp. 389–399.

Weatherhead, A.K. "Romantic Anachronism in *The Alexandria Quartet,*" in *Modern Fiction Studies.* X (Summer, 1964), pp. 128–136.

The Dark Labyrinth

Barrett, William. "Long Journey Inward," in *Atlantic Monthly.* CLIV (April, 1962), pp. 154–155.

Frazer, George S. *Lawrence Durrell: A Study.* Revised Edition. London: Faber and Faber, 1973, pp. 96–100.

Powell, L.C. "A Way of Saying Urgent Things," in *New York Times Book Review.* (February 18, 1962), pp. 5, 20.

Reavey, George. "Eight Characters in Search of an Exit," in *Saturday Review of Literature.* XLV (March 10, 1962), p. 24.

Weigel, John A. *Lawrence Durrell.* New York: Twayne, 1965, pp. 48–54.

Justine

Bode, Carl. "Durrell's Way to Alexandria," in *College English.* XXII (May, 1961), pp. 531–538.

Card, James. " 'Tell Me, Tell Me': The Writer as Spellbinder in Lawrence Durrell's *Alexandria Quartet,*" in *Modern British Literature.* I (1976), pp. 74–83.

Carruth, Hayden. " 'And I Shal Clynken Yow So Mery a Belle That I Shal Wakyn at this Company,' " in *Poetry.* XCIII (February, 1959), p. 5.

Decancq, Roland. "What Lies Beyond? An Analysis of Darley's 'Quest' in Lawrence Durrell's *Alexandria Quartet,*" in *Revue des Langues Vivantes.* XXXIV (1968), pp. 134–150.

DeMott, Benjamin. "Grading the Emanglons," in *Hudson Review.* XIII (Autumn, 1960), pp. 456–464.

Dobrée, Bonamy. "Durrell's Alexandrian Series," in *Sewanee Review.* LXIX (Winter, 1961), pp. 61–79.

Eskin, Stanley G. "Durrell's Themes in the *Alexandria Quartet,*" in *Texas Quarterly.* V (Winter, 1962), pp. 43–60.

Friedman, Alan W.   *Lawrence Durrell and* The Alexandria Quartet*: Art for Love's Sake.* Norman: University of Oklahoma Press, 1970, pp. 62–86.

Gossman, Ann.   "Love's Alchemy in the *Alexandria Quartet,*" in *Critique: Studies in Modern Fiction.* XIII (1971), pp. 83–96.

Hagopian, John V.   "The Resolution of the *Alexandria Quartet,*" in *Critique: Studies in Modern Fiction.* VII (Spring, 1964), pp. 97–106.

Kelly, John C.   "Lawrence Durrell: *The Alexandria Quartet,*" in *Studies.* LII (Spring, 1963), pp. 52–68.

Kruppa, Joseph E.   "Durrell's *Alexandria Quartet* and the Implosion of the Modern Consciousness," in *Modern Fiction Studies.* XIII (Autumn, 1967), pp. 401–416.

Lemon, Lee T.   "*The Alexandria Quartet*: Form and Fiction," in *Wisconsin Studies in Contemporary Literature.* IV (Autumn, 1963), pp. 327–338.

Mackworth, Cecily.   "Lawrence Durrell and the New Romanticism," in *Twentieth Century.* CLXVII (March, 1960), pp. 203–213.

Morcos, Mona L.   "Elements of the Autobiography in *The Alexandria Quartet,*" in *Modern Fiction Studies.* XIII (1967), pp. 343–359.

Proser, Matthew N.   "Darley's Dilemma: The Problem of Structure in Durrell's *Alexandria Quartet,*" in *Critique: Studies in Modern Fiction.* IV (Spring–Summer, 1961), pp. 18–28.

Read, Phyllis J.   "The Illusion of Personality: Cyclical Time in Durrell's *Alexandria Quartet,*" in *Modern Fiction Studies.* XIII (Autumn, 1967), pp. 389–399.

Weatherhead, A.K.   "Romantic Anachronism in *The Alexandria Quartet,*" in *Modern Fiction Studies.* X (Summer, 1964), pp. 128–136.

Mountolive

Bode, Carl.   "Durrell's Way to Alexandria," in *College English.* XXII (May, 1961), pp. 531–538.

Card, James.   " 'Tell Me, Tell Me': The Writer as Spellbinder in Lawrence Durrell's *Alexandria Quartet,*" in *Modern British Literature.* I (1976), pp. 74–83.

Decancq, Roland.   "What Lies Beyond? An Analysis of Darley's 'Quest' in Lawrence Durrell's *Alexandria Quartet,*" in *Revue des Langues Vivantes.* XXXIV (1968), pp. 134–150.

DeMott, Benjamin.   "Grading the Emanglons," in *Hudson Review.* XIII (Autumn, 1960), pp. 456–464.

Dobrée, Bonamy.   "Durrell's Alexandrian Series," in *Sewanee Review.* LXIX (Winter, 1961), pp. 61–79.

Eskin, Stanley G.   "Durrell's Themes in the *Alexandria Quartet,*" in *Texas Quarterly.* V (Winter, 1962), pp. 43–60.

Friedman, Alan W.   *Lawrence Durrell and* The Alexandria Quartet*: Art for Love's Sake.* Norman: University of Oklahoma Press, 1970, pp. 111–135.

Gossman, Ann.   "Love's Alchemy in the *Alexandria Quartet*," in *Critique: Studies in Modern Fiction.* XIII (1971), pp. 83–96.

Hagopian, John V.   "The Resolution of the *Alexandria Quartet*," in *Critique: Studies in Modern Fiction.* VII (Spring, 1964), pp. 97–106.

Kelly, John C.   "Lawrence Durrell: *The Alexandria Quartet*," in *Studies.* LII (Spring, 1963), pp. 52–68.

Kruppa, Joseph E.   "Durrell's *Alexandria Quartet* and the Implosion of the Modern Consciousness," in *Modern Fiction Studies.* XIII (Autumn, 1967), pp. 401–416.

Lemon, Lee T.   "*The Alexandria Quartet*: Form and Fiction," in *Wisconsin Studies in Contemporary Literature.* IV (Autumn, 1963), pp. 327–338.

Morcos, Mona L.   "Elements of the Autobiography in *The Alexandria Quartet*," in *Modern Fiction Studies.* XIII (1967), pp. 343–359.

Proser, Matthew N.   "Darley's Dilemma: The Problem of Structure in Durrell's *Alexandria Quartet*," in *Critique: Studies in Modern Fiction.* IV (Spring–Summer, 1961), pp. 18–28.

Read, Phyllis J.   "The Illusion of Personality: Cyclical Time in Durrell's *Alexandria Quartet*," in *Modern Fiction Studies.* XIII (Autumn, 1967), pp. 389–399.

Weatherhead, A.K.   "Romantic Anachronism in *The Alexandria Quartet*," in *Modern Fiction Studies.* X (Summer, 1964), pp. 128–136.

RICHARD EBERHART
(1904–   )

The Poetry of Eberhart

Aiken, Conrad. "Themes with Variations," in *New Republic*. CXII (April 2, 1945), pp. 451–453.

Arrowsmith, William. "Five Poets," in *Hudson Review*. IV (Winter, 1953), pp. 623–624.

Bishop, J.P. "Little Legacy," in *Collected Essays of J.P. Bishop*. New York: Scribner's, 1948, pp. 281–282.

Booth, Philip. "The Varieties of Poetic Experience," in *Shenandoah*. XV (Summer, 1964), pp. 62–69.

Carruth, Hayden. "Maturity and Responsibility," in *Poetry*. XCI (October, 1957), pp. 53–56.

Donoghue, Denis. "An Interview with Richard Eberhart," in *Shenandoah*. XV (Summer, 1964), pp. 7–29.

_____. "Richard Eberhart: The Visionary Farms," in his *Third Voice*. Princeton, N.J.: Princeton University Press, 1959, pp. 223–235.

Eberhart, Richard. "How I Write Poetry," in *Poets on Poetry*. Edited by H. Nemerov. New York: Basic Books, 1966, pp. 17–39.

Hall, James. "Richard Eberhart, the Sociable Naturalist," in *Western Review*. XVIII (Summer, 1954), pp. 315–321.

Hoffman, Daniel. "Hunting a Master Image: The Poetry of Richard Eberhart," in *Hollins Critic*. IV (October, 1964), pp. 1–12.

Mills, Ralph J. "Richard Eberhart," in *Contemporary American Poetry*. New York: Random House, 1965, pp. 9–31.

_____. *Richard Eberhart*. Minneapolis: University of Minnesota Press, 1966.

Roache, Joel. *Richard Eberhart: The Progress of an American Poet*. New York: Oxford University Press, 1971.

Rodman, Selden. "The Poetry of Richard Eberhart," in *Perspectives U.S.A.* X (Winter, 1955), pp. 32–42.

Thorslen, Peter L. "The Poetry of Richard Eberhart," in *Poets in Progress*. Edited by Edward B. Hungerford. Evanston, Ill.: Northwestern University Press, 1962, pp. 73–91.

Vasakas, Byron. "Eberhart: A Negative Report," in *Poetry*. LXXXV (November, 1954), pp. 106–108.

MARIA EDGEWORTH
(1767–1849)

The Absentee

Altieri, Joanne. "Style and Purpose in Maria Edgeworth's Fiction," in *Nineteenth-Century Fiction.* XXIII (December, 1968), pp. 265–279.

Butler, Marilyn. *Maria Edgeworth: A Literary Biography.* Oxford: Clarendon Press, 1972, pp. 374–378.

Flanagan, Thomas J.B. *Irish Novelists, 1800–1850.* New York: Columbia University Press, 1959, pp. 80–91.

Harden, O. Elizabeth M. *Maria Edgeworth's Art of Prose Fiction.* The Hague: Mouton, 1971, pp. 159–180.

Kooiman-Van Middendorp, Gerarda M. *The Hero in the Feminine Novel.* New York: Haskell House, 1966, pp. 43–48.

McHugh, R.J. "Maria Edgeworth's Irish Novels," in *Studies.* XXVII (Autumn, 1938), pp. 267–278.

Murray, Patrick. *Maria Edgeworth; a Study of the Novelist.* Cork: Mercier Press, 1971, pp. 31–32, 43–48, 83–84.

Newby, P.H. *Maria Edgeworth.* Denver: Swallow, 1950, pp. 67–73.

Newcomer, James. *Maria Edgeworth the Novelist, 1749–1849, a Bicentennial Study.* Fort Worth: Texas Christian University Press, 1967, pp. 19–21, 130–138.

Castle Rackrent

Altieri, Joanne. "Style and Purpose in Maria Edgeworth's Fiction," in *Nineteenth-Century Fiction.* XXIII (December, 1968), pp. 265–278.

Baker, Ernest A. *History of the English Novel,* Volume VI. London: Witherby, 1929, pp. 11–33.

Brookes, Gerry H. "The Didacticism of Edgeworth's *Castle Rackrent,*" in *Studies in English Literature, 1500–1900.* XVII (Autumn, 1977), pp. 593–605.

Butler, Marilyn. *Maria Edgeworth: A Literary Biography.* Oxford: Clarendon Press, 1972, pp. 352–360.

Colby, W.B. "An Early 'Irish' Novelist," in *Minor British Novelists.* Edited by Charles A. Hoyt. Carbondale: Southern Illinois University Press, 1967, pp. 13–31.

Doubleday, Neal F. *Variety of Attempt: British and American Fiction in the Early Nineteenth Century.* Lincoln: University of Nebraska Press, 1976, pp. 7–18.

Edwards, Duane. "The Narrator of *Castle Rackrent*," in *South Atlantic Quarterly.* LXXI (1972), pp. 124–129.

Flanagan, Thomas J.B. *Irish Novelists, 1800–1850.* New York: Columbia University Press, 1959, pp. 69–79.

Harden, O. Elizabeth M. *Maria Edgeworth's Art of Prose Fiction.* The Hague: Mouton, 1971, pp. 43–71.

McHugh, R.J. "Maria Edgeworth's Irish Novels," in *Studies.* XXVII (Autumn, 1938), pp. 267–278.

Murray, Patrick. *Maria Edgeworth; a Study of the Novelist.* Cork: Mercier Press, 1971, pp. 50–52.

Newby, P.H. *Maria Edgeworth.* Denver: Swallow, 1950, pp. 39–47.

Newcomer, James. "*Castle Rackrent*: Its Structure and its Irony," in *Criticism.* VIII (November, 1966), pp. 170–179.

_____. "The Disingenuous Thady Quirk," in *Studies in Short Fiction.* II (1964), pp. 44–50.

_____. *Maria Edgeworth the Novelist, 1749–1849, a Bicentennial Study.* Fort Worth: Texas Christian University, 1967, pp. 17–21, 66–69, 144–167.

Solomon, Stanley J. "Ironic Perspective in Maria Edgeworth's *Castle Rackrent*," in *Journal of Narrative Technique.* II (1972), pp. 68–73.

Teets, Bruce. "Introduction," in *Castle Rackrent.* By Maria Edgeworth. Coral Gables, Fla.: University of Miami Press, 1964, pp. 1–31.

WALTER D. EDMONDS
(1903–   )

The Works of Edmonds

Edmonds, Walter D. "A Novelist Takes Stock," in *Atlantic Monthly*. CLXXII (July, 1943), pp. 73–77.

Gay, R.M. "The Historical Novel: Walter D. Edmonds," in *Atlantic Monthly*. CLXV (May, 1940), pp. 656–658.

Kohler, Dayton. "Walter D. Edmonds: Regional Historian," in *English Journal*. XXVII (January, 1938), pp. 1–11.

McCord, David. "Edmonds Country," in *Saturday Review of Literature*. XVII (December 11, 1937), pp. 10–11.

Nyren, Dorothy. "Walter Edmonds," in *A Library of Literary Criticism; Modern American Literature*. Edited by Dorothy Nyren. New York: Frederick Ungar, 1960, pp. 154–156.

Whicher, George Frisbie. "Loopholes of Retreat," in *The Literature of the American People; An Historical and Critical Survey*. Edited by Arthur H. Quinn. New York: Appleton-Century-Crofts, 1951, pp. 890–891.

Wyld, Lionel D. "At Boyd House: Walter Edmonds' York State," in *English Record*. XX (1969), pp. 89–92.

———. "Canallers in *Waste Land*: Considerations of *Rome Haul*," in *Midwest Quarterly*. (1963), pp. 335–341.

———. "Fiction, Fact and Folklore: The World of *Chad Hanna*," in *English Journal*. LVI (May, 1967), pp. 716–719.

LONNE ELDER III
(1931–   )

Ceremonies in Dark Old Men

Bigsby, C.W.E. "Lonne Elder III: An Interview," in *The Black American Writer*, Volume II. Edited by C.W.E. Bigsby. Deland, Fla.: Everett/Edwards, 1969, pp. 219–226.

Conner, John W. "Lonne Elder, III: *Ceremonies in Dark Old Men*," in *English Journal*. LIX (1970), p. 593.

Jeffers, Lance. "Bullins, Baraka, and Elder: The Dawn of Grandeur in Black Drama," in *College Language Association Journal*. XVI (1972), pp. 32–48.

Lee, Dorothy. "Three Black Plays: Alienation and Paths to Recovery," in *Modern Drama*. XIX (1976), pp. 397–404.

GEORGE ELIOT
(1819–1880)

Adam Bede

Adam, Ian. *George Eliot.* New York: Humanities, 1969, pp. 10–12, 34–37, 57–63, 85–88.

———. "The Structure of Realisms in *Adam Bede*," in *Nineteenth-Century Fiction.* XXX (September, 1975), pp. 127–149.

Colby, Robert A. "Miss Evans, Miss Mulock, and Hetty Sorrel," in *English Language Notes.* II (1965), pp. 206–211.

Creeger, George R. "An Interpretation of *Adam Bede*," in *Journal of English Literary History.* XXIII (September, 1956), pp. 218–238. Reprinted in *George Eliot: A Collection of Critical Essays.* Edited by George R. Creeger. Englewood Cliffs, N.J.: Prentice-Hall, 1970, pp. 86–106.

Diekhoff, J.S. "The Happy Ending of *Adam Bede*," in *Journal of English Literary History.* III (1936), pp. 221–227.

Edwards, Michael. "A Reading of *Adam Bede*," in *Critical Quarterly.* XIV (1972), pp. 205–218.

Fyfe, A.J. "The Interpretation of *Adam Bede*," in *Nineteenth-Century Fiction.* IX (1954), pp. 134–139.

Goode, John. "*Adam Bede*," in *Critical Essays on George Eliot.* Edited by Barbara Hardy. New York: Barnes & Noble, 1970, pp. 19–41.

Halperin, John. *Egoism and Self-Discovery in the Victorian Novel: Studies in the Ordeal of Knowledge in the Nineteenth Century.* New York: Burt Franklin, 1974, pp. 126–143.

Harvey, W.J. "The Treatment of Time in *Adam Bede*," in *Anglia.* LXXV (1957), pp. 429–440.

Herbert, Christopher. "Preachers and the Schemes of Nature in *Adam Bede*," in *Nineteenth-Century Fiction.* XXIX (1975), pp. 412–427.

Hussey, M. "Structure and Imagery in *Adam Bede*," in *Nineteenth-Century Fiction.* X(1955), pp. 115–129.

Jones, R.J. *George Eliot.* Cambridge: Cambridge University Press, 1970, pp. 6–18.

Knoepflmacher, Ulrich Camillus. *George Eliot's Early Novels: The Limits of Realism.* Berkeley: University of California Press, 1968, pp. 89–127.

———. "The Post-Romantic Imagination: *Adam Bede*, Wordsworth and Milton," in *Journal of English Literary History.* XXXIV (December, 1967), pp. 518–540.

Kooiman-Van Middendorp, Gerarda M. *The Hero in the Feminine Novel.* New York: Haskell House, 1966, pp. 96–123.

Krieger, Murray. "*Adam Bede* and the Cushioned Fall: The Extenuation of Extremity," in *The Classic Vision: The Retreat from Extremity in Modern Literature.* Baltimore: Johns Hopkins Press, 1971, pp. 197–220.

Lerner, Laurence. *The Truthtellers: Jane Austen, George Eliot, D.H. Lawrence.* New York: Schocken, 1967, pp. 33–40, 89–92, 141–143.

Liddell, Robert. *The Novels of George Eliot.* New York: St. Martin's, 1977, pp. 33–50.

Martin, Bruce K. "Rescue and Marriage in *Adam Bede*," in *Studies in English Literature, 1500–1900.* XII (1972), pp. 745–763.

Paterson, John. "Introduction," in *Adam Bede* (Riverside Edition). Boston: Houghton Mifflin, 1968.

Roberts, Neil. *George Eliot: Her Beliefs and Her Art.* Pittsburgh: University of Pittsburgh Press, 1975, pp. 63–83.

Thale, Jerome. *The Novels of George Eliot.* New York: Columbia University Press, 1959, pp. 14–35.

Van Ghent, Dorothy. "On *Adam Bede*," in *The English Novel: Form and Function.* New York: Holt, Rinehart and Winston, 1953, pp. 172–181. Reprinted in *A Century of George Eliot Criticism.* Edited by Gordon S. Haight. Boston: Houghton Mifflin, 1965, pp. 281–285.

Wiesenfarth, Joseph. "*Adam Bede* and Myth," in *Papers on Language and Literature.* VIII (1972), pp. 39–52.

Daniel Deronda

Adam, Ian. *George Eliot.* New York: Humanities, 1969, pp. 28–33, 52–56, 77–84, 104–111.

Bagley, John. "The Pastoral of Intellect," in *Critical Essays on George Eliot.* Edited by Barbara Hardy. New York: Barnes & Noble, 1970, pp. 133-150.

Bedient, Calvin. *Architects of the Self: George Eliot, D.H. Lawrence, and E.M. Forster.* Berkeley: University of California Press, 1972, pp. 57–68.

Beebe, Maurice. " 'Visions are Creators': The Unity of *Daniel Deronda*," in *Boston University Studies in English.* I (Autumn, 1955), pp. 166–177.

Carroll, David R. "The Unity of *Daniel Deronda*," in *Essays in Criticism.* IX (October, 1959), pp. 369–380.

Cirillo, Albert R. "Salvation in *Daniel Deronda*: The Fortunate Overthrow of Gwendolen Harleth," in *Literary Monographs.* I (1967), pp. 203–243.

Fisch, H. "Daniel Deronda or Gwendolen Harleth?," in *Nineteenth-Century Fiction.* XIX (March, 1965), pp. 345–356.

Fricke, Douglas C. "Art and Artists in *Daniel Deronda*," in *Studies in the Novel.* V (1973), pp. 220–228.

Gottfried, Leon. "Structure and Genre in *Daniel Deronda*," in *The English Novel in the Nineteenth Century: Essays on the Literary Mediation of*

Human Values. Edited by George Goodin. Urbana: University of Illinois Press, 1972, pp. 164–175.

Halperin, John. *Egoism and Self-Discovery in the Victorian Novel: Studies in the Ordeal of Knowledge in the Nineteenth Century.* New York: Burt Franklin, 1974, pp. 162–192.

Jackson, Arlene M. "*Daniel Deronda* and the Victorian Search for Identity," in *Studies in the Humanities.* III (1972), pp. 25–30.

Jones, R.T. *George Eliot.* Cambridge: Cambridge University Press, 1970, pp. 97–116.

Kearney, John P. "Time and Beauty in *Daniel Deronda*: 'Was she beautiful or not beautiful?,' " in *Nineteenth-Century Fiction.* XXVI (1971), pp. 286–306.

Leavis, F.R. "George Eliot's Zionist Novel," in *Commentary.* XXX (October, 1960), pp. 317–325. Reprinted as Introduction in *Daniel Deronda.* New York: Harper, 1961.

Liddell, Robert. *The Novels of George Eliot.* New York: St. Martin's, 1977, pp. 162–182.

Preyer, Robert. "Beyond the Liberal Imagination: Vision and Unreality in *Daniel Deronda,*" in *Victorian Studies.* IV (September, 1960), pp. 33–54.

Martin, Graham. "*Daniel Deronda*: George Eliot and Political Change," in *Critical Essays on George Eliot.* Edited by Barbara Hardy. New York: Barnes & Noble, 1970, pp. 133–150.

Roberts, Neil. *George Eliot: Her Beliefs and Her Art.* Pittsburgh: University of Pittsburgh Press, 1975, pp. 183–219.

Robinson, Carole. "The Severe Angel: A Study of *Daniel Deronda,*" in *Journal of English Literary History.* XXXI (September, 1964), pp. 278–300.

Sedgley, Anne. "*Daniel Deronda,*" in *Critical Review.* XIII (1970), pp. 3–19.

Smalley, Barbara. *George Eliot and Flaubert: Pioneers of the Modern Novel.* Athens: Ohio University Press, 1974, pp. 198–216.

Sudrann, Jean. "*Daniel Deronda* and the Landscape of Exile," in *Journal of English Literary History.* XXXVII (1970), pp. 433–455.

Swann, Brian. "George Eliot's Ecumenical Jew, or, The Novel as Outdoor Temple," in *Novel.* VIII (1974), pp. 39–50.

Thale, Jerome. *The Novels of George Eliot.* New York: Columbia University Press, 1959, pp. 121–136.

Witemeyer, Hugh. "English and Italian Portraiture in *Daniel Deronda,*" in *Nineteenth-Century Fiction.* XXX (March, 1976), pp. 477–494.

Felix Holt, Radical

Adam, Ian. "Character and Destiny in George Eliot's Fiction," in *Nineteenth-Century Fiction.* XX (September, 1965), pp. 127–144.

Bedient, Calvin. *Architects of the Self: George Eliot, D.H. Lawrence, and E.M. Forster.* Berkeley: University of California Press, 1972, pp. 70–79.

Carroll, David R. *"Felix Holt:* Society as Protagonist," in *Nineteenth-Century Fiction.* XVII (December, 1962), pp. 237–252. Reprinted in *George Eliot: A Collection of Critical Essays.* Edited by George R. Creeger. Englewood Cliffs, N.J.: Prentice-Hall, 1970, pp. 124–140.

Harvey, W.J. *The Art of George Eliot.* New York: Oxford University Press, 1969, pp. 25–27, 132–135, 215–219.

Horowitz, Lenore Wisney. "George Eliot's Vision of Society in *Felix Holt, the Radical,"* in *Texas Studies in Literature and Language.* XVII (1975), pp. 175–191.

Jones, R.T. *George Eliot.* Cambridge: Cambridge University Press, 1970, pp. 43–56.

Kooiman-Van Middendorp, Gerarda M. *The Hero in the Feminine Novel.* New York: Haskell House, 1966, pp. 96–123.

Kroeber, Karl. *Styles in Fictional Structure: The Art of Jane Austen, Charlotte Brontë, George Eliot.* Princeton, N.J.: Princeton University Press, 1971, pp. 135–139.

Lerner, Laurence. *The Truthtellers: Jane Austen, George Eliot, D.H. Lawrence.* New York: Schocken, 1967, pp. 47–52, 139–141, 237–241.

Levine, George. "Introduction," in *Felix Holt, the Radical.* New York: Norton, 1970, pp. ix-xxi.

Liddell, Robert. *The Novels of George Eliot.* New York: St. Martin's, 1977, pp. 102–122.

Myers, William. "Politics and Personality in *Felix Holt,"* in *Renaissance and Modern Studies.* X (1966), pp. 5–33. Reprinted in *Literature and Politics in the Nineteenth Century.* Edited by John Lucas. London: Methuen, 1971, pp. 108–125.

Rance, Nicholas. *The Historical Novel and Popular Politics in Nineteenth-Century England.* London: Vision, 1975, pp. 120–136.

Roberts, Neil. *George Eliot: Her Beliefs and Her Art.* Pittsburgh: University of Pittsburgh Press, 1975, pp. 127–144.

Smalley, Barbara. *George Eliot and Flaubert: Pioneers of the Modern Novel.* Athens: Ohio University Press, 1974, pp. 190–193.

Sprague, Rosemary. *George Eliot: A Biography.* New York: Chilton, 1968, pp. 230–241.

Thale, Jerome. *The Novels of George Eliot.* New York: Columbia University Press, 1959, pp. 87–105.

Thomson, Fred C. *"Felix Holt* as Classic Tragedy," in *Nineteenth-Century . Fiction.* XVI (June, 1961), pp. 47–58.

————. "The Genesis of *Felix Holt*," in *PMLA*. LXXIV (December, 1969), pp. 576–584.

————. "The Legal Plot in *Felix Holt*," in *Studies in English Literature, 1500–1900*. VII (Autumn, 1967), pp. 691–704.

————. "Politics and Society in *Felix Holt*," in *The Classic British Novel*. Edited by Howard M. Harper, Jr. and Charles Edge. Athens: University of Georgia Press, 1972, pp. 103–121.

Tomlinson, T.B. "Love and Politics in the Early-Victorian Novel," in *Critical Review* (Melbourne). XVII (1974), pp. 134–138.

Vooys, Sijna de. *The Psychological Element in the English Sociological Novel of the Nineteenth Century*. New York: Haskell House, 1966, pp. 64–70.

Williams, Raymond. *Culture and Society, 1780–1950*. New York: Columbia University Press, 1958, pp. 102–109.

Wright, Walter F. "George Eliot as Industrial Reformer," in *PMLA*. LVI (1941), pp. 1107–1115.

Middlemarch

Adam, Ian. *George Eliot*. New York: Humanities, 1969, pp. 21–28, 45–52, 71–77, 97–104.

Anderson, Quentin. "George Eliot in *Middlemarch*," in *The Pelican Guide to English Literature*, Volume VI. Edited by Boris Ford. New York: Penguin Books, 1958, pp. 274–293. Reprinted in *George Eliot: A Collection of Critical Essays*. Edited by George R. Creeger. Englewood Cliffs, N.J.: Prentice-Hall, 1970, pp. 141–160. Also reprinted in *A Century of George Eliot Criticism*. Edited by Gordon S. Haight. Boston: Houghton Mifflin, 1965, pp. 313–324.

Armstrong, Isobel. "*Middlemarch*: A Note on George Eliot's 'Wisdom,'" in *Critical Essays on George Eliot*. Edited by Barbara Hardy. New York: Barnes & Noble, 1970, pp. 116–132.

Beaty, J. Middlemarch *from Notebook to Novel: A Study of George Eliot's Creative Method*. Urbana: University of Illinois Press, 1960.

Blake, Kathleen. "*Middlemarch* and the Woman Question," in *Nineteenth-Century Fiction*. XXXI (December, 1976), pp. 285–312.

Carroll, David R. "Unity Through Analogy: An Interpretation of *Middlemarch*," in *Victorian Studies*. II (1959), pp. 305–316.

Coles, Robert. *Irony in the Mind's Life: Essays on Novels by James Agee, Elizabeth Bowen, and George Eliot*. Charlottesville: University Press of Virginia, 1974, pp. 154–204.

Daiches, David. *George Eliot:* Middlemarch. Great Neck, N.Y.: Barron's, 1963.

Ferris, Sumner J.   "*Middlemarch*: George Eliot's Masterpiece," in *From Jane Austen to Joseph Conrad: Essays Collected in Memory of James T. Hillhouse.* Edited by Robert C. Rathburn and Martin Steinman. Minneapolis: University of Minnesota Press, 1958, pp. 194–207.

Hagan, John.   "*Middlemarch*: Narrative Unity in the Story of Dorothea Brooke," in *Nineteenth-Century Fiction.* XVI (June, 1961), pp. 17–31.

Hardy, Barbara.   "*Middlemarch* and the Passions," in *This Particular Web: Essays on* Middlemarch. Edited by Ian Adam. Toronto: University of Toronto Press, 1975, pp. 3–21.

Harvey, W.J.   "The Intellectual Background of the Novel: Casaubon and Lydgate," in Middlemarch: *Critical Approaches to the Novel.* Edited by Barbara Hardy. New York: Oxford University Press, 1967, pp. 25–37. Reprinted in *The Victorian Novel: Modern Essays in Criticism.* Edited by Ian Watt. New York: Oxford University Press, 1971, pp. 311–323.

Jones, R.T.   *George Eliot.* Cambridge: Cambridge University Press, 1970, pp. 57–96.

Kettle, Arnold.   *An Introduction to the English Novel,* Volume I. London: Hutchinson, 1951, pp. 171–190.

Kitchel, Anna Theresa.   *Quarry for* Middlemarch. Berkeley: University of California Press, 1950.

Knoepflmacher, Ulrich Camillus.   *Laughter and Despair: Readings in Ten Novels of the Victorian Era.* Berkeley: University of California Press, 1971, pp. 168–201.

Liddell, Robert.   *The Novels of George Eliot.* New York: St. Martin's, 1977, pp. 123–161.

Lyons, Richard S.   "The Method of *Middlemarch*," in *Nineteenth-Century Fiction.* XXI (June, 1966), pp. 35–47.

Roberts, Neil.   *George Eliot: Her Beliefs and Her Art.* Pittsburgh: University of Pittsburgh Press, 1975, pp. 145–182.

Schorer, Mark.   "Fiction and the 'Matrix of Analogy,'" in *Kenyon Review.* XI (Autumn, 1949), pp. 539–559. Reprinted in *A Century of George Eliot Criticism.* Edited by Gordon S. Haight. Boston: Houghton Mifflin, 1965, pp. 270–278.

————.   "The Structure of the Novel: Method, Metaphor and Mind," in Middlemarch: *Critical Approaches to the Novel.* Edited by Barbara Hardy. New York: Oxford University Press, 1967, pp. 12–24.

Stallknecht, Newton P.   "Resolution and Independence: A Reading of *Middlemarch*," in *Twelve Original Essays on Great English Novels.* Edited by Charles Shapiro. Detroit: Wayne State University Press, 1960, pp. 125–152.

Thale, Jerome,   *The Novels of George Eliot.* New York: Columbia University Press, 1959, pp. 106–120.

Willey, Frederick. "Appearance and Reality in *Middlemarch*," in *Southern Review.* V (1969), pp. 419–435.

Williams, Raymond. *The English Novel: From Dickens to Lawrence.* London: Chatto and Windus, 1970, pp. 87–94.

The Mill on the Floss

Adam, Ian. *George Eliot.* New York: Humanities, 1969, pp. 12–18, 37–41, 63–68, 88–94.

Auerbach, Nina. "The Power of Hunger: Demonism and Maggie Tulliver," in *Nineteenth-Century Fiction.* XXX (September, 1975), pp. 150–171.

Buckler, William E. "Memory, Morality, and the Tragic Vision in the Early Novels of George Eliot," in *The English Novel in the Nineteenth Century: Essays on the Literary Mediation of Human Values.* Edited by George Goodin. Urbana: University of Illinois Press, 1972, pp. 149–159.

Buckley, Jerome Hamilton. *Season of Youth: The Bildungs-roman from Dickens to Golding.* Cambridge, Mass.: Harvard University Press, 1974, pp. 95–115.

Carroll, David R. "An Image of Disenchantment in the Novels of George Eliot," in *Review of English Studies.* XI (1960), pp. 29–41.

Colby, Robert Alan. *Fiction with a Purpose: Major and Minor Nineteenth Century Novels.* Bloomington: Indiana University Press, 1967, pp. 213–255.

Drew, Elizabeth A. *The Novel: A Modern Guide to Fifteen English Masterpieces.* New York: Norton, 1963, pp. 127–140.

Ermarth, Elizabeth. "Maggie Tulliver's Long Suicide," in *Studies in English Literature, 1500–1900.* XIV (1974), pp. 587–601.

Goldfarb, Russell M. "Robert P. Warren's Tollivers and George Eliot's Tullivers," in *University Review.* XXXVI (1970), pp. 209–213.

————. "Warren's Tollivers and Eliot's Tullivers, II," in *University Review.* XXXVI (1970), pp. 275–279.

Hagan, John. "A Reinterpretation of *The Mill on the Floss*," in *PMLA.* LXXXVII (1972), pp. 53–63.

Haight, Gordon S. "Introduction," in *The Mill on the Floss* (Riverside edition). Boston: Houghton Mifflin, 1961, pp. v-xix. Reprinted in *A Century of George Eliot Criticism.* Edited by Gordon S. Haight. Boston: Houghton Mifflin, 1965, pp. 339–348.

Hardy, Barbara. "*The Mill on the Floss*," in *Critical Essays on George Eliot.* Edited by Barbara Hardy. New York: Barnes & Noble, 1970, pp. 42–58.

Higdon, David Leon. "Failure of Design in *The Mill on the Floss*," in *Journal of Narrative Technique.* III (1973), pp. 183–192.

Jones, R.T. *George Eliot.* Cambridge: Cambridge University Press, 1970, pp. 19–30.

Knoepflmacher, Ulrich Camillus. *George Eliot's Early Novels.* Berkeley: University of California Press, 1968, pp. 162–220.

———. *Laughter and Despair: Readings in Ten Novels of the Victorian Age.* Berkeley: University of California Press, 1971, pp. 109–136.

Levine, George. "Intelligence as Deception: *The Mill on the Floss*," in *PMLA.* LXXX (September, 1965), pp. 402–409. Reprinted in *George Eliot: A Collection of Critical Essays.* Edited by George R. Creeger. Englewood Cliffs, N.J.: Prentice-Hall, 1970, pp. 107–123.

Liddell, Robert. *The Novels of George Eliot.* New York: St. Martin's, 1977, pp. 51–71.

Molstad, David. "*The Mill on the Floss* and *Antigone*," in *PMLA.* LXXXV (1970), pp. 527–531.

Paris, Bernard J. *A Psychological Approach to Fiction: Studies in Thackeray, Stendhal, George Eliot, Dostoevsky, and Conrad.* Bloomington: Indiana University Press, 1974, pp. 165–189.

———. "Toward a Revaluation of George Eliot's *The Mill on the Floss*," in *Nineteenth-Century Fiction.* XI (June, 1956), pp. 18–31.

Roberts, Neil. *George Eliot: Her Beliefs and Her Art.* Pittsburgh: University of Pittsburgh Press, 1975, pp. 85–106.

Thale, Jerome. *The Novels of George Eliot.* New York: Columbia University Press, 1959, pp. 36–57.

Williams, Ioan. *The Realist Novel in England: A Study in Development.* London: Macmillan, 1974, pp. 178–182.

Romola

Allott, Miriam. "George Eliot in the 1860's," in *Victorian Studies.* V (December, 1961), pp. 93–108.

Allott, Miriam and Geoffrey Tillotson. "*Romola* and *The Golden Bowl*," in *Notes and Queries.* CXCVIII (1953), pp. 124–125, 223.

Bullen, J.B. "George Eliot's *Romola* as a Positivist Allegory," in *Review of English Studies.* XXVI (1975), pp. 425–435.

Carroll, David R. "An Image of Disenchantment in the Novels of George Eliot," in *Review of English Studies.* XI (1960), pp. 29–41.

Conrad, Peter. *The Victorian Treasure-House.* London: Collins, 1973, pp. 124–127.

Fleishman, Avrom. *The English Historical Novel: Walter Scott to Virginia Woolf.* Baltimore: Johns Hopkins Press, 1971, pp. 155–163.

Harvey, W.J. *The Art of George Eliot.* New York: Oxford University Press, 1969.

Huzzard, John A. "In Defence of *Romola*," in *George Eliot Fellowship Review.* VII (1976), pp. 22–26.

————. "The Treatment of Florence and Florentine Characters in George Eliot's *Romola*," in *Italica*. XXXIV (1957), pp. 158–165.

Knight, Grant C. *The Novel in English*. New York: Richard R. Smith, 1931, pp. 187–198.

Kooiman-Van Middendorp, Gerarda M. *The Hero in the Feminine Novel*. New York: Haskell House, 1966, pp. 96–123.

Lerner, Laurence. *The Truthtellers: Jane Austen, George Eliot, D.H. Lawrence*. New York: Schocken, 1967, pp. 243–249.

Levine, George. "*Romola* as Fable," in *Critical Essays on George Eliot*. Edited by Barbara Hardy. New York: Barnes & Noble, 1970, pp. 78–98.

Liddell, Robert. *The Novels of George Eliot*. New York: St. Martin's, 1977, pp. 85–101.

Myers, William. "George Eliot: Politics and Personality," in *Literature and Politics in the Nineteenth Century*. Edited by John Lucas. London: Methuen, 1971, pp. 108–122.

Parlett, Mathilde. "George Eliot and Humanism," in *Studies in Philology*. XXVII (1930), pp. 25–46.

Peterson, Virgil A. "*Romola*: A Victorian Quest for Values," in *West Virginia University Philological Papers*. XVI (1967), pp. 49–62.

Poston, Lawrence, III. "Setting and Theme in *Romola*," in *Nineteenth-Century Fiction*. XX (March, 1966), pp. 355–366.

Rance, Nicholas. *The Historical Novel and Popular Politics in Nineteenth-Century England*. London: Vision, 1975, pp. 104–120.

Roberts, Neil. *George Eliot: Her Beliefs and Her Art*. Pittsburgh: University of Pittsburgh Press, 1975, pp. 119–126.

Robinson, Carole. "*Romola*: A Reading of the Novel," in *Victorian Studies*. VI (September, 1962), pp. 29–42.

Sambrook, A.J. "The Natural Historian of Our Social Classes," in *English*. XIV (Summer, 1962), pp. 130–134.

Sprague, Rosemary. *George Eliot: A Biography*. New York: Chilton, 1968, pp. 202–222.

Sullivan, Walter J. "Piero di Cosimo and the Higher Primitivism in *Romola*," in *Nineteenth-Century Fiction*. XXVI (1972), pp. 390–405.

Thale, Jerome. *The Novels of George Eliot*. New York: Columbia University Press, 1959, pp. 70–86.

Silas Marner

Adam, Ian. *George Eliot*. New York: Humanities, 1969, pp. 18–21, 94–97.

Allen, Walter. *George Eliot*. New York: Macmillan, 1964, pp. 118–127.

Buckler, William E. "Memory, Morality, and the Tragic Vision in the Early Novels of George Eliot," in *The English Novel in the Nineteenth Century: Essays on the Literary Mediation of Human Values.* Edited by George Goodin. Urbana: University of Illinois Press, 1972, pp. 159–163.

Carroll, David R. "*Silas Marner*: Reversing the Oracles of Religion," in *Literary Monographs.* I (1967), pp. 165–200.

Dunham, Robert H. "*Silas Marner* and the Wordsworthian Child," in *Studies in English Literature, 1500–1900.* XVI (1976), pp. 645–659.

Fairlay, E. "The Art of George Eliot in *Silas Marner*," in *English Journal.* II (1913), pp. 221–230.

H., J. "The Schoolteacher's Novel: *Silas Marner*," in *Saturday Review of Literature.* XV (March 20, 1937), p. 13.

Haddakin, Lilian. "*Silas Marner*," in *Critical Essays on George Eliot.* Edited by Barbara Hardy. New York: Barnes & Noble, 1970, pp. 59–77.

Heilman, Robert B. "Return to Raveloe: Thirty-Five Years After," in *English Journal.* XLVI (1957), pp. 1–10.

Jones, R.T. *George Eliot.* Cambridge: Cambridge University Press, 1970, pp. 31–42.

Knoepflmacher, Ulrich Camillus. *George Eliot's Early Novels.* Berkeley: University of California Press, 1968, pp. 221–259.

Law, Frederick Houk. "*Main Street* and *Silas Marner*," in *Independent.* CVIII (1922), pp. 263–265.

Liddell, Robert. *The Novels of George Eliot.* New York: St. Martin's, 1977, pp. 72–84.

Martin, Bruce K. "Similarity Within Dissimilarity: The Dual Structure of *Silas Marner*," in *Texas Studies in Literature and Language.* XIV (1972), pp. 479–489.

Milner, Ian. "Structure and Quality in *Silas Marner*," in *Studies in English Literature, 1500–1900.* VI (1966), pp. 717–729.

Parson, Coleman O. "Background Material Illustrative of *Silas Marner*," in *Notes and Queries.* CXCI (1946), pp. 266–270.

Pauncz, Arpad. "The Lear Complex in World Literature," in *American Imago.* XI (1954), pp. 50–83.

Quick, Jonathan R. "*Silas Marner* as Romance: The Example of Hawthorne," in *Nineteenth-Century Fiction.* XXIX (1974), pp. 287–298.

Roberts, Neil. *George Eliot: Her Beliefs and Her Art.* Pittsburgh: University of Pittsburgh Press, 1975, pp. 107–118.

Squires, Michael. *The Pastoral Novel: Studies in George Eliot, Thomas Hardy, and D.H. Lawrence.* Charlottesville: University Press of Virginia, 1974, pp. 86–105.

Swann, Brian. "*Silas Marner* and the New Mythus," in *Criticism.* XVIII (1976), pp. 101–121.

Thale, Jerome. *The Novels of George Eliot.* New York: Columbia University Press, 1959, pp. 58–69.

Thomson, Fred C. "The Theme of Alienation in *Silas Marner,*" in *Nineteenth-Century Fiction.* XX (June, 1965), pp. 69–84.

Wisenfarth, Joseph. "Demythologizing *Silas Marner,*" in *Journal of English Literary History.* XXXVII (1970), pp. 226–244.

T. S. ELIOT
(1888–1965)

Ash Wednesday

Blackmur, R.P. "T.S. Eliot from *Ash Wednesday* to *Murder in the Cathedral*," in *The Double Agent*. New York: Arrow, 1935, pp. 184–218. Reprinted in *T.S. Eliot: A Selected Critique*. Edited by Leonard Unger. New York: Rinehart, 1948, pp. 236–262.

Brooks, Cleanth and Robert Penn Warren. "The Reading of Modern Poetry," in *American Review*. VIII (February, 1937), pp. 442–449.

Chiari, Joseph. *T.S. Eliot, Poet and Dramatist*. London: Vision, 1972, pp. 75–81.

Drew, Elizabeth. *T.S. Eliot, The Design of His Poetry*. New York: Scribner's, 1949, pp. 98–117.

Duncan–Jones, Elsie E. "*Ash Wednesday*," in *T.S. Eliot, A Study of His Writings by Several Hands*. Edited by B. Rajan. London: Dennis Dobson, 1947, pp. 37–56.

Gorman, William J. "Eliot's *Ash Wednesday*," in *Inlander*. XI (November, 1930), pp. 5–10.

Headings, Philip R. *T.S. Eliot*. New York: Twayne, 1964, pp. 70–92.

Kenner, Hugh. *The Invisible Poet: T.S. Eliot*. New York: McDowell, McDowell, Oblensky, 1959, pp. 261–275.

Leavis, F.R. "T.S. Eliot," in *New Bearings in English Poetry*. London: Chatto and Windus, 1932, pp. 75–132. Reprinted in *T.S. Eliot: A Selected Critique*. Edited by Leonard Unger. New York: Rinehart, 1948, pp. 195–215.

Matthiessen, F.O. *The Achievement of T.S. Eliot*. New York: Oxford University Press, 1959, pp. 114–123.

Morrison, Theodore. "*Ash Wednesday*: A Religious History," in *New England Quarterly*. XI (June, 1938), pp. 266–286.

Pottle, Frederick A. *The Idiom of Poetry*. Ithaca, N.Y.: Cornell University Press, 1941, pp. 86–92.

Ross, Malcolm Mackenzie. "Conclusion: The Firmament Arrested," in *Poetry and Dogma*. New Brunswick, N.J.: Rutgers University Press, 1954, pp. 249–251.

Schneider, Elisabeth. *T.S. Eliot: The Pattern in the Carpet*. Berkeley: University of California Press, 1975, pp. 108–128.

Seyppel, Joachim. *T.S. Eliot*. New York: Frederick Ungar, 1972, pp. 71–74.

Smith, Grover. *T.S. Eliot's Poetry and Plays*. Chicago: University of Chicago Press, 1956, pp. 135–158.

Southam, B.C. *A Guide to the Selected Poems of T.S. Eliot.* New York: Harcourt, Brace and World, 1968, pp. 111–116.

Spender, Stephen. *T.S. Eliot.* New York: Viking, 1975, pp. 127–133.

Stein, Arnold. *Answerable Style.* Minneapolis: University of Minnesota Press, 1953, pp. 132–134.

Tate, Allen. "On *Ash Wednesday*," in *Reactionary Essays.* New York: Scribner's, 1936, pp. 210–222. Also in his *Collected Essays.* Denver: Alan Swallow, 1959, pp. 341–349. Reprinted in *T.S. Eliot: A Selected Critique.* Edited by Leonard Unger. New York: Rinehart, 1948, pp. 289–295. Also reprinted in *T.S. Eliot: A Collection of Critical Essays.* Edited by Hugh Kenner. Englewood Cliffs, N.J.: Prentice-Hall, 1962, pp. 129–135.

Traversi, Derek. *T.S. Eliot: The Longer Poems.* New York: Harcourt Brace Jovanovich, 1976, pp. 55–84.

Unger, Leonard. *T.S. Eliot: Moments and Patterns.* Minneapolis: University of Minnesota Press, 1966, pp. 41–68. Also in *T.S. Eliot: A Selected Critique.* Edited by Leonard Unger. New York: Rinehart, 1948, pp. 349–394.

Ward, David. *T.S. Eliot Between Two Worlds.* London: Routledge and Kegan Paul, 1973, pp. 148–163.

Williamson, George. *A Reader's Guide to T.S. Eliot.* New York: Noonday, 1953, pp. 168–185.

Wilson, Edmund. "T.S. Eliot," in *Axel's Castle.* New York: Scribner's, 1931, pp. 93–131. Reprinted in *T.S. Eliot: A Selected Critique.* Edited by Leonard Unger. New York: Rinehart, 1948, pp. 170–194.

The Cocktail Party

Arrowsmith, William. "Notes on English Verse Drama (II): *The Cocktail Party*," in *Hudson Review.* III (Autumn, 1950), pp. 411–430.

Barber, C.L. "The Power of Development," in *The Achievement of T.S. Eliot.* By F.O. Matthiessen. New York: Oxford University Press, 1959, pp. 213–243.

Broussard, Louis. *American Drama: Contemporary Allegory from Eugene O'Neill to Tennessee Williams.* Norman: University of Oklahoma Press, 1962, pp. 78–84.

Browne, E. Martin. *The Making of T.S. Eliot's Plays.* London: Cambridge University Press, 1969, pp. 172–248.

Donoghue, Denis. *The Third Voice: Modern British and American Verse Drama.* Princeton, N.J.: Princeton University Press, 1959, pp. 114–137.

Gardner, Helen. "The Comedies of T.S. Eliot," in *Sewanee Review.* LXXIV (January–March 1966), pp. 153–175. Reprinted in *T.S. Eliot: The Man and His Work.* Edited by Allen Tate. New York: Delacorte, 1966, pp. 159–181.

Gassner, John. *The Theatre in Our Times.* New York: Crown, 1954, pp. 267–281.

Headings, Philip R.   *T.S. Eliot*. New York: Twayne, 1964, pp. 143–160.

Heilman, Robert B.   "*Alcestis* and *The Cocktail Party*," in *Comparative Literature*. V(Spring, 1953), pp. 105–116.

Hovey, Richard P.   "Psychiatrist and Saint in *The Cocktail Party*," in *Literature and Psychology*. IX (Summer–Fall, 1959), pp. 51–55. Reprinted in *Hidden Patterns: Studies in Psychoanalytic Literary Criticism*. Edited by Leonard F. and Eleanor B. Manheim. New York: Macmillan, 1966, pp. 230–242.

Jones, David E.   *The Plays of T.S. Eliot*. Toronto: Toronto University Press, 1960, pp. 123–154.

Lawlor, John.   "The Formal Achievement of *The Cocktail Party*," in *Virginia Quarterly Review*. XXX (Summer, 1954), pp. 431–451.

McLaughlin, John A.   "A Daring Metaphysic: *The Cocktail Party*," in *Renascence*. III (Autumn, 1950), pp. 15–28.

Melchiori, Giorgio.   "Eliot and the Theatre," in *English Miscellany*. IV (1953), pp. 187–233. Reprinted in *The Tightrope Walkers: Studies of Mannerism in Modern English Literature*. London: Routledge and Kegan Paul, 1956, pp. 145–149.

Mudford, P.G.   "T.S. Eliot's Plays and the Tradition of 'High Comedy,' " in *Critical Quarterly*. XVI (Summer, 1974), pp. 127–140.

Murry, John Middleton.   *Unprofessional Essays*. London: Cape, 1956, pp. 162–172.

Porter, Thomas E.   "The Old Woman, the Doctor, and the Cook: *The Cocktail Party*," in *Myth and Modern American Drama*. Detroit, Mich.: Wayne State University Press, 1969, pp. 53–76.

Rahv, Philip.   "T.S. Eliot: The Poet as Playwright," in *Image and Idea: Twenty Essays on Literary Themes*. London: Weidenfeld and Nicolson, 1957, pp. 196–202. Reprinted in *The Myth and the Powerhouse*. New York: Farrar, Straus and Giroux, 1965, pp. 185–192. Also reprinted in *Literature and the Sixth Sense*. Boston: Houghton Mifflin, 1969, pp. 345–350.

Smith, Carol H.   *T.S. Eliot's Dramatic Theory and Practice from* Sweeney Agonistes *to* The Elder Statesman. Princeton, N.J.: Princeton University Press, 1963, pp. 147–183.

Smith, Grover.   *T.S. Eliot's Poetry and Plays*. Chicago: University of Chicago Press, 1974, pp. 214–227.

Spanos, William V.   *The Christian Tradition in Modern British Verse Drama*. New Brunswick, N.J.: Rutgers University Press, 1967, pp. 220–224.

Spender, Stephen.   *T.S. Eliot*. New York: Viking, 1975, pp. 212–216, 220–222.

Unger, Leonard.   "Laforgue, Conrad, and T.S. Eliot," in *The Man in the Name: Essays on the Experience of Poetry*. Minneapolis: University of Minnesota Press, 1956, pp. 211–215. Reprinted in *T.S. Eliot: Moments and Patterns*. Minneapolis: University of Minnesota Press, 1966, pp. 103–156.

Ward, David. *T.S. Eliot Between Two Worlds.* London: Routledge and Kegan Paul, 1973, pp. 205–213.

Wimsatt, W.K. "Eliot's Comedy," in *Sewanee Review.* LVIII (Autumn, 1950), pp. 666–678. Reprinted in *Hateful Contraries: Studies in Literature and Criticism.* Lexington: University of Kentucky Press, 1965, pp. 184–200.

The Confidential Clerk

Bellow, Saul. "Pleasures and Pains of Playgoing," in *Partisan Review.* XXI (May, 1954), pp. 313–315.

Bentley, Eric. "Old Possum at Play," in *What Is Theatre? Incorporating the Dramatic Event and Other Reviews, 1944–1967.* New York: Atheneum, 1968, pp. 141–145.

Broussard, Louis. *American Drama: Contemporary Allegory from Eugene O'Neill to Tennessee Williams.* Norman: University of Oklahoma Press, 1962, pp. 84–88.

Brown, Spencer. "T.S. Eliot's Latest Poetic Drama," in *Commentary.* XVII (April, 1954), pp. 367–372.

Browne, E. Martin. *The Making of T.S. Eliot's Plays.* London: Cambridge University Press, 1969, pp. 249–294.

Colby, Robert A. "Orpheus in the Counting House: *The Confidential Clerk,*" in *PMLA.* LXXII (September, 1957), pp. 791–802.

Dobrée, Bonamy. *The Lap and the Lute.* London: Cass, 1964, pp. 122–141.

Donoghue, Denis. *The Third Voice: Modern British and American Verse Drama.* Princeton, N.J.: Princeton University Press, 1959, pp. 138–157.

Findlater, Richard. "The Camouflaged Drama," in *Twentieth Century.* CLIV (October, 1953), pp. 311–316.

Gardner, Helen. "The Comedies of T.S. Eliot," in *Sewanee Review.* LXXIV (January–March, 1966), pp. 153–175. Reprinted in *T.S. Eliot: The Man and His Work.* Edited by Allen Tate. New York: Delacorte, 1966, pp. 159–181.

Gerstenberger, Donna. "T.S. Eliot: Toward Community," in *The Complex Configuration: Modern Verse Drama.* Salzburg, Austria: Universität Salzburg, 1973, pp. 69–74.

Harding, D.W. "Progression of Theme in Eliot's Modern Plays," in *Kenyon Review.* XVIII (Summer, 1956), pp. 337–360. Reprinted in *Experience into Words: Essays on Poetry.* New York: Horizon Press, 1964, pp. 132–162.

Headings, Philip R. *T.S. Eliot.* New York: Twayne, 1964, pp. 160–164.

Jones, David E. *The Plays of T.S. Eliot.* Toronto: Toronto University Press, 1960, pp. 155–178.

Melchiori, Giorgio. "Eliot and the Theatre," in *English Miscellany.* IV (1953), pp. 187–233. Reprinted in *The Tightrope Walkers: Studies of Man-*

nerism in Modern English Literature. London: Routledge and Kegan Paul, 1956, pp. 248–255.

Murry, John Middleton. *Unprofessional Essays*. London: Cape, 1956, pp. 172–182.

Smith, Carol H. *T.S. Eliot's Dramatic Theory and Practice from* Sweeney Agonistes *to* The Elder Statesman. Princeton, N.J.: Princeton University Press, 1963, pp. 184–213.

Smith, Grover. *T.S. Eliot's Poetry and Plays*. Chicago: University of Chicago Press, 1974, pp. 228–243.

Spanos, William V. *The Christian Tradition in Modern British Verse Drama*. New Brunswick, N.J.: Rutgers University Press, 1967, pp. 224–230.

Tynan, Kenneth. *Curtains: Selections from the Drama Criticism, and Related Writings*. New York: Atheneum, 1961, pp. 57–59.

Unger, Leonard. "Laforgue, Conrad, and T.S. Eliot," in *The Man in the Name: Essays on the Experience of Poetry*. Minneapolis: University of Minnesota Press, 1956, pp. 219–226. Reprinted in *T.S. Eliot: Moments and Patterns*. Minneapolis: University of Minnesota Press, 1966, pp. 103–156.

Ward, David. *T.S. Eliot Between Two Worlds*. London: Routledge and Kegan Paul, 1973, pp. 213–217.

Weales, Gerald. *Religion in Modern English Drama*. Philadelphia: University of Pennsylvania Press, 1961, pp. 183–206.

Weedon, William S. "Mr. Eliot's Voices," in *Virginia Quarterly Review*. XX (Autumn, 1954), pp. 610–613.

Weightman, J.G. "Edinburgh, Elsinore and Chelsea," in *Twentieth Century*. CLIV (October, 1953), pp. 306–308.

The Elder Statesman

Boardman, Gwenn R. "Restoring the Hollow Man," in *Review*. IV (November, 1962), pp. 35–45.

Browne, E. Martin. *The Making of T.S. Eliot's Plays*. London: Cambridge University Press, 1969, pp. 307–344.

Dobrée, Bonamy. *The Lamp and the Lute*. London: Cass, 1964, pp. 141–149.

Donoghue, Denis. *The Third Voice: Modern British and American Verse Drama*. Princeton, N.J.: Princeton University Press, 1959, pp. 158–168.

Fleming, Rudd. "*The Elder Statesman* and Eliot's 'Programme for the Metier of Poetry,'" in *Wisconsin Studies in Contemporary Literature*. II (Winter, 1961), pp. 54–64.

Gardner, Helen. "The Comedies of T.S. Eliot," in *Sewanee Review*. LXXIV (January–March, 1966), pp. 153–175. Reprinted in *T.S. Eliot: The Man and His Work*. Edited by Allen Tate. New York: Delacorte, 1966, pp. 159–181.

Headings, Philip R. *T.S. Eliot.* New York: Twayne, 1964, pp. 143–160.

Jones, David E. *The Plays of T.S. Eliot.* Toronto: Toronto University Press, 1960, pp. 179–209.

Kenner, Hugh. "For Other Voices," in *Poetry.* XCIV (October, 1959), pp. 36–40. Reprinted in *T.S. Eliot: A Collection of Critical Essays.* Edited by Hugh Kenner. Englewood Cliffs, N.J.: Prentice-Hall, 1962, pp. 187–191.

Kermode, Frank. "What Became of Sweeney?," in *Spectator.* CCII (April 10, 1959), p. 513.

Kirk, Russell. *Eliot and His Age.* New York: Random House, 1972, pp. 403–410.

Langbaum, Robert. "The Mysteries of Identity as a Theme in T.S. Eliot's Plays," in *Virginia Quarterly Review.* XLIX (Autumn, 1973), pp. 560–580.

Salmon, Christopher and Leslie Paul. "Two Views of Mr. Eliot's New Play," in *Listener.* LX (September, 1958), pp. 340–341.

Sarkar, Subhas. *T.S. Eliot the Dramatist.* Calcutta, India: Minerva, 1972, pp. 227–257.

Sena, Vinod. "Henrick Ibsen and the Latest Eliot," in *Literary Criterion.* VI (1965), pp. 19–25.

Smith, Carol H. *T.S. Eliot's Dramatic Theory and Practice from* Sweeney Agonistes *to* The Elder Statesman. Princeton, N.J.: Princeton University Press, 1963, pp. 214–239.

Smith, Grover. *T.S. Eliot's Poetry and Plays.* Chicago: University of Chicago Press, 1974, pp. 244–248.

Spanos, William V. *The Christian Tradition in Modern British Verse Drama.* New Brunswick, N.J.: Rutgers University Press, 1967, pp. 230–238, 241–251.

Spender, Stephen. *T.S. Eliot.* New York: Viking, 1975, pp. 190–197, 220–221.

Stanford, Derek. "T.S. Eliot's New Play," in *Queen's Quarterly.* LXV (Winter, 1959), pp. 682–689.

Tynan, Kenneth. *Curtains: Selections from the Drama Criticism and Related Writings.* New York: Atheneum, 1961, pp. 220–222.

Ward, David. *T.S. Eliot Between Two Worlds.* London: Routledge and Kegan Paul, 1973, pp. 217–222.

Wasson, Richard. "The Rhetoric of Theatre: The Contemporaneity of T.S. Eliot," in *Drama Survey.* VI (Spring, 1968), pp. 231–243.

Weales, Gerald. "The Latest Eliot," in *Kenyon Review.* XXI (Summer, 1959), pp. 473–478.

Weightman, J.G. "After Edinburgh," in *Twentieth Century.* CLXIV (October, 1958), pp. 342–344.

The Family Reunion

Barber, C.L.   "T.S. Eliot After Strange Gods," in *Southern Review*. VI (Autumn, 1940), pp. 387–416. Reprinted in *T.S. Eliot: A Selected Critique*. Edited by Leonard Unger. New York: Rinehart, 1948, pp. 415–443.

Belli, Angela.   *Ancient Greek Myths and Modern Drama*. New York: New York University Press, 1969, pp. 51–70.

Bodkin, Maud.   *The Quest for Salvation in an Ancient and a Modern Play*. London: Oxford University Press, 1941.

Broussard, Louis.   *American Drama: Contemporary Allegory from Eugene O'Neill to Tennessee Williams*. Norman: University of Oklahoma Press, 1962, pp. 73–78.

Browne, E. Martin.   *The Making of T.S. Eliot's Plays*. London: Cambridge University Press, 1969, pp. 90–151.

Donoghue, Denis.   *The Third Voice: Modern British and American Verse Drama*. Princeton, N.J.: Princeton University Press, 1959, pp. 94–113.

Gardner, Helen.   *The Art of T.S. Eliot*. New York: Dutton, 1959, pp. 139–157.

Hamalian, Leo.   "Wishwood Revisited," in *Renascence*. XII (Summer, 1960), pp. 167–173.

Headings, Philip R.   *T.S. Eliot*. New York: Twayne, 1964, pp. 112–118.

Jones, David E.   *The Plays of T.S. Eliot*. Toronto: Toronto University Press, 1960, pp. 82–122.

Matthiessen, F.O.   *The Achievement of T.S. Eliot*. New York: Oxford University Press, 1958, pp. 165–174.

Melchiori, Giorgio.   "Eliot and the Theatre," in *English Miscellany*. IV (1953), pp. 187–233. Reprinted in *The Tightrope Walkers: Studies of Mannerism in Modern English Literature*. London: Routledge and Kegan Paul, 1956, pp. 136–145.

Murry, John Middleton.   *Unprofessional Essays*. London: Cape, 1956, pp. 154–162.

Palmer, Richard E.   "Existentialism in T.S. Eliot's *The Family Reunion*," in *Modern Drama*. V (September, 1962), pp. 174–186.

Peter, John.   "*The Family Reunion*," in *Scrutiny*. XVI (September, 1949), pp. 219–230.

Ransom, John Crowe.   "T.S. Eliot as Dramatist," in *Poetry*. LIV (August, 1939), pp. 264–271.

Read, Herbert.   *The True Voice of Feeling: Studies in English Romantic Poetry*. London: Faber and Faber, 1953, pp. 139–150.

Scott, Nathan A.   *Rehearsals of Discomposure: Alienation and Reconciliation in Modern Literature*. London: John Lehmann, 1952, pp. 229–237.

Sena, Vinod. "Eliot's *The Family Reunion*: A Study in Disintegration," in *Southern Review*. III (Autumn, 1967), pp. 895–921.

Smith, Carol H. *T.S. Eliot's Dramatic Theory and Practice from* Sweeney Agonistes *to* The Elder Statesman. Princeton, N.J.: Princeton University Press, 1963, pp. 112–146.

Smith, Grover. *T.S. Eliot's Poetry and Plays.* Chicago: University of Chicago Press, 1974, pp. 196–213.

Spanos, William V. *The Christian Tradition in Modern British Verse Drama.* New Brunswick, N.J.: Rutgers University Press, 1967, pp. 184–218.

Spender, Stephen. *T.S. Eliot.* New York: Viking, 1975, pp. 206–211, 221–222.

Styan, J.L. *The Dark Comedy.* Cambridge: Cambridge University Press, 1968, pp. 158–166.

Ward, David. *T.S. Eliot Between Two Worlds.* London: Routledge and Kegan Paul, 1973, pp. 197–205.

Four Quartets

Blamires, Harry. *Word Unheard: A Guide Through Eliot's Quartets.* London: Methuen, 1969.

Bradford, Curtis. "Footnotes to 'East Coker,' " in *Sewanee Review*. LII (Winter, 1944), pp. 169–175. Reprinted in *T.S. Eliot:* Four Quartets. Edited by Bernard Bergonzi. Nashville, Tenn.: Aurora, 1970, pp. 57–63.

Chiari, Joseph. *T.S. Eliot, Poet and Dramatist.* London: Vision, 1972, pp. 81–104.

Davie, Donald. "T.S. Eliot: The End of an Era," in *Twentieth Century*. CLIX (April, 1956), pp. 350–362. Reprinted in *T.S. Eliot: A Collection of Critical Essays*. Edited by Hugh Kenner. Englewood Cliffs, N.J.: Prentice-Hall, 1962, pp. 192–206. Also reprinted in *T.S. Eliot:* Four Quartets. Edited by Bernard Bergonzi. Nashville, Tenn.: Aurora, 1970, pp. 153–167.

De Masirevich, Constance. *On the* Four Quartets *of T.S. Eliot.* New York: Barnes & Noble, 1953.

Donoghue, Denis. "T.S. Eliot's *Quartets*: A New Reading," in *Studies*. LIV (Spring, 1965), pp. 41–62. Reprinted in *T.S. Eliot:* Four Quartets. Edited by Bernard Bergonzi. Nashville, Tenn.: Aurora, 1970, pp. 212–238.

Drew, Elizabeth. *T.S. Eliot, The Design of His Poetry.* New York: Scribner's, 1949, pp. 140–200.

Flint, R.W. "The *Four Quartets* Reconsidered," in *Sewanee Review*. LVI (Winter, 1948), pp. 69–81. Reprinted in *T.S. Eliot:* Four Quartets. Edited by Bernard Bergonzi. Nashville, Tenn.: Aurora, 1970, pp. 107–118.

Gardner, Helen. *The Art of T.S. Eliot.* New York: Dutton, 1950, pp. 36–56. Reprinted in *T.S. Eliot:* Four Quartets. Edited by Bernard Bergonzi. Nashville, Tenn.: Aurora, 1970, pp. 119–138.

Harding, D.W. "Little Gidding," in *Scrutiny*. XI (Spring, 1943), pp. 216–219. Reprinted in *T.S. Eliot: A Collection of Critical Essays*. Edited by Hugh Kenner. Englewood Cliffs, N.J.: Prentice-Hall, 1962, pp. 125–128.

Headings, Philip R. *T.S. Eliot*. New York: Twayne, 1964, pp. 119–142, 170–171.

Kenner, Hugh. *The Invisible Poet: T.S. Eliot*. New York: McDowell, McDowell, Oblensky, 1959, pp. 289–323. Reprinted in *T.S. Eliot:* Four Quartets. Edited by Bernard Bergonzi. Nashville, Tenn.: Aurora, 1970, pp. 168–196.

Leavis, F.R. "Eliot's Later Poetry," in *Scrutiny*. XI (Summer, 1942), pp. 60–71. Also in his *Education and the University*. London: Chatto and Windus, 1943, pp. 87–104. Reprinted in *T.S. Eliot: A Collection of Critical Essays*. Edited by Hugh Kenner. Englewood Cliffs, N.J.: Prentice-Hall, 1962, pp. 110–125.

Matthiessen, F.O. *The Achievement of T.S. Eliot*. New York: Oxford University Press, 1959, pp. 177–197. Reprinted in *T.S. Eliot:* Four Quartets. Edited by Bernard Bergonzi. Nashville, Tenn.: Aurora, 1970, pp. 88–106.

Ross, Malcolm Mackenzie. "Conclusion: The Firmament Arrested," in *Poetry and Dogma*. New Brunswick, N.J.: Rutgers University Press, 1954, pp. 249–251.

Schneider, Elisabeth. *T.S. Eliot: The Pattern in the Carpet*. Berkeley: University of California Press, 1975, pp. 168–208.

Seyppel, Joachim. *T.S. Eliot*. New York: Frederick Ungar, 1972, pp. 91–102.

Smith, Grover. *T.S. Eliot's Poetry and Plays*. Chicago: University of Chicago Press, 1956, pp. 251–300.

Spender, Stephen. *T.S. Eliot*. New York: Viking, 1975, pp. 158–167, 169–184.

Stead, C.K. "The Imposed Structure of the *Four Quartets*," in *The New Poetic*. London: Penguin, 1964, pp. 170–185. Reprinted in *T.S. Eliot:* Four Quartets. Edited by Bernard Bergonzi. Nashville, Tenn.: Aurora, 1970, pp. 197–211.

Sweeney, James Johnson. "East Coker: A Reading," in *Southern Review*. VI (Spring, 1941), pp. 771–791. Reprinted in *T.S. Eliot: A Selected Critique*. Edited by Leonard Unger. New York: Rinehart, 1948, pp. 395–414. Also reprinted in *T.S. Eliot:* Four Quartets. Edited by Bernard Bergonzi. Nashville, Tenn.: Aurora, 1970, pp. 36–56.

Traversi, Derek. *T.S. Eliot: The Longer Poems*. New York: Harcourt Brace Jovanovich, 1976, pp. 85–214.

Ward, David. *T.S. Eliot Between Two Worlds*. London: Routledge and Kegan Paul, 1973, pp. 223–288.

Weitz, Morris. "T.S. Eliot: Time as a Mode of Salvation," in *Sewanee Review*. LX (Winter, 1952), pp. 48–64. Reprinted in *T.S. Eliot:* Four Quartets. Edited by Bernard Bergonzi. Nashville, Tenn.: Aurora, 1970, pp. 138–152.

Williamson, George. *A Reader's Guide to T.S. Eliot*. New York: Noonday, 1953, pp. 205–236.

"Gerontion"

Bailey, Ruth. *A Dialogue on Modern Poetry.* London: Oxford University Press, 1939, pp. 9–31, 38–39.

Chiari, Joseph. *T.S. Eliot, Poet and Dramatist.* London: Vision, 1972, pp. 46–51.

Daiches, David. "Some Aspects of T.S. Eliot," in *College English.* IX (December, 1947), pp. 117–120.

Douglas, Wallace, Roy Lamson and Hallet Smith. *The Critical Reader.* New York: Norton, 1949, pp. 125–130.

Drew, Elizabeth. *T.S. Eliot, The Design of His Poetry.* New York: Scribner's, 1949, pp. 47–57.

Gross, Harvey Seymour. "T.S. Eliot: 'Gerontion,'" in *The Contrived Corridor.* Ann Arbor: University of Michigan Press, 1971, pp. 32–44.

Headings, Philip R. *T.S. Eliot.* New York: Twayne, 1964, pp. 45–52.

Holbrook, David. *Lost Bearings in English Poetry.* New York: Barnes & Noble, 1977, pp. 58–100.

Kenner, Hugh. *The Invisible Poet: T.S. Eliot.* New York: McDowell, McDowell, Oblensky, 1959, pp. 124–141.

Leavis, F.R. "T.S. Eliot," in *New Bearings in English Poetry.* London: Chatto and Windus, 1932, pp. 79–87. Reprinted in *T.S. Eliot: A Selected Critique.* Edited by Leonard Unger. New York: Rinehart, 1948, pp. 195–215.

Matthiessen, F.O. *The Achievement of T.S. Eliot.* New York: Oxford University Press, 1959, pp. 62–63.

Patterson, Gertrude. *T.S. Eliot: Poems in the Making.* New York: Barnes & Noble, 1971, pp. 125–133.

Ransom, John Crowe. "'Gerontion,'" in *T.S. Eliot: The Man and His Work.* Edited by Allen Tate. New York: Delacorte, 1966, pp. 133–158.

Rochat, Joyce. "T.S. Eliot's 'Companion' Poems: Eternal Question, Temporal Response," in *Contemporary Review.* CCXXVII (August, 1975), pp. 73–79.

Rosenthal, M.L. and A.J.M. Smith. *Exploring Poetry.* New York: Macmillan, 1955, pp. 638–644.

Schneider, Elisabeth. *T.S. Eliot: The Pattern in the Carpet.* Berkeley: University of California Press, 1975, pp. 45–58.

Seyppel, Joachim. *T.S. Eliot.* New York: Frederick Ungar, 1972, pp. 26–28.

Smith, Grover. *T.S. Eliot's Poetry and Plays.* Chicago: University of Chicago Press, 1956, pp. 57–66.

Southam, B.C. *A Guide to the Selected Poems of T.S. Eliot.* New York: Harcourt, Brace and World, 1968, pp. 43–47.

Spender, Stephen. *T.S. Eliot.* New York: Viking, 1975, pp. 59–76.

Unger, Leonard. *T.S. Eliot: Moments and Patterns.* Minneapolis: University of Minnesota Press, 1966, pp. 21–22, 74–75.

Vickery, John Britten. " 'Gerontion': The Nature of Death and Immortality," in *Arizona Quarterly.* XIV (Summer, 1958), pp. 101–115.

Ward, David. *T.S. Eliot Between Two Worlds.* London: Routledge and Kegan Paul, 1973, pp. 58–67.

Wheelwright, Philip. "A Contemporary Classicist," in *Virginia Quarterly Review.* IX (January, 1933), pp. 155–160.

Williamson, George. *A Reader's Guide to T.S. Eliot.* New York: Noonday, 1953, pp. 106–113.

Williamson, Mervyn W. "T.S. Eliot's 'Gerontion': A Study in Thematic Repetition and Development," in *Texas Studies in English.* XXXVI (1959), pp. 110–126.

"The Hollow Men"

Blackmur, R.P. "T.S. Eliot," in *Hound and Horn.* I (March, 1928), pp. 203–205.

Chiari, Joseph. *T.S. Eliot, Poet and Dramatist.* London: Vision, 1972, pp. 71–74.

Drew, Elizabeth. *T.S. Eliot, The Design of His Poetry.* New York: Scribner's, 1949, pp. 91–97.

Drew, Elizabeth and John L. Sweeney. *Directions in Modern Poetry.* New York: Norton, 1940, pp. 134–136.

Foster, Genevieve W. *"Archetypal Imagery of T.S. Eliot,"* in *PMLA.* LX (June, 1945), pp. 576–578.

Fussell, Paul, Jr. "The Gestic Symbolism of T.S. Eliot," in *Journal of English Literary History.* XXII (September, 1955), pp. 198–201, 203.

Gillis, Everett A., Laurence V. Ryan and Friedrich W. Strothmann. "Hope for Eliot's Hollow Men?," in *PMLA.* LXXV (December, 1960), pp. 635–638.

Headings, Philip R. *T.S. Eliot.* New York: Twayne, 1964, pp. 70–72, 92–95.

Holbrook, David. "The Lack of a Creative Theme," in *Lost Bearings in English Poetry.* New York: Barnes & Noble, 1977, pp. 58–100.

Kenner, Hugh. *The Invisible Poet: T.S. Eliot.* New York: McDowell, McDowell, Oblensky, 1959, pp. 183–194.

Kinsman, Robert S. " 'The Hollow Men,' " in *Explicator.* VIII (April, 1950), item 48.

Leavis, F.R. "T.S. Eliot," in *New Bearings in English Poetry.* London: Chatto and Windus, 1932, pp. 75–132. Reprinted in *T.S. Eliot: A Selected Critique.* Edited by Leonard Unger. New York: Rinehart, 1948, pp. 195–215.

Schneider, Elisabeth. *T.S. Eliot: The Pattern in the Carpet.* Berkeley: University of California Press, 1975, pp. 99–107.

Seyppel, Joachim. *T.S. Eliot.* New York: Frederick Ungar, 1972, pp. 60–61.

Smith, Grover. *T.S. Eliot's Poetry and Plays.* Chicago: University of Chicago Press, 1956, pp. 99–109.

Southam, B.C. *A Guide to the Selected Poems of T.S. Eliot.* New York: Harcourt, Brace and World, 1968, pp. 97–108.

Spender, Stephen. *T.S. Eliot.* New York: Viking, 1975, pp. 123–127.

Stanford, Donald L. "Two Notes on T.S. Eliot," in *Twentieth Century Literature.* I (October, 1955), pp. 133–134.

Strothmann, Friedrich W. and Lawrence V. Ryan. "Hope for T.S. Eliot's 'Empty Men,' " in *PMLA.* LXXIII (September, 1958), pp. 426–432.

Symes, Gordon. "T.S. Eliot and Old Age," in *Fortnightly.* CLXIX (March, 1951), pp. 191–192.

Unger, Leonard. *T.S. Eliot: Moments and Patterns.* Minneapolis: University of Minnesota Press, 1966, pp. 25–26, 104–105, 112–114.

Vickery, John B. "Eliot's Poetry: The Quest and the Way," in *Renascence.* X (Autumn, 1957), pp. 8–9.

Ward, David. *T.S. Eliot Between Two Worlds.* London: Routledge and Kegan Paul, 1973, pp. 144–148.

Williamson, George. *A Reader's Guide to T.S. Eliot.* New York: Noonday, 1953, pp. 154–162.

Worthington, Jane. "The Epigraphs to the Poetry of T.S. Eliot," in *American Literature.* XXI (March, 1949), pp. 14–15.

"The Love Song of J. Alfred Prufrock"

Adams, Robert. *Strains of Discord: Studies in Literary Openness.* Ithaca, N.Y.: Cornell University Press, 1958, pp. 112–113.

Basler, Roy P. *Sex, Symbolism, and Psychology in Literature.* New Brunswick, N.J.: Rutgers University Press, 1948, pp. 203–221.

Berryman, John. "Prufrock's Dilemma," in *The Freedom of the Poet.* New York: Farrar, Straus, 1976, pp. 270–278.

Blackmur, R.P. "T.S. Eliot," in *Hound and Horn.* I (March, 1928), pp. 209–212.

Blum, Margaret Morton. "The Fool in 'The Love Song of J. Alfred Prufrock,' " in *Modern Language Notes.* LCCII (June, 1957), pp. 424–426.

Brooks, Cleanth and Robert Penn Warren. *Understanding Poetry.* New York: Henry Holt, 1950, pp. 433–444. Reprinted in *The Creative Reader.* Edited by R.W. Stallman and R.E. Watters. New York: Ronald Press, 1954, pp. 881–885.

Chiari, Joseph. *T.S. Eliot, Poet and Dramatist.* London: Vision, 1972, pp. 36–41.

Drew, Elizabeth. *T.S. Eliot, The Design of His Poetry.* New York: Scribner's, 1949, pp. 31–37.

Engle, Paul and Warren Carrier. *Reading Modern Poetry.* Chicago: Scott, Foresman, 1955, pp. 167–174.

Everett, Barbara. "In Search of Prufrock," in *Critical Quarterly.* XVI (1974), pp. 101–121.

Kenner, Hugh. *The Invisible Poet: T.S. Eliot.* New York: McDowell, McDowell, Oblensky, 1959, pp. 3–12.

Patterson, Gertrude. *T.S. Eliot: Poems in the Making.* New York: Barnes & Noble, 1971, pp. 109–118.

Rochat, Joyce. "T.S. Eliot's 'Companion' Poems: Eternal Question, Temporal Response," in *Contemporary Review.* CCXXVII (August, 1975), pp. 73–79.

Schneider, Elisabeth. *T.S. Eliot: The Pattern in the Carpet.* Berkeley: University of California Press, 1975, pp. 22–33.

Seyppel, Joachim. *T.S. Eliot.* New York: Frederick Ungar, 1972, pp. 15–34.

Smith, Grover. *T.S. Eliot's Poetry and Plays.* Chicago: University of Chicago Press, 1956, pp. 15–20.

Spender, Stephen. *T.S. Eliot.* New York: Viking, 1975, pp. 7–8, 31–38, 90–91.

Tschumi, Raymond. *Thought in Twentieth-Century English Poetry.* London: Routledge and Kegan Paul, 1951, pp. 127–132.

Turner, W.A. "The Not So Coy Mistress of J. Alfred Prufrock," in *South Atlantic Quarterly.* LIV (October, 1955), pp. 516–522.

Ward, David. *T.S. Eliot Between Two Worlds.* London: Routledge and Kegan Paul, 1973, pp. 12–23.

Weitz, Morris. *Philosophy of the Arts.* Cambridge, Mass.: Harvard University Press, 1950, pp. 94–107, 145.

Williamson, George. *A Reader's Guide to T.S. Eliot.* New York: Noonday, 1953, pp. 57–69.

Wilson, Edmund. "T.S. Eliot," in *Axel's Castle.* New York: Scribner's, 1931, pp. 93–131. Reprinted in *T.S. Eliot: A Selected Critique.* Edited by Leonard Unger. New York: Rinehart, 1948, pp. 170–194.

Wimsatt, William Kurtz. "Prufrock and Maud: From Plot to Symbol," in *Hateful Contraries.* Lexington: University of Kentucky Press, 1965, pp. 201–212.

Wormhoudt, Arthur. "A Psychoanalytic Interpretation of 'The Love Song of J. Alfred Prufrock,' " in *Perspective.* II (Winter, 1949), pp. 109–117.

Murder in the Cathedral

Adair, Patricia M. "Mr. Eliot's *Murder in the Cathedral*," in *Cambridge Journal*. IV (November, 1950), pp. 83–95.

Adams, John F. "The Fourth Temptation in *Murder in the Cathedral*," in *Modern Drama*. V (February, 1963), pp. 381–388.

Bodkin, Maud. *Studies of Type Images*. London: Oxford University Press, 1951, pp. 128–135.

Boulton, J.T. "The Use of Original Sources for the Development of a Theme: Eliot in *Murder in the Cathedral*," in *English*. XI (Spring, 1956), pp. 2–8. Reprinted in *Twentieth Century Interpretations of* Murder in the Cathedral. Edited by David R. Clark. Englewood Cliffs, N.J.: Prentice-Hall, 1971, pp. 74–79.

Donoghue, Denis. *The Third Voice: Modern British and American Verse Drama*. Princeton, N.J.: Princeton University Press, 1959, pp. 76–93.

Fergusson, Francis. "*Murder in the Cathedral*: The Theological Scene," in *The Idea of a Theater*. Garden City, N.Y.: Doubleday, 1949, pp. 222–234. Reprinted in *Twentieth Century Interpretations of* Murder in the Cathedral. Edited by David R. Clark. Englewood Cliffs, N.J.: Prentice-Hall, 1971, pp. 27–37.

Gardner, Helen. *The Art of T.S. Eliot*. New York: Dutton, 1959, pp. 133–139.

Gerstenberger, Donna. "The Saint and the Circle: The Dramatic Potential of an Image," in *Criticism*. II (Fall, 1960), pp. 336–341.

Hathorn, Richmond Y. *Tragedy, Myth, and Mystery*. Bloomington: Indiana University Press, 1962, pp. 195–216.

Headings, Philip R. *T.S. Eliot*. New York: Twayne, 1964, pp. 106–112.

Jones, David E. *The Plays of T.S. Eliot*. Toronto: Toronto University Press, 1960, pp. 50–81.

Kenner, Hugh. *The Invisible Poet: T.S. Eliot*. New York: McDowell, McDowell, Oblensky, 1959, pp. 276–285.

Krieger, Murray. *The Classic Vision: The Retreat from Extremity in Modern Literature*. Baltimore: Johns Hopkins University Press, 1971, pp. 337–362. Reprinted in *The Shaken Realist*. Edited by Melvin J. Friedman and John B. Vickery. Baton Rouge: Louisiana State University Press, 1970, pp. 72–99.

Martz, Louis L. *The Poem of the Mind*. New York: Oxford University Press, 1966, pp. 105–124. Reprinted in *T.S. Eliot: A Selected Critique*. New York: Rinehart, 1948, pp. 444–462. Also reprinted in *Twentieth Century Interpretations of* Murder in the Cathedral. Edited by David R. Clark. Englewood Cliffs, N.J.: Prentice-Hall, 1971, pp. 15–26.

Mason, William H. *Murder in the Cathedral*. Oxford: Blackwell, 1962.

Peacock, Ronald. *The Poet in the Theatre.* London: Routledge and Kegan Paul, 1946, pp. 1–20.

Peter, John. *"Murder in the Cathedral,"* in *Sewanee Review.* LXI (Summer, 1953), pp. 362–383. Reprinted in *T.S. Eliot: A Collection of Critical Essays.* Edited by Hugh Kenner. Englewood Cliffs, N.J.: Prentice-Hall, 1962, pp. 155–172.

Shorter, Robert N. "Becket as Job: T.S. Eliot's *Murder in the Cathedral*," in *South Atlantic Quarterly.* LXVII (Autumn, 1968), pp. 627–635. Reprinted in *Twentieth Century Interpretations of* Murder in the Cathedral. Edited by David R. Clark. Englewood Cliffs, N.J.: Prentice-Hall, 1971, pp. 86–93.

Smith, Carol H. *T.S. Eliot's Dramatic Theory and Practice from* Sweeney Agonistes *to* The Elder Statesman. Princeton, N.J.: Princeton University Press, 1963, pp. 91–111.

Smith, Grover. *T.S. Eliot's Poetry and Plays.* Chicago: University of Chicago Press, 1974, pp. 180–195.

Spanos, William V. *The Christian Tradition in Modern British Verse Drama.* New Brunswick, N.J.: Rutgers University Press, 1967, pp. 81–104.

Spender, Stephen. *T.S. Eliot.* New York: Viking, 1975, pp. 197–206.

Styan, J.L. *The Elements of Drama.* Cambridge: Cambridge University Press, 1960, pp. 135–140.

Ward, David. *T.S. Eliot Between Two Worlds.* London: Routledge and Kegan Paul, 1973, pp. 180–197.

Weales, Gerald. *Religion in Modern English Drama.* Philadelphia: University of Pennsylvania Press, 1961, pp. 189–194.

The Waste Land

Aiken, Conrad. "An Anatomy of Melancholy," in his *A Reviewer's ABC.* New York: Meridian Books, 1958, pp. 176–181. Reprinted in *T.S. Eliot: The Man and His Work.* Edited by Allen Tate. New York: Delacorte, 1966, pp. 194–202. Also reprinted in *A Collection of Critical Essays on* The Waste Land. Edited by Jay Martin. Englewood Cliffs, N.J.: Prentice-Hall, 1968, pp. 52–58. Also reprinted in *T.S. Eliot:* The Waste Land. Edited by C.B. Cox and Arnold P. Hinchliffe. Nashville, Tenn.: Aurora, 1970, pp. 91–99.

Brooks, Cleanth. *"The Waste Land:* Critique of the Myth," in his *Modern Poetry and the Tradition.* Chapel Hill: University of North Carolina Press, 1939, pp. 136–172. Reprinted in *T.S. Eliot, A Study of His Writings by Several Hands.* Edited by B. Rajan. London: Dennis Dobson, 1947, pp. 7–36. Also reprinted in *T.S. Eliot: A Selected Critique.* Edited by Leonard Unger. New York: Rinehart, 1948, pp. 319–348. Also reprinted in *Storm over* The Waste Land. Edited by Robert E. Knoll. Chicago: Scott, Foresman, 1964, pp. 58–87. Also reprinted in *A Collection of Critical Essays on* The Waste

Land. Edited by Jay Martin. Englewood Cliffs, N.J.: Prentice-Hall, 1968, pp. 59–86. Also reprinted in *T.S. Eliot:* The Waste Land. Edited by C.B. Cox and Arnold P. Hinchliffe. Nashville, Tenn.: Aurora, 1970, pp. 128–161.

Craig, David. "The Defeatism of *The Waste Land,*" in *Critical Quarterly*. II (1960), pp. 241–252. Reprinted in *Storm over* The Waste Land. Edited by Robert E. Knoll. Chicago: Scott, Foresman, 1964, pp. 122–135. Also reprinted in *T.S. Eliot:* The Waste Land. Edited by C.B. Cox and Arnold P. Hinchliffe. Nashville, Tenn.: Aurora, 1970, pp. 200–215.

Dobrée, Bonamy. "T.S. Eliot," in *The Lamp and the Lute*. Oxford: Clarendon Press, 1929, pp. 107–133.

Drew, Elizabeth. *T.S. Eliot, The Design of His Poetry*. New York: Scribner's, 1949, pp. 58–90.

Gardner, Helen. *The Art of T.S. Eliot*. New York: Dutton, 1950, pp. 86–98.

Headings, Philip R. *T.S. Eliot*. New York: Twayne, 1964, pp. 49–69.

Hough, Graham. "Imagism and Its Consequences," in *Reflections on a Literary Revolution*. Washington, D.C.: Catholic University Press, 1960, pp. 1–40. Reprinted in *Storm over* The Waste Land. Chicago: Scott, Foresman, 1964, pp. 98–121.

Kenner, Hugh. *The Invisible Poet: T.S. Eliot*. New York: McDowell, McDowell, Oblensky, 1959, pp. 145–152. Reprinted in *Storm over* The Waste Land. Edited by Robert E. Knoll. Chicago: Scott, Foresman, 1964, pp. 2–7. Also reprinted in *T.S. Eliot:* The Waste Land. Edited by C.B. Cox and Arnold P. Hinchliffe. Nashville, Tenn.: Aurora, 1970, pp. 168–199.

Kermode, Frank. "A Babylonish Dialect," in *T.S. Eliot: The Man and His Work*. Edited by Allen Tate. New York: Delacorte, 1966, pp. 231–243. Reprinted in *T.S. Eliot:* The Waste Land. Edited by C.B. Cox and Arnold P. Hinchliffe. Nashville, Tenn.: Aurora, 1970, pp. 224–235.

Korg, Jacob. "Modern Art Techniques in *The Waste Land,*" in *Journal of Aesthetics and Art Criticism*. XVIII (June, 1960), pp. 456–463. Reprinted in *A Collection of Critical Essays on* The Waste Land. Edited by Jay Martin. Englewood Cliffs, N.J.: Prentice-Hall, 1968, pp. 87–96.

Leavis, F.R. "*The Waste Land,*" in *New Bearings in English Poetry* [1932]. Ann Arbor: University of Michigan Press, 1960, pp. 75–91, 112–132. Reprinted in *T.S. Eliot: A Selected Critique*. Edited by Leonard Unger. New York: Rinehart, 1948, pp. 195–215. Also reprinted in *T.S. Eliot: A Collection of Critical Essays*. Edited by Hugh Kenner. Englewood Cliffs, N.J.: Prentice-Hall, 1962, pp. 89–103. Also reprinted in *Storm over* The Waste Land. Edited by Robert E. Knoll. Chicago: Scott, Foresman, 1964, pp. 24–38.

Martin, Jay. "T.S. Eliot's *The Waste Land,*" in *A Collection of Critical Essays on* The Waste Land. Edited by Jay Martin. Englewood Cliffs, N.J.: Prentice-Hall, 1968, pp. 1–14.

Matthiessen, F.O.   *The Achievement of T.S. Eliot.* New York: Oxford University Press, 1959, pp. 36–41, 46–52. Reprinted in *Storm over* The Waste Land. Edited by Robert E. Knoll. Chicago: Scott, Foresman, 1964, pp. 39–57. Also reprinted in *T.S. Eliot:* The Waste Land. Edited by C.B. Cox and Arnold P. Hinchliffe. Nashville, Tenn.: Aurora, 1970, pp. 108–127.

Patterson, Gertrude.   *T.S. Eliot: Poems in the Making.* New York: Barnes & Noble, 1971, pp. 134–168.

Schneider, Elisabeth.   *T.S. Eliot: The Pattern in the Carpet.* Berkeley: University of California Press, 1975, pp. 59–91.

Schwartz, Delmore.   "T.S. Eliot as the International Hero," in *Partisan Review.* XII (Spring, 1945), pp. 199–206. Reprinted in *T.S. Eliot: A Selected Critique.* Edited by Leonard Unger. New York: Rinehart, 1948, pp. 43–50. Also reprinted in *Storm over* The Waste Land. Edited by Robert E. Knoll. Chicago: Scott, Foresman, 1964, pp. 88–96. Also reprinted in *A Collection of Critical Essays on* The Waste Land. Edited by Jay Martin. Englewood Cliffs, N.J.: Prentice-Hall, 1968, pp. 97–104.

Scott, Nathan.   "T.S. Eliot: A Contemporary Synthesis," in *Rehearsals of Discomposure.* New York: King's Crown Press, 1952, pp. 178–228.

Shapiro, Karl.   "The Death of Literary Judgment," in *In Defense of Ignorance.* New York: Random House, 1960, pp. 35–60. Reprinted in *Storm over* The Waste Land. Edited by Robert E. Knoll. Chicago: Scott, Foresman, 1964, pp. 136–154.

Smith, Grover.   *T.S. Eliot's Poetry and Plays.* Chicago: University of Chicago Press, 1956, pp. 72–98.

Spender, Stephen.   *T.S. Eliot.* New York: Viking, 1975, pp. 100–121.

Traversi, Derek.   *T.S. Eliot: The Longer Poems.* New York: Harcourt Brace Jovanovich, 1976, pp. 9–54.

Ward, David.   *T.S. Eliot Between Two Worlds.* London: Routledge and Kegan Paul, 1973, pp. 68–141.

Williams, Helen.   *T.S. Eliot:* The Waste Land. London: Edward Arnold, 1973.

Williamson, George.   *A Reader's Guide to T.S. Eliot.* New York: Noonday, 1953, pp. 118–154.